ABSTRACTS OF DEEDS

1784-1813

Vol. 1

ELEANOR SMITH DRAUGHON

Southern Historical Press, Inc.
Greenville, South Carolina

Please direct all correspondence and orders to:

www.southernhistoricalpress.com
or
**SOUTHERN HISTORICAL PRESS, Inc.
PO BOX 1267
Greenville, SC   29601
southernhistoricalpress@gmail.com**

ISBN #0-89308-598-7

Printed in the United States of America

INTRODUCTION

Duplin County is located in the southeastern section of North Carolina and was formed in 1750 from New Hanover County. In the year 1800 the County was bounded by the counties of Jones, Lenoir, New Hanover, Onslow, Sampson and Wayne. Part of New Hanover was annexed to Duplin in 1751, and in 1777 part of Duplin was annexed to Johnston County. A major change involved the formation of Sampson County from Duplin in the year 1784. The county seat of Duplin is Kenansville.

The earliest deed books, being eight in number, remain in the Sampson County Courthouse; however, photo copies of these eight books have in recent years been acquired by the Duplin County Register of Deeds Office. Dr. Max R. Peterson, Jr. has published abstracts of the first three of these eight deed books, entitled Abstracts of Sampson-Duplin Deeds, Book 1-3 (ca. 1750 to ca. 1774).

The original deed books for Duplin County in the courthouse at Kenansville begin with Book 1A (1784-1788). This publication includes Book 1A as well as Book 3A (1794-1809) and Book 4A (1804-1813). There is no book known as Book 2A. Some deeds in Book 1A (1784-1788) are dated earlier than 1784, and one is dated after 1788. These deeds are as follows: 1766(p. 529), 1771 (p. 264), 1777(pgs. 58 & 59), 1779(pgs. 263, 274, 334 & 355), 1803 (p. 267).

The date of each deed is noted in these abstracts as well as the month and year each was probated. The page numbers listed at the beginning of each deed abstract refer to the page of the deed book on which the actual deed begins and not the page number of this manuscript.

Some of the deeds deal with land sold in other counties in N. C. and out-of-state. These include Onslow Co. (Book 1A 383), Sampson Co. (Book 1A 467, 515; Book 3A 167, 291, 361, 510, 512), Darlington Co., S. C. (Book 1A 529), Davidson Co., Ohio (Book 3A 12, 22), Davidson Co., Tenn. (Book 3A 118, 119), Norfolk Co., Va. (Book 4A 489) and Williamson Co., Tenn. (Book 4A 521).

Each person's name and every place mentioned in the deeds are included in these abstracts, as well as the beginning point of each piece of land. Names at the heading of each deed for the grantor is recorded the way the grantor signed his or her name; and, where the grantor made his or her mark, this is noted in parenthesis. Additional spellings of names for the grantor or grantee are also listed.

The Index combines the three deed books under each person's name. The book numbers such as 1A, 3A and 4A are listed only once followed by the pages on which the name appears.

In the Negro Slave Index the given name of the slaves is listed under both the grantor and the grantee.

One should search the indexes thoroughly for various spellings of surnames as well as for given names. A list of various spellings of some of the surnames of Duplin County are listed at the end of the list of abbreviations. Surnames are listed in all capital letters for "an easy glance".

Eleanor Smith Draughon

Route 2, Box 681-B
Chapel Hill, North Carolina 27514

Publisher's Note

    In presenting this volume to the public the Duplin County Historical Society, as publisher, wishes to record its gratitude to the one who made it possible, Mrs. Eleanor Smith Draughon, of Chapel Hill, whose ancestry includes the Smith and allied families of Duplin. Mrs. Draughon read all of the Duplin deeds abstracted here and carefully prepared all of the text, including the indices, and typed the finished manuscript for publication.

    The result is a work of inestimable value to everyone whose heritage includes the individuals whose names are recorded here and to everyone who is interested in the social and economic history of these times in this place. The painstaking care with which the manuscript was prepared merits our highest respect.

The Research Committee
DUPLIN COUNTY HISTORICAL SOCIETY
P. O. Box 130
Rose Hill, N. C. 28458

1 October 1983

TABLE OF CONTENTS

ABBREVIATIONS

A = acres
& = and
adj = adjoining
admr = administrator
admx = administratrix
afsd = aforesaid
atty = attorney
beg = beginning
BS = both sides
CC = Clerk of Court
clk = clerk
co = county
cont = containing
CS = county surveyor
C. Sur. = county surveyor
Ct. = court
dau = daughter
dec'd = deceased
Dist = district
D. Sec. = district secretary
D. Sur. = district surveyor
E = East
ES = East side
Esqr. = Esquire
Exr. = executor
Exx. = executrix
furn = furniture
Gov. = Governor
husb = husband
impr == improvement
incl = including

LW & T = last will and testament
N = North
NE = Northeast
no = number
NS = North side
of same = same county and state
p = page
pds = pounds
planta = plantation
poss = possession
proc = proclamation money
prop = property
P. Sec. = private secretary
Regr. = Registrar
S = South
sd = said
SE = Southeast
sec = secretary
shff = sheriff
shill = shillings
sic = intentionally so written; original
Sp. Sur. = special surveyor
SS = South side
Sup. Ct. = Superior Court
sur = surveyor
W = West
Wit = witnesses
WS = West side
yds = yards
yrs = years

Below is a list of variations of spellings of some of the most common surnames found in Duplin County.

ADKINSON-ADKISON-ATKINSON
ALBERSON-ALBERTSON
ALLAN-ALLEN
BAREFIELD-BARFIELD-BEARFIELD
BLANCHARD-BLANSARD-BLANSHARD
BLOODWORTH-BLUDWORTH
BOURDEN-BOWDEN
B. HURST-BROADHURST
COMMINS-CUMINGS-CUMMINGS
DEVER-DEVOUR
DICKSON-DIXON
EVERS-AVERS
GARRASON-GARRISON
GOAR-GOORE-GORE
GRADDY-GRADY
HAINS-HAYNES
JERNIGAN-JOURNEGAN
JOHNSON-JOHNSTON
KNOWLES-NOLES

LANEAR-LANIER
LEDDON-LIDDON
LEE-LEIGH
LITTLE-LYTLE
MATHIS-MATTHEWS-MATTHIS
MONDS-MUNDS
PEARCE-PEARSE-PIERCE
REAVES-REEVES-REVES
RHODES-ROADS
SCARLES-SEARLES-SURLS
SHOALER-SHOLAR-SHOLER
SMITH-SMYTH(E)
STALLIN-STALLINGS
STOAKS-STOKES
STRICKLAND-STRICKLING
SUL(L)IVAN-SUL(L)IVEN
SUL(L)IVANT-SUL(L)IVENT
THOMPSON-THOMSON-TOMSON
WADKINS-WATKINS

p. 1   WILLIAM HOUSTON, SENR. of Duplin Co. to EDWARD HOUSTON, 13 May 1784, for $1, a tract of 360A on the ES of the Northeast River of Cape Fear, being part of 840A granted to HENRY McCULLOH, ESQR. 3 Mar 1745, & later granted to WILLIAM HOUSTON, ESQR. May 1780, beg. at a stake on the river GRIFFETH HOUSTON'S lower corner & runs with his line S & N to a water oak & gum in Bridle Branch. WILLIAM HOUSTON & his wife to have lifetime rights on sd. land. Wit: CHARLES WARD, JOSEPH BRAY, SEN. July Ct. 1784.

p. 2   BENJAMIN RHODES to JACOB RHODES, both of Duplin Co., 13 July 1784, for 100 pds. specie 400A on the NS of Limestone below where the road crosses sd. Limestone, beg. at a water oak & gum near THANKFUL HICKS' line on the swamp, granted to BENJN. RHODES by patent. Wit: JOHN WOODWARD, JOSEPH T. RHODES. July Ct. 1784.

p. 3   JESSE OATES & LOWHAMAH (X) OATES his wife to MATHEW MASON, planter, all of Duplin Co., 9 Apr 1783, for 75 pds. specie 295A on the NS of Goshen Swamp, beg. at a sweet gum on the NS of sd. swamp, running N to a small red oak in GOODMAN'S line. Wit: STEPHEN KING. July Ct. 1784.

p. 5   JOHN SULLIVAN, planter, to ELIZABETH SULLIVAN, both of Duplin Co., 20 Oct 1782, for 4 pds. State money 100A on the Huckleberry Pond & head of Bee Branch & Little Marsh, to JOHN SULLIVAN'S old corner. Wit: FLOOD FOLEY, MOSES TEEL, CASEN (X) HARRIS. July Ct. 1784.

p. 6   MIKEL (W) MERRIT to ROBERT MERRIT, both of Duplin Co., 10 Mar 1784, for 48 pds. specie 150A on the SS of Stewart's Creek, granted to sd. MERRIT by patent, one half of sd. land given to sd. MIKEL by deed by sd. ROBERT MERRIT, beg. in the mouth of the branch at 2 large pines in the mouth of Cook's Marsh, along BARTREW BRYAN's line along the swamp joining JOSHUA LEE'S line. Wit: NOTHIAL MERRIT, JACOB MERRIT. July Ct. 1784.

p. 8   JOSEPH WILLSON to RICHARD WILLIAMS, both planters of Duplin Co., 13 Jan 1783, for 200 pds. specie 200A between himself & Muddy Creek, it being the upper half of 400A granted to CHARLES COX 20 Apr 1744 by patent & divided between the widow of CHARLES COX dec'd & the child ANN COX, orphan of sd. COX. Wit: JOHN WILLIAMS, STEPHEN WILLIAMS. July Ct. 1784.

p. 9   JACOB WELLS to SHADRACK STALLINGS, both of Duplin Co., 20 July 1784, for 20 pds. specie 25A on the ES of Ben's Creek, beg. at a maple in the edge of the swamp at the mouth of a small branch at the ford at an old Beaver Dam, to a small pine at sd. STALLINGS own corner, being part of the contents of a patent granted to ELIJAH BOWEN & later conveyed to JACOB WELLS. Wit: WILLIAM GOFF, EDWARD DICKSON. July Ct. 1784.

p. 11   THOMAS (T) CUMMINGS to ABRAHAM GLISSON, both of Duplin Co., 5 Oct 1782, for 40 pds. 200A on the ES of the Northeast Branch Cape Fear River opposite the mouth of Rockfish Creek, incl. a survey formerly made for JOB ROINGTON, beg. at a black jack on the river bank at HERRINGTON'S upper corner, being the contents of a patent granted to sd. CUMMINGS 22 July 1774. Wit: DENIS GLISSON, SAML. HOWARD. July Ct. 1784.

p. 13   SHADRACK STALLINGS to WILLIAM WELLS, both of Duplin Co., 20 July

1784, for 20 pds. spécie 50A on the ES of Bens Creek, a branch of Rockfish Creek & on BS of the Reedy Branch, beg. at a white oak on the lower edge of the branch on JACOB WELLS' line. Wit: EDWARD DICKSON, WILLIAM GOFF. July Ct. 1784.

p. 14   NATHANIEL (z(.) MERRIT to NOTHIEL MERRIT, both of Duplin Co., 9 Aug 1782, for 13 pds. current money of N. C. 100A on BS of Cliff's Marsh, beg. at a pine on JEREMIAH HORN'S line. Wit: WILLIAM (M) MERRIT, JACOB SELLERS. July Ct. 1784.

p. 16   WALTER BRYANT (BRYAN) to AARON HODGESON, both planters of Duplin Co., 10 Apr 1784, for 55 pds. proc 200A a little above McREE'S landing above the mouth of Rockfish Creek on BS of Mill Creek, incl. his impr., beg. at a cypress near WILLIAM JONES' line. Wit: JOHN (I) EVERS, JUNR., ELIZABETH (E) EVERS, JOHN EVERS. July Ct. 1784.

p. 17   DAVID (R) REES to THOMAS WEEKS, 25 Mar 1783, a deed of gift for sundry items, consisting of notes, bonds, horses, cattle, money, beds & furn. THOMAS WEEKS' sister SABRA married DAVID REES. Wit: AUSTIN BEESLEY, MARY BEESLEY. July Ct. 1784.

p. 18   WILEY GURGANUS to ABSALOM MERCER, both planters of Duplin Co., 10 Feb 1783, for a mare, bridle, saddle & 16 pds. 200A on the ES of the Northeast, & WS of Limestone Creek & BS of Cabbin Swamp, patented by WILLIAM MERCER 1779, beg. at a pine WS of the swamp, crossing Poley Bridge Branch & Cabbin Swamp. Wit: JOHN WHEEDEN, WILLIAM (ơ) MARCER. July Ct. 1784.

p. 19   AUSTON BEESLEY to ALEXANDER DICKSON, both of Duplin Co., 4 Aug 1782, for 20 pds. spécie 113A on the ES of Maxwell Swamp on BS of Lawrey's Branch, beg. at a post by the head of sd. branch, a corner of the patent, & to SOLOMON BEESLEY'S corner, being part of the contents of a patent granted to WILLIAM RIGSBEE, JOSEPH DICKSON & ALEXANDER DICKSON for 640A 25 July 1774. Wit: SOLOMON BEESLEY, JAMES DICKSON. July Ct. 1784.

p. 20   WILLIAM HOUSTON, SEN. of Duplin Co. to WILLIAM HUBBARD, 13 May 1784, for $1 a tract of 325A on the ES of the Northeast River, being part of a tract of 840A granted to HENRY McCULLOH 3 Mar 1745 & granted to WILLIAM HOUSTON, ESQR. May 1780, beg. at a gum on the East Branch of the Cape Fear River. Wit: W. DICKSON, SAML. HOUSTON. July Ct. 1784.

p. 21   WILLIAM HOUSTON, SENR. of Duplin Co. to GRIFFETH HOUSTON, 13 May 1784, for $1 a tract of 256A on the ES of the Northeast River of Cape Fear, being part of 840A granted to HENRY McCULLOH, ESQR. 3 Mar 1745, later granted to WILLIAM HOUSTON, ESQR. May 1780, beg. at a maple & ash on the branch of Cape Fear River, WILLIAM HUBBARD'S lower corner. WILLIAM HOUSTON & wife to have use of wood on sd. land for their planta. Wit: CHARLES WARD, JOSEPH BRAY, SENR. July Ct. 1784.

p. 23   DAVID (X) TUCKER to JOHN TUCKER, both of Duplin Co., 17 June 1783, for 15 pds. spécie 150A on the SS of Stewart's Creek, on the head of Clear Run above Cook's Mill incl. sd. Mill Branch. Wit: AMBORAS ENZER, JAMES FAISON. July Ct. 1784.

p. 24   SAMUEL HOWARD to SHADRICK STALLINGS, both of Duplin Co., 17 Jan 1783, for 40 pds. specie 100A on the SS of Maxwell's Swamp on BS of Parson's Branch, beg. at a small pine at a large fallen down white oak DAVID SLOAN'S corner, being the contents of a patent granted to SHADRICK STALLINGS. Wit: JOSEPH DICKSON, JANE DICKSON. July Ct. 1784.

p. 25   JOHN LITTLE to STEPHEN WILLIAMS, both of Duplin Co., 22 Apr 1784, for 45 pds. specie 200A on the NS of Rockfish Creek, beg. at a white oak on JOSEPH WILLIAMS' line. Wit: DAVID WILLIAMS, JOHN (W) WILLIAMS. July Ct. 1784.

p. 27   LEMON DUNN of Duplin Co. to URIAH GURGANUS of Onslow Co., 29 Jan 1784, for 100 pds. specie 175A on Maple Branch, beg. at a maple in the side of Maple Swamp. Wit: LAM. DUNN, RICHARD COOPER. July Ct. 1784.

p. 28   WILLIAM BURTON, planter, to JESSE NORRIS, both of Duplin Co., 16 Jan 1784, for 12 pds. 150A on the WS of the Northeast River, on the upper side of Oaky Branch, beg. at a water oak in the mouth of Paul's Branch on GEORGE DAUGHERTY'S line, to WILLIAM JONES' line, to 2 pines by the old Rawling Road, to a stake in the Grassy Branch Pocosin, to GEORGE DAUGHERTY'S corner. Wit: JHON (B) BRALY, JHON (W) WOOD, JOHN EVARS. July Ct. 1784.

p. 30   J. PEARSALL (JAMES), High Shff. of Duplin Co. to WILLIAM DUNCAN of same, 3 Sep 1784, for 35 pds. 180A in 2 tracts: (1) 80A being part of a tract of 300A formerly granted to WILLIAM TEAGUE & since became the prop of ANDREW BASS which fell to HERMON BASS, oldest son & heir of sd. BASS dec'd, situated on the SS of the Northeast Swamp; (2) 100A adj. the 1st tract, beg. at a pine by EDMUND DUNCAN'S line, to a white oak by BASS' line, to a pine by SOLOMON'S line, formerly patented by THOMAS DRAPER & by him sold to ANDREW BASS & later became the prop of HERMON BASS. The Court of Duplin Co. awarded 60 pds. plus cost of 3 pds. 16 shill. 9 pence to THOMAS HOOKS for damages in a suit against HERMON BASS, owner of sd. 180A, which was sold for 35 pds. at public auction to WILLIAM DUNCAN 2 Sep 1783. Wit: DANIEL GLISSON, EDWD. PEARSALL. July Ct. 1784.

p. 33   JOHN HALSO, planter, to STEPHEN HALSO his brother, both of Duplin Co. 1 July 1784, 100A on the ES of the Northeast River on the NS of Cypress Creek & BS of Halso Swamp & part of his own land, beg. at a stake at his own planta. Wit: JOHN LANIER, ROBERT COX, HENRY HALSO. July Ct. 1784. (Deed of gift)

p. 34   JOHN MAGEE to EBENEZAR GARRISON, both of Duplin Co., 13 Dec 1783, for 30 pds. specie 135A on the ES of Northeast Branch of Cape Fear River & on a certain branch of Muddy Creek known by the name of Marsh Branch, being part of the planta. whereon sd. GARRISON now lives on & the SS of sd. Marsh Branch, beg. at a gum & to the back patent line of JOHN MAGEE dated 22 Dec 1779, & to JAMES BLAKS corner. Wit: CHARLES BOSTICK, WILLIAM FARRIOR. July Ct. 1784.

p. 35   JOHN (ꝛ) WATKINS of New Hanover Co. to THOMAS CARR of Duplin Co., both planters, 13 June 1782, for 87 & one half spanish milla dollars 147A on the WS of the Six Runs, being part of a tract cont. 450A granted by patent 22 July 1774 to ARTHUR PITMAN, beg. at a red oak in GAVIN'S line, to Turkey Cock Branch, to a oak on the Short Branch to BYRD LANNEARE'S line. Wit: W. SHARPLES,

DEMPSEY (O) PITMAN. July Ct. 1784.

p. 38   ARTHUR (X) MATHEWS to REUBEN EZZELL, both of Duplin Co., 16 Feb 1784, for 7 pds. 10 shill. specie 125A on the ES of Stewart's Creek & on the NS of Miller's Mill Swamp, being part of a survey of 250A, beg. at a pine by the swamp, the 4th & last corner of sd. survey. Wit: AUSTIN BEESLEY, WILLIAM (W) BUSH. July Ct. 1784.

p. 39   DAVID HALL to THOMAS CRUMPTON, both of Duplin Co., 2 Mar 1784, for 50 pds. specie 340A in 3 tracts: (1) 150A on the branches of Rockfish Creek, granted to sd. CRUMPTON 27 Oct 1782, beg. at a pine on the WS of Burrell Hill Branch at CLIFTON BOWEN'S corner, to a pine on BENJAMIN LANIER'S line; (2) 150A being part of 300A patented to sd. CRUMPTON 29 Oct 1782, beg. at a white oak on the ES of Burrell Hill Branch, the last corner of sd. patent; (3) 40A being part of 100A granted by patent to sd. HALL, beg. at a red oak, the upper corner of sd. 100A on the ES of Burrell Hill Branch. Wit: JOSEPH DICKSON, JOHN (🜨) COOK, EDWARD DICKSON. July Ct. 1784.

p. 41   WILLIAM (8) MERCER to JOHN MURROW, both of Duplin Co., 10 Apr 1783 for 20 pds. specie 100A on the ES of the Northeast River & N of Limestone Swamp on BS of Tapman's Branch, a drain of Horse Branch. Wit: HICK MILLS, WILLIAM NETHERICK. July Ct. 1784.

p. 42   WILLIAM WHITFIELD, JUNR. of Weane [sic] Co. to JAMES HERRING of Dobbs Co., 19 Aug 1782, for 30 pds. specie 200A on the NS of the Northeast of Cape Fear & on BS of Poley Bridge Branch & on BS of the main road incl. ROBERTS' impr., being a patent granted by RICHARD CASWELL, ESQR. to MICHALL WILKINS 17 Dec 1778 for 200A which sd. WILKINS deeded to WILLIAM WHITFIELD. Wit: JOHN ROOTS, JOHN (+) STANDLEY. July Ct. 1784.

p. 43   LEWIS BROCK to JEREMIAH PEARSALL, both of Duplin Co., 20 July 1784, for 75 pds. specie 266A on the branches of Rockfish Creek in 2 tracts: (1) 166A lying on BS of Taylors Creek, being the upper part of 270A patented by THOMAS KENAN, beg. at a pine & gum in the side of the Gallberry Branch; (2) 100A on the ES of Taylors Creek joining the 1st tract, beg. at a pine N of the Creek his old corner of the afsd. land. Wit: ROBERT TWILLEY, J. ROADS. July Ct. 1784.

p. 45   BAKER (X) BOURDEN of Hanover [sic] Co. to JOHN BRADLEY of Duplin Co., 11 Feb 1784, for 20 pds. specie 300A on the NS of Goshen Swamp & on the White Oak Swamp, beg. at a pine on the edge of WILLIAM BIZZELL'S line, to a stake on WILLIS CHERRY'S line, being the contents of a patent granted to sd. BOURDEN 29 Oct 1782. Wit: PATRICK NORRIS, RICHARD BRADLEY. July Ct. 1784.

p. 47   JOHN (ye) GOFF to RICE MATTHEWS, both planters of Duplin Co., 21 Feb 1783, for 25 pds. specie 100A on the NS of Beaverdam & running to the upper line, to a white oak by the Mill Branch. Wit: JONATHAN PARKER, WILLIAM GOFF. July Ct. 1784.

p. 48   THOMAS (T) PHIPS to LEWIS THOMAS, both planters of Duplin Co., 13 Mar 1784, for 10 pds. 50A, beg. at a sweet gum in Mahunga Swamp along a line of

marked trees agreed upon between sd. PHIPS & sd. THOMAS, to a bay tree about
the middle of a pond, being part of a tract of 200A held by a deed granted to sd.
THOMAS PHIPS by GOV. MARTIN dated 4 Mar 1774. Wit: FELIX FREDERICK,
JONATHAN THOMAS. July Ct. 1784.

p. 50   SAMUEL (*?*) WARD to ROBERT BROCK, both of Duplin Co., 15 Nov 1783,
for 10 pds. specie 320A whereon the sd. BROCK now lives on the head of the Poley
Branch between the Northeast & Goshen Swamp, beg. at a stake in the center of 3
pines on the NS of Poley Branch near sd. BROCK'S house, to a pine on ARTHUR
HERRING'S line, to a pine on SULLIVAN'S line, being the upper half of a tract of
640A granted to sd. WARD by patent dated 1 Apr 1780. Wit: W. DICKSON, JOHN
DICKSON. July Ct. 1784.

p. 51   HENRY NEWKIRK to JOSEPH CANADA, both of Duplin Co., 30 Dec 1780,
for 13 pds. 150A on the ES of the Northeast River & NS of Limestone Swamp, beg.
at a maple in the edge of the swamp at ANTHONY LEWIS' line, to a pine THANK-
FUL HICKS' corner, granted to sd. NEWKIRK by RICHARD CASWELL, ESQR. by
patent dated 1 July 1779. Wit: ROBERT SOUTHERLAND, ABRAHAM NEWKIRK.
July Ct. 1784.

p. 53   WILLIAM (W) SAVAGE, ARTHUR SAVAGE, & MARTHA PERKINS of Duplin
Co. to NICHOLAS HUNTER of same, 10 June 1784, for 160 pds. 150A beg. at a
large red oak by the Grove Swamp where a former survey was began, along JOHN
MILLER'S old line of the marked trees, being the contents of a deed from MR. Mc
CULOCH to FRANCIS SAVAGE, SENR. Wit: ROBERT DICKSON, JNO. DICKSON.
July Ct. 1784.

p. 55   THOMAS WORLEY of Onslow Co. to ANTHONY MILLER of Duplin Co., 19
Feb 1784, for 400 pds. specie 570A in 2 tracts: (1) on the ES of the Northeast River
beg. at a pine sd. WORLEY'S & LOFTEN WORLEY'S dividing corner & along JOHN
MESSER'S old line, to a dividing corner between THOMAS WORLEY & JOHN WEED-
ING; (2) small survey joining the old lines beg. at a pine. Wit: LOFTIS WORLEY,
ANTHONY (A) JONES, JOHN WOODWARD. July Ct. 1784.

p. 57   NICHOLAS BRYAN to ANDREW WALLACE, both planters of Duplin Co.,
15 Oct 1783, for 30 pds. 58A lying on a branch of Stocking Head Swamp, beg. at a
poplar & black gum in the branch, to a pine by TIMOTHY MURPHY'S line. Wit:
JOSEPH COOK. July Ct. 1784.

p. 58   JOSEPH (*`?`*) JOHNSTON to FRANCIS JOHNSTON, both of Duplin Co., 30
May 1777, for 120 pds. proc. 228A, being on a branch of the Golden Grove Swamp,
being known as Buckskin Branch, lying on the head of sd. branch, beg. at sd.
JOHNSTON'S upper corner, being part of 71, 160 A granted to HENRY McCULLOCH
ESQR. by patent dated 3 Mar 1745. Wit: DAVID GREEN, JOHN JOHNSTON.
Jan. Ct. 1781.

p. 59   FRANCIS JOHNSTON, cooper, to DAVID GREEN, both of Duplin Co., 2
June 1777, for 20 pds. 228A, being on a branch of the Golden Grove Swamp, known
by name of Buckskin Branch, beg. at sd. JOHNSTON'S upper corner, being in part
of 71, 160A granted to HENRY McCULLOCH, ESQR. by patent dated 3 Mar 1745.
Wit: JOHN AUSTON, JOHN GREEN, CHARLES WARD. Jan. Ct. 1781.

p. 61   DENNIS (X) CANNON to KEDAR BRYAN, both of Duplin Co., 14 Sep 1784, for 100 pds. current money of N. C. 200A on the NS of Stewart's Creek & on the ES of Cow Marsh, beg. at a persimmon at the run of the Cow Marsh, down the sd. run as it meanders to Buck Hall Swamp along JOHN ADKINSON'S, JAMES WILLIAMS' corner, half the contents of a patent of 400A granted to BENJAMIN WILLIAMS by patent dated 29 Apr 1768. Wit: JOHN ARMSTRONG, ROBERT WILLIAMS. Oct. Ct. 1784.

p. 62   DAVID CANNON to KEDAR BRYAN, both of Duplin Co., 14 Sep 1784, for 70 pds. current money 200A on the NS of Stewart's Creek & on the ES of Buck Hall Swamp beg. at Cow Marsh Branch on DAVID THOMPSON'S old line, to a pine Mc CULLOCH'S corner, it being one half of a tract of 400A granted to BENJAMIN WILLIAMS by patent dated 29 Apr 1768, & since by a deed made over to DENNIS CANNON & by sd. CANNON to DAVID CANNON. Wit: W. SHARPLES, SAML. WILLIAMS. Oct. Ct. 1784.

p. 64   JOHN BECK, JUNR. of Wayne Co. to THOMAS GRAY of Duplin Co., atty. at law, 1 Aug 1784, for 500 pds. 3 tracts on the NS of Goshen Swamp: (1) 220A beg. at a black gum at the run of Goshen Swamp by the mouth of Grantham's Branch joining HINNARD'S & HAINS'ES lines, being part of 580A patented by ROBERT WARREN & conveyed to sd. BECK 21 Oct 1777; (2) 150A joining the 1st tract beg. at a pine by Grantham's Branch, sd. WARREN'S corner tree, & FRAZER'S line, granted to JONATHAN TAYLOR 24 May 1773 & by sd. TAYLOR deeded to sd. BECK 3 Nov 1776; (3) 50A beg. at a stake by 3 marked pines at sd. TAYLOR'S corner, along MICAJAH HILL'S line, & along the lines of GEORGE FRAZER, JOSEPH TURBUVILLE & sd. TAYLOR'S corner, granted 15 Dec 1778. Wit: SAMUEL SLOCUMB, EDMUND BLACKMAN. Oct. Ct. 1784.

p. 66   JAMES MORRIS & EASTER MORRIS to DANIEL HICKS, 16 Oct 1784, for 70 pds. 300A on the ES of the Six Runs & WS of Stewart's Creek on the head of the Marsh Branch that runs into WILLIAMS Mill Branch about half a mile above the mill. Wit: ROBERT WILLIAMS, JOHN DOUGLESS, THEOPHILUS WILLIAMS. Oct. Ct. 1784.

p. 67   JOHN SULIVANT of Duplin Co. to STEPHEN GUFFORD, 22 Nov 1782, for 100 pds. 200A in the fork of the Northeast & Goshen & on the head of a branch called Ned's Branch. Wit: ANDREW GUFFORD, JAMES GUFFORD. Oct. Ct. 1784.

p. 69   THEOPHILUS WILLIAMS to RALEY MILLS, both of Duplin Co., 26 Jan 1784, for 50 pds. specie 50A on the SS of the Bear Swamp on the Meeting Branch, beg. at a post oak on the WS of the Cattail Marsh, to CHARLES HINES' corner, being part of 350A purchased by FREDERICK BELL of HENRY McCULLOCH of his large survey. Wit: DAVID CANNON, WM. NEWTON. Oct. Ct. 1784.

p. 70   HANCOCK (H) HATCHER to DANIEL HICKS, 27 May 1784, for 50 pds. 50A on the WS of Buck Hall Swamp about a mile & half below the courthouse, being part of a piece of land patented by HENRY McCULLOCH & conveyed by him to DAVID THOMPSON dec'd, who willed to WILLIAM THOMPSON who conveyed to sd. HATCHER, beg. at a white oak on the branch of Buck Hall the sd. HATCHER'S & sd. HICKS' corner of a piece of land patented by sd. HICKS, & running down the sd. branch to Buck Hall Swamp, to a stake on HICKS' line of a piece of land patented by JOSEPH WILLIAMS. Wit: THOMAS HICKS, SOLOMON HINES. Oct. Ct. 1784.

p. 72   THEOPHILUS WILLIAMS, High Shff of Duplin Co. to KILBY FAISON of same, 1 Nov 1784, for 90 pds. specie 400A being the prop of HENRY EUSTACE Mc CULLOCH, heir at law to the estate of HENRY McCULLOCH (now confiscated), which sd. 400A is on the ES of the Six Runs & the upper side of Gaylor's Branch, beg. at a water oak & white oak on the bank of the Six Runs Creek at JAMES FAISON'S lower corner, JOSEPH HERRING'S line & joining DANIEL NANCE'S & CURTIS IVEY'S land. The Court awarded 481 pds. 5 shill, plus cost of 2 pds. 6 shill to WILLIAM McCANNE for debt & damages in a suit against HENRY EUSTACE Mc CULLOCH, owner of the sd. land which was purchased by sd. KILBY FAISON at a public auction 1 Nov 1782. Wit: MICHAEL J. KENAN, JAMES THOMPSON. Oct. Ct. 1784.

p. 74   PHILLIP (P) ROUSE & ELIZABETH MARY ROUSE, his wife, cannot live happily together. They agree to a separation with PHILLIP giving his wife all the prop. that he got from her at the time of their marriage, consisting of stock, furn., & household items, etc. Dated 4 Oct 1784. Wit: WM. BEST, JAS. EVANS, ELIZABETH (𝒴) ROUSE. Oct. Ct. 1784.

p. 75   THEOPHILUS WILLIAMS, High Shff of Duplin Co. to JOHN SULLIVEN of same, 19 Nov 1782, for 15,000 pds. current money 200A in the fork of the Northeast & Goshen & on the head of a branch called Ned's Branch, being the land of WILLIAM HINES. The Court awarded 29,600 pds. plus costs of 3 pds. 12 shill. 7 pence to sd. SULLIVEN for debt in a suit against sd. HINES, sd. SULLIVEN being the highest bidder for the land at a public auction held 16 July 1782. Wit: MARY (W) MUNK, ANDREW GUFFIRD. Oct. Ct. 1784.

p. 77   ELIZABETH (✚) ELLIOT to JAMES WRIGHT, both of Duplin Co., 3 Aug 1784, for 20 pds. 320A on BS of the main head branches of Mahunga, beg. at a pine FELIX FREDERICK'S corner tree, to a pine joining ROBERT WILKINSON'S line, being part of the contents of a patent granted to WILLIAM ELLIOT for 640A dated 9 Nov 1779. Wit: WILLIAM NEWTON, PATRICK NEWTON, JOHN NEWTON. Oct. Ct. 1784.

p. 79   JAMES LOCKHART to NICHOLAS HUNTER, both of Duplin Co., 11 Sep 1784, for 55 pds. currency of N. C. 612A on the WS of the Northeast Branch of the Cape Fear on the back of the WIDOW BURTON'S land opposite the mouth of Limestone Creek, beg. at a pine on the SS of Persimmon Swamp about a mile from the river, to a stake in the Great Pocoson, to a pine near JACOB HANCHEY'S land, patented to JOHN RUTHERFORD, ESQR. 28 Oct 1765. Wit: HUGH McCANNE, JAMES PICKET. Oct. Ct. 1784.

p. 80   RICHARD PARKER to HENRY PICKET, both of Duplin Co., 5 May 1783, for 10 pds. specie 25A, being part of the 200A where the sd. PARKER now lives & where the late SOLOMON PARKER died, on the NS of Muddy Creek, beg. at a gum at sd. NS of the creek & adj. HENRY PICKET'S line. Wit: JAS. LOCKHART, LEWIS GOFF. Oct. Ct. 1784.

p. 82   WILLIAM (✚) SULLIVEN to JOHN SULLIVEN, JUNR., both of Duplin Co., 21 Apr 1783, for 90 pds. specie 400A in the fork of the Northeast & Goshen & on the head of Outlaw's Marsh, beg. at a stake JOHN SULLIVEN'S corner on the NS of Outlaw's Marsh & crossing Ground Nut & Narrow Marsh Branch, to a stake on JOHN

SULLIVEN'S line. Wit: DEMPSEY TAYLOR, CASEN (X) HARRIS, NATHAN (N) BULLARD. Oct. Ct. 1784.

p. 84   ELIJAH (X) BOWEN to SAMUEL SOWELL, both of Duplin Co., 10 July 1784, for 12 pds. 100A on the ES of the Northeast between the Great Branch & Matthews Branch incl. his impr. Wit: SHADRICK SOWELL, WILLIAM ROBERTS. Oct. Ct. 1784.

p. 85   DANIEL HERRING to STEPHEN HERRING, both of Duplin Co., 25 Oct 1783, for 110 pds. specie 3A on the NS of Goshen Swamp & on BS of Herring's Branch incl. a grist mill on it, the sd. DANIEL HERRING having had an order of the Court for the sd. mill Aug 1766. Wit: ARTHUR HERRING, WILLIAM O'DANIEL, ALEX.(+) O'DANIEL. Oct. Ct. 1784.

p. 86   JOSEPH WINFIELD of Wayne Co. to BENJAMIN COKWELL of Duplin Co., 18 Aug 1784, for 20 pds. specie 150A on the NS of the Northeast Marsh & NS of the Horsepen Pocoson, granted to sd. JOSEPH WINFIELD 17 Dec 177?. Wit: URH. BLANSHARD, SAMUEL ROGERS. Oct. Ct. 1784.

p. 88   SAMUEL (℈) WARD to WILLIAM HARRIS HAMES, both of Duplin Co., 20 Oct 1784, for 20 pds. specie 200A on the Northeast Swamp joining WILLIAM DUN- CAN'S & REUBEN JONSON'S [sic] line, beg. at a pine on REUBEN JOHNSTON'S corner & DRAPER'S line. Wit: JOHN BRADLEY, HARDY REAVES. Oct. Ct. 1784.

p. 88   JOHN SULLIVEN, JUNR. of Duplin Co. to JAMES HERRING of Dobbs Co., 29 Feb 1784, for 40 pds. current money 300A in the fork of the Northeast & Goshen & the branch called Ned's Branch, beg. at a stake JOHN SULLIVEN'S corner on the NS of Outlaw's Marsh, WILLIAM SULLIVEN'S line. Wit: JONATHAN (X) TAYLOR, REBEKAH (X) BULLARD. Oct. Ct. 1784.

p. 90   JAMES (H) TAYLOR of Duplin Co. to ABSALOM LANGSTON of Wayne Co., 3 Oct 1782, for 30 pds. specie 160A on a branch of Buck Marsh called Cabbin Branch. Wit: LEWIS HINES, ISAAC HINES, THOMAS JOHNSON. Oct. Ct. 1784.

p. 91   ABSALOM LANGSTON to WILLIAM WILKINS, both of Duplin Co., 20 Dec 1783, for 40 pds. specie 160A on a branch of Buck Marsh called Cabbin Branch. Wit: LEWIS HINES, ELIZABETH (X) KENT (?). Oct. Ct. 1784.

p. 92   CLIFTON (℮) BOWEN to JOHN BLANTON, both planters of Duplin Co., 2 Oct 1783, for 20 pds. proc 100A on the WS of the Northeast River & on the N. S. of Doctors Creek, beg. at a pine on his line of another survey. Wit: ELIJAH (℮) BOWEN, DANIEL ALDERMAN. Oct. Ct. 1784.

p. 94   JAMES RAWLINS to JOHN BLANTON, both planters of Duplin Co., 3 Oct 1783, for 20 pds. proc. a tract on the NS of Doctors Creek, a branch of Rockfish Creek. Wit: ELIJAH (℮) BOWEN, DANIEL ALDERMAN. Oct. Ct. 1784. (Acreage not listed.)

p. 95   JONATHAN (+) TAYLOR to BENJAMIN HERRING, both of Duplin Co., 14 Oct 1783, for 40 pds. specie 200A between the Northeast & Goshen on the head of one of Ned's Branches called the Rice Ground Branch, patented by sd. TAYLOR 4 May 1769. Wit: WILLIAM O'DANIEL, CHARITY (X) HERRING. Oct. Ct. 1784.

28. BEST, JOHN (CR.035.801.1/A-13)
10 May 1798 - Jul Term 1799
wife HANNAH all of my estate & at her death my Executors to rais out of my
Estate before it is divided so much as will pay my seven oldest Children
who have married and left the sum of ten shillings - that is to say PATTY,
BENJAMIN, JOHN, REBECCA, ELISABETH, ABSOLUM & HOWEL; residue to be divided
between my three youngest sons HENRY, ETHELDRED & REDDIN; son HENRY to
have lower part of land where it Joins ROBERT WILLIAMS; son ETHELDRED
upper part where it Joins CHARLES WARD; son REDDEN the middle or Centar
part of my Land which Contains my buildings & other improvements
extrs: sons BENJAMIN & ABSOLEM
wit: EDWD PEARSALL, HENRY BEST
                    signed: John ✗ Best

29. BEST, PRUDENCE (CR.035.801.1/3-120)
2 Mar 1859 - Jul Term 1867
dau. ELISABETH who has continued to live with & take care of me my Loom
and all its fixteres, 1 Cow & Calf, 1 Sow & Pigs and all Household &
Kitchen firniture; residue divided amongst my children JACOB, BARBARA
GRADY, REBEKAH GRADY & ELISABETH
extr: dau. ELISABETH
wit: JERE. PEARSALL, JEMIMA H. PEARSALL
                    signed: Prudence ✗ Best

30. BEST, REDDEN (CR.035.801.1/2-115)
15 Jul 1851 - Apr Term 1857
son BENJAMIN 150 acres adj. land whereon I live, ABSALEM BEST, HARPER
WILLIAMS & the main run of Nahonja Swamp; son WILLIAM H. 150 acres adj.
land given to son BENJAMIN, one grindstone & one sorrel colt which he now
claims; daus. MARTHA & ELLEN K. 34 acres whereon I now live including my
dwelling House, all out houses and other improvements, negro named Statira
& her child Mary, all fowls & poultry, 2 mares or horses, 1 cart, all tools,
saddle, bridle, Household & kitchen furniture, all crops and provisions at
hand; daus. now married BETSEY, the wife of JAMES BROWN, HANNAH wife of
MORRIS GUY, POLLY wife of THOMAS PHILLIP & SUSAN wife of ALEXR. CHAMBERS
$50 each; sons ABSALOM & HOWEL 50¢ each which seems together with the
advancements they have had from me will make theirs a fair and equitable
portion
extr: son WILLIAM H.
wit: JOHN J. KELLY, ROBERT STOKES
                    signed: Redden ✗ Best

31. BEST, WILLIAM (CR.035.801.1/A-44)
20 Oct 1790- Jan Term 1791
wife CATHIRINE use of all my estate until son JOHN is of age or marries
and she to raise & school my children [not named] at the Descretion of my
Executors and when each child comes of age or marries shall recieve a part
of my estate
extrs: wife CATHERINE, JAMES KENAN, WILLIAM FREDERICK
wit: G. MORREY [?], CHA. WARD, FELIX FREDERICK
signed: Wm Best

p. 108   SUTTON BYRD of Craven Co., S. C., planter, to LEWIS THOMAS of Duplin Co., planter, 15 Jan 1785, for 40 pds. in gold & silver 210A, beg. at a black
gum in Nahunga Swamp on the NS, beging the corner of a tract formerly laid off for
JESSE JERNAGAN, but now LEWIS THOMAS' corner. (Mentions MR. MOLTEN'S
line & POWELL'S field) The sd. 210A was conveyed from HENRY McCULLOCH,
ESQR. to SUTTON BYRD (date not given). Wit: JAS MIDDLETON, DAVID MID-
DLETON. Jan. Ct. 1785.

p. 110   SAMUEL SOWELL to JOHN BARNET, both planters of Duplin Co., 15 Jan
1785, for 40 pds. currency 100A on the ES of the Northeast between the Great &
Matthew Branches, incl. the impr. where the WIDOW BOWING [sic] formerly lived,
being the land patented by ELIJAH BOWEN & from him deeded to sd. SOWELL.
Wit: GEORGE SMITH, SHADRICK SOWELL. Jan. Ct. 1785.

p. 112   JAMES MOORE to THOMAS HILL, both of Duplin Co., 3 Mar 1785, for
125 pds. current money of N. C. 98A beg. at a gum & white oak on the run of Bear
Swamp, the dividing corner between the sd. MOORE & JOHN MOORE, it being part
of a tract formerly deeded from HENRY EUSTACE McCULLOCH to JOHN MOORE
& since by the L. W. & T. of the sd. JOHN MOORE became the prop. of sd.
JAMES MOORE, being subdivided & laid off for him agreeable to the will of sd.
JOHN MOORE. Wit: W. DICKSON, THOS. ROUTLEDGE. Apr. Ct. 1785.

p. 114   JAMES PEARSALL of Duplin Co. to the CHAIRMAN OF THE COURT OF
DUPLIN CO., 21 Jan 1785, for 5 pds. current money, 4A of land on PEARSALL'S
planta. on the Grove, for the purpose of building a courthouse prison & stocks for
the use of Duplin Co., which tract begins at a sweet gum on the edge of sd. PEAR-
SALL'S Spring Branch 50 feet below the spring. Wit: W. DICKSON, P. BALLERD.
Jan. Ct. 1785.

p. 115   ALEXANDER LANE to WILLIAM KENAN, both planters of Duplin Co., 5
Nov 1784, for 500 pds. specie 430A, being the land whereon the sd. LANE now
lives, on the SS of Nahunga Swamp, beg. at a stake at the run of the swamp & runs
to GEORGE COOPER'S line, along EPHRAIM BOYD'S line, LEWIS THOMAS' corner formerly ABRAHAM MOLTEN'S corner. Wit: THOMAS HILL, JOHN HILL.
Jan. Ct. 1785.

p. 117   JAMES WILLIAMS & wife ELEE (A) WILLIAMS to JAMES GILLESPIE, all
of Duplin Co., 4 Dec 1784, for 330 pds. specie 500A, beg. at a red oak on the SS
of Marsh Branch by the head of a small branch, being a tract purchased by sd.
WILLIAMS of HENRY McCULLOH, ESQR. 7 Nov in the 7th yr. of the reign of
GEORGE III. Wit: JAMES JAMES, JOHN ARMSTRONG, JOHN DUGLESS.
Jan. Ct. 1785.

p. 119   MARGARET (X) NEW, widow, to JOHN HILL, both of Duplin Co., 3 Jan
1785, for 16 pds. current money 200A on the SS of Goshen Swamp, it being the land
& planta. whereon the sd. MARGARET now lives & which she holds by virtue of the
L. W. & T. of her late husb. JOHN NEW dec'd for the term of her own life. Wit:
WM. KENAN, EDWARD HARRIS. Jan. Ct. 1785.

p. 121   JAMES KENAN to ANDREW THALLY, both of Duplin Co., 8 Jan 1785, for
80 pds. specie currency of N. C. 640A on the WS of the Northeast Branch of the
Cape Fear River on BS of Maxwell Swamp & on the road from Sarecta to the WELCH

tract, beg. at a white oak on the SE side of the swamp, it being the contents of a
patent granted 8 June 1739 to ELIAZER ALLEN, ESQR. dec'd, & conveyed by the
Exrs. of MRS. SARAH ALLEN late of New Hanover Co. dec'd to JOHN THALLY 23
Feb 1763, & from sd. THALLY to JAMES KENAN 18 June 1770. Wit: WM. KENAN,
ABRAHAM MOLTEN. Jan. Ct. 1785.

p. 122   WM. HURST (WILLIAM) to WILLIAM BURNUM, both of Duplin Co., 18 Aug
1784, for 50 pds. specie money 150A in 2 tracts: (1) 100A on the NS of Goshen
Swamp, being part of a tract patented by JOHN BECK 27 Apr 1767 & part of sd. land
patented by JOHN CARTER 6 Nov 1779, beg. at a white oak & maple in the fork of
Rattlesnake & North Prong; (2) 50A being part of 300A patented by JOHN CARTER 6
Nov 1779, beg. at a white oak WILLIAM UNDERHILL'S corner, to WIGGIN'S corner.
Wit: JAMES OATES, THOMAS WIGGINS, WYATT OATES. Jan. Ct. 1785.

p. 123   THOMAS WIGGINS, planter, to NATHANIEL KINNARD, bricklayer, both
of Duplin Co., 5 Jan 1785, for 15 pds. specie money 40A on the NS of Goshen Swamp,
beg. at a stake at the mouth of Tylor's Branch, to a white oak KINNARD'S corner,
WM. STEPHENS' line to the beg. Wit: WILLIAM HURST, JOHN BECK, WILLIAM
BECK. Jan. Ct. 1785.

p. 125   WILLIAM (A) ALLEN to ROBERT DICKSON, both of Duplin Co., 11 Sep
1784, for 30 pds. 300A on BS of a branch of Island Creek known by the name of
Cook's Creek, incl. the planta. whereon WILLIAM ALLEN now lives. Wit: CADER
HARRELL, JOHN DICKSON. Apr. Ct. 1785.

p. 126   THOMAS TAYLOR, planter, to ELISHA JONES, both of Duplin Co., 25 Aug
1784, for 20 pds. specie money 325A on the SS of the Northeast Swamp & on the
drains of Rattlesnake Branch, beg. at a white oak at CONSTANTINE WHITFIELD'S
corner, to a white oak ANTHONY JONES' corner, to a stake on HENRY GOODMAN'S
line. Wit: JAMES GOODMAN, STEPHEN JONES. Jan. Ct. 1785.

p. 128   TIMOTHY (X) MURPHY to JAMES PEARSALL, ESQR., both of Duplin Co.,
17 Jan 1785, for 100 pds. current money of N. C. 2 pieces of land: (1) 200A
granted to sd. MURPHY by patent dated 4 Dec 1744, on the WS of the Northeast
Branch of Cape Fear River near Elder Branch, beg. at a large white oak near the
head of Stocking Head Branch; (2) 100A, being part of a tract of 200A granted by
patent to JACOB & HENRY WELLS between JOHN MILLER'S land on Stocking Head
Branch & TIMOTHY MURPHEY'S own line, whereas by indenture dated 3 Jan 1764
by deed was executed, WILLIAM LAYCOCK then of Duplin Co. sold & conveyed unto
the sd. MURPHY. Wit: JAMES LOCKHART, DANIEL TEACHY. Jan. Ct. 1785.

p. 130 CHARLES (M) MERRIT to BENJAMIN EZZELL, both of Duplin Co., 22 Dec
1784, for 20 pds. current money of N. C. 100A on the ES of Stewart's Creek, being
part of 3 surveys, beg. at a pine the 3rd corner of his 150A survey to HENRY
HOLLINGSWORTH'S corner, & part of another new survey to a stake by a blue pond
on the sd. line of sd. survey, to a pine & black jack at the corner by the Juniper
Pond. Wit: ARTHUR (X) MATHEWS, WILLM. KNIGHT. Jan. Ct. 1785.

p. 131   ANDREW (Ⓓ) WILSON to JOHN GREEN, both planters of Duplin Co., 16
Sep 1783, for 45 pds. current money 150A on the SS of Goshen Swamp on a branch of
Maple Swamp, incl. his own impr., beg. at a red oak by his field, as by patent 25
Sep 1766. Wit: ISAAC HUNTER, NICHOLAS ROUTLEDGE. Apr. Ct. 1785.

p. 133   RICHARD MUNDS of Duplin Co. to EDWARD CARTER of Dobbs Co., 18
Oct 1784, for 100 pds. specie 300A on the N of the Northeast & in the fork of Buck
Marsh & Poley Bridge Branch, beg. at a pine on his own line, to a stake on JESSE
PIPKIN's line, to a stake on the run of Buck Marsh on RODGER'S line. Wit:
STEPHEN BRADDY, SOLOMON CARTER. Apr. Ct. 1785.

p. 134   WILLIAM GRADDY to SOLOMON CARTER, both of Duplin Co., 5 Feb
1782, for 20,000 pds. currency of N. C. 100A on the SS of Matthews Branch, being
the planta. where WILLIAM BOWEN formerly lived. Wit: RICHARD (X) MUNDS,
JAMES BOURN, ELISABETH GRADDY. Apr. Ct. 1785.

p. 136   THEOPHILUS (T) SWINSON to JOHN MATCHET, both of Duplin Co., 22
Mar 1785, for 55 pds. current money 250 acres on the SS of Goshen Swamp, beg. at
the mouth of the Briery Branch marked trees M. B. & W. B., to a pine ANTHONY
MILLER'S & GEORGE MILLER'S corner, JOSEPH WELLS' corner, the upper tract
of land granted to BENJAMIN FULSAM 1767. Wit: CHAS. WARD, ANTHY.
MILLER. Apr. Ct. 1785.

p. 136   LEWIS BARNES to ANTHONY JONES, both of Duplin Co., 13 Feb 1785,
for 14 pds. land (acreage not given) on the ES of the Northeast River on BS of the
road & Burncoat Swamp, beg. at a stake in the swamp ANTHONY JONES' corner,
to a pine along SAMUEL JONES' line, along ADAMS' line, to a pine on the edge of
Cow Hole Branch, to a pine on GEORGE SMITH'S line. Wit: ANTHONY MILLER,
FREDERICK SMITH. Apr. Ct. 1785.

p. 137   WILLIAM MAGEE of Duplin Co. to JOHN MAGEE (co. not given) 23 Nov
1784, 75 pds. specie 400A on the Marsh Branch joining Muddy Creek where the sd.
WILLIAM MAGEE formerly lived in 3 planta. to wit: (1) on the SS of Marsh Branch;
(2) on the NS of same branch where JOHN MAGEE'S store is; (3) one in the fork of
same branch, being the tracts of land that WILLIAM MAGEE bought of JOHN
WOODWARD. The sd. 400A joined the lines of JOHN WOODWARD, JACOB BROWN,
RICHARD KEEN, EBENEZAR GARRISON. Wit: WILLIAM FARRIOR, ANDREW
LAWS, JOHN FARRIOR. Apr. Ct. 1785.

p. 139   ABNER QUIN of Cartright [sic] Co. to WILLIAM NETHERCUT of Duplin
Co., 4 Sep 1783, for 30 pds. specie 100A on the NS of Limestone Swamp & on BS
of Cabbin Branch incl. his impr., beg. at a post on the ES of sd. branch, CHARLES
MUMFORD'S corner & ANTHONY MILLER'S line, formerly granted to sd. QUIN by
patent dated 1 July 1779. Wit: CALEB (X) QUIN, WILLIAM NETHERCUT. Apr.
Ct. 1785.

p. 141   FREDERICK GLISSON to JESSE BROCK, both planters of Duplin Co., 6
Dec 1783, for 20 pds. 100A on the NS of Goshen Swamp on the Mill Branch, beg. at
a black gum by the run in sd. branch, to a stake on WILLIAM TAYLOR'S line, to a
pine on WILLIAM PARKER'S line. Wit: JOHN SWINSON, JOHN ROGERS. Apr.
Ct. 1785.

p. 143   WILLIAM ROUTLEDGE & ESTHER ROUTLEDGE his wife of New Hanover
Co. to EDWARD PEARSALL of Duplin Co., 11 June 1785, for 225 pds. specie,
251A on the NS of the Grove Swamp incl. part of 3 surveys: (1) part of a survey of
JOHN MILLER, JUNR.; (2) part of a survey of 100A sold by HENRY EUSTACE Mc
CULLOCH to EDWARD MATCHET; (3) part of a patent of 140A granted to WILLIAM

ROUTLEGE. The sd. 3 pieces of land beg. at a maple on the NS of Grove Swamp
below the bridge called McCulloch's Maple Corner, along the main road with
SMITH'S line to the run of Mill Branch, divided as follows: (1) 100A by deed dated
8 Sep 1767 from JOHN MATCHET to WILLIAM ROUTLEDGE; (2) 100A by deed
dated 23 Aug 1768 from JOHN MILLER, JUNR. to WILLIAM ROUTLEDGE; (3) 141A
being part of a patent granted to sd. ROUTLEDGE. Wit: JAMES PEARSALL,
NICHOLAS ROUTLEDGE. July Ct. 1785.

p. 145   WILLIAM STOKES of Duplin Co. to MAJOR CROOM of Dobbs Co., 1 Dec
1784, for 100 pds. money of N. C. 72A being part of a tract of land granted to
MICHAEL & ROBERT DICKSON, beg. at a water oak on the 1st line of sd. patent
standing at the south of the dividing line made between sd. CROOM & STOKES.
Wit: JOHN NEIL, JOSHUA CROOM. July Ct. 1785.

p. 147   ABRAHAM KORNEGAY of Jones Co. to WILLIAM WHITFIELD, SENR. of
Wayne Co., 17 July 1785, for 40 pds. specie 200A in 2 tracts: (1) 100A on the NS
of the Northeast Swamp patented by GEORGE KORNEGAY 13 Oct 1745; (2) 100A,
same location as the 1st tract, granted to sd. GEORGE KORNEGAY 27 Sep 1756.
Wit: BRYAN WHITFIELD, NM. WHITFIELD. July Ct. 1785.

p. 149   LEWIS GRADDY of Duplin Co. to WILLIAM WHITFIELD, JUNR. of Wayne
Co., 11 Dec 1783, for 160 pds. current money 148A on the SS of the Northeast
Branch of Cape Fear & on the ES of the Beaverdam Branch, incl. the planta. where-
on the sd. GRADDY liveth. Wit: MICHAEL (O) GLISSON, WILLIAM WHITFIELD,
JOSEPH WHITFIELD. July Ct. 1785.

p. 150   HENRY HOLLINGSWORTH of Sampson Co. to HARDY CARROLL of Duplin
Co., 25 Mar 1785, for 80pds. 196A on BS of Stewart's Creek, beg. at a pine then
running along the giving line of the patent to a branch called Enzor's Branch. Wit:
CHARLES (M) MERRIT, JAMES HOLLINGSWORTH, ARTHUR (A) MATTHEWS.
July Ct. 1785.

p. 151   RICHARD (T) WILLIAMS to ABRAHAM ANDREWS, both of Duplin Co., 31
July 1784, for 100 pds. specie 100A on the ES of the Northeast Branch of Cape Fear
River on Muddy Creek at a place called Stafford's Folley, being part of a tract
granted to FRANCIS BRICE by patent dated 1745. Wit: NICHOLAS FENNEL,
ROBERT SOUTHERLAND. July Ct. 1785.

p. 153   STEPHEN WILLIAMS to ABRAHAM ANDREWS, both of Duplin Co., 31
July 1784, for 50 pds. specie 50A on a branch of Muddy Creek joining the planta.
he lives on, being part of a survey of land granted to RICHARD WILLIAMS by patent
dated 13 Oct 1765. Wit: NICHOLAS FENNEL, ROBERT SOUTHERLAND.
July Ct. 1785.

p. 155   FREDERICK BEARFIELD to ANDREW GUFFORD, both planters of Duplin
Co., 29 Jan 1785, for 10 pds. specie 100A beg. at a pine in SNIPES' former line to
the head of the Mare Branch, formerly granted to JESSE BEARFIELD. Wit:
STEPHEN GUFFORD, JAMES HERRING. July Ct. 1785.

p. 156   ROBERT MERRIT to ANDREW NEELEY, both of Sampson Co., 2 Mar
1785, for 35 pds. a tract (acreage not given) on the NS of Doctors Creek, a prong
of Rockfish Creek, on BS of the Iron Mine Branch, beg. at a pine on GEORGE

HEARS'ES line. Wit: JACOB (S) SELLERS, NATHIEL MERRIT. July Ct. 1785.

p. 157   RICHARD (T) WILLIAMS, planter, to JEREMIAH WILLIAMS, both of
Duplin Co., 15 Jan 1784, for 150 pds. current money of N. C. 75A being part of a
planta. whereon sd. RICHARD WILLIAMS purchased from JOSEPH WILLSON, beg.
at a red oak, to a corner tree of BARNET BROCK'S. Wit: JOHN (Ŧ) PARKER,
CHARLES (X) GOAFF, JOSEPH WILLSON. July Ct. 1785.

p. 159   JAMES PEARSALL & wife ZILPHA PEARSALL of Duplin Co. to JAMES
JAMES, planter of same, 19 July 1785, for 45 pds. currency 45A in 2 tracts: (1)
20A patented by sd. PEARSALL 10 Nov 1784 on the WS of the Northeast Branch of
Cape Fear River & NS of Maxwell Swamp on the head of Elder Branch, beg. at a
pine ROBERT DICKSON'S corner on JOHN McCULLOH'S line; (2) 25A on the SS of
the Grove Swamp & the SS of Pasture Branch granted to sd. PEARSALL 1 July 1779,
beg. at a pine at the sd. PEARSALL'S own line, to ROBERT MILLER'S line, to a
pine on sd. McCULLOH'S line by ROBERT CLUGSTON'S line. Wit: JOHN CARR,
JAMES EVANS. July Ct. 1785.

p. 161   ADAM PLATT to MOSES HANCHEY, both of Duplin Co., 2 Oct 1779, for
100 pds. currency 100A on the NS of Maxwell Swamp above the mouth of Stocking
Head, beg. at a pine near to HENRY GILLMAN'S line, being the contents of a patent
granted to the sd. PLATT 26 Oct 1767. Wit: JACOB WELLS, HICKS MILLS.
July Ct. 1785.

p. 162   JACOB FUSSELL of Philadelphia, Pa., by his atty. TIMOTHY BLOOD-
WORTH to WILLIAM DUFF of Duplin Co., 10 Apr 1784, for 40 pds. proc. 360A in
2 tracts: (1) 300A beg. at a poplar tree on a branch near the line of BENJAMIN
FUSSELL'S land near Rockfish Creek; (2) 60A beg. at a stake in Rockfish Road.
Wit: JOHN DUFF, THOMAS DEVAN, JUNR. July Ct. 1785.

p. 164   JOHN PARKER to WILLIAM BEVAN, both of Duplin Co., 10 May 1785,
for 20 pds. specie of N. C. 160A on the WS of Rockfish Creek, incl. JOHN PARK-
ER'S survey that joins DANIEL BOWEN'S line & EDWARDS' survey, beg. at a holly
in the mouth of Cabbin Branch & patented by sd. PARKER 29 Oct 1782. Wit: JOHN
BONNEY, JOSEPH BEVAN. July Ct. 1785.

p. 165   JAMES EVANS to GEORGE MALLARD, both of Duplin Co., 1 Jan 1785,
for 5 pds. currency 50A on the WS of the Northeast River & on BS of Platts Branch,
a drain of Horse Branch, beg. at a pine ABSALOM STRICKLAND'S corner, to a
large pine by JAMES MIDDLETON'S line. Wit: ROBERT DICKSON, JAMES
DICKSON. July Ct. 1785.

p. 166   JAMES MAXWELL to JAMES McINTIRE, both of Duplin Co., 1 Dec 1784,
for 95 pds. specie 300A in 2 tracts: (1) 100A on the WS of the Northeast Branch of
Cape Fear River on Horse Branch, being the contents of a patent granted to
JOSEPH DUKES 1 Apr 1780; (2) 200A(same location), beg. at a white oak GEORGE
MALLARD'S corner, ARTHUR STOKES' corner, DUKE'S line & JAMES GILLES-
PIE'S line, also being the contents of a patent dated 1 Apr 1780. Wit: STEPHEN
TILLMAN, JOHN NEIL. July Ct. 1785.

p. 167   WILLIAM SOUTHERLAND to ABRAHAM NEWKIRK, both of Duplin Co.,
14 Mar 1785, for 500 pds. 75A on the ES of the Northeast River & on the SS of

Limestone Creek, beg. at a birch on the WS of sd. creek at FRANCIS BRYCE'S lower corner, to a pine at SAMUEL JOHNSTON'S line, to JOHN ATKIN'S corner, being part of a tract granted to WILLIAM FOLSOM by patent dated 3 Sep 1766 & conveyed from him to PHILL SOUTHERLAND who conveyed to sd. WILLIAM SOUTHERLAND. Wit: NATHANL. McCANNE, DANIEL SOUTHERLAND, NICHOLAS ROUTLEDGE. July Ct. 1785.

p. 170   JONATHAN (X) DAVIS to DAVID DAVIS his son, both of Duplin Co., for "natural love and affection" & 20 shill. specie, 1 Mar 1784, 50A on the SS of Rockfish Creek, being part of a patent for 300A granted to JAMES COOK. Wit: JOSEPH DICKSON, JOHN LITTLE, JOHN (Ŧ) BLANTON. July Ct. 1785.

p. 171   JOHN COOK to EMANUEL BOWZER, both of Duplin Co., 23 Apr 1785, for 10 pds. current money of N. C. 250A on the SS of Bland Creek, beg. at a pine the 2nd corner of the patent & FREDERICK WELLS' corner & HENRY ALLEN'S, being part of the contents of a patent granted to sd. COOK 10 Nov 1784. Wit: JAMES PEARSALL, JOSEPH DICKSON. July Ct. 1785.

p. 172   JAMES WILLIAMS, SENR. to AUSTEN BEESLEY, both of Duplin Co., 4 Apr 1785, for 5 pds. 50A on the branches of Maxwell Swamp, being the western part to half of a survey of 100A granted to JAMES MIDDLETON 22 July 1774, beg. at a pine sapling SOLOMON BEESLEY'S corner on the 1st line of the patent, by Lawrey's Branch, beyond DICKSON'S & RIGSBEE'S corner, to SOLOMON BEESLEY'S corner. Wit: SOLOMON BEESLEY, DORATHY WILLIAMS. July Ct. 1785.

p. 174   ABRAHAM BEESLEY of New Hanover Co. to THOMAS HEATH of Duplin Co., 20 Dec 1784, for 20 pds. current money of N. C. 83A on the SS of Maxwell Swamp on BS of the main road, beg. at a white oak & 4 pines on the swamp side BEESLEY'S corner. Wit: JAMES (Ŧ) HEATH, WILLIAM (W) BUSH. July Ct. 1785.

p. 175   ANDREW (A) WALLACE to TIMOTHY MURPHY, both of Duplin Co., 10 Mar 1785, for 30 pds. 58A on a branch of Stocking Head, beg. at a poplar & black gum in the branch, to a pine by sd. MURPHY'S line. Wit: NICHOLAS BRYAN. July Ct. 1785.

p. 176   ABRAHAM BEESLEY of New Hanover Co., planter, to JOSEPH WILLSON of Duplin Co., 10 Feb 1785, for 4 pds. current money 100A on the SS of Maxwell Swamp & the NS of Parson's Branch & Cabbin Branch, incl. Taylor's Meadow, beg. at a pine the 3rd corner of JAMES WALLACE'S survey, crossing the Indian Grave Branch, granted to sd. BEESLEY 4 Nov 1784. Wit: JACOB (B) BEBERRT, JAMES (Ŧ) WALLACE. July Ct. 1785.

p. 178   JAMES (X) WALLACE (JUNR.), planter, to JOSEPH WILLSON, both of Duplin Co., 10 Dec 1784, for 26 pds. 180A in 2 tracts: (1) 80A being part or half of 60 acres patented by ROBERT DICKSON 26 Oct 1767 & conveyed by sd. DICKSON to ANDREW WALLACE 1 Jan who deeded to JAMES WALLACE 19 Feb 1778, lying on the SS of Maxwell Swamp & NS of Cabbin Branch & Parson's Branch; (2) 100A in Duplin Co. on the SS of Maxwell Swamp & NS of Cabbin & Parson's Branches, being patented by JAMES WALLACE 19 Nov 1784, part of 200 acres, also on BS of Indian Grave Branch, beg. at a pine on his own line a little above his house, above ROBERT STONE'S corner. Wit: JACOB (B) BEBBERRT, WILLIAM (M) PHILLMAN. July Ct. 1785.

p. 180   JOSEPH WILLSON, planter, to JAMES WALLACE, both of Duplin Co., 10
Dec 1784, for 30 pds. current money of N. C. 250A on the ES of the Northeast
Branch of Cape Fear between Limestone Creek & Muddy Creek in 2 tracts: (1) 100A
joining CHARLES COX & FREDERICK GREGG, patented by PRESIDENT MATTHEW
ROWAN 27 Feb 1754, beg. at a pine sd. GREGG'S corner at the river, near sd.
COX'S corner; (2) 150A joining the 1st tract on the ES of the Northeast Branch of
Cape Fear River, beg. at a water oak on the river bank JOHN BROCK'S lower cor-
ner, to sd. COX'S corner. Wit: JACOB (B) BEBERET, WILLIAM (M) PHILLMET.
July Ct. 1785.

p. 182   STEPHEN BAREFIELD to DAVID CANNON, JUNR., both of Duplin Co.,
16 Nov 1785, for 250 pds. specie 42A on the SS of the Northeast & Rattlesnake
Branch adj. the lines of ELIJAH JONES, JACOB KORNEGAY & ANTHONY JONES
in 4 tracts: (1) 121A on the SS of the Northeast Swamp in the fork of Rattlesnake
Branch, being part of a survey patented by JOHN CONNERLY 2 Apr 1751, beg. at a
small pine in the branch below ANTHONY JONES' field, which lands descended from
sd. CONNERLY to his son CULLEN CONNERLY, who deeded to JESSEE BARE-
FIELD who deeded to CONSTANTINE WHITFIELD 11 Mar 1775; (2) 100A beg. at a
white oak on the SS of the Northeast on Rattlesnake Branch, granted by patent to
EDWARD ROLLINS 29 Sep 1753; (3) 100A adj. the 2nd tract granted by patent to
SOLOMON BAREFIELD 15 Mar 1756, beg. at a pine, a corner tree of his former
survey near Rattlesnake Branch. The last 2 tracts sold & conveyed by WILLIAM
GRADDY & JESSE BAREFIELD to CONSTANTINE WHITFIELD. (4) last tract 100A
on the SS of Rattlesnake Branch, joining the lines of the other lands, being part of a
tract of 200A granted to sd. WHITFIELD 24 May 1773, who deeded all 4 tracts of
421A by deed of gift to his dau. RACHEL GOODMAN 24 Sep 1778 & since from
HENRY GOODMAN & RACHEL his wife to TIMOTHY GOODMAN 24 Oct 1778 & sd.
TIMOTHY GOODMAN deeded to HENRY GOODMAN 26 Oct 1778 & sd. HENRY to
STEPHEN BAREFIELD 25 Oct 1785. Wit: WILLIAM SHARPLESS, ALEXR.
WILLSON. Jan. Ct. 1786.

p. 185   DAVID CANNON, JUNR. to JOHN GIBBS, both of Duplin Co., 11 Apr
1785, for 20 pds. current money 85A on the NS of Goshen Swamp joining the middle
run of sd. swamp & lying between the mouth of Cow Hole Branch & the mouth of
White Oak Branch, beg. at a white oak in the swamp, the upper corner of DENNIS
FOLEY'S survey, to JOHN GIBBS' corner. Wit: D. GLISSON, ALEXR. WILLSON.
Oct. Ct. 1785.

p. 187   ADAM (A) RUNCHEY, weaver, to JOHN COX, both of Duplin Co., 10 Aug
1785, for 30 pds. current money of N. C. 100A on a branch of Maxwell Swamp,
called Elder Branch, beg. at a water oak in Elder Swamp, to GEORGE POWELL'S
line, by patent granted to ADAM RUNCHEY 10 Nov 1784. Wit: JAMES DICKSON,
WILLIAM FLOWERS. Oct. Ct. 1785.

p. 188   SAMUEL (4) TANNER of Duplin Co. to WILLIAM WHITFIELD of Wayne
Co., 6 Oct 1785, for 30 pds. current money of N. C. 100A on the ES of the Northeast Branch of Cape Fear, being part of a patent granted to JESSE BAREFIELD for
200A 22 Dec 1770, beg. at a pine the 2nd corner of sd. patent near to a foard across
Rooty Branch above WILLIAM DANIEL'S planta., to THEOPHILUS WILLIAMS' land
to KORNEGAY'S line, to Smith's Branch, being the planta. where sd. TANNER now
lives which sd. TANNER bought from WILLIAM O'DANIEL 3 Feb 1785. Wit:
WILLIAM WHITFIELD, SARAH (X) BUTON [sic]. Oct. Ct. 1785.

p. 190   WILLIAM O'DANIEL to SAMUEL TANNER, both of Duplin Co., 3 Feb 1785, for 24 pds. specie money 100A on the NS of the Northeast of Cape Fear on the upper side of Smith's Branch lying between THEOPHILUS WILLIAMS' line & joining the sd. branch, being part of 200A taken up by JESSE BARFIELD joining KORNE-GAY'S line & STEPHEN BAREFIELD'S line. Wit: THOMAS TANNER, JOHN DURRELL. Oct. Ct. 1785.

p. 191   ROBERT DICKSON to MARTIN ROUSE, both of Duplin Co., 8 Oct 1784, for "the love of good will and affection" 100A whereon PHILLIP ROUSE now lives in Duplin Co. on the WS of the Northeast River & joining on the SS of Persimmon Swamp, beg. at a black gum on sd. swamp, along GARRISON'S line. Wit: W. DICKSON, JOHN DICKSON. Oct. Ct. 1785.

p. 192   THEOPHILUS WILLIAMS of Duplin Co. to WILLIAM WHITFIELD, SENR. of Wayne Co., 15 Oct 1785, for 50 pds. current money of N. C. 150A on the NS of the Northeast Marsh joining KORNEGAY'S line on the south & STEPHEN BEAR-FIELD'S on the east, beg. at a pine KORNEGAY'S corner in Bales' Branch, toward Rooty Branch, to a pine STEPHEN BARFIELD'S corner, to a white oak in KORNE-GAY'S line, being part of 300A granted by patent to JESSE BEARFIELD 15 Dec 1778 who conveyed to sd. WILLIAMS 24 Jan 1780, incl. the planta. & impr. whereon sd. WILLIAMS then lived. Wit: W. DICKSON, JOHN BRADLEY. Oct. Ct. 1785.

p. 194   GEORGE SMITH of Duplin Co., farmer, to JOHN HERRING of Dobbs Co., farmer, 5 Sep 1782, for 100 pds. in gold & silver 450A in 2 tracts on the SS of the Northeast Marsh & on BS of the Beaverdam Branch above RICHARD ROBERTS' land as was formerly, now LEWIS GRADDY'S: (1) 300A granted to WILLIAM GODWIN 7 Apr 1770; (2) 150A granted to GEORGE SMITH 1780, beg. at a hickory near SAMUEL JOHNSTON'S line on the Myrey Branch, to SAMUEL ROGERS' corner. Wit: JESSE CROOM, WILLIAM SMITH. Oct. Ct. 1785.

p. 195   JACOB KORNEGA to JOHN KORNEGA, both planters of Duplin Co., 23 Mar 1785, for 60 pds. 300A on the NS of the Northeast Branch of Cape Fear River & the SS, beg. at a white oak EDMUND DUNCAN'S corner, to JOHN KORNEGUS corner, along OWEN DANIEL'S line. Wit: EDMUND DUNCAN, JUNR., WILLIAM DUNCAN, ADAM REEVES. (Deed unsigned) Oct. Ct. 1785.

p. 197   REUBEN GREEN to FREDERICK WILLIAMS, both of Duplin Co., 14 Oct 1785, for 32 pds. 10 shill. specie 90A on the SS of Rockfish Creek incl. the sd. GREEN'S impr., beg. at a white oak supposed to be NATHANIEL MERRADITH'S corner, patented by REUBEN GREEN 1784. Wit: AARON WILLIAMS, JAMES RYAN. Oct. Ct. 1785.

p. 198   WILLIAM (W) BIZZEL to ELISHA JERNAGAN, both of Duplin Co., 19 July 1785, for 100 pds. specie 80A on the NS of White Oak Branch, beg. at a maple in sd. branch along BLANSHARD'S line, to a white oak & red oak on NICHOLAS BOURDEN'S line, to Hoop Pole Branch & White Oak Branch, patented to sd. WILLIAM BIZZEL. Wit: D. GLISSON, JOHN GIBBS. Oct. Ct. 1785.

p. 199   SHADRACK STALLINGS to DAVID SLOAN, both of Duplin Co., 4 June 1785, for 50 pds. specie 150A on BS of Parson's Branch, beg. at a dead white oak DAVID SLOAN'S corner, the 50A of the 150A on the SS of Maxwell Swamp & NS of Parson's Branch, beg. at a pine the corner of the remaining 100A. Wit: JAMES

DICKSON, WILLIAM WELLS. (Deed unsigned) Oct. Ct. 1785.

p. 201   MILLS MUMFORD to JOSEPH BRAY, SENR., both of Duplin Co., 4 Mar
1782, for 40 pds. (cash) 200A being part of a tract of 640A granted by patent to sd.
MUMFORD by ALEXANDER MARTIN 10 Nov 1784, beg. on Panther Swamp at the
mouth of Bryar Branch, to Stirrup Branch. Wit: SAMUEL HOUSTON, JUNR.,
JOSEPH BRAY. Oct. Ct. 1785.

p. 203   SHADRACK STALLINGS to DAVID SLOAN, both of Duplin Co., 4 June
1785, for 30 pds. specie 150A, beg. at a pine sd. to be sd. SLOAN'S corner, to a
gum in Sam's Branch, to a stake in the Pocoson. Wit: JAMES DICKSON,
WILLIAM WELLS. Oct. Ct. 1785.

p. 205   ABRAHAM (A) GLISSON to JAMES CHAMBERS, both of Duplin Co., 12
Oct 1785, for 210 pds. current money 500A in 5 tracts: (1) 50A granted to THOM-
AS KENAN by patent dated 28 Feb 1754 & later conveyed to JAMES KENAN who
deeded to sd. GLISSON 13 Jan 1778, lying on a branch of Maxwell called Cabbin
Branch; (2) 150A granted by patent 27 Apr 1767 to JAMES KENAN who conveyed to
sd. GLISSON 13 Feb 1778, sd. land being on the SS of Maxwell Swamp & on BS of
Cabbin Branch joining the 1st tract of 50A; (3) 100A on the WS of the Northeast
Branch of Cape Fear River & SS of Maxwell Swamp in the fork of Parson's Branch
& Cabbin Branch, beg. at a maple & ash at the run of Cabbin Branch by or near to
his corner of 150A patented by JAMES KENAN, joining WILLIAM TELMOT'S line,
granted by patent to ABRAHAM GLISSON 1 July 1779; (4) 100A patented 1 July 1779
by sd. GLISSON on the WS of the Northeast Branch of Cape Fear River on the SS of
Maxwell & Cabbin Branch, joining his own & JOHN HOLDON'S land; (5) 100A on the
WS of the Northeast Branch of Cape Fear River granted to sd. GLISSON 1 July 1779
on the SS of Maxwell & Cabbin Branch. Wit: JOSEPH DICKSON, JAMES
GILLESPIE. Oct. Ct. 1785.

p. 208   THEOPHILUS WILLIAMS of Duplin Co. to JAMES MORRIS of New Hanover
5 Aug 1785, for 500 pds. current money 901A in 4 tracts: (1) 101A on the head of
Bear Swamp joining WILLIAM GRIEG'S line & on BS of the main road, being part of
HENRY McCULLOCH'S large grant dated 3 Mar 1745 & deeded to CHRISTOPHER
BURCH 6 Oct in the 6th yr. of reign of George III., & which sd. BURCH conveyed to
DANIEL WILLIAMS 1 July 1774; (2) 200A joining the 1st tract granted to DANIEL
WILLIAMS 22 July 1774; (3) 300A joining above 2 tracts granted to sd. WILLIAMS
by patent dated 1 Apr 1780 (mentions GRIEG'S corner, WARD'S line & BELL'S
corner); (4) 300A granted 1 Apr 1780 (mentions GRIEG'S corner, ORSON BELL'S
corner, NEWTON'S line). All 4 tracts conveyed by DANIEL WILLIAMS to
THEOPHILUS WILLIAMS 2 Dec 1783. Wit: W. DICKSON, SAML. (S) WARD.
Oct. Ct. 1785.

p. 210   JAMES PEARSALL, High Shff. of Duplin Co., to EPHRAIM GARRASON
of same, 15 Oct 1785, for 25 pds. 1 shill. 100A on the NE side of Stocking Head
Branch joining JOHN MILLER'S line, being the contents of a patent granted to
JACOB HANCHEY 5 Dec 1769 & being the goods & chattels of WILLIAM EGERTON.
The Court awarded 20 pds. 10 shill. plus cost of 3 pds. 2 shill. 7 pence to JAMES
MIDDLETON for debt in a suit against WILLIAM EGERTON, & the sd. GARRASON
became the last & highest bidder of sd. 100A at a public auction held 10 Dec 1784.
Wit: JAMES GILLESPIE, JOSEPH DICKSON. Oct. Ct. 1785.

p. 213 WILLIAM SOUTHERLAND of Duplin Co. to SOLOMON CARTER (co. not given), 18 Jan 1785, for 30 pds. current money 150A on the ES of the Northeast on a branch called Mathews Branch & upon BS of the branch, incl. an old former survey made for ROBERT BISHOP, beg. at a small white oak on the SS of sd. branch & on the west edge of a Juniper Branch, BISHOP'S old corner, STEPHEN BRADDY'S line. Wit: DAVID GREEN, STEPHEN BRADDY. Oct. Ct. 1785.

p. 214 THOMAS CRUMPTON to DAVID HALL, both of Duplin Co., 18 July 1785, for 15 pds. current money of N. C. 150A on the WS of Burrill Hill Branch, beg. at a pine on the swamp side CLIFTEN BOWEN'S corner, BENJAMIN LANIER'S line, being the contents of a patent granted to sd. THOMAS CRUMPTON 29 Oct 1782. Wit: W. DICKSON, JOSEPH DICKSON. Oct. Ct. 1785.

p. 215 HARDY (H) REEVES, planter, to JOHN PROWSE, school master, both of Duplin Co., 27 Aug 1785, for 50 pds. specie 100A on the NS of Hurst Branch, being part of a tract granted to CHRISTOPHER BURCH 22 Feb 1764 & by him conveyed to JOSEPH BURCH who deeded to REUBEN WESTON, & by sd. WESTON to BURRILL BRANCH who deeded to HARDY REEVES. Wit: FRANCIS OLIVER, LEVIN WATKINS. Jan. Ct. 1786.

p. 217 JOHN FOLEY of George Town District, S. C. to FRANCIS OLIVER of Duplin Co., 29 Apr 1785, for 175 pds. specie 325A in 2 tracts: (1) 200A on the NS of Goshen Swamp & on Bear Marsh, beg. at a pine on sd. Marsh, being part of 300 acres granted to sd. FOLEY 17 Mar 1759; (2) 125A joining the 1st tract on BS of Bear Marsh between the 1st 200A & WESTON'S formerly, now BOURDEN'S lands, granted to sd. FOLEY by patent dated 23 Apr 1762. Wit: JOHN WRIGHT, LEVIN WADKINS, ARTHUR BIZZEL. Jan. Ct. 1786.

p. 219 ABRAHAM GLISSON to DAVID CANNON, both of Duplin Co., 7 Dec 1785, for 40 pds. 200A on the ES of the Northeast Branch of Cape Fear River opposite the mouth of Rockfish Creek, incl. a survey formerly made for JOAB HERRINGTON, the 200A being the contents of a patent granted to THOMAS CUMMINGS 27 July 1774. Wit: THOMAS JAMES, SARAH MOLTEN. Jan. Ct. 1786.

p. 220 JEREMIAH CHUBBUCK (co. not given) to THOMAS BENNET of sd. Co. (Duplin?), 28 Aug 1784, for 36 pds. 10 shill. specie 63A on the WS of White Oak Branch, being the land the sd. CHUBBUCK lived on, & between the sd. BENNET'S own land & JACOB MILLER'S land, beg. at a holly & a water oak on the run of White Oak Branch, along sd. BENNETT'S line, to a pine on JACOB TAYLOR'S line, to a white oak CHRISTOPHER BURCH'S corner, patented 1 Apr 1780 to sd. CHUB-BUCK. Wit: JOHN GIBBS, JACOB MILLARD. Jan. Ct. 1786.

p. 222 JOHN (M) WHITMAN to JOHN CRAWFORD, both of Duplin Co., 18 Jan 1785, for 50 pds. specie 141A on the NS of Maxwell Swamp joining the lines of HENRY GILLMAN & ADAM PLATT, beg. at a white oak in the fork of Maxwell & Stocking Head Swamp, to a pine ADAM PLATT'S corner, to a water oak on HENRY GILLMAN'S line, being the contents of a patent granted to sd. WHITMAN 1 July 1779. Wit: THOMAS ROUTLEDGE, JOSEPH T. RHODES. Jan. Ct. 1786.

p. 223 ELIJAH (6) BOWEN to MESHACK STALLINS, both of Duplin Co., 11 July 1785, for 20 pds. specie 50A on the NS of Rockfish Creek & on the ES of Fussell's Creek, beg. at a pine an old corner of another survey of sd. FUSSELL (1st name not given). Wit: JOSEPH DICKSON, WILLIAM WELLS. Jan. Ct. 1786.

p. 225   WILLIAM MOORE to FELIX FREDERICK, both of Duplin Co., 20 Oct 1785, for 100 pds. current money of N. C. 250A in 2 pieces: (1) 100A on the SS of Goshen Swamp & on a branch of Bear Branch joining HENRY McCULLOCH'S land, beg. at a hickory by his line, patented to THOMAS KENAN 4 Sep 1754; (2) 150A joining the 1st, beg. at a hickory above sd. WILLIAM MOOR'S corner, FELIX FREDERICK'S corner, JOHN MOOR'S corner, to a pine on THOMAS PHIP'S line, granted to sd. WILLIAM MOORE 10 Nov 1784. Wit: WILLIAM FREDERICK, WILLIAM SOUTHERLAND. Jan. Ct. 1786.

p. 226   EDWARD DICKSON to JAMES DICKSON, both of Duplin Co., 10 Aug 1785, 40 pds. current money of N. C. for 200A in 2 pieces: (1) 100A on Maxwell Swamp incl. the Beaverdam & some islands called Folley Islands, beg. at a water oak & 2 pines by Middle Branch; (2) 100A on Maxwell Swamp, beg. at a poplar on the run in Folly on MORGAN SWEENY'S line, WILLIAM RIGSBEE'S line, RICHARD WILLIAMS' line, about 150 yards above the mouth of Wolf Pit Branch, JOSEPH DICKSON'S line, granted to EDWARD DICKSON by patent dated 10 Nov 1784. Wit: LEWIS BARNES, ADONIJAH GARRASON. Jan. Ct. 1786.

p. 228   GEORGE SMITH to ANDREW GUFFORD, both of Duplin Co., 20 Aug 1785, for 15 pds. specie 75A on the SS of the Northeast Swamp, being part of a tract patented by BENJAMIN SNIPES 7 Dec 1769, in the fork of the Mirey Branch. Wit: JAMES GUFFORD, JAMES (Ŧ) DOBSON. Jan. Ct. 1786.

p. 229   JAMES CARR to WILLIAM CARR, both of Duplin Co., 17 Jan 1785, for 10 pds. specie 100A on the SS of Maxwell Swamp & both sides of Mirey Branch, beg. at a water oak by the swamp, to a black jack on BEN. WILLIAMS' line, being the contents of a patent dated 1 Apr 1780. Wit: JOHN CARR, DAVID SLOAN. Jan. Ct. 1786.

p. 230   FREDERICK (F) RIVENBARK to MESHACK STALLINS, both of Duplin Co., 24 Apr 1784, for 30 pds. specie 100A on the NS of Rockfish Creek on Perrey's Branch, being the same surveyed for JOHN RIVENBARK, joining BENJAMIN FUSSEL'S & THOMAS HILL'S lines. Wit: SHADRACK STALLINGS, WILLIAM JAMES. Jan. Ct. 1786.

p. 232   HENRY GOODMAN of Dobbs Co. to STEPHEN BAREFIELD of Duplin Co., 25 Oct 1785, for 250 pds. specie 421A in 4 tracts. (See Book 1A, p. 182 for the contents of this deed. Due to the length of this deed it will not be recorded here.) Wit: FREDERICK BARFIELD, JOHN (J) HANKS. Jan. Ct. 1786.

p. 235   MOSES (X) HANCHEY to JAMES MAXWELL, both of Duplin Co., 4 Aug 1785, for 6 pds. current money 100A on the NS of Maxwell Swamp about the mouth of Stocking Head, beg. at a pine near to HENRY GILLMAN'S line, being the contents of a patent granted to ADAM PLATT 26 Oct 1767 which sd. PLATT sold to sd. HANCHEY. Wit: WILLIAM CARR, D. BUNTING.   Jan. Ct. 1786.

p. 236   JOHN V. (VALENTINE) (₶) TAYLOR to HANDCOCK HATCHER, both of Duplin Co., 23 Nov 1784, for 7 pds. specie 100A on the ES of Buck Hall, beg. at a pine at a pond, to a pine called McCULLOCH'S corner. Wit: DANL. HICKS, SERENE HICKS. Jan. Ct. 1786.

p. 237   BAKER (B) BOWDEN (BOURDEN) of New Hanover Co., planter, to

WILLIAM TAYLOR, planter of Duplin Co., 7 Nov 1784, for 12 pds. specie 500A on
the NS of Goshen Swamp & on the head of Bear MARSH Branch, beg. at 3 pines on
JOHN WHITEHEAD'S line & sd. TAYLOR'S corner, to a bay in the Huckleberry
Pond on WESTEN'S line, to a pine in the head of Bear Marsh Branch, with BURREL
BRANCH'S line, to JESSE BARFIELD'S corner, to a stake on THOMAS TAYLOR'S
line, to a pine on JOHN WHITEHEAD'S line. Wit: SAMUEL BOWDEN (BOURDEN),
JAMES STANDLEY. Jan. Ct. 1786.

p. 239   DAVID CANNON to WILLIAM WARD, both of Duplin Co., 16 Jan 1786, for
40 pds. specie 105A on the WS of Bear Swamp, being the back part of a survey of
320A which sd. CANNON purchased at public sale, the prop. of HENRY EUSTACE
McCULLOCH, ESQR., beg. at a small white oak the corner tree of sd. CANNON'S
land, to JOHN STUCKEY'S line & along SAMUEL WARD'S line. Wit: WILLIAM
SHARPLESS, SAMUEL OATS. Jan. Ct. 1786.

p. 241   JOHN (J) DEVOUR (DEVER) of Duplin Co., planter, to JACOB KORNEGAY
(co. not given), 4 Jan 1786, for 10 pds. 100A on the head of Deep Gully Branch, beg.
at a water oak EDMUND DUNCAN'S new corner, to a white oak JACOB KORNEGAY'S
corner. Wit: EDMOND DUNCAN, STEPHEN JONES. Jan. Ct. 1786.

p. 242   AMBROSE ENZOR to JOSHUA BLAKE, both of Duplin Co., 3 Sep 1785, for
12 pds. specie 100A on a branch of Rockfish called Gum Branch, beg. at a pine in
the meadow. Wit: JACOB (𝄞) MATHEWS, WILLIAM KNIGHT, JOHN (⌓) COOK.
Jan. Ct. 1786.

p. 243   JOSEPH DICKSON (ESQR.) to LEWIS THOMAS, planter, both of Duplin Co.,
7 Jan 1786, for 60 pds. currency 330A, beg. at a stake in the head of a branch or
pond the last corner of EPHRAIM BOYD'S 100A survey, being a prong of Ashe
Branch, & along ALEXANDER LANE'S former line, but now WILLIAM KENAN'S
line & along JOHN GOAR'S [sic] line, & along the former line of ANDREW GUFFORD
but now JOHN BEST'S, & with ARTHUR BOYD'S line. Wit: ISAAC HUNTER,
NATHEN WALLER. Apr. Ct. 1786.

p. 246   WILLIAM BOYET to LEWIS THOMAS, both planters of Duplin Co., 4 Feb
1786, for 80 pds. current money 400A in 3 tracts: (1) 200A beg. at a pine on the
line formerly called ABRAHAM MOLTEN'S, but now LEWIS THOMAS', formerly
taken up by FELIX KENAN who conveyed the same to sd. BOYET; (2) 100A on the
WS of the Northeast River on the SS of Nahunga Swamp patented by sd. BOYET; (3)
100A on a branch of Nahunga Swamp above sd. BOYET'S planta. on BS of the road,
beg. at a pine in a pond his own corner, to STEPHEN POWELL'S line, patented by
sd. BOYET. Wit: JAS. KENAN, LEAVIN WADKINS, WARREN BLOUNT. Apr. Ct.
1786.

p. 248   JOSEPH GRIMES, millright, to SAMPSON GRIMES, planter, both of Duplin
Co., 18 Jan 1786, for 4 pds. specie money 100A on the NS of Goshen Swamp, beg. at
a cypress tree in Goshen Swamp at CHARLES WARD'S line, to a red oak on WES-
TON'S line, to a white oak on OUTLAW'S line, to a stake on SAMPSON GRIMES'
line, patent dated 10 Nov 1784. Wit: SNODON PEARCE, JOHN WHITEHEAD. Apr.
Ct. 1786.

p. 250   JOHN WHITEHEAD to JOHN WINDERS, both of Duplin Co., 1 Mar 1786,
for 80 pds. current money 500A in 3 tracts: (1) 200A beg. at a pine at the head of

Hall's Marsh, being the contents of a patent granted to JOSEPH GRIMES 19 Apr 1763 which sd. GRIMES sold to sd. WHITEHEAD; (2) 200A between Goshen Swamp & the Northeast on Wolfscrape Branch, beg. at a hickory on WESTON'S line on the SS of sd. branch, to a pine by the Wolf Pit, to a black jack near a drain of Hall's Marsh, to a pine in the edge of Panther Pocosin, being the contents of a patent granted to sd. WHITEHEAD 29 Oct 1782; (3) 100A on the NS of Goshen Swamp & on the drains of Hall's Marsh joining JAMES GRIMES' line & his own, beg. at a red oak GRIMES' line on the Half-way Branch, being the contents of a patent granted to sd. WHITEHEAD 29 Oct 1782. Wit: SAMPSON GRIMES, JAMES GRIMES, JOHN WINDERS, JUN. Apr. Ct. 1786.

p. 252   WILLIAM STEVENS to WILLIAM HURST, both of Duplin Co., 1 Apr 1785, for 250 pds. specie 324A on the SS of Goshen Swamp in 2 tracts: (1) 142A, beg. at 2 gums on the SS the run of Goshen Swamp, the upper corner of SAMUEL HERRING'S survey & runs along HERRING'S line to a hickory sd. STEVEN'S corner; (2) 182A beg. at the above mentioned 2 gums on the run of Goshen Swamp, to a white oak by a small branch WILLIAM BECK'S corner, down Long Branch as it meanders with the run till it empties into the run of Goshen Swamp. Wit: JOHN BECK, WILLIAM BECK, WILLIAM (+) BURNAM. Apr. Ct. 1786.

p. 254   WILLIAM (8) MERCER to FREDERICK SMITH, both planters of Duplin Co., 18 Mar 1786, for 8 pds. specie 50A on the ES of the Northeast & on the NS of Limestone Creek & on BS of Cabbin Branch, beg. at a pine & black jack on the WS of Cabbin Branch by a drain or a gully, up a branch called Hog Branch, being the upper part of 200A by patent granted to the sd. MERCER (date not given). Wit: LOFTIS WORLEY, STEPHEN BRADDY. Apr. Ct. 1786.

p. 255   SAMUEL (SA) ALBERSON & JOHN (A) ALBERSON, both of Duplin Co., to WINDEL DAVIS of Dobbs Co., 10 Apr 1786, for 50 pds. specie money 400A in 2 tracts: (1) SAMUEL ALBERSON'S part of 200A on the drains of the Great Branch joining the sd. JOHN ALBERSON'S line by his house & runs with his line crossing a drain of the Great Branch; (2) JOHN ALBERTSON'S part of 200A lying between the head of Poley Bridge Branch & the Beaverdam Branch, beg. at a hickory on EDWARD CARTER'S line. Wit: ISAAC HINES, JUNR., ISAAC HINES, MICHAEL (O) GLISSON, JESSE (T) PIPKIN. Apr. Term 1786.

p. 257   WM. (WILLIAM) KENAN, admr. of his father FELIX KENAN, ESQR., dec'd, late shff. of Duplin Co., to JESSE BROWN, planter of Duplin Co., 17 Jan 1786, 12 pds. for 100A. The sd. FELIX KENAN by virtue of a recovery & judgment in the Inferior Court of Duplin Co. against JAMES MOORE late of Duplin Co., did issue an execution for the afsd. sum of 12 pds. for the cost of a suit brought by ARCHABALD BELL, then of Duplin Co. The sd. FELIX KENAN by virtue of the execution did levy the same on a tract of land patented by JOHN BROWN on the NE side of Muddy Creek cont. 100A, beg. on the corner at the sd. creek, which sd. land is between the land now JOHN WOODWARD'S & JOHN MAGEE'S & the afsd. JESSE BROWN purchased the same for the debt & cost afsd. of the sd. FELIX KENAN. Wit: CATHERINE KENAN, ELIZABETH (X) CANNON. Apr. Ct. 1786.

p. 258   THEOPS. (THEOPHILUS) WILLIAMS to JOHN COOK, both of Duplin Co., 15 May 1785, for 60 pds. 100A on the SS of Bear Swamp & on the WS of Cattail Branch in 2 tracts: (1) 50A beg. at a post oak, to a poplar in the Gum Branch, CHARLES HINES' corner, down Gum Branch to the Meeting Branch, to a gum at the

mouth of Cattail Branch, being part of 300A purchased by FREDERICK BELL of
HENRY McCULLOCH out of his great tract of land, lying on the head of the Northeast & Black River; (2) 50A beg. at a pine in the head of a little branch, along a
line of marked trees to RAWLEY MILLS' back line to HARDY MALPUS' corner.
Wit: SAMUEL WARD, ALEX. DICKSON. Apr. Ct. 1786.

p. 260   SAML. (SAMUEL) ASHE of New Hanover Co., Gent., to JACOB BONEY
of Duplin Co., 8 Feb 1786, for 150 pds. current money of N. C. 400A on the NS of
Rockfish Creek on BS of the main road & Porter's Branch, being the contents of a
patent granted to JOHN PEACOCK 15 Feb 1737 & by sd. PEACOCK sold to JOHN
PORTER, beg. at a black oak or water oak on the creek bank, crossing the road &
Porter's Branch. Wit: SAM. ASHE, SHADK. STALLINGS. Apr. Ct. 1786.

p. 261   JOAB PADGET to ISAAC HUNTER, both of Duplin Co., 29 Dec 1783, for
10 pds. specie money 212 A on the NS of the Grove Swamp, beg. at a red oak
JAMES PEARSALL'S corner, to a red oak sd. ISAAC HUNTER'S corner, to a
gum NICHOLAS HUNTER'S corner in Horsepen Branch, to a pine SAMUEL CARR'S
corner, to a white oak JOAB PADGET'S corner, to a gum in Long Branch, being
part of 500A granted to JOAB PADGET. Wit: JOSEPH BRAY, ARTHUR STOKES.
Apr. Ct. 1786.

p. 263   THOMAS BURTON to JAMES EVANS, both planters of Duplin Co., 7 June
1779, for 100 pds. money of N. C. 400A on the WS of the Northeast Branch of Cape
Fear River, beg. at a pine standing in the woods on the NS of Persimmon Branch,
to a pine in CONDRICK WHITMAN'S line, to Boney's Branch, formerly surveyed for
WILLIAM BURTON. Wit: CHARLES BURTON, JOHN BURTON. Apr. Ct. 1786.

p. 264   FELIX KENAN, Shff. of Duplin Co. to THOMAS ROUTLEDGE of Duplin
Co., 5 Oct 1771, for 10 pds. 1 shill. 200A on a branch of Maxwell Swamp known by
the name of Stocking Head, being a parcel of 400A patented by JOHN MILLER 20
Nov 1744 & late the prop. of JOHN MILLER, SENR., which was sold to satisfy an
execution obtained by JOSEPH WILLIAMS & to whom the court awarded 5 pds. 10
shill. plus cost of 4 pds. 7 shill. 10 pence for debt in a suit against sd. MILLER.
THOMAS ROUTLEDGE became the last & highest bidder at a public auction held on
5 Oct 1771 for sd. 200 acres of land. Wit: CHARLES WARD, HUGH McCANNE.
Apr. Ct. 1785.

p. 266   JOHN (✠) COOK of Sampson Co. to WILLIAM KNIGHT of Duplin Co., 3
Sep 1785, for 6 pds. specie 50A between Stewarts Bridge & the head of Clear Run,
being part of sd. COOK'S 150A entry. Wit: JACOB (A) MATHEWS, JOSHUA (✠)
BLAKE, AMBORAS ENZOR. Apr. Ct. 1786.

p. 267   HARDY (✠) POWELL (SENR.) of Duplin Co., planter, to JOSEPH
STRINGFIELD of Duplin Co., 27 Oct 1803, for 150 pds. 400A in 3 tracts: (1) 200A
on which sd. POWELL lives, beg. on a pine & runs along JAMES BLAND'S line;
(2) 100A joining the first tract, beg. at a pine his corner of ELIJAH POWELL'S, to
a pine near JOHN ALDERMAN'S line; (3) 100 acres beg. at a pine his old corner of
the land he lives on along DANIEL HYSMITH'S line. HARDY POWELL & his wife
RACHEL POWELL to have use & occupation of all the lands during their natural
lives. Wit: WILLIAM BLAND, WM. ROBESON. Jan. Ct. 1804.

p. 268   WILLIAM HOUSTON, SENR. & EDWARD HOUSTON, both of Duplin Co. to

THE COMMISSIONERS of the town of Sarecta; namely, CHARLES WARD, JOHN HILL, DAVID MURDOCK, JAMES OUTLAW, SAMUEL HOUSTON, GEORGE MILLER, JOHN MATCHET, 15 July 1786, for 160 pds. 100A on the ES of the Northeast River, being part of 840A granted to HENRY McCULLOCH, Esqr. 3 Mar 1745 & thence granted to WILLIAM HOUSTON, Esar. May 1780, & being the same laid out for a town of Sarecta, beg. at a stake under the hill now the apple orchard, running down the river. Wit: JAMS. GILLESPIE, J. WALLACE, A. READ. July Ct. 1786.

p. 270   RICHARD SINGLETON to FREDERICK WELLS, both of Duplin Co., 16 Dec 1783, for 50 pds. specie 100A on a branch of Rockfish Creek called the North Branch, beg. on JOSEPH WILLIAMS' line at the run in the head of Mill Pond, to a pine at JOSEPH JAMES' line, to a water oak at the run of Bear Branch. Wit: EATHERENT ROCHELS, BENJAMIN WILLIAMS. July Ct. 1786.

p. 271   JOHN BECK (SENR.) to STEPHEN BECK, both of Duplin Co., 15 July 1786, for 200 pds. 278A on the SS of Goshen Swamp & the SS of Long Branch, beg. at a pine & runs north to a white oak standing in Long Branch in sd. JOHN BECK'S planta., to the fork of Long Branch & Body Branch, to HENRY McCULLOCH'S corner, to a small black oak near the head of Camp Branch. Wit: WILLIAM WILKINSON, MARY WRIGHT. July Ct. 1786.

p. 273.   JOHN BECK, planter, to WILLIAM BECK, both of Duplin Co., 17 July 1786, for 200 pds. currency of N. C. 86A on the SS of Goshen Swamp & on the NS of Long Branch near Slocumb's Branch, part of a tract patented by sd. JOHN BECK, beg. at a red oak & white oak sd. JOHN BECK'S corner, to WILLIAM STEVEN'S line. Wit: (none listed) July Ct. 1786.

p. 274   JAMES LOVE to JOHN BAPTIST SHEPHERD, both of Duplin Co., 10 Mar 1779, for 10 pds. current money of N. C. 100A on the head branches of Maple Swamp, a branch of Goshen Swamp, joining sd. LOVE'S own land & lands of PATRICK STEWART, ANDREW WILLSON, MR. McCULLOCH & FELIX KENAN, beg. at a hickory his own corner on PATRICK STEWART'S line, being the contents of a patent granted to sd. JAMES LOVE 4 Mar 1775. Wit: JOSEPH DICKSON, JAMES CARR. July Ct. 1786.

p. 276   JOHN BAPTIST SHEPHERD to ROBERT WILLIAMS, both of Duplin Co., 10 Feb 1784, for 70 pds. specie 100A on the head branches of Maple Swamp, a branch of Goshen Swamp, joining sd. WILLIAMS' own land, & the lines of PATRICK STEWART, JOHN GREER, MR. McCULLOCH & FELIX KENAN, being the contents of a patent granted to JAMES LOVE & by him deeded to sd. SHEPHERD. Wit: BENJAMIN BEST, GEORGE WILLIAMS. (MORNEN SHEPHERD also signed.) July Ct. 1786.

p. 277   JOHN (R) RIVENBARK of New Hanover Co. to DANIEL BONEY of Duplin Co., 9 July 1785, for 20 pds. current money of N. C. 100A in Duplin Co. on Farises Branch, beg. at a pine by sd. branch. Wit: WM (W) SAVAGE, DANIEL TEACHEY. July Ct. 1786.

p. 279   THOMAS WIGGINS to GEORGE HOLMS, both planters of Duplin Co., 9 Feb 1782, for 100 pds. specie 100 acres on the NS of Goshen Swamp & on the ES of Rattlesnake Branch beg. at a red oak. Wit: DANL. WILLIAMS, HARDY REAVES. July Ct. 1786.

p. 280   AARON WILLIAMS of Duplin Co. to JACOB WELLS (co. not given) 24 Jan
1785, for 25 pds. specie 100A on a branch of Rockfish called the Big Branch of
Fussel's Creek, beg. at a water oak at the run of sd. branch & to a pine on THOMAS
HILL'S line. Wit: ADAM PLATT, MESHACK STALLINS. July Ct. 1786.

p. 281   FREDERICK WELLS to AARON WILLIAMS, both of Duplin Co., 5 June
1786, for 12 pds. 15A on a branch of Rockfish Creek, beg. at a water oak at the run
of Taylor's Creek near the mouth of Deep Branch & along JOHN WALKER'S old line
to the main run of Taylor's Creek or the head of the Mill Pond, being part of a survey of land patented by the sd. WELLS in 1778. Wit: SHADRACK STALLINGS,
FREDERICK WILLIAMS. July Ct. 1787.

p. 283   AARON WILLIAMS to ADAM PLATT, both of Duplin Co., 24 Jan 1785, for
30 pds. specie 100A on a branch of Rockfish called the Big Branch of Fussel's
Creek, beg. at a pine on the WS of sd. branch. Wit: MESHACK STALLINGS,
JACOB WELLS. July Ct. 1786.

p. 284   HENRY (II) ALLEN (SENR.) to JAMES HALL, both of Duplin Co., 18 July
1786, for 16 pds. specie 50A being part of a tract of 131A patented by ZEBULON
HOLLINGSWORTH in 1763, lying on Muddy Creek, a branch of the Northeast River,
all that part on the WS of the swamp, beg. on the old line of sd. tract at the run of
the swamp & to a white oak at the mouth of the Broad Branch by JACOB BROWN'S
corner. Wit: JOSEPH T. RHODES. July Ct. 1786.

p. 285   JAMES McINTIRE to JOHN MALLARD, both of Duplin Co., 7 Mar 1785,
for 65 pds. current money of N. C. 100A on the WS of the Northeast Branch of
Cape Fear River on Horse Branch, being the contents of a patent granted to
JOSEPH DUKES 22 Nov 1746 & afterwards conveyed from the sd. DUKES' atty.
WILLIAM CARR to NICHOLAS PULLARD who deeded to PELEG ROGERS, SENR.
of Duplin Co. & from sd. ROGERS to JOHN ATKINS on 9 July 1768. Wit: PHILL
SOUTHERLAND, JOHN SOUTHERLAND. July Ct. 1786.

p. 287   JOHN WOODWARD to ELISHA WOODWARD, both of Duplin Co., _____
July 1786, for 50 pds. specie 320A on the ES of the Northeast & on BS of a prong of
Muddy Creek called Stevens Creek & the Pometo Pond Branch, which sd. 320A was
granted to JOHN WOODWARD by patent dated 1 July 1779. Wit: ABRAHAM
MOLTEN, JUNR., WILLIAM HOUSTON, JUNR.   July Ct. 1786.

p. 289   JAMES (Ŧ) ELLIS of Duplin Co., planter, to BENJAMIN LANIER (co.
not given), 21 Jan 1786, for 50 pds. specie 100A on the NS of Cypress Creek & BS
of the Great Branch, beg. at a pine at the side of Cypress Creek Swamp opposite
PARKER PEARCE'S land, patented by JOHN HALSO. Wit: JOHN LANIER, JESSE
LANIER, MARY (X) HALSO. July Ct. 1786.

p. 290   ARTHUR STOKES to JOHN MALLARD, both of Duplin Co., 29 May 1786,
for 60 pds. specie 120 acres in 2 tracts: (1) 80A on the Horse Branch, beg. at a
black gum in a pond & to a pine sapling on ANDREW McINTIRE'S line & to a white
oak JOSEPH DICKSON'S corner, patented 27 Apr 1767 to MATHEW CANADY; (2)
40A adj. the 80A on BS of Horse Branch, beg. at a red oak on the SS of the branch
his own corner, as patent doth appear. Wit: PHILL SOUTHERLAND, JOSEPH
MALLARD. July Ct. 1786.

p. 292   ABRAHAM NEWKIRK to HENRY NEWKIRK, both of Duplin Co., 18 July
1786, for 100 pds. specie 100A on the SS of Limestone Swamp, joining FELIX
KENAN'S & JAMES PATERSON'S & his own, beg. at a pine on his own line & to a
pine on sd. KENAN'S line, being a grant to sd. ABRAHAM NEWKIRK 10 Nov 1784.
Wit: DANIEL SOUTHERLAND. July Ct. 1786.

p. 294   AUSTIN BEESLEY 7 JAMES RODGERS to SOLOMON BEESLEY, all of
Duplin Co., 8 Apr 1786, for 50 pds. currency 151A on the WS of the Northeast
River & on BS of Maxwell Swamp, beg. at a pine on the NS of Reedy Meadow Branch,
on the edge of sd. branch SOLOMON BEESLEY'S corner & to a pine sd. AUSTIN
BEESLEY'S own corner & crossing Maxwell Swamp to ALEXANDER ARMSTRONG'S
line & down sd. swamp to the mouth of Reedy Meadow run. Wit: THOMAS CARL-
TON, ALEX. PORTER. Oct. Ct. 1786.

p. 296   LOIS (X) NEWTON & ABRAHAM NEWTON to JOHN LITTLE, both of Duplin
Co., 22 Feb 1786, for 25 pds. 100A on the NS of Farises Creek, beg. at a pine on
Gum Branch at the mouth of a small branch, it being part of 350A patented by
JACOB NEWTON in 1775. Wit: JOSEPH WILLIAMS, AARON WILLIAMS.
[Body of deed reads "LOUIS" NEWTON, with "his" mark "X".] Oct. Ct. 1786.

p. 297   LOIS (X) NEWTON & ABRAHAM NEWTON of N. C. (co. not given) to
JOHN LITTLE of N. C. (co. not given), 22 Feb 1786, for 25 pds. currency 85A on
the NS of Farizes Creek incl. ABRAHAM NEWTON'S impr., beg. at a water oak in
Gum Branch. Wit: JOSEPH WILLIAMS, AARON WILLIAMS. Oct. Ct. 1786.

p. 298   CHARLES (M) MERRIT to BENJAMIN EZZELL, both of Duplin Co., 13
Mar 1786, for 12 pds. current money of N. C. 50A on the ES of Stewart's Creek,
being part of the sd. MERRIT'S old survey of 150A whereon he now lives & part of
a new survey of sd. MERRIT'S of 100A granted 9 Nov 1784, beg. at a poplar in
MERRIT'S Branch at the mouth of the first branch below sd. MERRIT'S little field,
being sd. EZZELL'S corner of a deed of 100A purchased from sd. MERRIT & CO.,
adj. THOMAS JAMES' line. Wit: AUSTIN BEESLEY, THOMAS CARLTON. Oct.
Ct. 1786.

p. 300   J. PEARSALL, SHFF. to JOHN BONEY, both of Duplin Co., 18 Jan 1786,
for 10 pds. 200A on the SS of Maxwell Swamp opposite & above the mouth of Stocking Head Swamp & joining below sd. BONEY'S planta., it being the upper half of a
tract of land formerly granted by patent to HENRY GILMAN, beg. at a water oak &
gum RICHARD CHASSON'S corner on the NS of Maxwell Swamp, being the goods &
chattel lands & tenements of HENRY GILMAN, schoolmaster, late of Duplin Co.
The Court awarded 75 pds. plus cost & damages of 4 pds. 1 shill 9 pence to JOHN
BONEY for debt in suit against sd. GILMAN & JOHN BONEY became the last &
highest bidder for sd. 200A at a public auction held on 17 Oct 1784. Wit: JOSEPH
DICKSON, CHAS. WARD. Oct. Ct. 1786.

p. 302   J. PEARSALL (JAMES) to ROBERT DICKSON, both of Duplin Co., 18 July
1785, for 3 pds. current money of N. C. 80A on the WS of the Northeast Branch of
Cape Fear River, NS of Maxwell Swamp on the head of Eldar Branch, beg. at a red
oak ROBERT DICKSON'S corner in the fork of the far prong, to the patent corner on
CLUGSTON'S line & to a pine on JOHN McCULLOCH'S line & a patent corner on
ALEXANDER DICKSON'S old line, now ROBERT DICKSON'S line, being the contents
of a patent granted to sd. JAMES PEARSALL 10 Nov 1784. Wit: JOSEPH DICKSON,

W. DICKSON. Oct. Ct. 1786.

p. 304   ALEXANDER DICKSON to ROBERT DICKSON, both of Duplin Co., 11 Oct
1779, for 50 pds. currency 50A on BS of the main road & drains of Green Branch,
being part of 615A granted to ALEXANDER DICKSON dated (left blank), beg. at a
pine in Green Branch sd. ALEXANDER DICKSON'S line, to ROBERT DICKSON'S
line. Wit: DORATHY DICKSON, JAMES DICKSON. Oct. Ct. 1786.

p. 305   WATSON (W) BURTON & JAMES GILLESPIE to ROBERT DICKSON, all of
Duplin Co., 22 June 1780, for 5 pds. current money of N. C. 250A between Maxwell
Swamp & Elder Swamp & between HOLDEN'S & POWELL'S lines, beg. at a water
oak in Elder Swamp ROBERT DICKSON'S corner on PATRICK POWELL'S line, being
the contents of a patent granted to sd. WATSON BURTON & JAMES GILLESPIE 4
Mar 1775. Wit: WM. McGOWEN, WATSON BURTON. Oct. Ct. 1786.

p. 306   W. (WILLIAM) DICKSON & ROBERT DICKSON to WILLIAM DICKSON, all
of Duplin Co., 13 May 1785, for 50 pds. current money 540 acres on the WS of the
Northeast River, between Persimmon Swamp & Stocking Head Swamp on BS of Poley
Branch, beg. at a pine the corner of land sold to PHILLIP ROUSE, along JOHN
MILLER'S line, to ANDREW ROUSE'S line, which sd. 540 acres is part of a patent
granted to sd. WILLIAM DICKSON & ROBERT DICKSON for 640A 4 May 1769. Wit:
JOSEPH DICKSON, ARTHUR SAVAGE. Oct. Ct. 1786.

p. 307   W. (WILLIAM) DICKSON & ROBERT DICKSON to ROBERT DICKSON, all
of Duplin Co., 13 May 1785, for 50 pds. current money 250 acres on the WS of the
Northeast River above the mouth of Island Creek joining the Great Pocoson at a
place called Love's Island & joining the west corner of LAUGHLIN LOVE'S land,
beg. at a red oak in the head of a small branch, being the contents of a patent
granted to WILLIAM DICKSON & ROBERT DICKSON 26 Oct 1777. Wit: JOSEPH
DICKSON, ARTHUR SAVAGE. Oct. Ct. 1786.

p. 308   JAS. (JAMES) LOCKHART to LINCOLN SHEFFIELD, both of Duplin Co.,
22 Nov 1783, for 5 pds. specie 130A on the ES of the Northeast River, beg. at a
pine the 2nd corner of JESPER COX'S survey of 400A. Wit: JOSEPH DICKSON,
JOSEPH BROOKS. Oct. Ct. 1786.

p. 309   CHARLES MILLER of Duplin Co. to his dau. MARY MILLER (co. not
given) 7 June 1785, for "natural love & affection" a negro girl named DINAH about
10 yrs. old, one feather bed, furn., one lining wheel, one large wheel, one side
saddle, one pott, one skillet, six earthen plates, two bowls, & three tumblers.
Wit: SAMUEL HOUSTON, SARAH MILLER. Oct. Ct. 1786.

p. 310   JESSE (+) REGISTER of Johnston Co. to SHADRACK STALLINGS of Duplin Co., 24 Feb 1786, for 30 pds. specie 123A on the ES of Farises Creek, beg. at
a maple on the creek to a pine EDWARD DICKSON'S corner. Wit: WILLIAM
WELLS, JAMES CARR. Oct. Ct. 1786.

p. 312   JOHN WRIGHT to his son THOMAS WRIGHT, both of Duplin Co., 14 Oct
1786, for "natural love & affection" 400A in 2 tracts: (1) 250A on the SS of Goshen
Swamp, being part of the mannor planta. sd. JOHN WRIGHT now lives on joining
the dividing branch, beg. at a small water oak by the run of sd. branch to a white
oak by the place where the still commonly stands, to a pine by a pond the corner of

WILLIAM DICKSON'S land; (2) 150A on the SS of Goshen Swamp between Reedy
Branch & the head of Poley Branch, beg. at a pine the corner of ROBERT BIRD'S
land, to a pine on GILBERT McCALLAP'S line, to a pine on sd. JOHN WRIGHT'S
own line, being one half of a patent of 300A granted to sd. JOHN WRIGHT 15 Dec
1778. Wit: W. DICKSON, CHARLES HOOKS. Oct. Ct. 1786.

p. 314   GEORGE SMITH, planter, to WILLIAM SMITH, young man, both of Duplin
Co., 21 Mar 1786, for 50 pds. specie 250A on the ES of the Northeast on the head
of Burncoat & joining Dobbs Co. & at the head of the Tuckaho, it being part of 500
acres patented by the sd. GEORGE SMITH 1 July 1779 of which ROBERT EVERS had
part, joining BS of Cow Hole Branch, the sd. divided by a row of marked trees
almost cornering the sd. land, beg. at a pine by a pond that drains into Tuckaho,
crossing Burncoat, to the far corner next to Dobbs. Wit: JOHN ALBERSON,
MICHAEL (O) GLISSON. Oct. Ct. 1786.

p. 316   GEORGE SMITH to MICHAEL GLISSON, both planters of Duplin Co., 23
Mar 1786, 20 pds. currency money of N. C. 100A on the ES of the Northeast & on
the NS of Mathews Branch & the Wolf Pit Branch, joining DURHAM LEIGH'S &
SILVANUS PUMFREY'S lines, patented by DURHAM LEIGH, taken by execution on
the account of ELISHA BLACKSHER & sold by the High Sheriff of Duplin Co.,
THEOPHILUS WILLIAMS, to the highest bidder the sd. GLISSON. Wit: JOHN
ALBERSON, WILLIAM SMITH.

p. 317   ROBERT DICKSON to ALEXANDER DICKSON, both of Duplin Co., 11 Oct
1779, for 50 pds. currency 50A on the heads of Green Branch & Stalkinghead [sic]
Branch, being part of the contents of a patent granted to ROBERT DICKSON for 400A
4 Mar 1775. Wit: JAMES DICKSON, DORATHY DICKSON. Oct. Ct. 1786.

p. 318   JOSEPH WILLIAMS, planter, to DAVID WILLIAMS, both of Duplin Co., 27
Mar 1779, deed of gift for 150A on a branch of Rockfish Creek, beg. at a black jack
at JOHN WILLIAM'S upper corner, to the corner near JOSEPH JAMES', being part
of the land that JOSEPH WILLIAMS bought of JOHN WALKER, the NW corner of the
survey. Wit: JOSEPH WILLIAMS, JUNR., ELIAS JAMES, AARON WILLIAMS.
Oct. Ct. 1786.

p. 319   SAMUEL (+) TANNER of Duplin Co. to JESSE PIPKIN of Dobbs Co., 26
Nov 1785, for 5 pds. specie money 60A joining ISAAC HINES, JESSE PIPKIN &
RICHARD ROBERDS' lines, beg. at a pine HINES' line by a pond & runs with his
line. Wit: DANIEL HINES, ELIZABETH DAVIS. Oct. Ct. 1786.

p. 320   WILLIAM (X) WILKINS to LEWIS HINES, both of Duplin Co., 15 Jan 1784,
for 70 pds. specie money 200A on the NS of the Northeast & beg. at a pine on ISAAC
HINES' line, crossing Toms Branch, crossing the Great Savannah Branch. Wit:
ISAAC HINES, SAML. ALBERSON. Oct. Ct. 1786.

p. 321   JOHN (Ŧ) JONES to JOHN WEEDINGS, both of Duplin Co., 11 June 1783,
for 20 pds. specie 200A on the ES of the Northeast River & NS of Limestone Swamp
on BS of Cabbin Branch, beg. at a gum in the edge of Gum Swamp on THOMAS
QUIN'S line, to WILLIAM MERCER'S corner, ABNER QUIN'S line, to a pine on
ANTHONY LEWIS' line. Wit: WILLIAM MURROW, WILLIAM (W) NETHERCUT.
Oct. Ct. 1786.

p. 323   GEORGE WILLIS of Duplin Co., planter, to AMBROSE ENZOR of Sampson
Co., planter, 4 May 1786, for 70 pds. specie 150A on the WS of Rockfish Creek,
beg. at a cypress in the swamp, it being half the upper part of a 300A survey granted by ROBERT KNOWLES to JONATHAN WILLIS.   Wit: ELIJAH (E) BOWEN,
WILLIAM KNIGHT.   Oct. Ct. 1786.

p. 324   WEMBERK BONEY to ADONIJAH GARRISON, both of Duplin Co., 20 Sep
1780, for 20 shill. current money of N. C. 20A on the NS of Island Creek, being
part of a tract of 400A granted by patent to the sd. BONEY, beg. at a red oak JOHN
COOK'S corner on the edge of Island Creek, at the lower corner of JOHN MER-
CHANT'S planta., to a stake on sd. COOK'S line.   Wit: ROBERT DICKSON,
JAMES EVANS.   Oct. Ct. 1786.

p. 325   JOHN MARCHANT to ADONIJAH GARRISON, both of Duplin Co., 20 Sep
1785, for 60 pds. current money of N. C. 100A on the NS of Island Creek, incl. sd.
MARCHANT'S impr., being the sd. land the sd. MARCHANT purchased from JOHN
COOK of Island Creek in Jan 1782, beg. at a cypress in the edge of the swamp of
Island Creek at the mouth of the Island Branch above sd. MARCHANT'S planta., to
a pine in the edge of Love's Pocoson.   Wit: ROBERT DICKSON, NATHANIEL
McCANNE.   Oct. Ct. 1786.

p. 327   WILLIAM WHITFIELD (SENR.) of Wayne Co. TO WILLIAM WHITFIELD,
minor of Duplin Co., 30 July 1786, for 150 pds. specie 600A on the NS of the Northeast Branch in several tracts: (1) 150A being part of a tract attained by deed from
SAMUEL JOHNSTON, Esqr. & JEAN BLAIR, beg. on Jumping Run at the 7th or last
corner of JOHNSTON'S patent, to a drain that lies near midway between the sd.
WILLIAM WHITFIELD'S planta. & run, to the Northeast Creek, up to the creek to
JOHNSTON'S giving line; (2) 200A granted to WILLIAM WHITFIELD, SENR. 1 Apr
1780, beg. at a pine his old corner in Jumping Run, to a stake on SIMON DAVIS'S
line; (3) all the remaining part of a tract of 100A granted to sd. WHITFIELD 23 Feb
1754 that the sd. JOHNSTON'S land does not include; (4) 200A attained by deed from
WILLIAM O'DANIEL & SAMUEL TANNER, beg. at a pine on Jumping Run, to a pine
near Rooty Run, a corner tree of JESSE BARFIELD'S patent, to THEOPHILUS
WILLIAMS' line, to the 3rd corner of BARFIELD'S survey to KORNEGAY'S line, to
Smith's Branch & Jumping Run to the beg.; (5) all the land that lies to the WS of the
middle of the bottom that lies midway between the sd. WILLIAM WHITFIELD'S
planta. & Jumping Run that is within his line, cont. in the whole 600A.   Wit:
WILLIAM WHITFIELD, BUCKNER KILLEBREW.   Oct. Ct. 1786.

p. 328   WILLIAM WHITFIELD (SENR.) of Wayne Co. to his son-in-law BUCKNER
KILLEBREW (co. not given), 30 July 1786, for "the natural love good will & affec-
tion which I bear unto my beloved son WILLIAM WHITFIELD & at his request or
desire & for other good causes" 350A in 2 tracts on the NS of the Northeast of Cape
Fear: (1) 200A in 2 tracts each granted to GEORGE KORNEGAY 14 Oct 1749 & 27
Sep 1753; (2) 150A obtained by deed from THEOPHILUS WILLIAMS, beg. at a pine
KORNEGAY'S corner in Bailes Branch, toward Rooty Branch, to a pine STEPHEN
BARFIELD'S corner.   Wit: WM. WHITFIELD, WILLIAM WHITFIELD, minor.
Oct. Ct. 1786.

p. 329   AMOS (A) PARKER to AUSTIN BRYAN, both of Duplin Co., 13 Aug 1785,
for 10 pds. current money of N. C. 100A on the SS of Muddy Creek joining & between the lines of SOLOMON PICKETT, WILLIAM HOLLINGSWORTH & sd. BRYAN,

being part of the contents of a patent granted to STEPHEN HOLLINGSWORTH 21 June 1746 for 600A, which sd. 100A is known by the name of JONES' 100A survey, which is the lower third of a deed of 300A formerly sold by BENJAMIN EVANS to SOLOMON PARKER to AMOS PARKER. Wit: JOSEPH DICKSON, JOHN (X) BRICE. Oct. Ct. 1786.

p. 331 GEORGE SMITH (SENR.) of Duplin Co., planter, to ROBERT IVEY of Wayne Co., 31 Dec 1785, for 60 pds. specie 150A on Cow Hole Branch, being part of 500A patented by the sd. SMITH 1 July 1779, incl. the impr. where JAMES DOBSON now liveth, being divided by a row of marked trees almost cornering, beg. where SOLOMON CARTER'S line of his 100A joins the blazed trees, to the head of a branch of Burncoat, to a black gum near ADAMS' line. Wit: JOSIAH (X) STAFFORD, JAMES (⊥) DOBSON. Oct. Ct. 1786.

p. 332 GEORGE (O) COOPER (SENR.) to GEORGE COOPER, JUNR., both of Duplin Co., 19 Aug 1786, for 30 pds. current money of N. C. 97A on the SS of Nahunga Swamp lying in the fork of a branch that make out of sd. swamp by the upper end of JOHN B. SHEPPARD'S old field, part of the land purchased by sd. GEORGE COOPER, JUNR. from WILLIAM HALL, beg. at the fork of a branch where the two runs meet & runs up the branch by various courses with RICHARD COOPER'S line. Wit: RICHARD COOPER, FRANCES COOPER. Oct. Ct. 1786.

p. 334 WM. (WILLIAM) TAYLOR of Duplin Co., planter, to his dau. ELIZABETH TAYLOR of Duplin Co., 3 June 1779, for "natural love & affection" all that messuage or tenements, tract or tracts of land, with all houses, out houses, lands & c. Wit: WILLIAM GOODMAN, JOHN GIBBS, HENRY GOODMAN. Apr. Ct. 1787.

p. 335 WM. (WILLIAM) TAYLOR of Duplin Co. to his dau. ELIZABETH TAYLOR of Duplin Co., 3 June 1779, the following slaves, goods, & chattels: one negro man named ARTHUR, one named DARBY, one mulatto girl AMA, one negro girl SILVA, one named GEANEY, & one half of stock of every kind & one half of household goods & working tools. Wit: WILLIAM GOODMAN, JOHN GIBBS, HENRY GOODMAN. Apr. Ct. 1787.

p. 336 JOHN HOLDON, heir at law of JEREMIAH HOLDON, dec'd of Duplin Co., to JAMES CARR of Duplin Co., 7 Sep 1785, for 60 pds. specie 240A on the NS of Maxwell Swamp in 2 tracts, being the contents of a patent granted to sd. JEREMIAH HOLDEN 23 Feb 1754, & also the contents of a patent granted to sd. JOHN HOLDEN 29 Oct 1782, beg. at a maple & hornbeam on the run of Maxwell Swamp, to SHEFFIELD'S corner, ROBERT DICKSON'S corner, & JEREMIAH HOLDEN'S corner. Wit: ROBERT SLOAN, JOHN SLOAN. Jan. Ct. 1787.

p. 337 JOSEPH BRAY (SENR.) of Duplin Co., scrivenor, to JOHN WILLIAMS of Duplin Co., planter, 19 Sep 1786, for 40 pds. 200A, being part of a 640A tract granted to MILLS MUMFORD by ALEXR. MARTIN 10 Nov 1784, beg. on Panther Swamp at the mouth of Brice's Branch & to Stirrup Branch, & transferred to JOSEPH BRAY, SENR. by sd. MUMFORD 9 June 1786. Wit: JAMES PEARSALL, DANL. GLISSON. Jan. Ct. 1787.

p. 339 RICHARD PRESCOAT, farmer, to JOHN WILLIAMS, both of Duplin Co., 12 July 1786, for 80 pds. specie 150A on the ES of the Northeast River, granted to sd. PRESCOAT 25 July 1784, beg. at ALEXR. McCULLOCH'S corner on the NS of

Peter's Branch, that runs into Panther Swamp, & along McCULLOCH'S line to a
pine GEORGE SMITH'S corner Tree, to a maple in the Pocoson on the head of
Peter's Branch. Wit: LOFTIS WORLEY, GEORGE SMITH, JUN., ABSALAM
BOYET. Jan. Ct. 1787.

p. 340   JOHN TOMSON (THOMPSON) of Duplin Co., planter, to MOSES STANDLEY
of Wayne Co., planter, 29 Mar 1783, for 40 pds. specie 300A on the ES of the
Northeast River & on BS of the Great Branch, granted to sd. THOMPSON 10 Nov
1784, beg. at a pine on the SS of the branch on or near BIBBY BUSH'S line, crossing the Great Branch & the Spring Branch, to a pine in the NS of the Great Branch.
Wit: WM. WHITFIELD, LEWIS WHITFIELD, WILLIAM WHITFIELD. Jan Ct. 1787.

p. 342   NATHAN (X) NEWELL of Duplin Co., joiner, to MOSES STANDLEY of
Wayne Co., 29 Jan 1784, for 26 pds. specie 300A on the ES of the Northeast River &
on the NS of Mathews Branch as by patent dated 10 Nov 1784, beg. at a pine in sd.
Branch Bagges Bridge [sic], to a pine JAMES WILLIAMS' corner, to a pine near
Viney's Branch to a bay in Matthews Branch. Wit: WM. WHITFIELD, WILLIAM
(X) EDWARDS. Jan. Ct. 1787.

p. 344   JOSEPH DICKSON to JOHN BLANTON, both of Duplin Co., 18 July 1785,
for 10 pds. current money of N. C. 100A on the NS of the main Doctors Creek of
Rockfish on BS of a branch called the Deep Gully, beg. at a pine CLIFTON BOWEN'S
corner, being the contents of a patent granted to sd. DICKSON 10 Nov 1784. Wit:
SAMUEL CAUMAN, CLAUDIUS CARTRIGHT. Jan. Ct. 1787.

p. 345   JAMES LOCKHART, in behalf of his minor sons LILLINGTON LOCKHART
& JAMES LOCKHART, JUNR. of Duplin Co. to JOSEPH GRIMES (co. not given),
carpenter & millright, 5 Oct 1785, binds his sons for a term of 7 yrs. to begin from
the day of finishing & settling to work a certain saw mill now intended to be built by
the sd. JAMES LOCKHART & JOSEPH GRIMES at a place known as Muddy Creek in
Duplin Co. JOSEPH GRIMES to pay one half the expenses of building & keeping in
repair the sd. mill for the time mentioned & to receive half of the profit arising
from sd. mill. Wit: JAMES GILLESPIE, WILLIAM McCANNE. Jan. Ct. 1787.

p. 347   JOHN WINDERS, planter, to his son JAMES WINDERS, both of Duplin Co.,
18 Nov 1786, for "natural love & affection" 304A, being part of 71,160A formerly
granted to HENRY McCULLOCH & since by the sd. McCULLOCH conveyed to
WILLIAM CANNON & by sd. CANNON to the sd. JOHN WINDERS 18 Oct 1775, which
sd. 304A is in 2 tracts: (1) 204A beg. at a sweet gum in King's Branch, to a maple
on Wolf Branch, to a pine on McCULLOCH'S line of the great tract, crossing King's
Branch; (2) 100A joining the 1st tract on the SS of King's Branch & on BS of Wolf's
Branch, beg. at a hickory WILLIAM CANNON'S corner of the above granted land, to
a maple in Wolf's Branch, to a dogwood on HENRY CANNON'S line, being the contents of a patent granted to WILLIAM CANNON 16 Dec 1769. Wit: JAMES WARD,
JESSE SWINSON. Jan. Ct. 1787.

p. 349   JOHN WINDERS to JESSE SWINSON his son-in-law, both of Duplin Co., for
"natural love & affection", 11 Nov 1786, 100A near a place called Wolfscrape in the
fork of the Northeast of Cape Fear on the head of Bear Marsh, beg. at a pine below
sd. marsh, granted to JOSEPH WINDERS 3 Oct 1755 & now conveyed by the sd.
JOHN WINDERS to JESSE SWINSON. Wit: JAMES WARD, JOHN WINDERS, JAMES
WINDERS. Jan. Ct. 1787.

p. 350   ROBERT MERRIT of Sampson Co. to DAVID DAVIS of Duplin Co., 11 Nov 1786, for 23 pds. specie 200A on BS of Rockfish Creek, beg. at a pine DAVID DAVIS' corner SS the creek by a little branch, by JOHN WILLSON'S corner, crossing the creek along MEREDITH'S line, to a pine on JOSEPH WILLIAMS' line. Wit: JAMES RYAN, JAMES RAWLINGS. Jan. Ct. 1787.

p. 352   ABRAHAM NEWTON & LOIS (⊖) NEWTON of Duplin Co. to JAMES NEWTON & JOSHUA NEWTON (co. not given), 8 Jan 1787, for "the love good will & affection" 300A in 2 tracts: (1) 100A formerly patented by HENRY SKIBBOW, it being the same whereon the sd. JACOB NEWTON settled & improved, on Gum Branch & Pharises Creek; (2) 200A being part of a survey of 300A patented by JACOB NEWTON 1775. LOIS NEWTON to have the enjoyment of the sd. land during her natural life & at her decease to remain unto sd. JAMES NEWTON & JOSHUA NEWTON. Wit: AARON WILLIAMS, DANIEL ALDERMAN. Jan. Ct. 1787.

p. 353   ROBERT WILKINSON to LUKE WARD, both of Duplin Co., 30 Oct 1786, for 10 pds. current money 75A on the NS of Bear Swamp, joining on the back of sd. LUKE WARD'S own land, beg. at a black gum & white oak sd. WARD'S corner in a branch, to a new marked line between sd. WARD & JAMES WRIGHT. Wit: W. DICKSON, DANIEL GLISSON. Jan. Ct. 1787.

p. 355   JAMES MURRAY, SENR. to JAMES MURRAY, JUNR., both of Duplin Co., _____ 1787, for 60 pds. specie 100A whereon the sd. JAMES MURRAY, JUNR. now lives on the Northeast side of the Northeast Branch of Cape Fear River, beg. at a red oak in the sd. JAMES MURRAY'S line between his planta. & Ratliff's Branch, near the old meeting house, to a corner tree between the sd. JAMES MURRAY, SENR. & JESSE MURRAY'S former line, by a dividing line to WILLIAM PICKETT'S out corner, to a pine on a branch between the sd. PICKET'S & MURRAY'S planta., to a maple on the Mill Branch & up the Mill Dam to the afsd. JAMES MURRAY SENR!S survey. Wit: WILLIAM PICKET, WILLIAM (X) PICKET. Jan. Ct. 1787.

p. 356   DAN (X) BOWEN to ELIJAH BOWEN, both planters of Duplin Co., 19 Nov 1784, for 50 pds. specie 200A on the WS of Rockfish Creek, beg. at a red oak by the side of the creek, to a cypress in Rockfish Swamp, patented by DAN. BOWEN 1 Apr 1780. Wit: DAVID ALDERMAN, DANIEL ALDERMAN. Jan. Ct. 1787.

p. 358   ALEXR. DICKSON, planter, to JAMES CARR, both of Duplin Co., 29 Mar 1786, for 10 pds. currency of N. C. 100A on the NS of Maxwell Swamp joining & between JEREMIAH HOLDEN'S, ALEXANDER HOLDEN'S & ROBERT DICKSON'S. Wit: JAMES DICKSON, ANN DICKSON. Jan. Ct. 1787.

p. 359   JOHN JOHNSTON to HANNAH JOHNSTON, both of Duplin Co., 20 Dec 1783, for 100 pds. specie 250A between Goshen & the Grove on BS of Dark Branch & the main road incl. the 2 & 20 mile posts, beg. at a pine south edge the main road on BORTHICK GILLESPIE'S line, formerly ANTHONY MILLER'S line, being the 12th corner of a tract of 340A patented by BENJAMIN JOHNSTON 26 Sep 1760. Wit: JOSEPH DICKSON, ARCHABALD CARR. Jan. Ct. 1787.

p. 360   JOHN (✝) TUCKER to JOHN EVANS, both of Duplin Co., 3 Sep 1785, for 75 pds. specie 150A, it being part of DAVID TUCKER'S entry, beg. in the fork of Clear Run, to JACOB MATTHEWS' corner. Wit: JOHN MATHEWS, WILLIAM KNIGHT. Jan. Ct. 1787.

p. 361   JOHN MOLTEN, planter, to JOSEPH COX, JUNR., both of Duplin Co.,
4 Apr 1786, for 50 pds. currency of N. C. 250A on the WS of the Northeast River,
beg. at a maple gum & water oak in the edge of a bent of the River Swamp, being the
contents of a patent granted to the sd. MOLTEN 10 Nov 1784. Wit: JAMES DICK-
SON, BEN. DULANY. Jan. Ct. 1787.

p. 363   THOMAS (X) PICKET of New Hanover Co. to JOHN PARKER of Duplin Co.,
6 Nov 1786, for 50 pds. specie 50A on a branch of Cypress Creek joining WILLIAM
PICKET'S planta. line & JAMES MURROW'S planta. line, being SUSANAH HOOK'S
part of her father's land divided by the run of the sd. branch, her sister RUTH
having the other half of her father's land. Wit: WILLIAM SOUTHERLAND, JAMES
PICKET. Jan. Ct. 1787.

p. 364   HENRY BULLS of Johnston Co. to PATRICK NEWTON of Duplin Co., 8
Nov 1786, for 20 pds. specie 150A on the ES of Bear Swamp, joining sd. MAIRSES
land & THOMAS HILL'S land, beg. at a small pine FELIX FREDERICK'S line, by
RICHARD MAIRSES corner, being the upper part of a patent of 250A granted to
JOHN MOORE 1 July 1779. Wit: AUSTIN MOORE, JOHN HOWSMAN. Jan. Ct. 1787.

p. 365   RICE MATTHEWS to MESHACK STALLINGS, both of Duplin Co., 25 Feb
1786, for 100 pds. specie 200A on the waters of Rockfish & the WS of Fussel's
Creek, on BS of Pig Pen Branch, beg. at a gum in sd. branch MESHACK STALL-
INGS corner, to a pine ADAM PLATT'S corner. Wit: JACOB WELLS, WILLIAM
WELLS. Apr. Ct. 1787.

p. 367   WM. (WILLIAM) KENAN to FELIX FREDERICK, both planters of Duplin
Co., 20 Sep 1785, for 100 pds. current money 100A on BS of the Big Branch, beg.
at a white oak JOHN MOOR'S corner, along JOHN BELL'S line, as by patent dated
30 Sep 1768. Wit: CHRISTOPHER MARTIN, CHARLES BROWN. Apr. Ct. 1787.

p. 369   THOMAS CLARK of Brunswick Co. to SHADRACK STALLINGS of Duplin
Co., 24 Feb 1787, for 300 pds. specie 320A on a branch of Rockfish Creek known
by the name of Knowles' or James' Creek, beg. at a red oak marked ΞP. Wit:
JOHN HOWELL, JOHN HOLDON. Apr. Ct. 1787.

p. 371   THOMAS CLARK of Brunswick Co. to SHADRACK STALLINGS of Duplin
Co., 24 Feb 1787, for 40 pds. specie 50A between EVAN JONES' & THOMAS
CLARK'S land on a branch of Rockfish Creek. Wit: JOHN HOLDON, JOHN
HOWELL. Apr. Ct. 1787.

p. 372   REUBEN WESTON, planter, to SAMUEL BOWDEN (BOURDEN), taylor,
both of Duplin Co., 4 Apr 1785, for 50 pds. specie 320A on the NS of Goshen Swamp
& on the ES of Bear Marsh Branch, joining & between the lines of MOSES TYLER,
JOHN WINDERS, HENRY HOLLEY, & THOMAS BRADLEY, being part of a tract of
520A granted to the sd. WESTON 28 Feb 1775. Wit: WM. TAYLOR, JOSHUA
CHAMBLEE. Apr. Ct. 1787.

p. 374   ABSALUM (X) BOYET to JOHN WILLIAMS, both planters of Duplin Co.,
1 Mar 1786, for 62 pds. 10 shill. current money of N. C. 75A on the SS of Panther
Swamp, beg. at a spanish oak, MR. ALEXR. McCULLOCH'S line on Peter's
Branch, to Prescoat's Spring Branch, patented by sd. McCULLOCH 9 Oct 1749 &
transferred from him to JOHN WILLIAMS 9 Apr 1761 & from sd. WILLIAMS to

RICHARD PRESCOAT, & from sd. PRESCOAT to MAJOR CROOM who deeded to sd.
BOYET. Wit: LEWIS BARNES, HALL FAUNAU, LUTSON (S) STROUD. Apr. Ct.
1787.

p. 375   WILLIAM ANDERSON of Bertie Co. to PHILLIP WARD of Duplin Co., 21
Nov 1786, for 10 pds. current money, his distributive part of the estate of PHILLIP
WARD, late of Bertie Co., dec'd, which part belongs to him the sd. ANDERSON in
right of SARAH his wife, the dau. of sd. WARD dec'd, or in consequence of the
L. W. & T. of the sd. PHILLIP WARD dec'd, by which he devised negroes & their
increase, household furn., planta. tools, stock money or money at interest or any
other articles whatsoever, which is now in the poss. of MARY WARD, the widow of
the sd. PHILLIP WARD dec'd. Wit: WARREN BLOUNT, BENJAMIN BLOUNT.
Jan. Ct. 1787.

p. 377   JOHN McGEE of New Hanover Co. to JAMES GILLESPIE of Duplin Co.,
16 June 1787, for 230 pds. specie a woman slave named JUNO & her 2 children
DANIEL & SOLOMON & one negro boy named WILL, the child of my wench GRACE.
Wit: JOHN HOUSEMON, KILBY FAISON, SAML. SPENCER. Probated 18 Dec 1787.

p. 377   SAMUEL JOHNSTON, Exr. & JEAN BLAIR, Exx. of the L. W. & T. of
GEORGE BLAIR dec'd of Edenton in Chowan Co., N. C. & JOHN JOHNSTON of
Bertie Co. to FREDERICK BARFIELD of Duplin Co., 2 July 1780, for 47 pds. 4
shill. proc. 243A, being part of a tract of 3,000A taken up by SAML. JOHNSTON,
Esqr. in his lifetime & by him willed to SAMUEL JOHNSTON & JOHN JOHNSTON &
one undivided moiety thereof conveyed by the sd. SAMUEL JOHNSTON to GEORGE
BLAIR in his lifetime. Deed mentions WILLIAM WHITFIELD'S corner. Wit:
JOHN GRAY, JOSEPH HORNE. Probated 3 Nov 1787.

p. 379   JOHN (R) RIVENBARK of New Hanover Co. to JOHN BONEY of Duplin Co.,
17 Mar 1787, for 60 pds. N. C. money 100A on the Long Branch of Rockfish Creek,
beg. at a pine WIMBARK BONEY'S corner, to a pine by the Long Branch at WM.
CAISE'S line. Wit: DANIEL TEACHY, JACOB BONEY. Apr. Ct. 1787.

p. 380   CHRISTOPHER MARTIN to HENRY STOKES, both of Duplin Co., 25 Feb
1787, for 100 pds. specie 180A in 2 tracts: (1) 80A beg. at a bunch of bays on the
Miery Branch on WILLIAM HALL'S line, to a white oak in the Wolf Pond Branch;
(2) 100A beg. at a white oak in the Wolf Pond Branch his corner of the before men-
tioned survey, to a stake on JAMES FLEMMON'S line, to a stake on FELIX
KENAN'S line as by deed from WILLIAM HALL to sd. CHRISTOPHER MARTIN 4
Feb 1780 for the former tract & patent dated 9 Oct 1783. Wit: RICHARD COOPER,
ANDREW READ. Apr. Ct. 1787.

p. 382   HICKS MILLS to BENJAMIN DULANY, both of Duplin Co., 20 Mar 1787,
for 50 pds. specie 100A on the ES of the Northeast River & SS of Limestone Swamp
on the ES of Mill's Mill Branch, being part of 3 surveys beg. at a black gum in sd.
Mill Branch. Wit: JAMES MURROW, JOHN MURROW. Deed also signed by
ELIZABETH (O) MILLS. Apr. Ct. 1787.

p. 383   WILLIAM WILKINS to EDWARD CORNWALLACE DeBRUHL, both of
Duplin Co., 9 Feb 1780, for 3,000 pds. good & lawful money of N. C. 200A in
Onslow Co. in 2 tracts: (1) 100A on the SS of New River, beg. at a small gum by
the river side KIBBLE'S lower corner on the river above a branch or creek in a

field, to a pine in the WARD line of the tract, being land deeded from DANIEL
HICKS to WILLIAM WILKINS; (2) 100A deeded from JAMES KIBBLE to WILLIAM
WILKINS, beg. at a sweet gum by New River to JOHN WILLIAMSON'S corner. Wit:
FREDERICK BARFIELD, JAMES (卅) TAYLOR. Apr. Ct. 1787.

p. 385   WILLIAM GRADDY to ALEXANDER GRADDY, both planters of Duplin Co.,
16 Apr 1787, for 10 pds. specie 100A in the Northeast, beg. at a hickory in the back
line, part of a tract taken up by WILLIAM WILLIAMS & from him deeded to
RICHARD BUSH who deeded to sd. WILLIAM GRADDY, which sd. land was patented
by sd. WILLIAMS 6 Apr 1745. Wit: FREDK. GRADDY, WM. GRADY, JUNR.
Apr. Ct. 1787.

p. 386   ISAAC (Ŧ) DAWSON to ALEXANDER GRADDY, both planters of Duplin
Co., 16 Apr 1787, for 10 pds. specie 150A on the ES of the Northeast River & on the
NS of Burncoat Swamp, beg. at a gum in the side of the sd. swamp by JOHN
GRADDY'S corner, to the mouth of the Race Path Branch, patented 23 Dec 1779.
Wit: FREDK. GRADDY, WILLIAM GRADDY. Apr. Ct. 1787.

p. 387   GEORGE (O) COOPER to his son JOHN COOPER, both of Duplin Co., 20
Feb 1787, for "natural love & affection" 250A on the SS of Nahunga Branch, being
part of a tract the sd. GEORGE COOPER bought of WILLIAM HALL, beg. on the sd.
swamp at the mouth of a small branch dividing GEORGE COOPER'S planta. & the
sd. 250A. Also mentions the Miery Branch at CHRISTOPHER MARTIN'S corner.
Wit: BENJM. BEST., RICHARD COOPER. Apr. Ct. 1787.

p. 388 JAMES HURST (JUNR.) to LEVIN WATKINS, both of Duplin Co., for 35 pds.
specie 60A in 2 tracts: (1) 20A on the head of Cow Hole Branch, being the ES of a
patent granted to JAMES HURST, SENR. 23 Dec 1763; (2) 40A adj. the 1st 20A, on
the NS of Goshen Swamp & on the ES of Cow Hole Branch, joining & between JAMES
HURST, SENR. & JOHN FOLEY'S lines, beg. at a live oak at the run of Cow Hole
Branch, to a maple on FOLEY'S line, to a pine JOHN SHUFFIELD'S corner, along
JAMES HURST, SENR.'S line, granted to JAMES HURST, JUNR. 10 Nov 1784.
Deed dated 21 Jan 1785. Wit: FRANCIS OLIVER, GEORGE OUTLAW, JAMES
HURST. Apr. Ct. 1787.

p. 390   GEORGE OUTLAW to LEVIN WATKINS, both of Duplin Co., 16 Dec 1785,
for 85 pds. specie 125A on the NS of Goshen Swamp & on the ES of Cow Hole Branch,
beg. at a pine a corner tree near Cow Hole, the tree that is in VINING'S patent &
running across Cow Hole as the line runs to an oak near BLANSHARD'S corner, to
the mouth of Scantling Branch. Wit: FRANCIS OLIVER, ELISHA JERNAGAN.
Apr. Ct. 1787.

p. 392   JAMES HURST, planter, to LEVIN WATKINS, both of Duplin Co., 2 Apr
1786, for 6 pds. specie 5A on the NS of Goshen Swamp & on the drains of Cow Hole,
beg. at a spanish oak a corner of WILLIAM VINING'S patent, now belonging to the
sd. WATKINS, being part of a tract of 100A granted to sd. JAMES HURST 27 Dec
1763. Wit: FRANCIS OLIVER, SARAH (X) OLIVER. Apr. Ct. 1787.

p. 393   JOHN NEELE (NEALE) to ANDREW REED, both of Duplin Co., 14 Apr
1787, for 50 pds. specie 100A beg. in the run of Battle Branch on RICHARD
MILLER'S paten line, to the run of Dark Swamp, to River Swamp, to run of Battle
Branch. Wit: ROBERT LESTER, JOHN NEALE, JUNR. Apr. Ct. 1787.

p. 395   WILLIAM (X) PICKET (SENR.) to WILLIAM PICKET, JUNR., both of
Duplin Co., 13 Feb 1786, for 97 pds. 250A in 2 tracts: (1) 50A on the ES of Cape
Fear River known as the Indian Graves, beg. at a pine above the mouth of Cypress
Creek & running down the river swamp to a white oak in a branch, to a corner pine
in MURRAY'S line, to ROADS'ES[sic] old field; (2) 200A beg. at a water oak on the
bank of the river at the mouth of Cypress Creek, to a pine at HARP'S line. Wit:
JAMES MURRAY, JUNR., JAMES MURRAY, SENR. Apr. Ct. 1787.

p. 397   JEREMIAH (W) HULET to SOLOMON CARTER, both of Duplin Co., 14 Feb
1787, for 30 pds. current money 100A on the ES of the Northeast River & WS the
Beaverdam prong of Limestone, beg. at a water oak JOSEPH CANADAY'S upper
corner in a glade or drain 80 yards wide of the swamp, to a loblolly bay in Mirey
Branch, down the run of Limestone to JOSEPH CANADAY'S line. Wit: JAMES
PICKET, SOLOMON (S) PICKET. Apr. Ct. 1787.

p. 398   RICHARD BLACKLEDGE of Beaufort Co., merchant, to THOMAS GRAY,
Esqr. of Sampson Co., 5 Nov 1786, for 1,025 millea dollars, 5 negroes to wit: a
man DANY about 36 yrs., a negro lad ARON about 18 yrs., two negro women BETT
& NANCY each about 18 yrs. & a negro boy named BEN about 15 yrs. of age. Wit:
ARTHUR PIPKIN, HARRY GRAY. July Ct. 1787.

p. 399   JAMES MORRIS to WILLIAM BECK (co. not given), 28 Dec 1786, for
68 pds. 10 shill. & 50 barrels of good merchantable corn, a negro fellow called
JACOB. Wit: JOHN NICHOLS, RIGDOM BRYAN. July Ct. 1787.

p. 399   THEOPHILUS WILLIAMS to JOHN BARFIELD, both of Duplin Co., 19 Apr
1786, for 50 pds. current money one negro girl about 3 yrs. old named HANNAH,
dau. of THENER. Wit: FREDERICK BARFIELD, WILLIAM WHITFIELD. July
Ct. 1787.

p. 400   WILLIAM HURST, planter, to WILLIAM BECK, merchant, both of Wayne
Co., 24 Oct 1786, for 200 pds. specie money a negro fellow slave named LEWIS
about 21 yrs. of age. Wit: JOHN BECK, SAMUEL SLOCUMB. July Ct. 1787.

p. 400   LEVIN KING of Somerset Co., Md. to WILLIAM DICKSON of Duplin Co.,
28 Nov 1786, for 80 pds. current money of N. C. in gold & silver & 34 pds. in
paper currency, a negro man named STEPHEN 20 yrs. of age & a negro woman
named LYDIA about 60 yrs. of age. Wit: JAMES MORRIS, EDWARD DICKSON.
July Ct. 1787.

p. 401   JAMES KENAN, High Shff. of Duplin Co. to WILLIAM HUNTER of Duplin
Co., 19 July 1787, 257A on the NS of the Grove Swamp on Ash Branch in 2 tracts:
(1) 102A beg. at a bunch of ash trees growing out of an old stump by the Grove Run,
lower side of Ash Branch, to a white oak in a little branch HUNTER'S lower corner,
formerly MOLTEN'S corner, to SAMUEL BOYET'S corner, thence JOHN PHILLIP'S
line; (2) 150A beg. at a pine sd. HUNTER'S corner, formerly ABRAHAM MOLTEN'S
by a little drain of Ash Branch, to a pine by HUNTER'S lower corner. The Court
awarded 56 pds. 5 shill. 3 pence, plus cost & charges of 3 pds. 11 shill. 9 pence to
THOMAS JERNIGAN for damages in a suit against JESSE JERNIGAN, owner of
257A of above sd. land which was purchased of WILLIAM HUNTER for 10 pds. 10
shill. at public auction held 3 Mar 1787. Wit: THOS. GRAY. July Ct. 1787.

p. 404   WILLIAM (H) HUNTER of Duplin Co., planter, to ANDREW LAWS of Wayne

Co., 21 Aug 1786, for 80 pds. specie 200A on the WS of the Northeast River & on the WS of Persimmon Swamp between RUTHERFORD'S & McINTIRE'S lines, the 1st tract beg. at a white oak on the side of Persimmon Swamp & runs thence to a post RUTHERFORD'S corner, patented 22 July 1774, & the 2nd tract on the WS of the Northeast River & SS of Persimmon Swamp, beg. at a black gum & bay tree on the run of Persimmon Swamp, at ROBERT DICKSON'S corner. Wit: THOS. ROUTE-LEDGE. July Ct. 1787.

p. 405   LEWIS BARNES of Duplin Co. to BRYAN WHITFIELD of Dobbs Co., 14 Oct 1786, for 100 pds. specie 1,276A on Burncoat Swamp in 5 tracts: (1) 640A granted to ANTHONY WILLIAMS by patent; (2) 156A joining the 1st 640A, by patent granted to sd. BARNES, adj. & between the lands of LEWIS SMITH, MAXWELL, & THOMAS SHELTON & White Oak Swamp; (3) 200A granted by patent to sd. BARNES on the head of Burncoat & Panther Branches in & between the old Mill Branch, SAMUEL JONES' corner, JONES BOYETS' corner, MONTFORD'S & MAXWELL'S lines; (4) 100A patented to JOSEPH SUTTON on the NS of Burncoat in & between the mouth of Prescoat's Branch & ROBERT BEVERLY'S line; (5) 180A patented to JAMES OUTLAW lying on the NS of Burncoat Swamp in & between Prescoat's Branch, JOSEPH SUTTON'S line. Wit: ISAAC HINES, THOS. UZZELL, JOHN BARFIELD. July Ct. 1787.

p. 407   JOHN RHODES of Duplin Co. to CATHERINE TAYLOR, relict of the late WILLIAM TAYLOR dec'd (co. not given), 23 Apr 1787, for 100 peper corn to be paid unto sd. RHODES 1 Jan annually, if required, & the sd. RHODES farm lett unto the sd. CATHERINE TAYLOR, all the lands (acreage not given) on the NS of Goshen Swamp & on the ES of Bear Marsh, incl. the planta. whereon the sd. WILLIAM TAYLOR, Esqr. dec'd lived, which was given by deed of gift by sd. WILLIAM TAYLOR to his dau. ELIZABETH, now the wife of the sd. JOHN RHODES excepting 1A at the end of the Mill Dam & the privileges of the Mill Pond, unto the sd. CATHERINE TAYLOR during her natural life. Wit: SAMUEL BOWDEN, FRANS. OLIVER. July Ct. 1787.

p. 409   MILLS MUMFORD to THOMAS SHELTON, both of Duplin Co., 5 Jan 1787, for 16 pds. specie 100A patented by JAMES DOBSON 10 Nov 1784 which sd. DOBSON sold to sd. MUMFORD, between the Calf Marsh & White Oak, joining the sd. SHELTON'S line. Wit: LEWIS (X) BARFIELD, ANTHY. (A) JONES. July Ct. 1787.

p. 410   THEOPHILUS WILLIAMS, planter, to JAMES MORRIS, both of Duplin Co., 9 Feb 1787, for 75 pds. current money of N. C. 100A on the SS of Bear Swamp, being the land where RAWLEY MILLS formerly lived, beg. at a water oak WILLIAM GUY'S corner, at HARDY MALPAS' corner, to a white oak sd. MILLS' corner. Wit: W. DICKSON, D. GLISSON. July Ct. 1787.

p. 412   WILLIAM O'DANIEL of Duplin Co. to WILLIAM WHITFIELD of Wayne Co., 28 Dec 1785, for 40 pds. specie 200A on the NS of the NE Creek & WS of Jumping Run, beg. at a pine on Jumping Run Marsh a corner tree of JESSE BARFIELD'S patent dated 15 Dec 1778, to Rooty Branch, THEOPHILUS WILLIAMS' line, incl. part of the two patents of land & the planta. where CHARITY O'DANIEL formerly lived. Wit: JOHN IVEY, JOHN BARFIELD, BRYAN WHITFIELD. July Ct. 1787.

p. 414   JOEL WILDER to JESSE BROWN, both of Duplin Co., 25 Oct 1786, for 24 pds. specie 120A on a branch of Muddy Creek called Stephen's Swamp, being part

of a survey of land granted to JOSHUA LEE for 108A by a patent dated 1764, beg.
at the mouth of Jacob's Branch, a dividing line. Wit: WM. FARRIER, MARY (X)
FARRIER. July Ct. 1787.

p. 415   WILLIAM FOLSOM of Burk Co., Ga. to PHILL SOUTHERLAND of Duplin
Co., for 50 pds. specie 200A on the ES of the Northeast of Cape Fear River on BS
of Limestone Creek, beg. at a birch on the SS of the creek at FRANCIS
BRICE'S corner, & in & between SAMUEL JOHNSTON'S line, JOHN ATKINS' cor-
ner, formerly granted to the sd. FOLSOM 26 Sep 1766. Wit: WILLIAM SOUTHER-
LAND, STEPHEN BOWEN, NICHOLAS FENNEL. Dated 10 Dec 1784. July Ct. 1784.

p. 417   JAMES MILLS to WILLIAM HALL, both of Duplin Cp, 22 Mar 1787, for
30 pds. current money of N. C. 100A granted to sd. MILLS 1 Apr 1780, on the NS
of Maxwell Swamp & BS of Stocking Head, beg. at a white oak JOHN WHITMAN'S
corner, along ADAM PLAT'S line. Wit: JOSEPH T. RHODES, THOMAS ROUT-
LEDGE, JUNR. July Ct. 1787.

p. 418   ELIJAH (*AU*) BOWEN to MESHACK STALLINGS, both of Duplin Co., 15
Apr 1786, for 140 pds. specie 200A on the upper end of BENJAMIN FUSSEL'S land,
beg. at a stake in his cornfield, to a gum in Fussel's Creek. Wit: SHADRACK
STALLINGS, JOHN DUFF. July Ct. 1787.

p. 420   DAVID CANNON, planter, to JAMES MORRIS, both of Duplin Co., 29 Dec
1786, for 300 pds. current money 421A on the SS of the Northeast on Rattlesnake
Branch in 4 tracts: (1) 121A on the SS of the Northeast Swamp in the fork of sd.
branch, beg. at a small pine in a branch below ANTHONY JONES' field, being part
of a survey of 300A formerly granted by patent to JOHN CONNERLY dated 2 Apr
1751, which land descended from sd. CONNERLY to his son CULLEN CONNERLY
& since conveyed by sd. CULLEN CONNERLY to JESSE BARFIELD who sold sd.
land to CONSTANTINE WHITFIELD; (2) 100A on the SS of the Northeast on Rattlesnake Branch, which was formerly granted to EDWARD ROLLINS by patent dated
29 Sep 1753; (3) 100A adj. the 2nd piece formerly granted to SOLOMON BARFIELD
by patent dated 15 Mar 1756, the last 2 tracts being sold to CONSTANTINE WHIT-
FIELD by WILLIAM GRADDY & JESSE BEARFIELD; (4) 100A on the SS of Rattlesnake Branch & joining the lines of the other lands hereby granted, being part of a
tract of 200A granted to sd. WHITFIELD 24 May 1773. All 4 tracts of 421A was
conveyed from sd. WHITFIELD to his dau. RACHEL GOODMAN by deed of gift 24
Sep 1778 & since conveyed by a deed from HENRY GOODMAN & RACHEL his wife
to TIMOTHY GOODMAN who conveyed to sd. HENRY GOODMAN by deed of gift
dated 26 Oct 1778. HENRY GOODMAN deeded the same 421A to STEPHEN BEAR-
FIELD 25 Oct 1785 & sd. STEPHEN deed to DAVID CANNON 16 Nov 1785. Wit:
WILLIAM DICKSON, JOHN NICHOLS. July Ct. 1787.

p. 423   GEORGE (x) MALLARD to DANIEL MALLARD, both planters of Duplin
Co., 16 July 1787, for 50 pds. current money of N. C. 300A in 2 tracts: (1) 100A
on the WS of the Northeast River on Turkey Pen Branch, beg. at a chinquapin tree
at the river swamp, as by patent doth appear; (2) 200A between the mouth of Persimmon & the Grove Swamp, beg. at a red oak on JOHN MALLARD'S line, to a red
oak by CHARLES WARD'S line, to a water oak by Horse Branch. Wit: WILLIAM
SOUTHERLAND, ELIJAH MALLARD, PHILL SOUTHERLAND. July Ct. 1787.

p. 425   DAVID GREER of Duplin Co. to STEPHEN MILER, cooper of same, 28

Apr 1786, for 600 pds. good & lawfull money of N. C. 2 tracts of land: (1) 150A on the SS of Goshen Swamp, beg. at a lightwood stake by a pond formerly ANTHONY MILLER'S corner, to a dividing line between the sd. GREER & GEORGE MILLER, formerly laid off for sd. GREER by EDWARD COOLEY, to CHAMBERS' line, being the contents of a deed made by sd. COOLEY to the sd. GREER; (2) 80A on the SS of Goshen Swamp & joining the 1st piece, part of a patent of 260A formerly granted to ANTHONY MILLER & GEORGE MILLER, beg. at a litewood stake, the corner of the pst tract. Wit: CHAS. WARD, EDWARD SLOAN. July Ct. 1787.

p. 427   WILLIAM FARRIOR to JOAB PADGET, both of Duplin Co., 22 Jan 1788, for 150 pds. current money of N. C. 191A on the SS of Muddy Creek, incl. the planta. & impr. made by sd. FARRIOR & lately occupied by JOHN PARKER, it being part of the contents of 2 old surveys, one granted to ZEBULON HOLLINGS-WORTH for 150A dated 23 May 1757, which by sundry conveyances became the prop. of the sd. FARRIOR, & the other granted to JAMES FARRIOR, the patent dated 16 Apr 1765 & left to JOHN FARRIOR by his father, & conveyed from JOHN FARRIOR to WILLIAM FARRIOR. Deed mentions a corner between WILLIAM FARRIOR & JOB THIGPEN, Little Mirey Branch & JOHN FARRIOR'S planta. Wit: JOHN DICKSON, ROBERT BISHOP. Jan. Ct. 1788.

p. 429   WILLIAM MOOR (MOORE) to JOSEPH SMITH of Co. afsd. (Duplin?), 19 June 1787, for 150 pds. specie a negro woman named SILVY about 22 yrs. of age. Wit: ISAC HUNTER, THEOPHILUS WILLIAMS. Oct. Ct. 1787.

p. 429   ELIZABETH (O) HOLLINGSWORTH to JACOB HOLLINGSWORTH, both of Duplin Co., 15 Sep 1787, for 100 pds. specie a certain negro boy named TONEY about 15 yrs. of age, reserving of sd. negro to herself during her natural life, & after her decease to sd. JACOB HOLLINGSWORTH. Wit: SARAH HOLLINGS-WORTH, JOSEPH T. RHODES. Oct. Ct. 1787.

p. 430   GEORGE MORISEY (co. not given) to JAMES PEARSALL (co. not given), 17 Oct 1787, for 150 pds. a negro wench called NANCY. Wit: W. L. HILL, C. IVEY. Oct. Ct. 1787.

p. 430   THO. (THOMAS) GRAY to ELIAS JAMES, 25 May 1787, for 125 pds. specie one negro woman slave named NANNY about 16 yrs. of age. Wit: EDMD. BLACKMAN. (Probate date not given.)

p. 430   WM. (WILLIAM) McGOWAN to JAMES GILLESPIE, both of Duplin Co., 11 Nov 1785, for 11 1/4 A, a certain tract of 6 1/4 A on the SS of the Mill Branch, adj. & between the lands of the sd. McGOWAN & JAMES GILLESPIE. Wit: JOSEPH DICKSON, JAMES JAMES. Oct. Ct. 1787.

p. 432   MAJOR CROOM of Dobbs Co. to JAMES GILLESPIE of Duplin Co., 12 Oct 1787, for 170 pds. 172A in 2 tracts: (1) 100A on the WS of the Northeast Cape Fear between ANTHONY MILLER'S land & a place called Clarks Folly, adj. & between the lands of sd. MILLER & STEPHEN CLARING; (2) 72A, being part of a tract granted to MICHAEL DICKSON & ROBERT DICKSON adj. & between the lands of MAJOR CROOM & WILLIAM STOKES. Wit: MAJOR CROOM, JUNR., THOMAS UZZELL. Oct. Ct. 1787.

p. 433   MARTIN WELLS to NICHOLAS BRYAN (BRYANT), both of Duplin Co.,

15 Sep 1787, for 50 pds. specie currency of N. C. 150A on the WS of the Northeast Branch of Cape Fear River & on SS of Island Creek in 2 pieces, beg. at a maple the 1st station of his old survey of 160A, adj. & between the lines of HENRY ALLAN, JOHN COOK & JOHN PARKER & FREDERICK WELLS. Wit: JOHN HOLDON, FREDERICK WELLS. Oct. Ct. 1787.

p. 434   JOHN RHODES to HENRY McCULLOCH, PENELOPE McCULLOH & CATHERINE McCULLOH, all of Duplin Co., 24 Apr 1787, for 5 shill. specie, a tract (acreage not given) on the NS of Goshen Swamp & on the ES of Bear Marsh, cont. all the lands adj. to & incl. the planta. whereon the late WILLIAM TAYLOR, Esqr. dec'd lived, which was given by deed of gift by the sd. TAYLOR to his dau. ELIZABETH, now the wife of the sd. RHODES, excepting 1A joining the end of the Mill Dam & all the privileges of the Mill Pond, & also excepting a lease of the sd. land & tenements with every part & parcel thereof to CATHERINE TAYLOR, relict of the sd. WILLIAM TAYLOR, Esqr., made by the sd. RHODES bearing date 23 Apr 1787 during his life. Wit: SAMUEL BOWDEN, FRANS. OLIVER. Oct. Ct. 1787.

p. 435   JAS. KENAN (JAMES), Shff. of Duplin Co. to JOHN WALLER, JUNR. of Duplin Co., 19 Apr 1786, for 25 pds. 15 shill. 100A on the SS of Limestone Swamp & on BS of the main road, being the place where BENJAMIN SMITH, planter late of Duplin Co. dec'd formerly lived on, beg. at a pine on WALLER'S back line near the road, by the end of Halls Ave., which sd. KENAN exposed for sale on 16 Sep 1785 & JOHN WALLER, JUNR. became the highest bidder at public auction. The Court awarded 9 pds. 19 shill., plus cost and charges of 3 pds. 9 shill. 3 pence to STEPHEN WILLIAMS for debt & damages in suit against BENJAMIN SMITH, dec'd. Wit: WILLIAM DICKSON, W. LIGHTFOOT. Oct. Ct. 1787.

p. 437   ROBERT MERRIT of Sampson Co. to JAMES BLAND of Duplin Co., 10 Nov 1786, for 10 pds. 100A on BS of the Iron Mine Branch, beg. at a stake by a pine, a corner tree of a survey formerly patented by JOHN BLANTON. Wit: DAVID WILLIAMS, ROBERT ROLINS. Oct. Ct. 1787.

p. 439   JOHN WILLIAMS & CLOE (X) WILLIAMS his wife to AMOS JOHNSTON, all of Duplin Co., 11 Aug 1787, for 150 pds. current money of Carolina 100A on the Northeast Prong of Cape Fear incl. the planta. whereon ROBERT HOOKS formerly lived, became the property of RUTH HOOKS & SUSANNAH HOOKS, which sd. land by several conveyances became the prop. of sd. WILLIAMS, beg. at a large red oak at the last station or corner of the original patent, the dividing line between WILLIAM PICKET & MURRAY. Wit: JOB THIGPEN, WILLIAM FARRIOR, JOHN FARRIOR. Oct. Ct. 1787.

p. 440   JACOB (✠) MATHEWS, planter, to JOHN MATHEWS, both of Duplin Co., 18 Oct 1787, for 20 pds. lawful money, 190A on the SE side of Stewart's Creek & BS of Miller's Mill Swamp, beg. at a cypress on the NS of sd. swamp ARTHUR MATTHEWS corner, along DAVID TUCKER'S line, to a pine on the edge of a Clear Run Branch, to a pine on the edge of the Sand Hill Branch, the sd. 190A being the contents of a patent granted to JACOB MATHEWS 10 Nov 1784. Wit: JOHN EVANS, JAS. WILSON. Oct. Ct. 1787.

p. 441   JOHN WRIGHT to ROBERT BYRD, both of Duplin Co., 9 Oct 1787, for 5 pds. current money 150A on the SS of Goshen between the Reedy Branch & the heads of the Poley Branch, joining sd. BYRD'S own land, beg. at a pine ROBERTS'

old corner, to a pine in the Reedy Branch by THOMAS GRAY'S line, being the upper
half of a patent of 300A granted to sd. WRIGHT 15 Dec 1778. Wit: W. DICKSON,
STEPHEN BARFIELD. Oct. Ct. 1787.

p. 443   ANDREW (⊗) NEELY of Sampson Co. to JAMES BLAND of Duplin Co.,
28 Nov 1786, for 30 pds. 100A on a branch of Rockfish called the Iron Mine Branch,
beg. at a pine on GEORGE MERRIT'S line. Wit: JOSHUA (X) BLANTON, JOSHUA
HACKLEY. Oct. Ct. 1787.

p. 444   EBENEZER GARRISON, planter of Duplin Co. to JOHN McGEE of New
Hanover Co. & nigh Wilmington, 2 June 1787, for 30 pds. current money of N. C.
135A on the ES of the North Branch of Cape Fear River, & on it certain branch of
Muddy Creek, known by the name of Marsh Branch, it being the south of sd. Marsh
Branch, beg. at a small black gum below a small branch, running into the Marsh
Branch & Mill Pond, in the back part or line of JOHN MAGEE, bearing date 22 Dec
1770. Wit: WILLIAM FARRIOR, JUSTIS MILLER. Oct. Ct. 1787.

p. 445   SAMUEL BOWDEN of Duplin Co., taylor, to JESSE SWINSON, planter of
Duplin Co., 17 June 1785, for 25 pds. specie 160A on the NS of Goshen Swamp & the
ES of Bear Marsh, beg. at a pine JOHN WINDERS' corner, to HENRY HALLY &
THOMAS BRADLEY'S lines, to a place called the Calf Pen, being part of a tract of
320A & now transferred to sd. SWINSON. Wit: JOHN WINDERS, SENR., JOHN
WINDERS. Oct. Ct. 1787.

p. 447   CLAUDIUS CARTWRIGHT to JOHN BLANTON, both of Duplin Co., 29 Aug
1785, for 40 pds. current money of N. C. 300A on the SS of Rockfish & NS of
Doctor's Creek, beg. at a pine JOHN LITTLE'S corner tree, adj. & between the
lines of LITTLE & BLANTON & BLANTON'S other line patented by JOSEPH DICK-
SON. Wit: JANE DICKSON, JOSEPH DICKSON. Oct. Ct. 1787.

p. 448   THOMAS (T) PHIPS (PHIPPS), planter, to FELIX FREDERICK, taylor,
both of Duplin Co., 16 Oct 1787, for 12 pds. lawfull money, 2 tractsof 350A: (1)
150A being part of 200A held by the sd. PHIPPS by patent granted by GOV. MARTIN
5 Mar 1774, beg. at a small white oak in the edge of a pond, to a sweet gum in
Nahunga Swamp, it being the dividing line between sd. PHIPPS & LEWIS THOMAS,
as SUTTON BIRD'S line runs on the NS of the swamp to sd. PHIPP'S line; (2) 200A
on the NS of Nahunga Swamp adj. the 1st tract incl. WILLIAM MOOR'S pecoson,
beg. at a pine the sd. PHIPP'S corner & adj. WILLIAM MOORE'S & WILLIAM
ELLIOT'S corner, as by patent granted by GOV. CASWELL 1 Sep 1785. Wit:
WILLIAM BEST, ALEXANDER DICKSON. Oct. Ct. 1787.

p. 450   THOMAS BAKER of Great Pee Dee in S. C. to JOHN McGEE of Duplin
Co., 15 Oct 1784, for 13 pds. annuity 100A on the ES of the Northeast & upper side
of Cypress Creek & NS of the Gum Swamp, beg. at a white oak on BENTON WILLI-
FORD'S line, to JOSEPH HUTCHESON'S line, patented to sd. BAKER 29 Oct 1782.
Wit: JAMES LOCKHART, STEPHEN WILLIAMS, JOHN FARRIOR. Oct. Ct. 1787.

p. 452   JAMES WRIGHT of New Hanover Co. to JACOB WELLS, JUNR. of Duplin
Co., 8 Sep 1787, for 200 pds. 440A on the NS of Rockfish Creek, a place called
POTTER'S land, adj. & between HAWKINS' or DUFF'S line, JAMES PHEBUS' line,
& SHADRACK STALLINGS' line. ELIZABETH WRIGHT also signed the deed.
Wit: DANIEL TEACHY, JACOB BONY. Oct. Ct. 1787.

p. 454   JAMES PATERSON & JANE PATERSON of the Town of Fayetteville to
JAMES GILLESPIE of Duplin Co., 8 Jan 1787, for 120 pds. current money of N. C.
232A on the ES of the Northeast Branch of Cape Fear River, near the mouth of
Limestone on Maple Branch, being part of a larger tract of land granted by GEORGE
II. by letters patent dated 7 May 1754 to JOHN BROCK, which sd. BROCK conveyed
to FRANCIS BRICE who conveyed to DAVID MITCHELL, & sd. MITCHELL deeded
to JOHN BUNTING who conveyed to WILLIAM WARD late husb. of the sd. JANE
PATTERSON. Wit: JOSEPH T. RHODES, JOHN WAHH, DOLPHIN DAVIS. Oct.
Ct. 1787.

p. 456   CHARLES HOOTEN & his wife ANN HOOTEN of Bertie Co. to LEWIS
THOMAS of Duplin Co., 12 Aug 1785, for 200 pds. current money of N. C. 242A on
the head of the Grove Swamp, beg. at an ash on the main run of the sd. swamp.
Wit: JHONATHAN THOMAS, DEBORAH (X) PHIPS. Oct. Ct. 1787.

p. 457   JAMES PEARSALL, Shff. of Duplin Co. to JAMES JAMES of same, 20 Oct
1785, for 150 pds. 100A on the SS of the Grove Swamp & on the Middle Branch of
Frederick Mill Branch, it being the contents of a patent granted to PATRICK
POWELL, but now the lands & tenements of ARCHIBALD PEARCE. The Court
awarded 20 pds. 7 shill 10 pence, plus cost & charges of 3 shill 9 pence to ELISHA
CARROL for debt & damages in suit against sd. PEARCE, owner of sd. 100A,
which was purchased by JAMES JAMES at public auction 22 June 1785. Wit:
DANIEL GLISSON, JAMES WALLACE, JOHN ARMSTRONG. Oct. Ct. 1787.

p. 459   WILLIAM TAYLOR, planter, to his dau. ELIZABETH TAYLOR, both of
Duplin Co., 14 Jan 1779, for 100 pds. proc. 1,060A in 3 tracts: (1) 600A on the NS
of Goshen Swamp; (2) 100A on the NS of Goshen Swamp, beg. at a black oak JOHN
ROGERS' corner; (3) 360A NS of Goshen Swamp joining other lines of sd. WM.
TAYLOR, beg. at a white oak on Goshen Swamp near ROGERS' corner, to Bearskin
Branch, to the head of Poley Bridge Branch, with sd. TAYLOR'S other line, to a
pine in the side of Goshen Swamp. Wit: WILLIAM GOODMAN, JOHN GIBBS,
Oct. Ct. 1787.

p. 461   (Note: This page missing on microfilm. See Book 1A in Duplin Co.
           Courthouse.)

p. 462   "Duplin County. Be it remembered that the sd. WILLIAM TAYLOR is to be
ever intrusted with the two deeds of gift from him to his daughter for land and
negroes, goods & chattels & that the intent of the said deeds is to invest a proper
and lawfull right to hur of the land negros good & chattels, at or after his death, no
wise debaring the said WILLIAM TAYLOR of using or altering ye the deed or deeds
at his will and pleasure or selling or giving any part or all of ye premises mentioned in the deeds aforesaid, in witness whereof I have hereunto set my hand this "
Wit: WILLM. GOODMAN
      JOHN GIBBS   ELIZABETH TAYLOR
      HENRY GOODMAN

p. 462   (Note: This page missing on microfilm. See Book 1A in Duplin Co.
           Courthouse.)

p. 462   W. (WILLIAM) DICKSON to THEOPHILUS WILLIAMS, both of Duplin Co.,
19 July 1788, for 180 pds. current money, 2 negro slaves to wit: LIDIA about 24
yrs. of age, & Country Born, with her child a boy about 18 mos. named HAMLET.
Wit: THOS. GRAY, W. GRAY. July Ct. 1788.

p. 463   PHILL SOUTHERLAND to WILLIAM SOUTHERLAND, both of Duplin Co.,
20 Dec 1784, for 100 pds. 200A on the ES of the Northeast of Cape Fear River, on
BS of Limestone Creek, beg. at a birch on the SS of the creek FRANCIS BRICE'S
lower corner, & adj. & between the lines of SAMUEL JOHNSTON, JOHN ATKINS,
JEREMIAH FOULSOM,   the sd. 200A being granted to WILLIAM FOULSOM by
patent dated 26 Sep 1766. Wit: ROBERT SOUTHERLAND, ROBERT BISHOP. Oct.
Ct. 1787.

p. 465   RICHARD (X) MEARS to PATRICK NEWTON, both of Duplin Co., 11 Feb
1787, for 180 pds. current money of N. C. 148A in 2 tracts: (1) 98A on the SE side
of Bear Swamp between the WIDOW MOOR'S & THOMAS HILL'S planta., being part
of 440A which HENRY EUSTACE McCULLOCH formerly sold to JOHN MOORE 25
Mar 1764 & which sd. MOORE by his L. W. & T. dated 14 July 1771, the sd. 98A
bequeathed to sd. JOHN MOORE it being his equal division of the land lying below
the Spring Branch divided agreeable to sd. will between his sons JOHN MOORE &
JAMES MOORE; (2) 50A on the SE side of Bear Swamp joining on the bank of the
afsd. 98A, it being part of a patent granted to sd. JOHN MOORE for 200A dated 1
July 1779. Wit: JAMES WRIGHT, AUSTIN MOORE, ANDREW FREDERICK. Oct.
Ct. 1787.

p. 467   SAMUEL WEST to ELIAS JAMES, both planters of Duplin Co., 18 July 1787,
for 500 pds. lawfull money of N. C. 200A in Duplin Co. & Sampson Co. on the NS of
the main branch of Rockfish & Calips Meadows, granted by patent to WILLIAM
KNOWLES & at his decease fell by heirship to his brother JOHN KNOWLES who sold
sd. 200A to CLIFTON BOWEN who conveyed the same to SAMUEL WEST. Wit:
CHARLES JAMES, STEPHEN SMYTH. Oct. Ct. 1787.

p. 469   ABRAHAM NEWKIRK to WILLIAM SOUTHERLAND, both of Duplin Co.,
14 _____ 1785, for 500 pds. specie 280A entered by sd. NEWKIRK, warrant No.
1191, on the NS of Limestone Creek above the mouth of Gum Branch, beg. at a
burch [sic] on FOLSOM'S line. Deed mentions WILLIAM FULSOM'S old patented
land excepted, it being a tract of land granted to ABRAHAM NEWKIRK in 1784.
Wit: NICHOLAS ROUTLEDGE, NEITHNEL McCAUM, NICHOLAS FENNEL. Oct.
Ct. 1787.

p. 471   JAS. (JAMES) MORRIS to DANIEL CLARK, both of Duplin Co., 1 Aug
1787, for 300 pds. specie 421A in 4 tracts: (See Book 1A, p. 420, DAVID CANNON
to JAMES MORRIS, for this land description.) Wit: CHARLES BROWN, WM.
WHITFIELD, DAVID CLARK. Oct. Ct. 1787.

p. 474   JOHN JOHNS, planter, & his wife ISABLE JOHNS of New Hanover Co. to
JAMES JAMES, planter of Duplin Co., 10 Sep 1776, for 60 pds. proc. 54A on the
WS of the Northeast Branch of Cape Fear River opposite the mouth of Limestone
Creek between his own land & the river that he bought of WIDOW BURTON, to the
lower corner of the WIDOW BURTON'S line formerly JACOB HANCHEY'S line,
which land was granted to JOHN JOHNS by ARTHUR DOBBS, Governor, 16 Nov
1764. Wit: DAVID BLOODWORTH, THOMAS ARMSTRONG. Jan. Ct. 1788.

p. 476   JAMES (J.) CHAMBERS, to MICHAEL GLISSON, both planters of Duplin
Co., 5 July 1787, for 60 pds. specie 200A on the SS of the Northeast Swamp, the
lower end of the Great Marsh between Horsepen Branch & Sandy Run, beg. at a
pine DENNIS GLISSON'S corner, the same being patented by WILLIAM MOBLEY

16 Dec 1762. Wit: JOHN MATCHET, JANE (O) MATCHET. Jan. Ct. 1788.

p. 477   JAMES (J) CHAMBERS to MICHAEL GLISSON, both planters of Duplin Co.,
10 Nov 1787, for 60 pds. specie 300A on the SS of the Northeast in the fork between
Camp Branch & Outlaw's Mill Swamp, beg. at a pine near DENNIS GLISSON'S line,
sd. land patented by MICHAEL GLISSON 22 Dec 1770. Wit: JOHN MATCHET,
JANE (♫) MATCHET. Jan. Ct. 1788.

p. 478   JAMES (♯) HEATH to JOHN WATERS, both of Duplin Co., 29 Jan 1787,
for 155 pds. current money 460A on the WS of Maxwell Swamp in 4 tracts: (1) 100A
patented by ISAAC PARKER beg. at a turkey oak on the side of Frank's Creek; (2)
50A conveyed from ABRAHAM BEESLEY to ALEXR. ARMSTRONG 8 Sep 1776 beg.
at the run of Jamey's Branch on the BEESLEY'S upper line, to the 2nd corner of
sd. land BEESLEY bought from JAMES WILLIAMS; (3) 110A granted to ALEXR.
ARMSTRONG 1 Apr 1780, beg. at a red oak on the edge of Parker's Branch, being
the 1st station of 100A patented by ISAAC PARKER, to a black jack on ABRAHAM
BEESLEY'S line, AUSTIN BEESLEY'S line, to a white oak at the run of Armstrong's
Branch; (4) 200A granted to sd. ARMSTRONG 1 Apr 1780, beg. at an ash at the
run of Jamey's Branch on ABRAHAM BEESLEY'S line, as it meanders with
WILLIAMS' line. Wit: JOSEPH DICKSON, LEWIS THOMAS. Jan. Ct. 1788.

p. 480   WARREN BLOUNT & ANNIS (X) BLOUNT his wife to CULLEN CONNERLY,
all of Duplin Co., 22 Sep 1786, for 80 pds. currency money of N. C. a negro girl
named ESTHER about 7 yrs. old. Wit: ROBERT BYRD, JOHN CALEB. Jan. Ct.
1788.

p. 481   JOHN LITTLE to JOHN BLANTON, both of Duplin Co., 22 Mar 1787, for
10 pds. 86A on the NS of the Doctors Creek of Rockfish, beg. at a pine JAMES
RAWLINGS line. Wit: DAVID ALDERMAN, SARAH (X) ALDERMAN. Jan. Ct.
1788.

p. 482   THOMAS GREEN to JOHN WILLSON, both of Duplin Co., 7 Apr 1787, for
7 pds. specie 34 1/2 A on the NS of Rockfish Creek incl. the impr. whereon JOHN
WILLSON'S planta. lies, beg. at a red oak near the swamp on sd. GREEN'S line,
to a large red oak in sd. WILLSON'S field near the swamp, being part of a survey
of 82A granted to sd. GREEN 1 Apr 1780. Wit: ARON WILLIAMS, JAMES
ROLLINGS. Jan. Ct. 1788.

p. 483   JOHN WILLSON to THOMAS GREEN, both of Duplin Co., 7 Apr 1787, for
7 pds. specie 42A on the NS of the main creek of Rockfish, beg. at a white oak on
the east side of the Long Branch, & on his old line, being part of a survey of 100A
patented by the sd. WILLSON in 1782. Wit: AARON WILLIAMS, JAMES
RAWLINGS. Jan. Ct. 1788.

p. 485   ELEAZER (E) ROGERS to MOSES SHOLDERS, both of Duplin Co., 5 Oct
1787, for 40 pds. specie 150A on the ES of the Northeast River & on the Richland
Branch that makes into Holly Shelter Pocosin, beg. at a pine running S 150 poles
crossing the sd. branch to a red oak near the pocosin, thence E 160 poles to a gum
in a small branch, thence N 150 poles to a stake in the Cedar Pond, thence to the
beg. Wit: ROBERT COLE, JACOB LANIER, JOHN LANIER. Jan. Ct. 1788.

p. 486   ELIJAH (X) BOWEN to WILLIAM ALBERSON, both of Duplin Co., 6 Jan

1788, for 20 pds. specie money 100A on the waters of the Northeast River between the Great Branch & Matthews Branch on Poley Bridge Branch, which sd. 100A was taken up by sd. BOWEN. Wit: ISAAC HINES, WM. O'DANIEL, SAMUEL ALBERSON. Jan. Ct. 1788.

p. 487   AARON (A) HODGESON , planter of S. C. to BYRD LANIER of Duplin Co., 13 Jan 1787, for 30 pds. specie 100A on a branch of Cypress Creek incl. a place where CHARLES GOFF now lives, beg. at a white oak by the side of a small branch in or near FRANCIS BRICE'S line, the sd. land patented by JOSEPH HODESON in 1769. Wit: JOHN LANIER, WM. CROSBY, CHARITY (X) CROSBY. Jan. Ct. 1788.

p. 488   JOHN MAGEE of New Hanover Co., nigh the Town of Wilmington, to EBENEZAR GARRISON, planter of Duplin Co., 24 Aug 1787, for 35 pds. current money 50A on the Marsh Branch near Muddy Creek, it being part of 2 surveys of land patented by WILLIAM MAGEE & the other one patented by JOHN MAGEE, beg. at a red oak on the SS of the Mill Branch upon WILLIAM FARRIOR'S line, to a pine upon THOMAS BLAKE'S line, to WILLIAM FARRIOR'S corner. Wit: WILLIAM FARRIER, JUSTICE MILLER. Jan. Ct. 1788.

p. 489   HARDY (U) REAVES to THOMAS BRADLEY, both of Duplin Co., 24 Sep 1785, for 40 pds. 100A on the NS of Goshen Swamp & on the head of Bear Marsh near HURST old line, beg. at a black gum in the branch near HURST'S line, to the 3rd corner of the patent, to a white oak on the south prong of Hurst Branch, being part of a tract granted to CHRISTOPHER BIRK, patent dated 22 Feb 1764 & conveyed through several hands unto the sd. REAVES. Wit: FRANS. OLIVER, BAKER BOURDEN. Jan. Ct. 1788.

p. 491   WILLIAM NEWTON to WILLIAM WILKINSON, both of Duplin Co., 14 Jan 1788, for 250 pds. current money of N. C. 540A in 2 tracts: (1) 100A on the SS of Bear Swamp & on the lower side of the Meeting Branch, beg. at a sweet gum & poplar at the branch, to the black oak near the head of Thunder Bottom, to GEORGE HOMES' line, the sd. 100A being part of a tract of 360A conveyed by HENRY EUSTACE McCULLOCH, Esqr. to FREDERICK BELL, who conveyed the same to CHARLES HINES & which sd. HINES conveyed to sd. NEWTON; (2) 440A on the SS of Bear Swamp & on the head of the Meeting Branch & Gum Branch & adj. the afsd. 100A, beg. at a stake & small pine GEORGE HOMES' corner, to RAWLEY MILLS' corner, to HARDY MALPASS' corner, the sd. 440A being the contents of a patent granted to sd. NEWTON 15 Dec 1778. Wit: WILLIAM WILKINSON, SEN., ROBERT WILKINSON. Jan. Ct. 1788.

p. 494   JOHN (+) HAINS of Sampson Co., planter, to SAMUEL SLOCUMB of Duplin Co., 4 Dec 1787, for 150 pds. specie 250 acres in 2 tracts: (1) 150A whereon sd. HAINS lately lived on the NS of Goshen Swamp & on the ES of Grantham's Branch, beg. at a lightwood stake on the WS of the main road, along the lines of THOMAS GRAY & NATHANIEL KENNARD, which sd. tract was conveyed by deed 19 Apr 1777 from ROBERT WARREN to the sd. HAINS; (2) 100A on the head of Grantham's Branch & on BS of the main road, beg. at a pine MICAJAH HILL'S corner or JONATHAN TAYLOR'S line, along the lines of CHARLES WOOLF & PEREGRIM JOHNSTON, & MICAJAH HILL, which tract was granted by patent 15 Dec 1778. Wit: THOS. GRAY, DAVID SLOCUMB. Jan. Ct. 1788.

p. 495   DEMPSEY (+) WESTBROOK to JACOB TAYLOR, both of Duplin Co.,

____ Jan 1786, for 30 pds. specie money 100A on the Northeast Marsh & SS of Gum Branch, beg. at a pine on the marsh above BAILES' impr. Wit: FREDK. BARFIELD, JAMES TAYLOR. Jan. Ct. 1788.

p. 497   WILLIAM WILKINS to JACOB TAYLOR, both planters of Duplin Co., 6 Oct 1784, for 40 pds. specie 100A beg. at a dividing line of marked trees between sd. TAYLOR & DEMPSEY WESTBROOK & runs a west course to a pine, thence N 40 E 180 pole to a pine by a marsh, thence down sd. marsh to the sd. dividing line between WESTBROOK & TAYLOR, thence along sd. line to the beg. Wit: FREDERICK BARFIELD, JAMES (X) TAYLOR. Jan. Ct. 1788.

p. 498   THOS. (THOMAS) WRIGHT, Shff. to JAMES GILLESPIE of Duplin Co., 17 Dec 1787, for 366 pds. 10 shill. secured to be paid to WILLIAM LORD, formerly of Brunswick Co., dec'd, by sd. GILLESPIE, 5 negroes being the prop. of the estate of sd. LORD dec'd. , the negroes being KATE, MARIAH, SARAH, PEGGY, & HANNAH sold at vendue by direction of the sd. exrs. Wit: SAMUEL HOUSTON, J. P. Apr. Ct. 1788.

p. 499   CHARLES WARD, JOHN HILL, JAMES OUTLAW, SAMUEL HOUSTON, DAVID MURDOCK, GEORGE MILLER & JOHN MATCHET, commissioners appointed by the Act of Assembly passed 6 Jan 1787, for laying out the Town of Sarecta, 16 Oct 1787, for 2 pds. for each lott in hand paid to WILLIAM HOUSTON & EDWARD HOUSTON proprietors after sd. town by GRIFFITH HOUSTON, WILLIAM SOUTHERLAND, JEAN WORLEY & JOHN CHAMBERS, do exonerate acquit & discharge to JAMES WALLACE & ISRAEL BOURDEAUX all that messuage or part of the sd. town known by name in the plan of the sd. town by lot #7 drawn by WILLIAM SOUTHERLAND & by him sold to sd. WALLACE & BORDEAUX, lot #6 drawn by GRIFFETH HOUSTON & by him sold to sd. WALLACE & BORDEAUX, lot #26 drawn by JANE WORLEY & by her sold to sd. WALLACE & BORDEAUX, lot #27 drawn by JOHN CHAMBERS & sold to same in like manner. Wit: JAMES KENAN, ROBERT DICKSON, GEO. MORISEY. Apr. Ct. 1788.

p. 500   THOMAS (X) ADKISON (co. not given) to FREDERICK RIVENBARK (co. not given), 18 Mar 1786, for 50 pds. currency 70A in 2 tracts: (1) 50A beg. at the run of Buck Hall Swamp, near the Cow Branch; (2) 20A beg. at the run of Buck Hall at the mouth of Cow Branch, to Possom Run. Wit: KEDAR BRYAN, JESSE COLLINS. Jan. Ct. 1788.

p. 502   THEOPHILUS WILLIAMS to JOHN HART, both of Duplin Co., 12 Sep 1784, for 33 pds. current money 200A on the NS of Goshen Swamp incl. a place called the lake, beg. at a white oak on WESTON'S line, to a pine on HUSK'S line, to a pine HURST corner, to a water oak by HURST corner, in the edge of the Northeast Pocosin, being the contents of a patent for 200A granted to JESSE BARFIELD 1 Apr 1780 & conveyed from him to sd. WILLIAMS. Wit: DANIEL CLARK, STEPHEN BAREFIELD. Jan. Ct. 1788.

p. 504   HENRY HOLLEY of New Hanover Co. to RICHARD BRADLY of Duplin Co., 25 Aug 1786, for 45 pds. current money of N. C. 100A on the NS of Goshen Swamp & in the fork of Bear Marsh, beg. at a gum in the branch near JOHN SHEFFIELD'S line & running east along REUBEN WESTON'S line, being part of a tract granted to sd. WESTON & by him conveyed to the sd. HOLLY. Wit: JAMES BRADLY, WILLIS MOORE. Jan. Ct. 1788.

p. 505   JOHN WHITEHEAD to SAMUEL WARD, both planters of Duplin Co., 23 Oct 1786, for 1 pd. good & lawful money of N. C. 500A on the SS of the Northeast Swamp & SS of Poley Bridge Branch, beg. at a pine at REUBEN WESTON'S corner by a pond, on JOHN PORTER'S line at NELLY BAILS' corner, to the Wolfscrape Branch. Wit: BRINKLEY GLISSON, DAVID CANNON. Jan. Ct. 1788.

p. 507   ABRAHAM BEESLEY of New Hanover Co. to AUSTIN BEESLEY of Duplin Co., (date not given), for 12 pds. current money 100A on the main prong of Miller's Mill Branch on BS above the old dam, beg. at a black gum & an elm on the side of the Boiling Spring Run about 400 or 50 yards from the creek, adj. & between the lines of THOS. CARLTON & KNOX, being the contents of a patent granted to sd. ABRAHAM BEESLEY 10 Nov 1784. Wit: THOMAS CARLTON, JAMES BAKER. Jan. Ct. 1788.

p. 508   CULLEN CONNERLY to JAMES WRIGHT, both of Duplin Co., 31 Oct 1786, for 5 pds. current money 10A on the WS of Bear Swamp, joining the lands sd. WRIGHT bought of JOHN WARD & sd. CONNERLY'S own land, beg. at a red oak on CONNERLY'S line. Wit: W. DICKSON, DANIEL GLISSON. Jan. Ct. 1788.

p. 509   ALEXANDER PORTER, planter, to DAVID CARLTON, both of Duplin Co., 10 Jan 1787, for 20 pds. current money of N. C. 100A on BS of Wells' Swamp or branch of Miller's Swamp that empties into Stewart's Creek, beg. at a large white oak in Gum Branch, adj. & between the lines of JACOB WELLS in WELLS' Swamp, BEESLEY'S line, being sd. 100A granted to sd. PORTER 21 Sep 1785. Wit: AUSTIN BEESLEY, JOHN CARLTON. Jan. Ct. 1788.

p. 510   EDWARD DICKSON to JOHN JOHNSTON, both of Duplin Co., 15 Feb 1782, for 60 pds. specie 100A on the WS of Stewart's Creek by BENJAMIN JOHNSTON'S land, beg. at a red oak by sd. Stewart's Creek Swamp, being the contents of a patent granted to THOMAS JOHNSTON 5 Nov 1761 & afterwood conveyed by sd. JOHNSTON to MICAJAH BRUMLEY, who conveyed sd. 100A to EDWARD DICKSON. Wit: JOSEPH DICKSON, DAVID JONES, JUNR. Jan. Ct. 1788.

p. 512   ROBERT WILKINSON to JAMES WRIGHT, both of Duplin Co., 13 Oct 1786, for 10 pds. current money 75A on the NS of Bear Swamp & SS of Poley Bridge Branch, joining & between LUKE WARD'S & CULLEN CONNERLY'S lines, beg. at a small live oak in a small branch, a little above the main road, up the branch to a pine by the head of the pocosin, along JOHN WARD'S line, to a dividing line between sd. WRIGHT & LUKE WARD. Wit: W. DICKSON, DANIEL GLISSON. Jan. Ct. 1788.

p. 513   JAMES PEARSALL, Shff. of Duplin Co. to JESSE DARDEN of Sampson Co., 15 Aug 1785, for 26 pds. 3 shill. 287A on BS of Buck Hall Swamp, between the lines of JOHN ADKINSON, ROBERT HICKS, HANDCOCK HATCHER, JAMES THOMPSON, JOHN VALENTINE TAYLOR & KEDAR BRYAN. The Court of Duplin Co. awarded to JAMES LOCKHART (sum left out) for debt & damages in a suit against HENRY EUSTACE McCULLOCH, the late owner of the sd. 287A. JESSE DARDEN became the last & highest bidder at a public auction held 15 Aug 1785 . Wit: C. IVY, PETER WINNANTS. Jan. Ct. 1788.

p. 515   GEORGE FRAZAR of Duplin Co. to JOHN BECK, JUNR. of Wayne Co., 15 Apr 1788, for 2,000 pds. current money of N. C. 1,767A in 6 tracts: (1) 425A on the upper side of the head of Panther Swamp, beg. at a stake standing on the run

of sd. swamp, now in Sampson Co. the corner of another survey, at the mouth of
Persimmon Branch; (2) 400A on the SS of Goshen Swamp & on the WS of Panther
Swamp & on BS of a small branch called the Camp Branch, beg. at a maple & a gum
in the side of Goshen Swamp about a quarter of a mile above the mouth of Panther
Swamp, being the lower corner of another survey, to a black oak on HILLARY
HOOKS' line, along HENRY FAISON'S, it being a tract formerly belonging to HENRY
E. McCULLOCH & sold by the shff. in action of a writ of fieri facias against the
estate of the sd. McCULLOCH & purchased by the sd. FRAZAR & conveyed to him
by a shff. deed 13 July 1782; (3) 640A in Sampson Co. on the heads of Panther
Branches above YOUNG'S old road joining the Bear Pocosin, adj. & between the
lines of THOMAS GRAY, GEORGE FRAZAR & FELIX KENAN, being the contents of
a patent granted to NATHAN KING 4 Mar 1775 & which sd. KING deeded to sd.
FRAZAR; (4) 9A in Duplin Co. on the SS of the main branch of Panther, beg. at a
small white oak by the run of the sd. branch, a little below sd. FRAZAR'S own corner, being part of a marsh land sold & conveyed by JOHN CLARKE to the sd.
FRAZAR; (5) 200A in Sampson Co. on the head of a small branch leading into
Panther on the NS & on BS of YOUNG'S old path, beg. at a white oak sd. FRAZAR'S
corner tree, to a large pine near FELIX KENAN'S line, to a pine on the SS of a
branch of Panther, the sd. 200A being the contents of a patent granted to THOMAS
GRAY 22 July 1774 & conveyed to sd. FRAZAR by sd. GRAY; (6) 93A on the SS of
Goshen Swamp & on the NS of Panther Swamp on the head of Camp Branch, beg. at
a small pine sd. FRAZAR'S own corner, along HILLARY HOOKS' line, MR. Mc-
CULLOCH'S line, JOHN BECK'S line, being the contents of a patent granted to sd.
GEORGE FRAZAR 15 Dec 1778. Wit: JOSEPH GREEN, WM. BECK. Apr. Ct.
1788.

p. 520   THOMAS QUINN to JOHN WILLIAMS, both planters of Duplin Co., 10 Sep
1787, for 30 pds. good & lawful money of N. C₀ 100A on the NS of Limestone Creek
& on BS of Gum Swamp above ANTHONY LEWIS' land, incl. his impr., beg. at a
red oak on the ES of the swamp by MOSES STRAHORN'S line, the sd. 100A patented
by THOMAS QUINN 1 July 1779. Wit: CHAPLAIN WILLIAMS, JACOB WILLIAMS.
Apr. Ct. 1788.

p. 521   THOMAS QUINN, planter, to JOHN WILLIAMS, both of Duplin Co., 2 July
1787, for 80 pds. good & lawful money of N. C. 100A on Limestone Creek about 3
miles above WILLIAM THOMAS' place, granted & patented to FRANCIS GREGORY
10 May 1753, beg. at a white oak near the mouth of White Oak Branch. Wit:
CHAPLAIN WILLIAMS, JACOB WILLIAMS. Apr. Ct. 1788.

p. 522   THOMAS QUINN to JOHN WILLIAMS, 2 July 1787, for 40 pds, the crop on
the planta. where sd. QUINN now lives & 22 head of cattle & 35 head of hogs & the
greatest part of the cattle & all the hogs marked with an over square in each ear.
Wit: CHAPLAIN WILLIAMS, JACOB WILLIAMS. Apr. Ct. 1788.

p. 523   JOHN HILL of New Hanover Co. to STEPHEN MILLER of Duplin Co., 9
Apr 1788, for 115 pds. one negro girl names SARAH. Wit: JAMES MAXWELL.
Apr. Ct. 1788.

p. 523   JAMES KENAN to JAMES TORRANS, both of Duplin Co., 26 Feb 1788,
for 200 pds. current money of N. C. 320A in 2 tracts: (1) 80A on the NS of Turkey
Swamp, beg. at the edge of the main run of Turkey Swamp, formerly THOMAS
KENAN'S upper corner, now MICHAEL JOHNSTON KENAN'S upper corner, on the

edge of the main run of sd. swamp, being part of a 71,160 tract granted to HENRY McCULLOCH by patent dated 1745, & sd. HENRY McCULLOCH with HENRY EUSTACE McCULLOCH deeded the sd. land to MICHAEL J. KENAN in 1768, & the sd. MICHAEL JOHNSTON KENAN deeded to JAMES KENAN in 1779; (2) 240A on the NS of Turkey Swamp, beg. at a pine sd. MICHAEL J. KENAN'S corner tree & a corner of the 1st tract, to a gum in BENJAMIN JOHNSTON'S branch, the sd. 240A being part of 440A granted to sd. JAMES KENAN patent dated 17--. Wit: MOSES JONES, ALEXR. TORRANS. Apr. Ct. 1788.

p. 525   HEZEKIAH BLIZZARD of Duplin Co. to GEORGE OUTLAW of Darlington Co., S. C., 1 Feb 1788, for 30 pds. lawful money of N. C. 150A in Darlington Co., S. C., formerly Craven Co., bounded when taken up on all sides by vacant land & hath such shape courses & marks as the platt annexed to the patent doth represent, the sd. 150A granted to RICHARD BLIZZARD 10 Jan 1771. Wit: LEVIN WATKINS, FRANS. OLIVER. Apr. Ct. 1788.

p. 526   CHARLES MUMFORD to ROBERT COLE, both of Duplin Co., 1788 (no month or day listed), for 30 pds. currency 320A on the NS of Limestone Swamp on BS of Horse Branch, beg. at a cypress by the run of Limestone Swamp, by the mouth of Cabbin Branch, near Horse Branch, to a pine by a tar kiln, to a pine near Gum Branch by WILLIAM FOLSOM'S line, the sd. land granted to ANTHONY MILLER by a patent dated 22 July 1774 & conveyed from sd. MILLER to sd. MUM-FORD, & the sd. land also being WILLIAM NETHERCUT'S older patent land & a small point of sd. MUMFORD'S old patent. Wit: ROBIN SOUTHERLAND, PATIENCE SOUTHERLAND. Apr. Ct. 1788.

p. 529   JOHN JOHNS, planter, & his wife ISABLE JOHNS of New Hanover Co. to JAMES JAMES, planter of Duplin Co., 10 Sep 1766, for 60 pds. proc., 165A on the WS of the Northeast Branch of Cape Fear River, beg. at a white oak about 100 yards below Limestone Ford, which lands were granted to JACOB HANCHEY by GABRIEL JOHNSTON, Esqr., as by grant & patent dated 20 Apr 1745, & sd. HANCHEY conveyed to FRANCIS BRICE Dec 1746, & sd. BRICE deeded to PRISILLA BURTON 8 June 1758 & sd. BURTON deeded to JOHN JOHNS 26 June 1763, the sd. 165A once being in New Hanover Co., but now in Duplin Co. Wit: DAVID BLOODWORTH, THOS. ARMSTRONG. Jan. Ct. 1788.

p. 530   JOHN WARD to JAMES WRIGHT, both of Duplin Co., 13 Oct 1786, for 200 pds. current money of N. C. 330A in 2 tracts: (1) 165A on the NS of Bear Swamp opposite ROBERT WILKINSON'S planta., beg. at a pine on CULLEN CONNERLY'S line by BELLOT'S impr. Deed mentions LUKE WARD'S corner & the dividing cor- ner between JAMES WRIGHT & ROBERT WILKINSON. (2) 150A on the NW side of Bear Swamp between the 2 main roads, beg. at a pine near the head of Poley Bridge Branch, STEPHEN HERRING'S upper corner, adj. & along the lines of WILLIAM DICKSON & ROBERT WILKINSON. Wit: W. DICKSON, DANL. GLISSON. Jan. Ct. 1788. (Note: The body of the deed says total acreage is 310, the heading says 330A, but the 2 tracts total 315A.)

p. 533   THOMAS (T F) JOHNSTON to BENJAMIN JOHNSTON, planter, both of Duplin Co., 12 June 1775, for 40 pds. proc. 200A on Stewart's Creek, branch of Black River, beg. at a pine in FELIX KENAN'S line, MR. McCULLOCH'S line. Wit: JOHN ARMSTRONG, FRANCIS JOHNSTON. Jan. Ct. 1788.

p. 535   MICAJAH (✛) BRUMLEY to JOHN JOHNSTON, both planters of Duplin Co.,
10 Mar 1783, for 80 pds. specie 100A on the WS of Stewart's Creek above the mouth
of Buck Hall joining his own, JOHN BAPTIST SHEPHERD & ABRAHAM GLISSON'S
line, beg. at a pine at his own upper back corner of the land he lives on, patented by
THOMAS JOHNSTON, the sd. 100A being the contents of a patent granted to sd.
BRUMLEY & from him conveyed by virtue of this deed to JOHN JOHNSTON, JUNR.
Wit: JNO. MOLTEN, ABRAHAM MOLTEN. Jan. Ct. 1788.

p. 536   ANTHONY (A) JONES, planter, to LEWIS BARFIELD, both of Duplin Co.,
16 Apr 1788, for 30 pds. specie 120A on the ES of the Northeast River, on BS the
road & on the SS of Burncoat Swamp, beg. at a stake in the swamp at ANTHONY
JONES' corner, along SAMUEL JONES' line, it being part of 200A patented by
LEWIS BARNES 10 Nov 1784. Wit: GEO. SMITH, SENR., SAML. (✛) JONES.
Apr. Ct. 1788.

p. 538   ANTHONY (A) JONES to LEWIS BARFIELD, both planters of Duplin Co.,
16 Apr 1788, for 50 pds. specie 150A on the ES of the Northeast River & on the SS
of Burncoat Swamp on BS of the main road, beg. at a pine in sd. swamp, along
LEWIS BARNES' line, the sd. land being patented by ANTHONY JONES 10 Nov
1784. Wit: GEO. SMITH, SAML. (✓) JONES. Apr. Ct. 1788.

p. 539   JOHN TEACHEY to TIMOTHY TEACHEY, both planters of Duplin Co.,
7 Mar 1788, for 100 pds. specie 100A on BS of Little Rockfish Creek, beg. at a
pine on the WS of sd. Little Rockfish Swamp on the edge by WEMBIRK BONEY'S
line. ELIZABETH (E) TEACHEY signed the deed. Wit: MARTIN (X) HANCHEY,
DANIEL TEACHEY. Apr. Ct. 1788.

p. 541   JOSEPH DICKSON to JOHN BONEY, both of Duplin Co., 17 Apr 1788, for
50 pds. 150A on the Northeast side of Little Rockfish or Cummins' Creek, & on BS
of the main road joining the land known by the name of the Red House Land, beg. at
a pine a little east of the Red House Meadow, to RUTHERFORD'S corner. Wit:
THOMAS HOOK, DANIEL TEACHEY. Apr. Ct. 1788.

p. 542   JAMES MIDDLETON (SENR.) of Duplin Co. to his son DAVID MIDDLETON,
21 Apr 1788, for "the affection & good will" as well as 5 pds. current money of N.C.,
220A on the SS of the Grove Swamp, beg. at a maple at the mouth of Indian Spring on
the run of the Grove Swamp, GEORGE GIBBON'S corner, crossing the Wildcat Pond,
CANNON'S old corner, WILLIAM WILLIAMS' line, "being a full proportionate part
of my land of which I am at present possessed of in Duplin Co. agreeable to such
share as I propose for the rest of my family, & c.". Wit: JOSEPH DICKSON,
SARAH MIDDLETON. Apr. Ct. 1788.

p. 544   ELISHA FARLES (co. not given) to BIBBY BUSH of Dobbs Co., 10 Jan
1788, for 50 pds. 200A as by the patent doth appear, being the planta. that JOHN
SMITH now lives on, in the fork of the Great Branch, beg. at a pine in the Piney
Pond. Wit: ARCHAD. McDONALD, JAMES OUTLAW. Apr. Ct. 1788.

p. 545   ABSALOM (X) BOYET, planter of Dobbs Co. to OBADIAH WADE, planter
of Duplin Co., 1 Oct 1787, for 125 pds. current money of N. C. for sundry pieces
of land: 5A, it being the moiety of 150A which was purchased of MAJOR CROOM of
Dobbs Co., on the NS of a branch called Spring Branch near PRESCOT'S line & the
dividing line runs as the fence runs, being the bounds by which is mentioned in JOHN

WILLIAMS' deed for the moiety that ABSALOM BOYET sold to sd. WILLIAMS & whereon LUTSON STROUD did live & runs down the Spring Branch into Panther Swamp, thence up the sd. swamp & so incl. 70A on the NS with all buildings, etc., together with 100A more of wood land on the ES of the Northeast River, joining GEO. SMITH'S line, between the head of Panther Swamp & the dry pocosin, beg. at a pine sd. SMITH'S line. RHODEY (R) BOYET also signed the deed. Wit: THOS. QUINN, WILL. CROOM. Apr. Ct. 1788.

p. 547 JOHN (B) BALLARD, planter, to JESSE GREGORY, taylor, both of Onslow Co., 19 Sep 1787, a deed of gift for one feather bed & furn., one chest, one pot, one kettle, one skillet, one spice (?) mortar & pistol, carpenter tools, 3 cows & calves , a barren cow & one 3 yr. old heifer this spring. Wit: ALEX. NIELSON, HARDY (G) GREGORY. Apr. Ct. 1788.

p. 548 THOMAS (X) ADKISON of Duplin Co. to JAMES THOMPSON of Sampson Co., 15 Mar 1788, for 35 pds. current money 60A on BS of Buck Hall Swamp, beg. at a small pine his & sd. THOMPSON'S corner, adj. & between RIVENBARK'S line, the mouth of Cow Branch, KEDAR BRYAN, BENJAMIN WILLIAMS. Wit: JOSEPH DICKSON, JOHN KELLY. Apr. Ct. 1788.

p. 549 EBENEZAR GARRASON (co. not given) to JAMES PICKET of same (Duplin Co. ?), 19 Jan 1788, for 100 pds. one negro boy 8 yrs. old named SAM. Wit: JONATHAN PARKER. Apr. Ct. 1788.

p. 550 SARAH HURST to JOHN CLARK, both planters of Duplin Co., 1 Sep 1787, for 200 pds. specie money, one negro slave man named SEASOR about 25 yrs. of age. Wit: WILLIAM BECK, WILLIAM BECK, JUNR. Apr. Ct. 1788.

p. 550 PATRICK NEWTON to RICHARD MEARS, both of Duplin Co., 10 Feb 1787, for 120 pds. current money of N. C. one negro man named ADAM about 5 feet 6 in. high, well made, born in the West Indies & about 32 yrs. old. Wit: AUSTIN MOORE, BETSEY MOORE. Apr. Ct. 1788.

p. 551 JOHN HUSKE to WM. CARR, at Wilmington 12 Nov 1787, for 80 pds. current money being full payment for a negro girl named DAPHNE. Test. HUGH McCANNE. Apr. Ct. 1788.

p. 551 PATRICK NEWTON to WILLIAM WILKINSON, SENR., both of Duplin Co., 22 Apr 1788, for 70 pds. one negro girl named DIZEY between 3 & 4 yrs. old. Wit: DAVID BUNTING. Apr. Ct. 1788.

p. 552 JOHN MAGEE to JOHN FARRIER, both of Duplin Co., (date not given), for 120 pds. specie one negro boy named CEASAR. Test. WILLIAM SOUTHERLAND, JUSTIS MILLER. Apr. Ct. 1788.

p. 552 SHADRACK STALLINGS to JOHN WILLIAMS (cos. not given), 13 Jan 1788, for 20 pds. (acreage not given), land on the NS of Rockfish Creek, beg. at a large pine on an old line sd. to be PITMAN'S line, joining an old survey of 640A patented by JOHN PIDCOCK called PORTER'S land. Test. JOHN BONEY, JACOB BONEY. Apr. Ct. 1788.

p. 554   CHARLES WARD to CHARLES BROWN, both of Duplin Co., 28 Mar 1788, for 100 pds. current money of N. C. 330A in 2 tracts: (1) 230A on the ES of Mahunga Swamp between the two Mirey Branches, being part of the land sd. WARD bought of DAVID MURDOCK, beg. at an ash on Mahunga at the mouth of the upper Mirey Branch, to CHRISTOPHER MARTIN'S boundary; (2) 100A joining on the ES of the afsd. 230A, being part of the sd. WARD'S new survey, beg. at a red oak sd. WARD'S corner, to a water oak in Wolf Pond Branch, to a white oak CHRISTOPHER MARTIN'S corner, to CHARLES BROWN'S own line. Wit: JOSEPH DICKSON, J. PEARSALL. Apr. Ct. 1788.

p. 1   JOHN FARRIOR to JOSEPH JOHNSTON, both planters of Duplin Co., 3 Jan 1794, for 40 pds. specie currency of N. C. 200A on the ES of the Northeast River & SS of Muddy Creek on BS of the Great Branch, beg. at a pine by a pond. Wit: WILLIAM FARRIOR, LEMUEL (L.) WILLIAMS. Apr. Ct. 1794.

p. 2   JOHN (X) PUMPHRY of Duplin Co. to SOLOMON CARTER (co. not given), 7 Feb 1789, for 80 pds. specie money a tract (acreage not given) of land, it being one half of a piece of land left to the sd. PUMPHREY by his father SOLOMON PUMPHREY & the upper end of the land joining sd. CARTER'S line & mill being divided by a parcel of blazed trees about the middle of the old field & straight course to Mathews' Branch his own line. Wit: MICHAEL GLISSON, HEZEKIAH (**S**) BLIZZARD. Apr. Ct. 1794.

p. 3   WILLIAM FARRIOR to WILLIAM HALL, both of Duplin Co., 1 Apr 1794, for 150 pds. current money of N. C. 217A on the ES of the Northeast Branch of Cape Fear River below the mouth of Limestone Creek, beg. at a stake on the river bank below the bridge, adj. JAMES GILLESPIE, it being part of a patent of 580A granted to WILLIAM DICKSON, ARCHIBALD GILLESPIE & ANDREW McINTIRE 23 Dec 1763 & conveyed by sd. DICKSON to sd. FARRIOR 24 Feb 1791, excepting 14A for use of sd. FARRIOR for timbers for building & firewood which sd. 14A is joining on the river at & below Limestone Bridge. Wit: JOHN DICKSON, JOHN FARRIOR. Apr. Ct. 1794.

p. 5   DANIEL (X) COOK to JACOB WELLS, both of Duplin Co., 20 Nov 1792, for 80 pds. current money of N. C. 160A formerly patented by JOHN COOK SENR., late of Duplin Co. dec'd & by him sold to his son JOHN COOK JUNR. 27 Apr 1769, beg. at the 1st corner of the sd. patent at a red oak on the swamp side to the old patented corner, crossing Bear Branch with the patent line. Wit: JOSEPH DICKSON, ISAAC (**I**) JAMES, JOHN EVERS. Apr. Ct. 1794.

p. 6   STEPHEN BECK of Sampson Co. to WILLIAM BECK of Duplin Co., 1 Feb 1794, for 1,000 pds. specie 848A whereon the sd. STEPHEN BECK formerly lived & also sundry other tracts, thereto adj. & incl. the planta. whereon ELIZABETH BECK, widow of JOHN BECK, now lives, beg. at a stake at the run of Long Branch, a little below the main road, adj. McCANNE, FRAZOR, THOMAS GRAY, Slocumb Branch, OATS, the Long Pond, BECK'S old line, being the land conveyed to sd. STEPHEN BECK by deed & will of his father JOHN BECK dec'd, lying in Duplin & Sampson Cos. Wit: WILLIAM BECK, JUNR., JOHN BECK, JUNR., BIB (X) BUSH. Apr. Ct. 1794.

p. 8   THOS. (THOMAS) WRIGHT, Shff. of Duplin Co., by virtue of a writ of fieri facias to him directed from the Sup. Ct. of Law & Equity, held for the Dist. of Wilmington against the goods & chattels lands & tenements of LEWIS STUCKEY, did levy the same on a negro man named HARRY in the poss. of DAVID WRIGHT, claimed by the sd. STUCKEY. DAVID WRIGHT became the highest bidder in the sum of 15 shill. for the sd. negro on 16 Oct 1794. Wit: JOHN SHAW. Dated 20 Apr 1795. Apr. Ct. 1795.

p. 8   THOS. (THOMAS) WRIGHT, Shff. of Duplin Co., by virtue of a writ of fieri facias to him directed from the Sup. Ct. of Law, held for the Dist. of Wilmington against the goods & chattels, lands & tenements of LEWIS STUCKEY, did levy the same on a negro girl by the name of CLARY in the poss. of DAVID MIDDLETON, claimed by the sd. LEWIS STUCKEY & did advertise for sale his right of sd. negro girl CLARY on 18 Oct 1794 & THOMAS NORMENT became the highest bidder for sd. negro in the sum of 17 shill. Dated 20 Apr 1795. Wit: D. GLISSON. Apr. Ct. 1795.

p. 9   WM. (WILLIAM) DICKSON of Duplin Co. to his son WILLIAM DICKSON JUNR. (co. not given), 1 Aug 1793, for "natural love & affection", 146A on SS of Goshen Swamp on BS of the Poley Bridge Branch & on BS of the main road, beg. at a pine on the ES of a pond & WS of the main road & runs S to McCULLOCH'S lines, crossing Poley Branch, & adj. STEPHEN HERRING, being the contents of a patent granted to FREDERICK BELL 4 Mar 1775 & from him conveyed to WILLIAM DICKSON who deeded to his son WILLIAM DICKSON, JUNR., excepting 4A laid off & divided by sd. WILLIAM DICKSON to certain trustees as at lot for the purpose of building a meeting house for holding & performing divine worship. Wit: FREDK. BARFIELD, JAMES DICKSON, JUNR. July Ct. 1794.

p. 11   JOSEPH T. (THOMAS) RHODES of Duplin Co. to JACOB RHODES of Robeson Co., 1 Jan 1796, for 36 pds. 360A on the NS of Limestone Swamp, beg. at a white oak sd. JOSEPH F. RHODES corner of a survey of 140A, adj. JACOB RHODES, between the Bear & White Oak Pocosin, adj. FRANKS, the sd. 360A granted to sd. JOSEPH T. RHODES by patent dated 1 Sep 1785. Wit: TIMOTHY TEACHY, JAMES DICKSON. Jan. Ct. 1796.

p. 12   NATHANIEL McCANNE of Duplin Co. to THOMAS OVERTON of Moore Co. & JOHN BECK of Sampson Co., 22 Jan 1796 for 600 spanish milled dollars 2560A in Davidson Co. in the Territory of the U. S., Southwest of the Ohio, on the SS of Cumberland & on BS of the first creek above the mouth of Caney Fork on the SS of the ss. river, beg. at a maple & sycamore running up the river according to its meanders to a large elm on the bank of the river. Wit: WILLIAM DICKSON, GABL. HOLMES. Jan. Ct. 1796.

p. 13   WM. (WILLIAM) WHITFIELD of Wayne Co. to his loving dau. ELIZABETH KEITHLEY, now wife of JOHN KEITHLEY of Duplin Co., 11 Sep 1794, for "love, good will & affection" one negro girl named LINAY & one negro boy named DANIEL. Wit: BUCKNER KILLEBREW, JO. WHITFIELD. Apr. Ct. 1795.

p. 14   WILLIAM WHITFIELD (JUNR.) of Wayne Co. to loving dau. RACHEL HOUSE, now wife of JAMES HOUSE of Onslow Co., 6 Sep 1794, for "love, good will & affection" one negro girl named BINER & one negro boy named JACOB now in the poss. of sd. JAMES HOUSE & his wife RACHEL HOUSE in Onslow Co. Wit: JOHN KITHLEY, JO. WHITFIELD, BUCKNER KILLEBREW. Apr. Ct. 1795.

p. 14   WM. (WILLIAM) WHITFIELD JR. of Wayne Co., planter, to MARY KILLE- BREW his dau., now wife of BUCKNER KILLEBREW of Duplin Co., 10 Sep 1794, for "love, good will & affection" a negro woman named MILLIA & her children, one boy named FURNEY, one girl named WINNEY, one girl named ROSE & one negro boy named BEN & their increase, being now in the poss. of sd. KILLEBREW & his wife MARY. Wit: JOHN KITHLEY, JO. WHITFIELD. Apr. Ct. 1795.

p. 15   WM. (WILLIAM) McCANNE (JUNR.) of Duplin Co. to JOHN HOLDON of New Hanover Co., 4 Dec 1794, for 200 pds. specie 510A in 2 tracts to wit: (1) 410A on the WS of the Northeast River, incl. the planta. where the sd. McCANNE now lives, beg. at a white oak on the bank of the Northeast River, about 8 or 10 yds. below the mouth of Mill Branch (or Creek), a corner of a patent of 147A, with a line dividing JAMES MURRAY & McCANNE, being the contents of a patent of 200A in the Horseshoe patented by sd. McCANNE 20 Dec 1791, & also part of 3 other patents, 2 patented by sd. McCANNE (one for 147A, one for 80A dated 20 Dec 1791), & the 3rd patented by THOMAS JOHN 9 Mar 1754 & transferred by sd. JOHN to WILLIAM JONES & from JONES to sd. McCANNE; (2) 100A on the ES of the Northeast River & on BS of Wet-acre Branch, beg. at a white oak on the river bank near WILLIAMS' Camp, to a stake by the edge of a prong of the Holly Shelter Pocosin, to a stake on the bank of the river at a place called Wilson's Hole. Wit: GEORGE POWELL, WM. (A) ALLEN. Jan. Ct. 1796.

p. 17   JOHN COOK (J.C.) of Duplin Co., planter, to WILLIAM JONES of New Hanover Co., 12 July 1788, for 100 pds. good & lawful money of N. C. 205A on the WS of the Northeast River on the branches of Island Creek, beg. at a water oak in Immanuels Branch, thence the sd. EMMANUELS BOWZER'S line, to a stake at sd. COOK'S old corner of 160A, crossing the creek along JOHN AVERS' line, with JOHN COOK SENR.'S line. Wit: ANDREW THALLY, JOHN (+++) COX. Apr. Ct. 1795.

p. 18   JOHN HOUSMAN to JEREDIAH B. (BASS) FOLEY, both of Duplin Co., 20 Oct 1793, for 30 pds. specie money 100A on the NS of Goshen Swamp & joining ABSALOM WESTON'S Branch, beg. at a pine in a drain of sd. branch, to a large pine on JOHN WINDERS' line, to a hickory at the corner of the line patented by GEORGE OUTLAW. Wit: FLOOD FOLEY, JOHN FOLEY, STEPHEN FOLEY. July Ct. 1794.

p. 19   CHARLES HOOKS of Duplin Co. to his 2 sons THOMAS HOOKS & CHARLES HOOKS (infants), 23 Nov 1794, for "natural love & affection" 2 negro slaves to wit: BETTY a girl about 11 yrs. old & MERCY a girl about 1 yr. old with all their future increase to be equally divided between them, reserving for himself the use of the sd. slaves during his natural life unless sooner given up to his 2 sons my his own free consent. Wit: W. DICKSON, LEWIS DICKSON. Jan. Ct. 1795.

p. 20   JAMES KENAN to BENJAMIN JOHNSTON, both of Duplin Co., 17 Jan 1795, for 5 pds. current money 100A on the NS of Turkey Swamp, beg. at a pine SAMUEL GUY'S line, being part of a survey of 440A joining MICHAEL J. KENAN & ELIZABETH TORRANS' line. Wit: DAVID WRIGHT, SHADRACK STALLINGS. Jan. Ct. 1795.

p. 21   MICHAEL GLISSON to JAMES SMYTH, both of Duplin Co., 6 Dec 1794, for 300 pds. 550A on the WS of the Northeast of Cape Fear River, being part of the land sd. GLISSON purchased from JOHN JOHNSTON & the other part patented by sd. GLISSON, beg. at a cypress on the main run of the Northeast Swamp, sd. to be SAMUEL JOHNSTON'S lower corner, to a poplar in Horse Branch, to a pine WHITFIELD'S corner, to a stake in the Northeast Swamp on SAMUEL JOHNSTON'S line. Wit: WM. ALBERSON, DAVID SMYTH, EDWARD ALBERSON. Jan. Ct. 1795.

p. 22   JOHN BECK of Sampson Co. to WILLIAM SULIVEN of Duplin Co., 17 Feb 1796, for 600 spanish milled dollars 1280A being his one half share of 2560A which NATHANIEL McCANNE conveyed to sd. BECK of Sampson Co. & THOMAS OVERTON of Moore Co. on 22 Jan 1796 for same sd. sum, the sd. land being in Davidson Co. in the Territory of the U. S. Southwest of the Ohio. (see p. 12) Wit: WM. DICKSON, JOSEPH DICKSON, LEE SULIVEN. Apr. Ct. 1796.

p. 24   THOMAS NORMENT to REV. JOHN ROBESON, both of Duplin Co., 5 Mar
1795, for 300 pds. current money of N. C. 460A on BS of Kings Branch & on BS of
the main road, incl. a place called the Goose Pond, beg. at a red oak on the NS of
Kings Branch on JAMES WINDERS' line, to a black gum saplin on the run of Pritty
Branch by the road, to JOHN SOUTHERLAND'S line, being land formerly poss. by
FELIX KENAN, Esqr. & since by his son WILLIAM KENAN & now by sd. NOR-
MENT. Wit: WILLIAM DICKSON, JR., THOMAS WRIGHT. Apr. Ct. 1795.

p. 26   SAMUEL SOWELL of Duplin Co. to STEWART BARNET of Jones Co., 19
July 1794, for 15 pds. 100A being part of a 400A tract on the head of the Wolf Pit
Branch, beg. at a lightwood stump on a dividing line of sd. 400A & running to JOHN
STEWART'S corner. Wit: ELIAS BUTLAR, F. SOWELL. Apr. Ct. 1795.

p. 27   JOHN COOPER to BENJAMIN COOPER, both of Duplin Co., 20 Mar 1795,
for 200 pds. 250A on the SS of Nahunga Swamp, beg. on Nahunga at the mouth of a
small branch that divides the land that was GEORGE COOPER'S & sd. land running
up sd. branch, being a line of a tract that WILLIAM HALL sold to GEORGE
COOPER, to Miry Branch at CHRISTOPHER MARTIN'S corner. Wit: THOS. NOR-
MENT, JOSEPH COOPER. Apr. Ct. 1795.

p. 28   DAVID HALL to JOHN CARLETON, both of Duplin Co., 21 Apr 1795, for
100 pds. current money of N. C. 150A on the WS of Burwell Hill Branch, beg. at a
pine on the swamp side CLIFTON BOWEN'S corner, to BENJAMIN LANIER'S line,
being the contents of a patent granted to THOMAS CRUPTON dated 29 Oct 1782.
Wit: JAMES DICKSON, THOS. CARLETON. Apr. Ct. 1795.

p. 30   GEORGE KORNEGAY to JOHN KEATHLEY, both of Duplin Co., 25 May
1792, for 50 pds. current money 13A in the fork of the Northeast & Lewis Branch,
beg. at a pine sd. KORNEGAY'S lower corner on Lewis Branch, being part of a
patent granted to sd. KORNEGAY (date not given). Wit: W. DICKSON, DANIEL
KORNEGAY. Apr. Ct. 1795.

p. 31   SAMUEL WHALEY to LYBERN BASDEN, both planters of Duplin Co., 3 Jan
1795, for 157 pds. 10 shill. specie 200A in 2 tracts to wit: (!) 100A on the ES of
Lymestone [sic] between MORGAN SWEENEY'S & MOSES COX'S lines, beg. at a
poplar in Limestone Swamp near SWEENEY'S line, as by patent granted to JAMES
WHALEY 24 May 1773 & by him conveyed to JOSEPH THIGPEN 9 Feb 1793 & by him
to SAMUEL WHALEY 29 July 1793; (2) 100A on the ES of the Beaverdam of Limestone Swamp, joining the 1st tract & on BS of Gourd (?) Branch, beg. at a pine on
the line of the afsd. 100A, as by patent granted to SOLOMON COX 29 Oct 1782 & by
him conveyed to SAMUEL SOWELL & by him to JAMES WHALEY. Wit: JOHN
THIGPEN, THOS. QUINN, JOSEPH T. RHODES. Apr. Ct. 1795.

p. 32   DAVID WILLIAMS to AARON WILLIAMS, both of Duplin Co., 23 July 1794,
for 110 pds. specie 250A in 2 tracts to wit: (1) 100A on the WS of JOSEPH WILL-
IAMS' Mill Pond incl. the sd. DAVID WILLIAMS' impr. on Horse Branch, beg. at
a stake at the run of the creek where JOHN WILLIAMS' upper line corners, to the
back line of WALKER'S old survey & to the upper corner of sd. survey, to the run
of the Mill Creek, it being the NE corner of the survey of 640A that JOSEPH WILL-
IAMS bought of JOHN WALKER; (2) 150A on the WS of the main road, beg. at a
pine JOSEPH JAMES' corner the WS of the Richland Pond, to a pine CHARLES
JAMES' corner, to a pine ELIAS JAMES' corner, through JAMES' Pocosin. Wit:

JOSEPH WILLIAMS, AMBROSE SMITH. Apr. Ct. 1796.

p. 34   ABRAHAM POWELL of Pitt Co. to LEWIS THOMAS of Duplin Co., 9 Mar
1795, for 50 pds. 300A on the SS of Nahunga Swamp, beg. at a pine WILLIAM EL-
LIOT'S corner & adj. the lines of SUTTON BYRD, LEWIS THOMAS & WILLIAM
BOYD as by patent (date not given). Wit: BENJAMIN (X) JOHNSON, WILLIAM (X)
JOINER. Apr. Ct. 1795.

p. 35   DANIEL GLISSON, Shff., to STEPHEN MILLER, both of Duplin Co., 25 Dec
1793, for 32 pds. current money 100A formerly the property of WILLIAM HUBBARD
& part of the Sarecta survey granted to HENRY McCULLOCH by patent dated 3 Mar
1745 & afterwards granted to WILLIAM HOUSTON May 1780 & which sd. HOUSTON
granted to GRIFFITH HOUSTON who deeded to WILLIAM HUBBARD, beg. at a stake
on the river bank at EDWARD HOUSTON'S upper corner to the New River Pond.
The Court awarded 30 pds. 10 shill., plus cost of 4 pds. 17 shill. & 4 pence to
HENRY GOODMAN & HARRY GOODMAN, exrs. of TIMOTHY GOODMAN dec'd lately
of Lenoir Co., for damages in a suit against sd. HUBBARD, owner of the sd. 100A,
which was purchased by sd. MILLER for 32 pds. at public auction 8 Oct 1793. WIN-
STON CASWELL, Clerk of the Ct. of Lenoir Co. Wit: EDWD. PEARSALL, JAMES
CARR. Apr. Ct. 1795.

p. 38   JOB ROGERS, PELEG ROGERS, JAMES ROGERS & NICHOLAS ROGERS,
heirs of JAMES ROGERS dec'd to ANNE ROGERS, all of Duplin Co., 24 Jan 1793,
for 5 pds. current money of N. C. 200A on the SW side of Maxwell Swamp & on BS
of Carrs Branch, beg. at a pine & hickory on the SS of the branch, a little below the
mouth of Bee Tree Branch JOB ROGERS' corner, adj. JOHN RICHARDS, PELEG
ROGERS, a line of a survey patented by FREDERICK LEWIS, JOB ROGERS. Wit:
ROBERT MILLER, JOHN McCULLOCH, JOSEPH DICKSON. Apr. Ct. 1795.

p. 39   NATHANIEL (X) WELLS of Duplin Co. to WILLIAM FRAZAR (co. not given)
10 Feb 1795, for 20 pds. good & lawful money 50A incl. Persimmon Swamp, beg. at
a white oak HUNTER'S lower corner, SS the swamp, to LOCKHART'S corner. Wit:
HUGH McCANNE, RICHARD CHAISTEN. Apr. Ct. 1795.

p. 40   GEORGE BANNERMAN & PHEBE BANNERMAN of New Hanover Co. to
JOHN WILLIAMS, JUNR. of Duplin Co., 24 Jan 1794, for 118 pds. 10 shill. specie,
125A on the WS of JOHN WILLIAMS SENR'S Mill Creek & BS of the main road, beg.
at a large white oak marked with a great R, at the run of the creek a little below the
Mill Dam, being part of a survey of 200A patented by JOHN WILLIAMS in 1756.
Wit: BYRD WILLIAMS, ROBERT BANNERMAN. Apr. Ct. 1795.

p. 42   THOS. (THOMAS) WRIGHT, Shff. to BENJAMIN LANEAR & JACOB LANEAR,
all of Duplin Co., 22 Apr 1795, for 40 pds. 100A on Cypress Creek on the ES of the
Northeast Branch of Cape Fear River, being part of a survey of 400A patented by
JOHN ANCRUM, beg. at a pine NS of Cypress Creek, the 2nd corner of sd. patent,
as by survey made by JOSEPH DICKSON, Esqr. The court awarded 45 pds. 9 shill.
10 pence, plus cost of 5 pds. 7 shill. 2 pence to JAMES GILLESPIE, exr. of JAS.
GRIMES dec'd, for damages in a suit against CHARLES GRIMES, owner of the sd.
100A, which was purchased by sd. LANEARS for 40 pds. at public auction held 18
Apr 1795. Wit: WILLIAM SOUTHERLAND, JOB THIGPEN. Apr. Ct. 1795.

p. 43   JESSE (X) BRANCH to JAMES WOODARD, both of Duplin Co., 19 Sep 1793,

for 50 pds. current money 72A on the NS of Goshen Swamp & on the WS of the Mill
Branch, beg. at a black jack by the road near a pond, adj. PARKER & BRACKS
[sic] line, to a corner formerly made for JOHN ROGERS & along his line to the
main road, being part of a patent of 350A formerly granted to WILLIAM PARKER &
since by the LW & T of sd. PARKER to his wife SUSANNAH PARKER & since by
JOHN SWINSON & SUSANNAH his wife as of right in consequence of sd. LW & T of
sd. PARKER sold & conveyed to sd. BRANCH. Wit: FRANCIS OLIVER, ZACHA-
RIAH (X) TURNAGE. Apr. Ct. 1795.

p. 45   D. (DANIEL) GLISSON, Shff. of Duplin Co. to THOMAS NORMAN, 2 Feb
1793, for 350 pds. 1673A in Duplin Co. (location not given), sold at public auction
Feb 1793. The Court awarded 171 pds. 16 shill. 9 pence to GEORGE HOOPER,
exr. for ARCHIBALD McLAIN dec'd, merchant of Wilmington & 104 pds. 17 shill.
to CHARLES JURKES (?), merchant of Wilmington in 2 separate judgments against
THOMAS NORMAN & JOHN HILL, guardians of the heirs of FELIX KENAN. These
actions began at the June 1788 & June 1789 Terms of Court. Subsequent court
judgment in Sept 1792 resulted in the 1673A, granted formerly to FELIX KENAN by
virtue of sundry patents & deeds, being sold to sd. NORMAN. Wit: SAML. R.
JOCELYN. Apr. Ct. 1795.

p. 48   KENAN LOVE to THOMAS NORMENT, both of Duplin Co., 1 Apr 1795, for
15 pds. 125A on the NS of Nahunga, beg. at a maple at the run in Beaverdam FELIX
KENAN'S corner, now the sd. NORMENT'S & along his line to a pine by the side of
Rooty Branch, to the corner of JACOB TAYLOR'S land along his line, below the
mouth of Rooty Branch & across the run of Nahunga. Wit: THOS. WRIGHT, HENRY
CANNON. Apr. Ct. 1795.

p. 49   KENAN LOVE to THOMAS NORMENT, both of Duplin Co., 1 Apr 1795, for
80 pds. 260A on the NS of Nahunga Swamp below the mouth of Kings Branch, beg. at
a small white oak by the run of Nahunga Swamp, to a white oak FELIX KENAN'S
now sd. NORMENT'S corner, up the Long Branch, the sd. land patented by JAMES
LANE in 1793. (No witnesses given. Heading of deed says 250A.). Apr. Ct. 1795.

p. 50   DANL. (DANIEL) GLISSON, Shff. of Duplin Co. to THOMAS NORMENT (co.
not given), 6 May 1793, for 221 pds. 6 negroes to wit: CEASOR, PHILLIS, CLEAR-
RY, SALL, BOB & NANCE, the prop. of WILLIAM KENAN dec'd, by virtue of a
writ of fieri facias to sd. GLISSON, one at the suit of the exrs. of JAMES GARDNER
against the admrs. of WILLIAM KENAN dec'd & the other at the suit of JOHN &
RICHARD KAY   against the admrs. of sd. KENAN & others. Wit: THOMAS
WRIGHT. Apr. Ct. 1795.

p. 50   THOMAS WRIGHT, Shff of Duplin Co. to THOMAS NORMENT (co. not
given), 18 Apr 1795, by virtue of a writ of fieri facias from the Sup. Ct. of Halifax
Dist., at the suit of JOHN & RICHD. KAY against the admrs. of WILLIAM KENAN
namely, KEDAR BRYAN, THEOPHILUS WILLIAMS & WILLIAM HARRIS, to sell 5
negroes, the property of WILLIAM KENAN dec'd, to sd. NORMENT at public auction 18 Apr 1795 for the following sums to wit: GEORGE for 20 pds. 10 shill:,
DIANAH & GEORE [sic] her child for 30 pds., ADAM for 20 pds. 10 shill. &
GEORGE for 25 pds. 5 shill. Wit: D. GLISSON. Apr. Ct. 1795.

p. 51   THO. (THOMAS) WRIGHT,, Shff. of Duplin Co. to THOMAS NORMENT (co.
not given), 18 Apr. 1795, by virtue of a writ of fieri facias from the Sup. Ct. of

Halifax Dist. at the suit of WILKINSON against KENAN'S admrs. & did levy the same on 6 negroes the prop. of sd. KENAN dec'd (WILLIAM KENAN) to wit: BESS, BET, GINNE, MILLEY, POLLEY & PHIBBS. THOMAS NORMENT became the last & highest bidder for sd. negroes at a public auction for 120 pds. the 3rd Saturday in July last. Wit: DANL. GLISSON. Apr. Ct. 1795.

p. 52   LEAH (X) IVEY, widow, to NICHOLAS BOURDEN & FRANCIS OLIVER, planters, all of Duplin Co., 6 Nov 1794, for "natural Love & affection", a deed of gift for sundries (to wit): one negro boy called CASH, one negro girl called LUCY, all of stock of every kind, household goods & planta. tools, "reserving always unto the sd. LEAH IVEY her natural life & the natural life of JOHN AUSTON of the county & State afsd., in the full & peaceble poss. of the same." Wit: BAKER BOURDEN, READING STOKES. Apr. Ct. 1795.

p. 52   WM. (WILLIAM) McREE, Esqr. of Bladen Co., 24 Oct 1778, deposeth on oath that "between the year 1741 & 1745 he was at the running (?) of the dividing lines between his father WILLIAM McREE now dec'd & HUGH McALEXANDER dec'd & lines begun in the bottom of a branch near Woodard's Chase Creek (now Goshen Swamp) at a water oak, thence runs a course about S50W along the lane between the fields of sd. McREE dec'd & the field of the sd. McALEXANDER down the side of a small hill & over a little wet slash to a black oak, down a branch a course about E20S into the corner of a swamp, to a maple in the swamp, no more line being then run for the compliment of 500A & that sd. McREE dec'd never claimed any other line for sd. land & further this deponent doth sware [sic] that the 24th day of this Instant (October), that he was along the lines at the water oak corner first described & up the line to the 2nd place & c, & is fully satisfied they are the corners of lines surveyed for the above sd. McREE & McALEXANDER dec'd. Wit: THOS. ROUTLEDGE. Apr. Ct. 1795.

p. 53   CONSTANTINE WHITFIELD of Craven Co. to his dau. WINNEFORD MILLER, 25 Mar 1795, for "natural love & affection" 9 negroes to wit: DORATHA, JIMMIMA, DANIEL, ANNA, JACK, PEG, BEN, JACOB & AGNESS. (Heading of deed says STEPHEN MILLER). Wit: JAMES PEARSALL, JAMES WHITFIELD. Apr. Ct. 1795.

p. 54   JOHN COOPER of Duplin Co. to DAVID CARLTON (co. not given), 31 Jan 1795, hath bargained & sold in plain & open market (sum not given) one negro wench named RUTH. Wit: EDWARD DICKSON. Apr. Ct. 1795.

p. 54   CONST. (CONSTANTINE) WHITFIELD of Duplin Co. to his dau. FERABE PEARSALL (co. not given), 25 Mar 1795, for "natural love and affection" 8 negroes to wit: CLOE & her 5 children BUCK, CHARLOTTE, CHLOE, ARTHUR & DOLL & 2 other negroes PENNY & CHARLES. Wit: STEPHEN MILLER, JAMES WHITFIELD. (Heading of deed says JAMES PEARSALL rather than FEREBE PEARSALL) Apr. Ct. 1795.

p. 55   SHADRACK WOOTEN & WILLIAM WOOTEN, both of Lenoir Co. to STEPHEN MILLER of Duplin Co., 4 Oct 1793, for 210 pds. current money of N. C. one negro woman slave named PEGG about 19 yrs. old & her child a boy named HARRY about 9 mos. old & also one negro girl named MARY about 14 yrs. old. Wit: JAMES PEARSALL, DAVID NEWSOM. Apr. Ct. 1795.

p. 56   THOS. (THOMAS) JAMES (co. not given) to AUSTON BEESLEY of Duplin
Co., 18 Mar 1795, for $300 a negro man slave named LANCE (?) about 28 yrs. of
age. Wit: ABRAM MOLTEN. No probate date.

p. 56   JOHN HILL (co. not given) to THOMAS GARRISON (co. not given), 22 Apr
1795, for 100 pds. a negro girl named CLOE. Wit: THOS. NORMENT. No probate date given.

p. 56   THOS. (THOMAS) WRIGHT to GEORGE SMITH, JUNR., both of Duplin Co.,
27 Mar 1795, for 140 pds. current money of N. C. one negro man slave named
ROGER. Wit: LOFTIS WORLEY. No probate date given.

p. 57   JOSEPH COOPER of Duplin Co. to DAVID CARLTON (co. not given), 31
Jan 1795, hath bargained & sold in plain & open market (sum not given) for one
negro man named CUFF. Wit: EDWARD DICKSON. Apr. Ct. 1795.

p. 57   KENAN LOVE to WILLIAM WARD POLLOCK, both of Duplin Co., 4 Apr
1795, for 60 pds. one negro boy slave named PETER. Wit: URIAH BLANSHARD,
DANL. LOVE, MICHL. LOVE. Apr. Ct. 1795.

p. 58   JOHN (✝) ROGERS (SENR.) to JAMES WOODARD, both of Duplin Co., 19
Sep 1793, for 10 pds. current money 14A on the NS of Goshen Swamp, beg. at 3
small pines by the main road on WILLIAM PARKER'S line & runs along a concluded
line between the sd. PARKER & JOHN ROGERS to the main road, being part of a
patent of 530A granted to sd. PARKER & since conveyed by sd. PARKER to sd.
ROGERS. Wit: FRANCIS OLIVER, ZACHARIAH TURNAGE. Apr. Ct. 1795.

p. 59   JOHN COOK (J. C.) of Island Creek in Duplin Co. to BENJAMIN LEDDON
(co. not given), 22 Oct 1795, for $133 one negro woman slave named GRACE & all
her increase about 33 yrs. old. Wit: LAVIN WATKINS, JAMES REARDON. Oct.
Ct. 1795.

p. 60   JAMES MILLS, planter, to JAMES JONES, both of Duplin Co., 14 Jan
1795, for 160 pds. specie a negro girl slave called DAVID CATO. Wit: WM.
FREDERICK. Jan. Ct. 1795.

p. 61   MICHAEL (X) MENON (MINON) to MARY KORNEGAY (co. not given), 12
Sep 1796, for 40 pds. one black horse about 10 yrs. old, saddle, one filly about 1
yr. old, & 1 filly about 2 yrs. old. Wit: JAMES WATKINS, TIMOTHY SPENCE.
Oct. Ct. 1796.

p. 61   ANNE HOOPER of Hillsborough, Orange Co., widow, & JOHN INNIS (?)
CLARK of Providence, Rhode Island, merchant, to SHADRACK STALLINGS of
Duplin Co., 3 Apr 1793, for 300 spanish milled dollars 320A on a branch of Rockfish Creek, beg. at a pine, formerly the property of JAMES MURRAY, Esqr. dec'd,
granted to THOMAS CLARK 9 May 1783 & to others in part of their claims on the
estate of sd. MURRAY. Wit: HENRY WALTERS, THOS. H. HOOPER at Herring-
ham in New Hanover Co. DAVID STONE, Justice of the Sup. Ct. of Law & Equity.
Probated 14 May 1796.

p. 62   MICHAEL DICKSON of Pendleton Co., S. C. appoints JOHN DICKSON of
Duplin Co. his attorney, 12 Aug 1794, to sell a tract of land on the mouth of the

Golden Grove belonging to sd. MICHAEL DICKSON & the heirs of ROBERT DICKSON dec'd. Wit: JAMES DICKSON, JUNR., JOHN DICKSON. Jan. Ct. 1795.

p. 63   JOHN MATCHET of Duplin Co. to JOHN WORSLEY (co. not given), 8 Aug 1794, for 115 pds. current money of N. C. a negro lad named FRIDAY about 17 or 18 yrs. of age. Wit: GEORGE SMITH, SENR., WILLIAM CHURCHWELL. Jan. Ct. 1795.

p. 63   JOHN HILL (co. not given) to THOS. GARRASON, 22 Apr 1795, for 100 pds. a negro girl named CHLOE. Wit: THOMAS NORMENT. Apr. Ct. 1795.

p. 64   ARTHUR HERRING of the State afsd. to WILLIAM ALBERSON (co. not given), 15 Oct 1794, for 200 pds. good & lawful money 115A in 2 tracts to wit: (1) 65A in the fork of the Northeast & Goshen Swamp, being part of 200A granted by patent to SAMUEL RATLIFF in 1755; (2) 50A in the fork of the Northeast & Goshen Swamp & in the fork of McCULLOCH'S or BENJAMIN HERRING'S Branch, to WILLIAM KORNEGAY'S line. Wit: SAML. ALBERSON, OWEN O'DANIEL, HENRY GRADDY. Oct. Ct. 1794.

p. 65   NICHOLAS HUNTER of Duplin Co. to JAMES KENAN, JOHN JAMES, WILLIAM DICKSON, KEDAR BRYAN, THOMAS ROUTLEDGE, JOSEPH DICKSON & DAVID DODD, Esqrs. Trustees, elected by the Subscribers, 5 Sep 1785, for 8 pds. current money 8A for the building of a house for the purpose of keeping there at a school or seminary for the instruction of youth & their successors in trust of the other part, the sd. 8A on Savage Mill Branch, beg. at a small white oak on the WS of the sd. branch about 15 feet the NW side of Savage's Upper Spring, to a small hickory on sd. HUNTER'S line, thence his & McGEE'S line. Wit: ROBERT DICKSON, WM. BEST. Oct. Ct. 1794.

p. 66   THO. (THOMAS) WRIGHT, Shff. of Duplin Co. to SAMUEL HOUSTON, Esqr. 9 Aug 1794, for 16 pds. current money, by virtue of a writ of fieri facias to him directed against the chattels, lands & tenements of WILLIAM HUBBARD levied on a negro woman named CATO, late the prop. of sd. HUBBARD exposed to public sale 22 July and to which sd. HOUSTON became the highest bidder. Wit: DAVID WRIGHT. Oct. Ct. 1794.

p. 67   NATHANIEL McCANNE, THOS. (THOMAS) McCANNE & HUGH McCANNE, SENR. to WILLIAM BECK, merchant, all of Duplin Co., 21 Oct 1794, for 700 spanish milled dollars 300A on the SS of Goshen Swamp, beg. at a stake JOHN BECK'S lower corner in the run of Long Branch at the mouth of Bawdy Branch, a little below the road, to a water oak on the line of Panther survey, to a maple & black gum on the run of Goshen Swamp, being the contents of a survey which was deeded & conveyed by THEOPHILUS WILLIAMS, Esqr. to WM. McCANNE, SENR., pursuant to a court order in consequence of a judgment which sd. WILLIAM McCANNE, SENR. obtained against the estate of HENRY McCULLOCH, Esqr. & since by the LW & T of sd. WILLIAM McCANNE was bequeathed to sd. NATHANIEL, THOMAS & HUGH McCANNE to be divided between them agreeable to the directions of sd. will. Wit: DAVID MURDOCK, JOHN JOHNSTON. Oct. Ct. 1794.

p. 69   D. (DANIEL) GLISSON, Shff. of Duplin Co. to ELIZABETH WILKINSON, 16 Aug 1793, for 46 pds. a negro named Tom. The Court of Duplin Co. awarded 35 pds. 15 shill. to JAMES SPILLER, plus cost of 4 pds. 14 shill. 6 pence for damages

in suit against WILLIAM WILKINSON & ELIZABETH WILKINSON, admrs. of
ROBERT WILKINSON dec'd, the sd. ROBERT being the owner of sd. negro TOM,
to whom ELIZABETH WILKINSON became the highest bidder at public auction on
22 Dec 1792. Wit: W. WILKINSON, SENR., JOHN WILKINSON. Oct. Ct. 1794.

p. 71   J. (JOHN) HURST to MICAJAH BYRD, both of Duplin Co., 18 July 1794, for
140 pds. specie 2 negroes to wit: one called ANDREW about 50 yrs. of age, the
other a boy about 5 yrs. of age called SIMON. Wit: STEPHEN SNELL. Oct. Ct.
1794.

p. 71   JOHN HURST to CHARLES KING, both of Duplin Co., 20 Oct 1794, for 150
pds. current money one negro man named ANDREW or ANDY. Wit: LOAMMI
STEVENS. Oct. Ct. 1794.

p. 72   HENRY GOODMAN (co. not given) to SAMUEL HOUSTON, Esqr. (co. not
given), 14 Sep 1794, the sum not given, one negro man named WILL. Wit: DAVID
SMYTH, ISAAC HINES. Oct. Ct. 1794.

p. 72   JOHN TREADWELL of Sampson Co., 21 Oct 1794, to his two grandchildren
JOHN TREADWELL MOLTEN & ELIZABETH MOLTEN, children of ABRAHAM
MOLTEN SENR. & of his dau. ZILPHA MOLTEN dec'd, both of Duplin Co., for
"natural love & affection" 3 negro slaves to wit: one negro woman slave named
FRANCES or FRANKS & her increase & her 2 children or 2 girls named CENTIER
or CYNTHIA & CLARRISSA with their after increase. TREADWELL & ELIZABETH
under lawful age. Wit: JOSEPH DICKSON, ANNE DICKSON. Oct. Ct. 1794.

p. 73   JOHN WINDERS to JAMES KENAN, planters of Duplin Co., 20 Oct 1794,
for 50 pds. current money 600A on the NS of Goshen, beg. at a cypress tree in
Goshen Swamp at the run of JOHN NEWS' lower corner, by a branch above OUT-
LAW'S field, adj. ABSALOM WESTON, ALEXANDER ROUSE & ANDREW BASS.
Wit: SAMPSON GRIMES, EDWARD WINDERS, NANCY (X) GRIMES. Oct. Ct.
1794.

p. 75   W. (WILLIAM) WILKINSON SENR. to JACOB WILLIAMS, both of Duplin Co.,
30 Sep 1794, for 200 pds. good & lawful money of N. C. 230A on the WS of the Northeast River between the lines of BROCK RUTHERFORD & McINTIRE, beg. at a maple
gum & water oak in the edge of the bent of the river swamp, it being the contents of
a patent granted to JOHN MOLTEN 10 Nov 1794 & sold to JOSEPH COX JUNR. & by
him to his brother JOHN COX who sold to sd. WILKINSON. Wit: THOMAS GARRI-
SON, HUGH MAXWELL. Oct. Ct. 1794.

p. 76   RUTH (R) HALSO, widow & relict of STEPHEN HALSO dec'd, late of Duplin
Co., to JOHN HALSO of Duplin Co., 12 Apr 1794, for 10 pds. current money of
N. C. all her right, claim & demand of any part of her lated husb's. estate lying in
Duplin Co. Wit: JOHN LANIER, JAMES LANIER. Oct. Ct. 1794.

p. 77   CHRISTOPHER MARTIN of Duplin Co. to ALEXANDER FLEMING (co. not
given), 21 Oct 1794, for 100 pds. 129A on the Northeast Branch of Cape Fear River,
beg. in the Juniper Pond Branch in sd. FLEMING'S line & to Jumping Run. Wit:
BENJA. BEST, HENRY GRADDY. Oct. Ct. 1794.

p. 78   SAMUEL (X) RATLEFF of Duplin Co., planter, to WILLIAM McCANNE of

New Hanover Co., 14 Oct 1794, for 8 pds. current money of N. C. 200A on the WS of the Northeast River & binding upon the river, beg. at a cypress near the river, in the edge of Love's Pocosin, across DUNN'S land, being the contents of a patent granted to sd. RATLEFF 1 Apr 1780 & half of a survey granted to MARTAN DUNN 16 Apr 1770, the sd. RATLEFF being lawful owner of sd. land by his wife & partly by a bond given by his wife's sister dated 25 June 1789. Wit: WILLIAM McCANNE JUNR., RICHARD CHASTEN. Oct. Ct. 1794.

p. 79   DANIEL MURRAY, planter, to THOMAS BURTON, turner, both of Duplin Co., _____ 1793, for 50 pds. lawful money 150A on the ES of a branch of Cape Fear River commonly called the Laggoon, beg. at a cypress at the mouth of a large fish pond & joining to the sd. river, commonly called the Laggoon, below a place called the Indian Graves Neck, by a dividing between the place where NICHODEMUS THOMPSON JUNR. & THOMAS THOMPSON lived, to a large pine near an arm of the Great Pocosin, to SOLOMON THOMPSON'S corner, to JACOB THOMPSON'S landing & to JAMES MURRAY'S (JUNR.) line. Wit: ARTHUR MURRAY, WILLIAM JOHN-STON. Oct. Ct. 1794.

p. 81   MATTHEW (*JZ*) EDWARDS, planter, to JOHN WALLER, house joiner, both of Duplin Co., 21 Oct 1794, for 25 pds. lawful money 25A being part of 130A granted to AMOS WILLIAMS by patent dated 24 Sep 1754 & by him conveyed to sd. EDWARDS lying below the 2nd branch from sd. EDWARDS' dwelling house & just above the waggon ford on the SS of Limestone Swamp. Wit: NATHAN WALLER, ISAAC WHALEY. Oct. Ct. 1794.

p. 82   JAS. (JAMES) KENAN, Esqr. to HARDY PARKER, both of Duplin Co., 20 Oct 1794, for 30 pds. current money 146A on Emanuels Branch, a prong of Island Creek, being part of a tract of 1,000A granted to sd. KENAN by patent (date not given), beg. at a white oak JOHN PARKER'S beg. corner of his survey of 200A, to a pine near COOK'S line & nearly joining BOWZER'S line, to a pine JACOB WELLS' corner. Wit: JOSEPH DICKSON, SHADRACK STALLING. Oct. Ct. 1794.

p. 84   ARTHUR HERRING to MICHAEL GLISSON, both planters of Duplin Co., 7 Aug 1794, for 100 pds. 75A on BS of the drain of the Beaverdam that empties into the Northeast Marsh a little below OUTLAW'S road, beg. at a red oak on the branch his own corner, adj. JONATHAN KEITHLEY, GOFF, & GLISSON, being land patented by sd. HERRING 20 Dec 1791. Wit: OWEN O'DANIEL, WILLIAM KORNE-GAY. Oct. Ct. 1794.

p. 85   JAMES HOUSE of Onslow Co. to JAMES BALEY of Duplin Co. ____ day of Sep 1794 for 20 pds. specie, five hundred & ...eight acres on the SS of the North-east prong of Cape Fear River, being part of a survey granted to SAMUEL JOHN-STON in his lifetime for 3,000A & conveyed by will to SAMUEL JOHNSTON, JEAN BLAIR & JOHN JOHNSTON who deeded to sd. HOUSE through several conveyances to wit: 172A being part of one deed for 350A, beg. at a stake in the 5th line of sd. patent near the mouth of the Beaverdam & runs up the sd. Beaverdam across the patent to the 3rd line of sd. patent to the 3rd corner & from thence No. 23W with the 2nd line crossing the main road to a stake in sd. line JAMES OUTLAW'S corner, thence wtih OUTLAW'S line N53E crossing the sd. patent to a stake in the 5th line & from thence to the beg. & ...hundred & six A beg. at a stake in the Beaverdam Swamp in the 3rd line of sd. patent & runs with the 3rd line of the sd. patent S34E 280 poles to a stake... ?? E 350 poles across the patent...in the 5th line of sd.

patent thence with that line N3 W 180 poles to a stake, from thence to the beg. or
1st station. Wit: JOHN KEITHLEY, BUCKNER KILLEBREW. (A note made by
B. F. GRADY, Transcriber, that part of the original record cont. the foregoing
deed has been worn out & lost, viz. wherever a dotted blank occurs.) Oct. Ct.
1794.

p. 87   JAMES LANIER & ELIZABETH LANIER his wife to AMOS JOHNSTON, both
of Duplin Co., 2 Nov 1793, for 50 pds. 50A on the ES of the Northeast River & NS
of Cypress Creek, beg. at a pine WILLIFORD'S first corner, formerly JOSEPH
PEARCE'S, thence with sd. WILLIFORD'S open line N45 W 127 poles. "Note. The
balance of the original record of the foregoing deed has been worn out and lost."
B. F. GRADY, Transcriber.

p. 87   NATHAN WALLER to _____. Wit: WILLIAM DICKSON. Oct.
Ct. 1794. "Note. Balance of the original record of the foregoing deed has been
worn out & lost." B. F. GRADY, Transcriber.

p. 88   ROBERT COLE, felt maker, to JOHN BATTS, planter, both of Duplin Co.,
6 Sep 1794, for 50 pds. specie 200A on the ES of the Northeast & SS of Muddy Creek
incl. ...GOFF'S impr., beg. at a water oak S.S. of the Long Branch, to a pine in
FOUNTAIN'S line, to ABRAHAM ANDREWS' corner. Signed also by ELIZABETH
(૬) COLE. Oct. Ct. 1794. Wit: ...GARRISON, ...FOUNTAIN. "Note. Part
of the original record containing the foregoing deed has been worn out & lost."
B. F. GRADY, Transcriber.

p. 89   CHARLES GRIMES to WILLIAM PICKET, both planters of Duplin Co., 20
July 1794, for 30 pds. specie 100A on the ES of the Northeast River & upper side of
Cypress Creek & NS of the Gum Swamp, beg. at a white oak on BENTON WILLI-
FORD'S line & to JOSEPH HUTCHINSON'S line, being patented by THOMAS...,
dated 29 Oct 1782...him to JOHN McGEE & from him made...to JOSEPH GRIMES
& from him to sd. CHARLES GRIMES. Wit: ... (X) PICKET, ...LANIER. Oct.
Ct. 1794. (Note: Part of the original record cont. the foregoing deed has been
worn out & lost, no doubt, wherever a dotted blank occurs. E.S.D., author.)

p. 90   THOMAS GRAY of Sampson Co. to CHARLES KING of Duplin Co., ____day
of May 1794, for 200 pds. current money 200A on the NS of Goshen Swamp in 2
tracts to wit: (1) 110A (?) incl. the ... BECK formerly ...ROBERT WARREN'S old
patented line, POWELL'S line by POWELL'S fence (now cut down), to WARREN'S
outside patented line, JOHN HAIN'S corner; (2) 90A beg. at a water oak near sd.
ROBERT WARREN'S corner, to the back line of CHARLES WOLF'S patent, to a
prong of the Marsh Branch, to CALEB BECK'S line. Wit: J. BECK, J. BARFIELD
Oct. Ct. 1794. "Note. Part of the original record of the foregoing deed has been
worn out & lost (to wit) wherever a dotted blank occurs." B. F. GRADY, Transcriber.

p. 92   JOHN HOUSMAN to WILLIAM GRADDY, both of Duplin Co., 30 May 1794,
for 50 pds. 214A in the fork of Goshen & the Northeast joining JOHN GLISSON'S,
beg. at a red oak GLISSON'S corner, to MICAEL GLISSON'S line, crossing Sandy
Run, to a stake by Camp Branch Pocosin along the patented line to ABRAHAM
_____ to the Huckleberry Glade, to the mouth in Sandy Run, to JOHN GLISSON'S
corner, being part of a tract patented by sd. HOUSMAN 20 Dec 1791 & now from
him to sd. GRADDY. Wit: FREDK. GRADDY, DURHAM GRADDY. July Ct. 1794.

p. 93   EDWARD DICKSON to JESSE NORRIS, both of Duplin Co., 30 Apr 1794,
(sum not given) 300A on Mill Branch granted by patent to sd. DICKSON (date not
given), beg. at a bay in the edge of a pond, on an old (left out) of McREES, adj. the
lines of AARON HODGESON & RUTHERFORD. Wit: SAM EVANS, MARTIN (X)
HANCHY. July Ct. 1794.

p. 94   SAMUEL (S) WARD to WILLIAM DUNCAN, both of Duplin Co., 22 July
1792, for 10 pds. current money of N. C. 40A on the Calf Pasture Branch, being
part of the land formerly patented by sd. WARD in 1782, beg. at a black jack at
WILLIAM HARRIS HAINES' corner, consented upon by sd. HAINES & REUBEN
JOHNSTON, to Pasture Branch, adj. JOHNSTON & HAINES. Wit: ADAM REAVES,
JOHN (I) STUCKCA [sic], WILLIAM (R) HARRIS HAINES. July Ct. 1794.

p. 95   STEPHEN BARFIELD of Duplin Co. to JOHN BARFIELD of Sampson Co.,
22 July 1794, for 75 pds. current money of N. C. one negro boy named TONEY.
Wit: LEWIS BARFIELD. July Ct. 1794.

p. 95   JACOB WILLIAMS, Esqr., to THOMAS QUIN, planter, both of Duplin Co.,
17 Oct 1793, for 100 pds. lawful money 100A on Limestone Creek, beg. at a white
oak near the mouth of White Oak Branch. Wit: GEORGE MILLER, JOHN MURROW.
July Ct. 1794.

p. 96   JESSE GEORGE to SAMUEL EVANS, both of Duplin Co., 10 May 1794, (sum
not given) 266A on BS of Island Creek, being part of a tract of 300A granted to JOHN
EVANS by patent dated 29 Oct 1784, beg. at a stake on JOHN EVERS old line, to a
stake on THOMAS EVANS' line, from the corner in Spring Branch, it being a dividing line between JOHN EVERS & THOMAS EVANS. Wit: JNO. JAMES, THOS.
EVANS. July Ct. 1794.

p. 97   EDMUND DUNCAN to WILLIAM DUNCAN, both of Duplin Co., 12 Feb 1794,
for 3 pds. current money 25A on the SS of the Northeast Swamp of Cape Fear River,
it being part of a tract of land patented by sd. EDMUND DUNCAN in 1780, beg. at a
pine OWEN O'DANIEL'S corner, adj. JACOB KORNEGAY & JOHN KORNEGAY.
Wit: EDMUND DUNCAN, JUNR., GEORGE DUNCAN. July Ct. 1794.

p. 98   LEWIS SMITH to LUTSON STROUD, both of Duplin Co., 2 Nov 1793, for
20 pds. currency 25A being part of 150A patented by GEORGE SMITH SENIOR &
transferred from him to LEWIS SMITH 23 Apr 1762, beg. at the last corner pine
mentioned in the patent & runs the giving line to the run of White Oak as the patent
directs. Wit: JAMES BLOUNT TREWHITT, JAMES WILLIAMS. July Ct. 1794.

p. 100   EDMUND DUNCAN SENR. to GEORGE DUNCAN, both of Duplin Co., 15
Feb 1792, for 100 pds. 250A, it being part of the surveys of JOHN SPEARS, JACOB
GOODMAN & EDMOND DUNCAN, beg. at a poplar EDMUND DUNCAN'S corner in
the Northeast Swamp, adj. GOODMAN & JOEL SASSER'S corner. Wit: WILLIAM
DUNCAN, EDMUND DUNCAN JUNR. July Ct. 1794.

p. 101   GEORGE SMITH SENR. to ARTHUR STROUD, both planters of Duplin Co.,
20 Nov 1793, for 50 pds. currency 100A between White Oak & Brices (?), it being
part of 2 surveys patented by ANTHONY WILLIAMS & MILLS MUMFORD, beg. at
MUMFORD'S corner, & adj. THOMAS SHELTON & LUTSON STROUD. Wit: JAMES
BLOUNT TREWIT, JAMES WILLIAMS. July Ct. 1794.

p. 102   DAWSON (X) PICKET to JAMES PICKET SENR. , both planters of Duplin
Co. , 20 May 1794, for 6 pds. out of a certain judgment obtained by the afsd. JAMES
PICKET against the estate of SOLOMON PICKET dec'd, 10A on the ES of the North-
east River & SS of Muddy Creek, beg. at a litewood stake near the head of a small
branch which makes between the afsd. JAMES PICKET'S field & SOLOMON PICK-
ET'S dec'd, his old field & likewise in their dividing line, it being part of 150A
deeded to SOLOMON PICKET 14 Oct 1771 & by patent granted to STEPHEN HOL-
INGSWORTH 21 June 1746. Wit: WILLIAM McCANNE, WILLIAM PICKET. July
Ct. 1794.

p. 103   SHADRACK (S) SOWELL to ALEXANDER SAUNDERS, both of Duplin Co. ,
7 Sep 1793, for 50 pds. specie 400A on the NS of the Northeast River & NS of
Limestone & on the ES of Gum Branch, patented by WILLIAM FOLSOM, ABRAHAM
NEWKIRK & WILLIAM SOUTHERLAND in 3 separate patents joining each other,
beg. at the mouth of Gum Branch & adj. sd. FOLSOM, sd. SOUTHERLAND, sd.
NEWKIRK & also JEREMIAH FOLSOM. Wit: WILLIAM SOUTHERLAND, SAMUEL
SOWELL. July Ct. 1794.

p. 105   JOHN (X) DEAVER(or DAVICE) to STEPHEN JONES, both of Duplin Co. ,
20 Sep 1790, for 30 pds. specie money 200A on the SS of the Northeast between
Rattlesnake Branch & the head of ... Marsh, beg. at a pine BAKER BOWDEN'S corner & runs along JESSE BARFIELD'S line, along with sd. DEAVER'S own line, to
a pine ELIJAH JONES' corner. Wit: WILLIAM DUNKAN, JAMES GRIMES,
GEORGE DUNKAN. July Ct. 1794.

p. 106   PETER CARLTON to CHARLES STRICKLING, son of ABSOLEM STRICK-
LING, all of Duplin Co. , 16 Nov 1793, for 20 pds. current money of N. C. 106A on
BS of Maxfield [sic] Swamp, incl. the house & planta. where THOMAS BEESLEY
formerly lived, beg. at a pine at the run of Reedy Meadow & runs with JAMES
DICKSON'S line, to SOLOMON BEESLEY'S old corner, the sd. land being the con-
tents of a deed of sale from SOLOMON BEESLEY to PETER CARLTON 20 Feb 1787.
ABSOLOM STRICKLING & wife SARAH to have lawful claim to sd. land during their
natural lives. Wit: THOMAS CARLTON, JOHN CARLTON. Jan. Ct. 1795.

p. 107   WINDELL DAVIS to CHRISTOPHER BROWN, both of Lenoir Co. , 6 Aug
1793, 6 Aug 1793, for 150 pds. specie money 380A on the drains of the Great Branch
between Poley Bridge Branch & the Beaverdam Branch in 2 tracts to wit: (1) 200A
beg. at a hickory on EDWARD CARTER'S line patented Oct 1782; (2) 180A being
part of 200A taken up & patented by JOHN ALBERSON 21 Dec 1785, beg. at a pine
on his own line by his house & crossing a drain of the Great Branch to a hickory on
the side of the branch. Wit: ISAAC HINES, AUGUSTIN HINES. Jan. Ct. 1795.

p. 109   ABSOLOM STRICKLING & SARAH ($\mathcal{L}$) STRICKLING his wife (co. not
given) to PETER CARLTON (co. not given), 18 Nov 1793, a grant & free privilege
of 100A on James' Branch until sd. STRICKLING'S son RICHARD STRICKLING is
of age & then sd. CARLTON to have no more lawful claim for a privilege. Wit:
JOHN EVENS. Jan. Ct. 1795.

p. 109   JAS. (JAMES) OUTLAW of Duplin Co. to ISAAC HINES of Lenoir Co. , 3
Apr 1793, for 50 pds. specie money 350A on the SS of Poley Bridge Branch joining
MICHAEL WILKINS & EDWARD OUTLAW'S land, beg. at a stake on WILKINS' line
to a bay in Poley Bridge Branch, & E with sd. OUTLAW'S line, to SAMUEL

ALBERSON JUNR'S. line, patented by JAMES OUTLAW 11 July 1788. Wit: READ G. STOKES, EDWARD OUTLAW. Jan. Ct. 1795.

p. 110 JAMES (X) WILKINS, planter of Sampson Co. to BENJAMIN HERRING of Duplin Co., 4 Dec 1793, for 25 pds. specie money 200A on the NS of Goshen Swamp near the head of Ground Nut Branch, joining land entered by JOHN WHITFIELD, beg. at a white oak & pine by a meadow near HINES' line, along BEASANT BROCK'S line. Wit: ALEXANDER BENTON, WILLIS WILKINS. Jan. Ct. 1795.

p. 112 CHARLES GRIMES, planter, to ALEXANDER MOBLEY & his brother MORDECAI MOBLEY, planter, all of Duplin Co., 10 Dec 1792, for 20 pds. specie 175A being part of a track of 350A granted to NICHODEMUS THOMPSON 22 Dec 1768, beg. at a white oak on the river bank THOMPSON'S corner, sd. land transferred by sd. THOMPSON to LUKE BOWZER & from him to JOSEPH GRIMES who deeded to CHARLES GRIMES. Wit: SNODEN PEARSE, SIHON PICKET, ARCHA. PEARSE. Jan. Ct. 1795.

p. 113 WILLIAM (ᐊ) NETHERCUT of Onslow Co. to JOHN MURROW of Duplin Co., 20 Nov 1794, for 50 pds. specie 100A on the ES of the Northeast River & on a branch of the NS of Limestone known as Cabbin Branch, beg. at the run of Cabbin Branch on MESSER'S line, & adj. CALEB QUIN, MESSER, sd. NETHERCUT, ABNER QUIN, ANTHONY MILLER & MUMFORD. Wit: JOAB (X) PADGET, RENN NETHERCUT. Jan. Ct. 1795.

p. 114 ARTHUR HERRING of the province of New Georgia to ANDREW GUFFORD of Duplin Co., 20 Oct 1794, for 200 pds. specie 125A on the NS of Herrings Mill Swamp joining BENJAMIN HINES' line at the mouth of the Brock Branch on the NS of the marsh, to WILLIAM HINES' line, incl. the planta. where WILLIAM SHIVERS lived & another tract of 200A joining the first tract, beg. at a stake a corner of his old line, to HINES' corner. Wit: BENGEMON SNIPES, JOHN SULAVANT. Jan. Ct. 1795.

p. 116 EDWARD CARTER of Dobbs Co. to WILLIAM ROBERTS of Duplin Co., 3 Oct 1789, for 40 pds. specie money 75A on the ES of the Northeast & SS of the Great Branch, incl. the upper part of 200A taken up by sd. CARTER & patented 1 July 1779, being the remainder of sd. land where sd. ROBERTS now lives on. Wit: JOSHUA BENTON, RICHARD HART, ALEXANDER BENTON. Jan. Ct. 1795.

p. 117 BENJAMIN SNIPES to WILLIAM MANOR, both of Duplin Co., 2 Apr 1788, for 40 pds. specie money 100A patented 1 July 1779, on the NS of Goshen Swamp, by the E corner of the Maple Pond, incl. an impr. made by ARTHUR HERRING, beg. at a white oak & pine, to a black jack by the Maple Pond. Wit: JOHN (X) MAINOR, ELENDER (X) MAINER, WILLIAM BULLARD. Jan. Ct. 1795.

p. 118 BENJAMIN LIDDON & his wife SARAH LIDDON to THOMAS ROUTLEDGE SENR., Esqr., all of Duplin Co., 16 Jan 1797, for $2,000 a tract of 2560A in Davidson Co., Tenn. on the waters of Stones River, joining ARCHIBALD LYTLE & WILLIAM MITCHELL; which patent for sd. land was granted to SARAH ROUT-LEDGE, heiress at law of WILLIAM ROUTLEDGE, a lieutenant, now dec'd, she being now the wife of BENJAMIN LIDDON. Wit: JAMES KENAN, JAMES OUTLAW. Jan. Ct. 1797.

p. 119   THOMAS ROUTLEDGE SENR., Esqr. to BENJAMIN LIDDON, both of
Duplin Co., 17 Jan 1797, for 2,000 dollars 2560A in Davidson Co., Tenn. on the
waters of Stones River joining ARCHABALD LYTLE & WILLIAM MITCHELL,
granted to SARAH ROUTLEDGE, heiress at law to WILLIAM ROUTLEDGE, lieu-
tenant, dec'd, now the wife of BENJAMIN LIDDON & by sd. LIDDON & wife SARAH
conveyed to sd. THOMAS ROUTLEDGE. Wit: JAMES KENAN, JAMES OUTLAW.
Jan. Ct. 1797.

p. 120   THOMAS WRIGHT, Shff. of Duplin Co. to BENJAMIN LANIER (co. not
given), 12 Dec 1795, for 135 pds. 640A beg. at the head of Williams Branch near
the head of Rhodes' Swamp at a pine between the Dark Pond & HENRY RHODES'
Swamp, to a pine between the head of Milliners Branch & the Great Meadow, which
was granted by patent 23 Apr 1762 to JOHN ANCRUM & now sold in satisfaction of
his debts at public auction 12 Dec 1795 to sd. LANIER. New Hanover County Court
awarded at Feb. Ct. 1794 the sum of 1150 pds. 10 shill. 9 pence, plus cost, being
the residue of former judgement of 5250 pds. & cost of suit awarded in 1783 to the
exrs. of WILLIAM DRY for damages in a suit against the exrs. of JOHN ANCRUM.
Wit: SAML. R. JOCELYN. Jan. Ct. 1796.

p. 123   ROBERT (X) IVEY of Lenoir Co. to his loving dau. MARY HERRING of
Duplin Co., spinner, 6 Sep 1794, for one negro woman named DORCAS, for
"natural love & affection". Wit: MICHAEL HERRING, STEPHEN HERRING,
DANIEL HINES. Jan. Ct. 1795.

p. 124   RICHARD (X) ROBERTS (SENR.) to his son WRIGHT ROBERTS (cos. not
given), 13 Oct 1791, for "natural love & affection", all his cattle, hogs, horses &
stock of every kind, together with all his planta. tools & household furn. & all his
other things belonging to him alive or dead & in whose hands or poss. they can be
found. Wit: LEWIS HINES, ALEXANDER DANIEL. Jan. Ct. 1795. (RICHARD
ROBERTS & MARY his wife to enjoy use of all the within granted goods during their
natural lives.)

p. 125   ROBERT (X) IVEY (co. not given) to his dau. CHLOE HINES, spinner of
Duplin Co., 26 Sep 1794, for "love & affection" one negro girl named NANCE. Wit:
MICHAEL HERRING, LEWIS HERRING, ROBERT IVEY. Jan. Ct. 1795.

p. 125   BRYAN WHITFIELD of Lenoir Co. to JAMES WILLIAMS of Duplin Co., 10
Jan 1795, for 150 pds. 215A on the ES of the Northeast River on the NS of Panther
Swamp, beg. at a black jack on the WS of the road along SMITH'S or BARNES' line,
adj. LEWIS BARFIELD, MILLS MUMFORD, LEWIS SMITH, to a white oak in
White Oak Swamp, granted to SAMUEL JONES 10 Nov 1784 & conveyed from him to
BRYAN WHITFIELD. Wit: RICHARD _____, JAMES WILLIAMS. Jan. Ct. 1795.

p. 126   MICHAEL (X) SULIVAN to JAMES KENAN, both of Duplin Co., 30 Oct
1794, for 50 pds. current money of N. C. 250A on the NS of Goshen Swamp, beg. at
a cypress tree at the run in Goshen Swamp by JOHN NEW'S lower corner, to a pine
by a branch above OUTLAW'S planta., to ANDREW BASS' upper corner, being the
upper part of a tract of land patented by GEORGE OUTLAW & the same land the sd.
KENAN conveyed to WILLIAM SULIVAN who deeded to ABRAHAM GLISSON & from
him to ANDREW GUFFORD who deeded to MICHAEL SULIVAN. Wit: KENAN
LOVE, THOMAS KENAN. Jan. Ct. 1795.

p. 127   EDWARD DICKSON to ADAM PLATT, both of Duplin Co., 12 Feb 1791, for 15 pds. current money of N. C. 100A on the NS of Rockfish Creek & on BS of the big branch of Fussel's Creek, beg. at a gum in a small branch on the line of a survey patented by AARON WILLIAMS, to a stake by the Double Horsepen Pocosin, being the contents of a patent granted to sd. DICKSON 11 July 1788. Wit: DANIEL TEACHY, JACOB BONEY. Jan. Ct. 1793.

p. 129   ALEXANDER OUTLAW of Dobbs Co. to JAMES OUTLAW of Duplin Co., (date not given), for 150 pds. lawful money of N. C. 178A on the NES of Cape Fear River, beg. at a sweet gum in the swamp side, the upper or beg. corner of his old survey, to a sweet gum on ROGERS' line, to the main Northeast Branch at JOHN STEVENS' line, patented by ALEXANDER OUTLAW joining his old survey & granted 13 Oct 1765. Wit: ISAAC HINES, EDWARD OUTLAW, WILLIAM HINES. Jan. Ct. 1795.

p. 130   EDWARD DICKSON to SHADRACK STALLINGS of Duplin Co., 1 Feb 1792, for 50 pds. current money of N. C. 100A on the NS of Rockfish Creek on BS of the main road & joining CLARK'S land, beg. at a poplar in a small branch E of Bens Creek on THOMAS CLARK'S line, to the upper side of the road 4 poles from ANNE CLARK'S corner white oak, to a red oak at BLAKE'S line, to a pine on THOMAS CLARK'S line, being the contents of a patent granted to JAMES HARROLD 15 Dec 1778 & from him conveyed to sd. DICKSON 29 June 1782. (No witnesses listed) Jan. Ct. 1795.

p. 131   JAMES MORRIS, planter, to WILLIAM GUY, both of Duplin Co., 8 Nov 1794, for 50 pds. current money of N. C. 60A adj. GUY & the main road, beg. at a gum in the branch his & GUY'S corner, to a gum GUY'S corner & JOHN WARD'S corner in Hogpen Branch. Wit: JAMES WRIGHT, LUKE WARD, THOMAS GUY. Jan. Ct. 1795.

p. 133   WILLIAM GUY, planter, to JAMES MORRIS, both of Duplin Co., 8 Nov 1794, for 50 pds. current money of N. C. 25A that sd. GUY had of FREDERICK BELL on the SS of Bear Swamp, being part of 360A granted to sd. BELL by HENRY McCULLOCH by dated 10 Oct 1766 & also part of a large tract granted to sd. HENRY McCULLOCH by King GEORGE II 3 Mar 1745, being upon the branches of the Northeast of Cape Fear River & also on Black River & the branches thereof, which sd. 25A begins at CHRISTOPHER BURCH'S corner & ash on the run of Bear Swamp. Wit: JAMES WRIGHT, LUKE WARD, THOMAS GUY. Jan. Ct. 1795.

p. 135   DAVID BALES of Rythurford [sic] Co. to STEPHEN JONES of Duplin Co., 5 Jan 1795, for 84 pds. specie 210A beg. at a large pine at the side of JOHN PARKER'S corner & running down the branch sd. PARKER'S line to ANTHONY JONES' corner, to a pine in sd. PARKER'S line. Wit: DANIEL PARKER, PETER PARKER, LEWIS JONES. Jan. Ct. 1795.

p. 136   RICHARD (?his mark) ROBERTS (co. not given) to his son WRIGHT ROBERTS, 13 Oct 1791, for "love & affection" a parcel of land (acres not listed) on the ES of Buck Marsh, with sd. RICHARD ROBERTS & his present wife MARY ROBERTS having poss. & use of land during their natural lives. Wit: LEWIS HINES, ALEXANDER DANIEL. Jan. Ct. 1795.

p. 137   FRANCIS OLIVER to RICHARD BRADLEY, both of Duplin Co., 31 July

1794, for 30 shill. current money of N. C. 33A on the NS of Goshen Swamp & in the
fork of Bear Marsh, being part of a large tract granted to sd. OLIVER by patent
bearing date 2 Dec 1791, beg. at a scrub oak sd. OLIVER'S corner, by a path on sd.
BRADLEY'S own line. (Heading of deed says 23A). Wit: JEPTHA (X) DANIEL,
VICEY WADE. Jan. Ct. 1795.

p. 138   CHARLES JAMES to JOHN WATERS, both of Duplin Co., 4 Mar 1789, for
25 pds. current money of N. C. 50A on the WS of Rockfish Creek, beg. at a white
oak & ash on the edge of the creek 10 yards above the new road, to a pine on JOHN
GOFF'S line, touching JOSEPH BEVIN'S line. Wit: EDWARD DICKSON, ANNE
DICKSON. Jan. Ct. 1795.

p. 140   LEWIS PIPKIN of New Hanover Co. to JONATHAN KEITHLEY of Duplin
Co., 7 Jan 1794, for 50 pds. lawful money of N. C. 100A on the drains of Buck
Swamp, beg. at a black jack sd. PIPKIN'S corner on RICHARD ROBERTS' line, to
a stake on DANIEL HINES' line, patented 20 Dec 1794. Wit: ISAAC HINES, JOHN
PIPKIN. Jan. Ct. 1795.

p. 141   JESSE (X) PIPKIN of Lenoir Co. to JONATHAN KEITHLEY of Duplin Co.,
27 Jan 1794, for 45 pds. lawful money 250A in 2 tracts to wit: (I) 100A on Buck
Swamp joining THOMAS JONES' land, beg. at a pine on the ES of Buck Swamp &
patented 27 Apr 1767; (2) 150A on the ES of Buck Marsh joining his own land, beg.
at a gum on the run of Buck Swamp a little below the fork, to CARTER'S line, being
land taken up by sd. PIPKIN by patent dated 21 Sep 1784. Wit: ISAAC HINES, JOHN
PIPKIN. Jan. Ct. 1795.

p. 142   JOHN GOFF of Duplin Co. to JOHN HENNESEY (co. not given), 25 Feb
1793, for 10 pds., during his life or the lifetime of his wife SALLY, 100A on the WS
of a small branch that DAVID HENNESY lives on, joining the sd. DAVID HENNESY'S
line & WILLIAM FRYAR'S line, incl. the bridge where the sd. JOHN HENNESY is
building. Wit: DAVID HENESY. Jan. Ct. 1795.

p. 143   ALEXANDER OUTLAW of Dobbs Co. to JAMES OUTLAW of Duplin Co.
(date not given), for 250 pds. lawful money 118A on the NES of Cape Fear, beg. at
a gum, to a pine on the Northeast Swamp, being the planta. the sd. ALEXANDER
OUTLAW now lives on, patented by LUKE WHITFIELD 26 June 1746 & from sd.
WHITFIELD to ALEXANDER OUTLAW Apr 1753. Wit: ISAAC HINES, EDWARD
OUTLAW, WILLIAM HINES. Jan. Ct. 1795.

p. 144   LEONARD MILLS to JAMES MURRAY, both of Duplin Co., 9 Feb 1795,
for 100 pds. good money one negro man named MINGOW. Wit: WM. McCANNE.
July Ct. 1795.

p. 144   HENRY (H) FOUNTAIN (JUNR.) to HENRY FOUNTAIN SENR., both
planters of Duplin Co., for 10 pds. 100A on the ES of the Northeast River & the head
of the Long Branch joining ABRAHAM ANDREWS' line, beg. at a pine in the head of
a small branch ANDREWS' corner. Wit: ROBERT COTTELL, THOS. COTTELL.
Dated 15 Jan 1795. July Ct. 1795.

p. 145   LIDIA (X) JONES to JOHN WILKINS, both of Duplin Co., 19 Apr 1794, for
10 pds. 100A granted by patent to JAMES OUTLAW, Esqr., on the NS of the Northeast of Cape Fear & on the side of Buck Marsh, cont. 100A joining WILLIAM

GRADDY'S line, beg. at a maple in the head of sd. branch. Wit: CHRISTOPHER MARTIN, LEWIS MARTIN, ALEXANDER HERRING. (Heading of the deed says 200A, but the body of the deed reads 100A.) July Ct. 1795.

p. 146   CURLING SMITH to JAMES WINDERS, both of Duplin Co., 20 July 1795, for 35 pds. 52A on the SS of Goshen & NS of Kings Branch, beg. at a pine on the main road sd. SMITH'S corner, to a pine on the side of the Mill Branch on JAMES WARD'S line, to a pine on THOMAS HOOKS' line. Wit: C. HOOKS, KITTY HOOKS. July Ct. 1795.

p. 147   ANDREW GUFFORD to JESSE ELLISON, both of Duplin Co., 10 Nov 1791, for 80 pds. specie 200A on the NS of Goshen Swamp on a branch running out of the Northeast called Outlaw's Mill Branch, beg. at a small pine WILLIAM MAYNER'S line by a pond called the Open Pond, to SMITH'S line, crossing BARFIELD'S road. Wit: JONATHAN KEITHLEY, ARTHUR HERRING, MATTHEW WARD. July Ct. 1795.

p. 148   MATTHEW JOHNSTON of Wilmington, New Hanover Co. to ISAAC HALL of Duplin Co., 20 Oct 1794, for 55 pds. specie 150A on the NS of Rockfish Creek on the branch of Blake's Mill incl. Angels Schoolhouse & on BS of the Great Path, beg. at a pine a little E of the marsh called the Little Beaverdam & crossing KNOWLES' Marsh & the main swamp. Wit: FREDERICK WILLIAMS, THOS. REGISTER. July Ct. 1795.

p. 149   CHARLES JAMES, planter, to JOHN WATERS, both of Duplin Co., 26 Jan 1789, for 40 pds. specie 150A on the ES of Rockfish Creek, beg. at a poplar on the ES of the Swamp, being a tract granted by WILLIAM TRYON, Esqr. 27 Apr 1767. Wit: M. J. KENAN, ANN KENAN. July Ct. 1795.

p. 151   JACOB MILLARD to JESSE MILLARD, both of Duplin Co., 14 May 1795, for 64 pds. 100A on the ES of Dry Pond Branch, beg. at a white oak in the ES of Dry Pond Branch to CHRISTOPHER BURCH'S corner, to a pine in JAMES SMITH'S line. Wit: LAVIN WATKINS, HEZEKIAH MILLARD. July Ct. 1795.

p. 152   MARTIN (X) HANCHY to JOHN WHITMAN, both of Duplin Co., 20 Feb 1786, for 30 pds. currency 200A on the WS of the Northeast River below Island Creek & lower side of Oakey Branch, beg. at a pine on SAMPSON MOSELEY'S line, patented by ROBERT McREE (date not given). Wit: DANIEL TEACHY, JACOB TEACHEY. July Ct. 1795.

p. 153   JOHN GIBBS, admr. of CHRISTOPHER BURCH,dec'd of Duplin Co. to ZACHERIAH TURNAGE & TREACY his wife of Duplin Co., 17 July 1795, "that whereas sd. BURCH did on the 20Aug 1788 make & assign a bond unto TRECY WARREN (now the wife of sd. TURNAGE) for 50 pds. lawful money of N. C. binding him the sd. CHRISTOPHER BURCH & his admrs., to make unto the sd. TREACY WARREN a certain tract on White Oak Branch, joining his own, MILLARD'S & GIBBS' lines containing 10A & since laid off for sd. TURNAGE, beg. at a red oak a corner of the sd. BURCH'S patent on the WS of White Oak Branch & also a tract of 10A joining the 1st tract between the 1st 10A & White Oak Branch, beg. at a small red oak, to a corner of sd. GIBBS' patent on the run of White Oak, to the red oak in MILLARD'S field & thence with the 1st line of the 1st tract, the 2nd 10A being part of a tract granted to JOHN GIBBS & by him conveyed to sd. TURNAGE for 6 pds. Wit: FRANS. OLIVER, LAVIN WATKINS. July Ct. 1795.

p. 156   WILLIAM THOMAS (SENR.) to WILLIAM THOMAS JUNR., 10 Dec 1794, for 30 pds. specie 200A on the ES of the Northeast between Limestone & Muddy Creek on BS of the New River Road, beg. at a white oak HICKS MILLS' corner, granted to WILLIAM THOMAS dec'd by patent dated 26 Oct 1767 & conveyed to sd. WILLIAM THOMAS SENR. by the LW & T of sd. WILLIAM THOMAS dec'd. Wit: ROBERT SOUTHERLAND, JOSEPH T. RHODES. July Ct. 1795.

p. 156   GEORGE JERNIGAN HODOM, planter, to BARTHOLOMEW BURNS, both of Duplin Co., 15 Oct 1794, for 60 pds. good & lawful money of N. C. 85A on the SS of Hooks' Marsh, beg. at a pine JAMES GRIMES' corner, adj. JOHN WINDERS & sd. GRIMES. Wit: TIMOTHY SPENCE, JOHN GIBBS. July Ct. 1795.

p. 157   JACOB (8') POWELL of Brunswick Co. to JOHN GORE of Duplin Co., 2 Apr 1795, for 15 pds. 150A on the head of the drains of the Grove Swamp, beg. at a pine JONATHAN GORE'S corner, along WM. BOYT'S line, being land surveyed for JACOB POWELL in Aug 1782. Wit: JAMES REARDON, WILLIAM GOORE. July Ct. 1795.

p. 158   JAMES PADGET, georgey man, to RICHARD CHASTON, planter, both of Duplin Co., 25 Sep 1792, for the valuable consideration of one likely horse, 250A on the WS of the Northeast River & on the SS of Island Creek in 2 tracts to wit: (1) 150A being the contents of a patent granted to LAMUEL EVANS & conveyed by him to sd. PADGET, beg. at a white oak below COOK'S Branch above his upper field on the creek side; (2) 100A beg. at a pine DANIEL COOK'S corner, to a stake on sd. EVANS' line, to a pine WELLS' & JAMES KENAN'S corner, to a gum in JOHN COOK'S line, to a stake in DANIEL COOK'S line, being the contents of a patent granted to WILLIAM HALL SENR. 16 Nov 1790 & conveyed to sd. PADGET. Wit: JOHN GILMAN, WM. McCANNE. July Ct. 1795.

p. 160   GEORGE WILLIAMS to CURLING SMITH, both of Duplin Co., 24 Nov 1794, for 230 pds. specie 300A on the NS of the Grove Swamp & on BS of Carrs Branch, being part of 3 surveys, beg. at a cypress in the Grove Swamp near a field called GEORGE WILLIAMS' low field, to a pine on the ES of Carrs Branch, to a bay in the head of Gum Swamp, thence down between Gum Swamp & the Grove Swamp a straight line to a pine below the Five Runs to sd. WILLIAMS' lower line, to a cypress at the run of the Grove Swamp. Wit: HENRY STOAKES, JOHN (X) WILLIAMS. July Ct. 1795.

p. 161   HENRY (X) EZEL to BENJAMIN BELL, both of Duplin Co., 22 July 1794, for 50 pds. specie 100A in 2 tracts to wit: (1) 50A between Stewart's Creek Bridge & the head of Clear Run, beg. at a pine on the road, a W course to a pine at the branch; (2) another tract of 50A joining the 1st tract on the SS of Stewart's Creek on BS of Clear Run or Cooks Mill Branch, beg. at a pine DAVID TUCKER'S corner of his 350A survey, the N edge of the main road, to a water oak in a pond on JOHN COOK'S line, & with TUCKER'S old line. Wit: JOHN MATTHIS, L. STALLINGS. July Ct. 1795.

p. 163   CALEB (⊂) SULLIVENT of Anson Co. & ROBERT SULLIVENT (⊆) of Sampson Co. to MICHAEL SULLIVENT (co. not given), 16 Apr 1794 for 12 pds. 130A on the NS of Goshen Swamp & on the ES of Rooty Branch, beg. in the old line patented by JOHN SULLIVENT (little) at the NE corner of MICHAEL SULLIVENT'S 100A that JOHN SULLIVENT SENR. dec'd willed to sd. MICHAEL SULLIVENT.

Wit: SAMPSON GRIMES, MARRY (*uu*) ALBERSON, ELKANAH (8) SULLIVENT.
July Ct. 1795.

p. 165   CALEB (*♗*) SULLIVENT of Anson Co., planter, to SAMPSON GRIMES,
planter of Duplin Co., 16 Mar 1795, for 20 pds. 60A on the NS of Goshen Swamp &
WS of Absolams Branch, beg. at a hickory WM. B-LLARD'S corner, to a hickory on
STEPHEN HERRING'S old line, now JOHN HOUSEMAN'S line, patented 1 Apr 1780.
Wit: JOHN SULLIVENT, MICHAEL (X) SULLIVENT, NANCY (X) GRIMES. July
Ct. 1795.

p. 166   DANIEL GLISSON, Shff. of Duplin Co. to THOMAS NORMENT (co. not
given), 12 Jan 1792, for 74 pds. a negro girl named CLEARY, age about 9 yrs. The
Court awarded 1658 pds. 11 shill. 1/2 penny, plus cost, to JAMES KENAN & JOHN
HILL, admrs. of WILLIAM KENAN dec'd, for damages in a suit against THEO-
PHILUS WILLIAMS, JAMES MORRIS, JOHN STUCKEY & SAMUEL WARD, owners
of sd. negro belonging to the estate of JOHN STUCKEY. Wit: AARON WILLIAMS.
July Ct. 1796.

p. 167   ROGER ALDEN of New York City, N. Y., gentleman, to ROBERT
CHARLES JOHNSTON of same place, gentleman, 20 Apr.1796 for $10,000 lawful
money of the U. S. of America 18 tracts in Duplin & Sampson Cos. to wit: (1)
1,280A on the drains of Rockfish Creek, granted to ROGER ALDEN 1 Jan 1796 ;
(2) 5,120A on the head of Panther Swamp granted to sd. ALDEN 1 Jan 1796;   (3)
640A on the drains of Burncoat & Matthews Branch granted to sd. ALDEN 1 Jan
1796;   (4) 12,800A on the ES of the Northeast River on BS of Cypress Creek & Buck
Swamp & on the heads of Muddy Creek & Limestone & adj. the Onslow Co. line,
granted to sd. ALDEN 1 Jan 1796;   (5) 9,530A incl. the upper part of Holly Shelter
Pocosin, beg. at 3 pines the E station of JAMES CARAWAY'S survey of 79,184A on
the ES of the pocosin in the line which divides Duplin from New Hanover Co.,
granted to sd. ALDEN 1 Jan 1796;   (6) 3,200A on the WS of the NE River & in Love's
Pocosin, granted to sd. ALDEN 1 Jan 1796;   (7) 3,200A on BS of the Gourd Branch
& Cuffee Branch, incl. the Gourd Pocosin granted to sd. ALDEN 1 Jan 1796;   (8)
640A on the head of Fussels Creek on a branch of Rockfish, granted to sd. ALDEN
25 Feb 1796;   (9) 640A on the drains of Little Rockfish Creek in the pocosin, granted
to sd. ALDEN 25 Feb 1796.   These 9 tracts were located in Duplin Co. The following 9 tracts are for Sampson Co. (1) 20,000A on the ES of Black River (alias)
South River & WS of Little Cohera & on BS of the Great Swamp & the public road
leading from Fayetteville to New Bern, granted to sd. ALDEN 19 Mar 1796;   (2)
30,000A on the ES of Black River & WS of Little Cohera & on BS of the main road
leading from Campbell's Ferry on Black River to New Bern, granted to sd. ALDEN
19 Mar 1796;   (3) 11,950A between Little Cohera & Bearskin Swamp granted to sd.
ALDEN;   (4) 4,896A between Great Cohera & Little Cohera on BS of the old road,
granted to sd. ALDEN 19 Mar 1796;   (5) 4,502A on the ES of Bearskin Swamp on
BS of the old road granted to sd. ALDEN 19 Mar 1796;   (6) 2,266A on the ES of
South River on BS of the main road & adj. the county line, granted to sd. ALDEN
19 Mar 1796;   (7) 1110A on the ES of Black River granted to sd. ALDEN 19 Mar
1796;   (8) 557A between South River & Little Cohera, incl. part of Herrington's
Pocosin granted to sd. ALDEN 19 Mar 1796;   (9) 445A on BS of the main raod, incl.
Harrels Pocosin granted to sd. ALDEN 19 Mar 1796.   Wit: GEORGE JAMES, PHIL
T. DUNN.   Recorded 22 Apr 1796.before MATHEW CLARKSON, mayor of the city
of Philadelphia at the request of ROGER ALDEN.

p. 172   CORDEAL (X) JONES of Orangeburgh Dist., S. C., planter, to DEMP-
SEY JONES of same place, miller, 16 Nov 1796, for 7 pds. sterling money of S. C.
300A granted to CORDEAL JONES by patent dated 1789, on the ES of the Northeast
River & SES of the Back Swamp incl: LEVIN COVENTON'S house & planta. in the
fork of the Nine Mile & Back Swamp, beg. at a poplar & oak above the fork. Wit:
JOHN DUNNIN, JEREMIAH (X) McDALE, PHILIP (X) THOMAS. (Deed delivered
to DEMPSEY JONES in the Orangeburgh Dist. of S. C. with JOHN FANNING J. P.
Registered 18 July 1797 by JAMES DICKSON, Registrar.

p. 174   WILLIAM RIGBY (SENR.) to WILLIAM RIGBY JUNR., both of Duplin Co.,
17 July 1795, for 100 pds. 245A on the SS of the Horse Branch, beg. at a small
poplar & a gum in sd. branch, to a gum in a branch that runs into Marsh Branch, to
a large pine on the line of WILLIAM RIGBY'S 300A survey, along another line of sd.
patent to a lightwood post JAMES QUIN'S corner & along his line of trees to a pine &
persimmon tree at the run of Horse Branch, being part of a patent granted to WM.
RIGBY SENR. for 300A. Wit: JOSEPH DICKSON, BENJAMIN BEST. Oct. Ct.
1795.

p. 175   THOS. (THOMAS) NORMENT (co. not given) to JAMES BIZZELL (co. not
given), 22 Mar 1793, for 200 silver dollars a negro woman named HESTER. Wit:
WILLIAM DUNCAN, THOMAS McCULLOCH.

p. 176   WILLIAM MATCHETT to JAMES PEARSALL, both of Duplin Co., 24 June
1794, for 150 pds. good & lawful money of N. C. 128A being part of 2 surveys
patented by JOHN MATCHET, father to the sd. WILLIAM MATCHET, on the SS of
Goshen Swamp, beg. at a water oak on the run of Goshen Swamp & with sd. PEAR-
SALL'S own line, to JEREDIAH B. FOLEY'S corner. Wit: ALEXANDER
CHAMBERS, JEREMIAH PEARSALL. Oct. Ct. 1795.

p. 177   WILLIAM MATCHETT to JEREMIAH PEARSALL, both of Duplin Co., 24
June 1794, for 500 pds. good & lawful money of N. C. 463A on the SS of Goshen
Swamp adj. JAMES PEARSALL'S & JAMES CHAMBERS' lines, beg. at a gum on
the run of Goshen at CHAMBER'S corner, to a pine on FOLEY'S corner, which land
is part of 2 surveys patented by JOHN MATCHETT, father of sd. WILLIAM MAT-
CHETT. Wit: ALEXANDER CHAMBERS, J. PEARSALL. Oct. Ct. 1795.

p. 179   DAWSON PICKETT to WILLIAM PICKETT JUNR., both planters of Duplin
Co., 20 July 1795, for 25 pds. & a small tract of land, 300A on the ES of the Northeast River & NS of Cypress Creek, beg. at a red oak on the upper side Cypress,
below the main road & CHARLES GRIMES' corner, the first station of a patent of
400A patented by JOHN ANCRUM, to HOLLINGSWORTH'S line & adj. JAMES
PICKETT & WM. PICKET, being the contents of a patent granted to SOLOMON
PICKETT 31 Dec 1792, who having died intestate, DAWSON PICKETT became poss.
of the same as an absolute estate of inheritance in fee simple. Wit: HUGH Mc
CANNE, WILLIAM (X) COOK. Oct. Ct. 1795.

p. 180   JEREMIAH PEARSALL (co. not given) to JOHN NEALE JUNR. (co. not
given), 20 Oct 1795, for 190 pds. specie a negro woman slave CELIE & her 2
children PHEOBE & JO. Wit: JOHN JOHNSTON. Oct. Ct. 1795.

p. 181   ABRAHAM MOLTEN (JUNR.) of Duplin Co. to ALEXANDER FLEMMING
(co. not given), 18 Aug 1795, for 90 pds. good & lawful money of N. C. a negro

woman slave named JENNY or JANE about 23 yrs. old. Wit: THOS. ROUTLEDGE JUNR., BENJN. LIDDON. Oct. Ct. 1795.

p. 181   JESSE JERNIGAN of Sampson Co. to ZACHERIAH TURNAGE of Duplin Co. 10 May 1794, for 90 pds. good & lawful money of N. C. one negro boy about 12 yrs. old named JIM. Wit: JAMES WATKINS. Oct. Ct. 1795.

p. 182   WILLIAM SHAW of Onslow Co. to ISAAC THOMAS of Duplin Co., 8 Sep 1795, for 155 pds. of good & lawful money of N. C. one negro man named GIFT about 21 yrs. old. Wit: WILLIAM JONES, JOHN JONES. Oct. Ct. 1795.

p. 182   D. (DANIEL) GLISSON to SAMPSON GRIMES both of Duplin Co., 15 Oct 1795, for 150 pds. 240A on the NS of Goshen Swamp on a branch called ABSOLOMS Branch in 3 tracts to wit: (1) the 1st piece beg. at a hickory; (2) being the contents of 2 sundry pieces of land conveyed by REUBEN WESTON to JOHN HOUSMAN 10 Dec 1788, adj. ABSOLOM WESTON'S old line; (3) adj. Bullard's Branch, JOHN HOUSMAN'S old corner, WILLIAM BULLARD'S old line, sd. GRIMES' corner, Big Meadow Branch & OUTLAW'S old line, being the contents of a patent to REUBEN ... 20 Dec 1791 & sold by an execution as the prop. of sd. WESTON by THOMAS WRIGHT, Shff. to sd. GLISSON. Wit: THOS. WRIGHT, LEONARD MILLS. Oct. Ct. 1795.

p. 184   LEWIS SMITH, planter, to his son READING SMITH, single man, both of Duplin Co., 5 Oct 1795, for "love, good will & affection" 120A on the ES of the Northeast & on White Oak Branch, being the planta. whereon LEWIS SMITH lives, only with the exception for sd. LEWIS SMITH & his wife DOROTHY SMITH not to be interrupted during their natural lives of their house & firewood & what ground that they would want to tend. Wit: LOFTIS WORLEY, ISAIAH SMITH. Oct. Ct. 1795.

p. 185   WILLIAM (M) BATCHELDER to PHILLIP COVINGTON, both of Duplin Co., 14 Aug 1794, for 20 pds. current money of N. C. 100A on the SS of the Back Swamp & joining the boundary line between Duplin & Onslow Co. & incl. his planta., beg. at a gum in the edge of the Back Swamp on the county line, near ABE JONES' line, the sd. land being by patent (date not given). Wit: WM. PARADIN, SUSANAH (X) PARADIN. Oct. Ct. 1795.

p. 186   FRANCIS BLAKE of New Hanover Co. to WIMBRET BONEY of Duplin Co., 9 July 1795, for 110 pds. 320A above Rockfish Creek Bridge about one & one half miles, & on BS of the main road, beg. at a pine by the main rd. about 30 poles from the fork of the old road on CUMMINS old line, to RIVENBERG'S line, & adj. BONEY & BURDEAUS. Wit: ELIAS JAMES, JACOB BONEY. Oct. Ct. 1795.

p. 187   ABE JONES, planter, to CHRISTOPHER MASHBERN, shoemaker, both of Duplin Co., 10 Oct 1795, for 20 pds. current money 100A on the SS of the Back Swamp, granted to JOHN THALLY by patent 23 Dec 1763, beg. at a white oak by the side of the back swamp by his house. Wit: WILLIAM PARADIN. Oct. Ct. 1795.

p. 188   MARY (M) DOBSON to WILLIAM CHURCHWELL, planter, both of Duplin Co., 26 Sep 1795, for 10 pds. current money of N. C. 100A beg. at a stake in BARNES' line at Burncoat run, crossing the road from Burncoat to New Bern, to GEORGE VENTRESS & JOSIAH STAFFORD'S lines, being part of 200A granted to sd. MARY DOBSON 27 Oct 1791. Wit: DAVID GEORGE, JOSIAH (S) STAFFORD.

Oct. Ct. 1795.

p. 189   S-ADRACK STALLINGS to WILLIAM STOAKS, JUNR., both of Duplin Co.,
2 Oct 1795, for 24 pds. current money 50A on the WS of Bens Creek & on BS of 2
roads, beg. at a maple on the side of the creek on the line that divides JACOB
WELLS' & sd. STALLINGS land, adj. WILLIAM SWEATMAN'S & THOMAS CRUMP-
TON'S lines. Wit: JOSEPH DICKSON, CHA. WARDE. Oct. Ct. 1795.

p. 190   JACOB (X) WELLS to WILLIAM STOAKS JUNR, both of Duplin Co., 2 Oct
1795, for 73 pds. 10 shill. current money 150A on BS of Bens Creek & on BS of the
new road, beg. at a gum the ES of the creek on the side the high ground SHADRACK
STALLINGS' corner, to SWEATMAN'S corner, through the Beaverdam, down the
ES of the swamp with the high ground & STALLINGS' line. Wit: JOSEPH DICKSON
& CHA. WARD. Oct. Ct. 1795.

p. 192   SHADRACK STALLINGS to JAMES BONEY, both of Duplin Co., 25 Mar
1795, for 200 pds. 300A on the NS of Rockfish Creek in 2 tracts to wit: (1) 150A
incl. part of EDWARDS' old field on the main road, beg. at a white oak, water oak
& cypress at the mouth of a little branch that runs through the old field, the course
of JOHN PEACOCK'S old patent of 640A; (2) 150A on the NS of the creek on the
main road, beg. at a water oak on CUMMINGS' Creek on the line of the red house
land, to a pine BLAKE'S corner by the road, adj. STALLINGS' own line, WILLIAM
NEW, HICORY HILL. Wit: JACOB WELLS, JACOB BONEY. Oct. Ct. 1795.

p. 193   WILLIAM COLLENS of Onslow Co., planter, to STEPHEN HANDCOCK,
planter of Duplin Co., 1 Apr 1795, for 30 pds. specie 300A on the SS of Muddy
Creek & SS of Jumping Run, branch of Stafford's Swamp, beg. at a cypress on the
run of Jumping Run. Wit: CHARITY COLLENS, THOMAS (X) COLLENS,
JOSEPH JOHNSTON. Oct. Ct. 1795.

p. 195   LEAVIN (X) ALLEN to NICHOLAS BRYAN, both planters of Duplin Co.,
2 Feb 1796, for 40 pds. current money 100A on the Northeast River & on BS of
Island Creek Swamp, beg. at a pine the beg. corner of the old survey of which this
is a part & running across the swamp, being half of an old survey of land granted to
sd. SHUFFIELD 18 Apr 1771. Wit: ANDREW THALLY, AMOS SHUFFIELD. Apr.
Ct. 1796.

p. 196   JONATHAN (X) TAYLOR bound unto SOLOMON CARTER, both of Duplin
Co., 1 July 1785, in the sum of 250 pds. specie for 600A on the Beaverdam of
Limestone. Wit: EZEKIAH (X) BLIZZARD, JOHN (X) SMITH. Jan. Ct. 1796.

p. 197   SAMUEL (X) TANNER of Duplin Co. to WILLIAM WHITFIELD of Wayne
Co., 3 Feb 1796, for 65 pds. current money 100A on the NS of the Northeast
Swamp, being the land & planta. whereon sd. TANNER lives, beg. at a pine & run-
ning E to a poplar in a branch of Jumping Run, to a pine on DAVIS' line, along JOHN
DARELL'S line, being a patent granted by ALEXANDER MARTIN, Gov., to sd.
TANNER 20 Dec 1791. Wit: WM. WHITFIELD, THOS. ANDERSON. July Ct. 1796.

p. 198   J. (JOHN) BECK of Sampson Co. to GEORGE DREW of Duplin Co., 7 Jan
1794, for 250 pds. 249A being part of 2 parcels of land on the NS of Goshen Swamp,
patented by ROBERT WARREN & JONATHAN TAYLOR, beg. at a sweet gum on the
N run of Goshen about a quarter of a mile above the mouth of Granthams Branch,

adj. NATHANIEL KINNARD, ROBERT WARREN, STARLING POWELL, JONATHAN
TAYLOR, & GEORGE DREW. Wit: STARLING MADDRAY, CHARLES HOOKS.
Jan. Ct. 1796.

p. 199   JEDEDIAH BLANSARD of Duplin Co. to BRYAN WHITFIELD of Lenoir Co.,
19 Apr 1796, for 120 pds. current money 300A on the NS of the Northeast Branch of
Cape Fear in 2 tracts to wit: (1) 150A beg. at a stake in Juniper Branch in ALEX-
ANDER FLEMMING'S line, to DAVIS' line, to the mouth of Juniper Branch; (2)
150A, being part of a survey granted to WILLIAM KENAN, beg. at 2 pines sd.
FLEMMINGS' corner. Wit: WM. LEADE, WM. DICKSON. Apr. Ct. 1796.

p. 201   RIGHT (X) ROBERTS, RICHARD (X) ROBERTS & MARY (X) ROBERTS,
all of Duplin Co. to BRYAN WHITFIELD of Lenoir Co., ——July 1795, for 120 pds.
current money 250A on the NS of Buck Marsh, beg. at a pine in the first line of the
patent & adj. the lines of JESSE PIPKIN, ROGERS, & OUTLAW. Wit: ISAAC
HINES, JAMES OUTLAW, AL. KEATON. Apr. Ct. 1796.

p. 203   KEDAR BRYAN of Sampson Co. to THOMAS JAMES of Duplin Co., 25 Nov
1793, for 30 pds. specie 600A on the NS of Stewart's Creek & ES of the run of Buck
Hall Swamp, beg. at the run of Buck Hall at RIVENBARK'S Ford upon a large sweet
gum & white oak in sd. JAMES' corner, adj. JAMES GILLESPIE, JAMES WILLIAMS
& being the contents of a patent of 500A granted to BENJAMIN WILLIAMS (date not
given) & part of the contents of a patent of 200A granted to the afsd. WILLIAMS on
17 Oct 1782 for 100A. Wit: HENRY CANNON, JOHN BRYAN. Apr. Ct. 1797.

p. 205   A. (ABRAHAM) MOLTEN SENR. to THOMAS JAMES, Esqr., both of Duplin
Co., 19 Sep 1795, for 250 pds. current money of N. C. 1160A on the WS of Stewart's
Creek & BS of Buck Branch, being part of the land that was bequeathed by the LW &
T of ABRAHAM MOLTEN dec'd to his sons ABRAHAM & MICHAEL MOLTEN, beg.
at a gum in Buck Branch, an old corner of THOMAS JOHNSTON'S & ABRAHAM
GLISSON'S & along sd. GLISSON'S old line, it being now EDWARD DICKSON'S line,
to BRUMLEY'S old line, MOLTEN'S patent line, to MICHAEL MOLTEN'S corner,
formerly JAMES KENAN'S corner, to JAMES JOINER'S & JAMES PATTERSON'S
lines, to a gum in the mouth of Long Branch, & to THOMAS JOHNSTON'S corner.
Wit: STEVEN (X) VANN, MARY (X) VANN. Apr. Ct. 1797.

p. 206   JOHN HOUSEMAN of Duplin Co. to BRYAN WHITFIELD of Lenoir Co., 11
Feb 1794, for 30 pds. current money 112A on the NS of Goshen & SS of the North-
east, being part of a tract granted to sd. HOUSMAN for 158A on 6 Nov 1789, beg. at
a pine the 6th corner of sd. tract & runs to CARTER'S corner & BENJAMIN HERR-
ING'S line, being the given line to the beg., to a stake sd. HERRING'S corner,
thence around the lines of that part of sd. grant as was contracted to JAMES HERR-
ING so as to make the sd. HERRING 46 to the 6th corner of the tract. Wit: URIAH
BASS, ELISHA UZZEL. Apr. Ct. 1796.

p. 208   FRANCIS BLAKE of New Hanover Co. to WILLIAM BROWN of Duplin, 2
May 1795, for 112 pds. current money 200A patented by EVANS JONES on Rockfish
Creek on the SS, beg. at a gum by sd. creek or the main branch. Wit: THOMAS
WELLS, WILLIAM MATCHET. Jan. Ct. 1796.

p. 209   DRURY (X) HALL to LABEN WILLIAMS, both of Duplin Co., 29 Nov 1799,
for 50 pds. 118A beg. at an ash & elm in the mouth of the Rooty Branch on the run

of Batchelor's Branch. Wit: SAML. HOUSTON, CHARLES BOSTICK. Oct. Ct. 1794.

p. 211   WILLIS WILKINS to DEMPSEY WESTBROOK, both of Duplin Co., 15 Sep 1795, for 10 pds. 48A on the SS of Poley Bridge Branch, beg. at a pine on the NS of the branch, to WESTBROOK'S corner, to the Wolf Pond Branch, to GARRIS' corner. Wit: DANIEL HERRING, JOHN WHITEHEAD. Oct. Ct. 1795.

p. 212   WILLIAM EZZELL to JAMES KENAN, both of Duplin Co., 25 Feb 1792, for 80 pds. specie, 450A on the ES of the Northeast Branch of Cape Fear River, joining on the side of Angola or Holly Shelter Pocosin on BS of the Watry Branch, incl. DORMON DONOHOES' impr., beg. at a small red oak on the pocosin, to a pine on JOHNSTON'S line, being part of a 600A tract granted to JACOB JAMES (date not given). Wit: ROBERT MERRITT, THOS. KENAN. Apr. Ct. 1795.

p. 213   AUSTEN BRYAN, planter, to JACOB HARRELL & HENRY HARRELL, miners, both of Duplin Co., 20 Oct 1795, for 150 pds. 400A on Muddy Creek, which JACOB HOLLINGSWORTH dec'd in his lifetime took a bond of sd. BRYAN to purchase sd. land which sd. HOLLINGSWORTH dec'd left to sd. JACOB HARRELL & HENRY HARRELL to be equally divided between them. JACOB HARRELL to have the lower part down to the creek, & HENRY HARRELL to have the upper part, the land being on the ES of the Northeast of Cape Fear River & SS of Muddy Creek, being in 2 tracts to wit: (1) 312A being part of 640A granted by patent to STEPHEN HOLLINGSWORTH 21 June 1746, beg. at a hickory, poplar, & water oak SOLOMON PICKET'S corner on the given line in Muddy Creek Swamp, on a small Island; (2) 100A joining the above 300A patented by sd. BRYAN 31 Dec 1791, beg. at a holly on the edge of the creek on his own line, to HENRY PICKET'S corner, crossing the Bryary [sic] Branch & to JAMES PICKET'S line. Wit: JOSEPH DICKSON, JNO. HOLDON. Oct. Ct. 1795.

p. 215   NATHANIEL (NE) EDWARDS to DAVID SINGLETON, both planters of Duplin Co., 13 Nov 1788, for 50 pds. lawful money of N. C. 110A on the SS of the Miry Meadows, beg. at the Marsh Branch at a pine. Wit: JOHN GOFF, ABRAHAM NEWTON. Oct. Ct. 1795.

p. 216   JOHN COOK to JESSE BROWN, both of Duplin Co., 25 Apr 1795, for 60 pds. specie currency 75A on a branch of Muddy Creek, beg. at a white oak saplin by the side of the swamp, to JOSHUA LEE'S line, JOHN BROWN'S line, to the upper corner of a survey of land patented by RICHARD KEEN, being part of a patent granted to JOHN WOODWARD SENIOR, 7 May 1764. Wit: WILLIAM FARRIOR, DANIEL SOUTHERLAND. Oct. Ct. 1795.

p. 218   GEORGE SMITH to PHILLIP LEIGH, both of Duplin Co., 19 May 1787, for 100 pds. current money, a tract (acreage not given) on the SS of the Northeast of Cape Fear & on Mirey Branch, beg. at a poplar on sd. branch; also a parcel of land adj. thereunto, beg. at a black jack at ROGERS' corner, to the edge of Bales' Pocosin, being part of 200A patented by sd. SMITH 1780; a third tract of 300A beg. at a poplar ROGERS' corner, crossing the Miry Branch, to ALBERTSON'S line, to WM. ROGERS' corner; a 4th tract beg. at a hickory his own corner on the side of the swamp, a little above where the road crosses at the old mill, adj. GREGORY GOFF & STEPHEN GUFFORD, it being part of a tract patented by GEORGE SMITH 1782, "& by what as much as GODDIN'S older patent may take out of sd. land to be excepted."

Wit: WILIAM HUBBARD, FREDERICK GRADDY. Oct. Ct. 1794.

p. 220   JOHN HILL to FELIX HILL, both of Duplin Co., 5 Feb 1796, for 200
spanish milled dollars one negro man named DUBLIN. Wit: D. GLISSON, THOS.
HILL. Apr. Ct. 1796.

p. 220   NATHANIEL SPIVEY to SILAS CARTER, both of Duplin Co., 14 Oct 1796,
for 80 pds. specie a tract (acreage not given) on the SS of the Northeast, which sd.
JOSHUA BENTON sold to NATHANIEL SPIVEY, beg. at a post oak on JOHNSTON'S
line near the marsh, down to the head of the branch that divides the sd. land & ADIN
GAINES' land. Wit. JOHN CARTER, JAMES McFARLIN. Oct. Ct. 1796.

p. 221   JNO. (JOHN) HOLDON of New Hanover Co. to ROBERT SLOAN of Duplin
Co., 18 Jan 1796, for 200 pds. specie 340A in 3 tracts: (1) 150A on the SS of
Taylor's Branch (now called the Beaverdam), a prong of Maxwell Creek, beg. at a
black oak by the Beaverdam, patented by THOMAS HOLDON 22 Dec 1759, which sd.
JOHN HOLDEN became heir at law to; (2) 100A patented by sd. JOHN HOLDON 10
Nov 1784, beg. at a poplar in the head of Pig Pen Branch, his own & COMMINS'
corner; (3) 90A patented by JOHN HOLDON 1 July 1779, beg. at a maple JOHN
THALLY'S corner, crossing Beaverdam joining A. GLISSON'S line, to HOLDON'S
corner of his old survey. Wit: HOLDEN McGEE, JOHN BONEY. Jan. Ct. 1796.

p. 223   DAVID MURDOCK to BENJAMIN LIDDON, both of Duplin Co., 29 July
1795, for & in consideration of the rents & covenants herein after reserved & contained, 800A being all that planta. & lands lying & being at & round about the courthouse in Duplin Co., in 3 surveys (a lot formerly leased to DICKSON & ROUT-
LEDGE, lying on the SS of the courthouse lot excepted), to sd. LIDDON from 1 Mar
last during the term of 8 yrs. from thence next ensuing & fully to be completed &
ended, to be paid yearly to sd. MURDOCK 80 pds. current money of N. C. or in
spanish milled dollars at 10 sh. each to be pd. annually on 1 Mar. Wit: TH.
ROUTLEDGE, JR., JOHN MATCHET. Jan. Ct. 1796.

p. 225   THOS. (THOMAS) ROUTLEDGE SENR. to ANDREW McINTIRE, both of
Duplin Co., 1 Dec 1795, for 30 pds. current money of N. C. 150A patented 4 Mar
1774 on the WS of the Northeast River & on the NS of Persimmon Swamp, below
Riney Branch, beg. at a hickory on the edge of the swamp, the lower corner of sd.
McINTIRE'S survey joining BENTON'S line. Wit: JAMES McINTIRE, THOS.
JAMES JUNR. Jan. Ct. 1796.

p. 226   WM. McCANNE of New Hanover Co. to JAMES MURRAY JUNR. of Duplin
Co., both planters, 19 Sep 1794, for 50 pds. 180A on the WS of the Northeast River,
beg. at 3 large water oaks on the river bank near the rafting oar, just below an old
tar kiln bed, to a pine old WALTER BRYANT'S corner, along the line of a new survey patented by sd. McCANNE, to JOHN WHITMAN'S corner, along POWELL'S line
to the 3rd corner of another survey granted to sd. McCANNE, to FREDK. WELLS'
corner, incl. part of 2 new surveys granted to sd. McCANNE, & likewise part of an
old survey whereon THOMAS JONES formerly lived, deeded to sd. McCANNE &
cont. the sd. 180A. Wit: ISAAC (✝) JAMES, THOS. WRIGHT. Jan. Ct. 1796.

p. 227   HUGH McCANNE to THOMAS McCANNE, both of Duplin Co., 26 Aug 1795,
for 150 pds. lawful money 300A on the WS of the Northeast River & SS of Maxwell
Creek, incl. a place called the Landing Neck, beg. where Maxwell Creek empties

into the river, up the creek with SHUFFIELD'S line to a cypress & birch on the
creek run, which Ready Meadow makes out of sd. run at WM. McCANNE SENR'S.
corner, being the greater part of a tract of 400A granted to WILLIAM McCANNE
JR. by a patent dated 9 Oct 1783. Wit: NATHL. McCANNE & ROBT. SLOAN.
Jan. Ct. 1796.

p. 229   JOSEPH WETTS of Duplin Co. to ANDREW McINTIRE (co. not given), 18
Aug 1795, for "a valuable consideration" paid by JOSEPH DICKSON & JAMES Mc
INTIRE, 2 negro girls , one named LUCY 15 yrs. old & JUDITH about 10 yrs. of
age with their increase, "at the same time excepting my own & my wife ELIZA-
BETH'S natural lifetime in the sd. LUCY & JUDITH." Wit: J. PEARSALL,
JEREMIAH PEARSALL. Jan. Ct. 1796.

p. 229   THOMAS McCANNE to HUGH McCANNE JUNR., both of Duplin Co., 18
Apr 1795, for 150 pds. lawful money a negro man named SAM. Wit: JOHN GIL-
MAN, THOS. EVANS. Jan. Ct. 1796.

p. 230   LEWIS (X) HINES of Hanover (New Hanover) Co. to CHRISTOPHER LAW-
SON of Duplin Co., 10 Oct 1794, for 100 pds. 290A on the NES of Cabing [sic]
Branch in 2 tracts to wit: (1) 90A (?) beg. at a pine on sd. branch with the patent;
(2) 200A granted to sd. HINES by patent on the NS of the Northeast joining his own
land & on BS of Cabin Branch, beg. at a gum on sd. branch on his own line, near
WHITFIELD'S line. Wit: CHRISTOPHER MARTIN, WM. (H) HUNTER. July Ct.
1796.

p. 231   JOHN REEVES, planter of Duplin Co. to JOHN GIDDENS, planter of Wayne
Co., 1 Jan 1796, for 25 pds. current money of N. C. 67A on the head of a branch of
the Northeast, beg. at a small white oak by the side of the main road by the 9 mile
post, along ADAM REEVES' line, to a stake on BAKER'S line by Stout's Pond, being
part of a patent granted to sd. REEVES 17 Dec 1794. Wit: WILLIAM TAYLOR,
JESSE NORRIS. July Ct. 1796.

p. 232   WILLIAM DUNCAN to JOHN REEVES, both of Duplin Co., 1 Dec 1794, for
50 pds. 216A on the Northeast of Cape Fear on the upper side of Morises Branch,
beg. at a pine JACOB TAYLOR'S corner, to EDMOND DUNCAN'S line, along
BENJAMIN SELLARS' line, to TAYLOR'S line. Wit: JAMES GRIMES, EDMUND
DUNCAN. Jan. Ct. 1797.

p. 233   ADAM REEVES, planter of Wayne Co. to JOHN REEVES of Duplin Co., 18
Dec 1793, for 100 pds. current money 381A upon Morises Branch on BS & the NS of
the Northeast Swamp, beg. at a pine GEORGE POOL'S corner, to DANIEL SALMON
& EDMUND DUNCAN'S lines, being part of this land where the widow BASS formerly
lived, joining GEORGE KORNEGAY'S land, beg. at a pine, to a gum in Morises
Branch, a consented line to LASSESFRA'S [sic], a consented corner, to a stake on
the head line dividing ANDREW BASS' land from GEORGE KORNEGAY'S land, along
sd. DUNCAN'S line to the beg. Wit: JESSE REEVES, GEORGE DUNCAN. Jan. Ct.
1796.

p. 235   LEWIS MARTIN of Duplin Co. to NEEDHAM WHITFIELD of Lenoir Co.,
5 Oct 1796, for 40 pds. 147A on the NS of the Northeast & SS of Cabbin Branch,
being part of 2 surveys granted to WILLIAM KENAN & JESSE PEACOCK, beg. at a
pine KENAN'S 3rd corner & PEACOCK'S 2nd corner, & runs with PEACOCK'S line,

to a stake near a spring CHRISTOPHER LAWSON'S corner, W along PEACOCK'S line to a dividing line between MARTIN & FLEMMON, thence along that line S through PEACOCK & KENAN'S surveys, to the back line of KENAN'S surveys, then E along KENAN'S line to the beg. Wit: ALEX. FLEMMING, ROBERT DONNELL. Oct. Ct. 1796.

p. 236   CHARLES GRIMES (co. not given) to BYRD LANIER (co. not given), 4 Feb 1796, for 155 pds. 300A on the ES of Cape Fear, beg. at a red oak standing on the SS of Cypress Swamp just above Cypress Creek, to BENJAMIN & JACOB LANIERS' line, part of the same patent, incl. 300A of land patented by JOHN ANTHRAM 15 Nov 1762. Wit: WILLIAM WILLEFORD, BENJN. LANIER. Jan. Ct. 1797.

p. 238   DANIEL SOUTHERLAND to MOSES SHOALER, both of Duplin Co., 16 July 1796, for 109 pds. specie one negro boy named ARTHUR. Wit: JOHN SHOALER. Oct. Ct. 1796.

p. 238   JOHN BLAKLY, Deputy Marshal of N. C. District, to THOMAS NORMENT 2 Apr 1794, for $1155 11 negroes belonging to the estate of WILLIAM KENAN, the sd. negroes being BALAAM, FRIDAY, SAMPSON, HANAH, SOLLIS, DRURY, SILVIA, JOUNEY, ANNY, DUCK & STEPHEN, in obedience to the late Circuit Ct. of the N. C. Dist. at the suit of WILLIAM CLARK of Va. against the admrs. of WM. KENAN et al. Wit: MICHAEL MOLTEN. Jan. Ct. 1796.

p. 239   LEWIS THOMAS of Duplin Co. to SARAH OLIVER of New Hanover Co., 23 Nov 1795, an agreement & contract with the sd. SARAH OLIVER, widow of JOHN OLIVER dec'd, that "all her estate real & personal with part, parcel, profit, advantage or interest thereof shall as fully remain & be her own after we enter marriage as though we had never married forever, & shall remain hers & her heir free from me & my heirs or assigns without the least claim or interruption from either me or my heirs or assigns forever & the sd. SARAH OLIVER do in like manner agree with sd. LEWIS THOMAS that his estate, etc. shall remain his the sd. LEWIS THOMAS, & his heirs after their marriage as though they never had been married, & that her heirs to have no claim to sd. LEWIS' estate, & that sd. SARAH OLIVER to receive no more than a common support from sd. THOMAS during his natural life. Wit: JAMES REARDON, ISAAC OLIVER." Jan. Ct. 1796.

p. 240   JOHN LIVINGSTON of Wilmington, New Hanover Co., gentleman, & ANN LIVINGSTON his wife to JOHN COOPER, planter of Duplin Co., 16 Jan 1796, for 500 pds. current money of N. C. 718A in 3 tracts to wit: (1) beg. at a sweet gum on the Oaky Branch in the Grove Swamp, crossing sd. branch twice, crossing Pond Branch to a small water oak in Indian Camp Branch, conta. 285A; (2) 300A on the ES of the Grove Swamp, beg. at a water oak in the Indian Camp Branch at MOSES MOOR'S upper corner of the land he lives on, to BURWELL LANIERS' line, (3) 133A beg. at JESSE JERNIGAN'S lower corner on Ash Branch on the run of the Golden Grove & to a water oak on the run of Indian Camp Branch. Wit: LEE SULLIVAN, DANL. HARTWELL. Jan. Ct. 1796.

p. 242   JOHN HILL to ISAAC HUNTER, both of Duplin Co., 15 May 1786, for 90 pds. specie a negro girl named AMY about 10 yrs. of age. Wit: JAS. KENAN. Jan. Ct. 1796.

p. 243   JESSE HOWARD to JAMES BIZZEL, both of Duplin Co., 10 Nov 1794,

110 pds. current money of N. C. 2 negroes named BEN & ABRAHAM. Wit:
ARTHUR BIZZEL, WILLIAM FLOWERS. Jan. Ct. 1796.

p. 243   JOHN HOUSMAN of Duplin Co. to WILLIAM HUBBARD late of Duplin Co.,
15 Feb 1796, for 50 pds. specie 2 tracts in the fork of the Northeast & Goshen
Swamp to wit: (1) 44A being part of a survey patented by sd. HOUSMAN for 158A,
beg. at a stake the 2nd corner of afsd. survey to sd. HOUSMAN'S corner of a former
survey, to a stake in BRYAN WHITFIELD'S line; (2) 50A being part of a survey of
100A patented by sd. HOUSMAN 1789, beg. at WILLIAM ALBERTSON'S corner.
Wit: EDWARD PEARSALL, STEPHEN GUFFORD. Apr. Ct. 1796.

p. 245   JOSEPH T. (THOMAS) RHODES to JOHN FARRIOR, both planters of Duplin
Co., 16 Sep 1796, for 500 pds. lawful money 400A deeded to sd. RHODES by JOHN
McGEE 18 Dec 1787, on Muddy Creek on BS of the Marsh Branch & joining the sd.
creek swamp, beg. at a black gum in the creek below sd. branch & running N up the
creek to JOHN WOODWARD'S line, to JACOB BROWN'S lower corner, to RICHARD
KEAN'S corner on the SS of the branch, down the branch the SS to EBENEZAR
GARRISON'S lower line, to sd. KEAN'S old line. Wit: WM. FARRIOR, THOS.
WRIGHT. Oct. Ct. 1796.

p. 246   WILLIAM FARRIOR of New Hanover Co. to JOHN FARRIOR, planter of
Duplin Co., 1 Mar 1796, for 70 pds. specie 158A on the ES of the Northeast River,
joining JOHN JOHNS & WILLIAM McGEE. Wit: DANL. SOUTHERLAND, ED.
ARMSTRONG. Oct. Ct. 1796.

p. 248   CURLING SMITH to JOHN SOUTHERLAND, both of Duplin Co., 18 Jan
1797, for 125 pds. a negro woman named ISBEL about 25 yrs. old. Wit: D. (DAVIS)
WRIGHT. Apr. Ct. 1797.

p. 249   Hanover Co. (New Hanover). H. (HUGH) CAMPBELL to JAMES MURRAY,
27 Jan 1796, for $200 a negro girl named GRACE about 16 yrs. old. Wit: JOHN
FARRIOR. Apr. Ct. 1797. Registered Duplin Co.

p. 249   CHARLES (+) GOFF to JAMES MURRAY, both of Duplin Co., 26 Nov
1796, for 150 pds. current money of N. C. 130A on the WS of the Northeast Branch
of Cape Fear River, a little above the mouth of Rockfish Creek, beg. at a pine on
the back of the river, which in the patent is called McREE'S corner, to the mouth of
Mill Branch, up the branch to where WALTER BRYAN'S line crosses sd. branch,
being the contents of a part of 2 patents granted to sd. BRYAN, which land is on the
lower edge of sd. branch. Wit: JOHN FARRIOR, JOB THIGPEN. Apr. Ct. 1797.

p. 250   HENRY HALSEY (co. not given) to JOHN WOODWARD (co. not given), 13
Sep 1797, for 5 shill., a quit claim deed for 170A (location not given). (Bottom of
deed says "New Hanover County - let the same be registered.") Wit: WILLIAM
MIZZEL, JAMES DICKSON. (No probate date)

p. 251   JAMES DICKSON to JAMES MIDDLETON, both of Duplin Co., 12 Nov
1795, for 200 pds. good & lawful money of N. C. 450A on BS of Maxwell Swamp &
BS of Reedy Meadow (or JOHN MATCHET'S Branch), incl. the planta. whereon
SOLOMON BEESLEY formerly lived, being part of 6 surveys, beg. at a pine on the
edge of Reedy Meadow Run, JOHN WATERS' line (formerly ALEX. ARMSTRONG'S
line) to MATTHEW ROGERS' corner, to the 3rd corner of MATCHET'S survey of

150A, along a line patented by JOSEPH DICKSON, to a pine JAMES HEATH'S corner, to the run of Little Reedy Meadow, down the run of sd. branch with sd. HEATH'S line to the mouth, down main Reedy Meadow to the beg. Wit: ALEXR. DICKSON, DAVID SLOAN. July Ct. 1796.

p. 252   RENATUS (R) LAND to ALEXANDER SAUNDERS, both planters of Duplin Co., 17 July 1797, for 35 pds. current money of N. C. 230A on the ES of the Northeast River opposite the mouth of Island Creek, beg. at a water oak on the river bank & runs SE to a pine on the side of the Great Pocosin. Wit: AMOS JOHNSTON, WILLIAM JOHNSTON. July Ct. 1797.

p. 253   AARON WILLIAMS of Duplin Co. to ISAAC RAMSEY of Columbia Co., Ga., 16 Oct 1798, a deed of gift to for one negro boy named BOB & one negro girl named JENNEY. Wit: BENJM. LIDDON. Oct. Ct. 1798.

p. 254   SAMUEL SOWELL, constable of Duplin Co., to GEORGE SMITH JUNR. (co. not given), 20 Apr 1795, a planta. on the ES of the Northeast of Cape Fear River on the Tandam Branch, joining SMITH'S own land & LOFTIS WORLEY'S line, which land formerly belonged to CHARLES MILLER & his wife ELIZABETH MILLER &signed over by them to GEORGE MILLER JUNR. for the term of 10 yrs., which land was sold by virtue of an execution at the instance of HENRY HALSEY against GEORGE MILLER & sd. HALSEY became the highest bidder & purchased the same & by order of sd. HALSEY he defended the title of the sd. land to sd. SMITH for a period of 7 yrs. from the time of sd. sale. Wit: ROBERT SOUTHERLAND, WILLIAM THOMAS. July Ct. 1797.

p. 255   JOHN EVERS (SENR.), planter, to REUBEN MEEKS, both of Duplin Co., 10 Nov 1792, for 80 pds. specie 2 tracts on the SS of Island Creek & on BS of the main road to wit: (1) 100A beg. at a cypress in Island Creek above the deep bottom running a S course to a corner pine in the patent, to Paul's Branch, being one half of a patent granted to sd. AVERS 1 July 1798; (2) 50A of another patent granted to sd. AVERS 29 Oct 1782, beg. above the head of Paul's Branch on a black jack near an east course over the main road, being one half of a patent of 100A. Wit: WM. McCANNE, GEO. POWELL, SAML. EVANS. Apr. Ct. 1795.

p. 256   EDWARD DICKSON to ISAAC JAMES, both of Duplin Co., 20 Apr 1795, for 40 pds. 300A on the WS of the Northeast of Cape Fear & on the SS of Island Creek, beg. at a pine JACOB WALLACE'S line, lately MARTIN HANCHY'S, near a branch running out of Rattlesnake Pocosin, to JOHN COOK'S line, with the edge of the main road, to JOHN AVERS' line, to GEORGE DORHERTY'S corner. Wit: W. DICKSON, ELISHA (W) WILLEFORD.   Apr. Ct. 1795.

p. 258   JOSIAH (S) STAFFORD, planter, to HENRY GRADY, both of Duplin Co., 13 May 1796, for 100 pds. 500A on the ES of the Northeast River & on the head of Burncoat Swamp & BS of Cow Hole Branch, beg. at a pine by a pond that drains into Tuckahoe, crossing the branches of Burncoat & Cow Hole, to a gum in the Piney Woods, by the falling ground of Tuckahoe, by the line of Dobbs Co. to the beg., the sd. land patented by GEORGE SMITH 1 July 1779. Wit: ALLEN WOOTEN, JAMES GUFFORD, JOHN GRADY. July Ct. 1796.

p. 260   JAMES WILLIAMS to HENRY GRADY, both of Duplin Co., 29 Dec 1797, for 60 pds. 6/8 currency 200A on the ES of the Northeast River & the NS of

Matthews Branch, joining SOLOMON CARTER'S & MOSES STANDLEY'S lands, incl.
WM. BOWEN'S impr., beg. at a poplar sd. CARTER'S corner, at a poplar in the
mouth of the Juniper Branch, & runs with CARTER'S line to a pine on STANDLEY'S
line, to ELISHA BOWEN'S line, patented by THOMAS ROUTLEDGE, Esqr. 21 Sep
1785. Wit: EZEKIAL WILLIAMS, JOHN T. GRADY. Jan. Ct. 1798.

p. 261   CHARLES WARD, JOHN HILL, JAMES OUTLAW, SAMUEL HOUSTON,
DAVID MURDOCK, GEORGE MILLER & JOHN MATCHET, commissioners of the
town of Sarecta, to HENRY GRADY of Duplin Co., 3 Nov 1796, for 10 pds. currency
5 one half acre lots in Sarecta to wit: (1) No. 2 drawn by JOHN QUIN; (2) No. 17
drawn by JAMES OUTLAW; (3) No. 25 drawn by JAMES GRADY; (4) No. 34 drawn
by SAML. JOHNES [sic]; (5) No. 37 drawn by FRANCIS JOHNSTON. Wit: JACOB
WILLIAMS, WM. KORNEGAY. Jan. Ct. 1797.

p. 262   WILLIAM GRADY to ALEXANDER GRADY, both planters of Duplin Co.,
10 Oct 1797, for 11 pds. currency 11A in the fork of the Northeast River & Goshen,
it being the SW corner of a 640A survey granted to COMMANDER WILLIAMS &
surveyed 7 May 1738, "lying in & near the mouth", beg. at a red oak & runs N25E
45 poles to a pine, thence S84E 45 poles to a cypress, thence N25E 45 poles to the
beg. Wit: JAMES OUTLAW, HENRY GRADY. Oct. Ct. 1797.

p. 263   THO. (THOMAS) WRIGHT, Shff. to DANIEL SOUTHERLAND, both of Duplin Co., 2 Oct 1797, for 7pds. 10 shill. 6 pence 230A on the ES of the Northeast
River, being a place called the Eight Mile Bluff, being the contents of a patent
granted to NICHODEMUS THOMPSON 22 Dec 1768, which through several conveyances became the prop. of a certain RENATUS LAND & by him sold to SOLOMON
COX dec'd, late of Duplin Co. & by sd. COX to WILLIAM HALL 24 May 1788 & by
sd. HALL to JAMES PEARSALL, Shff. at the suit of JOHN McGEE versus SOLO-
MON COX & WILLIAM HALL, which land begins at a water oak below the impr. on
the river bank, to the Great Pocosin. The Superior Ct. of the Dist. of Wilmington
awarded to ALISIA (?) HASON (?) damages (sum not given) in suit against JOHN
McGEE, owner of the 230A purhcased by sd. SOUTHERLAND at public auction 23
Mar 1795. Wit: JOSEPH DICKSON, WM. DICKSON. Apr. Ct. 1798.

p. 265   THO. (THOMAS) WRIGHT, Shff. to WILLIAM GRADY, both of Duplin Co.,
18 Oct 1796, for 40 pds. 440A in 2 tracts to wit: (1) 400A joining on the Buck Marsh
Branches sd. GRADY'S other line, beg. at a black jack on the SS of Buck Marsh &
runs with his line, to a gum & birch in the Northeast Swamp, to a stake in the head
of Buck Marsh; (2) 40A joining GRADY'S own line, beg. at a gum OUTLAW'S corner on the SS of Rogers' Swamp, to MUND'S line, being part of 200A granted to sd.
JAMES WM. ROGERS. The Court awarded 400 pds. with costs to sd. GRADY,
"from an attachment given by JOSEPH DICKSON, Esqr." for damages in suit
against JAMES WM. ROGERS, owner of the sd. 440A, which sd. GRADY purchased
for sd. 40 pds. at public auction held on 13 Oct 1796. Wit: OWEN O'DANIEL,
FREDERICK GRADY, WM. ALBERSON. Oct. Ct. 1796.

p. 267   JACOB WILLIAMS to JAMES WALLACE, both of Duplin Co., 18 Aug 1795,
for 30 pds. current money of N. C. 185A on the ES of the Northeast River, beg. in
a swamp on JOSEPH T. RHODES' line, late FREDERICK GREIGS', now JACOB
WILLIAMS', on 2 black gums 56 poles from Butcher Bluff, being the half of a patent
granted to sd. RHODES for 400A patented 24 Oct 1786. Wit: HUGH McCANNE,
JEREMIAH WILLIAMS. Jan. Ct. 1796.

p. 269   JOHN HILL of Duplin Co. to his son FELIX KENAN HILL (co. not given),
18 Apr 1797, for "natural love & affection" 600A on the SS of Goshen River, beg. at
a cypress on the run of Goshen River at JOHN NEWS' corner, to a water oak on the
run of Stewart's Branch, to a poplar on the Long Branch. Wit: THO. NORMENT,
WM. BECK JUN. Apr. Ct. 1797.

p. 270   THOS. (THOMAS) WRIGHT, Shff. to BENJAMIN SNIPES, both of Duplin
Co., _____ Apr 1796, for 12 pds. 14 shill. 200A in 2 tracts to wit: (1) 100A on the
NS of Goshen Swamp joining the Maple Pond, a drain of Herring's Mill Swamp, beg.
at a black jack by sd. pond, being the contents of a patent granted to WM. HINES
1 July 1779; (2) 100A on the NS of Goshen Swamp on the branches of Herring Mill
Swamp joining the lands patented by GEORGE OUTLAW poss. by BENJAMIN SNIPES
& beg. at a gum in sd. branch on sd. line, adj. JOHN SILIVENT'S land, being the
contents of a patent granted sd. HINES 1 Apr 1780. Court charges of 8 pds. 14 shill.
9 pence,adjudged against RACHEL HINES & CHARITY HINES in their suit against
JOHN HOUSMAN, was ordered to be paid by the sale of sd. 200A owned by sd.
RACHEL & CHARITY HINES, & levied upon by OWEN O'DANIEL & sold to sd.
SNIPES at public auction held on 16 Oct 1795 by the sd. Shff. for 12 pds. 14 shill.
Wit: OWEN O'DANIEL, JEDEDIAH B. FOLEY. Apr. Ct. 1796.

p. 273   OWEN O'DANIEL (co. not given) to STEPHEN HERRING (co. not given),
both planters, 23 Dec 1794, for 320 pds. 300A on the NS of Goshen Swamp & ES of
sd. HERRING'S Mill Branch, incl. the planta. where sd. HERRING now lives, beg.
at the side of the Mill Pond down against the old tan troft log & joining the sd.
HERRING'S line, to the head of the Great WHIFIELD HERRING'S corner, to
GUFFORD'S corner, with the line of the sd. granted of OWEN O'DANIEL & BENJA-
MIN SNIPES' line to SNIPE'S corner, just by the foot of OUTLAW'S road, a corner
agreed on by DANIEL HERRING & ARTHUR HERRING SENR., which is now SNIPES'
corner, W to the head of a small branch & down sd. branch of sd. HERRING'S
Marsh, & down sd. marsh to the beg., being part of 3 patents. The 1st patent
granted to WM. WHITFIELD, the 2nd to DANIEL HERRING, & the 3rd. to OWEN
O'DANIEL, conveyed by deed from WM. WHITFIELD to ABRAHAM HERRING &
from ABRAHAM HERRING to DANIEL HERRING who deeded to OWEN O'DANIEL.
Wit: ALEXANDER DANIEL, BENJAMIN BRANCH. Jan. Ct. 1798.

p. 275   WILLIAM BULLARD to STEPHEN HERRING, both of Duplin Co., 18 Mar
1796, for 110 pds. current money of N. C. 122 1/2A on the NS of Goshen Swamp &
below Absolom's Branch in 2 tracts: (1) 100A beg. at a hickory the beg. tree of the
patent of the lower survey running down sd. branch to a water oak, to sd. HERR-
ING'S line, patented by sd. BULLARD 15 Nov 1762; (2) 22 1/2A beg. at a pine
SULLIVENT'S corner, to a gum in Absolom's Branch. Wit: OWEN O'DANIEL,
JOHN (X) GARRAS, THO.(X) WILLIAMS. Jan. Ct. 1798.

p. 276   JAMES WM. (WILLIAM) ROGERS of Duplin Co. to WILLIAM GRADY of
Dobbs Co., 29 Jan 1780, the sd. ROGERS bound unto sd. GRADY in the sum of
2,000 pds. good & lawful money of N. C. within a term of 12 months, for 200A
joining WHITFIELD'S line & sd. ROGERS' own line lying in the Great Creek. Wit:
ISAAC HINES, JAMES OUTLAW. Oct. Ct. 1797.

p. 276   ARTHUR HERRING to OWEN O'DANIEL, both of Duplin Co., 9 Feb 1797,
for 468 pds. 560A being part of several surveys, one taken up by EDWD. OUTLAW,
one by SAMUEL RATLIFF, one by GEORGE McCULLOCH, one by GREGORY GOFF,

& one by MICHAEL GLISSON, lying in the fork of the Northeast & Goshen Swamps, joining WILLIAM KORNEGY, JACOB GLISSON, WM. ALBERTSON & ANDREW GUFFORD, beg. in the 3rd line of the RATLIFF patent at a white oak WM. ALBERT-SON'S corner, to KORNEGAY'S line & SOLOMON CARTER'S corner, by the Gum Pond, to HOUSMAN'S old path, to the Little Mirey Branch, adj. JACOB GLISSON, JOHN'S Branch, & STEPHEN MILLER, incl. the planta. where sd. O'DANIEL now lives & the planta. called the Quarter Planta. Wit: ANDREW GUFFORD, STEPHEN GUFFORD. Apr. Ct. 1797.

p. 278   JOHN DURAL, planter, to his son DAVID DURAL, both of Duplin Co., 9 Sep 1797, for "love & affection" 100A on the NS of the Northeast Swamp, it being part of a survey granted to STEPHEN BARFIELD & by him conveyed to sd. JOHN DURAL, beg. at a red oak & runs along the patented line. Wit: JOHN WHITEHEAD, JOS. WHITFIELD. Jan. Ct. 1798.

p. 279   THOMAS WRIGHT, Shff. to JOHN GILMAN, both of Duplin Co., 17 Oct 1797, for 6 pds. 300A formerly granted by the Kings Patent to ELIZABETH BOW-SER & since conveyed by deed in writing from RICHARD THORN to sd. NATHANIEL LOVE, on the WS of the Northeast River in Mulberry Neck near Maxwell Creek, beg. at a lightwood tree near Gum Branch. The Superior Ct. of Wilmington Dist. awarded 190 pds. 1 shill 6 pence, plus cost of 12 pds. 2 pence to JOHN MURPHY, by a writ issued by JAMES MOORE, Clerk of Ct., to WILLIAM SOUTHERLAND, deputy, for damages in a suit against NATHANIEL LOVE, ISAAC BRINSON & JOHN BRINSON. The 300A of land was owned by NATHANIEL LOVE & "lived upon" by JOHN GILMAN who purchased land at public auction 23 Mar 1795. Wit: WM. DICKSON, CHARLES HOOKS. Oct. Ct. 1797.

p. 282   JAMES SMITH to JAMES OUTLAW, both of Duplin Co., 4 Mar 1782, for 83 pds. specie 40A on the NES of Cape Fear on the upper side of Jumping Run, beg. at a pine on the edge of the marsh, OUTLAW'S corner tree & runs down the swamp, to the mouth of Jumping Run, to ALEXANDER OUTLAW'S line, being the planta. that sd. SMITH now liveth upon, as by patent granted to JAMES SMITH 28 Feb 1775. Wit: WILLIAM GRADY, JAMES BOWEN, WILLIAM (X) WRAY. July Ct. 1796.

p. 285   JOHN SULLIVENT to RICHARD BRADLEY, both of Duplin Co., 10 Feb 1797, for 150 pds. lawful money of N. C. 240A on the NS of Goshen, beg. at a stake in the marsh, to a black gum, white oak & red oak on the edge of the high land & marsh where the 2nd branch joins the marsh on the upper side by the run, to a pine on the N edge of the main road, up the main road, by the corner of sd. SULLIVENT'S field, down the middle of the run of Mirey Branch, to a stake in HERRING'S marsh. Wit: SOUTHY RAPHEL, URIAH SULLIVENT. Jan. Ct. 1797.

p. 285   L. DORSEY (co. not given) to DAVID MIDDLETON of Duplin Co., 17 May 1797, for 100 pds. current money a negro boy named BALAM. Wit: J. MORAN, THOS. HOOKS. July Ct. 1797.

p. 285   ARCHIBALD CARR to GEORGE SMITH JUNR., both of Duplin Co., 26 Dec 1796, for 120 (left blank) a negro girl slave named CHANEY about 17 yrs. of age. Wit: JACOB WILLIAMS, JOHN JOHNSTON. Jan. Ct. 1797.

p. 286   THOMAS WRIGHT, Shff. to GEORGE SMITH, both of Duplin Co., 15 Jan 1798, for 2 pds. 3 shill. 80A on the ES of the Northeast River on the head of Tandam

& Cabin Branches, being the prop. of ANTHONY MILLER dec'd, beg. at a black
jack on DANIEL GREER'S line by sd. branch & adj. FREDERICK SMITH. Wit:
JACOB WILLIAMS, FREDERICK GRADY. Jan. Ct. 1798. JAMES KENAN
obtained a judgment of 21 pds. 13 shill., plus cost before WM. BECK, Esqr. for
debt against ANTHONY MILLER dec'd, owner of sd. 80A in poss. of WILLIAM
HUBBARD, admr. of ANTHONY MILLER, which 80A was purchased by GEORGE
SMITH at public auction 20 Apr 1797.

p. 288   JAMES THOMPSON of Sampson Co. to WILLIAM UNDERHILL of Duplin
Co., 6 Feb 1797, for 250 pds. current money of N. C. 448A on the WS of Buck Hall
in 3 tracts to wit: (1) 300A being the contents of a patent granted to ROBERT HICKS,
beg. at a water oak in a drain on McCULLAR'S line, to HANCOCK HATCHER'S line,
up Spring Branch, to a pine by the Mill Branch, to a pine ESTHER WILLIAMS' old
corner, deeded to sd. THOMPSON from ROBERT HICKS 2 Dec 1780; (2) 123A being
the contents of a deed from JESSE DARDEN to JAMES THOMPSON 7 Feb 1791, beg.
at a stake in the run of Buck Hall Swamp on sd. THOMPSON'S line, formerly
THOMAS ATKINSON'S line, to a pine, being the corner & line of a survey of 300A of
sd. THOMPSON'S patented by ROBERT HICKS on the SW side of sd. Buck Hall, to a
poplar in Spring Branch WILLIAM WARD'S corner, down the run of Buck Hall with
KEDAR BRYAN'S old line (now WILLIAM WARD POLLOCK'S line); (3) 25A also
being part of a tract of 60A from sd. ATKINSON to sd. THOMPSON 15 Mar 1788,
beg. at a maple on the run of Buck Hall by the mouth of the little or lower Spring
Branch, FREDERICK RIVENBARK'S open corner to ROBERT HOOKS' old corner.
Wit: ABNER HICKS, WILLIAM TUTON, KENAN LOVE. July Ct. 1797.

p. 291   WILLIAM WARD to JEDIDIAH BLANCHARD, both of Duplin Co., ___Jan
1795, for 225 pds. current money of N. C. 300A in Duplin & Sampson Cos. in 2
tracts to wit: (1) 150A beg. at a water oak, to McCULLOCH'S line & up the Spring
Branch to Buck Hall Swamp to the mouth of the Mirey Branch; (2) 150A on BS of
the main rd. on the drains of Buck Hall, beg. at a white oak, with HATCHER'S line,
along ROBERT HICKS' line, to BOON'S corner with D. HICKS' line. Wit: UR.
BLANCHARD, URIAH HINTON BLANCHARD. (Deed also signed by MARY (X)
WARD. Apr. Ct. 1795.

p. 292   JAS. (JAMES) THOMPSON, Esqr. of Sampson Co. to URIAH BLANCHARD
of Duplin Co., 21 Apr 1795, for 400 pds. current money of N. C. 500A on the drains
of Buck Hall Swamp, a branch of Stewart's Creek in 3 tracts to wit: (1) 200A being
part of a deed of 299A from HENRY McCULLAR to DAVID THOMPSON 8 Apr 1762,
beg. at a water oak in the head of Buck Hall Swamp, the 1st station in the afsd. deed
of 299A, at the run of a branch formerly the corner of WILLIAM THOMPSON'S 100A
survey, thence HANCOCK HATCHER'S corner & lastly WILLIAM WARD'S corner,
down the run of Buck Hall to the mouth of Spring Branch; (2) 200A being the contents
of a patent granted to JAMES THOMPSON 1 Apr 1780, beg. at a white oak & adj.
DANIEL HICKS & JAMES LANE; (3) 100A being the contents of a patent granted to
JAMES THOMPSON 10 Nov 1784 on the ES of Buck Hall, beg. at a white oak, a pine
& red oak, the last corner of the 200A patent afsd. to JAMES THOMPSON. Wit:
W. WILKINSON, DAVID CLARK. Apr. Ct. 1796.

p. 294   JAMES WATKINS to RICHARD BRADLEY, both planters of Duplin Co.,
22 Feb 1797, for 70 pds. lawful money of N. C. 145A on the NS of Goshen Swamp &
in the fork of Absalom's Branch, beg. at a gum in sd. branch a little below the
mouth of Bear Branch. Wit: DAVID KORNEGAY, FRANCIS OLIVER. Apr. Ct. 1798.

p. 296   JOSHUA BENTON to WILLIAM BENTON, both of Duplin Co., 17 Oct 1797, for 5 pds. 175A in 2 tracts to wit: (1)100A being part of a survey patented by JESSE BARFIELD & purchased from ANDREW GUFFORD 20 Feb 1787, beg. at a pine on SNIPES' former line, to Poley Pocosin, to the head of Mirey Branch; (2) 75A being part of a survey patented & purchased from sd. GUFFORD 12 Mar 1787, beg. at a jack & runs E to a poplar in a branch then N across the run of the Mirey Branch, up the sd. branch to the upper line of the sd. survey, along sd. line to the beg. Wit: SARAH HERRING, BENJAMIN HERRING. Oct. Ct. 1797.

p. 297   ABRAHAM CANNON of Duplin Co. to URIAH HINTON BLANCHARD (co. not given), 20 Mar 1797, for 175 pds. current money 260A between Buck Hall & Cow Marsh in 2 tracts to wit: (1) 177A being part of 400A formerly granted by patent to BENJAMIN WILLIAMS & c. ; (2) 83A being the contents of a patent granted to KEDAR BRYAN 16 Nov 1790. The first tract mentions "the old THOMPSON corner"; the 2nd tract mentions the corners of JAMES KENAN, TAYLOR, & BRYAN, formerly called McCULLOCH'S. Wit: URH. BLANCHARD, ABNER HICKS. Apr. Ct. 1797.

p. 298   JOSHUA CHAMBLES to ALEXANDER BENTON, both of Duplin Co., 7 Jan 1796, for 40 pds. specie money 100A beg. at a stake on SAMUEL WARD'S patented line, to a pine ARTHUR HERRING'S line, to SULLIVENT'S line, near a small branch of Poley Bridge & DEMPSEY WESTBROOK'S line, by a contracted line formerly between ROBERT BROCK & BEASANT BROCK, to WARD'S patented line, it being part of sd. land & the east end of it & joining the sd. BROCK'S survey, ROBERT BROCK & JESSE BROCK. Wit: NATHANIEL CHAMBLES, WILLIAM BENTON, JOSHUA BENTON. Apr. Ct. 1796.

p. 300   JAMES MIDDLETON SENR. to DAVID MIDDLETON, both of Duplin Co., 11 May 1797, for 25 pds. current money of N. C. 40A on the NS of the Grove Swamp above BENJAMIN PHILLIPS' land, beg. at a gum & maple on the Grove Creek sd. PHILLIPS' upper corner, joining along by GORE'S old fence, down the creek joining sd. DAVID MIDDLETON'S other land, being part of the land the sd. JAMES MIDDLETON bought from THOMAS & JOHN PHILLIPS & part bought from BENJAMIN BEST. Wit: JOSEPH DICKSON, DANL. NIXON. July Ct. 1797.

p. 301   ELIZABETH THOMPSON of Duplin Co., 4 Mar 1796, for "the kind love & affection that I have for my grandson WILLIAM THOMPSON, son of JOHN C. THOMPSON & MARY THOMPSON his wife" 100A lying on the Long Branch, beg. at a white oak. Wit: AUSTON MOORE, WM. ALBERTSON. Oct. Ct. 1797.

p. 302   ARTHUR HERRING to ANDREW GUFFORD, both of Duplin Co., 10 Feb 1796, for 70 pds. 200A in 2 tracts to wit: (1) 120A in the fork of the Northeast of Goshen Swamp, joining STEPHEN GUFFORD, OWEN O'DANIEL & JACOB GLISSON, beg. at a pine known by the name of the squat pine, near to a place known by the name of the Great Hogpen, being sd. O'DANIEL'S corner, running along a row of marked trees to a pine by the White Meadow, JACOB GLISSON'S corner, with GLISSON'S line to 3 small pines in a small branch called the Little Mill, OWEN O'DANIEL'S other corner, to a black jack at the foot of HOUSMAN'S old path; (2) 80A beg. at the same squat pine & near SOLOMON CARTER'S corner to 3 small spines by a pond, near to the Great Pond, to a pine on the head of GUFFORD'S branch. Wit: OWEN O'DANIEL, STEPHEN GUFFORD. Jan. Ct. 1797.

p. 303   MARY MURDOCK (co. not given) to JOHN O. POWELL (co. not given), 16
Oct 1797, for 509 pds. 813A in 3 tracts, 2 of which were formerly the prop. of
WILLIAM FLOWED (?) by virtue of a deed from HENRY USTUS [sic] McCULLOCH,
which sd. 2 tracts were seized by FELIX KENAN, Shff. of Duplin Co., by virtue of
a writ of fieri facias to him directed from the Superior Ct. of Duplin of the Dist. of
Wilmington, & by him sold to THOMAS ROUTLEDGE 20 July 1773 & later deeded to
JAMES JAMES 13 Oct 1773 who sold to JAMES PEARSALL 7 Dec 1778 & seized by
THOMAS WRIGHT, Shff. by virtue of a writ of fieri facias to him directed from the
Ct. of Craven Co. & by him sold to MARY MURDOCK 30 May 1797. The sd. 813A
consisting of 3 tracts to wit: (1) 330A, the courthouse lot being excepted & deducted,
lying on the SS of the Grove Swamp, beg. at an ash THOMAS ROUTLEDGE'S corner,
to a white oak on the Mill Branch, crossing the head of Pasture Branch; (2) 173A
beg. at an ash at the run of the swamp a corner of OBEDIAH EVENS' tract, to a
water oak on the run of the Grove Swamp; (3) 310A on the SS of the Grove Swamp,
incl. the Indian Grave on the main road, beg. at a pine MARY McCULLOCH'S corner on WILLIAM FREDERICK'S line, to ISAAC HUNTER'S line, to JAMES' corner,
to a white oak his corner in the Mill Swamp. Wit: MICHAEL MOLTEN, EDWARD
GRAHAM. Oct. Ct. 1797.

p. 305   THOMAS SHELTON to JONATHAN THOMAS, both of Duplin Co., 17 Nov
1795, for 25 pds. current money of N. C. 90A patented by JOHN GORE & sold to
sd. SHELTON, beg. at a water oak & gum between the Grove & Nahunga Swamp in
a pond, to LEWIS THOMAS' line, to EDWARD CANNON'S corner. Wit: REBECKAH
SHELTON, HENRY BEST. Jan. Ct. 1796.

p. 306   JOHN (⊥⊥) GORE & FRANCES GORE (Ƨ) his wife to JONATHAN
THOMAS, all of Duplin Co., 18 Jan 1796, for 150 pds. 410A in 4 tracts to wit: (1)
150A surveyed for EDWARD CANNON on 25 Mar 1768 by W. DICKSON, being on the
head of Gum Swamp & on its head branches, joining to DAVID CANNON SENR'S.
land, beg. at a pine JAMES MIDDLETON'S corner, formerly DAVID CANNON'S;
(2) 100A on a branch of the Grove Swamp, beg. at a pine on sd. GORE'S line, being
a tract that JONATHAN GORE deeded to sd. JOHN GORE; (3) 150A on the head
drains of the Grove Swamp, beg. at a pine JONATHAN GORE'S corner, along
WILLIAM BOYT'S corne, now LEWIS THOMAS' corner, being a tract surveyed for
JACOB POWELL 26 Aug 1789 by JOSEPH DICKSON; (4) 10A lying at EDWARD
CANNON'S old corner, along the giving line of the patent to the beg. of a tract of
land JOHN GORE had surveyed by JOSEPH DICKSON, being part of a tract surveyed
by JO DICKSON for JOHN GORE & then sold to THOMAS SHELTON by sd. GORE,
the same being a reserve that JOHN GORE made of 10A to himself when he sold it
to sd. SHELTON. Wit: JAMES REARDON, WILLIAM GORE. Jan. Ct. 1796.

p. 308   WILLIAM FARRIOR to WILLIAM HALL, both planters of Duplin Co., 20
Oct 1794, for 20 pds. current money of N. C. 400A on the ES of the Northeast on
the drains of Limestone Swamp & on BS of the main road, beg. at a pine a little W
of the road ELIJAH WALLER'S corner, being granted by patent to sd. FARRIOR 20
Dec 1791. Wit: JOHN McGEE, JAMES HALL. Apr. Ct. 1797.

p. 309   SAMUEL (S) WARD, planter, to ANDREW GUFFORD, both of Duplin Co.,
19 Jan 1796, for 30 pds. current money 220A on the heads of Poley Bridge Branch,
beg. at a stake & 3 pines on the NS of the branch, near ROBERT BROOK'S old field,
to a pine on JOHN SULLIVENT'S line, WESTBROOK'S corner a little above his
fish dam, to a pine on the giving line of SAMUEL WARD'S patent, being part of a

tract granted to sd. SAMUEL WARD by patent dated 1 Apr 1780, it being also that land that ROBERT BROCK formerly lived on, & which he sold to sd. GUFFORD. Wit: FREDERICK BARFIELD, WARREN BLUNT. Jan. Ct. 1796.

p. 311   THO. (THOMAS) WRIGHT, Shff. of Duplin Co. to MARY MURDOCK, widow of Craven Co., 30 May 1797, for 710 pds. a total of 763A belonging to DAVID MUR-DOCK dec'd, which sd. land is in 3 tracts: (1) 330A, the courthouse lot being excepted & deducted, on the SS of the Grove Swamp, beg. at an ash THOMAS ROUT-LEDGE'S corner, to a white oak on the Mill Branch, crossing the head of Pasture Branch; (2) 123A joining & opposite the 1st tract on the WS of the Grove Swamp, beg. at an ash at the run of the swamp, a corner of OBEDIAH EVENS' tract; (3) 310A on the SS of the Grove Swamp adj. the 1st tract, incl. the Indian Grave on the main road, beg. at a pine MARY McCULLOCH'S corner on WILLIAM FREDERICK'S line & adj. ISAAC HUNTER, JAMES' corner. Craven Co. Ct. awarded 509 pds., with cost of suit to JOHN OSBON POWELL by his guardian WILLIAM SHEPHERD, for damages in suit against MARY MURDOCK, admrx. of DAVID MURDOCK dec'd. ANDREW McINTIRE & NANCY his wife, & ARCHIBALD McCALEB, guardian to HANNAH, JAMES, DAVID, WILLIAM & ELIZABETH MURDOCK (minors) requested to appear in Mar. Ct. 1797 to "show cause if any... why the real estate of the sd. MURDOCK dec'd should not be sold to satisfy the afsd. judgment...". The 763A was sold at public auction on 30 May 1797 to sd. MARY MURDOCK. Wit: MICHL. MOLTEN, EDWARD GRAHAM. Oct. Ct. 1797.

p. 314   JAMES KENAN of Duplin Co. to JAMES MAXWELL, Esqr. of same, 31 Jan 1798, for 218 pds. current money of N. C. 2 negroes to wit: one negro boy named WILL about 14 yrs. old & one negro girl named HANNAH about 16 yrs. old. Wit: SUSANAH KENAN, D. L. KENAN. (Bill of sale acknowledged in open court to be registered, but no date of probate given.)

p. 314   JEREDIAH B. (BASS) FOLEY of Duplin Co. to JAMES RAPHAEL of same, 2 Oct 1798, for 40 pds. specie 100A patented by STEPHEN HERRING & conveyed by sd. HERRING to JOHN HOUSMAN who sold to sd. FOLEY, being between the North-east & Goshen Swamp on Absolom's Branch, beg. at a pine in a drain of sd. branch, to a large pine in JOHN WINDERS' line, to a hickory at the corner of land poss. by JONATHAN TAYLOR & patented by GEORGE OUTLAW, to a maple in the head of a drain about 100 yds. from sd. branch, down the drain & up the main branch the various courses to the beg. Wit: JOHN MATCHET, WILLIAM ALEC PIERCE. Jan. Ct. 1799.

p. 315   JON. (JOHN) HOUSMAN to JAMES RAPHAEL, both of Duplin Co., 17 Apr 1798, for 30 pds. lawful money of N. C. 12A on the NS of Goshen Swamp, beg. at a lightwood stake by sd. HOUSMAN'S line in a marshy meadow sd. to be SULLIVENT'S corner. Wit: JEREDIAH BASS FOLEY, ARCHABALD CARR. Jan. Ct. 1799.

p. 317   ARTHUR (X) STROUD to ABEL CROOM STROUD, both planters of Duplin Co., 16 Jan 1797, for 60 pds. specie 100A on White Oak Swamp, beg. at a lightwood stump, the 2nd corner of sd. patent, to a pine on THOMAS SHELTON'S line, down sd. swamp to the mouth of Spring Branch, a direct course to TREWIT'S corner, being part of 2 patents, one taken up by ANTHONY WILLIAMS of 93A, the other of 640A patented by MILLS MUMFORD & c. Wit: THOS. SHELTON, LOT STROUD. July Ct. 1797.

p. 318   BENJAMIN THOMPSON of Duplin Co. to LOTT CROOM of Lenoir Co., 20
Oct 1798, for 120 pds. 300A in 3 tracts: (1) 100A being part of BENJAMIN ADAMS'
& ANDREW ADAMS' patent, taken up by WILLIAM THOMPSON 1785, beg. at DAW-
SON'S corner on CARTER'S line; (2) 100A beg. at a pictured pine, to a stake on
GEORGE SMITH'S line, to a pine ES of Cow Hole Branch, LEWIS BARNES' line to a
pine BENJAMIN THOMPSON'S corner; (3) 100A being part of ANDREW ADAMS'
patent, the S end, beg. at a pictured pine & goes with BENJM. ADAMS' line to
BENJM. THOMPSON'S corner, to ISAAC DAWSON'S line, concluding the upper end
of ANDREW ADAMS' land from the dividing blazed trees. Wit: JAMES WILLIAMS,
JOHN THOMSON, SOLOMON CARTER. July Ct. 1799.

p. 319   MICHAEL GLISSON, planter, to JOHN GLISSON, both of Duplin Co., 23
Aug 1788, for 100 pds. specie 200A on the SS of the Northeast Swamp at the lower
end of the Great Marsh, between the Horse Pen Branch & Sandy Run, beg. at a pine
DENNIS GLISSON'S corner, the sd. land surveyed for WILLIAM MOBLEY, patent
bearing date 16 Dec 1769. Wit: GEORGE SMITH, FREDERICK GRADY. Jan. Ct.
1798.

p. 320   ELIZABETH THOMSON (co. not given) to her dau. BARSHEBA GIBBS (co.
not given), 16 Oct 1797, one feather bed, bedstead & furn., one pot, one spider,
one pair of stilards, one quart pot, one mare & all stock of cattle & all the rest of
household furn. Wit: ALEXR. GRADDY, HENRY GRADDY. Oct. Ct. 1797.

p. 321   STEPHEN JONES to LAVIN COVINGTON, both planters of Duplin Co., 14
Aug 1787, for 3 pds. 10 shill. specie, 150A being part of 300A, beg. at a poplar &
oak above the fork of the Nine Mile & Back Swamp, to a pine corner on LAVIN'S
branch. Wit: ABE JONES, MARY (X) ANDREWS. Oct. Ct. 1797.

p. 322   GEORGE MILLER of Duplin Co. to STEPHEN MILLER (co. not given), 19
May 1796, for 350 pds. current money, for slaves to wit: DARRY or DERRY born
6 July 1775, TOM born 31 Aug 1780, GLASGOW born 27 May 1779, BETTY or
BESSEY born 4 May 1787. Wit: JOSEPH DICKSON, ANNE PEARSALL. July Ct.
1796.

p. 322   JOB (X) ROGERS to EBENEZER SWINSON, both of Duplin Co., 25 Dec
1794, for 100 pds. good & lawful money of N. C. 200A on BS of Carr's Branch, beg.
at a pine & hickory on the SS of the branch a little below the mouth of Bee Tree
Branch, to a stake on HUDGESON'S line, along a line of 250A patented by FRED-
ERICK LEWIS, to a pine a little S of Carr's Branch. Wit: JAMES DICKSON,
JAMES (Ŧ) HEATH. Jan. Ct. 1796.

p. 324   JACOB (𝒫) WELLS to DAVID CARLTON, both of Duplin Co., 16 Jan 1796,
for 70 pds. good & lawful money of N. C. 57A on Yokey's Swamp, beg. at a pine on
the ES of sd. swamp, a corner of the patent, being the lower part of a tract of 640A
granted to sd. WELLS 10 Nov 1784. Wit: THOS. WRIGHT, KENAN LOVE. Jan.
Ct. 1797. (The heading of the deed says 75A.)

p. 324   GEORGE MILLER to STEPHEN MILLER, both of Duplin Co., 19 May 1796,
for 100 pds. current money sundry lands consisting of 845A to wit: (1) 260A beg.
at a water oak, up the river & Woodward's Chase Creek, reducting from the sd.
tract 240A that was formerly granted from GEORGE MILLER to EDWARD HOUSTON
& by sd. HOUSTON to STEPHEN MILLER, the sd. patent granted to WILLIAM

McREE 21 Sep 1741; (2) 86A being the 1/3 of a patent of 260A granted to ANTHONY
& GEORGE MILLER 1 Dec 1759 & being the balance of the patent of the reducting to
JOHN MATCHET & the sd. STEPHEN MILLER, their parts of the sd. patent, beg.
at a hickory the 2nd corner of HUGH McALEXANDER'S survey, along STEPHEN
MILLER'S survey, with JOHN MATCHET'S line; (3) 330A granted by patent to
ROBERT SLOAN 26 May 1757 between RICHARD MILLER'S & WILLIAM McREE'S
planta., beg. at a bay tree GEORGE MILLER'S corner, to a gum on the Northeast
River; (4) 25A granted by patent to GEORGE MILLER 9 Nov 1784 on the WS of the
Northeast River, beg. at a gum on the river bank sd. GEORGE MILLER'S corner of
land patented by ROBERT SLOAN; (5) 150A being part of a patent granted to HUGH
McALEXANDER 11 Apr 1745, beg. at a water oak in a Reedy Branch WILLIAM
McREE'S corner, along his line to a stake on the upper line of the patent to a water
oak in a pocosin the last corner of sd. McALEXANDER'S patent. (The heading of
deed states 851A as well as the contents of the deed, but the total acres for the 5
tracts makes out to be 845A.) Wit: JOSEPH DICKSON, ANNE PEARSALL. July
Ct. 1796.

p. 327   JOB (R) ROGERS, PELEG (X) ROGERS, JAMES (X) ROGERS, NICHOLAS
(X) ROGERS to ISABELLA ROGERS, all of Duplin Co., 16 Jan 1794, for 20 shill.
lawful money of N. C. to fulfill the desire & regquest of JAMES ROGERS their dec'd
father & for the promotion & advancement of the sd. ISABELLA their sister, 200A
on the SS of Carr's Branch, a prong of Maxwell Swamp & on BS of the main road,
beg. at a poplar & gum on the run of Carr's Branch at the mouth of Raccoon Branch,
PELEG ROGERS' corner, down the run of sd. branch, to the mouth of Poplar Branch,
THOMAS HEATH'S corner, up the run of sd. branch as it meanders to a water oak,
at the mouth of a glade sd. HEATH'S corner, up the gully with HEATH'S line,
BEESLEY'S old line, to the run of Raccoon Branch, to PELEG ROGERS' line to the
beg. Wit: JOSEPH DICKSON, WM. SOUTHERLAND. Oct. 1798.

p. 328   SAMUEL SOWELL to MICHAEL GLISSON, both of Duplin Co., 17 Feb 1795,
for 50 pds. current money of N. C. 200A on the ES of the Northeast River, it being a
part of a piece of land entered by sd. SOWELL 21 Sep 1785, beg. at LEE'S corner.
Wit: H. HALSEY, BENJN. HALSEY. Apr. Ct. 1798.

p. 329   DEMPSEY (X) WESTBROOK to WILLIS WILKINS, both of Duplin Co., 13
Mar 1795, for 20 pds. 48A on the SS of the Northeast & on the Poley Bridge Branch,
being part of a survey patented by sd. WESTBROOK 1791, beg. at a pine on the NS
of the Poley Bridge Branch sd. WESTBROOK'S corner, to the Wolf Pond Branch, to
a bay at GARRIS' corner. Wit: JOHN WHITEHEAD, SIKES (X) GARIS. Apr. Ct.
1795.

p. 331   THOMAS BURTON (co. not given) to CHARLES DARDEN of Duplin Co., 20
Apr 1795, for 50 pds. current money of N. C. 62A whereon sd. DARDEN now lives,
beg. at a gum in a branch below sd. DARDEN'S planta. & runs to the sd. corner of
the sd. patent survey, along sd. line to the 3rd corner, down the branch to the mouth
of another small branch & to the beg. Wit: ROBERT SOUTHERLAND, PETER
FREDERICK. Apr. Ct. 1795.

p. 332   SARAH IVEY, CLABORN IVEY & THOMAS ROUTLEDGE JUNR., admrs.
to the estate of CURTIS IVEY, Esqr. late of Sampson Co. to WILLIAM CARR of
Duplin Co., 26 July 1794, for the sum of _____ 300A on the WS of the Northeast
River & NS of Island Creek, BS of part of Open Branch, beg. at a pine JOHN

SLOAN'S line, lately WILLIAM ALLEN'S, a little above sd. SLOAN'S field, JOHN COOK'S line, near a small pocosin, to a stake in THOMAS' line, granted to sd. CURTIS IVEY dec'd as heir at law to WILLIAM ROUTLEDGE JUNR. dec'd by patent dated 16 Nov 1790. Wit: THOMAS ROUTLEDGE SENR. Apr. Ct. 1795.

p. 334   DANL. (N) BOWEN to AARON BOWEN, both of Duplin Co., 1 Jan 1795, for 25 pds. current money of N. C. 200A on the drains of Rockfish & in the fork of the Doctors Creek, beg. at a pine on CAMPBELL'S line, BLOODWORTH'S line. Wit: JOHN SHAW, SHADRACK STALLINGS. Apr. Ct. 1795.

p. 335   PETER GILSTRAP of Craven Co. to DAVID CARLTON of Duplin Co., (date not given), for 50 pds. specie 380A in the fork between Stewart's Creek & Miller's Swamp & on BS of Oakey & Holingsworth's Branches, survey incl. an old survey of 100A where he lives patented by JOHN ADKINSON, beg. at a white oak stump his own corner of 50A patented by ARCHIBALD CARR, across Holingsworth's Branch with CHARLES MERRIT'S line, near THOMAS CARLTON'S line, crossing Oakey Branch at the upper fork, to KNOX'S line dated 10 Nov 1784. Wit: AUSTIN BEASLEY, SAMUEL LAMBIRTH. Apr. Ct. 1795.

p. 336   JOHN McCALEB, planter, to DANIEL McCALEB, taylor [sic], both of Duplin Co., 27 June 1796, for 200 pds. current money 353A on the SS of Goshen Swamp & on BS of the Horse Pen Branch & on BS of the main road, incl. the planta. whereon WARREN BLOUNT now lives, beg. at a water oak & gum on the run of sd. branch, being the upper corner of the land formerly laid off for DANIEL GLISSON, to a white oak by a small branch at ROBERT BYRD'S line, to McCALEB'S old corner by the head of Gilbert's Branch, down sd. branch as it meanders to a stake in the mouth thereof on the run of Horse Pen Branch, being part of 2 surveys adj. each other on Horse Pen Branch to wit: one 278A sold by HENRY EUSTACE McCULLOCH to GILBERT McCALEB by deed dated 31 Mar 1767 & one tract of 300A granted to sd. GILBERT McCALEB by patent dated 4 Mar 1775, given by GILBERT McCALEB dec'd to sd. JOHN McCALEB oldest son & heir of sd. GILBERT McCALEB (except the dower or part thereof which ANNIS McCALEB now ANNIS BLOUNT, the widow of sd. GILBERT McCALEB dec'd is by law entitled to during her own life) which is herein excepted & reserved for her during her life. Wit: JOSEPH DICKSON JUNR., BRYAN BOWDEN. July Ct. 1796.

p. 338   BENJAMIN LANIER (JUNR.) to JOHN HALSO, both planters of Duplin Co., 18 Apr 1796, for 40 pds. specie 75A on the ES of the Northeast River & the upper side of Cypress Creek & SS of Halso's Swamp, beg. at a water oak in the Long Branch, to sd. HALSO'S old line, Wit: JAMES LANIER. July Ct. 1796.

p. 340   JOHN HALSO (co. not given) to LEWIS LANIER (co. not given), 20 Jan 1796, for 100 pds. 75A on the ES of the Northeast River & BS of Long Branch of Cypress Creek, beg. at a small pine his old corner of the land whereon he now lives S crossing the Long Branch, W crossing sd. branch, to a stake by his old corner, his old line to the beg. Wit: BENJA. LANIER, JAMES LANIER. July Ct. 1796.

p. 341   FREDERICK SULIVEN of Brunswick Co., N. C. & GEORGE JERNIGAN HODUM of Duplin Co. to JOSIAH OUTLAW (co. not given), 18 Feb 1793, (sum not given), 300A on the SS of Southerland's Marsh, beg. at the run of sd. marsh where HODOM'S line crosses the river, on or near MANOR'S Path, to a large pine near Manor's old field, to CASON HARRISON'S corner & along sd. HARRISON'S line to

Long Branch, it being the land whereon sd. OUTLAW now lives. Wit: WM. SULI-
VEN SENR., WM. SULIVEN JUNR. July Ct. 1796.

p. 342   EDWARD HOUSTON, planter, & MARY (*h*) HOUSTON his wife to STE-
PHEN MILLER, all of Duplin Co., 17 July 1796, for 150 pds. current money of
N. C. 335A in 2 tracts to wit: (1) 250A on the WS of Goshen Swamp & the Northeast
Branch of Cape Fear River where the sd. EDWARD HOUSTON lived formerly & SS
of Goshen Swamp, beg. at a water oak in a branch by the side of Goshen Swamp, the
1st station of GEORGE MILLER'S land, formerly patented by WILLIAM McREE;
(2) 85A beg. at a red oak above the main road where it crosses Goshen STEPHEN
MILLER'S corner, running down sd. swamp, thence White Oak Northeast River
Swamp, crossing the Northeast River to a stake STEPHEN MILLER'S corner, along
the sd. ... the sd. HOUSTON for STEPHEN MILLER, being part of a survey of 200A
patented by EDWARD HOUSTON 1 Apr 1780. Wit: JOHN MATCHET, JOHN NEIL
JUNR. July Ct. 1796.

p. 344   ANTHONY LEWIS to JOHN CHAMBERS, both of Duplin Co., 15 May 1796,
for 100 pds. specie 220A on the ES of the Northeast River & on the NS of Limestone
Swamp, which lands include the sd. LEWIS' impr., beg. at a pine in the fork of
Gum Branch, to a water oak at the creek in Limestone Swamp, down the sd. swamp,
up Gum Branch to the beg. cont. 200A; and also 20A being part of another survey
patented by sd. LEWIS of 50A, which joins the above mentioned survey of 200A &
bounded by them lines & the lines named in the deed from the sd. ANTHONY LEWIS
to JAMES HEIRS [sic] for 30A. Wit: JEREMIAH PEARSALL, JAMES CHAMBERS.
July Ct. 1796.

p. 349   JEPHTHA (X) DANIEL to ISAAC SPENCE, both planters of Duplin Co.,
26 Nov 1795, for 100 pds. current money 100A on the NS of Goshen Swamp & incl.
part of the place called the Lake Land, beg. at a white oak, the beg. of JOHN
SHEFFIELD'S land near Pompey's Pocosin & running a direct line to the center of
3 pines, marked formerly WESTON PRAIRSES [sic] corner, to HART'S line, to a
pine the beg. of the land JOHN HART sold to JESSE COOK & which the sd. SPENCE
now lives on, being half of a patent granted to JESSE BARFIELD 1 Apr 1780 &
conveyed through several hands unto sd. DANIEL. Wit: STEPHEN JONES,
TIMOTHY SPENCE. July Ct. 1796.

p. 351   JOHN AUSTIN, planter, to HOWEL BEST, both of Duplin Co., 8 June 1795,
for 80 pds. current money 200A where he formerly lived on the WS of the E branch
of the Cape Fear known by the name of Smith's Branch, being 2 surveys of 100A
each, beg. at a pine by the sd. branch the last corner of a survey of 100A deeded to
sd. AUSTIN by CHARLES GAVEN, to a stake near BENJAMIN JOHNSTON'S corner,
to a pine on ANTHONY MILLER'S line, being 2 surveys as afsd. & 100A deeded to
sd. AUSTIN by CHARLES GAVEN as afsd. bearing date 20 Apr 1757, the other 100A
patented by sd. AUSTIN 22 Jan 1793. Wit: EDWARD PEARSALL, ROBERT
WILLIAMS. July Ct. 1796.

p. 352   DANIEL SOUTHERLAND to ABRAHAM ANDREWS, both of Duplin Co., 15
Jan 1796, for 85 pds. specie one negro boy named SOLOMON. Wit: JOHN FARRIOR
BRYANT FARRIOR. July Ct. 1796.

p. 353   AMEY (X) STOAKS of Duplin Co. to WILLIAM GULLY (co. not given), 16
July 1796, for 110 pds. good & lawful money of N. C. one negro woman named

LETTIE about 17 yrs. of age. Wit: JESSE GULLY, JACOB TAYLOR. July Ct. 1796.

p. 353   JACOB BUTLER of Wilmington, N. C. to LEWIS THOMAS of Duplin Co., 26 Mar 1796, for 105 pds. one negro woman named SAL about 30 yrs. of age. Wit: WILLIAM CARLTON. July Ct. 1796.

p. 354   LEONARD MILLS, exr. to the estate of JAMES MILLS dec'd to MESHACK STALLINGS of Duplin Co., 13 Apr 1796, for 52 pds. 10 shill. a negro woman named PLEASANT. Wit: THOMAS EVANS. July Ct. 1796.

p. 354   WM. (WILLIAM) TUTON & JAS. (JAMES) KENAN, (no cos. given), to CULLEN CONNELY (co. not given), 20 Apr 1796, for 155 spanish milled dollars a negro boy named MOSES about 12 yrs. old. Wit: DAVID MIDDLETON, WILLIAM WARD POLLOCK. July Ct. 1796.

p. 355   RICHARD BARNES of Gates Co. to THOMAS BENNET of Duplin Co., 16 Nov 1795, for 137 pds. one negro man named STEPHEN. Wit: JAMES BIZZEL, HEZEKIAH MILLARD. July Ct. 1796.

p. 355   WILLIAM MIZELL SENR. to WILLIAM MIZELL JUNR., both of Duplin Co., 31 May 1796, for 80 pds. good & lawful money a negro boy named HARPER about 12 yrs. old. Wit: LEVY (I) MIZELL, LUKE MIZELL. July Ct. 1796.

p. 356   NATHAN FOUNTAIN to JOHN FARRIOR, both of Duplin Co., 29 June 1795, for 5 pds. current money of N. C. 30A on the SS of Muddy Creek on the side of Stafford's Swamp, being part of a tract of 150A granted to sd. FOUNTAIN by patent 16 Nov 1790, beg. at an ash on the run of Stafford's Swamp the upper corner of the patent, by HENRY FOUNTAIN'S corner, to the mouth of Stafford's Creek. Wit: JOSEPH DICKSON, WILLIAM FARRIOR. Oct. Ct. 1796.

p. 357   WILLIAM FARRIOR of New Hanover Co. to JOHN FARRIOR of Duplin Co., 1 Mar 1796, for 200 specie 150A on the Marsh Branch, a drain of Muddy Creek, being part of 3 surveys, granted to RICHARD REM(?), JOHN WOODWARD, & JOHN McGEE, beg. at a red oak in the fork of the Mill Branch, across the main prong of the Mill Branch to a stake, adj. BLAKE, DANIEL SOUTHERLAND & SHACKLE-FORD. Wit: DANIEL SOUTHERLAND, EDWARD ARMSTRONG. Oct. Ct. 1796.

p. 359   EBENEZAR (E) GARRISON to JOHN FARRIOR, both of Duplin Co., 14 Jan 1795, for 295 pds. current money of N. C. 590A on BS of Muddy Creek, beg. at a black gum in the edge of Muddy Creek Swamp, the 1st station of a survey of 200A patented by JOHN McGEE 22 Dec 1770, adj. sd. GARRISON & JOHN BLAKE, to a pine the corner of a survey of 450A patented by sd. McGEE 11 July 1788, to a corner of 100A patented by HENRY ALLEN, the corner of a survey patented by JOHN FARRIOR, to the corner of a survey of 150A patented by ZEBULON HOLLINGS-WORTH now the prop. of JOAB PADGET & JOB THIGPEN, adj. sd. THIGPEN & JOHN WOODWARD'S old corner. Wit: JOSEPH DICKSON, WILLIAM FARRIOR. Oct. Ct. 1796.

p. 361   THOMAS NORMENT of Duplin Co. to LEWIS JOHNSTON of Jones Co., 10 Oct 1798, for 500 pds. 976A (heading of deed says 966A), being in Duplin & Sampson Cos. on the head of Bear Swamp, being sundry surveys of former conveyances connected together, beg. on the run of Bear Swamp at the mouth of Cattail Branch, to a white oak on the WS of sd. branch JOHN COOK'S corner, in the edge of the Roughley [sic] field, to the back line of RAWLEY MILLS' 100A survey, WILLIAM NEWTON'S corner, to a pine ORSON BELL'S corner, to a pine WILLIAM GUY'S corner, to a stake in Hog Pen Branch to the main road leading to the old courthouse, down the run of the dividing branch to the main run of Bear Swamp to the beg. Wit: JOSEPH DICKSON, JUNR., DAVID HOOKS. Oct. Ct. 1798.

p. 362   AUSTON BEESLEY to DAVID QUIN, both of Duplin Co., 27 Jan 1795, for 150 pds. good & lawful money of N. C. 150A beg. at a pine the 4th corner of ALEXANDER HOLDON'S land, to ISOM SHEFFIELD'S corner in the swamp, to ANDREW WALLACE'S corner, the sd. land granted by patent 1 July 1779 to ALEXANDER DICKSON. Wit: JOHN MATHEWS, JACOB MATHEWS. Oct. Ct. 1796.

p. 363   ZACHERIAH TURNAGE of Duplin Co. to JOSHUA CHAMBLESS (co. not given), 15 July 1796, for 100 pds. lawful money a negro boy slave called JIM (?) about 14 yrs. Wit: FRANCIS OLIVER, JAMES WATKINS. Oct. Ct. 1796.

p. 364   GEORGE (C) MALLARD to ELIJAH MALLARD, both of Duplin Co., 15 Nov 1791, for 20 pds. good & lawful money 100A on the WS of the Northeast River patented by WILLIAM FREDERICK, beg. at JAMES MIDDLETON'S upper corner, on a drain of Horse Branch to ARTHUR STOAKS' corner. Wit: PHILL SOUTHER-LAND, JOSEPH MALLARD. Oct. Ct. 1796.

p. 365   DANIEL LOVE (co. not given) to THOMAS NORMENT (co. not given), 19 Oct 1796, for 100 pds. to be paid on or before the 25 Dec 1797, a negro boy slave named BEN. Wit: KENAN LOVE. Oct. Ct. 1796.

p. 366   THOMAS BARBER of Onslow Co. to GIDEON HAWKINS of Duplin Co., 19 Jan 1795, for 20 pds. specie 150A on BS of Muddy Creek, beg. at a pine SS of the Swamp, the swamp, the dividing corner between him & HILLARY BRINSON. Wit: HILLARY BRINSON, UZIAL HAWKINS. Oct. Ct. 1796.

p. 367   THOMAS WRIGHT, Shff. of Duplin Co. to BENJAMIN LANIER (co. not given), _____ Dec 1795, for 135 pds. 640A beg. at the head of Williams' Branch near the head of Rhodes' Swamp at a pine between the Dark Pond & HENRY RHODES' swamp, to a pine between the head of Miller's Branch & the Great Meadow. The County Ct. of New Hanover at Oct. Term 1783 had awarded 2550 pds. to the exrs. of WILLIAM DRY for judgment against the exrs. of JOHN ANCRUM. At Feb. Term 1795 it was adjudged that a residue of 1150 pds. 10 shill. 9 pence plus cost was due from the guardians of the heirs of sd. ANCRUM who were owners of the sd. 640A of land, purchased by sd. LANIER at public auction 12 Dec 1795. Wit: SAMUEL R. JOCELYN. Jan. Ct. 1796.

p. 369   SAML. (SAMUEL) ROGERS to his son RANDOLPH ROGERS, both of Duplin Co., 13 Nov 1795, for "natural love & affection" sundry lands to wit: (1) 300A on Cabbin Branch, beg. at a gum & run N27E 100 pole to a stake by an oak stump, thence S63E480 pole to a pine, thence S27W 100 poles to a pine, thence to the beg., being land which SAMUEL ROGERS purchased of WILLIAM LANE & HENRY ROBERTS; (2) 50A below the head of Clearing Branch joining the above, beg. at a small pine, patented by sd. SAMUEL ROGERS; (3) a tract (acreage not given) beg.

at a pine near the side of a large pond, to PHILLIP DAVIS' line, patented by
SAMUEL ROGERS. Wit: ROBERT DANNELL, LEWIS BRYAN. Apr. Ct. 1796.

p. 371   WILLIAM COLLINS, planter, & CHARITY (X) COLLINS to MOSES MANN-
ING, planter, all of Duplin Co., 16 Apr 1792, for 70 pds. specie 200A beg. at a
forked post oak on JOHN WILLIAMS' old line, & a 2nd piece of 85A patented by
HENRY SKIBBOW below RICHARD WILLIAMS' homeplace on Stafford's Branch,
being a branch of Muddy Creek, beg. at a white oak on sd. branch, to WILLIAMS'
corner. Wit: LYDIA MANNING, MERIT MANNING. Oct. Ct. 1796.

p. 372   JOHN CHAMBERS to WILLIAM CARR, both of Duplin Co., 15 Mar 1796,
for 100 pds. current money of N. C. 100A on a branch of Maxwell Swamp called
Alair Swamp, beg. at 4 peach trees in an old field, being part of 600A granted to
ROBERT WALKER of Wilmington by patent dated 7 June 1739. Wit: JAMES
MAXWELL, H. McCANNE. Oct. Ct. 1796.

p. 374   SAMUEL (X) MARTINDAL(E) to SAMUEL SOWELL, both of Duplin Co.,
24 Nov 1794, for 100 pds. specie 50A on the ES of the Northeast River & NS of
Limestone Swamp, between Gum Swamp & Cabbin Branch, one parcel of a tract
granted to ABNER QUIN by patent (date not given), beg. at a stake MUMFORD'S
corner, to a pine by ANTHONY LEWIS' corner; also part of one other tract consisting of 150A to sd. MARTINDALE by JOHN WEEDING joining the 1st 50A, beg.
at a gum in the edge of Gum Swamp on THOMAS QUINN'S line, to WILLIAM MESS-
OR'S corner, to ABNER QUINN'S line, to a pine on sd. LEWIS' line. Wit: JESSE
MEDFORD, ELIAS BUTLER. Oct. Ct. 1796.

p. 375   RICHARD HART & JOHN CARTER THOMPSON, both of Duplin Co. to
THOMAS TITTERTON of Lenoir Co., 13 Oct 1796, for 100 pds. lawful money 300A
on BS of Mathew's Branch, beg. at a maple in Rooty Branch, along JAMES
WILLIAMS' line, by JONES' corner, to a pine on the side of AZARIAH BRANCH, to
Reedy Branch, as by patent granted to WILLIAM THOMPSON 11 July 1788 & trans-
ferred by ELIZABETH THOMPSON, admrx. to the estate of WM. THOMPSON &
BENJAMIN THOMPSON to RICHARD HART SENR. & from him to his son the sd.
RICHARD HART. Wit: STEPHEN HERRING, BIBB (X) BUSH. Oct. Ct. 1796.

p. 376   WILLIAM (H) HUNTER & SARAH (M) HUNTER his wife to BENJAMIN
BEST, all of Duplin Co., 1 Jan 1796, for 200 pds. current money of N. C. 310A in
2 tracts to wit: (1) 150A on the NS of the Grove Swamp & over Ash Branch incl. sd.
HUNTER'S impr. where ABRAHAM MOLTEN formerly lived, beg. at a persimmon
tree at the mouth of Alexander's Branch, at the run of Ash Branch, to the run of the
Pine Log Branch, being part of a deed from STEPHEN MIDDLETON to sd. HUNTER
4 Oct 1783; (2) 160A joining the 1st 150A, beg. at a pine sd. HUNTER'S corner tree
by a little drain of Ash Branch sd. HUNTER'S corner, formerly ABRAHAM MOL-
TEN'S corner tree, being part of a deed from JAMES KENAN, Esqr. to sd. HUNTER
19 July 1787. The sd. 310A lying below the Pine Log Branch & down Ash Branch to
STEPHEN BROWN'S line at Alexander's Branch & to sd. BROWN'S line outward,
being the land the sd. HUNTER is poss. of in the 2 tracts of 150A & 160A. Wit:
JOSEPH DICKSON SENR., JAMES MIDDLETON. Oct. Ct. 1796.

p. 378   THOMAS PHILLIPS & JOHN PHILLIPS to JAMES MIDDLETON SENR., all
of Duplin Co., 27 Sep 1796, for 50 pds. current money 120A on the NS of the Grove
Swamp, being the upper part of a survey of land patented by ABRAHAM MOLTEN &

by him sold to JONATHAN GORE who deeded to JOHN PHILIPS dec'd, late of Duplin
Co., beg. at a pine in the line of the land which sd. MIDDLETON bought from BEN-
JAMIN BEST, to a black gum in the Grove Swamp & along the upper line of BENJA-
MIN PHILLIPS' land. Wit: JOSEPH DICKSON, BENJM. BEST. Oct. Ct. 1796.

p. 379   JOHN (W) WATERS to JOHN KNOWLES, both of Duplin Co., 16 Feb 1796,
for 100 pds. 230A in 3 surveys all lying on the main creek of Rockfish to wit: (1)
150A beg. at a poplar on the side of the swamp; (2) 50A on the SWS of Rockfish,
beg. at a white oak on the creek 10 yds. above the new road, to a pine on JOHN
GOOF'S (?) line, to JOSEPH BEVAN'S line; (3) 30A in the sd. Rockfish Swamp,
joining the old survey whereon the sd. WATERS now lives, beg. at a small sweet
gum on the ES of the lake a little above the house, to a poplar his old corner, to a
bay on the run of the creek to the 1st station. Wit: AARON WILLIAMS, MARY
WILLIAMS. Oct. Ct. 1796.

p. 381   MARY (M) DOBSON & REBECKAH (X) DOBSON her dau. of Duplin Co.,
to JACOB MEEKS of Duplin Co., 20 July 1796, for 50 pds. 100A beg. at a pine on
JOSIAH STAFFORD'S line on the NS of Cow Hole Branch, a corner of a survey
formerly BENJAMIN ADAMS', now the prop. of IVEY, to the corner of a survey of
200A patented by LEWIS BARNES, to Burncoat Swamp, up Burncoat to STAFFORD'S
line. Wit: THOMAS SHELTON, JAMES (B) BOYET. Oct. Ct. 1796.

p. 382   THOMAS HOOKS to JOHN SOUTHERLAND, both of Duplin Co., 12 Aug
1796, for 327 pds. 10 shill. current money 270A on the SS of Goshen Swamp on BS
of the main road joining & between King's Branch & Wild Cat Branch, beg. at a
black gum at the run of Wild Cat Branch by the old ford, adj. HENRY CANNON &
sd. HOOKS, to the dividing branch between CURLING SMITH'S boundary & the run
of Wild Cat Branch, being part of a survey which sd. HOOKS bought of WILLIAM
CANNON & part bought of HENRY CANNON & part patented by sd. HOOKS; one
small survey of 6A adj. the 270A on the NS of King's Branch, beg. at a pine on the
main road, to King's Branch, HENRY CANNON'S old line. Wit: WM. DICKSON,
SAML. HOUSTON. Oct. Ct. 1796.

p. 384   DEMPSEY (X) WESTBROOK to JOHN WHITEHEAD, both of Duplin Co.,
5 Feb 1795, for 20 pds. 22A on the SS of the Northeast, beg. at a pine the corner of
his own & sd. WHITEHEAD'S lands, to the Wolf Pond Branch, to the run of Poley
Bridge Branch. Wit: STEPHEN JONES, WILLIS WILKINS. Oct. Ct. 1796.

p. 385   ARTHUR STOAKES of Jones Co. to ELIJAH MALLARD of Duplin Co., 17
Aug 1792, for 20 pds. good & lawful money 100A on the SS of Horse Branch, beg.
at a pine near Horse Branch, to a water oak in the branch, to a pine near the landing path. Wit: PHILL SOUTHERLAND, GEORGE SMITH. Oct. Ct. 1796.

p. 386   JOHN (X) BATCHELDORE of Duplin Co. & ELISHA (X) WILLIFORD (co.
not given) to CHRISTOPHER BUTLER (co. not given) for 15 pds. current money,
30 Sep 1796, for 50A on the ES of the Northeast River & SS of Cypress Creek in the
fork of the Round About & the Watering Hole Branch, beg. at a black gum in the
Round About Branch & runs a direct line to a gum in the Watering Lake Branch.
Wit: SNODEN PEARCE, JOHN SHOLER. Oct. Ct. 1796.

p. 388   AMOUS (A) PARKER & ELISABETH (X) PARKER of Onslow Co. to
JAMES BATTS of Duplin Co., 1 Oct 1796, for 100 pds. specie 125A in 2 tracts to

wit: (1) 75A between Cypress Creek & Muddy Creek JAMES PICKETT'S line, beg. at a pine PICKETT'S line, through the Dark Pond to a water oak, to a stake PICKETT'S line; (2) 50A being part of a survey of land granted to HENRY ____ by patent & deeded by him to JAMES PICKETT who deeded to sd. PARKER, beg. at a pine the 4th corner of this survey from which this land is deducted & running to the 5th corner. Wit: JOHN (X) BATTS. Oct. Ct. 1796.

p. 389   JAMES BLOUNT TREWIT of Duplin Co. to HEZEKIAH DOBSON of same, both planters, 18 Jan 1798, for 55 pds. 100A on the ES of the Northeast & on the NS of Briery Branch, beg. at a gum at the run of Briery Branch, below the sd. MUM-FORD'S cornfield, to BLANK'S former corner & runs down the line that divides between GEORGE SMITH & sd. TREWIT to a holly in Panther Swamp, to the mouth of Briery Branch, being part of the land patented by WILLIAM BLAND & part of a survey patented by MILLS MUMFORD of which GEORGE SMITH had 200A. Wit: THOS. SHELTON, JAMES (c) HOLLAN, DAVID KING. Jan. Ct. 1799.

p. 390   EBENEZAR (G) GARRISON to JOHN FARRIOR, both planters of Duplin Co., 15 Sep 1796, for 50 pds. specie 200A on the NS of Muddy Creek on the head of the Mill Branch, beg. at a pine SS of the N prong of sd. branch, by a drain or sprout SHACKELFORD'S own & DANIEL SOUTHERLAND'S corner. Wit: WILLIAM FARRIOR, BRYANT FARRIOR. Oct. Ct. 1796.

p. 391   RICHARD CHASTEN to GEORGE GIBBONS, both of Duplin Co., 20 Dec 1795, for 45 pds. 250A on the WS of the Northeast River & lower side of Island Creek in 2 tracts to wit: (1) 150A beg. at a white oak below Cook's Branch above COOK'S upper field on the creek, to a water oak in a pond, to a gum saplin, to a stump by COOK'S field, being the contents of a patent granted to SAMUEL EVANS 10 Nov 1784; (2) 100A beg. at a pine DANIEL COOK'S corner, to a stake on SAMUEL EVAN'S line, to a large post oak EVANS' corner, with sd. EVANS' other line to a pine, adj. WELLS, JAMES KENAN, JOHN COOK, & DANIEL COOK, being the contents of a patent granted to WILLIAM HALL SENR. 16 Sep 1790. Wit: JOSEPH DICKSON, JOHN PHILLIPS. Jan. Ct. 1796.

p. 393   DEMPSEY (X) WESTBROOK, planter, to JOHN WHITEHEAD, both of Duplin Co., 3 Jan 1796, for 100 pds. specie 179A on the SS of the Poley Bridge Branch, being the place sd. WESTBROOK now lives on in 3 tracts: (1) 110A beg. at white bay in a small branch on JOHN SULLIVAN'S line, to the given line of SAMUEL WARD'S patent, to a pine on the NS of the branch, which land was conveyed by ROBERT BROCK to sd. WESTBROOK by deed 3 Jan 1786, & which sd. WESTBROOK sold to SAMUEL WARD who sold to DEMPSEY WESTBROOK Jan 1796; (2) 31A joining the 1st tract beg. at a bay in the Wolf Pond Branch, to a pine sd. WEST-BROOK'S corner, being land sold & conveyed by SIKES GARRIS to sd. WESTBROOK 4 May 1793; (3) 48A joining the 1st & 2nd tract, beg. at a pine on the NS of the branch at WESTBROOK'S corner, to the Wolf Pond Branch, up the branch to GARRIS' corner a bay being land conveyed by WILLIS WILKINS to sd. WESTBROOK 15 Sep 1795. Wit: STEPHEN JONES, WILLIS WILKINGS. Oct. Ct. 1796.

p. 395   THOMAS BARBER of Onslow Co. to UZZIEL HAWKINS & his wife SARAH (co. not given) for "love & good will", 12 July 1794, 100A on the ES of the North-east of Cape Fear River on the head of Muddy Creek, beg. at a pine in the edge of a branch & up the swamp, patented 1792. Wit: HILLARY BRINSON, ABSALOM BARBER. Oct. Ct. 1796.

p. 396   THOMAS BARBER of Onslow Co. to HILLARY BRINSON of Duplin Co.,
planter, 6 Jan 1795, for 22 pds. current money 150A on BS of Muddy Creek, being
the lower part of a survey of 300A granted to sd. BARBER 31 Dec 1792, beg. at a
red oak at the mouth of Half-Way Branch, to HAWKINS' line. Wit: UZZIEL
HAWKINS, GIDEON HAWKINS. Oct. Ct. 1796.

p. 397   THOMAS BRADLEY, planter, to EDWARD WINDERS, bachelor, both of
Duplin Co., 1 Sep 1796, for 175 pds. current money 200A on the NS of Goshen
Swamp & on Bear Marsh Branch in 2 tracts to wit: 100A beg. at a black gum at
HENNET'S old corner in Bear Marsh, to a pine ISAAC SPENCE'S corner, to a
white oak in Bear Marsh Branch, being part of a large tract granted to CHRISTO-
PHER BURCH & conveyed by deeds through several hands unto sd. BRADLEY; (2)
100A beg. at a pine near the head of Bear Marsh Branch, to a white oak JESSE
SWINSON'S corner, to a pine sd. SWINSON'S other corner on the great path leading
from sd. SWINSON'S to THOMAS BRADLEY'S, being part of a tract formerly
granted to REUBEN WESTON & sold by him to sd. BRADLEY. Wit: JESSE SWIN-
SON, FRANCIS OLIVER. Oct. Ct. 1796.

p. 399   JOSHUA CHAMBLESS to ZACHARIAH TURNAGE, both of Duplin Co., 15
July 1796 for 285 pds. 310A on the NS of Goshen Swamp & on the ES of Bear Marsh
in 2 tracts to wit: (1) 150A beg. at a stake on JONATHAN TAYLOR'S line standing
in Bear Marsh & runs along his line a S course to a small branch, to a small
branch in WILLIAM GOODMAN'S line that runs between the sd. GOODMAN &
SAMUEL BOWDEN, only 1A of the 150A excepted whereon the meeting house stands
which is reserved for the use thereof forever; (2) 160A beg. at a stake at or near
the last mentioned corner of the old patent, along GOODMAN'S line. Wit: FRANCIS
OLIVER, JAMES WATKINS, JESSE MILLARD. Oct. Ct. 1796.

p. 401   STEPHEN BARFIELD to PETER PARKER, both of Duplin Co., 2 Aug 1796,
for 100 pds. current money 130A in 2 tracts to wit: (1) 100A on the SS of the Northeast Swamp, being part of a tract of land patented by JOHN PARKER 25 Apr 1764,
beg. at a pine sd. PETER PARKER'S corner, to a pine on DANIEL GLISSON'S
line; (2) 30A joining the 1st tract & JONATHAN PARKER'S land, beg. at a poplar
in a small branch, running with his line to PETER PARKER'S line, to BALES'
corner. Wit: DANIEL PARKER, JONATHAN (X) PARKER. Oct. Ct. 1796.

p. 402   JAMES KENAN & JOHN HILL, admrs. of the estate of WILLIAM KENAN
dec'd, both of Duplin Co. to ARTHUR HERRING of same, 8 June 1793, for 350 pds.
current money of N. C. 2 tracts to wit: (1) 200A in the fork of the Northeast &
Goshen, beg. at a red oak below ROUSE'S line on JONES' Branch, being a grant to
SAMUEL RATLIFF Feb 1754; (2) 425A from ARTHUR HERRING SENR. to FELIX
KENAN dec'd, part of a survey of 550A, beg. at a water oak in the Great Branch
JOHN GLISSON'S corner, along the patent with sd. GLISSON'S line, to a pine being
both GLISSON'S & the patent corner, to ALEXANDER ROUSE'S line, to GEORGE
McCULLOCH'S line, down Great Branch Run. Wit: WILLIAM ALBERSON,
JOSEPH KORNEGAY. Oct. Ct. 1796.

p. 404   MILLS MUMFORD to WILLIAM CHURCHWELL, planter, both of Duplin
Co., 13 Feb 1796, for 20 pds. currency 50A beg. at a black jack at the head of a
small branch on the SS of the head prong of Burncoat, along a line of marked trees
eastwardly to FREDERICK JONES' line, incl. the impr. where sd. MUMFORD
lives, being part of 150A patented by ANTHONY JONES. (Deed also signed by

ELIZABETH (E) MUMFORD.) Wit: JAMES WILLIAMS JUNR., JOB LEARY.
Jan. Ct. 1797.

p. 406   WILLIAM McCANNE to CHARLES GOFF, both of Duplin Co., 19 Jan 1796,
for 150 pds. current money of N. C. 130A on the WS of the Northeast Branch of
Cape Fear River a little above the mouth of Rockfish Creek, beg. at a pine on the
bank of the river which in the patent is called the McREE'S corner, up the river to
a large white oak at the mouth of Mill Branch, up the branch to where WATTY
BRYAN'S line crosses the sd. branch of a 200A survey, & with that line to the corner, along the line of the 100A survey, it being the contents of 2 patents granted to
sd. BRYAN which land lies on the lower side of sd. branch. Wit: ANDREW Mc
INTIRE, MARTIN (X) HANCHEY. Jan. Ct. 1797.

p. 407   WILLIAM WILKINSON to JAMES WRIGHT, both of Duplin Co., 17 Jan
1797, for 300 pds. current money of N. C. 400A beg. at a black gum on the run of
the Great Branch at the mouth of the dividing branch a little above the new road, up
the run of the dividing branch, to a pine on JAMES REARDON'S line, to a white oak
FELIX FREDERICK'S corner, to a water oak in the Great Branch JOHN MOOR'S
old corner, being part of sundry tracts formerly poss. by ROBERT WILKINSON, on
the SS of Bear Swamp, & since the sd. WILKINSON'S death divided among his heirs,
one being WILLIAM WILKINSON. Wti: WM. DICKSON, THOS. WRIGHT. Jan. Ct.
1797.

p. 409   WILLIAM SULLIVEN to LEWIS THOMAS, both of Duplin Co., 5 Mar 1796,
for 500 pds. current money 479A in 3 tracts to wit: (1) 237A on the SS of Goshen
Swamp, being the place where the sd. SULLIVAN now lives on, beg. at a sweet gum
JOHN WARD'S corner in the side of Goshen Swamp, along WARD'S line to a pine his
corner, to a pine at JOHN HILL'S corner; (2) 206A in the low grounds of Goshen
Swamp, beg. at a cypress by a run in the sd. swamp & runs to a maple on JOHN
HILL'S corner, up the swamp with SULLIVEN'S own line, to a sweet gum his &
JOHN WARD'S corner, to a white oak CURLING SMITH'S corner, with SMITH'S line
to a maple & a cypress at JOHN WINDER'S corner; (3) 36A on the SS of Goshen
Swamp, beg. at a pine the corner of JOHN ROBINSON'S land, to a pine JOHN HILL'S
corner. (TABITHA (|) SULLIVEN, wife of WILLIAM SULLIVEN, was privately
examined before JOSEPH DICKSON J.P. on 16 Aug 1796 & was willing to relinquish
her right of dower or thirds in sd. land to be conveyed to LEWIS THOMAS.)
Wit: WM. DICKSON, JAMES WARD, WILLIAM ALBERSON. Jan. Ct. 1797.

p. 412   WIMBARK BONEY to DANIEL TEACHEY, both planters of Duplin Co., 16
Jan 1797, for 20 pds. specie 100A on the drains of Little Rockfish, being part of a
tract that sd. DANIEL TEACHEY SENR. bought of JOHN REATHERFORD [sic] &
conveyed by deed to sd. BONEY, beg. at a pine an old corner of HEDGES' patent.
Wit: TIMOTHY TEACHEY, JOHN BONEY. Jan. Ct. 1797.

p. 414   BESANT (B) BROCK to JAMES GRIMES, both planters of Duplin Co., 20
Oct 1796, for 17 pds. specie money 85A on the NS of Goshen Swamp on the heads of
Goshen Branch & the Northeast Branch, beg. at a lightwood tree & pine by the
Horse Pen Pocosin, HEZEKIAH _____ corner, to a pine by SILAS CARTER'S cor-
ner, to JOHN WHITEHEAD'S corner at the old path to a black jack, to BARFIELD'S
road to WHITEHEAD'S other corner. Wit: SAMPSON GRIMES, BATHSHEBA (X)
GRIMES. Jan. Ct. 1797.

p. 415   ADONIJAH GARRISON of New Hanover Co. to THOMAS GARRISON of
Duplin Co., 5 Jan 1797, for 20 pds. good & lawful money 50A on the WS of the
Northeast River & NS of Maxwell Swamp & on the Sand Hill Branch, beg. at a poplar
& gum in the branchNICHOLAS BRYAN'S corner, to ROBERT DICKSON'S line.
Wit: H. MAXWELL, PHILL SOUTHERLAND. Jan. Ct. 1797.

p. 416   JOHN GIBBS, planter, to LEVEN WATKINS, both of Duplin Co., 23 Oct
1789, for 5 shill. 19A on the NS of Goshen Swamp, between Cow Hole & Bear
Marsh, being part of a tract patented by BAKER BOWDEN & by him sold to JOHN
GIBBS, beg. at a stooping hickory BOWDEN'S corner tree, with his line to a stake
in a field, to a pine sd. GIBB'S line. Wit: FRANS. OLIVER, JOS. WATKINS.
Jan. Ct. 1797.

p. 417   JOHN DANIEL, planter, to HEZEKIAH MILLARD, wheelright, both of
Duplin Co., 17 Dec 1796, for 200 pds. current money 130A on the NS of Goshen
Swamp & on both heads of Fryer's Branch, incl. his impr., beg. at a red oak on
THOMAS WIGGINS' (now MICHAEL KENARD'S line), along JOHN BECK'S &
WILLIAM UNDERHILL'S lines, formerly granted by patent to sd. DANIEL 29 Oct
1782. Wit: WARREN BLOUNT, RICHD. BRADLEY. Jan. Ct. 1796 (should be 1797)

p. 419   LOVE SAVAGE to THOMAS GARRISON, both of Duplin Co., 15 Oct 1796,
for 50 pds. good & lawful money 100A on BS of Sand Hill Branch, incl. ANDREW
ROUSE'S old impr., beg. at a gum at the run of Sand Hill Branch, GEORGE
ROUSE'S corner, near WILLIAM DICKSON'S line, to a stake on JACOB WILLIS'
line. Wit: HENRY MAXWELL, PHILL SOUTHERLAND. Jan. Ct. 1797.

p. 420   JAMES THOMPSON of Sampson Co. to FREDERICK RIVENBARK of Duplin
Co., 2 Feb 1790, for 40 pds. current money 45A on BS of Buck Hall Swamp, being
part of a tract purchased by sd. THOMPSON of THOMAS ATKINSON, beg. at a
water oak in a small drain about 30 yds. from the SW corner of an old field cleared
by LEWIS SPIKERMAN on THOMAS ATKINSON'S land & about 30 yds. W of a white
oak, a corner of the land sd. THOMPSON purchased of sd. ATKINSON, to a stake
RIVENBARK'S corner, to the run of Buck Hall, to the mouth of Cow Marsh, up the
meanders of the run of Cow Marsh to an old dead persimmon KEDAR BRYAN'S
corner, to a red oak BRYAN'S corner, to a stake in the swamp side, to the run of
Buck Hall & down the run to a maple at the old ford at the mouth of the drain, up the
drain to the beg. Wit: C. IVEY, MARY (M) WILLIAMS. Jan. Ct. 1797.

p. 421   JOHN BRADLEY (SENR.), planter, to his son JOHN BRADLEY JUNR.,
both of Duplin Co., 24 Jan 1797, for "natural love & affection" 117A on the NS of
Goshen Swamp & SS Dry Pond Branch, being the same planta. whereon JOHN
DANIEL formerly lived, beg. at a white oak by the run in Dry Pond Branch by
WILLIAM HURST'S upper corner & runs along his line to a lightwood stake his other
corner by the old path, to a pine JOSEPH WADE'S old patented corner, along the
patented line to a white oak by the run in Dry Pond Branch by the old patent corner,
down the sd. branch with the patented line to the beg., being part of a patent of 340A
granted to JOSEPH WADE 10 Apr 1761 & sold by sd. WADE to sd. DANIEL & by
him to JOHN BRADLEY SENR. Wit: BETSEY (?) PATTERSON, WILLIAM
DICKSON. Apr. Ct. 1797.

p. 423   ARTHUR SAVAGE of New Hanover Co. to HARDY PARKER of Duplin Co.,
18 Oct 1796, for 55 pds. current money of N. C. 100A in the fork of Rockfish Creek

& Fussel's Creek, beg. at a water oak on the bank of Fussel's Creek above his planta., being a tract granted to SIMON RIVENBARK by patent dated 21 Feb 1783. Wit: SHADRACK STALLINGS, JACOB WELLS. Jan. Ct. 1797.

p. 425   SOLOMON CARTER of Duplin Co. to EDWARD CARTER & his son ELISHA CARTER (no co. given), 18 Sep 1797, a deed of gift of 150A, being part of 3 patents, to be lent to EDWARD CARTER during his natural life & then to ELISHA CARTER, son of EDWARD CARTER & RACHAEL his wife, the sd. 150A being on the ES of the Northeast of Cape Fear, some of it being the 1st part of a tract taken up by WILLIAM WILLIAMS by patent dated 6 Apr 1745 & some of a patent taken up by ANTHONY WILLIAMS & some part of another patent taken up by SOLOMON CARTER by patent dated 1768. The 1st patent mentioned beg. at the ES of a large Cypress Swamp, beg. at a red oak by the swamp side, to ISAAC DAWSON'S corner, to DAVID CARTER'S line, to the run of the little marsh, to a persimmon corner, with some marked trees upon the swamp in the given line of ANTHONY WILLIAMS & to the 1st corner of sd. WILLIAMS' land to the beg. (The other beg. lines for the 2 remaining patents not mentioned.) Wit: JOHN DEAVER, HEZEKIAH BLIZZARD. Jan. Ct. 1799.

p. 426   THOMAS WRIGHT, Shff. to SOLOMON CARTER, planter, both of Duplin Co., 6 July 1798, for 25 pds. 640A lying on the Beaverdam of Limestone, beg. at a black jack near the head of a drain called the Horse Pen Branch & adj. JOHN WILLIAMS, patented 12 Nov 1784. The Court awarded 250 pds., plus cost of 3 pds. 18 shill. 11 pence to sd. CARTER for debt in a suit against JONATHAN TAYLOR, owner of sd. 640A levied on by OWEN O'DANIEL, Shff. Deputy, purchased by sd. CARTER at public auction held 6 July 1798. Wit: THOMAS ROUTLEDGE, OWEN O'DANIEL.

p. 429   SIMON (X) RIVENBARK of Duplin Co. to ARTHUR SAVAGE of New Hanover Co., 29 Mar 1796, for 100 pds. current money of N. C. 100A in the fork of Rockfish & Fussel's Creek, beg. at a water oak on the bank of Fussel's Creek above his planta., to a holly at Rockfish Creek, being a grant to sd. RIVENBARK 21 Feb 1783. Wit: WILLIAM JAMES, BENJAMIN FUSSELL. Jan. Ct. 1797.

p. 430   THOMAS HOOKS to JAMES WINDERS, both of Duplin Co., 10 Sep 1796, for 75 pds. 108A on the SS of King's Branch, being a part subdivided from sundry grants & deeds of conveyances belonging to sd. HOOKS, beg. at a holly & sweet gum in King's Branch on CHARLES HOOKS' line, along THOMAS HOOKS' patent line to a pine his corner, to HENRY CANNON'S old corner, to a poplar in King's Branch, the dividing corner between him & JOHN SOUTHERLAND, up King's Branch to sd. SOUTHERLAND'S other corner. Wit: CHARLES HOOKS, SUSANAH HOOKS. Jan. Ct. 1797.

p. 431   JOHN (X) PARKER of New Hanover Co. to STEPHEN HANCOCK of Duplin Co., planter, 14 Dec 1796, for 30 pds. lawful money of N. C. 300A on BS of the cedar prong of Muddy Creek, beg. at a white oak SS of the swamp JAMES WHALEY'S 4th corner of his 200A survey, to a pine JOHN FARRIOR'S corner, to HENRY FOUNTAIN'S line, to a gum bay & holly his corner NS the swamp, which land was granted to JOHN PARKER by patent in 1790. Wit: NATHAN FOUNTAIN, HENRY (H) FOUNTAIN. Jan. Ct. 1797.

p. 433   ZACHERIAH (ʃ.) TURNAGE to JAMES WATKINS, both planters of Duplin

Co., 17 Jan 1797, for 60 pds. current money of N. C. 140A on the NS of Goshen
Swamp & in the fork of Absolom's Branch, beg. at a gum in sd. branch a little below
the mouth of Bear Branch, being the land sd. TURNAGE bought of ROBERT SULLI-
VENT. Wit: BRYAN BOWDEN. Jan. Ct. 1797.

p. 434   MESHACK STALLINGS, hatter, to WILLIAM JAMES, planter, both of
Duplin Co., 9 Oct 1790, for 360 pds. N. C. currency 550A on a branch of Rockfish
called Fussel's Creek in 5 tracts to wit: (1) 200A beg. at a stake in BENJAMIN
FUSSEL'S cornfield, conveyed to the sd. STALLINGS from ELIJAH BOEN 15 Apr
1786; (2) 100A near BENJAMIN FUSSEL & THOMAS HILL'S lines, beg. at a white
oak, conveyed to sd. STALLINGS by FREDERICK RIVENBARK 24 Apr 1784; (3)
100A between Fussel's Creek & Taylor's Creek, beg. at a white oak & red oak
WILLIAM JAMES' corner, to JOSEPH WILLIAMS' line, RICE MATHEWS' line,
granted by patent to sd. STALLINGS 10 Sep 1785; (4) a tract (acreage not given)
on the ES of Fussels Creek, beg. at a pine an old corner of another survey of sd.
FUSSEL'S, conveyed to sd. STALLINGS by ELIJAH BOEN 11 July 1785; (5) 100A
being 1/2 of 200A conveyed to the sd. STALLINGS by deed from RICE MATTHEWS
25 Feb 1786 on the WS of Fussel's Creek & BS of Pig Pen Branch. Wit: STEPHEN
SMYTH, WILLIAM JAMES. Jan. Ct. 1797.

p. 437   LEWIS BARFIELD of Sampson Co. to BRYAN WHITFIELD of Lenoir Co.,
28 Dec 1796, for 100 pds. current money 154A on the SS of the Northeast Marsh
between Reedy Branch & Gum Branch, being part of a tract granted to JESSE BAR-
FIELD 22 Dec 1770, beg. in the 1st line of sd. grant in JOHNSTON'S line. Wit:
BRYAN WHITFIELD, WILLIAM CROOM, DAVID SMITH. Jan. Ct. 1797.

p. 438   THOMAS WRIGHT, Shff. to HILLARY BRINSON, both of Duplin Co., 17 Jan
1797, for 5 pds. specie 350A being patented by JOHN WOODWARD SENR. & being
on BS of the Half-way Branch, a prong of Muddy Creek, incl. STEPHEN BROWN'S
impr., beg. at a pine near to a pocosin, adj. HILLARY BRINSON & GIDEON HAW-
KINS & WILDER. The Court awarded 5 pds. to HILL WILLIAMS of Onslow Co. for
damages in a suit against JOHN WOODWARD, owner of 350A. (ELISHA (X) WOOD-
WARD assigns his right.) Wit: MOSES MANNING, JOHN FARRIOR, C. HOOKS.
Jan. Ct. 1797.

p. 440   JEREMIAH PEARSALL to WILLIAM MATCHET, both of Duplin Co., 25
Aug 1794, for 313 pds. current money of N. C. 6 tracts to wit: (1) 110A being part
of a patent formerly granted to THOMAS KENAN, beg. at a pine in the SS of Taylor's
Creek, a branch of Rockfish Creek called LUVES BROOKS' corner, to a gum in the
side of Gaulberry Branch sd. BROOKS' corner; (2) 150A beg. at 2 pines, the lower
corner of the 1st tract to the E of Taylor's Creek, along FREDERICK WILLIS' line,
along JOSEPH WILLIAMS' line, the 1st 2 tracts of land being the contents of a deed
from DANIEL SOUTHERLAND to sd. PEARSALL 1 Feb 1783; (3) 166A being part
of a patent granted to THOMAS KENAN on BS of Taylor's Creek, beg. at a pine &
gum in the side of the Gautberry Branch; (4) 100A beg. at a pine NS of Taylor's
Creek, the old corner of the afsd. land described in the 3rd tract, the 3rd & 4th
tract conveyed by deed from LEWIS BROCK to sd. PEARSALL 20 July 1784; (5)
350A granted to sd. PEARSALL 5 Nov 1787, beg. at a bay tree near the Mud Ford
sd. PEARSALL'S corner of a survey of 130A, to a pine on FREDK. WELLS' line,
to a pine on his old line of land patented by THOMAS KENAN, to a corner of a piece
of land patented by LEWIS BROCK, to a pine EDWARD DICKSON'S corner, to a
pine by the double Horse Pen Pocosin; (6) 130A on the ridge between the double

Horse Pen Pocosin & the pocosin of Taylor's Creek, beg. at a bay tree near the Mud Ford his corner of 350A, to a pine by the double Horse Pen Pocosin, being the contents of a patent granted to JEREMIAH PEARSALL 11 July 1788. Wit: JOSEPH DICKSON, ROBERT SOUTHERLAND. Jan. Ct. 1797.

p. 442   SAMUEL ALBERSON to JAMES MATHEWS, both planters of Duplin Co., 16 Oct 1785, for 29 pds. specie 200A on the ES of the Northeast River between Mathews Branch & the Great Branch, beg. at a pine on EDWARD CARTER'S line, patented 20 Mar 1780, it being the planta. where JAMES _____ formerly lived. Wit: ISAAC HINES, JOHN ALBERSON. Jan. Ct. 1797.

p. 443   WILLIAM (W) PICKET to AMOS JOHNSTON of Duplin Co., 11 June 1796, for 50 pds. N. C. currency 200A on the ES of the Northeast River & SS of Cypress Creek, beg. at a pine sd. JOHNSTON'S line, to a pine by a branch HERRING'S line, to sd. JOHNSTON'S line to the beg. Wit. MOSES SHOLER, WILLIAM JOHNSTON. Jan. Ct. 1797.

p. 444   DANIEL TEACHEY to DANIEL BONEY, both of Duplin Co., 16 Jan 1797, for 20 pds. specie 100A on BS of the E prong of Little Rockfish, beg. at a pine the W side of a branch, to JESSE GEORGE'S line, the sd. 100A granted 10 Nov 1784 to sd. TEACHEY. Wit: JACOB TEACHEY, TIMOTHY TEACHEY. Jan. Ct. 1797.

p. 446   JAMES GILLESPIE of Duplin Co., exr. of EDWARD JOHN JAMES & AGUSTUS CARTER to NICHOLAS SANDLIN, planter of Duplin Co. in order to satis-fy debts of the estate sold at public auction 13 Sep 1794, for 27 pds. 100A owned by sd. CARTER. The sd. 100A was patented by HENRY GILMAN & by him transferred to AARON HODGESON who deeded to sd. CARTER, & was exposed for sale by JOSEPH WILLSON, deputy shff. of Duplin. DANIEL SOUTHERLAND became the highest bidder for sd. land & sd. SOUTHERLAND sold to NICHOLAS SANDLIN. Wit: THO. ROUTLEDGE, DAVID MIDDLETON.

p. 447   MARTIN KORNEGY (co. not given) to WILLIAM DUNKIN (co. not given), 26 May 1796, for 35 pds. one negro girl LEUCY. Wit: JOHN KORNEGY. Apr. Ct. 1797.

p. 448   WILLIAM MIZEL SENR. of Duplin Co. to LEVI MIZEL (co. not given), 26 Aug 1796, for 25 pds. good & lawful money a negro boy named DICK about 7 or 8 yrs. old. Wit: LUKE MIZEL, MARK (X) MIZEL. Jan. Ct. 1797.

p. 448   BENJAMIN HARDESTY of Cartrite (Carteret) Co. to SARAH MURRAY (co. not given), 12 Dec 1796, quit claim to a negro girl TAMER. Wit: AMOS JOHNSON, WILLIAM JOHNSON. Jan. Ct. 1797.

p. 449   ABRAHAM MOLTEN to THOMAS KENAN, both of Duplin Co., 1 July 1796, for $500 a negro fellow named BEN & a negro woman named CEALAH. Wit: KENAN LOVE. Jan. Ct. 1797.

p. 449   THOMAS NORMENT (co. not given) to THOMAS GARRISON of Duplin Co., 17 Jan 1797 for 150 pds. current money a negro man named TONEY about 25 yrs. of age, 5 feet 8 inches high, a good sound negro & c. Wit: ADONIJAH GARRISON. Jan. Ct. 1797.

p. 450   WILLIAM MIZELL (SENR.) of Duplin Co. to MARK MIZELL (co. not
given) 26 Aug 1796, for 50 pds. good & lawful money a negro boy named JACK
5 months old. Wit: LUKE MIZELL, LEVI (M) MIZELL. Jan. Ct. 1797.

p. 450   THO. (THOMAS) WRIGHT, Shff. of Duplin Co. to SAMUEL DUNN (co. not
given) 3 Sep 1796, for 125 pds. "a certain negro boy named JACK about 13 yrs. old
of the property of JAMES MORRIS". The Court of Duplin Co. awarded 801 pds. 10
shill., plus cost of 42 pds. 3 shill. to JAMES KENAN & JOHN HILL, admr. of
WILLIAM KENAN for damages in a suit against THEOPHILUS WILLIAMS, JAMES
MORRIS, JOHN STUCKEY & SAMUEL WARD to satisfy a judgment sd. negro boy
was sold to sd. DUNN. Wit: WILLIAM POLLOCK. Jan. Ct. 1797.

p. 451   THOMAS (X) PHILIPS to FELIX FREDERICK, both of Duplin Co., 1 Dec
1794, for 5 pds. 7 shill. a bill of sale for sundries, formerly the prop. of SAMUEL
GUY dec'd, consisting of a heiffer 3 yrs. old, one cooper's jointer, one axe, one
grubbing hoe, drawing knife, one feather bed with one sheet. Wit: JOHN NEWTON.
Jan. Ct. 1797.

p. 452   LEWIS THOMAS to THEOPHILUS PEACOCK, both of Duplin Co., 13 July
1793, for 35 pds. current money of N. C. 100A on the WS of Stewart's Creek, beg.
at a small black oak by the head of a small branch, being the contents of a patent
granted to ABRAHAM MOLTEN 28 Aug 1759 & conveyed by him to BURREL LANIER
who deeded to sd. THOMAS. Wit: THOS. SHELTON, CHARLES JAMES. July Ct.
1797.

p. 453   BENJAMIN DULANEY to JAMES MIDDLETON, both of Duplin Co., 3 Apr
1788, for 40 pds. current money 100A on the WS of the Northeast River, beg. at a
gum on the run of Horse Branch the sd. MIDDLETON'S corner. Wit: JOHN
MALLARD, PHILL SOUTHERLAND, MOSES (X) HANCHEY. Apr. Ct. 1797.

p. 455   MICHAEL GLISSON to THOMAS DALE, both of Duplin Co., 12 July 1796,
for 107 pds. 10 shill. 285A in 2 tracts to wit: (1) 175A on BS of the old mill or
Beaverdam Swamp, being part of the contents of a patent granted to GEORGE
SMITH for 300A dated 29th of Oct, beg. at a hickory the 1st station of the original
patent, adj. the lines of GOFF, STEPHEN GUFFORD, SMITH, JONATHAN
KEITHLEY; (2) 100A on the SS of the Northeast Marsh & on Mirey Branch, beg. at
a red oak his corner on ANDREW GUFFORD'S line & adj. his own line, ROGERS'
corner, being part of a patent granted to GEORGE SMITH 29 Oct 1782. Wit: ABEL
DALE, EDWD. ALBERTSON. Apr. Ct. 1797.

p. 457   WILLIAM ALBERSON to SAMUEL ALBERSON, both of Duplin Co., 15 Apr
1797, for 200 pds. 297A in 2 tracts to wit: (1) 100A on the ES of the Northeast
below the Great Meadow on Sam's Branch joining of SAMUEL ALBERSON'S land,
beg. at a black jack & adj. SAMUEL ALBERSON'S line & to a pine by his corner,
with his other line to the beg.; (2) 197A beg. at a white oak on his own line,
supposed to be on SAMUEL ALBERSON'S line & adj. BARNETT'S or OUTLAW'S
corner & MICHAEL WILSON'S line. Wit: WM. DICKSON, JAMES DICKSON JUNR.
Apr. Ct. 1797.

p. 458   JOHN McCULLOCH to WILLIAM HUNTER, both of Duplin Co., 13 July
1796, for 30 pds. current money of N. C. 100A on the head of Pasture Branch & on
BS of the main road, incl. sd. McCULLOCH'S former residence, beg. at a black

jack, the 2nd line of the patent, a little NW of a branch called Pole Cat Branch adj.
the lines of ALEXANDER DICKSON & JAMES JAMES, being 1/2 of a patent of 200A
granted to sd. McCULLOCH 9 Oct 1783. Wit: JOSEPH DICKSON, ANN MURDOCK.
Apr. Ct. 1797.

p. 460   OBEDIAH WADE to JESSE WILLIAMS, both of Duplin Co., 19 July 1796,
for 150 pds. current money of N. C. 175A in 2 tracts to wit: (1) 75A on the ES of
the Northeast River of Cape Fear & on the SS of Panther Swamp, beg. on a branch
called Spring Branch near PRESCOAT'S line, being part of a tract of 150A that
ABSOLEM BOYETT bought of MAJOR CROOM; (2) 100A on the head of Panther
Swamp, beg. at a pine GEORGE SMITH'S line. Wit: BENJN. LIDDON, GEO.
EUST. HOUSTON. Apr. Ct. 1797.

p. 461   JOEL WILDER of Onslow Co. to HILLARY BRINSON of Duplin Co., 1 Jan
1796, for 30 pds. current money 300A on the NS of Muddy Creek, beg. at a pine,
being a patent granted to sd. BRINSON 21 Sep 1785. Wit: JOSEPH DICKSON,
NATHL. McCANNE. Apr. Ct. 1797.

p. 462   JOHN FLEMMING to ALLEN FLEMMING, both of Duplin Co., 18 Apr 1797,
for 100 pds. 92A on the SS of Mahunga, beg. at a bunch of bays on the run of Mirey
Branch, to the corner of JAMES FLEMMING'S old survey & adj. the lines of
THOMAS FINLEY. Wit: WM. DICKSON. Apr. Ct. 1797.

p. 463   ANDREW GUFFORD to PETER WATKINS, both of Duplin Co., 24 Jan
1797, for 80 pds. 144A being part of 2 surveys patented by SAMUEL WARD & JESSE
BROCK on the Poley Bridge Branch, beg. at a pine WESTBROOK'S corner & adj.
the lines of sd. WARD, BROCK, & WHITEHEAD. Wit: C. HOOKS, LEAVEN
WATKINS. Apr. Ct. 1797.

p. 465   STEPHEN HANCOCK & SARAH HANCOCK to WILLIAM HUNTER, all of
Duplin Co., 2 Mar 1797, for 80 pds. current money of N. C. 300A on the SS of
Muddy Creek & SS of Jumping Run, a branch of Stafford Swamp, beg. at a cypress
on the run of Jumping Run, being a patent granted to WILLIAM COLLINS 10 Nov
1790 & sold to STEPHEN HANCOCK. Wit: MOSES MANNING, JOB HUNTER.
Apr. Ct. 1797.

p. 466   MICHAEL MOLTEN to ABRAHAM MOLTEN SENR., planter, both of Duplin Co., 20 Sep 1791, for 150 pds. currency of N. C. 640A bequeathed to sd.
MICHAEL MOLTEN by his father ABRAHAM MOLTEN dec'd on the ES & WS of
Back Branch & WS of Stewart's Creek, after a dower of SARAH MOLTEN for life is
excepted. Wit: JOSEPH DICKSON, THOMAS ROUTLEDGE JR. Apr. Ct. 1797.

p. 468   CHARLES WARD to JOSEPH MALLARD, both of Duplin Co., 10 Mar 1797,
for 100 pds. good & lawful money 200A above the mouth of Horse Branch, beg. at a
gum in the swamp, to a pine on the SS of sd. branch to a gum in the river swamp.
Wit: PHILL SOUTHERLAND, STEPHEN MIDDLETON. Apr. Ct. 1797.

p. 469   THOS. (THOMAS) BURTON of New Hanover Co. to PHILL SOUTHERLAND
of Duplin Co., 10 Dec 1792, for 10 pds. good & lawful money, 56A on BS of the
mouth of Persimmon, beg. at a pine CONDRICK WHITMAN'S lower corner, by a
drain near WILLIAM BURTON'S upper line. Wit: JAMES MIDDLETON, POLLY
(X) SOUTHERLAND. Apr. Ct. 1797.

p. 470   JOHN WHITEHEAD to PETER WATKINS, both of Duplin Co., 20 Feb 1797,
for 25 silver dollars 21A on the SS of the Northeast, beg. at a bay & maple in the
fork of Poley Bridge Branch, to the corner of sd. WHITEHEAD'S & WESTBROOK'S
survey, to a gum commonly called WESTBROOK'S corner, in the S prong of Poley
Bridge. Wit: EDWARD (X) WHITEHEAD, JOHN (W) WHITEHEAD. Apr. Ct.
1797.

p. 471   JOHN COOK of Duplin Co. to his son REUBEN COOK of Maulsborough
[sic] Co., S. C., 10 Feb 1797, for "natural love & affection" land in Duplin Co.
(acreage not given- REUBEN'S name recorded once as RICHARD). Wit: JAMES
MORRIS, BENJM. (B) JOHNSTON, THOMAS (T) COOK. Apr. Ct. 1797.

p. 472   KENAN LOVE to THOMAS NORMENT, both of Duplin Co., 12 Nov 1796,
for $275 land (acreage not given) descended to sd. LOVE from WILLIAM KENAN
dec'd of Duplin Co., & which sd. LOVE purchased from DANIEL LOVE 26 Oct
1796, & which descended to sd. DANIEL LOVE from WILLIAM LOVE dec'd & likewise of JAMES LOVE as by deed dated 26 Oct 1796, & which sd. KENAN LOVE
purchased from WILLIAM TUTON 27 Oct 1796, & which land did descend to sd.
KENAN LOVE & his wife SUSANAH by the death of sd. WILLIAM KENAN. Wit:
FELIX KENAN HILL, ABRAM MOLTEN. Jan. Ct. 1799.

p. 474   KENAN LOVE of Duplin Co. to JAMES PRICE, Esqr. of New Hanover Co.,
6 Feb 1796, for 500 pds. current money of N. C. 320A on the SS of Turkey Swamp,
known by the name of the "Old Courthouse", beg. at a gum on sd. swamp, being the
lands JOSEPH WILLIAMS purchased from HENRY McCULLOCH Esqr. Wit:
MICHAEL MOLTEN, THOMAS FENLEY. Apr. Ct. 1796.

p. 475   JOHN BURGWIN of New Hanover Co., planter, to MESHACK STALLINGS,
planter of Duplin Co., 5 Mar 1798, for $300, 300A situated on the NS of Rockfish &
within half a mile of the sd. creek bridge & on the WS of the Northeast Branch of
Cape Fear, beg. at a white oak. JOHN BURGWIN had purchased this land at public
auction on 5 Nov 1792 held by Shff. DANIEL GLISSON, who levied on the land
"having been conveyed from WILLIAM FARIS to ROBERT McKEE, by him to
WILLIAM CASE & by him to " JOSEPH BLAKE, who was party to a judgment for
2016 pds. 16 shill. 1 penny awarded to SAMUEL SPANN, formerly of Bristol (merchant), from WILLIAM MOSELEY & HENRY TUCKER, heirs at law in right of their
wives of JOSEPH BLAKE & WALTER BLAKE both dec'd. Wit: SHADRACK
STALLINS, ISAAC BOURDEAUX. Apr. Ct. 1798.

p. 477   JACOB JOHNSTON of Jones Co. to ARCHIBALD THOMAS of Duplin Co.,
8 Jan 1802, for $300, 385A being part of the 4 patents, 3 to HENRY MARTINDALE,
one for 150A, 2 for 100A each, all of which were granted 25 Oct 1779, & 7th & 8th
of Mar 1780, & the 4th tract granted to MARTIN PHILYAW for 250A 18 Jan 1796,
beg. at a stooping pine SAMUEL WHALEY'S corner, to an old tar kiln bed near
MARY GRAHAM'S old house, to the 13th corner from the beg. of sd. PHILYAW'S
grant, crossing Meadow Branch to his other corner, to a pine his last corner, in
JAMES MASHBURN JUNR'S. line, with his line to the run of Meadow Branch, down
the meanders of sd. branch to the mouth thereof (on Limestone Creek), to SAMUEL
WHALEY'S corner. Wit: CHARLES BOSTICK, JNO. B. HALL. Jan. Ct. 1802.

p. 479   OWEN O'DANIEL, 16 Mar 1799, a patent of 10A for 30 shill. for every
100A, signed by WILLIAM R. DAVIE, Esqr. of Raleigh, W. WHITE, Sec., D.

CASWELL, D. Sec. True copy by THOMAS ROUTLEDGE for J. DICKSON, Esqr. Grant No. 1553. The 10A on the NS of Goshen Swamp, beg. at a white oak in STEPHEN MILLER'S line, adj. JACOB GLISSON, his own, & the Quarter Place.

p. 480   JOHN BONEY, 2 Sep 1807, a patent of 25A for 50 shill. for every 100A, signed by B. KORNEGAY, surveyor. Grant No. 1911. The 25A beg. on the Long Branch & the Iron Mine prong, beg. at a pine JESSE GEORGE'S corner, adj. TEACHEY & sd. BONEY. Wit: BENJAMIN WILLIAMS, Esqr. Gov. at Raleigh, 28 Nov 1807. WM. M. WHITE, D. Sec.

p. 481   WILLIAM CARR, 20 July 1808, a patent of 425A for 50 shill. every 100A, surveyed by B. KORNEGAY & recorded by JOHN STALLINGS, D. Sur. Grant No. 1924. The 425A joining sd. CARR'S own land on the SS of Maxwell Swamp, beg. at a pine his own corner. Entered 15 Mar 1808. Wit: DAVID STONE, Esqr. Gov. at Raleigh 17 Dec 1808. WM. M. WHITE, Private Sec. A true copy by THOMAS ROUTLEDGE for J. DICKSON, Regr.

p. 482   WILLIAM CARR, 17 Dec 1808, a patent for 55A entered 15 Mar 1808, surveyed by B. KORNEGAY & JOHN STALLINGS, D. Sur., on the SS of Maxwell Swamp near the mouth of Reedy Meadow Branch, beg. at a sweet gum his corner, thence running on the WS of sd. branch, to a pine below the Huckleberry Springs. Wit: DAVID STONE, Esqr. Gov. at Raleigh, WM. M. WHITE, Private Sec.. A true copy by THOMAS ROUTLEDGE for J. DICKSON, Regr.

p. 483   HENRY KORNEGAY to JOHN JONES, both of Duplin Co., 23 May 1808, for $120, 46A on the SS of the Northeast Swamp, beg. at a sweet gum in sd. swamp CONNERLY'S old corner & sd. JONES' corner, adj. sd. JONES, WHITFIELD, & Rattlesnake Run, being the lower part of a patent granted to sd. CONNERLY & deeded to JESSE BARFIELD who deeded to JACOB KORNEGAY 11 Mar 1777, & since by division of the estate of JACOB KORNEGAY dec'd fell to his heir HENRY KOR- NEGAY. Wit: B. KORNEGAY, THOMAS JONES, SHADRACK JONES. Oct. Ct. 1808.

p. 485   JOHN GIBBS (JUNR.) to JESSE MILLARD, both of Duplin Co., 25 Apr 1808, for 220 silver dollars 55A on the NS of Goshen Swamp & WS of White Oak Branch, beg. at a stake his own corner near the road & his own house, adj. JOSEPH DICKSON'S line, being part of a patent granted to CHRISTOPHER BURCH for 100A. Wit: B. KORNEGAY, WM. CHERRY. Oct. Ct. 1808.

p. 486   NANCY (૨) MILLS to BENJAMIN CHASTEN, both of Duplin Co., 30 June 1808, for 175 barrels of turpentine 3 pieces of land on the WS of the Northeast River & in Maxwell Swamp & on the SS of sd. swamp to wit: (1) 56A beg. at a white bay tree RICHARD CHASTEN'S corner in the edge of a little branch of Maxwell, adj. ROBERT DICKSON & CHASTEN; (2) also that part or moriety of land of 100A granted to HENRY GILMAN 15 Feb 1764 & deeded from him to ISAAC HUNTER who deeded to JAMES MIDDLETON who deeded to RICHARD CHASTEN dec'd, husband of sd. NANCY MILLS, the sd. CHASTEN dec'd having willed to his son JOSEPH CHASTEN & from him to the sd. NANCY MILLS, which piece of land is the lower part of the afsd. patent & which was by the will of RICHARD CHASTEN dec'd, being divided by a branch running into Maxwell Creek near Crawford's footway; (3) 100A adj. the above willed in like manner, beg. at a small pine on CHASTEN'S line, adj. sd. CHASTEN, ROBERT DICKSON & JOHN THALLY. NANCY MILLS to have a life

estate on the last 100A tract for the term of her natural life. THOS. PHILLIPS.
Oct. Ct. 1808.

p. 488   JOHN ROBERTS of Duplin Co. to JAMES HERRING of Wayne Co., 7 May
1808, for $120, 96A on the head of Cabbin Branch being part of a patent granted to
RANDOLPH ROGERS 18 Dec 1797 for 340A & part of a patent granted to EDWARD
OUTLAW 1 Apr 1780, for 100A & afterwards transferred to ROGERS', beg. at a
black jack the 5th corner of ROGERS' patent, adj. SIMON HERRING, ROGERS,
& OUTLAW, & which sd. ROGERS sold to sd. ROBERTS. Wit: JAMES BOURDEN,
WM. WHITFIELD JR. Oct. Ct. 1808.

p. 489   JAMES WILLIAMS to LOFTON NETHERCUT, both of Duplin Co., 16 Aug
1806, for 115 silver dollars 200A in 2 tracts to wit: (1) 150A being part of 200A
granted to LEWIS BARNES, beg. at a stake in Burncoat; (2) 50A being part of a
patent granted to ANTHONY JONES for 150A, beg. at a stake in the run of Burncoat
& crossing ANTHONY'S Branch. Wit: HENRY GRADY, JOHN MAXWELL, ISAIAH
SMITH. Oct. Ct. 1808.

p. 490   DAVID WILLIAMS to DAVID BAZIN(BAZEN), both of Duplin Co., 29 Feb
1807 for $90, 100A beg. at a large pine marked "B" in a pond the WS of the Big
Branch of the Doctors Creek, adj. the lines of SMYTH & BLANTON & BLANTON'S
Branch, & up sd. branch to a pine near the bay marked "W". Wit: JOHN MATTHIS,
JOHN WILLIAMS. Oct. Ct. 1808.

p. 491   JOHN HOUSTON to LEWIS ASHTON THOMAS, both of Duplin Co., 1 Aug
1808, for $800 lawful money of the U. S. 400A on the ES of the Northeast of Cape
Fear River, beg. at a cypress on the river bank at Bull Bluff, beg. the sd.
HOUSTON'S share of his father's lands & laid off as such 5 Oct 1807. Wit: SAM.
HOUSTON, JOSEPH T. RHODES. Oct. Ct. 1808.

p. 493   JOHN HOUSTON to JAMES WILLIAMS, both of Duplin Co., 20 Sep 1808,
(sum not given), 846A being the land formerly the prop. of ROBERT TWILLY in the
fork of the Northeast River & Limestone Creek in 7 tracts to wit: (1) 150A being the
contents of a patent granted to FRANCIS BRICE 23 Feb 1750; (2) 191A being the
contents of a patent granted to GEORGE BELL 27 Apr 1767 adj. the 1st tract & adj.
the lines of SOUTHERLAND & FOLSOM; (3) 20A being the contents of a patent
granted to JAMES CONNER 29 Oct 1782 adj. the above lands, beg. at a pine
TWILLY'S corner, Jumping Run & ANTHONY MILLER; (4) 100A being the contents
of a patent granted to HENRY BISHOP 26 Oct 1767, beg. at a pine JOHN ATKINS' &
adj. FRANCIS BRICE'S line; (5) 75A being the contents of a patent granted to
ARCHIBALD GILLESPIE & adj. the above lands, beg. at a hickory in the low ground
below JACOB MURRAY'S old seat of a house; (6) 100A being a patent granted to
ROBERT TWILLY 21 Sep 1785, beg. at a cypress on the river bank JOHN ATKINS'
corner; (7) 210A being part of a patent granted to sd. TWILLY 29 June 1801 beg. at
a cypress WILLIAM HALL'S corner, adj. TWILLY'S own line & SOUTHERLAND'S
old line. Wit: H. GRADY, JOHN CANADY. (Deed also signed by CATHARINE
HOUSTON.) Oct. Ct. 1808.

p. 495   JAMES (J) PICKETT, planter of Duplin Co. to his son HENRY PICKETT
(co. not given), 18 Sep 1807, for 70 pds. 146A on the WS of the Northeast River
opposite & below the mouth of Muddy Creek, beg. at the mouth of Muddy Creek over
against it, on the WS of the Northeast River on a water oak, along a new line sur-

veyed for sd. JAMES PICKETT, adj. DANIEL MURRAY, being of the land sd.
JAMES PICKETT lives on & part of a new survey taken up round DANIEL MURRAY.
Wit: JOHN McCANNE, DANIEL MURPHY. Oct. Ct. 1808.

p. 496   JAMES (J.) PICKETT, planter, to his son JOHN PICKETT, both of Duplin
Co., 18 Sep 1807, for 60 pds. 120A on the WS of the Northeast River & upon the
river below sd. JAMES PICKETT'S landing, beg. on the river bank near the mouth
of Long Fish Pond, adj. DANIEL MURRAY'S upper corner, across the river at the
Bees Nest. Wit: JOHN McCANNE, DANIEL MURPHY. Oct. Ct. 1808.

p. 498   PETER PARKER to JOHN JONES, both of Duplin Co., 18 Feb 1808, for 40
pds. specie 40A on the SS of the Northeast & on a prong of Rattlesnake Branch, it
being part of a survey of 170A patented by JOHN PARKER & by him to son DANIEL
PARKER who deeded to sd. PETER PARKER, beg. at a white oak in sd. branch
DeBRUHL'S old corner & runs along sd. JONES' own line & sd. PARKER'S line.
Wit: B. KORNEGAY, THOMAS DAIL, THOMAS JONES. Oct. Ct. 1808.

p. 499   MATTHEW (M) EDWARDS of Duplin Co. to JOHN PADGET (co. not given),
7 Sep 1808, for 60 pds. specie one mulatto boy slave 6 yrs. old named SANDERS.
Wit: LEVEN WALLER, JOAB (X) PADGET, JAMES (X) COSTON. Oct. Ct. 1808.

p. 500   JOHN OUTLAW of Duplin Co. to HENRY GRADY (co. not given) 16 Jan
1808, for 200 pds. a negro girl named DOL about 15 yrs. old. Wit: WM. WHIT-
FIELD. Oct. Ct. 1808.

p. 500   J. PEARSALL (co. not given) to JOHN OUTLAW (co. not given), 22 July
1807, for $200 a negro girl named DOLL about 14 yrs. of age. Wit: J. HALL.
Oct. Ct. 1808.

p. 501   J. (JAMES) GUFFORD to WILLIAM CREEK, both of Duplin Co., 8 Oct
1808, for $50 lawful money of N. C. 100A, beg. at a stake on SAMUEL WARD'S
patent line, adj. ARTHUR HERRING, SULIVAN'S line, & to a small pine on a small
branch of Poley Bridge & DEMPSEY WESTBROOK'S line, to a contracted line formerly between ROBERT BROCK & BESANT BROCK, down to the sd. WARD'S
patented line, it being the E end of the land & joining the BROCK survey, ROBERT
BROCK'S & JESSE BROCK'S. Wit: BENJAMIN HERRING SENR., B. GLISSON,
BENJAMIN HERRING JUNR. Oct. Ct. 1808.

p. 502   BENJA. (BENJAMIN) HERRING SENR. to WILLIAM CREECH his son-in-
law & SALLY his wife & dau. of BENJAMIN HERRING, all of Duplin Co., '8 Oct
1808, for "natural love & affection", 200A on the NS of Ground Nut, beg. at a shrub
oak at the head of a small branch, to BENTON'S corner. Wit: B. GLISSON, J.
GUFFORD, BENJAMIN HERRING. Oct. Ct. 1808.

p. 503   STEPHEN HERRING to DANIEL MURPHY, both of Duplin Co., 31 Oct
1804, for 125 silver dollars 100A on the waters of Rockfish, beg. at a maple at the
mouth of Peg's Marsh Branch, adj. the lines of MOORE, TIMOTHY MURPHY &
JOHN MATTHIS, to MATTHIS'S Mill Branch, being part of a survey of 300A granted
by patent to WILLIAM MURPHY dec'd. Wit: THOMAS LANIER, TIMOTHY
MURPHY. Oct. Ct. 1808.

p. 505   JAMES (J) PICKETT to HENRY PICKETT, both of Duplin Co., 8 Oct 1808, for $80, 80A on the WS of the Northeast River, beg. at a hickory his own corner on the river bank, adj. the lines of HENRY BOWZER & MURPHY, it being part of a tract granted to ROGER ALDEN for 3200A in 1796 & by him conveyed to ROBERT C. JOHNSTON. Wit. H. McCANNE, GIBSON SLOAN. Oct. Ct. 1808.

p. 506   THOMAS GRIMES (SENR.) to WILLIAM GRIMES, both of Duplin Co., 3 Oct 1808, for $100, 100A beg. at a pine in the edge of Halls Marsh & adj. the lines of WINDERS & JAMES GRIMES, it being a part of 250A survey patented by HUGH GRIMES dec'd & fell by heirship to JOSEPH GRIMES & by heirship again to THOMAS GRIMES SENR. Wit: DANIEL JONES, LEWIS GRIMES. Oct. Ct. 1808.

p. 507   WILLIAM WARD of Sampson Co. to JOHN GOFF SENR. of Duplin Co., 10 Feb 1808, for $150, 80A on a branch of Rockfish called the Thick Branch, beg. at a pine in the sd. Thick Branch at the mouth, being a corner tree for sd. WARD & AUGUSTIN JONES & ABRAHAM NEWTON, adj. the White Meadow of WARD'S old corner. Wit: JOHN MATTHIS, SHADRACK STALLINGS. Oct. Ct. 1808.

p. 509   DANIEL MURPHY to JOHN VANN (JUNR.), both of Duplin Co., 27 July 1807, for $125, 100A on the waters of Rockfish, beg. at a maple at the mouth of Pegs Marsh Branch, adj. the lines of MOORE, TIMOTHY MURPHY, & JOHN MATTHIS, to MATTHIS'S Mill Branch, it being part of a survey of 300A granted by patent to WILLIAM MURPHY dec'd bearing even date. Wit: THO. LANIER, STEPHEN HERVY (?). Oct. Ct. 1808.

p. 510   SAML. (SAMUEL) STANFORD to CULLEN CONNERLY, both of Duplin Co., 16 Nov 1808, for $1500, 1006A in Duplin & Sampson Cos. on the head waters of Bear Swamp in 2 tracts: (1) 886A beg. in the run of Bear Swamp in a run of a branch which runs between RAWLEY'S field & GUY'S field & adj. the lines of RAWLEY MILLS (formerly WILLIAM NEWTON'S), ORSON BELL, WILLIAM GUY, to Hog Pen Branch, to the Great Road sd. GUY'S corner, to the old courthouse, to the Drinking Branch, being a part of sundry surveys; (2) 120A beg. at a small pine near the main road in his own line & adj. THOMAS KENAN'S new survey, a pine in the county line, BLOUNT'S corner, JOURNEGAN'S line, JO OSBURN'S field. Wit; WILLIAM HALL JUNR., ISAAC DUNKAN. Jan. Ct. 1809.

p. 512   JOHN BECK to LEVI BORDEN, both of Duplin Co., 25 Oct 1808, for 112 milled dollars 112 1/2A in Duplin & Sampson Cos. on the Long Branch, beg. at a stake JOSEPH KORNEGAY'S new corner, to a cole [sic] kiln on WILLIAM BECK SENR'S. line & adj. EASON, BECK, & JOSEPH KORNEGAY'S back line. Wit: WM. BECK JR., WM. BEHURST. Jan. Ct. 1809.

p. 513   MANUEL CARTER to SAMUEL DAVIS, both of Duplin Co., 9 Feb 1808, for $100, 100A on the ES of the Northeast Swamp & SS of Matthews Branch, adj. JAMES SMYTH & the JOHNSTON land & others, being part of a patent taken up by SOLOMON CARTER in 1782. Wit: EDWARD ALBERSON, STEPHEN GRAY. Jan. Ct. 1809.

p. 514   JANE HILL to BENJAMIN HODGES, both of Duplin Co., 24 Nov 1808, for $2,000, 796A beg. at a maple at the mouth of the Long Branch on the SS of Goshen Swamp, adj. MIDDLETON, Stewart's Branch, ANDREW HURST, ROBINSON'S land (WILLIAM K. HALL'S land) & THOMAS, being one entire survey of land conveyed by deed to JOHN HILL by FELIX KENAN of 240A 20 Jan 1773, one of 350A patented by JOHN HILL 29 Oct 1782 & part of 235A granted to sd. JOHN HILL 29 Oct 1782, all conveyed by the LW & T of JOHN HILL dec'd to the sd. JANE HILL. Wit: FELIX K. HILL, CHARLES HOOKS, W. SIKES. Jan. Ct. 1809.

p. 515   EDWD. (EDWARD) ALBERSON of Duplin Co. to CONSIDER BUSHEE of Lenoir Co., 12 Jan 1809, for 20 pds. 66A beg. at a pine, BUSBEE'S corner W of the White Pond, to RACHEL DAVIS' corner, to TARREN'S line. Wit: A. KEATON, D. ALBERSON. Jan. Ct. 1809.

p. 516   JOHN PARKER of Duplin Co. to ALEXANDER PARKER his son (co. not given), 27 July 1807, (sum not given) 100A on the ES of Rockfish Creek, beg. at a persimmon on the bank of Rockfish Creek PETER YOUNG'S corner, to WILLIAM PARKER'S corner. (ANN (A) PARKER also signed the deed.) Wit: JACOB WELLS, WILLIAM PARKER. Jan. Ct. 1809.

p. 517   JAMES BOURDEN to JOHN ROBERTS, both of Duplin Co., 27 May 1808, for $84, 21A beg. at a maple in the Cabbin Branch, adj. JOHN ROBERTS' line, being part of a patent for 118A granted to JEDEDIAH BLANSHARD 8 Dec 1802 & transferred to GEORGE THOMAS who deeded to sd. BOURDEN. Wit: WM. WHITFIELD JUNR., WILLIS HINES, LEVIN WATKINS. Jan. Ct. 1809.

p. 518   NM. (NEEDHAM) WHITFIELD to his dau. SALLY, wife of BENJAMIN HATCH, all of Wayne Co., 8 Nov 1808, for "natural love & affection", 587A in 3 tracts to wit: (1) 240A being part of a patent granted to PHILIP STONE for 400A dated 1767 & transferred from JAMES JONES TO LEWIS HINES 22 Sep 1774 & from sd. HINES to CHRISTOPHER LAWSON; (2) 200A being a patent granted to LEWIS HINES 10 Oct 1794 & from sd. LAWSON to NEEDHAM WHITFIELD 1 July 1797, beg. at a pine on the NS of Cabbin Branch, adj. LEWIS HINES; (3) 147A being part of a patent granted to JESSE PEACOCK for 100A dated 21 Sep 1785 & part of a patent granted to WILLIAM KENAN, beg. at a pine KENAN'S 3rd corner & PEACOCK'S 2nd corner, to a dividing line between MARTIN & FLEMMONS. Wit: JESSE COTTON, JAMES GRIMSLEY. Jan. Ct. 1809.

p.520   DANIEL SOUTHERLAND to JOHN GOUFF, both of Duplin Co., 9 Mar 1806, for 10 pds. lawful money of N. C. 200A on the ES of the Northeast River, beg. at ALEXANDER PICKETT'S & JACOB BROWN JUNR.'S & running a straight line to the beg. corner, to LINCOLN SHUFFIELD'S beg. corner of a patent granted to WILLIAM FARRIOR for 300A 17 Dec 1792, & adj. JAMES PICKETT & THOMAS PICKETT. Wit: AUSTON BRYAN, SAMUEL SOUTHERLAND. 2 July 1807 "I JOHN GAUGH do assign over my right in this deed to AUSTON BRYAN for value received." Wit: JESSE (X) SCARBOROUGH. Jan. Ct. 1809.

p. 521   JOHN GIBBS (SENR.) to CHARLES GIBBS, both of Duplin Co., 17 Jan 1809, for 200 pds. one wench & child by the name of PEGGY & ABBY, the wench aged about 22 & the child about 7 months. Wit: JAMES WATKINS, WILLIAM WATKINS. Jan. Ct. 1809.

p. 522   CHARLES WILLIAMS to SAMPSON GRIMES, both of Duplin Co., 5 May 1808, for $300 a negro boy named ROGER about 13 yrs. old. Wit: EMD. DUNKAN, JESSE GRIMES. Jan. Ct. 1809.

p. 522   JOHN WILSON to BENJAMIN HODGES, both of Duplin Co., 14 Nov 1808,

for $600 a negro wench named VIOLET about 25 yrs. of age & a girl CHLOE about
9 yrs. of age. Wit: D. HOOKS, W. SIKES, A. HERRING. Jan. Ct. 1809.

p. 523   ROBERT PARKER of Nansemond Co., Va. to BRYAN MINCY of Duplin
Co., 19 Feb 1807, for $312.50 good & lawful money of Va. a negro girl named
NELLY about 15 yrs. old. Wit: CHARLES WILLIAMS, EDY WILLIAMS. Jan. Ct.
1809.

p. 523   JESSE WILLIAMS of Duplin Co. to JOSEPH TAYLOR of Lenoir Co., 25
Aug 1808, for $50, 7A beg. at a white oak & sower [sic] wood in Peter's Branch, to
the mouth of Stroud's Branch. Wit: ELIJAH SMITH, JNO. TAYLOR, WILLIAM
TAYLOR. Jan. Ct. 1809.

p. 525   JOHN VANN to REDICK WATSON, both of Duplin Co., 22 Oct 1808, for
160 silver dollars 100A on the waters of Rockfish, beg. at a maple at the mouth of
Pegs Marsh Branch, adj. the lines of MOORE, TIMOTHY MURPHY, JOHN
MATTHIS & to the run of MATTHIS' Mill Branch, being part of 300A granted by
patent to WILLIAM MURPHY dec'd. Wit: SCOTT VANN, THO. LANIER. Jan. Ct.
1809.

p. 526   ELIJAH SMITH of Duplin Co. to JOSEPH TAYLOR of Lenoir Co., 26 Aug
1808, for $700, 234A beg. on the ES of the Northeast River & on the SS of Panther
Swamp, beg. at a red oak at ALEXANDER McCULLOCH'S corner on the NS of
Peter's Branch, that runs into Panther Swamp & runs along McCULLOCH'S line to
Stroud's Branch, to a poplar in Spring Branch, down Peter's Branch to Panther
Swamp, to McCULLOCH'S upper line reverse, to GEORGE SMITH'S to RICHARD
PRESCOTT'S corner tree, to a maple in the pocosin, on the head of Peter's Branch,
down the branch, the various courses to the beg. Wit: JESSE WILLIAMS, JOHN
TAYLOR, WILLIAM TAYLOR. Jan. Ct. 1809.

p. 527   PHILL SOUTHERLAND to his son-in-law STEPHEN WILLIAMS, both of
Duplin Co., 11 Aug 1808, for "natural good will & affection" 130A on the NS of
Persimmon Swamp, beg. at a black gum at the run of Persimmon, WILLIAM
HALL'S corner, WHITMAN'S old corner, down the main road to the run of Persim-
mon, up the run to the beg. Wit: JAS. RAPHAEL. Jan. Ct. 1809.

p. 528   BRYAN BRANCH & SARAH (X) BRANCH his wife to JOHN WILSON, all of
Duplin Co., 17 Jan 1809, for 180 pds. current money of N. C. 148A on the SS of the
Northeast Swamp & on Rattlesnake Branch in 2 tracts to wit: (1) 70A beg. at a gum
in Rattlesnake JOHN JERNIGAN'S lower corner & to ANTHONY JONES' line; (2)
78A in the Piney Woods on the Great Branch, beg. at a hickory WINDERS' old corner, to a pine in the Great Branch, to JOHN JERNIGAN'S corner, along the 40A
survey crossing the Wolf Scrape Branch. The 2 tracts being part of the lands owned
& poss. by ELISHA JERNIGAN dec'd, late of Duplin Co., & laid off by the Court of
Duplin to SALLY JERNIGAN (now SALLY BRANCH), one of the daus. & heirs of the
sd. ELISHA JERNIGAN as her share of her father's land as by record April Term
of Court 1807. Wit: WM. DICKSON. SALLY BRANCH privately examined &
signed the deed of her own free will 17 Jan 1809. Signed by J. HALL, J.P.,
B. BOURDEN, J.P. Jan. Ct. 1809.

p.531   ARCHIBALD THOMAS to THOMAS CANADAY, both of Duplin Co., 29 Jan
1803, for $32, 100A on the ES of the Northeast River between Limestone & Muddy

Creek on the New River Road, beg. at a stake in the 2nd line, being part of 200A granted to WILLIAM THOMAS SENR. & conveyed from him to WILLIAM THOMAS JUNR. & from him to his son WILLIAM THOMAS who deeded to sd. ARCHIBALD THOMAS. Wit: ROBERT SOUTHERLAND, PHILL SOUTHERLAND JUNR. Jan. Ct. 1809.

p. 533   ANTHONY DREW to OWEN CONNERLY, both of N. C. (co. not given), 26 Oct 1808, for 150 pds. 100A in 2 tracts to wit: (1) 50A on the SS of Bear Swamp & WS of Cattail Branch, conveyed by THEOPHILUS WILLIAMS 15 May 1785 to JOHN COOK SENR. & by sd. COOK to REUBEN afsd (REUBEN not mentioned before), beg. at a post oak, to a poplar in the Gum Branch, CHARLES HINES' corner, down the branch to the Meeting Branch, to a gum at the mouth of Cattail Branch, being part of 300A purchased by FREDERICK BELL of H. McCULLOCH; (2) 50A beg. at a pine in the head of a little branch, to RAWLEY MILLS' back line, to HARDY MALPUS' corner. Wit: C. HOOKS, LEWIS TINER. Jan. Ct. 1809.

p. 534   ELISHA (W) WILLAFORD, planter of New Hanover Co. to DAVID EVANS of same, 3 Jan 1809, for $270, 200A on the WS of the Northeast of Cape Fear in 2 tracts to wit: (1) 150A on the SS of Island Creek, beg. at a cypress stump on sd. Island Creek, running near the mouth of Paul's Branch, to a dividing line between sd. WILLAFORD & ZACHARIAH WHITE, to a black oak in the side of the upper survey of 100A patented by JOHN EVERS; (2) 50A on the NS of Island Creek, beg. at the lower corner of sd. EVERS' old survey at a cypress in the S edge of Island Creek, adj. JOHN COOK. Wit: JAS. PEARSALL JUNR., THOMAS EVANS. Jan. Ct. 1809.

p. 536   MANUEL CARTER to THOMAS GRADY, both of Duplin Co., 6 Mar 1804, for $450, 250A on the ES of the Northeast & in the fork of the Northeast & Matthews Branch in 2 tracts to wit: (1) 100A being the contents of a survey granted to GEORGE SMITH for 100A 6 Mar 1759, beg. at a red oak in the fork of the Northeast & Matthews Branch, near EDWARD CARTER'S line, & adj. DURHAM LEIGH; (2) 150A granted to SYLVANUS PUMPHRY, beg. at a white oak near sd. branch & adj. SMITH & LEIGH, excepting what SAMUEL DAVIS' 200A survey takes off & the 150A lying E of the Wolf Pitt Branch. Wit: ELISABETH GRADY, HENRY GRADY. Jan. Ct. 1809.

p. 537   JOSIAH COTTLE to ROBERT COTTLE, both of Duplin Co., 31 Dec 1808, for 100 pds. specie 100A on the NS of Muddy Creek, beg. at a red oak on sd. creek below sd. COTTLE'S, adj. PICKETT, to a cypress in Muddy Creek Swamp, being part of 200A patented by JOHN McGEE & from him conveyed to EBENEZAR GARRISON who deeded to WILLIAM McGEE & from him to CHARLES GAUGH who sold to ROBERT COTTLE, & then sold by HUGH McCANNE, Shff. for taxes to AUSTIN BRYAN who sold to JOSIAH COTTLE. Wit: JAMES PICKETT, HENRY PICKETT. Jan. Ct. 1809.

p. 539   EDWARD PEARSALL & W. G. (WILLIAM GUY) to JOHN MAXWELL (cos. not given), 26 Sep 1808, for $275 a negro girl named CLARENDER about 13 yrs. of age. Wit: WM. GUY JUNR., DANIEL LOVE KENAN. Apr. Ct. 1809.

p. 539   NATHAN FOUNTAIN to WILLIAM HUNTER SENR., both of Duplin Co., 18 Nov 1808, both of Duplin Co. for $540 a negro man named EMERY. Wit: WM. HOLLINGSWORTH. Apr. Ct. 1809.

p. 540   JOHN COOPER to JOSEPH GILLESPIE, both of Duplin Co., 29 Mar 1809, for $304 a negro boy named ALFRED, being sound & healthy & aged 12. Wit: JONES DICKSON. Apr. Ct. 1809.

p. 540   JACOB WOOD of Onslow Co. to JAMES WILLIAMS of Duplin Co., 2 Jan 1808, for 200 pds. a negro boy named ABRAM about 20 yrs. old. Wit: MERRIT MANNING. Apr. Ct. 1809.

p. 541   GEORGE KORNEGAY (SENR.) to his son BASIL KORNEGAY, both of Duplin Co., 16 Apr 1807, for "natural love & affection" 1230A in 2 tracts to wit: (1) 1100A on the Northeast Swamp & BS of Grays Branch, being the land sd. GEORGE KORNEGAY now lives on, incl. the household furn., & planta. & all the land the sd. GEORGE KORNEGAY SENR. poss. between Lewis' Branch & GEORGE KORNEGAY JUNR., beg. at a pine on Lewis' Branch, his own & WHITFIELD'S & runs their dividing line to the Northeast Swamp, adj. GEORGE DUNCAN, EDMUND DUNCAN JUNR. & GEORGE KORNEGAY JUNR., & up Arthurs' Branch to REAVES' line, adj. THOMAS BROWN & WILLIAM HARRIS' old line; (2) 130A on BS of Lewis' Branch joining the other in the Big Field, it being the contents of a patent granted to sd. GEORGE KORNEGAY SENR. Wit: DANL. KORNEGAY, JOHN KORNEGAY. (No probate date given.)

p. 542   WM. (WILLIAM) TURNAGE of Green Co. to JAMES WADE of Duplin Co., 8 Dec 1808, for $450, 300A on the NS of the Northeast Swamp & on Poley Bridge Branch, beg. at a stake & gum in sd. branch, to the beg. corner of a patent granted to JOEL HINES for 240A, to a pine near the co. line, to a gum in Wolf Branch near the fork of the same & the Buck Pond Branch, to the back line of the survey, being part of a survey granted to MATTHEW WARD for 120A & part of a survey formerly belonging to ISAAC HINES & by sd. WARD conveyed to the sd. TURNAGE. Wit: BASIL KORNEGAY, JESSE TURNAGE, M. WILKINS. Apr. Ct. 1809.

p. 544   WM. (WILLIAM) TUTON of Sampson Co. to JOHN HARGROVE of same, 10 Oct 1808, for $600, 380A on the SWS of Maxwell Swamp, beg. at a poplar on the run of the creek a little below the mouth of Jamy Branch, adj. CHARLES HIGGINS, PELEG ROGERS & down the run of Carr's Branch & up the run of Maxwell Swamp to the beg. Wit: FELIX K. HILL, WM. BECK JUNR. Apr. Ct. 1809.

p. 545   SAMUEL HERRING to MAJOR SCARLES, both of Duplin Co., 19 Apr 1808, for 120 pds. 200A on the NS of the Northeast Swamp & WS of Lewis' Branch, incl. the house & planta. where sd. SCARLES now lives, beg. at a poplar, pine & water oak on sd. branch, adj. HERRING'S old corner & being the whole of a survey. granted to EZEKIAL WATSON for 200A by RICHARD CASWELL 1778. Wit: ALEXANDER DICKSON, BASIL KORNEGAY. Apr. Ct. 1809.

p. 547   JOHN HILL & his mother JANE HILL of Duplin Co. to NATHAN L. DAVIS of Edgecombe Co., 19 Jan 1809, for $800, 447A being a part of 2 tracts that JOHN HILL gave to his sons JOHN HILL & JAMES HILL, the land might have been lands that FELIX KENAN gave to his dau. JANE HILL, the former donation made at the request of sd. JANE HILL, though she had not signed the former deed nor does freely sign her right over with her sd. son & was divided by a committee of Col. WM. DICKSON, WILLIAM BECK, Esqr., DANIEL GLISSON, THOMAS WRIGHT, DAVID HOOKS & BASIL KORNEGAY, surveyor, which was done at Apr. Ct. 1808, the sd. 474A lying on the SS of Goshen & NS of Nahunga, beg. at a water oak on

Nahunga, a little below the mouth of Stewart's Branch, to CHARLES MORRIS' line,
formerly NEW'S line. Wit: JAMES REARDON, ANDREW HURST, CHARLES
MORRIS. Apr. Ct. 1809.

p. 548   D. L. (DANIEL LOVE) KENAN, Shff. of Duplin Co. to BASIL KORNEGAY
(co. not given), 10 Dec 1807, for 23 pds. 100A at a public auction held 10 Dec 1807,
the sd. land being the prop. of GEORGE HAYS as levied on by WILEY GARNER,
constable of Duplin Co., to satisfy a judgment obtained by BASIL KORNEGAY &
ROBERT KORNEGAY, to the amount of 20 pds. 3 shill., plus cost of 1 pd. 18 shill.
3 pence for damages in a suit against sd. HAYS for a certain debt & damages. The
sd. 100A beg. at a pine in the edge of a Little Horse Pen Branch, to THOMAS
AYRES' corner. Wit: DANL. KORNEGAY, J. KORNEGAY. Apr. Ct. 1809.

p. 549   BENJAMIN (X) SUTTON of Lenoir Co. to JOHN ROBERTS of Duplin Co.,
____Dec 1807, (sum not given), 39 3/4A on the SS of the Great Branch, beg. at the
fun of the Great Branch, with exception of building a mill across sd. branch, which
sd. SUTTON has liberty to do where most convenient whatever. Wit: WILLIAM
ROBERTS, SANDERS (X) THOMPSON. Apr. Ct. 1809.

p. 550   ALEXANDER CARTER to HENRY GRADY, both of Duplin Co., 5 Dec 1806,
for $120, 100A on the ES of the Northeast & SS of Matthew's Branch, being part of a
patent granted to SOLOMON CARTER for 360A, beg. at the beg. of sd. patent at a
maple on the run of Matthew's, a little above the main road, along RICHARD SAN-
DERS' line, to WS of Davis' Branch. Wit: THOMAS GRADY, JAMES STEWART.
Apr. Ct. 1809.

p. 551   FRED. (FREDERICK) GRADY to HENRY GRADY, both of Duplin Co., 7
Apr 1808, for $60, 100A in the NE of Cape Fear, being part of a patent granted to
WILLIAM WILLIAMS for 640A deeded to sd. FREDERICK GRADY by his father
WILLIAM GRADY, beg. at a stake A. GRADY JUNR.'S corner in the 3rd line of sd.
patent, adj. A. GRADY SENR. & A. GRADY JUNR. Wit: ALEXANDER GRADY
SENR. & ALEXANDER GRADY JUNR. Apr. Ct. 1809.

p. 552   D. (DURHAM) GRADY of Wayne Co. to ALEXANDER GRADY JUNR. of
Duplin Co., 4 Oct 1806, for $750, 222A in the fork of the Northeast & Burncoat, beg.
at a gum on the edge of the Northeast Swamp at the mouth of Burncoat, sd. to be
WILLIAM ALBERSON'S line, to LEWIS BARFIELD'S corner, to a stake on the run
of Burncoat to a white oak near the road leading from BARFIELD'S to KORNEGAY'S
Bridge on the Northeast, to the head of Saw Pit Branch, granted to FREDERICK
GRADY for 175A, to FREDERICK GRADY'S old corner of a 175A survey. Wit:
HENRY GRADY, F. GRADY, ELISHA GRADY. Apr. Ct. 1809.

p. 554   ALEXANDER GRADY (SENR.) to HENRY GRADY, both of Duplin Co., 15
Nov. 1808, for $500, 161A in the fork of the Northeast of Cape Fear & Goshen in 2
tracts to wit: (1) 150A granted to JOHN PICKSON below the mouth of Camp Branch,
above ALEXANDER ROUSE'S land, to a large pine in the Northeast at the mouth of
Housman's Branch; (2) 11A being part of a patent granted to WILLIAM WILLIAMS
for 640A adj. the 1st, beg. at a stake the 4th corner of sd. survey. Wit: THO.
GRADY, ALEXANDER GRADY JUNR. Apr. Ct. 1809.

p. 555   FRED. (FREDERICK) GRADY to ALEXANDER GRADY JUNR., both of
Duplin Co., 17 Apr 1808, for $60, 100A on the Northeast of Cape Fear, being part

of a patent granted to WILLIAM WILLIAMS for 640A & deeded by his father to
WILLIAM GRADY to sd. FREDERICK GRADY, beg. at a stake in the 2nd line of sd.
patent A. GRADY SENR.'S corner. Wit: H. GRADY, ALEXANDER GRADY SENR.
Apr. Ct. 1809

p. 556 ALEX. (ALEXANDER) CARTER to HENRY GRADY, both of Duplin Co.,
5 Mar 1808, for 23 pds. 23A on the NS of Matthews Branch, beg. at a poplar in the
Juniper, the beg. of sd. GRADY'S 200A survey, patented by THOMAS ROUTLEDGE,
to Matthews Branch, along the side of the branch incl. all high lands down to the
same to the mouth of the Juniper. Wit: EDWARD ALBERSON, JAMES STEWART.
Apr. Ct. 1809.

ADDENDA to BOOK 3A

p. 345   NATHAN FOUNTAIN to HENRY FOUNTAIN JR., both of Duplin Co., 29
June 1795, for 190 pds. current money of N. C. 2 tracts to wit: (1) 144A granted
to WILLIAM SOUTHERLAND 23 May 1757 on the ES of the Northeast Branch of Cape
Fear River on Cedar(?) Branch, beg. at a gum on Muddy Creek Swamp near the
mouth of Cedar Swamp or branch; (2) 100A being part of one other survey of 150A
granted by patent to NATHAN FOUNTAIN 16 Nov 1790, beg. at a cypress on the N
run of Muddy Creek the 1st station of the patent, to a white oak the corner of 100A
patented by HENRY FOUNTAIN SENR., adj. NATHAN FOUNTAIN'S line of a survey
of 144 A patented by sd. SOUTHERLAND, to JOHN FARRIOR'S corner, to a cypress
at the mouth of Stafford's Swamp, down the swamp of Muddy Creek to where AUSTIN
BRYAN'S line leaves the sd. survey. Wit: JOSEPH DICKSON, JOHN FARRIOR.
July Ct. 1796.

p. 347   JOSEPH BEVA(E)N to WILLIAM BEVEN, both of Duplin Co., 25 May 1796,
for 30 pds. 250A on the WS of the main creek of Rockfish, beg. at a holly at the
mouth of Cabbin Branch, JOHN PARKER'S corner, to a stake in Rockfish Swamp,
patented by JOSEPH BEVEN 1782. Wit: FREDK. WILLIAMS, STEPHEN WILLIAMS.
July Ct. 1796.

p. 348   STEPHEN WILLIAMS to HANNAH BATTS, both of Duplin Co., 11 Feb
1796, for 12 pds. specie 50A on the ES of the Northeast River & on the NS of the
Back Swamp & on BS of the Round Meadow Branch, beg. at a pine on sd. branch.
(Deed also signed by JACOB WILLIAMS) Wit: JAMES (X) WALLIS, SARAH (X)
WILLIAMS. July Ct. 1796.

p. 1   JOHN (𝓜) GOFF (SENR.) to his son THOMAS GOFF, both of Duplin Co., 13
May 1804, for "love good will & affection" one negro man named Dick. Wit: JOHN
GOFF, RICHARD JOHNSTON. Apr. Ct. 1809.

p. 1   DAVID SLOAN to ISOM NORRIS, both of Duplin Co., 18 Oct 1808, for $100
46A on the SS of Island Creek, beg. at a water oak at the run of sd. creek. Wit:
JOHN WHITMAN, JOHN STALLINGS. Apr. Ct. 1809.

p. 2   JONATHAN (X) BROOKS to WILLIAM PICKITT, both of Duplin Co., 26 Jan
1808, for $75 lawful money of N. C. 230A on the ES of the Northeast River opposite
the mouth of Island Creek, beg. at a water oak on the river bank below the mouth of
sd. creek & runs to a pine on the side of the Great Pocosin. Wit: FREDK.
PICKETT, ARTHUR MURRAY. Apr. Ct. 1809.

p. 4   DAVID CARTER to HENRY GRADY, both of Duplin Co., 30 Jan 1806, for
$500, 235A on the ES of the Northeast River & below Matthews Branch & on BS of
Davis' Branch in 3 tracts to wit: (1) 100A being the contents of a patent granted to
RICHARD SANDERS, beg. at a red oak on the falling grounds of Davis' Branch, sd.
GRADY'S corner; (2) 100A being part of a patent granted to SOLOMON CARTER for
400A & joining the 1st piece, beg. at a stake & 2 pine saplins in the sd. SANDERS'
line, LAWRENCE THOMPSON'S corner; (3) 35A being part of a patent granted to
WILLIAM WILLIAMS for 640A, the sd. piece being known by the name of the DAVID
NEW Ground , beg. at a poplar in a branch that divides between sd. GRADY &
ELISHA CARTER. SOLOMON CARTER, father of sd. DAVID CARTER to have use
of the planta. in the fork of Davis' Branch where JAMES STEWART lives during his
natural life. Wit: ALEXANDER GRADY, ASA (X) HALL. Apr. Ct. 1809.

p. 5   THOMAS GRADY to HENRY GRADY, both of Duplin Co., 15 Nov 1808, for
$450, 250A on the ES of the Northeast of Cape Fear & in the fork of the Northeast &
Matthews Branch in 2 tracts to wit: (1) 100A being the contents of a survey granted
to GEORGE SMITH for 100A 6 Mar 1759, beg. at a red oak in the fork of the Northeast & Matthews Branch near EDWARD CARTER'S line adj. DURHAM LEIGH; (2)
150A granted to SYLVANUS PUMPHRY joining the 1st piece, beg. at a white oak
near Mathews Branch, adj. DURHAM LEIGH (with exception of what SAMUEL
DAVIS' old survey takes off & all that part of the PUMPHREY survey lying ES the
Wolf Pit Branch). Wit: ALEXANDER GRADY SENR.,ALEXANDER GRADY JUNR.
Apr. Ct. 1809.

p. 6   THOMAS COLE, planter, to WILLIAM PICKETT, both of Duplin Co., 15 Apr
1809, for 20 pds. currency 100A on the ES of the Northeast of Cape Fear River on
the NS of Lanier's Swamp, it being part of 2 surveys, the 1st patented by JOSEPH
GRIMES 19 May 1787; the 2nd patented by THOMAS COLE 9 Aug 1805, being his
surplus within his own lines, beg. at JOHN LANIER'S corner on the sd. COLE'S own
line & adj. BENTON WILLEFORD. Wit: ASA MURRAY, FREDERICK PICKETT.
Apr. Ct. 1809.

p. 8   Land Division of BENJAMIN SNIPES dec'd, 2 Jan 1809, being 679A valued to
$1341 into 9 parts, each child's share amounting to $149, 5 shares of the above land
being purchased by STEPHEN HERRING. ZILPHA ASBURY, ELIZABETH
WILLIAMS, SILLER SUMMERLIN, WILLIAM SNIPES & RACHEL SUMMERLIN are
heirs of BENJAMIN SNIPES dec'd. The committee laid off for sd. HERRING by his
own consent 269A valued at $941, which contains 4 separate pieces of land to wit:

(1) 153A being part of a survey patented by DANIEL HERRING 2 Nov 1764;   (2) 85A
joining the 1st piece conveyed to the sd. dec'd by ARTHUR HERRING;   (3) 18A joining the above land conveyed to the sd. dec'd by WILLIAM ALBERSON;   (4) 13A
patented by sd. SNIPES which land includes the dower of the widow of sd. SNIPES &
is distinguished in the surveyor's plats for the division of the lands of sd. estate by
No. 1, then the sd. STEPHEN HERRING stands indebted to the minor heirs of sd.
SNIPES the sum of $196 for his over proportion of land property. The other part of
the lands belonging to the minor heirs laid off by lott. BENJAMIN SNIPES drew
110A valued at $100 lying near Goshen, being the lower part of the land known as the
Sulivan survey, & being No. 3 in the surveyor's plat, the estate indebted to sd.
SNIPES in the sum of $49 for his deficiency in land prop. JOSEPH SNIPES drew
100A valued at $100, being the upper part of the sd. SULIVAN survey, known as No.
2, & sd. JOSEPH SNIPES indebted to the estate in the sum of $49 for his deficiency
in land property. NANCY SNIPES drew 100A valued at $100, being the N end of a
survey of 200A patented by the dec'd on BS of the Little Marsh, distinguished in the
plat as No. 4, then the estate stands indebted to sd. NANCY SNIPES for her
deficiency in the land prop. in the sum of $49. KITTY SNIPES drew 90A valued at
$100, lying on the S end of the above mentioned survey, on BS of the Little Marsh,
distinguished in the plat as No. 5, then the estate stands indebted to KITTY SNIPES
for her deficiency in land prop. the sum of $49. Signed by EDWARD ALBERSON,
CHRISTOPHER LAWSON, JOSEPH WHITFIELD.   2 Jan 1809.

p. 10   SAMUEL BOURDEN JUNR. to BRYAN BOURDEN, both of Duplin Co., 1
Dec 1807, for $700, 220A on the drains of White Oak Swamp, cont. part of several
old patents, beg. at a black jack BRYAN BOWDEN'S corner, with an old line marked
& established, a dividing line between NICHOLAS BOURDEN & JAMES HURST, by
the edge of MUND'S pocosin, to Hoop Pole Pocosin, adj. JAMES BIZZEL. Wit:
ROBERT DICKSON, FREDERICK SIKES. July Ct. 1808.

p. 11   TH. (THOMAS) ROUTLEDGE of New Hanover Co. to JAMES GILLESPIE of
Duplin Co., 4 June 1804, for $300 a negro man slave named POMPEY about 21 yrs.
old. Wit: EDWARD PEARSALL, AARON MORGAN. Apr. Ct. 1809. THOMAS
ROUTLEDGE received $300 from NATHAN WALLER 26 July 1809 for full payment
of sd. negro. The above was a mortgage bill of sale. Wit: JOHN McGOWEN,
AARON MORGAN.

p. 12   Patent No. 1917 surveyed 19 Sep 1808 for FREDERICK SMITH SENR. 46A
on the ES of the Northeast River, beg. at a gum on the side of the same below the
mouth of Goshen at Pates (?) Hole. Entered 19 Jan 1808. Issued by BENJAMIN
WILLIAMS, Governor, 1 Dec 1808. WILLIAM M. WHITE, D. Sec.

p. 14   BENJAMIN HATCH of Wayne Co. to WILLIS HINES of Duplin Co., 25 Nov
1808, for 375 pds. 587A on the NS of the Northeast Swamp & on BS of the Cabbin
Branch in 3 tracts to wit: (1) 240A being part of a patent granted to PHILLIP
STONE for 400A in 1767 & transferred from JAMES JONES to LEWIS HINES 22 Sep
1774 & from sd. HINES to CHRISTOPHER LAWSON; (2) incl. a patent granted to
sd. HINES for 200A on 10 Oct 1794 & then from sd. LAWSON to NEEDHAM WHIT-
FIELD 1 July 1797, beg. at a pine on the NES of Cabbin Branch, STONE'S corner,
adj. LEWIS HINES, to the beg. of HINES' patent a gum in Cabbin Branch; (3) 147A
being part of a patent granted to JESSE PEACOCK for 100A dated 21 Sep 1785 &
part of a patent granted to WILLIAM KENAN, beg. at a pine KENAN'S 3rd corner &
PEACOCK'S 2nd corner, to a line known to be a dividing line between MARTIN &

FLEMMONS & through PEACOCK'S & KENAN'S surveys. Wit: B. KORNEGAY,
WM. WHITFIELD JUNR. July Ct. 1809.

p. 16   TH. (THOMAS) ROUTLEDGE to HOPKIN WILLIAMS, both of Duplin Co., 17
July 1809, for $100 lawful money of U. S. 200A on the SS of Persimmon Branch,
beg. at a gum on the swamp edge by RUTHERFORD'S corner & adj. WHITMAN'S old
line, patented by THOMAS ROUTLEDGE SENR. 28 Aug 1795 & by him willed to the
sd. THOMAS ROUTLEDGE. Wit: PHILL SOUTHERLAND, HILLERY BISHOP.
July Ct. 1809.

p. 17   SAMUEL BOWDEN SENR. to his son HENRY BOURDEN, both of Duplin Co.,
30 Mar 1809, for "love good will & affection" 260A on the ES of Bear Marsh, beg.
at the mouth of a small branch called TURNEGE'S, to a stake on the open line in a
drain of Mill Branch & adj. BENJAMIN BOURDEN, to the run of Bear Marsh, being
the land whereon the parties now reside. The sd. SAMUEL BOURDEN SENR. & his
wife CATHERINE BOURDEN to have the use & privilege of the same during their
lives. Wit: JESSE SWINSON, BENJAMIN BOURDEN. July Ct. 1809.

p. 18 · C. (CHARLES) HOOKS to JOSHUA MERCER, 27 Mar 1809, for $60, 100A
being part of the land commonly called the STONE land, on the NS of Cabbin Branch,
beg. at the run of Cabbin Branch where GEORGE MILLER'S lower line strikes the
branch below his mill, adj. FREDERICK SMITH'S line of his 50A purchased off the
200A STONE Survey, except 1A at the end of GEORGE MILLER'S Mill Dam. Wit:
JAMES REARDON, DAVID HOOKS. July Ct. 1809.

p. 19   WILLIAM (X) HUNTER (SENR.) to STEPHEN BROWN JUNR., both of
Duplin Co., 20 Aug 1808, for $170, 160A in 2 tracts to wit: (1) 100A beg. at a gum
on the S of the Cedar prong of Muddy Creek on the run, being part of a tract of 200
A granted to JAMES WHALEY by patent dated 16 Nov 1790; (2) 60A adj. the 1st,
beg. at a stake the 3rd corner of the above patent of 200A, adj. STEPHEN HAN-
COCK to the Big Branch, to HILLERY BRINSON'S, granted to sd. HUNTER by patent
29 Nov 1803. Wit: ELIZABETH (E) MILLER, JOSEPH T. RHODES. July Ct. 1809.

p. 21   JESSE WILLIAMS to MATTHEW EDWARDS, both of Duplin Co., 8 Mar
1809, for $350 lawful money of the U. S. 260A on the WS of Limestone Swamp in 2
tracts to wit: (1) 100A beg. at a water oak at the run of Limestone marked for
JOHN HUMPHREY'S corner, granted to JAMES GILLESPIE by patent 29 Oct 1782 &
by him conveyed to LEMUEL WILLIAMS 1791 & by sd. WILLIAMS to JESSE
WILLIAMS 27 Sep 1805; (2) 160A adj. the 1st tract, beg. at a poplar MATTHEW
EDWARDS' corner, to the run of Limestone Swamp, patented by JOHN HUMPHREY
16 Nov 1784 & by him conveyed to LEMUEL WILLIAMS 1 Sep 1791. Wit: WILLIAM
HUNTER JUNR., JOSEPH T. RHODES. July Ct. 1809.

p. 22   WILLIAM DUNN of New Bern, Craven Co. to SAMUEL DUNN of Duplin Co.,
6 July 1809, for $2,000, 828A on the SS of Panther Swamp, beg. at an old blown
down gum & 3 small white oaks where the main road crosses Panther Branch, adj.
CLARK'S old line, to a large water oak in the branch, called the dividing branch in
the planta., to SAMUEL DUNN'S line, to the line of CLARK'S new survey & adj.
WILLIAM WHITFIELD, to a black gum on the run of the Doctors Branch to the run
of Panther Branch, being the contents of a deed from JAMES CLARKE to SAMUEL
DUNN. Wit: D. L. KENAN, C. HOOKS. July Ct. 1809.

p. 24   JACOB WELLS SENR. to WILLIAM CARR, both of Duplin Co., 20 May
1809, for $200, 155A in 2 tracts to wit: (1) 50A patented by FREDERICK WELLS
on the WS of the Northeast on BS of Island Creek, beg. at a pine by a gully HENRY
ALLEN'S corner, SS of the creek; (2) 105A adj. the sd. survey, beg. at a pine &
adj. HARDY PARKER'S corner. Wit: TH. ROUTLEDGE, JOHN. SLOAN. July Ct.
1809.

p. 25   WILLIAM HALL JUNR. to SAMUEL STANFORD, both of Duplin Co., 16
Nov 1808, for 700 spanish milled dollars 558 1/4 A on BS of Elder Swamp, beg. at
a water oak in sd. swamp sd. HALL'S lower corner, joining the lower side of
JAMES DICKSON'S old field, to a small pine the corner of WM. HALL SENR'S deed
from JAMES DICKSON, to the run of the main prong of Buck Branch, to a water oak
at the end of JAMES DICKSON'S old ditch, up a branch called Persimmon Gully, to
the old corner of PHAREZ' [sic] & DOUGLAS' lands, the old deed line joining
BUSH'S land. Wit: CULLEN CONNERLY, ISAAC DUNKAN. July Ct. 1809.

p. 27   ANTHONY DREW of Sampson Co. to HARDY CARROL of Duplin Co., 29
May 1809, for $124, 124A on the NWS of Storgs Creek & on the NS of Inser's
(Enzor's) Branch, beg. at a pine HENRY HOLLINGS(WORTH) corner, adj. the Mill
Swamp. Wit: WM. POLLOCK, DANIEL WEST, WILLIS CARRELL. July Ct. 1809.

p. 28   FOUNTAIN WILLIAMS of Jones Co. to MANUEL CARTER of Duplin Co.,
6 July 1808, for 57 pds. 10 shill. current money of N. C. 200A on BS of the
Beaverdam Swamp of Limestone, beg. at a white oak a little below the mouth of
Brandy Branch. Wit: THOS. QUIN, DAVID KING. July Ct. 1809.

p. 29   ALEXANDER GRADY SENR. to HENRY GRADY, both of Duplin Co., 15
Mar 1804, for the sum of 140 acres[sic] 140A in the Northeast Swamp, being part of
a patent granted to WILLIAM WILLIAMS for 640A dated 6 Apr 1745, beg. at a gum
sd. HENRY GRADY'S corner at the mouth of the dividing branch a little E of the
Dry Island, adj. HENRY GRADY & A. GRADY. Wit: THO. GRADY, HENRY
JOHNSTON, JOHN GRADY. July Ct. 1809.

p. 30   D. (DANIEL) GLISSON to BRYAN GLISSON (cos. not given), 20 Feb 1806,
for 125 pds. lawful money 180A on the head of Horse Pen Branch, Juniper & Sandy
Run, beg. at a pine on the head of Horse Pen, adj. SMITH, GOFF, to a black gum
on the drain of Duck Pond, to a black jack near the head of Sandy Run. Wit:
SAMUEL SMYTHE, B. KORNEGAY. July Ct. 1809.

p. 31   JOHN CHAMBERS to JAMES COSTON, both of Duplin Co., 1 Jan 1808, for
45 pds. current money of N. C. 100A on the ES of Elder Swamp & on BS of the main
road, beg. at a lightwood tree near the main road. Wit: HUGH McCANNE, JOHN
THALLY.

p. 32   MICHAEL BONEY to WILLIAM STREET, both of Duplin Co., 3 Mar 1806,
for $100, 300A being part of 2 tracts on the ES of the Northeast River patented by
WILLIAM McCANNE & MICHAEL BONEY, beg. at a stake on the bank of the river
at a place called WILSON'S hole, running with McCANNE'S old patent line, to a
stake by the edge of a prong of Holly Shelter Pocosin, ASA MURRAY'S corner, to
the upper end of Sturgeon Hole on the bank of the river. Wit: TIMOTHY TEACHEY
& ASA MURRAY. July Ct. 1809.

p. 33   THOMAS (X) BELL of Duplin Co. to JOSHUA BLANTON of Sampson Co.,
22 Feb 1805, for 300 pds. good & lawful money of N. C. 207A part of a tract of land
formerly belonging to JOHN BELL, the father of THOMAS BELL, on the waters of
Rockfish, beg. at a maple at the run of GOFF'S Beaverdam, runs thence as the
dividing line between JOHN BELL & THOMAS BELL, to a poplar in a prong of Black
Branch. (JANE BELL also signed the deed.) Wit: PETER CARLTON, WILLIAM
WARD. July Ct. 1809.

p. 35   JOHN SELLARS of New Hanover Co. to ABRAHAM NEWTON of Duplin Co.,
17 Mar 1806, for $400 lawful money of N. C. one negro woman named LUCE 16 yrs.
of age. Wit: JOHN HUFHAM. July Ct. 1809.

p. 36   JOHN DICKSON of Cumberland Co., by virtue of a power of attorney for
WILLIAM BROWN of Duplin Co., to JOSEPH BRICE of Duplin Co., 9 May 1809, for
$250 a negro woman slave named JINNEY. Wit: JOHN VANN, J. FREDERICK.
July Ct. 1809.

p. 36   W. ROBINSON (co. not given) to ABRAHAM NEWTON (co. not given), 12
Aug 1808, for $300 a negro boy called BALAM about 12 yrs. old. Wit: WILLIAM
STOAKS. July Ct. 1809.

p. 37   AA. (AARON) MORGAN of Duplin Co. to his son JAMES W. MORGAN (co.
not given), 25 Feb 1807, for $300 a legacy from JAMES GILLESPIE dec'd, being a
negro girl named PHEBE about 17 yrs. of age. Wit: ED. ARMSTRONG, THOS.
SHEPHERD. July Ct. 1809.

p. 37   DANIEL MURPHY of Duplin Co. to JOSEPH BRICE (co. not given), 6 Feb
1808, for $500 a negro man named Ceasar. Wit: WM. (X) HOWE, JOHN EVANS,
JOHN MATTHIS. July Ct. 1809.

p. 38   JAMES DEVANE of New Hanover Co. to ISAAC HALL of Duplin Co., 12 Apr
1809, for $200 a negro girl by the name of MARS (?) yrs. old. Wit: WM. DEVANE
& JOHN B. DEVANE. July Ct. 1809.

p. 39   JOHN HILL to JANE HILL, both of Duplin Co., 3 Dec 1808, for $325 a
negro boy slave named TOBY about 13 yrs. old. Wit: FELIX K. HILL, J. W.
BARFIELD. July Ct. 1809.

p. 39   A. (ABRAM) KORNEGAY SENR. of Jones Co. to BASIL KORNEGAY (co. not
given), 6 June 1807, for 100 pds. a negro boy named WILL. Wit: JOSEPH KORNE-
GAY, WILLIAM KORNEGAY JUNR. July Ct. 1809.

p. 40   HARDY (X) POWELL (SENR.) to JOSEPH STRINGFIELD, both of Duplin
Co., 17 Mar 1809, for $100 all stock with increase, consisting of one horse, 8
cattle, all hogs & sheep, household furn. & planta. tools, with exception of sd.
POWELL having use of the above during his natural life. Wit: WILLIAM BLAND,
JOHN JOHNSTON. July Ct. 1809.

p. 41   C. (CHARLES) HOOKS of Duplin Co. to JACOB LOCHON of same, 15 Apr
1809, for $40, 100A on the ES of Cabbin Branch, beg. at GEORGE MILLER'S upper
line in sd. branch, adj. WILLIAM HOUSTON & FREDERICK SMITH. Wit: JAMES
REARDON, DAVID HOOKS. July Ct. 1809.

p. 42   JESSE SMITH to OWEN O'DANIEL, both planters of Duplin Co., 1 Sep 1806,
for $450, 230 A being part of 3 surveys patented by ALEXANDER McCULLOCH,
THOMAS WORLEY & ANTHONY MILLER, joining FREDERICK SMITH SENR.,
JONES SMITH, LOFTIS WORLEY & STEPHEN MILLER, beg. at a pine in a drain
on DAVID GREER'S lines , running along a row of marked trees made by
FREDERICK SMITH SENR. & LOFTIS WORLEY to divide the land between JESSE
SMITH & JONES SMITH, that was left them by their father GEORGE SMITH, down
to the Northeast Swamp, to THOMAS WORLEY'S upper corner, to the mouth of
Tandam Branch near CS. (CHARLES?) MILLER'S swamp field, adj. FREDERICK
SMITH & GREER. Wit: WM. KORNEGAY JUNR., DAVID KORNEGAY. July Ct.
1809.

p. 43   EDMUND DUNCAN (JUNR.) to BASIL KORNEGAY, both of Duplin Co., 9
Feb 1809, for $700 250A on BS of the Northeast Swamp in 2 tracts to wit: (1) 226A
beg. at GEORGE DUNCAN'S corner, adj. JOHN KORNEGA & GEORGE KORNEGAY;
(2) 24A on BS of sd. swamp joining the 1st & above the same, beg. at a red oak sd.
KORNEGAY'S corner on the SS of sd. swamp, near the main road & runs with the
other line across the sd. swamp, adj. GEORGE KORNEGAY. The sd. 2 tracts
afsd. being the land that was devised by the LW & T of WILLIAM DUNCAN dec'd to
his son EDMOND DUNCAN. Wit: HENRY BOWDEN. July Ct. 1809.

p. 45   JOHN (Ŧ) GOORE SENR. of Duplin Co. to JONATHAN GOORE (co. not
given), 5 Aug 1806, for $110, 110A on the NS of Back Branch & the WS of Stewart's
Creek, beg. at a maple, laurel bay & sweet gum in Back Branch, JAMES PATTER-
SON'S upper corner, by & with a line of a survey of 580A patented by ABRAHAM
MOLTEN dec'd. Wit: JAMES REARDON, JAMES WARD, JAMES (X) WINDERS.
July Ct. 1809.

p. 46   JOHN HALSO to ALEXANDER MEREDY, both of Duplin Co., 13 Apr 1809,
for 25 pds. 25A joining HALSO'S line, beg. at a black gum on the SS of HALSO'S
Swamp, to a water oak in the Long Branch. Wit: JAMES LANIER, JOHN LANIER.
July Ct. 1809.

p. 47   WILLIAM (ſ) TUCKER to AMOS TUCKER, both of Duplin Co., 16 Oct
1809, for 100 pds. lawful money 150A in Halifax Co. on BS of HARRIS' Branch,
beg. at a corner pine AMOS HARRIS' corner, to a corner elm in HARRIS' Branch.
Wit: JACOB MATTHIS, JACOB MATTHIS JUNR. Oct. Ct. 1809.

p.48   THOS. (THOMAS) QUINN to his dau. CELIA BROCK, wife of JOHN BROCK,
all of Duplin Co., 14 Oct 1809, for "pur love & affection", 54A on the ES of White
Oak Branch, beg. at a pine on a small branch on the ES of White Oak Branch adj.
THOMAS QUINN, being part of a 150A plot granted to sd. QUINN in 1784. Wit:
LEWIS HALL, LOFTEN QUINN. Oct. Ct. 1809.

p. 49   FREDERICK JONES of Montgomery Co., Tenn. & NATHANIEL PRICE &
BARBARA PRICE, both of Duplin Co. to JOHN JONES SENR. of Duplin Co., 14 Sep
1809, for $250, 129A on the SS of Rattlesnake Swamp & the WS of Great Branch,
where the widow now lives, beg. at a stake on the patent line & on WILLSON'S line,
adj. SAMUEL JONES, SOLOMON JONES, only excepting 1/3 part of the same,
incl. the house & planta. where sd. widow MARY JONES, relict of ANTHONY
JONES dec'd now lives during her natural life, & afterwards to sd. JOHN JONES.
Wit: B. KORNEGAY, SOLOMON JONES. JOSEPH WHITFIELD & BASIL

KORNEGAY, Justices of Duplin Co., privately examined BARBARA PRICE, who
gave her consent with her husband of her own free will & accord & without any
obligation of her husband to assign sd. deed to JOHN JONES. Oct. Ct. 1809.

p. 51   JOHN PARKER (SENR.) of Duplin Co., planter, to his son WILLIAM PAR-
KER (co. not given), 10 May 1808, a deed of gift for 100A on the NS of Rockfish
Creek, beg. at a cypress in the Big Branch about 50 rod above PARKER'S old mill,
up the W prong of the branch to the head to PARKER'S upper line, adj. PETER
YOUNG, JACOB WELLS & JACOB BONEY. Wit: JOSEPH WILLIAMS, AMBROS
SMITH. Oct. Ct. 1809. (ANN (PA) PARKER also signed the deed.)

p. 52   MATTHEW WARD of Duplin Co. to WILLIAM TURNAGE of Green Co., 4
Feb 1808, for 476 pds. 670A on Poley Bridge, a branch of the Northeast, in 2 tracts
to wit: (1) 550A beg. at a stake in sd. branch & runs to the beg. corner of a patent
granted to JOEL HINES for 240A, to a corner of a 300A survey conveyed by deed
from ISAAC HINES to sd. WARD, the corner of a patent granted to ISAAC HINES for
100A, exclusive of a piece of 50A which is covered upon by part of a patent belonging
to JAMES OUTLAW; (2) 120A being part of a patent granted to JOEL HINES for
240A, beg. at a pine on the hill of Poley Bridge Branch, adj. OUTLAW. Wit:
BASIL KORNEGAY, JOHN OUTLAW, JESSE JESSE TURNING. Oct. Ct. 1809.

p. 54   ARCHIBALD THOMAS to PHILL SOUTHERLAND, both of Duplin Co., 3 Sep
1808, for $25, 100A on the ES of the Northeast River, between Limestone & Muddy
Creek on the New River Road, beg. at a large white oak & runs with the 1st line of
the old patent & adj. THOMAS CANNADAY, being part of a tract of 200A patented by
WILLIAM THOMAS SENR. Wit: THOMAS CANNADAY, HILLERY BISHOP. Oct.
Ct. 1809.

p. 56   LEVIN WATKINS, planter, to his son JESSE WATKINS, both of Duplin Co.,
21 Apr 1806, for "natural love & affection" 55A on the SS of the Northeast & WS of
the Mirey Branch, beg. at a black gum in the Miery Branch by BEN SNIPES' corner,
adj. BARFIELD & STEPHEN GUFFORD. Wit: WM. WATKINS, JOHN WATKINS.
Oct. Ct. 1809.

p. 57   LEVIN WATKINS to JESSE WATKINS, both of Duplin Co., 15 July 1809, for
600 silver dollars 300A on the NS of Goshen Swamp, beg. at a water oak & gum on
the run of Goshen, ISAIAH ROGERS' corner, to a pine on the edge of Bearskin, adj.
ASA ROGERS & JOEL ROGERS. Wit: JOHN WATKINS, LEVIN WATKINS JUNR.
Oct. Ct. 1809.

p. 58   HENRY SOUTHERLAND to KILLIS NEWKIRK, both of Duplin Co., 21 Mar
1808, (sum not given) 60A on the ES of the Northeast River, beg. at a large pine
near the run of Maple Branch, one of the dividing line trees between BROCK &
BRICE, being part of a tract of 640A granted to JOHN BROCK by patent dated 17 May
1754 & fell from him by heirship to BARNET BROCK & from him to DAVID BROCK
& from sd. BROCK to sd. SOUTHERLAND. Wit: DANIEL SOUTHERLAND, WIM-
BECK BONEY. Oct. Ct. 1809.

p. 60   WILLIAM MATHIS (MATTHEWS) of Rutherford Co., Tenn. to JACOB
MATTHEWS JUNR. of Duplin Co., 16 Sep 1809, for $150, 150A beg. in the fork of
the branch of Clear Run, adj. JACOB MATTHEWS' own corner tree at the head of the
branch, being part of DAVID TUCKER'S entry. Wit: THOMAS CARLTON, THO.

126   DUPLIN DEEDS, BOOK 4A

(X) BROOKS. Oct. Ct. 1809.

p. 61   JOSEPH T. RHODES to his son JAMES THOMAS RHODES, both of Duplin Co., 26 Aug 1809, for "love & affection" 264A on the SS of Goshen & WS of Bear Swamp, being part of 2 surveys in 2 tracts to wit: (1) 215A beg. at a black gum on the run of Bear Swamp, a corner tree of DAVID HOOKS' land & runs along his line, to the upper corner of a survey HENRY CANNON formerly bought of HENRY EUSTACE McCULLOCH, to HODGES' planta. & adj. LEWIS THOMAS, along his line to a cypress & hornbeam at his lower corner on the run of Bear Swamp; (2) 49A adj. the 1st tract on the NS, beg. at a pine on the road side in the line dividing the land of sd. JOSEPH T. RHODES & DAVID HOOKS, to a white oak in BENJAMIN HODGES' line, the 3rd corner of the 1st tract, being part of a tract of 365A deeded to JOSEPH T. RHODES by FREDERICK BARFIELD 8 Aug 1801. Wit: WILLIAM COX, SUSANAH HARRIS. Oct. Ct. 1809.

p. 63   MARTIN KORNEGAY to BRYAN KORNEGAY & LUKE KORNEGAY, all of Duplin Co., 2 Aug 1806, for 350 pds. current money of N. C. 150A being part of the estate of JACOB KORNEGAY dec'd, incl. the grist mill & planta. & being the lands of the allotted & adjudged by certain commissioners appointed by the County Court to divide the lands of sd. JACOB KORNEGAY dec'd & which division included in the sd. 150A the full share then allotted and laid off to the sd. MARTIN KORNE-GAY & WILLIAM DUNCAN & the sd. division being sanctioned by the Court & recorded at July Term 1796. Wit: MICHAEL WILKINS, ABRAM KORNEGAY. Oct. Ct. 1809.

p. 64   JAMES (+) HARRELL to JAMES PICKETT, both of Duplin Co., 29 May 1809, for $300, 280A on the SS of Muddy Creek in 2 tracts to wit: (1) 200A beg. at a poplar, water oak & hickory on a small Island in Muddy Creek in the giving line of an old patent granted to STEPHEN HOLLINGSWORTH 21 June 1746 & runs up sd. swamp along the old line; (2) 80A taken out of 200A according to quatity & quality, 100A belonging to the above recited patent was deeded by AUSTEN BRYAN to JACOB & HENRY HARRELL; the other 100A was granted to AUSTEN BRYAN & transferred in the same manner to the same person. Wit: H. McCANNE, DANL. (X) TEACHEY. Oct. Ct. 1809.

p. 65   JAMES PICKETT to DAWSON PICKETT, both planters of Duplin Co., 21 Nov 1804, for 100 pds. 150A on the WS of the Northeast River & BS of Muddy Creek in 2 tracts, beg. at a red oak on the bank of the river, to SOLOMON PICKETT'S lower corner, incl. a small piece of land formerly sold to JAMES PICKETT by DAWSON PICKETT cont. 10 or 12 A, crossing Muddy Creek & down sd. creek to the mouth of the river, excluding 3A of land on the side of the river lately sold by sd. JAMES PICKETT to ARTHUR B. GREGORY, incl. his storehouse at the landing being only 1/2A wide from the river bank, being part of a survey granted to sd. JAMES PICKETT 22 Jan 1773 & 10A deeded to sd. JAMES PICKETT 17 May 1794, in the whole estimated at about 150A. Wit: JOHN (X) PICKETT, WILLIAM PICKETT. Oct. Ct. 1809.

p. 67   JOS. (JOSEPH) GREEN to LOVE KENAN, both of Duplin Co., 5 Mar 1809, for 800 pds. 420A in Duplin Co. in 2 tracts to wit: (1) 320A on the SS of Turkey Swamp, known by the name of Duplin Old Court House, beg. at a green oak on Turkey Swamp; (2) 100A on a branch of Turkey on BS of the main road about half a mile from the Old Court House, beg. at a pine formerly JOSEPH WILLIAMS' corner.

Wit: THOMAS MOLTEN, B. HODGES. Oct. Ct. 1809.

p. 68   NICANOR (X) JAMES, planter, to DAVID WHITMAN, both of Duplin Co.,
12 Aug 1809, (sum not given), 120A being part of a patent for 147A to WILLIAM
McCANNE, lying on the ES of Mill Branch & on the WS of the Northeast Branch of
Cape Fear River, beg. at a pine on GEORGE POWELL'S line, adj. JOHN WHITMAN,
JOSEPH HODGESON, JOHN HOLDEN & POWELL. Wit: WILLIAM MALLARD,
JOHN WHITMAN JR. Oct. Ct. 1809.

p. 69   JACOB (𝓔)WAIDE to ROBERT BISHOP JUNR., both of Duplin Co., 25 Apr
1807, for $20, 100A on the ES of the Northeast River & ES of Gum Swamp, a branch
of Limestone Swamp, beg. at a white oak THO. QUINN'S corner, adj. JOHN
WILLIAMS. Wit: ROBERT SOUTHERLAND, PHILL SOUTHERLAND JNR. Oct.
Ct. 1809.

p. 71   JOHN KORNEGAY, planter of N. C. to STEPHEN JONES (co. not given),
26 Jan 1809, for 10 pds. 10 shill. 10 1/2 A on the SS of Deep Gully Branch, beg. at
a hickory JOHN JONES' corner, to a water oak in Deep Gully Branch, adj. JOHN
JONES. Wit: HENRY KORNEGAY, ISAAC (X) SPENCE. Oct. Ct. 1809.

p. 72   LEWIS HALL to STEPHEN MILLER, both of Duplin Co., 21 Jan 1806, for
100 pds. 140A on the NS of Gray's Run, beg. at a white oak & gum in the edge of sd.
run, to BURWELL land, to a pine the corner of land patented by SAMUEL CHAM-
BERS, adj. sd. CHAMBERS & THOMAS MATCHETT. Wit: JOHN WILKINSON,
JACOB WILLIAMS. Oct. Ct. 1809.

p. 73   BRYAN KORNEGAY, planter of Duplin Co. to STEPHEN JONES (co. not
given), 10 Jan 1809, for 50 pds. 100A being part of a patent that of 250A, the sd.
100A being on the head of Deep Gully Branch, beg. at a water oak in Deep Gully
Branch STEPHEN JONES' corner, along a line of marked trees to sd. JONES' other
corner, joining JOHN KORNEGAY. Wit: HENRY KORNEGAY, NANCY (Ŧ)
JONES. Oct. Ct. 1809.

p. 75   JACOB KORNEGAY to BASIL KORNEGAY, both of Duplin Co., 10 Jan 1808,
for $55,50A on the NS of the Northeast Swamp & on BS of Bails Branch, beg. at a
large pine on the ES of sd. branch ABRAHAM KORNEGAY'S corner, to a pine in
Camp Pocosin, joining WHITFIELD & GEORGE KORNEGAY, being the contents of
a patent granted to sd. JACOB KORNEGAY by his Excellency NATHANIEL
ALEXANDER 24 Nov 1806. Wit: READEN BOURDEN, THO. PRICE. Oct. Ct.
1809.

p. 76   JOHN GIBBS (SENR.), planter, to his son CHARLES GIBBS, both of Duplin
Co., 20 Jan 1806, for "natural love & affection" 354A on the NS of Goshen Swamp
between & on BS of Cow Hole & White Oak Branches, beg. at a black gum & maple
in Cow Hole Swamp, JOHN GIBBS JUNR.'S corner along WATKINS & his own line
fence, to MILLARD'S fence, crossing White Oak, to a spanish oak on JOHN GIBBS
JUNR.'S line. Wit: LEVIN WATKINS, JOHN GIBBS, JAMES WATKINS. Oct. Ct.
1809.

p. 78   JOHN WILSON to SARAH OLIVER, both of Duplin Co., 2 Aug 1809, for
$250 lawful money of N. C. a negro girl named JUDY about 14 yrs. of age. Wit:
JAS. WATKINS, JOHN OLIVER. Oct. Ct. 1809.

p. 79   LN. (LEVIN) WATKINS to ARCHIBALD BRANCH, both of Duplin Co., (date
not given) for $400 a negro girl named SALLY about 15 yrs. of age. Wit: JNO.
WATKINS. Oct. Ct. 1809.

p. 79   CONSTANT (X) CARTER to ALEXANDER CARTER, both of Duplin Co., 29
Aug 1809, in consideration of a bond for maintaining sd. CONSTANT CARTER
during her natural lifetime, a bill of sale for 26 cattle. Wit: EDWD. ALBERSON,
DAVID KING. Oct. Ct. 1809.

p. 80   JOHN (/) GOFF SENR. to ELIZABETH (X) HENNECY, both of Duplin Co.,
7 Feb 1807, a marriage contract witnesseth, that "the sd. JOHN GOFF SENR. hath
agreed to & with sd. ELIZABETH HENNECY if she would marry him & live with
him as man & wife & treat him well at all times in old age & infinnity & not run him
in debt at any time unless by consent of the sd. JOHN GOFF & him in his proper
senses & continues with him sd. JOHN GOFF during his natural life & for the above
performance of her the sd. ELIZABETH HENNECY...all the remainder & residue
of my estate at my decease after pay...all my just debts." Wit: JOHN HUFHAM,
L. STALLINGS. Jan. Ct. 1810.

p. 81   NEEDHAM (X) GARNER to NATHAN GARNER, both of Duplin Co., 9 Dec
1809, for 100 pds. 85A beg. at a persimmon tree on the SS of the Northeast, a little
below sd. planta. adj. JONAS SWINSON, LEWIS HERRING, 1st prong of the Reedy
Branch & JOHNSTON. Wit: JOS. WHITFIELD, SIMEON GARNER. Jan. Ct. 1810.

p. 82   ZILPHA BYRD of Duplin Co. to her loving children PEARCY, BENJAMIN,
NANCY & WILLIAM BYRD of same, 11 Mar 1807, for "love good will & affection"
a negro boy named CHARLES. Wit: JOHN HUFHAM, ELIZABETH CUMMINGS.
Jan. Ct. 1810.

p. 83   ELIJAH SHEPARD of Onslow Co. to LEVI SHOALER of Duplin Co., 9 Jan
1809, for $50, 300A on the SS of Cypress Creek & ES of the Northeast of Cape Fear,
beg. at a pine by an old tar kiln bed that was made by JOSEPH GRIMES, joining
FRANCIS BLAKE, sd. SHOALAR'S corner of another survey, the sd. 300A patented
by MOSES SHOLAR. Wit: FREDERICK PICKETT, JAMES PICKET. Jan. Ct. 1810.

p. 84   ISAAC (Ŧ) JAMES, planter, to REUBEN NORRIS, both of Duplin Co., 18
Jan 1809, for $150 current money 100A on the WS of the Rattlesnake Pocosin, beg.
at a large pine by the pocosin on JOHN COOK'S line, being granted by a patent to sd.
JAMES 29 Oct 1752. Wit: DANIEL GEORGE, ASA MURRAY. Jan. Ct. 1810.

p. 85   JAMES EVANS to THOMAS GARRISON, both of Duplin Co., 1 Apr 1809, for
20 pds. good & lawful money 19 1/2 A, beg. at a black gum in Sand Hill Branch.
Wit: DANIEL L. KENAN, JOHN BRYAN. Jan. Ct. 1810.

p. 86   BENJAMIN HERRING of Duplin Co. to EDWARD CREECH & his wife MARY
of Lenoir Co., his son-in-law & dau., 23 Dec 1809, for "natural love & affection"
163A on the SS of Ground Nut sd. HERRING'S Mill Branch, beg. in Ground Nut, to
the back line, to a stooping white oak on the side of the branch, joining HINES. Wit:
WILLIAM CREECH, SARAH CREECH. Jan. Ct. 1810.

p. 87   JAMES WATKINS to JESSE WATKINS, both of Duplin Co., 5 Aug 1805, for
$150 a negro girl named SPICE about 8 yrs. Wit: JOHN WATKINS. Jan. Ct. 1810.

p. 87   WM. (WILLIAM) BROWN, constable, a bill of sale, by virtue of an execution
to him directed in favor JACOB MUNK versus WILLIAM DEVANE, levied on & sold
a certain negro boy by the name of LINKHORN, the prop. of WILLIAM DEVANE, at
which sale JOHN BLOODWORTH was the highest & last bidder in the sum of $5.
Dated 5 July 1806. Wit: MAURICE FENNEL. Jan. Ct. 1810.

p. 88   WM. (WILLIAM) BROWN, constable, a bill of sale, by virtue of sundry
executions to him directed against WILLIAM DEVANE, levied on & sold 3 negroes
named TEANEY, BECK & NANCY, the prop. of sd. DEVANE, at which sale JOHN
BLOODWORTH was the highest & last bidder, now in consideration of the sd. last
bid of $120. Dated 9 Dec 1806. Wit: MAURICE FENNEL. Jan. Ct. 1810.

p. 88   WM. (WILLIAM) BROWN to JOHN D. BLOODWORTH, 2 Mar 1807, a certain
parcel of negroes by the names of NAN, EMANUEL, ABRAHAM, EDY, SERENA &
BOB, the prop. of WILLIAM DEVANE, for the sum of $148.50. Wit: AUGUSTIN
JONES. Jan. Ct. 1810.

p. 89   STEPHEN MASSEY & BETHIA (X) MASSEY to ALEXANDER GRADY JUNR.,
all of Duplin Co., 27 Dec 1805, for 124 silver dollars 104A in 2 tracts to wit: (1)
94A on the WS of the Northeast, beg. at a pine on the edge of a marsh on JAMES
CHAMBERS' line, above the mouth of Sandy Run, joining GRADY'S line, the same
being granted to ISAAC DAWSON 30 July 1779; (2) 10A being part of a patent &
joining the 1st tract, beg. at a stake on the run of Sandy Run where the 250 pole line
crosses it. Wit: JS. KORNEGAY, WILLIAM (X) ALPHIN. Jan. Ct. 1810.

p. 90   READIN POPE of Duplin Co. to JACOB LASSITER, Esqr. of Greene Co.,
2 Sep 1809, for $2,000, 777A in 2 tracts: (1) 600A on the SS of the Northeast & on
a branch called the Poley Bridge, beg. at a gum in sd. Northeast his & STANLEY'S
corner, to a pine in a meadow on READEN BOWDEN'S line, being the contents of
several patents granted to JESSE BARFIELD & FREDERICK BARFIELD & since by
several conveyances became the prop. of NICHOLAS & JAMES BOWDEN & from
them conveyed to sd. POPE; (2) 177A on the SS of the Northeast & WS of Poley
Bridge, beg. at a pine on the Mill Pond above the house on the old patent line, incl.
the house, planta. & mill whereon sd. POPE now lives. Wit: BLANEY HARPER
JUNR., CHARLES H. HARPER. Jan. Ct. 1810.

p. 92   WILLIAM DUNKAN(DUNCAN), planter of Jones Co. to JOHN FLOWERS of
Wayne Co., 25 Aug 1809, for 289 pds. 15 shill. currency 230A on the SS of the
Northeast Swamp, beg. at an ash in the Northeast near a footway & runs up the
meanders of sd. swamp, to a gum JACOBS' corner. Wit: DANL. KORNEGAY,
JACOB DUNKAN. Jan. Ct. 1810.

p. 93   NEEDHAM (N) GARNER (SENR.) & WILEY GARNER to NATHAN GARNER,
all of Duplin Co., 28 July 1809, for $228, 115A on the SS of the Northeast Swamp &
NS of Reedy Branch, beg. at a gum in the 1st prong of sd. branch on the old patent
line, being part of a patent granted to LUTSON STROUD for 250A & since by several
conveyances became the prop. of NEEDHAM & WILEY GARNER. Wit: MILES
SCARBOROUGH, SIMEON GARNER. Jan. Ct. 1810.

p. 95   JAMES GUFFORD & STEPHEN GUFFORD (cos. not given) to BRYAN
GLISSON of Duplin Co., 19 Nov 1808, for 150 pds. 240A on the drains of Goshen
Swamp & on BS of Goshen Road, beg. at a sweet gum in GUFFORD'S Branch just

below the road, to a maple in the Cows Branch. Wit: STEPHEN HERRING, WM. HERRING. Jan. Ct. 1810.

p. 96   S. (SHADRACK) STALLINGS to WILLIAM STALLINGS, both of Duplin Co., 12 Jan 1810, for 300 pds. 2 negro boys, one named CLABORN about 15 yrs. & one named BILL about 5 yrs. Wit: W. ROBINSON, JAS. KENAN. Jan. Ct. 1810.

p. 96   ABSOLAM BEST, Patent No. 1952, 13 Nov 1810, for 21A on the WS of the Northeast River & on the SS of Beaverdam Branch, beg. at a pine near his corner & runs with ROBERT WILLIAMS' line , to a pine on ROBERT JOHNSTON'S line. Signed by JOHN FARRIOR, Sur. Countersigned by DAVID STONE, his Excellency, WILLIAM WHITE, Sec.

p. 97   HENRY FOUNTAIN, Patent No. 1958, (date not given), for 46A on the ES of the Northeast River & on the SS of Muddy Creek Swamp, beg. at a pine ROBERT COLE'S & NATHANIEL FOUNTAIN'S corner, to a pine on HENRY FOUNTAIN'S line. Signed by JOHN FARRIOR, Sur., DAVID STONE.

p. 97   BENJAMIN LANIER, Patent No. 1969, 7 Nov 1811, for 51A on the ES of the Northeast River & on the SS of Muddy Creek, beg. at a sweet bay on the WS of the Great Branch in HENRY PICKETT'S old line, thence with HOLLINGSWORTH'S line, to a bunch of small pines in the edge of sd. branch WILLIAM PICKETT'S corner. Assigned by F. PICKETT, Dist. Sur., H. MAXWELL, C.S., BENJAMIN SMITH, WILLIAM WHITE, Sec.

p. 97   ALEXANDER CARTER, Patent No. 1950, (date not given), for 40A on the ES of the Northeast River & on the NS of Panther Swamp, just below CARTER'S Bridge, beg. at a dead pine CHERRY'S corner & runs with ALDEN'S line, to CHRISTOPHER LAWSON'S corner, to a pine on SAMUEL JONES' line, to WORLEY'S line & CHERRY'S corner. Assigned by D. STONE, JOHN FARRIOR, C.S., by WILLIAM WHITE, Sec.

p. 98   STEPHEN GRAHAM, Patent No. 1967, 13 Nov 1811, entered 16 July 1811, for 52A on the drains of Persimmon & FREDERICK'S Mill Branch, beg. at a pine the 5th corner of a 200A patent granted to WILLIAM FREDERICK, to an old pine in the cleared land FREDERICK'S corner. HUGH MAXWELL, Sur. Assigned by BENJM. SMITH. WILL HILL, Sec.

p. 98   WILLIAM (X) FREDERICK & JOHN BEST to STEPHEN GRAHAM, all of Duplin Co., 6 June 1811, for $200, 75A beg. at the run of FREDERICK'S Mill Swamp in the main road that leads from JAMES' across roads to Limestone Bridge, to a white oak in the fork of the Miery Branch, to a white oak at the run of Mill Swamp, up the sd. swamp to the beg. Wit: THOMAS MOLTON, GEORGE TIPLER. July Ct. 1811.

p. 99   WILLIAM (X) FREDERICK to STEPHEN GRAHAM, both of Duplin Co., 11 June 1811, for $34.80, 175A in 2 tracts to wit: (1) 50A on the ES of Jening's Branch or sd. FREDERICK'S Mill Branch, beg. at a pine May pole & gum in sd. branch on BEST'S line, to PEARSE'S old corner, now GABRIEL JAMES' corner, to a gum & white oak ISAAC HUNTER'S corner now JOHN HUNTER'S; (2) 125A beg. at a black jack on the side of Sand Hill Pocosin, to the WS of Jenny's Branch, to ELIZABETH BEST'S new corner. Wit: GEORGE TIPLER, JANE FREDERICK. July Ct. 1811.

p. 101   F. (FREEMAN) WOODS, HANNAH WOODS, JAS. (JAMES) MURDOCK, DA.
(DAVID) MURDOCK, WM. (WILLIAM) MURDOCK & ELIZABETH MURDOCK of
Craven Co. to ANDREW McINTIRE of Duplin Co., 23 Mar 1811, for $3,000, 763A
in 3 tracts to wit: (1) 330A on the SS of the Grove Swamp on which the Court House
is situated (the Court House Lott excepted), beg. at an ash THOMAS ROUTLEDGE'S
corner, running with their dividing line to a white oak in the Mill Branch, crossing
the head of Pasture Branch to a black oak; (2) 123A on the NS of the Grove, beg. at
an ash in the run of the swamp a corner of OBADIAH EVANS' tract; (3) 310A on the
SS of the Grove incl. the Indian Grave on the main road beg. at a pine MARY
McCULLOCH'S corner, on WILLIAM FREDERICK'S line, joining ISAAC HUNTER &
JAMES, excepting from the last tract about 50 or 60A conveyed by MARY MURDOCK
to WILLIAM McGEE. Wit: M. STEVENSON, THOMAS BROWN. HANNAH WOODS
was privately examined before J. L. TAYLOR, Justice of the Sup. Ct. that she
executed the sd. land freely & voluntarily, without any manner of coercion from her
husband FREEMAN WOODS or any other person. Proved 24 May 1811.

p. 103   FREDERICK SMITH, Patent No. 1937, 30 Nov 1809, for 50 shill. for every
100A granted, 123A on the ES of the Northeast River, beg. at a pine his own corner
on the SS of Hog Branch, to a stake WILLIAM A. HOUSTON'S corner, to a pine
DAVID GREER'S corner. Surveyed by F. PICKETT 27 July 1809. Entered 19 Jan
1808. DAVID STONE, Esqr. Gov. WILL WHITE, Sec.

p. 104   BENJAMIN SNIPES, Division of Land in 3 plats. The 1st plat represents
the division of 269A laid off to STEPHEN HERRING in 4 tracts to wit: (1) 153A
purchased by BENJAMIN SNIPES dec'd from ARTHUR HERRING 12 Feb 1778; (2)
85A joining the 1st purchased by sd. SNIPES of sd. HERRING & by him from
ALEXANDER OUTLAW; (3) 18A joining the above conveyed by WILLIAM ALBERSON
to sd. SNIPES as the above figures are laid down, reference being had to the original
will more fully appear & c., incl. the house & planta; (4) 13A (not described).
The 2nd plat represents the division of 202A belonging to the estate of BENJAMIN
SNIPES dec'd as follows: No. 2 to JOSEPH SNIPES an heir of sd. dec'd, 102A on
the NS of Goshen Swamp, the western part of a 400A tract granted to JOHN SULI-
VANT 4 May 1769, beg. at a pine near BULLARD'S old field; (2) No. 3 to BENJA-
MIN SNIPES JUNR., being 100A beg. at a stake the 2nd corner of JOSEPH SNIPES'
division & joining OUTLAW'S line & HERRING'S corner. The 3rd plat represents
No. 4 to NANCY SNIPES, being 110A beg. at a pine on the side of Manor's Branch,
the beg. corner of sd. patent, to a stake in the old line, to a stake in the head of
Fawn Skin Branch. No. 5 on the 3rd plat to KITTY SNIPES for 90A beg. at a pine
the 2nd corner of NANCY SNIPES' & crossing Little Marsh Branch & joining
HERRING'S line. All 3 plats surveyed by B. KORNEGAY 14 Dec 1809. Jan. Ct.
1810.

p. 106   JOHN (X) BEST to ROBERT MIDDLETON, both of Duplin Co., 25 Jan
1810, for $2.50, 3A beg. at a maple at the run of Dennis's Branch, formerly
BENJAMIN BEST'S corner, now MIDDLETON'S corner. Wit: BENJN. BEST.
Jan. Ct. 1810.

p. 107   STEPHEN GUFFORD to JAMES JERNIGAN, both of Duplin Co., 4 Mar
1809, for 200 pds, 200A on the NS of Goshen Swamp & being part of the MOBLEY
survey, beg. on the back line in Goshen Swamp, running a straight line to the
mouth of the Great Branch, joining GEORGE KORNEGAY, LEWIS GLISSON & sd.
GUFFORD, being part of 3 surveys (MOBLEY, JOHN GLISSON & WILLIAM

GOODWIN'S. Wit: GEO. J. HODUM, DANL. JERNIGAN. Apr. Ct. 1810.

p. 108   JAMES WATKINS to LEVIN WATKINS, both of Duplin Co., 19 Mar 1804,
for 200 pds. good & lawful money of N. C., 150A on the NS of Goshen Swamp & on
Cow Hole Branch, beg. at a maple & poplar in the sd. branch JAMES HURST'S
lower corner, joining JOHN FOLEY, BAKER BOWDEN, GEORGE OUTLAW, to a
water oak in the Scantling Branch known by the name of the Foley Place, the sd.
150A granted by patent to LEVIN WATKINS 10 Nov 1754. Wit: JESSE WATKINS,
JOHN WATKINS. Apr. Ct. 1810.

p. 110   LEVI (L. M.) MIZELL to JOHN BUSH, both of Duplin Co., 17 Sep 1808,
for $110 current money of N. C. 150A on the NS of Maxwell Swamp & WS of Alder
[Elder] Swamp, beg. at a pine a corner of land granted to ALEXANDER DICKSON'S
(now JAMES DICKSON'S) line to his corner joining ALEXANDER HOLDON, RIGBY,
RICHARD WILLIAMS. Wit: JAMES DICKSON, WM. (X) MIZELL. Apr. Ct. 1810.

p. 111   B. (BRYAN) GLISSON to WILLIAM HUDGINS (cos. not given), 17 Apr
1810, for 140 pds. lawful money 180A on the head of Horsepen Branch, Juniper
& Sandy Run, beg. at a pine on the head of Horsepen joining SMITH, GOFF, to a
black gum in a drain of Duck Pond, to a black jack near the head of Sandy Run.
(No witnesses) Apr. Ct. 1810.

p. 112   JESSE GEORGE to JOHN BONEY, both of Duplin Co., 28 Oct 1809, for
$600, 284A on the ES of Little Rockfish on Cummins' Creek & on the NS of Kizor's
Branch, being part of 2 surveys of land, patented by JACOB WELLS in 3 tracts to
wit: (1) 134A beg. at a bay tree & gum in Kizor's Branch, on the patent line of the
lower survey joining JOHN BONEY; (2) 100A on the ES of Little Rockfish & the
main road , beg. at a pine on or near the old line patented by JACOB WELLS,
joining RUTHERFORD & McREE; (3) 50A in Rockfish Neck, beg. at a pine on
RUTHERFORD'S line, joining McREE, the corner of GEORGE'S 100A survey. Wit:
TIMOTHY TEACHEY, JACOB BONEY. Apr. Ct. 1810.

p. 114   H. (HUGH) McCANNE, late Shff. of Duplin Co. to DAVID CARLTON of
same, 29 Feb 1804, 320A for 174 pds. 13 shill. & one penny, at public auction 24
Apr 1803, in 3 tracts to wit: (1) 200A formerly granted to ALEXANDER ARM-
STRONG, beg. at an ash on the run of JAMES' Branch on ABRAM BEESLEY'S line
& the corner of another survey of sd. ARMSTRONG, to a red oak the corner of the
old 100A survey patented by ISAAC PARKER joining WILLIAMS' old line, to a water
oak in JAMES' Branch; (2) 100A formerly granted to ISAAC PARKER, beg. at a
turkey oak on the side of ARMSTRONG'S Branch, formerly called FRANK'S Branch;
(3) 20A joining the 1st piece, beg. at an ash in JAMES' Branch, the corner of the
200A survey, to the line of the 100A patented by ISAAC PARKER, to a turkey oak on
the edge of PARKER'S Branch, to ABSALOM STRICKLAND'S corner. The Sup. Ct.
of Wilmington Dist. awarded 133 pounds 3 shill & one penny to JAMES W. WALKER
for damages in suit against JAMES KENAN & also, 169 pounds 8 shill. & one penny
to ELIZABETH SIMPSON for damages in suit against HOLDEN McGEE. The Shff.
afsd. levied on 200A land "deeded from CHARLES JAMES to the sd. HOLDEN Mc-
GEE" & on 100A "formerly granted to ISAAC PARKER" & on 20A "joining the first"
totaling the 320A sold to DAVID CARLTON afsd. Wit: JOHN MAXWELL, JOSEPH
BRICE. Apr. Ct. 1810.

p. 116   FOUNTAIN WILLIAMS of Jones Co. to THOMAS JOHNSTON of Duplin Co.,

4 Nov 1809, for $150, 156A on the ES of the Beaverdam prong of Limestone Creek in 2 tracts to wit: (1) 106A beg. at a large white oak by the swamp & mouth of Cypress Branch, patented by ETHELDRED GREGORY in 1762; (2) 50A beg. at a gum & white bay on the sd. creek joining his own, THOS. QUINN, patented by LEWIS WILLIAMS in 1792. Wit: LOFTIN QUINN, STEPHEN (ſ) BROCK. Apr. Ct. 1810.

p. 118   WILLIAM (W) BUSH to his loving son JOHN BUSH, both of Duplin Co., 28 May 1806, for "natural love good will & affection" 170A in 2 tracts to wit: (1) 120A on BS of Maxwell Swamp, being part of 200A granted to WILLIAM RIGBY 25 July 1774, beg. at a maple on Maxwell Swamp in ALEXANDER HOLDEN'S line, joining WILLIAM HALL & crossing the Beaverdam; (2) 50A joining the above formerly granted to KEDAR HARRELL 10 Nov 1784, beg. at a pine on the SWS of Maxwell Swamp on the lower side the 2nd branch below the bridge, joining WILLIAM RIGBY, & PEARCE'S line (now SWINSON'S line). Wit: JAMES DICKSON, JONES DICKSON. Apr. Ct. 1810.

p. 119   PETER CARLTON to DAVID CARLTON, both of Duplin Co., 15 Aug 1805, for 100 pds. current money of N. C. 100A on the WS of Maxwell Swamp between ARMSTRONG'S Branch & Jamey's Branch, being part of the land that ALEXANDER ARMSTRONG sold to JOHN WATERS & by sd. WATERS to CHARLES JAMES, beg. at an ash tree on the run of JAMES' Branch, to ARMSTRONG'S Branch, joining McGEE & JAMES, to a pine an old corner of a survey of 200A patented by JAMES WILLIAMS & with sd. WILLIAMS' old line now PETER CARLTON'S line. Wit: JOHN WILKINSON, JOHN SWINSON. Apr. Ct. 1810.

p. 120   WILLIAM WATTS JONES, atty. at law of Wilmington to STEPHEN GIBBONS of Duplin Co., 4 Jan 1810, for 90 pds. 160A on the WS of the Northeast River on the branches of Island Creek, beg. at a water oak in Emanuel's Branch, joining EMMANUEL BOWZER, JOHN COOK'S old corner of 160A, JOHN AVER, JOHN COOK SENIOR'S line, to a stake at the confluence of Island Creek & Emanuel's Branch,   patented by JOHN COOK JUNR. & sold to WILLIAM JONES & afterwards by the Shff. of Duplin for the taxes & purchased by WILLIAM WATTS JONES. Wit: VINE ALLEN. Apr. Ct. 1810.

p. 122   JOHN WHITMAN (JUNR.) to JAMES WHITMAN, both of Duplin Co., 31 Mar 1810, for 50 pds. specie 50A on the WS of the Northeast River, beg. at a stake on his father's old line, joining JESSE NORRIS, JAMES MURRAY. Wit: ASA MURRAY, HENRY HULET. Apr. Ct. 1810.

p. 123   WILLIAM WORSLEY of Edgecombe Co. to CHRISTOPHER LAWSON of Duplin Co., 25 Jan 1808, for $174 current money of N. C. 230A on the NS of Panther Swamp in 2 tracts to wit: (1) 200A patented by SAMUEL JONES, beg. at 3 little pines on GEORGE SMITH'S line ES of a small branch, joining the Mill Swamp, the Blue Pond, NANCY BOWEN'S line to sd. SMITH'S line, to the run of Panther Swamp, to the lower line of the patent of the GEORGE SMITH survey. (The 2nd tract not described) Wit: OWEN O'DANIEL, H. GRADY. Apr. Ct. 1810.

p. 124   MARTIN (X) HANCHY to JAMES HARRELL, both of Duplin Co., 17 Feb 1810, for $360, 330A in 2 tracts to wit: (1) 200A beg. at a stake; (2) 130A the 8th & last corner of LEWIS THOMAS' survey of 500A, to a pine in the N edge of Pency Island, crossing Little Creek, to 2 bays by a thick Gaulberry Pond or Pocosin.

Wit: JOHN WHITMAN JUNR., BENJAM. (B) BRADSHAW. Apr. Ct. 1810.

p. 126   STEPHEN (ʃ) BROWN to JOHN PHILLIPS, both of Duplin Co., 10 Feb
1810, for $600, 155A on the SS of the Grove Swamp in 2 tracts to wit: (1) 105A beg.
at a bay in Buck Branch, to a dogwood & gum at the run of the Grove Swamp, to a
gum on Horse Branch, to the mouth of Buck Branch; (2) 50A being part of the
estate of WILLIAM RIGBY dec'd on the SS of the Grove Swamp, beg. at the lower
corner of the widow's dower on the run & runs with sd. line, to the run of Horse
Branch. Wit: ISAAC MIDDLETON, JOSEPH BRAY. Apr. Ct. 1810.

p. 127   J. (JAMES) HALL, Shff. to DAVID CARLTON, both of Duplin Co., 13 Oct
1804, for 165 pds. 13 shill. & 7 pence, 310A levied on by sd. Shff. & sold at public
auction to sd. CARLTON on 4 Nov 1803, which sd. land belonged to HOLDER
McGEE & HENRY CANNON. The Sup. Ct. of the Dist. of Wilmington awarded 165
pds. 13 shill. & 7 pence & costs to ELIZABETH SIMPSON for damages in suit
against sd. HOLDEN McGEE & others. The sd. 310A beg. at a poplar on the edge
of WILLIAM McGEE'S Mill Pond, about 60 yds.,above the Mill Pond, to an ash on
the run of ARMSTRONG'S or CHARLES JAMES' Branch, to WILLIAM McGEE'S
upper corner, to ARMSTRONG'S line of another survey, to a gum & maple at the
run of Maxwell, down the run as it meanders to the head of the Mill Pond, down the
pond to the beg. Wit: D. GLISSON & JOHN HUNTER. Apr. Ct. 1810.

p. 129   REUBEN NORRIS & JACOB TEACHEY (JUNR.) to JAMES HARRELL,
all of Duplin Co., 7 Feb 1810, for $150, 100A on Island Creek, beg. at a water oak
DAVID SLOAN'S corner on the run of Island Creek, running thence as SLOAN'S &
HANCHEY'S lines. Wit: JOHN WHITMAN JR., HENRY (H) ROUSE. Apr. Ct.
1810.

p. 130   WILLIAM THOMAS (SENR.) of Duplin Co. to his son ARCHIBALD
THOMAS, 24 Jan 1810, for 25 silver dollars & for "natural love & affection..."
a negro man slave named DENNIS, now in poss. of JOHN E. HUSSEY & by him
claimed for the heirs of ISAAC THOMAS dec'd & which sd. WILLIAM THOMAS
received from his father WILLIAM THOMAS dec'd in consequence of his LW & T,
giving to each of his the sd. WILLIAM THOMAS SENR.'S children a negro child in
rotation as they should be born of his negro woman slave PHILLIS & in consequence
of his dau. MARENDA dying under age of maturity & in her infancy, sd. WILLIAM
THOMAS SENR. deeds to his son the sd. ARCHIBALD THOMAS, the sd. MARENDA
having had a right & claim in rotation of sd. negro PHILLIS' increase. Wit:
WILLIE THIGPEN, REDICK (o) BROWN, JOHN THIGPEN. Apr. Ct. 1810.

p. 131   RICHARD (X) STRICKLAND to DAVID CARLTON, 26 Jan 1808, for 20 pds.
good & lawful money 24 1/2 A on the WS of Maxwell Swamp & on the SS Jammy's
Branch, being part of a grant of 100A granted to ABRAHAM BEESLEY, patented 1
Apr 1780, beg. at a white oak at the run of sd. branch sd. STRICKLAND'S corner
& joining DAVID CARLTON. (SARAH STRICKLAND also signed the deed - her
mark left blank.) Wit: SHADRACK CARLTON, MATTHEW (X) STRICKLAND.
Apr. Ct. 1810.

p. 132   HENRY GRADY to GEORGE F. KORNEGAY, both of Duplin Co., 5 Mar
1810, for $250, 250A in the fork of the Northeast River & Goshen in 2 tracts to wit:
(1) 150A granted to JOHN PICKNER below the mouth of Camp Branch, above
ALEXANDER ROUSE'S land, beg. at a pine by the marsh joining sd. ROUSE &

HOUSMAN'S Branch, except what WILLIAM WILLIAMS' survey of 640A & 100A patents now owned by FREDERICK GRADY on the mouth of Camp Branch may take off of the sd. 150A survey; (2) 100A beg. at a stake the 4th corner of sd. patents & runs with the giving line of sd. patent, joining A. GRADY SENR., A. GRADY JUNR. Wit: THOS. KING, LEWIS JONES. Apr. Ct. 1810.

p. 133   SAMUEL DUNN of Duplin Co. to JAMES DUNN of Sampson Co., 1 Dec 1809, for $1250, 415A on the SS of Panther Swamp, it being part of the land the sd. SAMUEL DUNN purchased from JAMES CLARK, beg. at a water oak, black gum & maple on the S edge of Panther Swamp at WILLIAM WHITFIELD'S line about 150 yds. above the upper end of the planta. where JAMES CLARK formerly lived. Wit: CHARLES HOOKS JUNR., WILLIAM DUNN. Apr. Ct. 1810.

p. 135   W. (WILLIAM) CHASTEN to BENJAMIN CHASTEN, both of Duplin Co., 29 Aug 1809, for $70, 35A beg. at a black gum on the main road in Cabbin Branch, to MRS. CHASTEN'S garden & RICHARD CHASTEN, being a patent granted to WILLIAM CHASTEN 27 Nov 1805. Wit: DAVID BROCK, JACOB (X) HARREL. Apr. Ct. 1810.

p. 136   JACOB MATHIS (JUNR.) to JAMES BUTLER, both of Duplin Co., 23 Dec 1809, for $150, 150A in the fork of the branch of Clear Run & being part of DAVID TUCKER'S entry. Wit: ABRAHAM JAMES, EDMUND MATTHIS. Apr. Ct. 1810.

p. 137   WILLIAM (X) KNOWLES of Duplin Co. to JOHN BONEY (co. not given), 13 Jan 1810, for $25, 44A on the SS of Mill Branch on the WS of the Northeast River, beg. at a bay in a small branch, along the old line, to a pine in a pond, the old corner, to a pine in small branch, from thence to the beg. Wit: TIMOTHY TEACHEY, R. HENRY. Apr. Ct. 1810.

p. 138   JAMES CHURCHWELL to WILLIAM CHURCHWELL, both of Greene Co., 2 Apr 1810, for $20, 36A on Burncoat, beg. at a stake on the run of sd. Burncoat SILAS CARTER'S corner, joining WILLIAM CHURCHWELL & SMITH, being land which descended to sd. JAMES CHURCHWELL by the death of his father WILLIAM CHURCHWELL. Wit: TH. HOLLIDAY, BENAJAH DIXON. Apr. Ct. 1810.

p. 139   WM. (WILLIAM) WATTS JONES of Wilmington, Atty. at law to WIMBRICK BONEY of Duplin Co., 15 Jan 1810, for $160, 640A being the lower or SE part of a survey of 1000A, beg. at a red oak & white oak one of the corners of the old patent near JESSE GEORGE'S land, being patented by WILLIAM JONES & sold by the Shff. of Duplin Co. for taxes & purchased by WILLIAM WATTS JONES. Wit: DANIEL BONEY, C. SHAW. Apr. Ct. 1810.

p. 140   J. (JOHN) D. BLUDWORTH to BRITAIN POWELL, both of Duplin Co., 7 Sep 1807, for $260 lawful money of N. C. a negro girl named LUNER about 15 yrs. of age & her increase. Wit: JOHN HUFHAM. Apr. Ct. 1810.

p. 141   WM. (WILLIAM) ALBERSON to SAMUEL ALBERSON, both of Duplin Co., 16 Jan 1794, for 200 pds. good & lawful money of N. C. 275A in 2 tracts: (1) 75A in the fork of the Northeast & Burncoat Swamp, being part of a tract of 125A granted by patent to LEWIS POWELL 30 Mar 1754, incl. the Island between the E & W runs of Burncoat Swamp & the NE bridge where the sd. ALBERSON'S new field now is & c., beg. at a stake in the run of Burncoat Swamp the upper line of the patent, joining

LEWIS BARFIELD'S line; (2) 200A on BS of the Northeast Swamp incl. the bridge near the mouth of Burncoat Swamp & part of the great road, beg. at a white oak the 1st station of 200A patented by GEORGE SMITH on the open line of his old survey of 125A joining WILLIAM KORNEGAY & his own, being the contents of a patent granted to WILLIAM HUBBERD 11 July 1788. Wit: THOMAS WRIGHT, SHADK. WOOTEN. Apr. Ct. 1804.

p. 143   NEEDHAM (N) GARNER to SIMEON GARNER, both of Duplin Co., 5 Dec 1807, for 20 pds. current money of N. C. for 6 head of cattle, 5 head of hogs, 1 feather bed & furniture, 5 barrels of corn, 2 stocks of fodder & all my household goods & working tools. Wit: MOSES STANLEY, NICHOLAS (X) BOWDEN. Apr. Ct. 1810.

p. 143   J. (JOHN) WILSON to BENJAMIN HODGES, both of Duplin Co., 4 Apr 1810, for $450 2 negroes, one wench named LINTZ about 16 yrs. of age & her child a girl about 2 yrs. old called FILLIS & their future increase, "reserving to my grand- mother SUSANAH HOOKS the use of sd. negroes during her natural life." Wit: ALEXR. HERRING. Apr. Ct. 1810.

p. 144   WILLIAM KORNEGY (SENR.) of Duplin Co. to his beloved son GEORGE FISHER KORNEGAY (co. not given), 22 Apr 1806, for "natural love & affection" a negro woman named HAGAR & her child BEN, to take poss. of them immediately after his death & the death of his wife ELIZABETH KORNEGAY * if the sd. GEORGE FISHER KORNEGAY should die without lawful heirs of his body, the sd. negro woman & her child & increase to return to the brothers & sisters of the sd. GEORGE F. KORNEGAY. Wit: EDWARD ALBERSON, FRED. GRADY. Apr. Ct. 1810.

p. 145   JAMES WHITBEE (co. not given) to JOHN MAXWELL (co. not given), 7 Mar 1810, for $325 a negro boy named SIMEON about 14 yrs. old. Wit: JOHN THALLEY. Apr. Ct. 1810.

p. 145   BENJA. (BENJAMIN) BEST to JOHN PHILLIPS, both of Duplin Co., 31 Oct 1808, for 150 pds. a negro girl slave named SARAH about 10 yrs. of age. Wit: JOSEPH BRAY, CATHARINE QUINN. Apr. Ct. 1810.

p. 146   JOHN WILKINSON of Duplin Co. to his children JAMES CLARK WILKIN- SON, MARY JANE WILKINSON, ELIZABETH ANN WILKINSON & HARRIET WIL- KINSON, 16 July 1810, for "natural love & affection" the following negroes to wit: LEW 18 yrs. old, MINT about 16 yrs of age, LUCE about 8 yrs. of age & VIRGIL about 1 yr. old, they being the children of a certain negro woman named SYLVIA. Wit: JAMES McGOWEN, JAMES HALL. July Ct. 1810.

p. 147   JOSEPH (X) SCREWS to JESSE SCREWS, both of Duplin Co., 23 Jan 1810, for $38, 150A on the SS of Cypress Creek, adj. his own land whereon he now lives, beg. at a stake E edge of a branch his own line & corners on the line of New Han- over Co., to a water oak in Dog Branch, patented by JOSEPH SCREWS in 1794. Wit: MOSES MANNING, JAMES SCREWS, NATHAN (W) BEAGLIN. July Ct. 1810.

p. 148   JOSEPH (X) SCREWS to JAMES SCREWS, both of Duplin Co., 23 Jan 1810, for $38, 150A on the ES of Cypress Creek & BS of Cabbin Branch, beg. at a stake JESSE SCREW'S corner, joining JESSE SCREWS, being part of a patent

granted to JOSEPH SCREWS in 1794. Wit: MOSES MANNING, NATHAN (𝑤/)
BEAGLIN. July Ct. 1810.

p. 149   WILLIAM GLISSON & Mary (X) GLISSON (co. not given) to LEVIN WAT-
KINS of Duplin Co., 17 July 1810, for 30 pds. current money of N. C. 40A on the
NS of Goshen Swamp, beg. at a lightwood stake the 2nd corner of BENNITT MILL-
ARD'S division of sd. land on the back line near the road, joining JESSE MILLARD'S
division to the given line on the run of Goshen, being the middle division of a tract
sold & conveyed by ASA ROGERS to HEZEKIAH MILLARD of 150A & since in conse-
quence of the death of the sd. HEZEKIAH MILLARD, persuant to an order of the Co.
Ct. of Duplin, directing a subdivision of all the lands owned & poss. by the sd.
MILLARD at the time of his death to be made amongst his several children, claiming
their equal division of their sd. dec'd father's lands & the sd. 40A herein above
describes, being surveyed & valued was drawn by MARY MILLARD, dau. of sd.
HEZEKIAH MILLARD & now the wife of the sd. WILLIAM GLISSON. Wit: DAVID
WRIGHT, LEVIN WATKINS JUNR. July Ct. 1810. MARY GLISSON was privately
examined by DAVID WRIGHT, J. P. & B. BOURDEN, J. P. & declared she signed
the above deed of her own free will & consent 16 July 1810.

p. 151   NATHAN FOUNTAIN of Duplin Co. to MILES THIGPEN of Jones Co., 29
Nov 1809, for $300, 125A in 2 tracts to wit: (1) 50A on the ES of the Northeast
River & on the SS of Muddy Creek, beg. at a pine the 4th corner of the survey from
which this land was deeded, being granted to HENRY PICKETT & deeded from him
to JAMES PICKETT who deeded to AMOS PARKER & from sd. PARKER to JAMES
BATTS who deeded to JEREMIAH WILLIAMS & from him to sd. FOUNTAIN; (2) 75A
beg. at a pine on PICKET'S line WILLIAMS' corner, through the Dark Ponds to a
water oak, to a stake on PICKET'S line. The last 75A was sold from CHARLES
GOFF to AMOS PARKER who deeded to JAMES BATTS & from sd. BATTS to JERE-
MIAH WILLIAMS & from him to NATHAN FOUNTAIN. Wit: JOB THIGPEN, MARY
FOUNTAIN. July Ct. 1810.

p. 152   WIMBRICK BONEY to JOHN BONEY, both of Duplin Co., 8 June 1810, for
$140, 70A on the WS of Little Rockfish, beg. at a pine his lower corner on the SW
side of sd. swamp adj. BLAKE. Wit: T. TEACHEY, JOHN STALLINGS. July Ct.
1810.

p. 153   MAURICE MOORE of N. C. (co. not given) to DAVID HOOKS of Duplin Co.,
4 Oct 1807 for 1200 silver dollars 250A on the NS of Bear Swamp in 2 tracts to wit:
(1) 225A beg. at a water oak at the mouth of a small branch about 1/4 mile from the
main road, joining MICHAEL BYRD, GILBERT McCALOP'S back line, the lower
line of sd. McCALOP'S old survey to the run of Horse Pen Branch; (2) 25A joining
the above survey incl. the planta. on the SS of the main road where JOHN BYRD formerly lived, beg. at a hickory on the bank of the run of Gilbert's Branch & runs
thence a dividing line with NEEDHAM BLOUNT'S line, to the run of Horsepen
Branch, to the mouth of Gilbert's Branch to the beg. Wit: C. HOOKS, ANN HOOKS.
July Ct. 1810.

p. 155   NEEDHAM BLOUNT to DAVID HOOKS, both of Duplin Co., 13 July 1810,
for $700, 188A in 2 tracts to wit: (1) 103A between Goshen Swamp & Bear Swamp on
the SS of Poley Bridge Branch & on the WS of the road, beg. on McCALEP'S old line,
joining BRANCH, BLOUNT & McCALEB'S old corner; (2) 85A adj. the former tract
where GILBERT McCALEB lived of the land formerly sold & conveyed from HENRY

EUSTACE McCULLOCH to GILBERT McCALEB, beg. at a stake in the run of Horse Pen Branch in the main roads, joining MAURICE MOORE'S boundary to the turn of the road, thence a dividing line between sd. BLOUNT to sd. MOORE, to a hickory on a bank on the run of Gilbert's Branch, to McCALEB'S old corner, joining WM. BRANCH, MATTHEW BRANCH, to a black gum in the fork of Horse Pen Branch. Wit: D. WRIGHT, L. DICKSON. July Ct. 1810.

p. 156   JACOB MATHIS (JUNR.) to AUSTIN BEESLEY, both of Duplin Co., 13 July 1810, for $50, 50A on the SS of Miller's Swamp on BS of Spring Branch, incl. the Alligator Pond, beg. at the upper end of the Big Hucklebury Pond at sd. BEES-LEY'S elbow corner on a pine, to an agreed corner on a line patented in 1784 by JACOB MATHIS SENR. Wit: DAVID (X) TUCKER, JOSEPH (X) MATHIS. July Ct. 1810.

p. 157   EDWARD (X) ERWIN to LOFTIS NETHERCUT, both of Duplin Co., 11 Jan 1808, for $150, 146A being part of a survey of 500A, by patent granted to GEORGE SMITH on the ES of the Northeast on the head of Burncoat Swamp, beg. at a pine by a pond that drains into Tuckahoe, across the head of Burncoat to a black gum in a branch of sd. swamp ... to the beg. Wit: CHRISTOPHER LAWSON, MARTIN ERWIN. July Ct. 1810.

p. 158   JACOB MINSHEW to JESSE TURNAGE, both of Duplin Co., 16 Aug 1808, for $320, 250A on the SWS of Cabbin Branch, beg. at a pine on the SES of sd. branch PHILIP STONE'S patent corner, which land includes part of a patent granted to sd. STONE & part of a patent granted to sd. LANGSTON, incl. the houe and planta. whereon he now lives. Wit: B. KORNEGAY, JAMES WATKINS. July Ct. 1810.

p. 160   THOS. (THOMAS) BARNARD of Pasquotank Co. to DR. LEVI BORDEN, 21 Apr 1810, for $800 good & lawful money 5 negroes to wit: a negro woman slave named SUCKY about 26 yrs. of age, with her 4 children; namely, one girl LYDIA about 7 yrs, one boy PASIS about 5 yrs, one girl JANE about 2 yrs. one girl LUCY about 5 months. Wit: COLIN SHAW, WM. BECK JR. July Ct. 1810.

p. 160   DD. (DAVID) WILLIAMS, constable of Duplin Co. to JOHN HUFHAM, 12 May 1809, for $276.86, "by virtue of 3 executions, JAMES CORBED vs. against JOHN D. BLUDWORTH, amounting to $74.94, also one morgage vs. JOHN HUF-HAM against sd. BLUDWORTH, amounting to $200, levied on & sold 7 negroes to wit: NAN, EADE, EMANUEL, NANCY, ABRAHAM, LINKHAM, BOB, being the prop. of JOHN D. BLUDWORTH, at which sale JOHN HUFHAM, Esqr. became the highest bidder. Wit: MAURICE FENNEL, WM. DEVANE. July Ct. 1810.

p. 161   ELISHA POWELL & FRANCES (X her mark) DEVANE, both of New Hanover Co. to ABRAHAM NEWTON of Duplin Co., 2 Mar 1810, for $250 lawful money of N. C. a negro girl NAN about 10 yrs. of age & her increase. Wit: HOWARD HARLEY, JAMES NEWTON. July Ct. 1810.

p. 161   DANIEL ALDERMAN to his son ELISHA ALDERMAN, both of Duplin Co., 11 Apr 1810, for "love, good will & affection" all the lands in his poss. on a branch of Rockfish called Pharis's Creek "which quantity courses & distances he doth here omit" with reservation that sd. DANIEL ALDERMAN & his wife SARAH ALDERMAN shall have a full free right & privilege to the sd. lands, planta. house & etc. during their natural lives. Wit: JAMES NEWTON, DAVID ALDERMAN. July Ct. 1810.

p. 163   FELIX K. HILL (co. not given) to JOSEPH GREEN of Wayne Co., 20 Oct 1807, for $3,200, 425A in 2 tracts to wit: (1) 300A on the SS of Long Branch, beg. at a maple on the run of sd. branch, adj. WILLIAM BECK & WILLIAM BROAD-HURST; (2) 125A on the SS of Long Branch & ES of Goshen Swamp below WILLIAM BROADHURST'S planta., beg. at a black gum & ash on the main run of Goshen Swamp, joining sd. BECK'S corner & BROADHURST. Wit: A. HURST, RO. G. GREEN, WILLIS SIKES. July Ct. 1810.

p. 164   D. L. (DANIEL LOVE) KENAN, Shff. to LEWIS BARFIELD, both of Duplin Co., 1 Jan 1810, for 22 shill. & 6 pence 99A lying on Bear Marsh, beg. at a stake on the 1st line of a surveyof 100A laid off by order of the Co. Ct. of Duplin for HENRY McCULLOCH. The sd. land was surveyed by BASIL KORNEGAY, Esqr. of sd. Co. & LEWIS BARFIELD became the bidder for sd. land at public auction, the taxes for the sd. land being unpaid for the year 1807. Wit: JOHN WHITEHEAD. July Ct. 1810.

p. 165   LUKE WARD of Smith Co., Tenn. to JAMES WRIGHT of Duplin Co., 1 June 1810, for $917, 300A in 2 tracts to wit: (1) 225A beg. at a large maple at the run of Bear Swamp, the mouth of Hog Pen Branch; (2) 75A beg. at a black gum & white oak a corner of the above survey, to a new marked line made for a dividing line between LUKE WARD & JAMES WRIGHT, thence along sd. line a westwardly course to the main road, joining sd. WRIGHT. Wit: CH. HOOKS, ANN HOOKS. July Ct. 1810.

p. 167   BENJAMIN HERRING (SENR.) to his son BENJAMIN HERRING JUNR., 25 Nov 1808, for "natural love & affection" 229A in 2 pieces to wit: (1) 227A on the WS of Herring Branch, beg. at a gum & joining CREECH; (2) 2A joining the lower cor-ner of the afsd. land on the ES of sd. branch, the 2A for privilege for a mill. Wit: ALEX O'DANIEL, BENJN. (X) CREECH. Jan. Ct. 1810.

p. 168   WILLIAM (X) BROCK to his son JAMES BROCK, both of Duplin Co., 9 May 1810, for "natural love & affection" 100A on the ES of the Beaverdam prong of Limestone Creek, beg. at a red oak the 2nd corner of a survey of 40A belonging to LEWIS BROCK, to a corner formerly made for LOTT GREGORY'S 200A survey & joining JOHNSTON'S line. Wit: LOFTIN QUINN, THOMAS (T) JOHNSTON. July Ct. 1810.

p. 169   FELIX K. HILL of Sampson Co. to JAMES WINDERS of Duplin Co., 1 Feb 1810, for $10, 10A on the SS of Goshen Swamp & head of Cross Branch, beg. at the 3rd corner of JOHN WARD'S land about 100 yds. E of MRS. GREGORY'S old house & joining GREGORY & WARD. Wit: CHARLES HOOKS, ANN HOOKS. July Ct. 1810.

p. 170   ROBERT SOUTHERLAND to ROBERT BISHOP, both of Duplin Co., 11 Aug 1809, for 5 pds. specie 30A on the SS of Limestone Swamp, beg. at a pine BISHOP'S corner, to a poplar in the Miery Glade in SWINSON'S line, to ROBERT BISHOP'S corner, being part of 200A of land patented by sd. ROBERT SOUTHERLAND. Wit: DAVID SOUTHERLAND, PHILL SOUTHERLAND. July Ct. 1810.

p. 172   WILLIAM POLLOCK, Patent No. 1570, 16 Mar 1799, for 50 shill. for

every 100A, 56A on the ES of Buck Hall, a branch of Stewart's Creek, beg. at a
pine, adj. JOHN VALENTINE TAYLOR, JAMES THOMPSON, JAMES KENAN &
surveyed by JOSEPH DICKSON. Wit: W. R. DAVIE, Esqr. Gov. Signed by WILL
WHITE, Sec. & T. MALONE, P. Sec.

p. 173   LEWIS BARFIELD, Patent No. 1913, 1 Dec 1808, for 50 shill. for every
100A, 7A on the ES of Bear Marsh & on the NS of the main road joining his own &
TURNAGE'S lines, beg. at a stake his & sd. TURNAGE'S corner in their field.
Entered 9 Dec 1807 & surveyed by BASIL KORNEGAY 8 Sep 1808. Wit: BENJAMIN
WILLIAMS, Esqr. Gov. WM. M. WHITE, Dist. Sec.

p. 173   ISAAC DUNKAN to LEMUEL CHERRY, both of Duplin Co., 2 Mar 1810,
for $1150, 300A beg. at a white oak by the run of the Northeast & running up a
branch that makes out of Thunder Swamp Pocosin, to sd. DUNKAN'S old patent corner, joining JOHNSTON & FRANCIS OLIVER, to a sweet gum in the Northeast Pocosin. Wit: WM. BIZZELL, JESSE BIZZELL. July Ct. 1810.

p. 175   HARDY CARRELL to WILLIS CARRELL, both of Duplin Co., 26 June 1810,
for $200, 295A on BS of Stewart's Creek, beg. at a pine on the WS of the marsh at
JOSEPH BOWEN'S old corner, joining CHARLES MERRITT & all that part of a new
survey of sd. HARDY CARRELL called the surplus land contained in sd. old lines of
above mentioned lands. Wit: ZEBULON HOLLINGSWORTH, DANIEL WEST. July
Ct. 1810.

p. 176   ELIJAH (( ) BOWEN to WILLIAM KNOWLS, both of Duplin Co., 15 Jan
1806, for 10 shill. specie 44A on the Mill Branch on the SS of sd. branch, on the WS
of the Northeast River, beg. at a bay in sd. branch, to a pond, the old corner, down
the run of sd. branch to the beg. Wit: JOHN STALLINGS, JOHN BONEY. July Ct.
1810.

p. 177   B. (BENJAMIN) HODGES to JESSE MILLER, both of Duplin Co., 13 Jan
1809, for $800, 200A on the NS of Goshen Swamp & BS of Dry Pond Branch, beg. at
a black gum in sd. branch, JACOB TAYLOR'S & sd. MILLER'S corner & runs their
dividing line to a stake in sd. MILLER'S field, along THOMAS BENNET JUNR.'S
line, adj. GULLY & DICKSON, the sd. 200A being where WILLIAM CHERRY formerly lived. Wit: LEWIS TINER, JOHN BRADLEY, WM. CHERRY. Jan. Ct.
1810.

p. 179   C. (CHARLES) HOOKS to OWEN O'DANIEL, both of Duplin Co., 18 Apr
1809, for $45, 391A on the ES of the Northeast lying on the waters of the Indian
Branch, Poley & Tandam Branches, being part of a patent granted to DAVID GREER
of 640A & conveyed from him to HENRY HALSEY who conveyed to sd. HOOKS, beg.
at a pine called the stooping pine on the NS of the Indian Branch, running the course
of the patent, to a corner of STEPHEN MILLER'S which he made on the line when he
run out of his 249A, out of the same patent, which he purchased at public auction,
thence the course of MILLER'S line to his other corner, to a pine below the marsh
of Tandam Branch to the 2nd line of the patent, to a spruce pine the 3rd corner of
the patent to the beg. Wit: WILLIAM McGEE, DAVID KORNEGAY. July Ct. 1810.

p. 180   ABEL CROOM STROUD of Duplin Co. to ABSALOM BOYETT of Lenoir
Co., both planters, 6 May 1809, for $100 specie 100A on the White Oak Swamp, beg.
at a lightwood stump the 2nd corner of sd. patent adj. THOMAS SHELTON, to the

mouth of Spring Branch & joining TRUET, being part of 2 patents; one taken up by ANTHO. WILLIAMS of 93A, the other by MILLS MUMFORD for 640A. Wit: WM. H. HERRING, WM. ALBERTSON. Jan. Ct. 1810.

p. 181   JNO. (JOHN) WILLIAMS (co. not given) agent for THO. BARNARD (co. not given) to JOSEPH GILLESPIE (co. not given), 19 Apr 1810, for 225 spanish milled dollars for one negro girl named MIRRIAM 10 yrs. of age. Wit: A. McINTIRE, THOMAS MOLTON. July Ct. 1810.

p. 182   JAMES HALL (co. not given) to JAMES DICKSON (co. not given), 18 July 1810, for $337.50 a negro girl named CATE about 18 yrs. of age. Wit: S. HOUSTON. (D. L. KENAN also signed the deed) July Ct. 1810.

p. 182   JAMES DEVANE of New Hanover Co. to ISAAC HALL of Duplin Co., 27 Apr 1810, for $340, 2 negroes to wit: LUCY about 40 yrs. of age & BURR, a boy about 6 yrs. of age. Wit: JNO. HUFHAM, J. MONK. July Ct. 1810.

p. 183   EDWARD FRANKLIN to JONATHAN JOHNSTON, both of Duplin Co., for $200 lawful money one negro boy named CALEB about 6 yrs. of age. Wit: ABRAHAM NEWTON. Dated 18 June 1810. July Ct. 1810.

p. 183   THOS. (THOMAS) GOFF to SHADRACK STALLINGS, both of Duplin Co., 22 Apr 1810 (sum not given) a negro fellow named DICK about 38 yrs. of age. Wit: JOHN STALLINGS, WILLIAM STALLINGS. July Ct. 1810.

p. 184   ISAAC DUNKAN (co. not given) to LEMUEL CHERRY (co. not given), 2 Mar 1810, for 100 pds. good & lawful money of N. C. one negro boy named JIM about 6 yrs. of age. Wit: GEORGE CHERRY, WM. BIZZELL. July Ct. 1810.

p. 184   AARON MORGAN to DAVID MIDDLETON, both of Duplin Co., 31 July 1810, for $1250 current money of N. C. 500A on the SS of Stewart's Creek, beg. at a sweet gum on the run of the sd. creek, at the mouth of Camp Branch, being part of a survey purchased by JAMES GILLESPIE from JOHN JOHNSTON & by the exrs. of sd. GILLESPIE sold to AARON MORGAN. Wit: JOSEPH GILLESPIE, SUSAN GILLESPIE. Oct. Ct. 1810.

p. 186   EDWARD ALBERSON, Patent No. 1946, 6 Dec 1809, for 50 shills. for every 100A 165A on the head of the Great Branch, beg. at a pine WINDOL DAVIS' corner joining DAVIS, BUSHEE, RACHEL DAVIS, LARRANCE, SAMUEL SOWELL. Entered 17 Jan 1809, surveyed by SAMUEL DAVIS. Countersigned by JOHN FARRIOR, Sur. Wit: DAVID STONE, Esqr. Gov., WILL WHITE, Sec.

p. 187   ABRAHAM JOHNSTON, Patent No. 1939, for 50 shills. for every ___A, 15A on the NS of Calf Pasture Branch, beg. at a maple in the run of sd. branch, to a pine in the edge of a marsh in NORRIS' line, joining KORNEGAY & REUBEN JOHNSTON. Entered 17 Jan 1809. Surveyed by JOHN FARRIOR 11 Nov ___. Wit: DAVID STONE, Esqr., WILL WHITE, Sec., WM. M. WHITE, P. Sec.

p. 188   JOHN (X) COOPER SENR. of Onslow Co. to JOHN COOPER JUNR. of Duplin Co., 15 Apr 1809, for $2,000, 485A on the NS of the Grove Swamp, beg. at an ash on the run of the Grove at BENJAMIN BEST'S lower corner, joining STEPHEN BROWN'S house, to a bunch of bays in Sandy Branch about 30 yds. below the road, up the run of Silver Branch as it meanders to a pine in the head of sd. branch, joining ANDREW STOAKES, HOGAN HUNTER & COOPER'S own corner, to a pine on Rocky Branch & down sd. branch as it meanders to the mouth in the Grove. Wit: JOHN PHILLIPS, SAMUEL MIDDLETON. Oct. Ct. 1810.

p. 189 WILLIAM MATTHIS to JACOB MATHIS JUNR., both of Duplin Co., 5 Mar 1807, for 100 pds. current money of N. C. 170A on the SES of Stewart's Creek & on BS of Miller's Mill Swamp, being part of a survey, beg. at a cypress on the NS of sd. swamp, ARTHUR MATHIS' corner, along DAVID TUCKER'S line to a pine on the edge of Clear Run Branch, to a water oak at the Poley Causway, being the contents of a patent granted to JACOB MATTHIS SENR. 10 Nov 1784. Wit: JOHN MATTHIS, HENRY PORTER. Oct. Ct, 1810.

p. 190 ALEX(ALEXANDER) CARTER of Duplin Co. to CONSIDER BUSHEE of Lenoir Co., 20 Feb 1810, for $30, 30A on the waters of Matthews Branch, beg. at a black jack BUSHEE'S corner & runs along his line to JONATHAN NICKENS' line & along his line to the run of the nigh prong of Long Branch, up sd. branch to BUSHEE'S other line where it crosses sd. branch. Wit: ED. ALBERSON, HEZE-KIAH (X) BLIZZARD. Oct. Ct. 1810.

p. 191 ABRAHAM JOHNSTON of Duplin Co. to JESSE NORRIS of Wayne Co., 18 May 1810, for 11 pds. 5 shill. 15A on the NS of the Northeast Swamp & on the NS of the Calf Pasture Branch, beg. at a maple on the run of sd. branch, to a pine in the edge of a marsh on NORRIS' line, adj. KORNEGAY & REUBEN JOHNSTON, sd. land entered 17 Jan 1809 & patented by ABRAHAM JOHNSTON. Wit: DM. GRADDY & JOHN (X) ROUCE. Oct. Ct. 1810.

p. 193 ISAAC (Ŧ) SPENCE, planter of Duplin Co. to GILES THOMAS LOFTIN of Lenoir Co., 9 Oct 1810, for $574.50 good & lawful money of N. C. 193A on BS of the road between Goshen & the Northeast, incl. a place called the Lake Savannah & the planta. whereon the sd. ISAAC SPENCE now lives, it being land formerly patented by JESSE BARFIELD & part of a small survey patented by sd. SPENCE, beg. at a pine by his fence a corner of the ____ he sold to JOHN SCREWS & runs with sd. SPENCE'S old line along his fence, along BARFIELD'S old line to a pine stump of his corner, then along BARFIELD'S other line, to a white oak in the Northeast Pocosin his corner, joining OLIVER, to a stake in the Lake Meadow, JOHN SCREW'S corner. Wit: WM. DICKSON. Oct. Ct. 1810.

p. 195 MICHAEL WILKINS (SENR.) to GEORGE KORNEGY SENR., both of Duplin Co., 1 Oct 1803, for 95 pds. 350A in 3 tracts to wit: (1) 150A on the ES of the Northeast & BS of the Horse Pen Branch, incl. the house & planta. whereon he now lives joining sd. KORNEGAY'S line, beg. at a water oak & gum in sd. branch on sd. KORNEGAY'S line; (2) 100A beg. at the before mentioned stake on KORNEGAY'S line, the last corner of the afsd. survey & runs with his old line to a pine KORNE-GAY'S corner; (3) 100A joining the afsd., beg. at a pine the 4th corner of the old survey, joining JOHN KETHLEY, KORNEGAY, SAMUEL HERRING & the edge of Cypress Meadow. Wit: SAMUEL HERRING, JOSEPH WHITFIELD. Oct. Ct. 1810.

p. 197 BRYAN (X) MINSHEW & his wife PATSEY (X) MINSHEW & JOHN (X) PEAL to SAMUEL BOWDEN JUNR., all of Duplin Co., 14 Mar 1807, for $500, 214A on the NS of the Northeast Swamp & BS of the main road joining the Juniper Pond, incl. the house & plnata. where sd. MINSEY now lives, it being the land

descending to them by heirship from DAVID PEAL dec'd, beg. at a stake in COX'S
Meadow, along NATHANIEL PRICE'S line, joining ROBERTS' corner, to a black
jack near ROGERS' old path, to a pine in the Currant Pond, along WINFIELD'S old
line to the beg. Wit: JAMES BOWDEN, JAS. WHITFIELD. Oct. Ct. 1810.

p. 198   JAMES WILLIAMS to JESSE WILLIAMS, both of Duplin Co., 31 Dec 1810,
for 250 pds. 150A on BS of Muddy Creek, beg. at a sweet gum, white oak & pine
sapling by an old red oak stump in the edge of a Cypress Pond, the 1st station of
STEPHEN HOLLINGWORTH'S old survey, to a dividing line between SOLOMON
PICKETT & WILLIAM HOLLINGSWORTH.   (NANCY WILLIAMS also signed the deed)
Wit: (none given). Apr. Ct. 1811.

p. 199   STEPHEN GUFFORD, planter, to JESSE OUTLAW, both of Duplin Co.,
17 Dec 1802, for 25 pds. 54A between the Northeast & Goshen Swamp & on the ES of
Hall's Marsh, joining BRYANT SULLIVANT & his own line, beg. at a pine SULI-
VANT'S corner. Wit: JESSE SWINSON, J. GUFFORD. Oct. Ct. 1810.

p. 201   SAM. (SAMUEL) EVANS to JAMES MORRIS, both of Duplin Co., 29 Sep
1810, for $50, 18A on the NS of Rockfish Creek on a branch called Boney's Branch,
beg. at a pine by JACOB BONEY'S line. Wit: JACOB WELLS, JOHN BLANTON.
Oct. Ct. 1810.

p. 202   GEORGE JOURNEGAN HODAM to JAMES JOURNEGAN, both of Duplin Co.,
_____1804, for "love good will & affection" 70A beg. at a pine in a prong of
SOUTHERLAND'S Marsh on NEW'S line & joining DUNCAN. Wit: B. KORNEGAY,
JESSE SWINSON. Oct. Ct. 1811.

p. 203   CASON (X) HARRIS to JESSE OUTLAW, both of Duplin Co., 10 Feb 1802,
for 41 pds. current money 100A on BS of SOUTHERLAND'S Marsh, beg. at the run
where JOHN NEW'S line crosses sd. marsh, up sd. marsh to the mouth of Long
Branch joining JOHN SULIVANT'S line where it crosses the branch & joining
MOLPHER'S & along his line to JOHN NEW'S line. Wit: LEWIS GRIMES, GEORGE
J. HODUM. Oct. Ct. 1810.

p. 204   HENRY (X) BEST to FRANCIS WILLIAMS, both of Duplin Co., 20 Feb
1806, for 142 pds. current money of N. C. 100A on the Beaverdam Swamp & on a
branch called the Spring Branch, incl. the sd. BEST'S impr. where the newly
settled, beg. at a pine & water oak in the head of Spring Branch. Wit: BENJAMIN
BEST, THO. PHILLIPS. Oct. Ct. 1810.

p. 206   EPHRAIM (X) BOYET to FRANCIS WILLIAMS, both of Duplin Co., 24 Apr
1810, for 230 pds. 170A on the NS of the Grove Swamp & BS of the main road, beg.
at the mouth of Rocky Branch & runs down the run of the Grove Swamp as it meanders to the mouth of Oaky Branch. Wit: B. BEST, J. COOPER. Oct. Ct. 1810.

p. 207   D. L. (DANIEL LOVE) KENAN, Shff. of Duplin Co. to WILLIAM CARR
(co. not given), 18 Apr 1809, for $55.50, 100A bid off by EDWARD ARMSTRONG
for sd. CARR at public sale, the sd. land on Doctor's Creek, beg. at a cypress in
the creek swamp, JAMES RAWLING'S corner. A certain judgment was obtained by
EZEKIAL DUNCAN against HENRY COOK & execution issued thereon which was for
want of any goods & chattels of sd. HENRY COOK, levied on the sd. 100A, which
judgment was returned to the Ct. of Duplin, whereon a vendition as exponas issued

from the Clk. of Ct. & directed to sd. Shff. to expose sd. land for public sale. Wit:
EDWARD ALBERSON. Oct. Ct. 1810.

p. 208   JOSIAH (*9*)OUTLAW to JAMES JOURNEGAN, both of Duplin Co. , 20 Aug
1801, for 60 pds. current money 165A on the NS of Goshen Swamp & ES of Halls
Marsh, being part of a tract of 300A granted by patent to JOHN SULLIVAN, beg. at
a lightwood tree near a meadow his own corner, down the run of the Long Branch as
it meanders to where his line of the new survey crosses sd. SOUTHERLAND'S
Marsh a little below JOSIAH OUTLAW'S old house, incl. JOSIAH OUTLAW'S impr.
Wit: OWEN O'DANIEL, HAMPTON SULIVENT. Oct. Ct. 1810.

p. 210   JOHN JERNIGAN, planter, to JACOB GILMORE, both of Duplin Co. , 7
Oct 1809, for 200 pds. current money of N. C. 153A in 2 tracts to wit: (1) 80A in
the Piney Woods on the head of the Great Branch, beg. at a pine THOMAS
TAYLOR'S old corner adj. BLIZZARD'S old line; (2) 73A on Rattlesnake Swamp,
beg. at a gum in sd. swamp JESSE JOURNEGAN'S lower corner below the field &
runs along his dividing line to a stake on ANTHONY JONES' line, thence along the
dividing line between him & his sister SALLY BRANCH. The 2 tracts being the sd.
JOHN JOURNEGAN'S share of the lands of his dec'd father ELISHA JOURNEGAN &
also 1/3 of his father's lands which were laid off to ZILPHA JOURNEGAN, the
widow of the sd. ELISHA JOURNEGAN by her dower in sd. lands, which will be sd.
JOHN JERNIGAN'S after the death of sd. ZILPHA. Wit: WM. FREDERICK JUNR. ,
JOHN GULLY. Oct. Ct. 1810.

p. 212   WILLIAM JAMES (SENR.) to JAMES MURRAY, both of Duplin Co. , 5 May
1810, for $250, 150A on the ES of Fussel's Creek, beg. at a water oak at the run of
Fussel's Creek at the mouth of a small branch, joining RIVINGBARK'S corner at the
run of Pery Branch. Wit: JOHN STALLINGS, DANL. JAMES. Jan. Ct. 1811.

p. 213   DD. (DAVID) WILLIAMS, constable of Duplin Co. to ABRAHAM NEWTON
(co. not given), 9 Nov 1810, for $395.35, "by virtue of sundry executions to me
directed in favor of sd. NEWTON, LEVI MERRIT & JOSEPH BRICE to sell 4
negroes by the name of HESTER, PAT, SIMON & JUDE at public auction. " Wit:
MAURICE FENNEL. Jan. Ct. 1811.

p. 214   DD. (DAVID) WILLIAMS, constable of Duplin Co. to ABRAHAM NEWTON
(co. not given), 28 Dec 1810, for $61.10, "by virtue of sundry executions to me
directed in favor of sd. JAMES DEVANE & sd. NEWTON, to sell a negro named
JOHN at public auction." Wit: AMBROS SMITH, ENOCH NEWTON. Jan. Ct. 1811.

p. 214   JOHN FLOWERS, Patent No. 1951, 26 Nov 1810, for 210A on the SS of the
head of the Northeast Branch, incl. part of the impr. of WILLIAM DUNKAN dec'd,
beg. at a gum & white oak at the run of sd. branch, to a small white oak supposed
to be JACOB DUNKAN'S corner. Surveyed 25 Aug 1810 by JOHN FARIOR, Sur.
Assigned by DAVID STONE. WM. WHITE, Sec.

p. 215   MICHAEL GLISSON, Patent No. 1956, 26 Nov 1810, for 200A on the NS of
the Northeast & BS of Matthews Branch, beg. at a stake his corner on the NS of
Matthews Branch, about 1/2 a mile above CARTER'S Mill Dam, to a maple CAR-
TER'S corner on Matthews Branch above the road & with sd. CARTER'S line to a
water oak on an island in Matthews Branch, joining HENRY GRADY on the side of
the Northeast, to GLISSON'S own corner, to CARTER POMPHREY'S corner, to

CARTER'S Mill Pond, to CARTER'S other corner, to the beg. Surveyed by C. HOOKS 20 Oct 1800. Assigned by DAVID STONE. WM. WHITE, Sec.

p. 216   MICHAEL GLISSON, Patent No. 1976, 3 Dec 1811, for 80A on the ES of the Northeast River & NS of Matthews Branch, beg. at a pine H. GRADY'S corner of a 200A survey, adj. EDWARD ALBERSON, SAMUEL DAVIS, CARTER & H. GRADY. Surveyed 13 July 1811 by H. GRADY, Dist. Sur. & JOHN FARIOR, Sur. Assigned by BENJ. SMITH. WILL HILL, Sec.

p. 216   ROBERT BISHOP (JUNR.) to WILLIS BISHOP, both of Duplin Co., 21 Jan 1811, for $100, 100A on the ES of the Northeast River & ES of Gum Swamp, a branch of Limestone Swamp, beg. at a white oak THOMAS QUINN'S corner, joining JOHN WILLIAMS. Wit: MOSES MANNING, PHILL SOUTHERLAND JUNR. Jan. Ct. 1811.

p. 217   JOHN MATTHIS to JOHN D. BLUDWORTH (cos. not given), 14 Mar 1809, for $42, "by virtue of sundry executions to me delivered against WILLIAM DE-VANE have levied the same on a negro man named HARTWELL, commonly called BLAKE, the prop. of sd. DEVANE which negro the sd. DEVANE mortgaged to JOHN CARLTON after the execution was levied, having again got the sd. negro into poss., I have exposed him to public sale for the purpose of satisfying the above execution & JOHN D. BLUDWORTH became the highest & last bidder." Wit: JUNIUS BLUDWORTH, ABRAHAM NEWTON. July Ct. 1811.

p. 218   J. D. (JOHN D.) BLUDWORTH of Duplin Co. to JUNIUS BLUDWORTH (co. not given), 19 Dec 1810, for $130 a negro man named JACK, formerly the prop. of THOMAS DEVANE dec'd. Wit: JOHN PAGE, JOHN JOHNSON. July Ct. 1811.

p. 219   JOHN D. BLUDWORTH of Duplin Co. to JUNIUS BLUDWORTH of New Hanover Co., 12 Sep 1809, for $400 a negro man slave named BLAKE. Wit: MAURICE FENNEL, EDWARD FENNEL. July Ct. 1811.

p. 219   BRYAN WHITFIELD of Lenoir Co. to JOSEPH SPEARS HARDIE of Greene Co., 1 Jan 1807, for 83 pds. current money 83A on the NS of the Northeast Branch of Cape Fear River in 2 tracts to wit: (1) 72A being part of a tract of 100A granted to JESSE BARFIELD 17 Dec 1778, beg. on the 2nd line of the sd. tract where KOR-NEGAY'S line crosses, near Bale's Branch & joining KORNEGAY; (2) 11A granted to BUCKNER KILLEBREW 28 Aug 1795, beg. at a white oak in the run of Bale's Branch & joining KORNEGAY. Wit: JAMES YOUNG, AB. CROOM, MICHL. BELLOON. Oct. Ct. 1809. JOS. G. WRIGHT J.S.C.L.E.

p. 221   JOHN GOODING & MARY GOODING his wife of Craven Co. to HANNAH WOODS, JAMES MURDOCK, DAVID MURDOCK, WILLIAM MURDOCK & ELIZA-BETH MURDOCK, orphans of _____, (co. not given), 29 Jan 1806, for 750 pds. 813A in 3 tracts to wit: (1) 330A (the Court House Lot excepted) on the SS of the Grove Swamp, beg. at THOMAS ROUTLEDGE'S corner near the run of the swamp, down the dividing line to a white oak in the Mill Branch, crossing the head of Pasture Branch; (2) 173A joining & opposite the 1st tract on the NS of the Grove Swamp, beg. at an ash in the run of the swamp, a corner of OBADIAH EVANS' tract; (3) 310A on the SS of the Grove, incl. the Indian Grave on the main road, beg. at a pine MARY McCULLOCH'S corner on WILLIAM FREDERICK'S line, joining ISAAC HUNTER, JAMES & a white oak his corner in the Mill Swamp & WILLIAM

FREDERICK (excepting from the last described tract about 50 or 60A conveyed by the sd. MARY, their MARY MURDOCK to WILLIAM McGEE) provided always & this conveyance is made upon that express condition, that if all or any of the above parties of the 2nd part, or any for them shall hereafter claim any share or portion in the personal estate of the late JOHN OSBURN POWELL, then this conveyance shall be void as to such person who may make such claim in the above premises, shall go to the use & benefit of JAMES DICKSON, admr. of sd. JOHN OSBURN POWELL. Wit: HANNAH BROWN, CHRISTOPHER W. MASTERS. The above deed was probated 30 Jan 1806 at New Bern & JOHN LOUIS TAYLOR, J. S. C. & C. privately examined MARY GOODING who consented for her husb. to sell sd. land.

p. 223   JOHN JOHNSTON to ANDREW McINTIRE, both of Duplin Co., 8 Nov 1804, for 17 pds. 19 shill. current money of N. C. 50A on the NS of the Grove Swamp & in Gum Branch, beg. at a water oak in a drain on the WS of Gum Swamp. Wit: JOHN WILKINSON, JOHN MURROW JNR.

p. 224   JOHN HUNTER to ANDREW McINTIRE, both of Duplin Co., 25 Oct 1804, for 36 pds. current money of N. C. 72A on the NS of the Golden Grove Swamp, beg. at a cypress on the N run of sd. swamp. Wit: H. McCANNE, JEREMIAH PEARSALL. Apr. Ct. 1805.

p. 226   WILLIAM CARR to WILLIAM WRIGHT RIVENBARK, 20 Dec 1809, for $85 200A on the NS of Doctors Creek, beg. at a cypress in the creek swamp JAMES RAWLINS' corner. Wit: WILLIAM GREER, SAMUEL COX. July Ct. 1811.

p. 227   FREDERICK (F) RIVENBARK to JOHN GORE, both of Duplin Co., 11 Sep 1810, for $120 current money of N. C. 22A in the fork of Cow Marsh & Buck Hall, beg. at a sweet gum. Wit: AARON MORGAN, WILLIAM GORE. Jan. Ct. 1811.

p. 228   ROBERT (X) PEAL to NATHAN BRACKSTON, both of Duplin Co., 29 Oct 1810, for $95, 109A on the NS of the Northeast Swamp, beg. at a juniper in the Juniper Pond, ROGERS' old corner, at present JOHN ROBERTS', it being the 2nd corner in the 2nd lot, in the division of the lands of DAVID PEAL dec'd, joining PRICE, BOURDEN (formerly MINSEY), being part of a survey conveyed by deed from NATHAN PEAL to sd. DAVID PEAL & in the division of sd. PEAL'S estate was laid off to sd. ROBERT PEAL. Wit: B. KORNEGAY, SAMUEL SMITH. July Ct. 1811.

p. 229   JO. (JOSEPH) GILLESPIE & DAVID GILLESPIE, exrs. of the L. W. & T. of JAMES GILLESPIE dec'd to AARON MORGAN, 7 May 1805, for $3,554, principle & interest, 1440A on a branch of Black River known by the name of Stewart's Creek in 2 tracts to wit: (1) 840A purchased of JOHN JOHNSTON who sold to JAMES GILLESPIE 10 Dec 1787; (2) 600A on the ES of Stewart's Creek, on the heads of KENAN'S Branch, beg. at a pine the lower side of sd. branch his own corner of 100A patented by BENJAMIN JOHNSTON, to the corner of 240A patented by FELIX KENAN, to a supposed corner of a 200A survey patented by JOSEPH WILLIAMS & joining THOMAS CARLTON. Wit: SHADRACK STALLINGS, THO. WRIGHT. Jan. Ct. 1811.

p. 231   REUBEN NORRIS to EDWARD STREET, both of Duplin Co., 12 Jan 1811, for $100, 100A on the WS of the Northeast River on the NS of Island Creek & on BS of the Mill Branch, beg. at 2 pines, joining LEWIS THOMAS & JOHN EVERS. Wit:

THOMAS EVANS, DAVID EVANS. July Ct. 1811.

p. 232   ELIZABETH (✗) KNOWLES, EMANUEL (X) KNOWLES & JAMES (X)
KNOWLES to BENJAMIN FUSSEL, all of Duplin Co., 28 Apr 1810, for $100 lawful
money 100A on a branch of Rockfish called Reedy Branch, beg. at a pine on
MESHACK STALLINGS' line, joining WALLACE & STALLINGS. Wit: BYRD
WILLIAMS, ZILPHA WILLIAMS. July Ct. 1811.

p. 233   BENJAMIN DUFF to JACOB WELLS, both of Duplin Co., 5 Feb 1811, for
$196, 88A on the SES of Fussel's Creek, beg. at a water oak & black gum HAW-
KINS' beg. corner at the run of sd. creek. Wit: BONEY WELLS, STEPHEN (S)
MILLS. July Ct. 1811.

p. 234   WILLIAM (X) KNOWLS to STEPHEN MILLS, both of Duplin Co., 19 Sep
1805, for $150 lawful money of N. C. 125A on the lower side of Fussel's Creek &
on the NS of Rockfish Creek, beg. at a white oak on the WS of Harry's Branch,
JOHN HAWKIN'S line, by BENJAMIN FUSSEL'S line, cont. by patent 250A, for 1/2
of sd. patent being the 125A afsd. on the SS of the main road whereon sd. KNOWLS
now resides. Wit: WM. W. RIVENBARK, MARK (X) BOWEN. July Ct. 1811.

p. 236   CHARLES KING of Duplin Co. to THEOPHILUS BARFIELD of Wayne Co.,
23 Jan 1811, for $3,500 current money of N. C. 1000A on the NS of Goshen Swamp,
beg. at 2 small sweet gums at the mouth of Blount's Branch where it empties into
Friar's Branch, joining WIGGINS' old corner in Friar's Branch & also joining
ROUSE, KING, WARREN, POWELL, FLOWERS & BURNHAM, to a lightwood stump
in Edy's Pocosin & down sd. pocosin as it meanders to the head of Blount's Branch.
Wit: JOHN ELIOT, JOHN SMITH. July Ct. 1811.

p. 237   JONATHAN KEITHLEY to his son RICHARD KEITHLEY, both of Duplin
Co., 8 Aug 1810, for "natural love & affection" 170A beg. at a poplar on the run of
a small branch of the Mirey Branch & joining JOHNSTON'S line to the run of sd.
branch, up the Little Branch to the beg. Wit: SM. DAVIS, RACHEL KETHLEY.
Oct. Ct. 1810.

p. 238   JANE (X) SOUTHERLAND to GEORGE SOUTHERLAND, both of Duplin
Co., 15 Oct 1810, for $75, 110A being 1/2 of the tracts of land on the SS of King's
Branch, it being the sd. JANE'S right as heir at law equal with sd. GEORGE to her
father JOHN SOUTHERLAND dec'd real estate to wit:(1) 200A beg. at a red oak in
the SS of the Pritty Branch WILLIAM McCURDY'S corner, joining FELIX KENAN,
LEWIS THOMAS & McCURDY, patented 10 Nov 1784 by JOHN SOUTHERLAND; (2)
20A beg. at a water oak in a pond his own corner on KENAN'S line, joining LEWIS
THOMAS & with SOUTHERLAND'S own line to the beg., patented by sd. SOUTHER-
LAND 16 Mar 1799. Wit: C. HOOKS, A. HURST. Oct. Ct. 1810.

p. 239   DANIEL (X) WOOD to JOHN GREEN, both of Duplin Co., 9 Apr 1807, for
$130 lawful money 100A on BS of a branch of Rockfish called the Pig Pen Branch,
beg. at a pine to a stake in the edge of Redy Branch, to a stake on the old line & to
the other old line the ES of Pig Pen Branch. Wit: WM. W. RIVENBARK, TIMO-
THY GREEN. Oct. Ct. 1810.

p. 241   JOHN THIGPEN to BRYTHAL THIGPEN his son, both of Duplin Co., 6 Oct
1810, for "love & affection" 194A on BS of the Beaverdam prong of Limestone Creek,

beg. at a maple on the side of the swamp, joining THOMAS QUINN'S beg. corner,
to small pines in the line near a small branch between JOHN THIGPEN'S &
THOMAS QUINN'S fences, down the branch as it meanders to the White Oak Branch,
to the main road, across the swamp to WALLER'S line & his 4th corner, to the run
of Limestone, up the run to the beg., being part of 2 surveys, one patented by
SOLOMON COX 29 Oct 1782; the other by sd. THIGPEN 24 Dec 1798. Wit: JOS. T.
RHODES, JAMES HALL. Oct. Ct. 1810.

p. 242   WIMBERK BONEY to TIMOTHY TEACHEY SENR., both of Duplin Co., 28
June 1810, for 500 pds. or $1,000, 497A in 2 tracts to wit: (1) 200A on the WS of
the Northeast River & N of Rockfish Creek lying on Little Rockfish the NS, being
part of a survey of land that DANIEL TEACHEY SENR. bought of JOHN RUTHER-
FORD & conveyed to sd. WIMBERK BONEY SENR., beg. at a poplar on the NS of
Little Rockfish near the Iron Mine Branch in the mouth of a small branch, joining
WILLIAM BONEY & JOHN BONEY'S lines to a corner of a 70A survey & that line to
a pine at the side of Little Rockfish Swamp; (2) 100A joining the same on the WS of
sd. survey, beg. at a pine 40 yds. from the corner, on or near the old line, to the
beg.; (3) 197A on the drains of Harry's Branch, beg. at 2 small short leafed pines,
JACOB WELLS JUNR.'S corner. Wit: JOHN STALLINGS, JOHN BONEY. Oct. Ct.
1810.

p. 243   DANL. (DANIEL) SOUTHERLAND to NICHOLAS SANDLIN, both of Duplin
Co., 1 Jan 1810, for $200, 267A on the ES of the Northeast River, beg. at 3 gums
on the run of a branch with AUSTON BRYAN'S line, to a pine formerly called
DANIEL SOUTHERLAND'S corner, joining BRYANT FARRIOR, WILLIAM FARRIOR.
Wit: ROBERT SOUTHERLAND, PHILL SOUTHERLAND SENR. Oct. Ct. 1810.

p. 245   EPHRAIM (X) BOYT to ARTHUR BOYT, both of Duplin Co., 25 Nov 1797,
for 57 pds., 57A on the NS of the Grove Swamp, beg. at a gum in the mouth of
Dark Pond Branch, joining the back line of EPHRAIM BOYT'S 100A survey. Wit:
BENJAMIN BEST, JOHN BEST. Oct. Ct. 1810.

p. 246   DAVID GARRISON to LOVE SAVAGE, both of Duplin Co., 17 Jan 1810, for
35 pds. 100A between Persimmon & Stocking Head Branches, beg. at a pine
ROUSE'S corner, joining JACOB HANCHEY & JOHN MILLER, being part of a patent
granted to WILLIAM DICKSON & ROBERT DICKSON for 640A 4 May 1769. Wit:
PHILL SOUTHERLAND, RACHEL (X) JOHNSTON. July Ct. 1811.

p. 247   THO. (THOMAS) KENAN & D. L. (DANIEL L.) KENAN to AUSTON BEE-
SLEY, all of Duplin Co., 20 Sep 1810, for 40 cents per acre 431A on the heads of
the branches of Rockfish & Beesley's Mill Swamp, beg. at a stake & runs with
DAVID CARLTON'S line, joining SHADRACK STALLINGS. THOMAS KENAN &
D. L. KENAN acting exrs. of the L. W. & T. of JAMES KENAN, Esqr. dec'd.
Wit: H. JAMES, S. STALLINGS. Oct. Ct. 1810.

p. 248   JOHN THIGPEN to WILEY THIGPEN his son, both of Duplin Co., 6 Oct
1810, for "love & affection" a deed of gift for 218A on a branch of Limestone Swamp,
a little above the Watering Hole, beg. at a pine ROBERT WHITE'S 3rd corner,
joining WALLER & the main road towards Limestone, to 2 marked pines on the SS
of the road, to sd. WHITE'S 2nd corner, being the contents of a patent granted to
ELIJAH WALLER for 200A & 18A of a tract of 200A patented by sd. THIGPEN 16
Mar 1799. Wit: JOSEPH T. RHODES, JAMES HALL. Oct. Ct. 1810.

p. 249   JAMES KINNARD of Duplin Co. to SOLOMON ROUSE of Lenoir Co., 28 Nov 1804, for 1130 pds. current money, 635A on the NS of Goshen in 6 tracts to wit: (1) 40A beg. at a stake at the mouth of Tyler's Branch, joining KING, sd. KINNARD, the mouth of White Oak Branch; (2) 100A being a patent granted to JOHN WILLIAMS 20 June 1746, incl. the planta. whereon JOSEPH SANDERFER now lives; (3) 60A beg. at an ash & maple in the main run of Goshen Swamp by WIGGINS' upper corner, joining sd. KINNARD, to a white oak in Grantham's Branch, joining JOHN BECK, granted to JOHN BECK & sold to sd. KINNARD'S father by WILLIAM, JOHN & STEPHEN BECK, heirs of their father JOHN BECK; (4) 185A beg. at a black gum on the run of Goshen Swamp & along JONATHAN TAYLOR'S line, being the lower part of a tract of 580A granted to ROBERT WARREN 21 Apr 1764; (5) 150A beg. on the WS of the main road & runs along POWEL'S line to Grantham's Branch & joining KINNARD, being part of the afsd. patent granted to ROBERT WARREN; (6) 100A beg. at MICAJAH HILL'S corner on JONATHAN TAYLOR'S line, joining CHARLES WOLF & PEREGRINE JOHNSTON, granted to JOHN HAYNES by patent dated 15 Dec 1778. Wit: CHARLES KING, HENRY (H) ROUSE, B. ROBIN HOOD. Oct. Ct. 1810.

p. 251   FREDK. (FREDERICK) GRADY to his dau. SALLY OUTLAW, both of Duplin Co., 20 Nov 1809, a negro girl named ANAKY & all her increase, to hold after his death & not before without his consent. Wit: DURHAM GRADY, ELISHA GRADY. Oct. Ct. 1810. (A deed of gift)

p. 252   JNO. (JOHN) WILLIAMS (co. not given) to WILLIAM PICKET (co. not given), 21 Apr 1810, for 5 spanish milled dollars one negro boy named SAM, one named JERRY & one negro woman named FANNY. Wit: THO. MOLTEN, A. McINTIRE. Oct. Ct. 1810.

p. 253   MICHAEL BONEY (co. not given) to ASA MURRAY (co. not given), 15 Oct 1810, for $450 a negro boy named JIM about 14 yrs. of age. Wit: WM. (X) SWEETMAN, AMOS (X) SHUFFLE. Oct. Ct. 1810.

p. 253   FREDK. (FREDERICK) GRADY to his dau. CHARITY GRADY, both of Duplin Co., 20 Nov 1809, a negro girl named SUCKY & all her increase if any, to hold after his death & not before without his consent. Wit: DURHAM GRADY, ELISHA GRADY. Oct. Ct. 1810. (A deed of gift)

p. 254   FREDK. (FREDERICK) GRADY to his dau. ELIZABETH GRADY, both of Duplin Co., 20 Nov 1809, a deed of gift for a negro girl named ROSE & all her increase if any, to hold after his death & not before without his consent. Wit: DURHAM GRADY, ELISHA GRADY. Oct. Ct. 1810.

p. 255   JONATHAN THOMAS to MARTHA BOYET, both of Duplin Co., 1 May 1810, for 40 pds. 48A beg. at a willow in a drain of Ash Branch, to a dead pine formerly LEWIS THOMAS' corner & joining BLACKMORE. Wit: BENJA. BEST, SARAH BEST. Jan. Ct. 1811.

p. 256   ABEL (Z) DAIL (DEAL) to his son ISAAC DEAL, _____1810, for "natural love & affection" 273A in 3 tracts to wit: (1) 54A on the SS of the Northeast Marsh & on the ES of the Miery Branch, beg. at a poplar on sd. branch, incl. the place where the sd. ABEL DEAL now lives, being the contents of a patent granted to SAMUEL ROGERS; (2) 29A joining the 1st, beg. at a black jack the corner of sd. ROGERS' survey, adj. GODWIN'S corner of the land JONATHAN KETHLEY now lives on, to a

stake in the side of Bales' Pocosin, to a black jack on ROGERS' line, being part of
a tract patented by GEORGE SMITH; (3) 190A on the SS of the Northeast Marsh on
BS of the Mirey Branch joining the land sd. DEAL now lives on, beg. at a poplar
the beg. corner of SAMUEL ROGERS' survey, crossing the sd. branch, adj.
SAMUEL ALBERSON, ROGERS, GEORGE SMITH'S old line in Mirey Branch, being
part of a patent of 300A granted to GEORGE SMITH 29 Oct 1782. The sd. ABEL
DEAL & MARY DEAL his wife to have their lifetime rights on sd. land. Wit:
ELIZABETH DAIL, RICHARD KEITHLEY. Jan. Ct. 1811.

p. 258   JOHN JOHNSTON to STEPHEN MILLER, both of Duplin Co., 21 Jan 1811,
for 25 pds. 42A on the WS of the Northeast River, being part of a survey patented
by BENJAMIN JOHNSTON, beg. at a pine or the SS of the main road joining the
land the sd. MILLER purchased of BORTHWICK GILLESPIE. Wit: A. HURST,
JO. GILLESPIE. Jan. Ct. 1811.

p. 259   WILLIAM (X) WOOD & MARY (X) WOOD to ADAM TAYLOR, all of Duplin
Co., 29 Dec 1810, for $20 (acreage not given) land on the ES of the Northeast
River between Cypress Creek & Holly Shelter on Poley Bridge Branch, beg. at a
pine near the road, to a stake in the center of 3 pines, crossing the road to a white
oak in the branch by a large poplar, thence to the beg., being land patented by
WILLIAM ROGERS in 1782 & fell to sd. MARY WOOD by heirship & to the sd.
WOOD by marriage. Wit: BENJAMIN PADGET, CHARLES ( )) PEARCE. Jan.
Ct. 1811.

p. 260   JOHN THIGPEN, DICY (X) THIGPEN, ANNICE (X) THIGPEN, WILEY
THIGPEN & BRYTHAL THIGPEN, heirs in part of the estate of the sd. ALLEN
THIGPEN dec'd, the sd. JOHN THIGPEN being the admr. of sd. ALLEN THIGPEN
dec'd, to DAVID WILKINS, all of Duplin Co., 31 Dec 1810, for $300 lawful money
of U. S. 100A on the SS of Limestone Creek, being part of 3 surveys formerly the
prop. of HICKS MILLS & by him conveyed to BENJAMIN DULANY who conveyed to
ALLEN THIGPEN 2 Dec 1805, beg. at a gum in a branch by the planta. now occupied
by the widow of HICKS MILLS, being part of the estate of ALLEN THIGPEN dec'd &
sold for the benefit of the heirs. Wit: ABRAHAM HALL, WILLIAM NATHERCUT.
Jan. Ct. 1811.

p. 261   MARK (W) ROGERS to NEEDHAM WATERS, both of Duplin Co., 14 Jan
1811, for $357.60, 140A on the NS of Goshen Swamp, incl. the drains of Fryar's
Branch, beg. at a gum on the run of the branch sd. ROGERS' corner, adj.
WILLIAM BURNHAM & BRYAN. Wit: WILLIAM BECK JUNR., THOMAS WRIGHT.
Jan. Ct. 1811.

p. 262   JAMES HALL of Duplin Co. to EZLER KILPATRICK of Lenoir Co., 7 Nov
1810, for 450 pds. 548A in 3 tracts to wit: (1) 368A beg. at a stake on the river
bank below the bridge, adj. JOHN BROCK, it being part of a patent of 580A granted
to WILLIAM DICKSON, ARCHIBALD GILLESPIE & ANDREW McINTIRE bearing
date 23 Dec 1763; (2) 80A on the ES of the Northeast River, beg. at a holly, hornbeam & an old cypress on the river bank supposed to be on BROCK'S line, adj.
JAMES GILLESPIE; (3) 100A on the ES of the Northeast River, beg. at a pine
ABRAHAM NEWKIRK'S corner on the old line of the 580A survey patented by
GILLESPIE, DICKSON & McINTIRE, adj. BROCK'S corner of a survey of 150A.
One acre of the 1st mentioned survey to remain for the use & purpose of keeping up
a house of worship as also an exception of WILLIAM SOUTHERLAND'S stock having

the liberty of ranging on sd. 100A last mentioned during the sd. SOUTHERLAND'S life & no longer. Wit: JOHN HUNTER, JOHN BEST. Jan. Ct. 1811.

p. 265   WM. (WILLIAM) HOLLINGSWORTH, BENJAMIN LANIER, JOHN LANIER, JAMES LANIER, JESSE LANIER, ELIZABETH LANIER & MARY ANN LANIER, heirs of LEWIS LANIER dec'd (co. not given) to JOHN RAINER (co. not given), 20 Sep 1810, for 5 pds. 200A possessed of LEWIS LANIER dec'd; one piece patented by JOHN HALSO, 75A, part of one piece patented by BENJAMIN LANIER 75A, cont. in the whole 200A. (Deed reads as though the acreage may be only 175A.) Wit: JAMES LANIER. Jan. Ct. 1811.

p. 266   ADAM (A) PLATT to WILLIAM BROWNING, both of Duplin Co., 20 July 1810, for $20, 100A on the NS of Rockfish Creek on BS of the Big Branch of Fussel's Creek, beg. at a gum in a small branch on the line of the survey patented by AARON WILLIAMS, crossing the Big Branch, to a stake by the Double Horsepen Pocosin, being the contents of a patent granted to sd. EDWARD DICKSON 11 July 1788 & from him to ADAM PLATT. Wit: WM. McCANNE, JOHN McCANNE. Jan. Ct. 1811.

p. 267   LEWIS BARFIELD, planter, to LEWIS HERRING, both of Duplin Co., 16 Nov 1810, for $75, 99 3/4A on the head of Bear Marsh, being part of a tract of 500A granted to BAKER BOURDEN, beg. at the 3rd corner from the beg. of sd. survey at a pine in the head of Bear Marsh, patented 29 Oct 1782. Wit: LN. (LEVIN) WATKINS, LEWIS HINES, PETER WATKINS. Jan. Ct. 1811.

p. 268   DICKSON SULIVAN to SAMPSON GRIMES, both of Duplin Co., 21 Jan 1811, for $11, 10A on the NS of Goshen Swamp & ES of Rooty Branch, beg. at a gum in a small branch in the patent line. Wit: JAS. DICKSON, W. SOUTHERLAND, PHILL SOUTHERLAND JR. Jan. Ct. 1811.

p. 269   DAVID BROCK, planter, & his wife PENELOPE (X) BROCK to RAWLEY LEBERRY, all of Duplin Co., 13 Sep 1808, for 101 pds. 90A on the Rooty Branch, beg. at a poplar in sd. branch, being a tract of land which fell to PENELOPE SULLIVAN, the wife of DAVID BROCK & now sold by the sd. PENELOPE & DAVID BROCK her husband to the sd. LEBERRY. Wit: JESSE SWINSON, JOHN (X) BROCK. Jan. Ct. 1811.

p. 270   JAMES WATKINS of Duplin Co. to his dau. POLLY WATKINS (co. not given), 22 Dec 1810, a deed of gift for one negro boy named JACK about 17 yrs. of age. Wit: D. HOOKS. Jan. Ct. 1811.

p. 271   JAMES WATKINS to DAVID HOOKS, both of Duplin Co., 19 Dec 1810, for 150 pds. a negro boy named DANIEL about 12 yrs. Wit: PATRICK BRYAN. Jan. Ct. 1811.

p. 272   JAMES WATKINS to JOSEPH DICKSON, both of Duplin Co., 29 Dec 1810, for $300 a negro girl named BIDDY about 13 yrs. of age. Wit: JNO. WATKINS. Jan. Ct. 1811.

p. 272   LOTT BATTLE, admr. of FREDERICK BATTLE dec'd (cos. not given) to NATHAN FOUNTAIN (co. not given), 21 Jan 1811, for $600 by note, 6 months credit, 3 negro slaves AHF, SERENA & JAMES. Wit: JOB THIGPEN. Jan. Ct. 1811.

p. 272   JONATHAN JOHNSTON to JOHN HUFHAM, both of Duplin Co., 1 Sep 1810, for $200 lawful money one negro boy by the name of CALEB about 6 yrs. of age. Wit: (none listed) Jan. Ct. 1811.

p. 273   SAML. (SAMUEL) ALBERSON to SARAH ALBERSON, both of Duplin Co., (date not given), for 150 pds. one negro girl named MOURNING. Wit: EDWARD ALBERSON, DAVID ALBERSON. Jan. Ct. 1811.

p. 273   STEPHEN GRANT of Wayne Co. to ALEXANDER CARTER of Duplin Co., 28 Dec 1810, for $400 3 negro slaves to wit: CHERRY about 30 yrs., BRYANT her child 2 yrs., MILLY of the age of 5 weeks. Wit: EDWARD ALBERSON, J. T. BRYAN. Jan. Ct. 1811.

p. 274   ABRAHAM NEWKIRK of New Hanover Co. to JOSEPH KENEDY of Duplin Co., 18 July 1809, for 150 pds. 199A on the WS of the Northeast River in 2 tracts to wit: (1) 100A beg. at a pine on the river bank BLAKE'S corner & adj. COX; (2) 99A beg. at a red oak in the 1st line of the above & runs with WILLIAM or DAVID GILLESPIE'S line, being the greater part of a grant to GILLESPIE for 100A dated 22 Dec 1768. Wit: LOFTEN QUINN, JOSEPH MALLARD. Jan. Ct. 1811.

p. 275   JOHN BRITTON of Onslow Co. to NEWMAN EDWARDS of Duplin Co., 25 Apr 1810, for $70 lawful money of the U. S. 150A on the ES of the Northeast of Cape Fear River & NS of Little Limestone & BS of Wild Cat Branch, beg. at a holly at the run of Wild Cat Branch MATTHEW EDWARD'S corner, to a small pine on the NW edge of Cuffer Branch, adj. JAMES WHALEY, patented by sd. BRITTON 31 Sep 1785. Wit: FREDERICK WOOD, HENRY WOOD. Jan. Ct. 1811.

p. 276   JOHN HUFHAM & J. (JOHN) D. BLUDWORTH to ISAAC HALL, all of Duplin Co., 8 Mar 1810, for $190 a negro girl named NAN about 6 yrs. of age. Wit: EZEKIAL (X) MERRIT. Jan. Ct. 1811.

p. 277   JAMES WATKINS of Duplin Co. to BETSEY WATKINS (co. not given), 11 Jan 1811, for "natural love & affection" one negro girl named SPICY about 14 yrs. of age. Wit: D. HOOKS, ALEX. HERRING. Jan. Ct. 1811.

p. 278   NICHOLAS BOURDEN to BRYAN BOURDEN, both of Duplin Co., 10 Sep 1810, for $325 lawful money of N. C. 2 negro children slaves to wit: a boy named KEDAR 4 yrs. old & a girl named ROSE about 3 yrs. old. Wit: READIN BOURDEN & SIMEON GARNER. Jan. Ct. 1811.

p. 279   AMOS JOHNSTON HARRIS, planter, to JESSE LANIER, both of Duplin Co., 11 Dec 1810, for $100, 125A joining his own line, consisting of all the land sd. HARRIS is now possessed of on the SS of the Long Branch, incl. 2 surveys patented by AMOS JOHNSTON, part of a survey patented by JAMES LANIER, part of a survey patented by ROBERT LAND, beg. at a poplar JESSE LANIER'S own corner. Wit: NATHAN WALLER, JAMES LANIER, JOHN (X) LANIER. Jan. Ct. 1811.

p. 279   DAVID CARLTON to ARCHIBALD CANADA, both of Duplin Co., 5 June 1809, for 14 pds. 18A on the WS of Maxwell Swamp, beg. at a pine sd. CARLTON'S corner. Wit: A. MORGAN, JESSE JONES. Jan. Ct. 1811.

p. 281   WILLIAM (H) HUNTER (SENR.) to JESSE BROWN, both of Duplin Co.,

30 Oct 1810, for $200 lawful money of the U. S. 100A on the ES of the W prong of Muddy Creek, beg. at a pine in JOHN BROWN'S old patent, now sd. HUNTER'S, to a chinquapin in the bent of Jacob's Branch, on sd. JESSE BROWN'S former line, adj. WOODWARD'S & LEA'S lines to the W edge of Jacob's Branch, being part of 2 surveys, one patented by JOSHUA LEA & one by JOHN WOODARD for 270A. Wit: ISAAC BROWN, HOWEL HUNTER. Jan. Ct. 1811.

p. 282   WM. (WILLIAM) PICKETT to JOHN FARRIOR SENR., both planters of Duplin Co., 20 Dec 1810, for $257.50, 250A on the NS of Muddy Creek & BS of the Long Branch in 2 tracts to wit: (1) 150A beg. at a pine; (2) 100A beg. at a black jack on the back line on THOMAS PICKET'S line, being part of a 300A patent granted to JOHN McGEE 22 July 1774 lying in the NW corner of sd. patent. (The heading of the deed says 450A.) Wit: JOHN FARRIOR JUNR., F. PICKETT. Jan. Ct. 1811.

p. 283   JAMES BONEY to MESHACK STALLINGS, both of Duplin Co., 9 June 1807, for $25, 25A beg. at a lightwood stump, a corner of the red house land. Wit: ROBERT TATE, WRIGHT BONEY. Jan. Ct. 1811.

p. 284   H. (HENRY) GRADY to ALEXANDER CARTER, both of Duplin Co., 5 Mar 1808, for 23 pds. 23A on the NS of Mathews Branch, beg. at a poplar in the Juniper the beg. of a survey granted to THOMAS ROUTLEDGE. Wit: EDWARD ALBERSON & JAMES STEWART. Jan. Ct. 1811.

p. 285   JESSE (*9*) BROWN to DREW HALL, both of Duplin Co., 6 Nov 1810, for 20 pds. lawful money of the U. S. 100A on the SS of Steven's Swamp, beg. at a holly at the run of the sd. swamp, being part of a tract surveyed for sd. BROWN. Wit: ISAAC WHALEY, ISAAC BROWN. Jan. Ct. 1811.

p. 286   JOHN KORNEGAY, planter, to BASIL KORNEGAY, both of Duplin Co., 8 June 1810, for $2,000, 700A in 2 tracts to wit: (1) 550A on the SS of the Northeast Swamp, beg. at a white oak in the sd. Northeast Swamp EDMOND DUNCAN'S old corner, adj. HENRY KORNEGAY, JACOB DUNCAN; (2) 150A on the head of the Northeast Swamp & Deep Gully Branch, beg. at a pine a corner of ELIJAH JONES, to a white oak in Little Pocosin, being the contents of a deed from sd. JONES & BENJAMIN WESTON to JACOB KORNEGAY SENR. & by sd. KORNEGAY'S estate laid off to GEORGE KORNEGAY who conveyed to sd. JOHN KORNEGAY. Wit: JOHN OLIVER, LEWIS BARFIELD. Apr. Ct. 1811.

p. 288   JOHN KORNEGAY to BASIL KORNEGAY, both of Duplin Co., 13 Apr 1811, for 50 pds. 40A on the head of the Northeast Swamp, beg. at a white oak ISAAC SPENCE'S corner & runs also JACOB KORNEGAY'S old line, adj. DUNCAN'S old line, JACOB KORNEGAY'S other old corner, to a white oak in the pocosin, being part of a survey granted to ISAAC SPENCE & by him conveyed to JOHN KORNEGAY. Wit: ELISHA JONES, ABRAHAM JOHNSTON. July Ct. 1811.

p. 289   NATHAN WALLER to ISOM LANIER, both of Duplin Co., 21 Dec 1809, for $30, 100A on the Back Swamp & on the ES of the Northeast River, beg. at a sweet bay & maple & loblolly bay in the edge of the swamp a little below an old field & about a mile below the mouth of the Horsepen Pocosin Branch, as by patent granted to sd. WALLER 20 Dec 1789. Wit: JAMES LANIER, HOSEA LANIER. Jan. Ct. 1811.

p. 290   CHARLES (( ) BOSTICK to JAMES HALL JUNR., both of Duplin Co., 14
Apr 1808, for $20 lawful money of the U. S. 22 1/2A on the SS of Stephen Swamp,
being part of a tract of 200A granted to ELISHA WOODWARD (date not given), beg.
at an ash on the run of Stephen Swamp in sd. BOSTICK'S line. Wit: JOSEPH T.
RHODES, NATHAN WALLER. Jan. Ct. 1811.

p. 291   NANCY (X) QUINN (co. not given) to her 5 children (names not given),
6 Jan 1809, a deed of gift for all her property consisting of a cow & yearling, a 3
yr. heifer & their increase, 2 beds, steads & furn., 10 heads of hogs, one woolen
wheel, one linen wheel, one pot, one pewter dish, one pewter bason, 6 pewter
plates, one tin bucket, one ax, weeding hoe, loom, washing tub, water pail, piggen
keeler, chest, 2 baskets & "some other articles too tedious to mention." Wit:
DANIEL STEWART, JAMES STEWART. Apr. Ct. 1811.

p. 292   NICHOLAS (X) BOURDEN to his son BRYAN BOURDEN, both of Duplin
Co., 10 Sep 1810, a deed of gift for "natural love & affection" a negro girl named
HANNAH. Wit: READIN BOURDEN, SIMEON GARNER. July Ct. 1811.

p. 293   JOHN PARKER (SENR.) to WILLIAM KNOWLS, both of Duplin Co., 26
Jan 1804, for 50 pds. lawful money of N. C. 250A on the lower side of Fussel's
Creek & on the NS of Rockfish Creek, beg. at a white oak on the WS of Harry's
Branch in JOHN HAWKINS' line by BENJAMIN FUSSEL'S line, to a pine by the
Great Road. Wit: ALEXANDER PARKER, WM. PARKER. July Ct. 1811.

p. 294   JAMES (X) HOLLAND SENR. to his son JAMES HOLLAND JUNR., both
of Duplin Co., 25 July 1810, for "natural love & affection", a deed of gift, 50A beg.
at the 5th corner of a patent granted to JONES BOYET, a pine in or near BARNES'
line at the head of the Calf Marsh, adj. SAMUEL JONES & DOBSON'S land. Wit:
JOHN TAYLOR, JOS. TAYLOR. July Ct. 1811.

p. 295   DANL. (DANIEL) SIMMONS of Jones Co. to BASIL KORNEGAY of Duplin
Co., 4 May 1811, for $500 a certain negro man named ROBIN. Wit: WM.
SIMMONS, THOS. DILLARD. July Ct. 1811.

p. 296   J. (JACOB) RHODES of Robeson Co. to JOSEPH T. RHODES of Duplin Co.,
24 Jan 1806, for 2 pds. current money of N. C. 50A on the NS of Limestone Swamp,
beg. at a pine the 2nd corner of sd. JOSEPH'S 100A survey in the upper line of
BENJAMIN RHODES dec'd 150A survey, adj. JOSEPH T. RHODES & BENJN.
RHODES 150A survey, being part of 640A patented to sd. JACOB RHODES 15 Dec
1802. Wit: NATHAN WALLER, DELILAH (+) HARDESTY. July Ct. 1811.

p. 297   GEORGE F. KORNEGAY to ALEXANDER O'DANIEL, both of Duplin Co.,
14 Apr 1810, for $275, 120A in the fork of the Northeast & Goshen, beg. at a pine
known by the name of the Squat Pine, NS of the main road ALEX. O'DANIEL'S corner, adj. JOHN GLISSON JUNR. & STEPHEN GUFFORD near the White Meadow,
the Little Miery Branch, GLISSON'S other corner & ALEX. O'DANIEL. Wit: H.
GRADY, ALEXANDER GRADY. July Ct. 1811.

p. 298   WILLIAM JAMES (JUNR.) to JONES McGANUS, both of Duplin Co., 2 Dec
1804, for $6, 3A on the ES of Harry Branch, a branch of Rockfish, beg. at the run
of sd. branch at a bay. Wit: JACOB WELLS, STEPHEN (X) MILLS. July Ct.
1811.

p. 299   HENRY NEWKIRK to KILLIS NEWKIRK, both of Duplin Co., 16 July 1811, for $400, 180A on the ES of the Northeast Branch of Cape Fear River, beg. at a water oak, the dividing line between JOHN BRICE & GEORGE BRICE in a branch, adj. DANIEL SOUTHERLAND. Wit: B. FARRIOR, T. H. BRICKELL. July Ct. 1811.

p. 300   BENNAJAH KING to GEORGE F. KORNEGAY, both of Duplin Co., 13 Sep 1806, for $250, 120A in the fork of the Northeast & Goshen Swamp, joining STEPHEN GUFFORD, JACOB GLISSON, OWEN O'DANIEL & ALEX. O'DANIEL, beg. at a pine known by the name of the Squat Pine NS of the main road O'DANIEL'S corner, adj. JOHN GLISSON JUNR., STEPHEN GUFFORD, the White Meadow, the Little Miery Branch, GLISSON'S other corner, ALEX. O'DANIEL & O'DANIEL'S other corner. Wit: OWEN O'DANIEL, ISAAC KORNEGAY. July Ct. 1811.

p. 302   HENRY GRADY to ISAIAH SMITH, both of Duplin Co., 4 Feb 1807, for $36.68, 50A on the ES of the Northeast & on the drains of Burncoat, it being part of a patent granted to SAMUEL JONES for 100A dated 20 Dec 1791, beg. at a stake on the run of the Middle Branch where the 1st line of sd. patent crosses it, adj. MAXWELL. Wit: KEZIAH (X) SMITH, JOHN MAXWELL. July Ct. 1811.

p. 302   JACOB BROWN (SENR.) of Duplin Co. to his son JACOB BROWN JUNR., (co. not given), 26 Apr 1811, for $200 and "natural love & affection" a negro girl named DILCE about 10 yrs. of age. Wit: JEREMIAH WALLICE, ELIJAH (X) MALLARD. July Ct. 1811.

p. 303   HENRY GRADY to JOHN MAXWELL, both of Duplin Co., 4 Feb 1807, for $36.68, 50A on the ES of the Northeast & on the drains of Burncoat, it being part of a patent granted to SAMUEL JONES for 100A dated 20 Dec 1791, beg. at a stake on the run of the Middle Branch where the 1st line of sd. patent crosses it & adj. BARNS' line. Wit: KEZIAH (X) SMITH, ISAIAH SMITH. July Ct. 1811.

p. 304   THOMAS BENNET (JUNR.) to JESSE GULLY, both of Duplin Co., 1 Mar 1811, for $8, 2A on the NS of Goshen Swamp, beg. at a pine near GULLY'S house, near BENNETT'S new ground, joining SIMON BRADLEY. Wit: JOHN GULLY, WILLIAM DANIEL. July Ct. 1811.

p. 305   AARON CUMMINS of Sampson Co. & GEORGE (X) CUMMINS of Duplin Co. to JAMES MURRAH of Duplin Co., 6 Mar 1811, for $100 lawful money 150A on the ES of the Northeast River, opposite AARON HODGESON'S & McCANN'S planta. WS of sd. river, beg. at a cypress & maple on the river bank, same course & near a black jack cut down IVEY SMITH'S corner formerly THOMAS CUMMINS'..., being a patent granted to THOMAS CUMMINS. Wit: JOHN HUFHAM, NATHAN SMITH. Apr. Ct. 1811.

p. 306   WATSON (W) BURTON to JOHN WILKINSON, both of Duplin Co., 18 Feb 1811, for $107, 107A joining the lands of sd. BURTON, WILKINSON & HOGAN HUNTER, beg. at a pine, to a bay in Horse Branch & up sd. branch to sd. HUNTER'S corner on the run of sd. branch. Wit: HOGAN HUNTER. Apr. Ct. 1811.

p. 307   STEPHEN GRAY to ALEXANDER CARTER, both of Duplin Co., 7 July 1807, for 150 milled dollars 150A on the Great Branch, beg. at a red oak & runs across Beaverdam & adj. WILLIAM ROBERTS' corner, taken up by BIBEY BUSH by

deed to EDWARD CARTER & from him to LODWICK GRAY & by heirship to
STEPHEN GRAY. Wit: EDWARD ALBERSON, BARNET STEWART. Apr. Ct.
1811.

p. 309   JAMES HALL to STEPHEN WILLIAMS, both of Duplin Co., 4 Dec 1810,
for 75 pds. 100A beg. at a cypress & pine on the run of Persimmon Swamp, joining
HANCHEY & WHITMAN. Wit: DANIEL SOUTHERLAND. Apr. Ct. 1811.

p. 309   THOS. (THOMAS) BROWN of New Bern to BENJAMIN COOPER of Duplin
Co., 1 Jan 1810, for $146, 318A on the SS of Nahunga Swamp & on BS of the Miery
Branch, beg. at an ash on the run of Nahunga Swamp, at the mouth of the upper
Miery Branch, up the E prong of sd. branch called the Wolf Pond Branch, BENJA-
MIN COOPER'S line, to a white oak on his back line, thence up sd. branch to a
pine & water oak near the Wolf Pond, thence through sd. pond to a pine, thence to a
red oak, the beg. corner of the 100A survey, thence some course to a pine in the
lower Miery Branch, down sd. branch to a black gum on the run of Nahunga up sd.
run as it meanders to the beg. Wit: CHARLES HOOKS, A. McINTIRE. Apr. Ct.
1811.

p. 311   JOHN HUNTER to NATHAN FOUNTAIN, both of Duplin Co., 15 Apr 1811,
for $500 one negro woman named PENNY & child PHILIP. Wit: JAMES LANIER.
Apr. Ct. 1811.

p. 311   GEORGE F. (FISHER) KORNEGAY to ISAAC KORNEGAY, both of Duplin
Co., 10 Mar 1808, for $270, 100A in the fork of the Northeast & Goshen Swamp,
beg. at a hickory on the NES & running S65W to the main road, up the road to a
small pond on the SS of the road to where ISAAC KORNEGAY'S line crosses the sd.
road, adj. McCULLOCH, WILLIAM KORNEGAY JUNR. & WILLIAM KORNEGAY
SENR. Wit: WILLIAM KORNEGAY JR., LEWIS GLISSON. Apr. Ct. 1811.

p. 312   STEPHEN GUFFORD to ISAAC KORNEGAY, both of Duplin Co., 14 Sep
1807, for $225, 180A in the fork of the Northeast & Goshen, beg. at a water oak in
the E prong of the Great Branch on GEORGE F. KORNEGAY'S line, to the Squat
Pine, to a maple in the W prong of the sd. Great Branch, down sd. branch to its
junction with the E prong, up run of sd. prong to the beg. Wit: BRYAN GLISSON,
GEORGE F. KORNEGAY. Apr. Ct. 1811.

p. 313   WM. (WILLIAM) H. HALSEY, ANN SOPHIA HALSEY & C. (CARLETON)
WALKER, guardian of the infant children of HENRY HALSEY dec'd to WILLIAM
A. HOUSTON, (cos. not given), 12 Feb 1811, for $240, 100A on the ES of the North-
east River & NS of Limestone Swamp, on the heads of Indian Run & Poley Branch,
beg. at a pine the 3rd corner of DAVID GREEN'S land, joining WILLIAM HUBBARD
& JOHN WHEEDEN. Wit: S. HOUSTON, JOHN HOUSTON. Apr. Ct. 1811.

p. 315   LEWIS (B) BARFIELD (SENR.) to ANN BARFIELD his dau., both of Duplin
Co., 15 Mar 1811, for "natural love & affection" 195A on Burncoat Swamp, joining
BURWELL WILLIAMS & others, beg. on the NS of Burncoat in FREDK. GRADY'S
line, joining BEVERLY'S survey, DEBREWHL'S branch, CHRISTOPHER LAWSON,
JAMES GRADY, FREDERICK GRADY (Sadler), FREDK. GRADY SENR., being part
of 4 surveys. Wit: OWEN O'DANIEL, LEWIS BARFIELD JR. Apr. Ct. 1811.

p. 316   ISAAC (⌶) SPENCE to JOHN SCREWS, both of Duplin Co., 6 Apr 1807, for $40, 20A on the NS of Goshen Swamp, joining the lines of sd. SPENCE, WILLIAM UNDERHILL & lands belonging to the estate of JOHN SHUFFIELD dec'd, beg. at a stake in the center of 3 pines in the edge of Pompy's Pocosin. Wit: BRYAN BOURDEN, ELISHA (X) SPENCE, WILLIAM (𝒰) UNDERHILL. Apr. Ct. 1811.

p. 317   ANNY (X) WILLIAMS to JOSEPH WILLIAMS JUNR., both of Duplin Co., 27 Aug 1810, for $200, 78A on BYRD WILLIAMS' Mill Creek, it being the part of land that she drew of her father's estate, being the planta. whereon her father JOHN WILLIAMS lived & died, beg. at a black jack & joining JOSEPH WILLIAMS' old field to WILLIAMS' Mill Creek. Wit: JNO. HUFHAM, WILLIAM BROWN. Apr. Ct. 1811.

p. 318   BENJAMIN (X) JOINER of Duplin Co. to JOHN GOORE SENR. (co. not given), 10 May 1806, for $110, 110A on the NS of Back Branch & WS of Stewart's Creek, beg. at a maple, laurel bay & sweet gum in Back Branch, JAMES PATTERSON'S upper corner, with the line of a survey of 580A patented by ABRAHAM MOLTEN dec'd. Wit: JAMES REARDON, JONATHAN GOORE. Apr. Ct. 1810.

p. 319   LEWIS (B) BARFIELD (SENR.) to LEWIS BARFIELD JUNR., both of Duplin Co., 15 Mar 1811, for $200, 200A on the ES of the Northeast of Cape Fear & on Lawhorn Branch, joining FREDK. SMITH & LEWIS BARFIELD JUNR.'S lines, beg. at a pine BARFIELD'S corner of a survey patented by GEORGE SMITH, joining THOMAS WORLEY & by JOHN WILLIAMS' line. Wit: OWEN O'DANIEL, ANNA BARFIELD. Apr. Ct. 1811.

p. 320   LEWIS (B) BARFIELD (SENR.) to his dau. POLLY BARFIELD, both of Duplin Co., 15 Mar 1811, for "good will & natural love & affection" 150A on Burncoat Swamp, joining WRIGHT BARFIELD & BURWELL WILLIAMS, beg. at a short strawed pine on the NS of Burncoat on FREDK. GRADY'S line near the main road, along the main road across Burncoat to the forks of the road, along a row of marked trees to the back line of Beverly survey, along the back line to a large pine BURWELL WILLIAMS' corner & WRIGHT BARFIELD'S line & with his line to the run of Burncoat & up the run to ALEXANDER GRADY JUNR.'S line, along his line to a white oak near the main road, to FREDK. GRADY SENR.'S line to the beg., being part of 3 surveys incl. the cleared land between the main road & WRIGHT BARFIELD'S line. Wit: OWEN O'DANIEL, LEWIS BARFIELD JR. Apr. Ct. 1811.

p. 321   MARY MIDDLETON to ISAAC MIDDLETON, both of Duplin Co., 13 Aug 1810, for 30 pds. 270A on the SS of Miller's Swamp, being the manor planta. whereon the late JAMES MIDDLETON dec'd lived, the 1/10 part of sd. land claimed by MARY MIDDLETON. Wit: JOHN HUNTER, ED. HUNTER. Apr. Ct. 1811.

p. 322   SAMUEL SOWELL to RICHARD SWINSON, both of Duplin Co., 9 Feb 1809, for $150, 323A on the NS of Limestone Swamp & between Cabbin Branch & Gum Branch, beg. at a gum on the wedge of Gum Swamp, adj. THOMAS QUINN, WM. MERCER, ABNER QUINN, MUMFORD, ANTHONY LEWIS & JOHN JONES, it being part of a tract of land granted to JOHN JONES of 250A & part of a tract granted to ABNER QUINN & part of a tract granted to MILLS MUMFORD & 31A granted to sd. SOWELL. Wit: PHILL SOUTHERLAND JR., THOMAS CANADAY. Apr. Ct. 1811.

p. 324   ISAAC MIDDLETON, Exr. to the will of RICHARD NORMAN, of Duplin

Co. to SAMUEL MIDDLETON (co. not given), 19 Jan 1809, for $23, 9A on the ES of
Pasture Branch, beg. at a white oak & water oak in sd. branch, joining JAMES
WILLIAMS. Wit: JOHN HUNTER, ANN CHAMBERS. Apr. Ct. 1811.

p. 325   WM. (WILLIAM) ALBERSON to DAVID ALBERSON, both of Duplin Co., 13
Feb 1811, for 500 pds. lawful money 266A in 3 tracts to wit: (1) 100A beg. at a gum
KORNEGAY'S corner on sd. ALBERSON'S line, to Dempsey Island, joining LEWIS
BARFIELD & KORNEGAY patented 19 Oct 1803; (2) 70A beg. at a pine on
FREDERICK GRADY'S line, to a bay in the mouth of Burncoat Swamp, patented by
WILLIAM ALBERSON 7 Sep 1802; (3) 96A beg. at a gum sd. GRADY'S corner on
ISAAC KORNEGAY'S line, joining WILLIAM ALBERSON & ISAAC KORNEGAY,
patented to WILLIAM ALBERSON 13 Dec 1806. Wit: SAML. ALBERSON, EDWD.
ALBERSON. Apr. Ct. 1811.

p. 327   GIDEON ARTHUR to JOSEPH BROOKS, both of Duplin Co., 20 Nov 1810,
for 215 pds. lawful money of N. C. 194A in 2 tracts to wit: (1) 164A on the SS of
Maxwell Swamp & in the fork between Maxwell Swamp & Cabbin Branch, it being the
contents of a patent granted to ANDREW THALLY by patent dated 18 Nov 1794, beg.
at a persimmon & gum on Maxwell Run by ROBERT SLOAN'S corner; (2) 30A joining the 1st piece, being part of 150A granted to THOMAS CUMMINS by patent dated
1 Apr 1780, beg. at a white oak & black jack the 1st station of sd. CUMMINS' survey, joining ROBERT SLOAN & sd. CUMMINS' patent. Wit: JOHN MAXWELL,
JOHN THALLY. Apr. Ct. 1811.

p. 329   JEREMIAH PEARSALL to JAMES PEARSALL, both of Duplin Co., 10 Mar
1806, for 2,000 spanish milled dollars 623A in 4 tracts to wit: (1) 463A on the SS
of Goshen Swamp adj. JAMES PEARSALL & JAMES CHAMBERS, beg. at a gum on
the run of Goshen CHAMBERS' corner, joining JEDEDIAH B. FOLEY; (2) 70A beg.
at a pine sd. JEREMIAH PEARSALL'S own corner, it being the corner of 20A conveyed by deed from JOHN MATCHETT to BENJAMIN FOLSOM 22 Jan 1764, joining
JOSEPH WELTS' line, the corner of sd. FOLEY'S survey of 40A, being part of a
100A survey granted to BENJAMIN FOLSOM 30 Oct 1765 & a small part next to
WELTS' line granted to JOHN MATCHETT JUNR. 29 Oct 1782; (3) 40A granted to
sd. FOLEY 16 Mar 1799, beg. at a pine JAMES CHAMBERS' corner, joining
SAMUEL CHAMBERS' line & JEREMIAH PEARSALL'S corner, thence his line
formerly MATCHETT'S; (4) 50A granted to sd. JEREMIAH PEARSALL by patent
16 Mar 1799, beg. at a lightwood or pine stump, the corner of a survey of 150A
patented by SAMUEL CHAMBERS, joining J. B. FOLEY'S corner & JAMES CHAM-
BERS. (Heading of deed says total acreage is 640A.) Wit: TH. ROUTLEDGE,
ED. PEARSALL, STEPHEN MILLER. Apr. Ct. 1811.

p. 331   STEPHEN GUFFORD to ISAAC KORNEGAY, both of Duplin Co., 14 Sep
1807, for $70, 73A in the fork of Goshen & the NE, beg. at a maple in the W prong
of the Great Branch a little below the main road. Wit: BRYAN GLISSON, GEORGE
F. KORNEGAY. Apr. Ct. 1811.

p. 332   WILLIAM JOHNSON (JOHNSTON) to LEVI SHOLAR, both of Duplin Co.,
15 Dec 1810, for 50 pds. 100A on the ES of the Northeast of Cape Fear, beg. at a
black gum in the Long Branch in BLAKE'S line, joining HOLDEN'S & JOHNSTON'S
corners, patented by NORRIS & conveyed from him to BLAKE who conveyed to
BURGWIN & from sd. BURGWIN to JAMES LANIER who deeded to sd. WILLIAM
JOHNSTON. Wit: FREDK. PICKETT, ISOM SHOLAR. Apr. Ct. 1811.

p. 333   TIMOTHY (X) BRYANT to WILLIAM SWETMAN, 10 Nov 18--, for $30,
11A on the drains of Rockfish, beg. at a poplar & maple sd. SWETMAN'S corner, at
the run of Dugles Branch, to a pine by the Celligroves Spring. Wit: AARON
WILLIAMS, ISAAC (X) CALL. Apr. Ct. 1811.

p. 334   JESSE TURNAGE to THOMAS WILSON, both of Duplin Co., 27 Oct 1810,
for 217 pds. 10 shill. current money of N. C. 251A on the NS the Northeast on the
Cabin Branch. Wit: LEWIS HERRING, JOEL HINES. Apr. Ct. 1811.

p. 335   DAVID ALBERSON to WILLIAM KORNEGAY, both planters of Duplin Co.,
17 Apr 1811, for 50 pds. lawful money of N. C. 100A in the Northeast Swamp, beg.
at a gum WILLIAM KORNEGAY'S corner & sd. ALBERSON'S line & runs with his
own line E through the Dempsey Island, joining LEWIS BARFIELD & KORNEGAY.
Wit: JONES DICKSON, EDWARD PEARSALL. Apr. Ct. 1811.

p. 336   WILLIAM (X) RHODES & TAYLOR RHODES to BENJAMIN BOURDEN, all
planters of Duplin Co., 6 Feb 1810, for $60, 140A on the NS of Goshen Swamp &
near the head of Bear Marsh, being part of a survey of 500A granted to BAKER
BOURDEN 29 Oct 1782, beg. at 3 pines the beg. corner of sd. patent & runs with the
same...to a bay in Huckleberry Pocosin, the old corner & joining WHITEHEAD'S
line. Wit: HENRY BOURDEN, STEPHEN DUNKAN. Apr. Ct. 1811.

p. 338   D. (DANIEL) L. KENAN, Shff. to JOSEPH MERCER, both of Duplin Co.,
18 Feb 1811, for taxes & charges amounting to $2.25 for an acre less than the sd.
tract for 99A on the NS of Limestone Swamp & NS of Poley Branch, which taxes on
sd. land was unpaid for for the year 1809, to which land sd. MERCER became the
purchaser, the sd. tract beg. at a pine his own corner. Wit: JAMES HALL,
SAMUEL CHERRY. Apr. Ct. 1811.

p. 339   ZACHARIAH TURNAGE to his beloved nephew NEEDHAM BLOUNT, both
of Duplin Co., 12 Feb 1811, for "natural love & affection" a negro boy named
DANIEL about 30 months of age. TREACY (S) TURNAGE also signed the deed.
Wit: CULLEN CONNERLY, FANNY (S) TURNAGE. July Ct. 1811.

p. 340   SIMON BRADLEY to ELISHA HERRING, both of Duplin Co., 15 May 1811,
for $1,060 good & lawful money of N. C. 212A on the NS of Goshen Swamp & on
Maple Branch, beg. at a pine sd. BRADLEY'S & JOSEPH DICKSON'S upper corner,
above the head of Maple Branch, joining CASTELLOW'S old line, WILLIAM DICK-
SON, BRADLEY'S old corner & JOSEPH DICKSON, being part of sundry tracts of
land formerly purchased of by JOHN BRADLEY & since by him conveyed to the sd.
SIMON BRADLEY. Wit: WM. DICKSON, JONES DICKSON. Oct. Ct. 1811.

p. 342   MAJOR (X) SEARLES to BRYAN MINSHEW, both of Duplin Co., 23 Mar
1809, for 160 pds. 6 shill. & 3 pence 300A in 2 tracts to wit: (1) 200A beg. at a
pine in sd. SEARLES' field, near the house, down the run of Rooty Branch to
DUREL'S line, to a dividing line between sd. SEARLES & DAVID DUREL, being
part of a survey of 300A patented by STEPHEN BARFIELD 9 Oct 1782; (2) 100A
beg. at a pine called SAMUEL TANNER'S corner & runs to a pine by sd. SEARLES'
field, to the Rooty Branch, joining KORNEGAY, to a bunch of bays in the head of the
Hog Pen Branch, in the old line a new corner made for BRYAN WHITFIELD, to a
black jack in the old line on the side of the Little Sand Hill Pocosin, being part of a
survey of 180A patented by JOHN DURAL 16 Mar 1799. Wit: CHARLES WILLIAMS,

EDY WILLIAMS. July Ct. 1811.

p. 343   JESSE GULLY to ELISHA HERRING, both of Duplin Co., 6 July 1807, for
$1895,25, 361A on the NS of Goshen Swamp, incl. the planta. whereon sd. GULLY
now lives, beg. at a maple on the run of Goshen, WILLIAM DICKSON'S upper corner above GULLY'S Marsh adj. BRADLEY, CASTELLOW, WILLIAM BECK, Mc
CANNE, THOMAS BENNET, JOSEPH DICKSON, being part of sundry parcels of
land conveyed to sd. GULLY. Wit: WM. DICKSON. July Ct. 1811.

p. 346   JOHN (X) SCREWS to GILES T. LOFTEN, both of Duplin Co., 10 Oct
1811, for $71, 20A on the NS of Goshen Swamp, being part of a tract formerly
ISAAC SPENCE'S, adj. the land of WILLIAM UNDERHILL & lands belonging to the
estate of JOHN SHUFFIELD dec'd, beg. at a stake in the center of 3 pines in the
edge of Pompy's Pocosin, joining SPENCE near the old path & along SHUFFIELD'S
line to the beg. Wit: JOSEPH OSBURNE. Jan. Ct. 1812.

p. 347   MARTHA (M) BENNET to her niece SALLY JONES, the wife of BENNET
JONES, both of Duplin Co., 18 Dec 1810, a deed of gift for "natural love & affection" a negro girl named SILLA & a negro boy named BILL, one chest & one table,
all my wearing apparel, my young mare. Wit: JOHN ELIOT, MARY ELIOT. July
Ct. 1811.

p. 348   MARTHA (M) BENNET to SUSANNAH JONES, the dau. of BENNET &
SALLY JONES, all of Duplin Co., 18 Dec 1810, a deed of gift for "natural love &
affection" a negro boy NAT & one bed & furn. Wit: JOHN ELIOT, MARY ELIOT.
July Ct. 1811.

p. 348   MARTHA (M) BENNET to MARTHA JONES, dau. of BENNET & SALLY
JONES, all of Duplin Co., 18 Dec 1810, a deed of gift for "natural love & affection"
a negro girl BETS & one bed & furn. Wit: JOHN ELIOT, MARY ELIOT. July Ct.
1811.

p. 349   WINDEL DAVIS to BENJAMIN SUTTON, both of Duplin Co., 4 Feb 1811,
for 63 pds. 7 shill. & 6 pence 85A on the waters of the Great Branch, joining ROUSE
& SUTTON, beg. at a large pine, to a dead pine fallen down, or the center of 3
pines that is newly marked, to the center of 3 black jacks, to a black oak, to the beg.
Wit: JESSE HARDY, JAMES DAVIS. (No date of probate given)

p. 350   FRANCIS WILLIAMS of Duplin Co. to SILAS CARTER of Onslow Co., 23
Jan 1811, for 150 pds. good & lawful money of N. C. a negro woman named CHLOE
about 35 yrs. old. Wit: JAMES GUFFORD. July Ct. 1811.

p. 350   "The following indorsement was overlooked, until the registration of the
foregoing was closed - but is as follows - I hereby indorse the within Bill of Sale to
THOMAS CANADAY for value recd. by me 24 Jan 1811." Signed SILAS CARTER.
Wit: ROBERT SOUTHERLAND.

p. 351   DAVID GILLESPIE & JOSEPH GILLESPIE, exrs. of the L. W. & T. of
JAMES GILLESPIE, late of Duplin Co. dec'd, to HOGAN HUNTER, 16 July 1811,
for $150, 400A on the WS of the Northeast Branch of Cape Fear River, between the
Grove & Horse Branch, beg. at a black gum, MATTHEW CANADY'S beg. corner,
joining McINTIRE & JOB HUNTER. Wit: JONES DICKSON, SAMUEL STANFORD.
July Ct. 1811.

p. 352   HUGH McCANNE, Patent No. 1853, 19 Dec 1805, for 43A on the WS of the
Northeast River on & in Maxwell Pocosin, beg. at a bay in the E edge of sd. pocosin
on DAVID BROCK'S line, joining HOOKS. Entered 16 Apr 1805. Surveyed 24 Oct
1805 by B. KORNEGAY, C. Sur. ALEX MARTIN, Sp. Sur. WILL WHITE, Sec.

p. 352   HUGH McCANNE, Patent No. 1852, 19 Dec 1805, for 30A on the NS of
Maxwell Swamp, beg. at a pine BROCK'S corner, joining JOHN MATCHETT &
HUNTER. Entered 19 Feb 1805. Surveyed 7 Aug 1805 by B. KORNEGAY, Sur.
A. WILLIAMS, Dist. Sur. ALEX MARTIN, Sp. Sur. WILL WHITE, Sec.

p. 353   HUGH McCANNE, Patent No. 1735, 5 Dec 1801, for 200A on the NS of the
Northeast River & ES of Maxwell, beg. at a pine on Maxwell Pocosin below the
Cypress Pond, joining NATHL. McCANNE, SHUFFIELD, COX & BROCK. Entered
22 Apr 1801. No. 1208 entered 25 Sep 1800. No. 1271 entered Apr 1801. WILL
WHITE, Sec. B. WILLIAMS, Sp. Sur.

p. 353   HUGH McCANNE, Patent No. 1888, 29 Nov 1806, for 50A on BS of Maxwell
Swamp, joining NATHANIEL McCANNE'S & THALLEY'S old line, beg. at a pine near
a pocosin on THALLEY'S old line, crossing sd. swamp to a pine McCANNE's corner.
Entered 22 Oct 1805. WILL WHITE, Sec. Signed by NATHL. ALEXANDER.

p. 354   DAVID GILLESPIE & JOSEPH GILLESPIE, exrs. of JAMES GILLESPIE,
16 July 1811, a deed of gift as requested by the L. W. & T. of JAMES GILLESPIE
late of Duplin Co. dec'd "that the boy SONE bequeathed to my grandson JAMES
GILLESPIE be sold with my other chattel property that otherwise disposed of & the
sum of $300 appropriated to the purchase of a female slave to him & his heirs for-
ever." The sd. DAVID & JOSEPH GILLESPIE conveys to JAMES GILLESPIE,
grandson of JAMES GILLESPIE dec'd a female slave called MERIAN. Wit: ANN
QUINN. July Ct. 1811.

p. 355   MICHAEL BONEY of New Hanover Co. to JAMES CUMINGS of Duplin Co.,
11 Apr 1814, for $500 a negro man LIP. Wit: JOHN BONEY, WRIGHT BONEY.
July Ct. 1811.

p. 355   D. (DANIEL) L. KENAN, Shff. to JOSEPH T. RHODES, both of Duplin Co.,
17 Dec 1811, a negro slave named ARTHUR, aged 40. The Sup. Ct. of New Hanover Co. awarded 131 pds. 2 shill. & 3 pence, plus 12 pds. to GEORGE BRICE in
the name of HENRY NEWKIRK, for debt & damages in suit against JOHN FELIX
RHODES, owner of sd. negro ARTHUR, who was sold to WILLIAM SOUTHERLAND
for JOSEPH T. RHODES. Wit: JAMES REARDON. July Ct. 1812.

p. 356   ELISHA POWELL to JOHN D. BLUDWORTH, both of Duplin Co., 19 May
1810, for $300 a negro man named JACK about 60 yrs. of age. Wit: JOHN
HUFHAM. July Ct. 1811.

p. 357   D. (DANIEL) L. KENAN, Shff. of Duplin Co. to MERRIT MANNING (co.
not given), 17 July 1811. The Court awarded 60 pds. 10 shill., plus 4 pds. to
EDWARD McGOWEN for debt, and awarded 31 pds. 16 shill. to THOMAS HENDER-
SON for debt owed by MOSES MANNING, owner of 3 tracts of land which was purchased by MERRIT MANNING for 96 pds. 6 shill. at public auction held on 28 Jan
1808. The sd. land in 3 pieces to wit: (1) 200A beg. at a forked post oak; (2) tract
(acreage not given) patented by HENRY SKIBBOW, beg. at a white oak on Stafford's

Swamp, beg. at a blown down white oak, his corner of 200A patented by JOHN WILLIAMS, to a gum the run of Jumping Run, then up to Calf Branch, up Calf Branch to the line of his 200A survey. Wit: (not listed) July Ct. 1811.

p. 358   S. (SHADRACK) STALLINGS to his son WILLIAM STALLINGS, both of Duplin Co., 1 Jan 1810, for "natural love & affection" 800A being in several tracts & parts of tracts, beg. at an ash & maple in the run of Murphey's Creek, formerly Faris's Creek, at the old ford of sd. creek, joining BRICE, STOAKES, CRUMPTON & SWEATMAN, to the ES of the main road. Wit: AA. (AARON)MORGAN, HUGH MAXWELL. July Ct. 1811.

p. 360   JOHN FARRIOR SR., planter, to his loving dau. & son, PATTY & FRED-ERICK PICKETT, all of Duplin Co., 23 Jan 1812, a deed of gift for a negro woman & negro boy named DOLL & GEORGE. Wit: JOHN FARRIOR JR., JOHN BISHOP. Apr. Ct. 1812.

p. 361   JACOB BONEY to WIMBRICK BONEY, both of Duplin Co., 17 Nov 1806, for 10 shill. 197A in the head drains of Harry's Branch, a branch of Rockfish, beg. at 2 small short leafted pines JACOB WELLS JUNR.'S corner. Wit: TIMOTHY TEACHY, WILLIAM BONEY. Oct. Ct. 1810.

p. 362   JANE (X) LEWIS (co. not given) to STEPHEN WALLACE of Duplin Co., 5 Oct 1811, for 25 pds. 50A which fell to sd. JANE LEWIS by the death of her father ANDREW COX of Duplin Co. dec'd, it being the upper half of 100A granted to ANDREW COX by patent dated 27 Apr 1767, beg. at a stake in the 2nd line of the patent, it being the dividing corner of the other half of sd. 100A which fell to his sister PEGGY COX, since sold to JAMES WALLACE cont. 50A. Wit: NATHANIEL WALLER, JAMES CHAMBERS. Oct. Ct. 1811.

p. 363   WILLIAM CREECH of Duplin Co. to NEEDHAM WHITFIELD of Wayne Co., 22 Feb 1810, for 25 pds. 160A granted by patent to DAVID DURAL 28 Nov 1805 & from him to WILLIAM CREECH, on the NS of the Northeast on BS of the main road, beg. at a pine SAMUEL TANNER'S corner, joining WHITFIELD in the edge of Horsepen Pocosin & joining KORNEGAY, going through the Sand Hill Pocosin. Wit: JOSEPH WHITFIELD, BENJAMIN HERRING. Oct. Ct. 1811.

p. 364   PETER CARLTON to WILLIAM BLAND JUNR., both of Duplin Co., 15 Feb 1811, for 131 1/2 spanish milled dollars 131 1/2 A on the SS of the Doctors Creek, beg. at a water oak. Wit: JOHN (X) ALDERMAN, JOHN STALLINGS. Oct. Ct. 1811.

p. 365   BRYAN (X) MINSHEW of Wayne Co. to ROBERT PEAL of Duplin Co., 17 Jan 1811, for $390, 100A on the NS of the Northeast River, being part of 2 tracts to wit: (1) the 1st piece (acreage not given) beg. at a pine ROBERT SIRLS' field, near the sd. BRYAN MINSHEW, down the run of Rooty Branch to DURAL'S line, to the dividing line of sd. SIRLS & DANIEL DURAL, being part of a survey of 300A patented by STEPHEN BARFIELD 9 Oct 1782; (2) the 2nd piece (acreage not given) beg. at a pine SAMUEL TANNER'S corner joining sd. SIRLS' field, now BRYAN MINSHEW'S, joining KORNEGAY, with the patent line to a small pine & a bunch of bays in the Hog Pen Branch, in the old line, a new corner made for BRYAN WHIT-FIELD, to a black jack in the old line on the side of the Little Sand Hill Pocosin, being part of a survey of 180A patented by JOHN DURAL 16 Mar 1799. Wit: ____

WHITFIELD, J. T. BRYAN. Oct. Ct. 1811.

p. 367   JAMES (X) ROGERS to PELEG ROGERS, both of Duplin Co., 4 Dec 1807, for $24, 50A on the head of Gum Branch, beg. at a hickory DAVID CARLTON'S corner, joining EBENEZAR SWINSON, PELEG ROGERS & HENRY PORTER. Wit: BENJAMIN CHASTEN, BENETER CRANFORD. Oct. Ct. 1811.

p. 368   D. (DANIEL) L. KENAN, Shff. of Duplin Co. to ALEXANDER WELLS (co. not given), 22 Mar 1811. The Court awarded judgment (amount not given) to the exrs. of the late JAMES KENAN, Esqr. for damages in suit against JACOB WELLS & MICHAEL BONEY. The Shff. levied on 1028A of land "of the said JACOB" which was purchased by ALEXANDER WELLS for $200 at public auction held 25 Aug 1810. The sd. land beg. at a pine in the fork of Cabbin Branch, joining FREDERICK WELLS, crossing Island Creek & joining JOHN PARKER'S line. Wit: JONES DICKSON. Oct. Ct. 1811. (The heading of deed says 128A.)

p. 369   JAMES BOURDEN to JOHN ROBERTS, both of Duplin Co., 22 Nov 1810, for $40, 10 1/2A being part of a patent granted to JEDEDIAH BLANCHARD 8 Dec 1802 for 118A on the ES of the Cabbin Branch, a prong of the Cape Fear River, beg. at a maple in sd. branch, joining JOHN ROBERTS & RACHEL HUGHS. Wit: SAMUEL BOURDEN, EDMD. WHITFIELD. Oct. Ct. 1811.

p. 370   SAMUEL DAVIS to RICHARD BLANTON, both of Duplin Co., 25 Nov 1802, for 70 pds., 71A on the WS of the main creek of Rockfish, beg. at a water oak on the Creek Bank his own corner, joining CAMPBELL, patented 1784. Wit: TIMOTHY TEACHEY, JACOB BONEY. Oct. Ct. 1811.

p. 371   JAMES BOURDEN to RACHEL HUGHS, both of Duplin Co. 22 Nov 1810, for $382.50, 153A on the ES of the Cabbin Branch, a prong of the Northeast of Cape Fear, first being part of a patent granted to CHRISTOPHER MARTIN 16 Mar 1799 & by his & his son ABRAHAM MARTIN'S heirs conveyed the same parcel of land to GEORGE THOMAS, beg. at a pine in the Cabbin Branch near a place called DAVIS' Spring, joining NEEDHAM WHITFIELD'S corner & a line of JEDEDIAH BLANCHARD'S patent granted to him 8 Dec 1802 & secondly a part of the sd. patent granted to sd. BLANCHARD going on from sd. red oak WHITFIELD'S corner to a hickory WHITFIELD'S corner, joining JOHN ROBERTS, the last patent conveyed from JEDEDIAH BLANCHARD to GEORGE THOMAS & both parcels of land conveyed by deed from sd. THOMAS to JAMES BOURDEN. Wit: NM. WHITFIELD, SAMUEL BOURDEN, EDMD. WHITFIELD. Oct. Ct. 1811.

p. 372   JACOB BROWN, Patent No. 1947, 26 Nov 1810, for 92A on the SS of Stevens Swamp, beg. at a pine CHARLEY BOSTICK'S corner & joining JOSEPH T. RHODES. Entered 27 Mar 1810. Signed by DAVID STONE. WM. WHITE, Sec.

p. 373   LEWIS GRIMES, Patent No. 1983, 3 Dec 1811, for 84A beg. at a pine SAMUEL WARD'S & SILAS CARTER'S corner, joining LOD. OUTLAW, JAMES JOURNEGAN & sd. WARD. Entered 15 Nov 1810. Signed by BENJA. SMITH. WM. HILL, Sec.

p. 373   BENJAMIN SUTTON, Patent No. 1914, 1 Dec 1808, for 40A on BS of the Beaverdam Branch, adj. his own & JOHN ROUSE'S lines, beg. at a black jack his own corner. Entered 10 Dec 1807. Signed by B. WILLIAMS. WILL WHITE, Sec.

p. 373   WILLIAM FARRIOR, Patent No. 1960, 6 Dec 1810, for 22A on the ES of the Northeast River & on the NS of Muddy Creek, beg. at a pine his own corner & JAMES PICKETT'S corner. Entered 17 Oct 1809. Signed by B. SMITH. WM. WHITE, Sec.

p. 374   THOMAS GARRISON, Patent No. 1978, 3 Dec 1811, for 100A on the drains of Stocking Head & Sand Hill Branch, beg. at a pine NICHOLAS BRYANT'S corner. Entered 16 Apr 1811. Signed by B. SMITH. WILL WHITE, Sec.

p. 374   STEPHEN LANIER, Patent No. 1979, 3 Dec 1811, for 10A on the ES of the Northeast River & NS of Cypress Creek, beg. at a gum at the run of Cypress Creek. Entered 27 Mar 1810. Signed by BENJ. SMITH. WILL WHITE, Sec. STEPHEN LANIER paid 5 shill. for sd. 10A received by the Treasury Office 19 Nov 1811 as by Entry Taker's Certificate No. 1815, filed on 19 Nov 1811 by S. GOODWIN, Comptroller. Signed by STEPHEN HAYWOOD for JOHN HAYWOOD, P. Sec.

p. 375   JOHN HUFHAM to DAVID WILLIAMS, both of Duplin Co., 30 Jan 1811, for #350 lawful money of N. C. a negro boy named LINKHAM about 13 yrs. of age. Wit: JOHN MATTHIS. Apr. Ct. 1812.

p. 375   J. (JOHN) D. BLUDWORTH to JOHN BLUDWORTH, both of Duplin Co., for $1250, 1 Jan 1810, 6 negroes named NAN, LINKHAM, ABRAHAM, EADE, MANUEL & NANCE. Wit: MAURICE FENNEL, EDMOUND FENNEL. July Ct. 1812.

p. 376   ALEXANDER GRADDY (SENR.) of Duplin Co. to FREDERICK GRADY (Neuse) of Duplin Co., 10 Dec 1810, for $250, 154A on the ES of the Northeast of Cape Fear & on the NS of Burncoat, beg. at a black gum in the edge of Burncoat JAMES GRADY'S corner, just below the mouth of Long Branch, on the ES of the Long Branch opposite OUTLAW'S old ford, to a black gum in the run of the Tarkiln Branch, joining FREDERICK GRADY SENR. 'S line & LEWIS BARFIELD'S corner on the edge of Burncoat. Wit: WM. GRADY, ALEX GRADY JR., HENRY GRADY. July Ct. 1811.

p. 377   JACOB GILMORE of Duplin Co. to JOEL HINES of Lenoir Co., 18 Jan 1812, for $280 a negro girl slave named CLARRISSA about 8 yrs. of age, healthy, sound & sensible. Wit: JOHN GULLY. Jan. Ct. 1812.

p. 377   ED. (EDWARD) ARMSTRONG to SNODON PEARCE, both of Duplin Co., _____ Oct 1807, for $30, 270A being part of a tract of land patented by GEORGE LILLINGTON on the SS of Cypress Creek, beg. at a pine on Poley Bridge Branch, to the Watering Hole Branch & along SHOLAR'S line. Wit: WM. PICKETT, FREDK. PICKETT. Jan. Ct. 1812.

p. 379   WILLIAM (X) MUNDS & SARAH (SALLY) MUNDS his wife of Duplin Co., to SAMPSON GRIMES (co. not given), 27 July 1811, for $86, 93A on the NS of Goshen Swamp, patented by JOHN SULIVENT (little) & conveyed by him to JOHN SULIVAN SENR. who conveyed to MICHAEL SULIVAN, then fell by lott the 5th to SALLY MUNDS, wife of WILLIAM MUNDS, at the division of the sd. MICHAEL SULIVAN'S lands. The 93A beg. at a large pine on sd. GRIMES' line. Wit: LEWIS BARFIELD, TIMOTHY SPENCE. SARAH MUND acknowledged that she signed the above deed of her own free will & accord 21 Jan 1812 before DAVID WRIGHT & JOHN

BECK, Justices of the Peace. Jan. Ct. 1812.

p. 380   ISAAC PIPKIN to ARCHELAUS PIPKIN, both of Lenoir Co., 23 Nov 1811, for $200, 185A in 2 tracts to wit: (1) 125A on the waters of the Northeast, patented for JOHN ROBERTS, beg. at a pine on ISAAC HINES' line; (2) 60A joining the 1st piece surveyed for SAMUEL TANNER, patent dated 9 Oct 1783, beg. at a pine on HINES' line by a pond, joining JESSE PIPKIN'S line & ROBERTS' line. (Heading of the deed reads 60A.) Wit: ELISHA PIPKIN, EDMD. WHITFIELD.

p. 381   MM. (MALCOM) McALLISTER to ABRAHAM NEWTON, both of Duplin Co., 1 Dec 1811, for $600 lawful money 180A on the WS of Rockfish Creek, beg. at a stake in the run of Bruvers (?) Myre Meadow Branch, being part of 2 surveys, one of which was patented by DAN BOWEN in the year 1780, the other granted by patent to JOHN GOFF 29 Oct 1782. Wit: JOHN HUFHAM, NANCY HUFHAM. Jan. Ct. 1812.

p. 382   THOMAS ROBINSON of Sampson Co. to WILLIAM HIGHSMITH of Duplin Co., 25 Oct 1811, for $33 a negro woman named PAT about 20 yrs. of age & her child named SAPHIRA & their increase. Wit: WILLIAM BLAND. Jan. Ct. 1811.

p. 383   WILLIAM SOWELL of Cumberland Co. to EDWARD ALBERSON of Duplin Co., 15 Oct 1810 for 10 pds. 200A on or near the head of the Great Branch, incl. JOHN SMITH'S impr., beg. at a poplar in a small branch, taken up by SAMUEL SOWELL & left to be sold by his exrs. which sd. WILLIAM SOWELL became the purchaser & now sells to sd. ALBERSON. Wit: ROBERT SOUTHERLAND, J. KORNEGAY. Jan. Ct. 1812.

p. 384   JAS. (JAMES) K. HILL to JAMES WADE, both of Duplin Co., 26 July 1810, for $500, 510A in 2 tracts to wit: (1) 150A on the SS of Goshen Swamp, beg. at the mouth of Stewart's Branch, up the sd. branch as it meanders to the Flag Marsh, up the branch that makes out of the Flag Marsh, to the run of Nahunga Swamp, down the run to the beg; (2) 360A in the fork of Nahunga & Goshen Swamps, beg. at a water oak in Nahunga Swamp, the corner of FELIX KENAN'S 400A survey, now belonging to NATHAN L. DAVIS, to a pine on JOHN NEW'S lines now belonging to CHARLES MORRIS, on the main run of Goshen Swamp & down the run of sd. swamp as it meanders to the mouth of the main run of Nahunga Swamp & up the run of Nahunga as it meanders , it being CHARLES WARD'S boundary to the beg. Wit: JAMES REARDON, FELIX K. HILL, NATHAN (X) L. DAVIS. Jan. Ct. 1812.

p. 386   ALEXANDER GRADDY (SENR.) to his son ALEXANDER GRADY JUNR., both of Duplin Co., 10 Dec 1810, for "affection I bear to him as my son" & for the sum of 50¢, 100A being the half of a patent granted to ISAAC DAWSON for 200A, beg. at a pine HENRY GRADY'S corner on the open line of the sd. patent, joining LOTT CROOM & SUTTON'S branch, crossing the Maple String Branch. Wit: FREDK. GRADY, WM. GRADY, HENRY GRADY. Jan. Ct. 1812.

p. 386   READICK WORLEY to FREDERICK SMITH SENR., both of Duplin Co., 20 Nov 1811, for $580, 145A on the ES of the Northeast Swamp joining sd. SMITH & FREDERICK SMITH JUNR., beg. at a pine FREDERICK SMITH JUNR.'S corner near the Flaggy Bottom, to the mouth of the Stoop Hickory Branch, along the road to the Flaggy Bottom Branch, thence down sd. branch to FREDK. SMITH JUNR.'S line & with his line to the beg. Wit: O. O'DANIEL, L. BARFIELD. Jan. Ct. 1812.

p. 388   LOTT GREGORY of Sampson Co. to LOFTEN QUINN of Duplin Co., 18
Jan 1811, for $150 lawful money, 200A on the SWS of the Beaverdam of Limestone
Creek, about half a mile where the main road crosses sd. creek or Beaverdam
prong in 2 tracts to wit: (1) 100A beg. at a white oak on the side of the swamp joining SOLOMON COX'S line, granted to HENRY HULET by patent 29 Oct 1782 & by
him to JOHN FRANK who deeded to sd. GREGORY; (2) 100A adj. the 1st 100A,
patented by JOSEPH CANADAY & conveyed to sd. GREGORY by deed 30 Mar 1798.
Wit: JOSEPH T. RHODES, JOHN E. HUSSEY. Jan. Ct. 1812.

p. 389   EDWD. (EDWARD) ALBERSON to SAMUEL DAVIS, both of Duplin Co., 17
Oct 1810, for 10 pds. 200A on or near the head of the Great Branch, incl. JOHN
SMYTH'S impr., beg. at a poplar in a small branch, taken up by SAMUEL SOWELL
& left to be sold by his exrs. & WILLIAM SORRELL became the purchaser & he
sold to sd. ALBERSON who now sells to sd. DAVIS. Wit: SAMPSON GRIMES, A.
MAXWELL. Jan. Ct. 1812.

p. 390   JAMES HALL, Shff. to DANIEL LOVE KENAN, both of Duplin Co., 8 Aug
1805, 319A levied on by sd. HALL for the taxes due on sd. land for the year 1800 &
as the prop. of the heirs of JAMES SPITTER dec'd, which land was advertised for
sale on 10 May 1805. The sd. KENAN offered the sum of $5.50, that being the
division the same for 319A , that being the least number of acres any person on the
sd. day of sale would take to pay the afsd. sum. The sd. land beg. at a pine JAMES
KENAN'S corner in LEMUEL GUY'S line, to a pine sd. KENAN'S corner of a survey
patented by OWEN KENAN, that line to a pine on the SS of the main road in an
Island, to the line of a tract sold by HUGH McCANNE, Esqr. as the prop. of JAMES
ALLEN, Esqr. for the taxes due on the same. Wit: EDWARD HALL. Jan. Ct.
1812.

p. 391   JOHN McGOWEN to THOMAS MOLTEN, both of Duplin Co., 22 Jan 1812,
for $400 a negro boy slave named GEORGE MITCHEL. Wit: ANDREW McINTIRE.
July Ct. 1812.

p. 392   ALEXD. (ALEXANDER) CARTER to JONATHAN H. NICKINS, both of
Duplin Co., 10 Nov 1811, for $250, 146A on the ES of the Northeast & on the NS of
Matthews Branch, it being part of several surveys, beg. at a red oak on the NS of
Matthews Branch in the 4th line of a survey granted to WILLIAM SOUTHERLAND
for 150A, just at the head of CARTER'S mill pond, adj. EDWARD ALBERSON &
H. GRADY, to the run of Juniper Branch, to the run of Matthews Branch. Wit:
JAMES STEWART, OWEN O'DANIEL, JOHN (X) WARD. Apr. Ct. 1812.

p. 393   ALEXD. (ALEXANDER) CARTER of Duplin Co. to LEAH CARTER of
Lenoir Co., 27 Dec 1811, for $167.80, 118A on the ES of the Northeast & on the
NS of Matthews Branch, between the Juniper & the Long Branch, beg. at a poplar
in the Juniper Branch, the beg. of THOMAS ROUTLEDGE'S patent of 200A & adj.
BUSH'S line. Wit: H. GRADY, EDWARD ALBERSON. Apr. Ct. 1812.

p. 394   H. (HENRY) GRADY to ALEXANDER CARTER, both of Duplin Co., 25 Dec
1811 for $692.92, 250A on the ES of the Northeast & on the NS of Matthews Branch
in 2 tracts to wit: (1) 100A being part of a patent granted to GEORGE SMITH for
100A 6 Mar 1759, beg. at a red oak in the fork of the Northeast & Matthews Branch,
adj. SAML. DAVIS' line; (2) 150A being a patent granted to SYLVANUS PUMPHRY
& joining the 1st piece, beg. at a white oak near Matthews Branch, joining the line

of DURHAM LEIGH (now SAML. DAVIS'), except GEORGE SMITH'S old survey of
200A now SAMUEL DAVIS' may take off & all that part lying on the ES of the Wolf
Pit Branch. Wit: E. ALBERSON. Apr. Ct. 1812.

p. 395   A. (ANDREW) HURST to WILLIAM HURST, both of Duplin Co., 1 Feb 1812,
for $2,000, 600 1/2 A on the NS of Nahunga Swamp & WS of Kings Branch, beg. at
a water oak BLACKMORE'S corner on the run of Kings Branch, to a pine BLACK-
MORE'S beg. of his 420A survey, joining JOHN SOUTHERLAND & down the run of
Pritty Branch. Wit: (none listed) Apr. Ct. 1812.

p. 396   H. (HENRY) GRADY to ALEXANDER CARTER, both of Duplin Co., 9 Nov
1811, for $237.08 for 209A in 3 tracts to wit: (1) 175A being part of a patent granted
to THOMAS ROUTLEDGE for 200A, beg. at a poplar in Juniper Branch SOLOMON
CARTER'S corner & joining STANLEY; (2) 11A being the contents of a patent
granted to sd. GRADY 3 Nov 1800, beg. at a pine JOSEPH WINFIELD'S corner,
joining ED. ALBERSON'S line, CARTER & WINFIELD; (3) 23A being part of 2
patents, beg. at a poplar in the Juniper the beg. of THOMAS ROUTLEDGE'S 200A
survey, to Matthews Branch. (Heading of the deed says 211A.) Wit: JOHN DEVER
& E. ALBERSON. Apr. Ct. 1812.

p. 398   TIMOTHY MURPHY to JOHN STALLINGS, both of Duplin Co., 20 Apr
1807, (sum not given), a negro boy named STEPHEN about 18 or 19 years old. Wit:
S. STALLINGS, JOHN VANN. Apr. Ct. 1812.

p. 398   JACOB WELLS to ISAAC HALL, both of Duplin Co., 28 Nov 1811, for
$550 lawful money of N. C. a negro fellow named GEORGE about 20 yrs. of age.
Wit: DD. WILLIAMS, W. W. RIVENBARK. Apr. Ct. 1812.

p. 399   O. (OWEN) O'DANIEL (co. not given) to his dau. CHARITY KORNEGAY
(co. not given), 8 Aug 1811, a deed of gift for a negro girl named MILLEY her
lifetime & after her lifetime to the heirs of her body. Wit: FRED. SMITH. Apr.
Ct. 1812.

p. 399   D. (DANIEL) KENAN, Shff. of Duplin Co. to EDWARD ARMSTRONG (co.
not given), 20 Sep 1811, for $201, 275A at public auction held on 2 Sep 1811, levied
on by sd. KENAN & being in 2 tracts to wit: (1) 125A on the NS of Burncoat & BS of
Sutton's Branch, beg. at a lightwood stake the last corner of his old survey that was
patented by JOHN THOMSON, adj. B. THOMSON & DAVISON; (2) 150A deeded by
JOHN THOMPSON to JOHN JOHNSTON on the ES of the Northeast River & the NS of
Burncoat Swamp, beg. at a white oak & runs to a hickory, thence to HUMPHRY
WILLIAMS' corner, adj. JOHNSTON'S line in Sutton's Branch. The Sup. Ct. at
Edenton, Chowan Co. awarded 249 pds. 3 shill. & 9 pence, plus 10 pds. 16 shill.
for cost & damages to JOHN BURNSIDE & others, in a suit against JOHN JOHN-
STON'S admrs. JAMES WRIGHT & EDWARD PEARSALL, owners of the sd. 2 tracts
of land. Wit: SM. DAVIS, WILLIAM GLISSON. Apr. Ct. 1812.

p. 401   ED. (EDWARD) ARMSTRONG to SAMUEL DAVIS, both of Duplin Co., 2
Apr 1812, for $255, 275A on the ES of the Northeast & on the NS of Burncoat Swamp
on Sutton's Branch, known by the name of Johnston Place, in 2 tracts to wit: (1)
150A beg. at a white oak joining HUMPHRY WILLIAMS, JOSEPH SUTTON'S line in
Sutton's Branch; (2) 125A beg. at a lightwood post, the last corner of the 1st piece,
joining BENJAMIN THOMPSON, SOLOMON CARTER, WILLIAM THOMPSON, ISSAC

DAWSON. Wit: D. L. KENAN, WM. STREE. Apr. Ct. 1812.

p. 402   ALEXD. (ALEXANDER) CARTER to SAMUEL DAVIS, both of Duplin Co.,
17 Sep 1812, for $750, 250A on the ES of the Northeast River & on a branch called
Matthews Branch in 2 tracts to wit: (1) 100A beg. at a red oak near the mouth of sd.
branch, joining DAVIS' line; (2) 150A beg. at a red oak near the mouth of sd. branch
joining DAVIS' line; (2) 150A beg. at a white oak near or side of the branch, running
to the 2nd corner of the other survey, adj. DAVIS, to a red oak on the hill of the
Wolf Pit Branch, down the run to Matthews Branch. Wit: ALEXD. OUTLAW, JOHN
STEWART. July Ct. 1813.

p. 404   ISAAC JAMES to SAMUEL WEBB, both of Duplin Co., 19 Aug 1803, for
$60, 20A being part of a tract patented by JOHN EVERS, beg. at a pine near the main
road, near the round pocosin. Wit: ISOM NORRIS, NICANOR (X) JAMES. Oct. Ct.
1803.

p. 405   JESSE MILLARD to THOMAS BENNET JUNR., both of Duplin Co., 15 Feb
1809, for $300, 78A on Dry Pond Branch, beg. at a pine the old corner near the big
path on THOMAS BENNETT SENR.'S line, adj. this own & GULLY. Wit: BENJN.
HODGES, WM. GLISSON. Jan. Ct. 1812.

p. 406   JAMES LANIER, planter, to JAMES GARNER, both of Duplin Co., for $75,
150A on the NS of Cypress Creek, being part of a survey patented by JOHN LANIER
& from him willed to sd. JAMES LANIER, beg. at a pine on OBADIAH EDWARDS'
line on a path about 20 poles E of Hog Pen Branch, the beg. of the patent. Wit:
JOHN LANIER. Dated 28 Dec 1810. Jan. Ct. 1812.

p. 407   BENJAMIN HERRING to JOHN BLIZARD, both of Duplin Co., 1 Oct 1810,
for $60, 75A in Goshen Swamp, beg. at a cypress on the river in MILLER'S given
line, adj. JACOB GLISSON & JAMES PEARSALL. Wit: WM. KORNEGAY JR.,
JOHN MAINOR. Oct. Ct. 1812.

p. 408   WILLIAM GLISSON to JOHN BLIZARD, both of Duplin Co., 17 Sep 1812,
for $85, 17A in the fork of the Northeast River & Goshen, it being part of the MOB-
LEY survey, beg. at a pine about 1/4 mile NS of BLIZARD'S house. Wit: HENRY
GRADY, ALEX. O'DANIEL. Oct. Ct. 1812.

p. 409   STEPHEN GUFFORD to JOHN BLIZARD, both of Duplin Co., 3 Mar 1810,
for 172 pds. 10 shill. 120A on the NS of Goshen Swamp, being part of 3 patents,
patented by JACOB LAWHAUN, WILLIAM GODWIN & JACOB GLISSON, beg. at a
water oak ALEXANDER O'DANIEL'S corner near the corner of BLIZARD'S field, to
a black jack not far from STEPHEN GUFFORD'S house & adj. LEWIS GLISSON &
GEORGE F. KORNEGAY. Wit: WILLIAM KORNEGAY, AL. O'DANIEL. Oct. Ct.
1812.

p. 410   HAMPTON SULIVAN & JOHN SULIVAN to BRYAN GLISSON, all of Duplin
Co., 13 Nov 1812, for $371, 371A on the NS of Goshen at the Cross Roads, being
part of a patent granted to JOHN SULIVAN SENR. dec'd for 790A, beg. at a pine &
black jack the patent beg., adj. EZE. BRANCH'S corner, BROCK'S corner, to a pine
on the WS of the main road. Wit: HENRY GRADY, JOHN OUTLAW, A. BRANCH.
Apr. Ct. 1813.

p. 411   DAVID SMYTH of Lenoir Co. to his son SAMUEL SMYTH of Duplin Co.,
11 Apr 1806, for "natural love & affection", a deed of gift for 408A bought of JOHN
& MICHAEL GLISSON, lying on the SS of the Northeast of Cape Fear River, being
part of sundry grants joined together, the sd. 404A in 5 tracts to wit: (1) 285A beg.
at a pine near Horsepen Branch, to the run of Sandy Run Branch, adj. JAMES
SMYTH'S corner; (2) 50A beg. at a black jack DAVIS' corner, adj. the Horsepen
Branch, SMYTH'S own line & DAVIS' line; (3) 47A conveyed by WILLIAM GRADY
to the sd. DAVID SMYTH, beg. at a bay & pine sd. SMYTH'S corner by Sandy Run,
adj. JOHNSTON, JOHN GLISSON, DANIEL GLISSON (now BRYAN GLISSON); (4)
12A beg. at a white & red oak about 1/4 mile above the mouth of Sandy Run, sd.
SMYTH'S corner, adj. DAVIS, A. GRADY & sd. SMITH; (5) 4A beg. at a poplar in
Horsepen Branch, JAMES SMYTH'S corner, adj. WILLIAM GRADY, BRYAN GLIS-
SON. The last 2 pieces patented by JOHN GLISSON. Also 6A within the lines above
described. Wit: JAMES SMYTH, B. GLISSON. Jan. Ct. 1813.

p. 413   MORDECAI (X) MOBLEY (co. not given) to WILLIAM PICKETT SENR.
(co. not given), 16 Apr 1804, for 20 pds. 87 1/2 A beg. at a water oak on the river
bank NICODEMUS THOMPSON'S corner, to a dividing line across the land so as to
incl. half of 175A transferred by CHARLES GRIMES to ALEX MOBLEY & MORDE-
CAI MOBLEY, being part of a grant to the sd. THOMPSON for 350A. Wit: WILL-
IAM JOHNSON, ARTHUR MURRAY. Apr. Ct. 1804.

p. 415   WILLIAM HALL SENR. to THOMAS SHEPARD, both of Duplin Co., 11 Feb
1804, for 261 pds. 5 shill. current money of N. C. 372A in 2 tracts to wit: (1) 187A
incl. the buildings & planta. whereon sd. SHEPARD lives, lying on BS of Pasture
Branch, beg. on the NES of the branch on MIDDLETON'S line, joining MICHAEL
DICKSON, JAMES' line, to the main road in the run of Pasture Branch, to the run of
a branch at the lower corner of JOHN McCULLOCH'S old field at MICHL. DICKSON'S
corner, being part of 300A conveyed by deed from JAMES PEARSALL to JAMES
JAMES dated 20 Sep 1778; (2) 100A joining the 1st tract, lying on BS of the main
road, incl. the buildings where sd. SHEPARD now lives, being 1/2 of a tract of 200A
patented by JOHN McCULLOCH JUNR. & by him conveyed to WILLIAM HUNTER who
conveyed to THOMAS E. JAMES, beg. at a black jack in the 2nd line of the patent, a
little NW of a branch called Polleath, 26 poles from the 3rd corner of the patent,
crossing the branch & both main roads & joining McCULLOCH'S patent line, ALEX-
ANDER DICKSON'S line & JAMES JAMES' old line; (3) 20A lying on the head drains
of the far prong of Alder Swamp, being part of 100A patented by JAMES PEARSALL
10 Nov 1784, beg. at a pine ROBERT DICKSON'S corner, joining JOHN McCULLOCH
& ROBERT DICKSON; (4) 65A on both the main roads, being part of the 200A patented
by JOHN McCULLOCH JUNR., being the same 65A as laid off by CHARLES HOOKS,
Esqr. to THOMAS E. JAMES, being part of 100A sold by HUGH McCANNE, Shff. &
c. Wit: HEZK. MILLARD, WM. WILLIAMS. Apr. Ct. 1804.

p. 417   THOMAS E. JAMES to WILLIAM HALL SENR., both of Duplin Co., 11 Sep
1801, for 261 pds. 5 shill. current money of N. C. 372A in 4 tracts. (See the above
deed, p. 415, WILLIAM HALL SENR. to THOMAS SHEPARD for land description.)
Wit: HOLDEN McGEE, HENRY CANNON, THOMAS McGEE. Apr. Ct. 1804.

p. 419   TH. (THOMAS) ROUTLEDGE, planter, to EDWARD PEARSALL, both of
Duplin Co., 12 Feb 1789, for 215 pds. 200A in 2 tracts to wit: (1) 150A on the NS of
the Golden Grove, beg. at an ash below the bridge on the run of the Grove Swamp,
crossing Buckskin Branch, being a tract bought by the sd. ROUTLEDGE of MARGA-
RET EVANS, adj. the 1st tract, beg. on BS of Buckskin Branch, beg. at a pine

FELIX KENAN'S corner, joining MARGARET EVANS & FELIX KENAN. Wit:
DAVID MURDOCK, JOHN JOHNSTON. Oct. Ct. 1803.

p. 421   JOHN JOHNSTON to EDWARD PEARSALL, both of Duplin Co., 2 Jan 1796,
for 50 pds. specie 300A on BS of the main road, between the Grove Swamp & Carr's
Branch, being a survey patented by BENJAMIN JOHNSTON 16 Dec 1769, beg. at a
red oak JOHN MILLER'S 4th corner of his 150A survey joining sd. MILLER'S line
of his 300A survey, joining WILLIAM ROUTLEDGE & ARCHIBALD CARR. Wit:
J. PEARSALL, ARCHIBALD CARR. Oct. Ct. 1803.

p. 423   BENJ. (BENJAMIN) ELLIS to JAMES HOUSTON, both of Duplin Co., 26 Jan
1804, for $150, 11 lots in Sarecta, being Nos. 41, 49, 50, 28, 29, 30, 8, 18, 33,
40 & 45, agreeable to the plat & deed of sd. town as is recorded, with all buildings
& impr. upon the same made & done. Wit: JOHN HOUSTON, JNO. FELIX RHODES.
Apr. Ct. 1804.

p. 424   ISAAC (ⲧ) JAMES to JOHN WHITMAN, both of Duplin Co., 18 May 1805,
for 90 pds. specie 212A on the NS of Island Creek, it being a part of 2 surveys, beg.
at a gum on the run of sd. creek, at or just above Wyatt's Ford, to a stake in the
Great Desert, joining BONEY, JOHN COOK'S old corner, it being every part of the
land that sd. JAMES bought of MARTIN HANCHEY. Wit: JAMES WHITMAN, DAVID
WHITMAN. Oct. Ct. 1805.

p. 425   WILLIAM (R.) HARRIS & URIAH (N) HARRIS to SAMUEL HERRING, all of
Duplin Co., 12 Dec 1803, for 100 pds. 200A on the N side of the Northeast Marsh &
WS of Lewis' Branch, incl. his impr., beg. at a poplar, small pine & water oak in
the branch about 30 poles above SAMUEL HERRING'S corner, being land granted to
sd. HERRING from WILLIAM REVES. Wit: THO. REAVES, HARDY REAVES.
Apr. Ct. 1804.

p. 426   ARCHIBALD CARR to JOHN JOHNSTON, both of Duplin Co., 10 Jan 1799,
for 35 pds. specie 37A on the NS of the Grove Swamp & BS of Gum Branch, being a
part of a survey of land patented by GEORGE WILLIAMS 2 Mar 1775, beg. at a pine
below the pine, adj. CURLING SMITH. Wit: EDWARD PEARSALL, JED. B. FOLEY
& JACOB WILLIAMS. Oct. Ct. 1813.

p. 428   MICHAEL WILKINS of Duplin Co. to WILLIAM WHITFIELD of Wayne Co.,
1 Oct 1803, for $25, 75A on the ES of Lewis Branch, being part of a survey granted
to WILIE CARTER, beg. at a pine SAMUEL HERRING'S old line, the beg. corner of
sd. survey, to the sd. Lewis Branch. Wit: B. KORNEGAY, SAMUEL HEARING.
Apr. Ct. 1804.

p. 429   WHITFIELD HERRING (co. not given) to STEPHEN HERRING (co. not
given), both planters, 23 Oct 1796, for 15 pds. 50A on the NS of Goshen Swamp,
joining STEPHEN HERRING'S other line & being part of a patent granted to sd.
WHITFIELD HERRING, beg. at a hickory by the head of the Great Meadow across
the Bridge Branch, to a corner agreed on by ANDREW GUFFORD & the sd. HERR-
ING. Wit: OWEN O'DANIEL, GEO. L. ASBURY. Apr. Ct. 1804.

p. 431   JOHN SULIVENT (SENR.) to STEPHEN HERRING, both of Duplin Co., 13
July 1803, (sum not given), 25A on Herrings Marsh, joining BENJAMIN SNIPES,
GUFFORD & HERRING, beg. at a white oak BENJAMIN SNIPES' corner, on the main

road about 1/2 mile from Herring's Marsh. Wit: LEWIS SULIVENT. Apr. Ct. 1804.

p. 432   GEORGE (T) THOMAS, planter of Wayne Co. to SOLOMON CARTER of Duplin Co., 19 Sep 1801, for $25 in silver 85A in the fork & on BS of Brandy Branch on the ES of the Beaverdam of Limestone, beg. at a pine on the edge of a small drain of Brandy Branch, adj. LEWIS WILLIAMS' corner (formerly LOTT GREGORY) to a pine in Buck Pocosin. Wit: CHRISTOPHER LAWSON, LEWIS STROUD. Oct. Ct. 1803.

p. 433   URIAH (N) HARRIS to GEORGE HASE, both of Duplin Co., 29 Dec 1803, for 69 pds. 10 shill. 100A on the SS of Little Horsepen Branch incl. the Water Hole, beg. at a pine THOMAS AYRS' corner, being granted to sd. HASE by HARDY REVES. Wit: SAMUEL HERRING, NEDHAM BASS. Apr. Ct. 1804.

p. 434   SAMUEL HERRING of Duplin Co. to WILLIAM WHITFIELD of Wayne Co., 19 July 1803, for 80 pds. current money 171A on the head branch of the Northeast on a branch called Lewis Branch, joining the Little Horsepen Branch in 2 tracts to wit: (1) 91A beg. at a black jack sd. HERRING'S 3rd corner of his 400A survey, to a poplar in Lewis Branch, joining JOHN HARRIS & along his line to the Little Horsepen Branch, it being a part of the afsd. 400A survey; (2) 80A joining the 1st tract of 91A, being a patent granted to ZACHERIAH HARRIS 22 Oct 1800 by his Excellency BENJAMIN WILLIAMS, beg. at a poplar in a small branch of Lewis' Swamp, being sd. HERRING'S corner, crossing the swamp to GEORGE KORNEGAY'S corner & along WATSON'S line. Wit: MICAJAH CASEY, WM. CASEY, WM. CULLEN COOK. Apr. Ct. 1804.

p. 436   ZECHARIAH (𝒴) HARRIS to SAMUEL HERRING, both of Duplin Co., 17 Feb 1803, for 40 pds. 80A on BS of Lewis Swamp, beg. at a poplar in a branch of Lewis Swamp, the beg. of EZEKIEL WATSON'S 200A survey & runs as SAMUEL HERRING'S line (now MICHAEL WILKINGS' line), crossing the swamp to GEORGE KORNEGY'S corner, to WATSON'S old line, the sd. land being entered 22 Oct 1800. Wit: HARDY (𝓎) REEVES, WM. (𝓌) HERRING, JESSE (X) NEWEL. Apr. Ct. 1804.

p. 437   HARDY (𝓡) REAVES to SAMUEL HERRING, both of Duplin Co., 14 Jan 1802, for 45 pds. 10 shill. 91A on Lewis Branch & joining the Little Horsepen Branch, beg. at a black jack a corner called SAMUEL HERRING'S corner, to a poplar in Lewis Branch called SAMUEL HERRING'S corner, joining JOHN HARRIS & along his line to the Little Horse Pen Branch. Wit: MAJOR (X) SARLS, THO. REVES. Apr. Ct. 1804.

p. 438   THO. (THOMAS) ROUTLEDGE SENOIR of Duplin Co. to BENJAMIN LIDDON (co. not given), 27 Dec 1799, for 225 pds. 3 negroes to wit: CLOE a wench about 18 yrs. old & her 2 children BILL & JOHN. Wit: JAMES HALL. Apr. Ct. 1800.

p. 439   FREDERICK BARFIELD to LEWIS BARFIELD, both of Duplin Co., 24 July 1799, for 520 pds. current money of N. C. 6 negro slaves to wit: ELLECK about 14 yrs. old, TOM about 13 yrs. old, NANCY about 7 yrs. old, DINAH about 30 yrs. old & her child LUCY about 3 yrs. old & her youngest child SMITH about 7 mos. old. Wit: WM. DICKSON. Apr. Ct. 1800.

p. 439   ANNIE (X) BROWN (co. not given) to NATHANIEL KINNARD (co. not given), 1 Feb 1795, for $100 a negro woman named PHEBE. Wit: JAMES KINNARD. Apr. Ct. 1800.

p. 440   WM. (WILLIAM) McGOWEN (co. not given) to STEPHEN HERRING (co. not given) 24 Jan 1799, for 90 pds. a negro girl called MARY. Wit: J. PEARSALL, EDWARD PEARSALL. Apr. Ct. 1800.

p. 440   BRYAN EDMUNDSON (co. not given) to FRANCIS OLIVER (co. not given), 31 Mar 1802, for $300 a negro boy called WILLIS about 10 yrs. old. Wit: JOSEPH DICKSON. Apr. Ct. 1804.

p. 441   STEPHEN B. HERRING of Duplin Co. to WILLIAM BRANCH (co. not given), ____Apr 1804, for $450 a negro boy named DAVIE about 19 yrs. of age. Wit: (none listed) Apr. Ct. 1804.

p. 441   J. (JOHN) BECK of Sampson Co. to WILLIAM DUNKIN of Duplin Co., 27 Feb 1795, for 75 pds. current money a negro woman slave named ROSE. Wit: JAMES BIZZEL, JOHN BRADLEY. Oct. Ct. 1800.

p. 442   EDWARD HOUSTON to his beloved dau. REBECKAH HOUSTON, both of Duplin Co., 5 Dec 1803, for "natural love & affection" a negro boy named LIMBRICK about 8 mos. old. MARY (X) HOUSTON also signed the deed. Wit: JACOB WILLIAMS, Esqr., JNO. FELIX RHODES. Proved in court by oath of JACOB WILLIAMS. Apr. Ct. 1804.

p. 442   HANCEL (I) IZZEL (EZZEL) to ELIAS JAMES, both of Duplin Co., 20 Feb 1811, for $100, 100A lying on Clark's Branch, beg. at a pine saplin PHILLIP MERRITT'S corner, joining ELIAS JAMES' line (formerly WILLIAM MERRITT'S), to WILLIAM MERRITT'S new entry & joining PHILIP MERETT'S corner. Wit: ABRAHAM JAMES, JAMES BUTLER. July Ct. 1812.

p. 445   JACOB GILMORE to JOHN GULLY, both of Duplin Co., 21 July 1812, for $50, 80A on the NS of Goshen Swamp & on the head of the Great Branch, beg. at a pine THOMAS TAYLOR'S old corner & adj. BLIZZARD'S old line. Wit: SOLOMON JONES. July Ct. 1812.

p. 445   MAURICE FENNEL & EDMOND FENNEL, both of Sampson Co. to JOSHUA BLANTON of Duplin Co., 14 June 1812, for $65, 100A beg. at a pine by a small pond on the ES of a new road, crossing a prong of Long Branch to a pine. Wit: THOMAS GOFF, AUSTIN JONES. July Ct. 1812.

p. 446   JAMES DICKSON of Duplin Co. to his loving son JAMES DICKSON JUNR. (co. not given), 1 May 1812, for "natural love good will & affection" a negro boy slave named AUSTON age 9 yrs. Wit: JOHN MAXWELL. July Ct. 1812.

p. 446   JAS. (JAMES) DICKSON (SENR.) of Duplin Co. to his loving son JAMES DICKSON JUNR. (co. not given), 1 May 1812, "for natural love good will & affection" a deed of gift for 470A in 3 tracts: (1) 250A on BS of Big Elder & Little Elder & WS of the main road leading from Duplin Court House to Rockfish Bridge, beg. at a pine SS of Little Elder, a corner of land sold by JOHN DICKSON to sd. JAMES DICKSON, adj. ROBERT DICKSON, SWINSON'S line by the run of Big Elder, SWINSON'S line to the corner of a survey belonging to ROBERT & WILLIAM DICKSON; (2) 120A sold by JOHN DICKSON to JAMES DICKSON, beg. at a pine SS of Little Elder Branch; (3) 100A joining the above, beg. at a pine ALEXANDER HOLDEN'S corner, adj. THOMAS MILLER, HARREL, ALEXR. DICKSON. Wit: JOHN MAXWELL. July Ct. 1812.

p. 448   WILLIAM (X) FREDERICK of Duplin Co. to his daus. CATHERINE HOUSTON, wife of JOHN HOUSTON, JANE TIPLER, wife of GEORGE TIPLER, MARY WILKINSON, wife of JOHN WILKINSON, NANCY & BETSY FREDERICK, 17 July 1812, for "natural love & affection" the following negroes to wit: To CATHERINE HOUSTON a negro girl named CHARLOTTE age 17 yrs; to JANE TIPLER a negro girl named MACE aged 12 yrs; to MARY WILKINSON a certain girl named MILLEY age 15 yrs; to NANCY FREDERICK a girl named MINERVA age 12 yrs.; to BETSEY FREDERICK a certain girl named PRESCILLA aged 9 yrs., reserving my life estate in the girl MILLY granted to my dau. MARY WILKINSON & if either of sd. daus. die without children, the negro granted to them to be equally divided among their surviving sisters. Wit: DANIEL L. KENAN, JOHN STEWART. July Ct. 1812.

p. 449   GEORGE WILLIAMS (co. not given) to EDWARD WILLIAMS (co. not given), 16 Oct 1811, for $25 a sorrel horse colt about one yr. old & upwards. Wit: GEORGE E. HOUSTON. July Ct. 1812.

p. 449   D. L. (DANIEL LOVE) KENAN, Shff. to JAMES WILLIAMS, both of Duplin Co., for $2.50, 99A of a 100A tract, being the property of NATHAN BATTS, lying in the waters of Muddy Creek, remaining due & unpaid for for the year 1809, which land was advertised by law to be sold at auction to be adjudged in part to the person offering to pay the taxes thereon, the sd. land lying on JOHN WILLIAMS' branch, a drain of Muddy Creek, joining sd. JAMES WILLIAMS' own line, beg. at a water oak of sd. branch by the ford, to a stake in the Long Branch, down the sd. courses of sd. branch to sd. WILLIAMS' branch to the beg., the sd. 99A surveyed 15 Nov 1811 by HUGH MAXWELL, Sur. Wit: JAS. HALL. July Ct. 1812.

p. 451   JESSE JONES to JOHN MILLER, both of Duplin Co., 22 Mar 1810, for $221, 127 3/4A on the SS of Big Ready Branch, beg. at a water oak in Big Ready Meadow Branch, to a gum in Little Ready Meadow Branch. Wit: JOSEPH GILLESPIE. July Ct. 1812.

p. 452   GEORGE J. HODAM to his son RALPH JOURNEGAN, planter, both of Duplin Co., 21 Mar 1804, for "natural love & affection" 122A beg. at a gum in the Outlaw Branch, joining SULIVAN, to 3 white bays in Rooty Branch, to the widow SULIVAN'S & his own corner a gum, to a pine on the head of Outlaw's Branch. Wit: JAMES JOURNEGAN. Apr. Ct. 1813.

p. 454   LEWIS BROCK, Patent No. 936, 21 Sep 1785, for 100A on Taylor's Creek, a branch of Rockfish, beg. at a pine a little N of the Creek, his own old corner formerly THOMAS KENAN'S. Signed by RD. (RICHARD) CASWELL.

p. 454   JOHN CARR, Patent No. 2008, 4 Dec 1812, 77A on the SS of Maxwell Swamp, beg. at a black gum on the run of Maxwell Swamp, joining CARR'S own corner. Signed by WILLIAM HAWKINS. Entered 20 July 1812.

p. 454   JOHN CARR, Patent No. 2009, 4 Dec 1812, 30A on the SS of Maxwell

Swamp, joining JAMES HARRELL'S line & BONEY'S old line. Entered 16 July 1811. Signed by WILLIAM HAWKINS.

p. 455   HARDY BIZZEL to JAMES BIZZEL, both of Duplin Co., 25 Feb 1811, for $700, 550A on the ES of White Oak Swamp, beg. at a white oak in the head of sd. swamp, to a gum in Thunder Swamp Pocosin, to a dead pine on an island, along his own line, to a pine near the main road, joining JACOB WHITEHEAD'S survey, to the Long Pond, with the dividing line, to White Oak Swamp at the mouth of a small branch, up sd. swamp to the beg., being the land & incl. the house & planta. whereon sd. HARDY BIZZEL now lives. Wit: JOHN BECK, JNO. WATKINS, GEO. BENNETT. (Heading of the deed says 450A.) Apr. Ct. 1812.

p. 456   JOHN FARRIOR to his son BRYAN FARRIOR, both of Duplin Co., 1 May 1801, "for natural love & affection" 420A on the branches of Muddy Creek, incl. the whole of a survey of 150A granted to JOHN MEGEE & part of several surveys granted to JOHN WOODWARD, RICHARD KEEN, DANIEL SOUTHERLAND & JOHN MEGEE, beg. at a gum in JOHN FARRIOR'S planta. in the SS of the Mill or Marsh Branch, joining sd. SOUTHERLAND & JOHN FARRIOR. Wit: HUGH McCANNE, JAMES BATTS. Apr. Ct. 1812.

p. 458   GEORGE (T) THOMAS, MARY (/) THOMAS, TIMOTHY (T) GOODMAN & ELIZABETH (/) GOODMAN of Lenoir Co. to EDWARD ALBERSON of Duplin Co., 4 Nov 1806, for 80 milled dollars 100A on the waters of the Northeast River, beg. at a stake in the marsh, joining SAMUEL DREW & JAMES MATTHIS, taken up by SAMUEL SOWELL & conveyed by deed to JOHN BARNET & from him as by heirship. Wit: ALLEN WOOTEN, SHAD. WOOTEN. Proven by oath of SAMUEL DAVIS. Oct. Ct. 1812.

p. 459   WILLIAM DICKSON to SAMUEL STANFORD, both of Duplin Co., 20 Jan 1813, for $1,025 lawful money 520A on BS of Elder Swamp, beg. at ROBERT DICKSON'S upper corner, crossing Little Elder, to a stake among 6 pines on a line called MURRAY'S line, being part of a deed from JAMES DICKSON to WILLIAM HALL SENR. for 1,570A dated 17 Oct 1797. Wit: JONATHAN THOMAS. July Ct. 1813.

p. 460   JOSEPH BROOKS, Patent No. 2036, 24 Nov 1813, for 52A on the waters of Island Creek, beg. at a red oak WILLIAM CARR & JAMES MALLARD'S corner to THOMAS' corner. Entered 24 Mar 1812. Signed WILLIAM HAWKINS.

p. 461   EDWARD PEARSALL, Patent No. 1751, 17 Sep 1802, for 100A on the WS of the Northeast River on the head of the Gum Swamp, joining JOHN JOHNSTON, GEORGE WILLIAMS, ARCHIBALD CARR, STEPHEN MILLER & McINTIRE. Entered 10 Jan 1794. Signed by B. WILLIAMS.

p. 461   EDWARD PEARSALL, Patent No. 1662, 14 Apr 1800, for 35A on the NS of the Grove, beg. at a pine DAVID MURDOCK'S corner, adj. PEARSALL, JOSEPH JOHNSTON. Entered 5 Oct 1785. Signed by B. WILLIAMS.

p. 461   EDWARD PEARSALL, Patent No. 1854, 19 Dec 1805, for 130A on the NS of Grove Swamp, beg. at a pine & gum where McCULLOCH'S maple corner formerly stood, below the bridge, to KENAN'S old corner. Entered 22 Nov 1804. ALEX. MARTIN, Sp. Sur. during the inability of the Gov.

p. 462   EDWARD PEARSALL, Patent No. 1747, 17 Sep 1802, for 50A on the NS of
the Grove Swamp, beg. at a pine DAVID MURDOCK'S corner, adj. JOSEPH JOHN-
STON'S. Entered 8 Jan 1800. Signed by B. WILLIAMS.

p. 462   ELISHA (X) CARTER of Washington Co., Va. to WINDEL DAVIS of Lenoir
Co., 20 Apr 1813, for $250, 150A on the ES of the Northeast & on the SS of Matthews
Branch, beg. at a pine on the side of the sd. swamp, to a white oak & red oak the
1st & last corner of the ANTHONY & WILLIAM WILLIAMS' survey, joining ISAAC
DAWSON'S corner, may include the Dry Island on the run of the dividing branch &
joining GRADY. RACHEL CARTER (wife of EDWARD CARTER & mother of
ELISHA CARTER) came before WILLIAM TATE, a J. P. for Washington Co. &
declared that her son ELISHA CARTER is 21 yrs. of age, being born on the 19 Apr
1792. Certified by sd. TATE on 20 Apr 1813. Wit: WILLIAM TATE, SAMUEL
DAVIS. July Ct. 1813.

p. 464   JOHN BUSH to SAMUEL STANFORD, both of Duplin Co., ___ Jan 1813,
for $41, 100A on the NS of Maxwell Swamp & WS of Eldar Swamp, beg. at a pine a
corner of land granted to ALEXANDER DICKSON (later JAMES DICKSON'S), joining
ROBERT DICKSON. Wit: JOHN MAXWELL, GEORGE McGOWEN. Apr. Ct. 1813.

p. 465   WILLIAM GRADDY to HENRY GRADY, both of Duplin Co., 29 Aug 1812,
for 12 pds. 15 shill. a bill of sale for a certain parcel of cattle to wit: 2 cows &
calves, one bull, a certain parcel of hogs cont. about 20 head & all of the residue of
my prop. that is in the hands of sd. HENRY GRADY. Wit: LEWIS HERRING, JOS.
WHITFIELD. July Ct. 1813.

p. 465   SAMPSON GRIMES to his son JESSE GRIMES, both of Duplin Co., 14 Jan
1813, for "natural love & affection" a deed of gift for 300A on the NS of Goshen
Swamp & on the WS of Absolam's Branch in 4 tracts to wit: (1) 60A beg. at a
hickory WILLIAM HERRING'S corner, joining STEPHEN HERRING'S old line &
JOHN HOUSMAN'S old line; (2) (acreage not given) on Absolam's Branch & Goshen
Swamp, beg. at a hickory on Goshen; (3) (acreage not given) beg. at WILLIAM
HERRING'S corner & beg. of a tract patented by WILLIAM BULLARD & also the
beg. of the 1st tract mentioned in the deed, to a pine ABSOLAM WESTON'S old
line, being the contents of a deed of 2 sundry pieces of land conveyed by REUBEN
WESTON to JOHN HOUSMAN, patent dated 10 Dec 1788; (4) (acreage not given)
between & joining the 2 other pieces afsd. mentioned, beg. at a pine stump in
Absolam's Branch, HOUSMAN'S old corner, WILLIAM BULLARD'S old line, now
WILLIAM HERRING'S line, joining SAMPSON GRIMES' old corner, to a maple in
Big Meadow Branch, thence OUTLAW'S old line to the beg., being the contents of a
patent granted to REUBEN WESTON 20 Dec 1791 & sold by execution as the prop. of
sd. WESTON by THOMAS WRIGHT, High Shff. of Duplin Co. to DANIEL GLISSON &
conveyed by GLISSON to SAMPSON GRIMES. The last 3 tracts totaling 240A with
the 1st tract of 60A, making a total of 300A, the 1st tract being patented 1 Apr
1780. Wit: LOFTEN QUINN, NATHAN WALLER, TIMOTHY SPENCE. July Ct.
1813.

p. 468   GEORGE (T) THOMAS, TIMOTHY (T) GOODMAN, MARY (T) THOMAS
& ELIZAB. (ELIZABETH) (X) GOODMAN all of Lenoir Co. to EDWARD ALBER-
SON of Duplin Co., 3 Nov 1806, for 20 milled dollars 100A on the waters of the
Northeast River, beg. at a red oak taken up by ELIJAH BOWEN & conveyed by deed
to SAMUEL SOWELL & from sd. SOWELL to JOHN BEVENT & from him by heir-

ship to the sd. THOMAS & GOODMAN. Wit: ALLEN WOOTEN, SHAD. WOOTEN. Proved in court by oath of SAMUEL DAVIS. Oct. Ct. 1812.

p. 469   JAMES ELLIS & his wife MARY ELLIS of Duplin Co. to MOSES MANNING of Onslow Co., 13 Oct 1790, for 80 pds. specie 85A on the ES of the Northeast Branch of Cape Fear River & lying on Stafford's Branch, beg. at a black gum in the swamp, to a pine by Spring Branch, along the patent line to the run of Stafford's Swamp & runs the run of the swamp to the patent line, being land patented by HENRY SKIBBOW in 1762. Wit: MOSES MANNING. Oct. Ct. 1793.

p. 470   LEWIS BARFIELD (JUNR.) to REDICK WORLEY, both of Duplin Co., 20 Nov 1811, (sum not given), 200A on the ES of the Northeast Swamp & on a small branch called Lawhorn's Branch, patented by LEWIS BARFIELD SENR. 24 Feb 1779, beg. at a pine near his own corner of land patented by GEORGE SMITH, joining THOMAS WORLEY'S corner by a pond & JOHN WILLIAMS' line to the beg. Wit: FRED. SMITH, O. O'DANIEL. Oct. Ct. 1812.

p. 471   THEOPHILUS DILLARD of Lenoir Co. to JOHN PEAL(E) (co. not given), 24 Jan 1811, for 100 pds. 129A on the NS of the Northeast Branch of Cape Fear River, beg. in the Juniper Pond Branch, the sd. PEAL'S line & runs with his line to a pine his corner, with sd. PEAL'S line again to his other corner, to Juniper Run & thence up the meanders of the run to Juniper Pond Branch, up the meanders of sd. Pond Branch to the beg. Wit: BRYAN (X) MINSHEW, JOHN WATSON. Oct. Ct. 1812.

p. 472   STEPHEN (S) MILLS, planter of Duplin Co. to JACOB WELLS, planter, (co. not given), 5 Mar 1812, for $120 lawful money 125A on the lower side of Fussel's Creek & on the NS of Rockfish Creek, beg. at a white oak on the WS of Horse Branch, to a pine by the Great Road. Wit: BYRD WILLIAMS, JOHN WILLIAMS. Oct. Ct. 1812.

p. 473   REUBEN JOHNSTON, Patent No. 715, 9 Nov 1784, for 150A between the head of the Northeast & Calf Pasture Branch, joining JACOB TAYLOR'S line, beg. at a pine TAYLOR'S corner & joining DUNCAN. Signed ALEX. MARTIN.

p. 473   P. (PETER) FREDERICK of Sampson Co. to WILLIAM BECK of Duplin Co., 3 Mar 1808, for 1600 milled dollars 200A on the NS of Panther Swamp where the sd. PETER formerly lived, adj. the lines of LEVI BORDEN & WILLIAM BECK SENR., beg. at a dead pine & small water oak, LEVI BORDEN'S corner on SAML. DUNN'S line & then runs a dividing line between sd. LEVI & sd. PETER to a lightwood stump & pine on the side of the road near WM. BECK SENR.'S fence sd. BECK'S corner, then with BECK'S line to a pine his other corner, then a dividing line between LEVI BORDEN'S & EASON'S land & the above mentioned premises, to a water oak on the run of Panther Swamp, then down the sd. run as it meanders to a pine on the road on SAML. DUNN'S line, thence with DUNN'S line to a frost oak on the WS & near the road, DUNN'S other corner, then with DUNN'S old marked line to the beg. Wit: FELIX K. HILL, JAMES FREDERICK. Jan. Ct. 1813.

p. 475   DAVID CARLTON, planter, to his loving son SHADRACK CARLTON, both of Duplin Co., 31 Mar 1812, for "love good will & affection" 484 1/2A in 5 pieces to wit: (1) beg. at an ash on the run of JAMES' Branch, on ABRAHAM BEESLEY'S line & the corner of another survey of sd. ARMSTRONG'S, to a red oak the corner

of the old 100A survey patented by ISAAC PARKER, to a poplar in ARMSTRONG'S
Branch & up the branch as it meanders with the WILLIAMS' old line, to a water oak
on JAMES' Branch; (2) beg. at a turkey oak on the side of ARMSTRONG'S Branch,
formerly called FRANK'S Branch; (3) tract joining the 1st, beg. at an ash in
JAMES' Branch, the corner of the 200A survey, thence the line of the 100A patented
by ISAAC PARKER, to a turkey oak on the edge of PARKER'S Branch, to a small
gum ABSOLAM STRICKLAND'S corner; (4) a tract beg. at an ash tree on the run
of Jimmy's Branch below a path, to a gum on the run of ARMSTRONG'S Branch,
down branch as it meanders with McGEE'S line to a white oak JAMES' lower corner,
to an old corner of a survey of 200A patented by JAMES WILLIAMS (now PETER
CARLTON'S line), to a gum on the run of Maxwell Swamp; (5) beg. at a white oak
at the run of Jimmy's Branch, RICHARD STRICKLAND'S corner. Wit: WM.
MALLARD, RICHARD (X) STRICKLAND. Oct. Ct. 1812.

p. 477   D. (DANIEL) GLISSON, Shff. of Duplin Co. to FREDERICK SMITH (SENR.),
(co. not given), for 100 pds. 300A on the ES of the Northeast River & below the
mouth of Panther Swamp in 2 tracts to wit: (1) 200A beg. at a water oak in the
mouth of a branch called the Live Branch, adj. WALKER'S line, it being part of a
400A survey granted to ROBERT WALKER in 1740; (2) 100A beg. at a red oak on
the line of the afsd. mentioned survey, granted to SAMUEL RATLIFF in 1750 known
by the name of Ratliff's Venture. The Court awarded 73 pds. 10 pence, plus 1 pd.
2 shill. & 9 pence for cost & charges to ARCHELAUS BRANCH for debt in suit
against FREDERICK SMITH, BENTLEY WESTON & LEWIS BARFIELD. The Shff.
levied on sd. 300A belonging to afsd. SMITH, which sd. SMITH purchased at public
auction 20 July 1812. Wit: LOFTEN QUINN, PHILL SOUTHERLAND JR. Oct. Ct.
1812.

p. 479   PHILL SOUTHERLAND, Patent No. 1738, 5 Dec 1801, for 200A on the WS
of the Northeast of Cape Fear River, beg. at a water oak on the river bank, about
30 yds. below the mouth of Persimmon Creek & sd. to be the corner of WILLIAM
BURTON'S survey of 56A, to a small white oak on CONRAD WHITMAN'S old survey
of 250A, adj. BEN DULANY & CHARLES WARD, to a water oak sd. WARD'S corner
on the river below the Tar Landing, down the river as it meanders to the beg.
(No. 204 entered 30 June 1778; No. 509 entered 3 Jan 1794, No. 1182 entered 2
July 1800) Signed by B. WILLIAMS.

p. 479   WILLIAM COWPER of Murfreesboro, Hertford Co., N. C. to SARAH &
MARY GRAHAM, both of Duplin Co., 31 Dec 1812, for $185 a negro girl named
MATILDA about 11 yrs. old. Wit: STEPHEN GRAHAM, W. P. MORGAN. July
Ct. 1813.

p. 480   D. (DANIEL) L. KENAN, Shff. of Duplin to DANIEL GLISSON of Duplin
Co., 20 Apr 1812, 49A for the sum of $3.69 for one acre less, for which land the
taxes remain due & unpaid for the year 1807 & 1808, the sd. land being advertised
by law & put up at auction to be adjudged in part to the person offering to pay the
public county & parish taxes thereon, with all charges for advertising the same for
the smallest part thereof & sd. GLISSON presented to the Shff. a plat made by
JOHN FARRIOR surveyor of sd. county with the courses & distances set forth &
certified under his hand & purchased sd. land which is on the NS of Goshen, beg.
at a pine formerly BENJAMIN KING'S corner near the White Meadow & JOHN
BLIZZARD's corner of the land he bought of STEPHEN GUFFORD, to a pine on the
ES of the Little Branch. Wit: JOHN HUNTER, J. HALL. Apr. Ct. 1812.

p. 481   SM. (SAMUEL) DAVIS to ALEXANDER CARTER, both of Duplin Co., 22
Feb 1813, for $6, 8A on the ES of the Northeast in Matthews Branch, incl. the mill,
beg. at a stake in the given line of 300A survey in the Mill Pond & runs to a stake in
the pond called PUMPHRY'S corner, to the run of the Wolf Pit Branch. Wit: SAM.
SMYTH, HOPHGIBAH TUTLE. July Ct. 1813.

p. 482   SAMPSON GRIMES to his son JAMES GRIMES, both of Duplin Co., 19 July
1813, for "natural love & affection" 170A on the NS of Goshen Swamp in 3 tracts to
wit: (1) 93A patented by Little JOHN SULLIVAN & conv. by him to JOHN SULLIVAN
SENR., who conveyed to MICHAEL SULLIVAN, then at the division of MICHAEL
SULLIVAN'S lands fell by lott the 6th to SALLY SULLIVAN, dau. of MICHAEL, then
to WILLIAM MONDS by a marriage with SALLY SULLIVAN, then conveyed by sd.
MONDS & SALLY his wife to SAMPSON GRIMES & now from sd. SAMPSON to his
son JAMES GRIMES. The sd. 93A beg. at a large pine in the outline of MICHAEL
SULLIVAN'S lands now belonging to the heirs of sd. SULLIVAN on SAMPSON
GRIMES' former line; (2) 17A patented by SAMPSON GRIMES 19 Dec 1805, beg. at
a pine in the edge of a meadow MILLEY SULLIVAN'S corner, along HAMPTON
SULLIVAN'S line, SAMPSON GRIMES' former line; (3) 60A on BS of Rooty Branch
& on BS of the main road, beg. at a gum in the wedge of Rooty Branch, GEORGE J.
HODAM'S corner. Wit: A. MAXWELL, NATHAN WALLER, JNO. HUFHAM. July
Ct. 1813.

p. 484   A. (ABRAHAM) MOLTEN SENR. to JAMES PATTERSON, both of Duplin
Co., 10 Nov 1792, for 70 pds. current money of N. C. 230A on the NS of the Back
Branch & WS of Stewart's Creek, beg. at a water oak & gum where the Long Branch
& Back Branch joins, joining THOMAS JOHNSTON, to the line of a survey of 300A
patented by ABRAHAM MOLTEN dec'd. Wit: JOHN JOHNSTON, DAVID SLOAN.
July Ct. 1813.

p. 485   ALEXANDER WELLS to ROBERT SLOAN, both planter of Duplin Co., 21
Apr 1812, for 142 pds. 10 shill. 289A on the head drains of Island Creek, it being
part of the lands formerly the prop. of JACOB WELLS, late of Duplin Co., which
was sold at public vendue by the Shff. of Duplin to the afsd. ALEXANDER WELLS,
which land begins at a lightwood stake at the head of a small branch or drains, near
the loose harbour & joining JOHN ALLEN. Wit: GIBSON SLOAN, JOHN
STALLINGS. July Ct. 1813.

p. 487   JOSEPH (X) BROOKS to ROBERT SLOAN, both of Duplin Co., 6 July
1812, for 125 pds. lawful money 194A in 2 tracts to wit: (1) 164A on the SS of Maxwell Swamp & in the fork between Maxwell Swamp & Cabbin Branch, it being the
contents of a patent granted to ANDREW THALLY dated 18 Nov 1794, beg. at a
persimmon & gum on Maxwell Run by ROBERT SLOAN'S corner; (2) 30A beg. at a
white oak & black jack to the 1st station of CUMMINGS' survey, to the run of Cabbin
to a stake in the run ROBERT SLOAN'S corner, with SLOAN'S line to a stake in the
run SLOAN'S other corner in the 3rd line of sd. CUMMINS' patent, thence the
patent line N to a stake in Maxwell Swamp, thence to the beg. Wit: WILLIAM
SWINSON, JOHN SHUFFIELD. July Ct. 1813.

p. 488   D. (DANIEL) GLISSON to ABRAHAM GLISSON, both of Duplin Co., 16 Jan
1813, for $250, 208A in the fork of Goshen & the Northeast & on the NS of Camp
Branch, beg. at a small pine & black gum on the run of Camp Branch, joining
HUDGENS' line, WM. GRADY'S corner, near the head of Sandy Run, THOMAS

GRADY'S corner, DAVID KORNEGAY'S corner, to a pine in the edge of the Camp Branch Pocosin KORNEGAY'S corner. Wit: WILLIAM HUDGENS, HERRING (X) GLISSON. July Ct. 1813.

p. 489   FREDERICK SIKES to WILLIS SIKES, both of Duplin Co., 29 Apr 1813, for $250, 100A in Norfolk Co., Va. on the road leading from Great Bridge to Northwest Landing, which land is bounded by the lands formerly owned by FRANCIS BRISSEE, JOSEPH SIKES & RICHARD SMITH. Wit: JAS. K. HILL, C. HOOKS. July Ct. 1813.

p. 490   JACOB BONEY to WILLIAM BONEY, both of Duplin Co., 3 June 1812, for $35, 20A being part of his old survey on the NS of Rockfish Creek & also on the NS of the main road in sd. county, beg. at a pine his corner of the old survey near Blake's Branch. Wit: JOHN GILMAN, JAMES BONEY. July Ct. 1813.

p. 491   D. L. (DANIEL LOVE) KENAN, Shff. of Duplin Co. to BENJAMIN HODGES (co. not given), for 81 pds. 12 shill. & 3 pence, 150A purchased by JOHN KORNE-GAY for sd. HODGES at public auction held 25 Aug 1810. On 6 Aug 1811 the Court awarded five judgments to sd. HODGES & one judgment to ARCHIBALD MURRAY & one judgment to JOHN WHITEHEAD for damages in separate suits against JAMES WATKINS, owner of the sd. 150A of land on the NS of Goshen Swamp & on the Cow Hole Branch, adj. the lands of LEVIN WATKINS, beg. at a maple & poplar in sd. branch, JAMES HUNTER'S lower corner, adj. JOHN FOLEY & JAMES BAKER BOWDEN'S line, GEORGE OUTLAW & LEVIN WATKINS. Wit: LEVI BORDEN, JAMES TINER, LEWIS TINER. July Ct. 1813.

p. 493   FRED. (FREDERICK) WORLEY & NANCY (X) WORLEY to FREDERICK SMITH SENR., all of Duplin Co., 25 Feb 1813, for $150, 50A on the ES of the North-east Swamp, being patented by HENRY McCULLOCH incl. the ANN HOUSTON field, beg. at a large pine on a drain above the WM. ANN HOUSTON field, to a water oak corner made by FREDERICK SMITH SENR., O. O'DANIEL & DREW SMITH, along a row of marked trees to a holly, gum & bull bay on the run of Tandam Run. Wit: CHRISTOPHER LAWSON, H. GRADY. NANCY WORLEY, wife of FREDK. WORLEY consented to the afsd. conveyance of her own free consent before HENRY GRADY & CHRISTOPHER LAWSON, Esqrs. July Ct. 1813.

p. 494   HUGH MAXWELL, Co. Sur. for 56A to EDMOND DUNCAN (co. not given), 28 May 1813, sd. 56A on the ES of Halls Marsh, it being part of a 500A survey patented by MALPASS & deeded to sd. DUNCAN by the heirs of DANIEL SULLIVAN, beg. at a white oak on the edge of Halls Marsh, JAMES GRIMES' corner. Chainbearers: JESSE OUTLAW, SOLOMON JONES. July Ct. 1813.

p. 494   C. (CHARLES) HOOKS to BENJAMIN HODGES, both of Duplin Co., 14 July 1813, for $900 4 negroes to wit: KEZZIAH, a woman about 25 or 26 yrs. of age; JERRY her son about 7 yrs. of age; PLEASANT her dau. about 4 yrs. of age; & VENUS her dau. about 1 yr. old. Wit: CADER SIKES, H. HODGES. July Ct. 1813.

p. 495   New Hanover Co. GEORGE TAYLOR & WILLIAM H. BEATTY, agent for HAYS G. WHITE to ABRAHAM NEWTON, (cos. not given), 14 Oct 1811, for $500 a negro fellow named LEWIS. Wit: AMBROSE SMITH. July Ct. 1813. Duplin Co.

p. 495   FREDERICK GRADDY of Duplin Co. to HENRY GRADY (co. not given),

10 Apr 1807, for 200 pds. a negro woman named BINER & her child CLOE. Wit:
JOSEPH WHITFIELD. July Ct. 1813.

p. 496   CHARLES (( ) KING to his beloved dau. NANCY KING, both of Duplin Co.,
28 June 1813, for "natural love & affection" a deed of gift for one feather bed &
furn., all stock of horses, cattle, hogs, planta. tools, household & kitchen furn. &
everything that belongs to sd. CHARLES KING " I do make one reserve, that is, my
lifetime of myself & my beloved wife J INNEA KING, we are to be supported as long
as we live & after our deaths, the whole of my estate to my beloved dau. NANCY
KING." Wit: JOHN JONES, WM. SNEAD. July Ct. 1813.

p. 497   JOHN DICKSON of Cumberland Co. to DAVID CARR of Duplin Co., 4 Apr
1812, for $60, 156A on the WS of the Northeast River of Cape Fear & NS of Max-
field Swamp, beg. at a pine WILLIAM CARR'S corner known by the name of the
Galberry Pond, being patented by FLORENCE McCARTY in a grant of 640A &
became the prop. of ROBERT DICKSON & by him conv. to JOHN DICKSON his son
18 Apr 1788. (Heading of deed says 595A, but this apparently an error & meant for
the following deed.) Wit: EDWARD PEARSALL & WILLIAM CARR. Apr. Ct.
1812.

p. 498   JOHN FARIOR (SENR.) to his son JOHN FARIOR JUNR., both of Duplin
Co., 17 Feb 1812, for "natural love & affection" 595A on the branches of Muddy
Creek, incl. part of several surveys, beg. at the run of the S prong of the Mill
Branch on BRYAN FARIOR'S line, runs with his line on the SS of the N prong,
joining BRYAN FARIOR'S corner, DANIEL SOUTHERLAND'S line, JOHN JOHN'S
line by a path, JACOB BROWN SENR. 'S corner, to the mouth of the Mill Branch.
Wit: F. PICKETT, WILLIAM FARIOR. Apr. Ct. 1812.

p. 500   DICKSON SULLIVANT to SAMPSON GRIMES, both of Duplin Co., 13 Dec
1812, for $35.60, 50A on the NS of Goshen Swamp on BS of Rooty Branch & BS of
the main road, beg. at a gum in the wedge of Rooty Branch, GEORGE JORNEGAN
HODAM'S corner. Wit: JESSE GRIMES, WILLIAM GRIMES. Jan. Ct. 1813.

p. 501   JOHN FARIOR to his son WILLIAM FARIOR, both of Duplin Co., 1 Aug
1810, for "natural love & affection" 330A on the branch of Muddy Creek, incl. part
of several surveys, beg. at 2 small white oaks on the SS of the S prong of the Mill
Branch, a little above the fork on BRYAN FARRIOR'S line, joining JAMES PICKETT
& NICHOLAS SANDLIN. Wit: JOHN FARIOR JUNR., FREDK. FARIOR, DAVID
FARIOR. Apr. Ct. 1812.

p. 502   WILLIAM HUDGINS, constable of Duplin Co. to CATHARINE BEST (co.
not given), 20 Oct 1804, for 20 pds. a negro girl CLOE, the prop. of WILLIAM
BEST. Wit: JAMES FREDERICK, JOHN RICHARDS, DANIEL MURPHY. Jan.
Ct. 1813.

p. 503   JOHN WHITMAN (JUNR.), TIMOTHY TEACHEY, NICANOR JAMES,
ANN (X) WHITMAN, heirs of JOHN WHITMAN dec'd to JAMES WHITMAN, all of
Duplin Co., 26 Dec 1812, for $119.40, 200A on the WS of the Northeast River
below Island Creek & lower side of Oaky Branch, beg. at a pine SAMPSON MOSE-
LEY'S line, patented by ROBERT McREE. Wit: EDWD. STREET, WILLIAM
STREET. Apr. Ct. 1813.

p. 504   ALEXANDER GRADY SENR. of Duplin Co. to his dau. WINNIFRED
GRADY (co. not given), 1 Feb 1812, a deed of gift for a negro girl named JINNEY
about 18 yrs. of age & her future increase, reserving the use of sd. negro to him
& his wife NANCY during their natural lives. If WINIFRED should die without heirs
the right of sd. negro JINNEY & her increase to be vested in all his daus. Wit:
H. GRADY, FREDK. GRADY SENR. Jan. Ct. 1813.

p. 504   JAMES LANIER to BYRD LANIER, both of Duplin Co., 26 Oct 1801, for
50 pds. 60A on the ES of the Northeast River & on the WS of Cypress Creek, being
part of a survey patented by BENTON WILLIFORD 14 May 1773, beg. at a black
gum in the edge of the Gum Swamp, near the mouth of Wolf Pit Branch. Wit:
MATTHEW (X) MASBURN, ESTHER (X) PICKETT. Oct. Ct. 1812.

p. 506   ED. (EDWARD) ARMSTRONG, admr. to the estate of DENNIS CANNON
dec'd (co. not given) to ABRAHAM CANNON (co. not given), 15 Dec 1811, a negro
girl slave named MILLEY about 11 yrs. of age, sd. ABRAHAM CANNON being the
last & highest bidder at public auction held for sale of sd. slave in order to defray
the debts of sd. DENNIS CANNON dec'd. (Sum not given for the transaction)
Wit: WILLIAM McGOWEN, JOHN HUNTER. Dated 23 July 1812. Jan. Ct. 1813.

p. 507   JAMES PICKET, heir at law of HENRY PICKETT of New Hanover Co. to
NATHAN FOUNTAIN of Duplin Co., 15 June 1802 (or 1812), for $300, 300A on the
ES of the Northeast River & on the SS of Muddy Creek, beg. at a lightwood stump
near the sd. FOUNTAIN'S fence, granted to HENRY PICKET by patent (date not
given). Wit: JOB THIGPEN, SIHON PICKETT. July Ct. 1812.

p. 508   JAMES (X) WALLACE to JEREMIAH WALLACE, both of Duplin Co.,
(date not given), for 50 pds. 200A on the ES of the Northeast River below Butcher's
Bluff, beg. in a swamp JOSEPH T. RHODES' line, late FREDERICK GRIGGS', now
the afsd. JAMES WALLACE'S, near Butcher's Bluff, being half of a grant to
JOSEPH T. RHODES for 400A bearing date 24 Oct 1786. Wit: JACOB BROWN,
JACOB WALLACE. July Ct. 1812.

p. 509   CHARLES (X) WARD, Esqr. to JAMES RAPHAEL, both of Duplin Co.,
22 Dec 1810, for $400 good & lawful money of N. C. 500A in 3 tracts to wit: (1)
100A on the WS of the Northeast Branch of Cape Fear River & below the mouth of
the Grove Swamp, beg. at a pine on JOB HUNTER'S line, near THOMAS WEBB'S
corner, to a water oak in the river swamp; (2) 100A joining the 1st tract, beg. at a
birch on the river, to a large maple DANIEL MALLARD'S corner, joining GILLES-
PIE, PHILL SOUTHERLAND; (3) 300A situated as the before mentioned tracts &
joining below, patented by sd. CHARLES WARD, Esqr., beg. at a gum & hickory on
the river bank, joining the lines of MALLARD, DELANY, WARD & TWILLEY. Wit:
ANDREW McINTIRE, SARAH A. WARD. Apr. Ct. 1813.

p. 511   NM. (NEEDHAM) WHITFIELD & EDMD. (EDMOND) WHITFIELD, exrs. of
the L. W. & T. of NEEDHAM WHITFIELD dec'd, late of Wayne Co., to WILLIAM
WHITFIELD SENR. of Wayne Co., 16 Dec 1812, for $1,080, 368A being the prop.
of sd. dec'd, beg. at a pine one of JOHN ROBERTS' corners, to a stake in the line
dividing this tract from LEWIS WHITFIELD'S land, incl. the planta. known as the
Forehand Place, being a patent granted to WILLIAM WHITFIELD SENR. 12 Mar
1773 for 100A, part of a patent granted to WILLIAM WHITFIELD SENR. 17 Aug
1779 for 200A, part of a patent to NEEDHAM WHITFIELD 4 Jan 1792 for 225A &

part of a new entry in the name of NEEDHAM WHITFIELD dec'd. Wit: HATCH
WHITFIELD, JNO. DEMPSEY. Jan. Ct. 1814.

p. 512   SAMUEL DAVIS, Patent No. 2034, 24 Nov 1813, for 10A lying on the ES
of the Northeast & on the NS of Matthews Branch, near the mouth, beg. at a white
oak near the swamp, the beg. of SILVENUS PUMPHREY'S 150A survey, joining
GEORGE SMITH & MICHAEL GLISSON. Entered 27 Nov 1811. Signed by W.
HAWKINS.

p. 513   SAMUEL DAVIS, Patent No. 2035, 24 Nov 1813, for 22A on the ES of the
Northeast & on the head of the Long Branch, beg. at a white oak, the beg. of
DANIEL SANDERS' 100A survey, joining H. GRADY & SOLOMON CARTER'S 400A
survey & SANDERS' line. Entered 21 Nov 1811. Signed by W. HAWKINS.

p. 513   JACOB LASSITTER of Greene Co. to DANIEL WITHERINGTON of Lenoir
Co., 23 Oct 1812, for $2800, 888A in 2 tracts to wit: (1) 600A beg. at a gum in the
Northeast, his & STANLEY'S corner, to a pine in a meadow on READING BOW-
DEN'S line, to the run of Poley Bridge, down the sd. meanders of the western edge
& joining the high land to the mouth or run of the sd. Northeast, being the contents
of several patents granted to JESSE BARFIELD & also to FREDERICK BARFIELD
& since by several conveyances down to the sd. WITHERINGTON by the sd.
LASSITTER; (2) 177A beg. at a pine on the Mill Pond above the house on the old
patent line, to the run of the Northeast, down the run to the Poley Bridge. Wit:
JNO. GATLIN, BARNEY WITHERINGTON. Oct. Ct. 1813.

p. 515   ALEXR. (ALEXANDER) GRADY SENR. to his grandson ALEXANDER
HAMPTON GRADY, both of Duplin Co., his grandson afsd. being the son of JOHN
T. GRADY, 15 Jan 1813, for 10 pds. 432A on the ES of the Northwest where sd.
ALEXANDER GRADY SENR. lives, beg. in the Race Path Branch HENRY GRADY'S
corner, to a pine his other corner a little E of the road leading from Sarecta to
White Hall, near the 8 mile post, joining GEORGE F. KORNEGAY'S corner, A.
GRADY JUNR.'S corner in Poke Island, to FREDK. GRADY SENR.'S corner, to a
gum F. GRADY'S (Neuse) corner, to his other corner in the Tar Kiln Branch, join-
ing JAS. GRADY'S line, reserving the entire use of the land to sd. ALEXANDER
GRADY SENR. & his wife ANNE during their natural life & the entire use of the
same after their deaths to JOHN T. GRADY & his wife EUNICE during their
natural lifetime, at the end of which the sd. ALEXANDER H. GRADY is to be poss.
of & seized of a little in fee simple to the sd. premises. Wit: HENRY GRADY,
ALEXR. GRADY JR., ALEXR. O. GRADY, ABNER GRADY, WHITFIELD GRADY.
Jan. Ct. 1813.

p. 516   NM. (NEEDHAM) WHITFIELD to WILLIAM WHITFIELD, both of Wayne
Co., 16 Nov 1813, for $100, 80A on the waters of Buck Swamp, beg. at a stake in
WILLIAM WHITFIELD'S line, a corner of WILLIAM HINES' new entry, being part
of a patent granted to sd. NEEDHAM WHITFIELD 19 Aug 1813. Wit: HATCH
WHITFIELD, EDMD. WHITFIELD. Jan. Ct. 1814.

p. 517   JAMES RAPHAEL, Patent No. 2030, 16 Nov 1813, for 15A on the WS of
the Northeast River, beg. at a birch on the river bank, a corner of his own 300A
survey. Entered 1 Jan 1813. Signed by WILLIAM HAWKINS.

p. 518   BENJAMIN BROWN, Patent No. 2013, 4 Dec 1812, for sum of 8/, 16A on

the SS of Persimmon Swamp, beg. at a pine on the S edge of Persimmon on BENJA-
MIN CHASON'S line, to HOPKIN WILLIAMS' line. Entered 16 Nov 1811. Signed by
WILLIAM HAWKINS.

p. 518   NEEDHAM WHITFIELD, Patent No. 2022, 19 Aug 1813, 80A on the NS of
the Northeast & on the waters of Buck Swamp, beg. at a stake in WILLIAM WHIT-
FIELD'S line, a corner of WILLIS HANES' new entry, to a black jack WILLIAM
WHITFIELD'S corner. Entered 20 Oct 1812. Signed by WILLIAM HAWKINS.

p. 518   PETER CARLTON to JOHN ALDERMAN JR., both of Duplin Co., 15 Feb
1811, for $201.35 of spanish coining (?) 201 3/4A on BS of the Doctors Creek, beg.
at a water oak at the run of sd. branch, to a pine it being a dividing line between
WILLIAM BLAND & JOHN ALDERMAN. Wit: WM. BLAND, JOHN STALLINGS.
Jan. Ct. 1812.

p. 519   DARLIN DAFFIN, Patent No. 2029, 16 Nov 1813, for 155A on the ES of the
Northeast River & on the NS of Angolar Pocosin, beg. at a black gum. Entered 23
Jan 1812. Signed by WILL HAWKINS.

p. 520   NICANOR MURRAY, Patent No. 2024, 16 Nov 1813, for 245A on the ES of
the Northeast River, beg. at a small sweet gum on the river bank, at the mouth of
Sandy Run just below Willson's Hole & runs with the meanders of the river bank to a
pine on sd. bank JAMES MURRAY'S corner, to his corner on the county line to a
dead pine on the edge of Holly Shelter Pocosin. Entered 23 Mar 1812. Signed by
WILL HAWKINS.

p. 520   ALEXANDER CARTER, Patent No. 2026, 16 Nov 1813, for 106A on the ES
of the Northeast of Cape Fear & on the SS of Matthews Branch, beg. at a white oak
on the NS of Davis' Branch HENRY GRADY'S corner & the beg. of a 400A survey
granted to SOLOMON CARTER, joining ISAAC DAWSON'S patent line, ADAMS &
WM. GRADY'S patent corner & SOLOMON CARTER'S 100A survey. Entered 20
July 1812. Signed by WILL HAWKINS.

p. 521   JOHN RICHARDS to WILLIAM B. HURST, both of Duplin Co., 25 Jan 1811,
for $340, 170A in Williamson Co., Tenn. on Nelson's Creek, a branch called the
East Branch of Harpeth River, beg. at a stake OBADIAH WARD'S corner, the beg.
corner of the sd. JOHN RICHARDS' 240A survey purchased from WILLIAM TUTON.
Wit: D. L. KENAN, JAMES THOMPSON. Apr. Ct. 1814.

p. 522   JOHN JONES SENR. to CATY DEAL, dau. of sd. JOHN JONES & wife of
ABEL DEAL, all of Duplin Co., 1 Sep 1813, for "natural love & affection" tract of
land (acreage not given) on the SS of the Northeast, beg. at the ford on Rattle Snake
Branch & runs with the path to a white oak, by a line of marked trees to the Big
Path leading from ANTHONY JONES' to sd. JOHN JONES', excepting sd. JOHN
JONES & his family to have use of all the cleared lands within sd. boundary,
houses, orchards, wood land, etc. for use of his family during his natural life &
then to the use & benefit of the sd. CATY DEAL her heirs & assigns forever. Wit:
DAVID WRIGHT, JACOB GILMORE. Oct. Ct. 1813.

p. 523   JOHN GILMAN, Patent No. 2025, 16 Nov 1813, for 161A on the drains of
Lathlins (?) Pocosin, beg. at a red oak DANIEL MURPHY'S & GILMAN'S own
corner. Entered 20 July 1812. Signed by WILLIAM HAWKINS.

p. 524   SUSANNA (φ) CARRAWAY of Wayne Co. to her beloved dau. NANCY
KORNEGAY of Duplin Co., 28 Nov 1812, for "natural love & affection" a deed of
gift for a negro girl named TEMP & her increase. Wit: BRYAN KORNEGAY,
LUKE KORNEGAY, NATHAN GARNER. Jan. Ct. 1814.

p. 524   AB. (ABRAHAM) KORNEGAY & LUKE KORNEGAY, planters, to HENRY
KORNEGAY, both of Duplin Co., 24 July 1812, for $200, 489A on the SS of the
Northeast Swamp, it being the dower that was laid off to MARY KORNEGAY, the
widow of JACOB KORNEGAY SENR. dec'd, incl. the house & planta. where the sd.
widow now lives - "To have & to hold all that part or portion of land that would fall
or descend to us the sd. LUKE & ABRAHAM KORNEGAY by heirship in the sd.
dower after the death of the sd. widow MARY KORNEGAY." Wit: BRYAN KORNE-
GAY, WM. HOLLAMAN. Jan. Ct. 1814.

p. 526   THOMAS McGEE to ALEXANDER DICKSON, both of Duplin Co., 8 May
1812, for $21, 474A on the drains of Maxwell Swamp on BS of Sauney's Branch, beg.
at a stake ALEXANDER DICKSON'S corner & THOMAS McGEE'S corner, on the
SS of Sauney's Branch. Wit: JOHN MILLER, JOHN (X) BRAY. Apr. Ct. 1813.

p. 527   JOSEPH BRAY to ALEXANDER DICKSON, both of Duplin Co., 16 Dec
1812, for $43, 86A on the drains of Maxwell Swamp on the NES of sd. swamp, beg.
at a water oak on the run of Reedy Meadow Branch. Wit: HUGH MAXWELL,
NICHOLAS (X) ROGERS. Apr. Ct. 1813.

p. 528   PATRICK NEWTON'S Land Division according to his L. W. & T.
(1) 82A incl. the planta. where MRS. ELEANOR NEWTON lives, beg. at a white
oak on the run of the Great Branch, sd. NEWTON'S upper corner & WILLIAM
FREDERICK'S corner at the mouth of a small branch at the lower end of his planta.,
adj. the lines of the old McCULLOCH survey which 82 A fell to the heirs of JAMES
NEWTON dec'd; (2) 144A to WILLIAM NEWTON, beg. at a small pine on the Little
Branch which runs along side of MRS. NEWTON'S planta. & on the side of her
avenue, to the run of the branch which divides MRS. NEWTON & THOMAS HILL'S
planta., down the run of sd. branch as it meanders to the run of Bear Swamp, up
the swamp till it meanders to the mouth of the Great Branch, thence up the run of
the Great Branch as it meanders to the mouth of the small branch, which divides
the two MRS. NEWTON'S planta. (incl. the old planta.); (3) 168A to MAJOR NEW-
TON, which leaves WM. NEWTON in debt to MAJOR NEWTON $50, his land being
in that proportion more valuable. The sd. 168A being in 3 tracts to wit: (1) 98A
beg. at a sweet gum on the run of Bear Swamp at the mouth of the Dividing Branch;
(2) 50A beg. at a black gum in a savanna, to a white oak a corner of the above survey, in the dividing branch (these 2 pieces include the planta. where JOHN MOORE
formerly lived; (3) 20A joining the 1st 2 pieces lying in Bear Swamp purchased
from PHILIP WARD, beg. at a sweet gum & white oak CONNERLY'S corner on the
run of Bear Swamp, joining THOMAS HILL'S line. Wit: C. HOOKS, Sur., D.
HOOKS. Signed by the Committee appointed to divide the lands of the dec'd.
ALEXR. HERRING, JAMES WRIGHT, DAVID WRIGHT.   Apr. Ct. 1814.

p. 530   FREDK. (FREDERICK) SMITH SENR. to ZACHEUS SMITH, both of Duplin
Co., 1 Sep 1812, for $1,000, 370A on the ES of the Northeast joining his own land &
OWEN O'DANIEL, incl. the planta. & lands bought of LOFTIS WORLEY & REDICK
WORLEY, beg. at a pine near the Northeast Swamp on the dividing line between him
& the heirs of CHARLES MILLER dec'd, across the main road near Tandam, to the

head of Lawhorn Branch, to a corner of his 500A, to ELIJAH SMITH'S corner,
thence with BARFIELD'S line to FREDERICK SMITH JUNR.'S line across the main
road to WALKER'S line, to SAMUEL RATLIFF'S corner, along a row of marked
trees with FREDERICK SMITH JUNR.'S line to the main swamp & then to the beg.
Wit: WM. A. HOUSTON, SELIATHE SMITH. Oct. Ct. 1812.

p. 531   ARCHELAUS (X) BRANCH (SENR.) of Duplin Co. to his son ARCHELAUS
BRANCH JUNR. (co. not given), 20 Oct 1812, for "natural love & affection" 110A on
the NS of Goshen Swamp near Herring's Marsh, beg. at a black gum in the Mainor
Branch on the OUTLAW line, being a tract that BENJAMIN SNIPES conveyed to
DANIEL GLISSON & again conveyed by sd. GLISSON to WILLIAMS who conveyed to
ARCHELAUS BRANCH SENR. on the WS of the Mainor Branch & on BS of Brock
Branch, joining the lands of ANDREW GUFFORD & BENJAMIN SNIPES, now belong-
ing to STEPHEN HERRING. Wit: JESSE GRIMES, ARTHUR BRANCH. Oct. Ct.
1812.

p. 532   DANIEL HICKS JR. of Sampson Co. to REUBEN BLANCHARD of Duplin
Co., 13 Jan 1809, for $508, 254A beg. at a sweet gum on the main road, to a water
oak on the run in Buck Hall, thence with the main road to the beg. (Heading of deed
says 220A) Wit: JAMES HICKS, NOAH (X) BLANCHARD. Oct. Ct. 1812.

p. 534   JAMES (X) FAISON of Sampson Co. to JAMES WEST of Duplin Co., 13
Jan 1810, for 150 pds. 200A in 2 tracts to wit: (1) 100A lying & being on the ES of
Stewart's Creek, beg. at a white oak, to a stake in the S prong of Possom Branch,
down sd. branch to Buck Hall Swamp, down sd. swamp to Stewart's Creek, being
land conveyed by deed to DANIEL WATKINS & from DANIEL WATKINS to JAMES
FAISON; (2) 100A in the fork of Stewart's Creek & Merit'S Mill Swamp, beg. at a
white oak on the side of the Swamp, granted to DAVID WATKINS 1 July 1779. Wit:
DANIEL WEST, HENRY FAISON. Oct. Ct. 1812.

p. 535. An indenture. Dated 30 Dec 1812. FEREBY (? her mark) STOCKS to
ALEXANDER SAUNDERS, both of Duplin Co., sd. FEREBY "agreeable to her own
desire agrees to indenture herself to sd. SAUNDERS for the term of 99 yrs. in
consideration of him letting her be free from her former master URIAH BLAN-
CHARD of sd. county & agrees to serve sd. SAUNDERS faithfully & honestly." Wit:
MARK ROGERS. Oct. Ct. 1813.

p. 536   WM. (WILLIAM) POLLOCK of Sampson Co. to HENRY BEST of Duplin Co.,
20 Oct 1812, for $990 for 330A on the NS of Buck Hall, beg. at a water oak on the
run of Buck Hall. Wit: FRANCIS WILLIAMS, MICHAEL BOYETT.

p. 537   FREDK. (FREDERICK) WELLS of Duplin Co. to his children THOMAS
WELLS, JACOB WELLS, ALEXANDER WELLS, ANN MITCHELL, MARY MATHIS
& SARAH PORTERVENT, 12 Sep 1803, for "natural love & affection" a deed of gift
for sundries to wit: one negro man DEVER, horse, hogs, sheep, poultry, working
tools, except one feather bed & furn. to his loving wife, lands to his son ALEX-
ANDER WELLS, one acre excepted where burying ground is, then remaining 482A;
to grandson FREDERICK WELLS 52A on the main road joining his father THOMAS
WELLS' line & WILLIAM BROWN'S line. "Those children is to take care of their
sister ELIZABETH WELLS & not let her come to public charge." Wit: WILLIAM
BROWN, ELIZABETH CUMMINGS, WILLIAM SMYTH. Oct. Ct. 1812.

p. 538   STEPHEN GUFFORD to ALEXANDER O'DANIEL, both of Duplin Co., 27 Apr 1808, for $113.25, 50A in the fork of the Northeast & Goshen Swamp, beg. at a pine STEPHEN GUFFORD'S corner, across the WADE planta...Wit: WILLIAM KORNEGAY JR., LEWIS JONES. Oct. Ct. 1812.

p. 539   JOHN JONES, planter of Duplin Co. to STEPHEN JONES (co. not given), 8 Aug 1812, for 200 pds. 100A on BS of the Deep Gully Branch, beg. at a hickory on the NS of sd. branch BASIL KORNEGAY'S corner, on the given line of a patent granted to JOHN SPEARS of 250A. Wit: JAMES JOHNSTON, ISAAC PIPKIN. Oct. Ct. 1813.

p. 541   JESSE WILLIAMS to REDICK WORLEY, both of Duplin Co., 20 Nov 1811, (sum not given) 54A on the ES of the Northeast Swamp & on Panther Swamp patented 1787, beg. at a pine a corner of survey, joining SMITH & LEWIS BARFIELD, cont. 75A, 21A excepted which is sold out of sd. patent to ELIJAH SMITH before this sale. Wit: OWEN O'DANIEL, LEWIS BARFIELD. Oct. Ct. 1812.

p. 542   JESSE (S) BRANCH to BENTLY WESTON, both of Duplin Co., 31 Jan 1811, for 150 pds. current money 218A in 2 tracts to wit: (1) 193A beg. at a pine opposite the head of the dividing branch that runs through the planta. & the 93A patented by ANTHONY WILLIAMS, it being part of 2 surveys & runs down the various courses of sd. branch to White Oak Swamp, to LEWIS SMITH'S line, to sd. SMITH'S other corner, to a holly & bay in Panther Swamp, joining MUMFORD'S old corner; (2) 25A being part of 150A patented by GEORGE SMITH SENR. 23 Apr 1762, being the last corner of the patent line & runs the giving line to a white oak as the patent calls for. Wit: CHRISTOPHER LAWSON, CHRISTOPHER LAWSON JR. Oct. Ct. 1812.

p. 543   JONATHAN KITHLY to DANIEL GLISSON, both of Duplin Co., 15 Jan 1814, for $28, 14A in the fork of Goshen & the Northeast on the SS of the Beaverdam on BS of the main road, beg. at 3 maples on the run of the Beaverdam above the main road, to a stake in the edge of the Beaverdam above the mouth of Juniper Branch. Wit: THOMAS DAIL, DANL. GLISSON JR. Jan. Ct. 1814.

p. 544   THOMAS DAIL to DANIEL GLISSON, both of Duplin Co., 15 Jan 1814, for $40, 37A in the fork of Goshen & the Northeast, on the SS of the Beaverdam on BS of the main road, beg. at 3 maples in the Beaverdam above the main road in JONATHAN KITHLEY'S line (now sd. GLISSON'S corner & runs to a stake in an old root KITHLEY'S corner, now GLISSON'S). Wit: JONATHAN KITHLEY, DANL. GLISSON JR. Jan. Ct. 1814.

p. 545   JNO. (JOHN) WATKINS, son of LEVIN WATKINS dec'd & JAMES REAR-DON, exrs. to the L.W. & T. of LEVIN WATKINS dec'd late of Duplin Co. to SARAH WATKINS, widow of sd. WATKINS dec'd, 1 Nov 1813, by JOHN INGRAM, Esqr. of Sampson Co., highest bidder & purchaser of sd. lands of WATKINS dec'd, in the sum of $4,150 in a note with approved security payable, in behalf of sd. widow, 664A on the NS of Goshen Swamp in 8 tracts to wit: (1) 192A beg. at a white oak at or near Cow Hole, until it comes to the corner of a 7A patent granted to LEVIN WATKINS 20 Dec 1799, which joins GIBBS' line to JESSE WATKINS' line, being part of a tract LEVIN WATKINS purchased of THOMAS GRAY dec'd 25 Feb 1777 & a part of the sd. 7A patent; (2) 42A beg. at a white oak & red oak WILLIAM BIZZEL'S, joining WATKINS & NICHOLAS BOWDEN, being a patent granted to

LEVIN WATKINS 29 Oct 1782; (3) 20A beg. at a pine at the run of Cow Hole Branch, being purchased from JAMES HURST JUNR. 21 Jan 1785, it being the ES of a patent granted to JAMES HURST 23 Dec 1763; (4) 40A on the NS of Goshen & ES of Cow Hole Branch, joining & between JAMES HURST SENR. & JOHN FOLEY, beg. at a live oak at the run of the sd. branch & joining JOHN SHUFIELD & the above 20A granted to JAMES HURST JUNR. 10 Nov 1784; (5) 85A between the head of Cow Hole Branch & Bear Marsh on the SS of Mund's Pocosin, beg. at a marked pine & stake by the road on JOHN FOLEY'S line, joining NICHOLAS BOWDEN, to a stake by the Little Pocosin, along the dividing line of marked trees to the beg., laid off for LEVIN WATKINS 3 May 1782 by COL. WILLIAM DICKSON out of JOHN SHUF-FIELD'S patent; (6) 80A beg. at a black jack at or near CARTWRIGHT'S given line, a path leading from the public road to sd. JAMES HURST SENR.'S, from thence to Cow Hole Branch, NICHOLAS BOWDEN'S corner, which LEVIN WATKINS purchased of sd. BOWDEN 2 Mar 1780; (7) 5A on the drains of Cow Hole, beg. at a spanish oak a corner of WILLIAM VINING'S patent, now belonging to the estate of LEVIN WATKINS dec'd, joining VINING & being part of 100A granted to JAMES HURST by patent dated 29 Dec 1763 & deeded from sd. HURST to sd. WATKINS dec'd 22 Apr 1786; (8) 200A on Mund Pocosin & head of white oak pocosin, beg. at a pine THOMAS GRAY'S corner at the lower end of Mund's Pocosin, joining REUBEN JOHNSTON, BIZZELL, BOWDEN & SHUFFIELD, being granted to LEVIN WATKINS 10 Nov 1784. Wit: C. HOOKS, Auctioneer; JOSEPH DICKSON, BRYAN BOURDEN. Jan. Ct. 1814.

p. 549   JOHN FONVILLE & his wife SARAH FONVILLE of Duplin Co. to LAVIN WATKINS of Craven Co., 17 Jan 1814, for $4,320, 664A in 8 tracts formerly belonging to LAVIN WATKINS dec'd, on the NS of Goshen Swamp. (See preceding deed, p. 545, JOHN WATKINS & JAMES REARDON to SARAH WATKINS, for land description of this 664A.) Wit: JAMES REARDON, JOHN WATKINS. Jan. Ct. 1814. SARAH FONVILLE signs the deed of her own free will & consent without any compulsion or request of her sd. husband JOHN FONVILLE, before D. WRIGHT & JOHN HUNTER on 18 Jan 1814. [SARAH FONVILLE no doubt the former wife of LEVIN WATKINS dec'd whose will was proven Oct. Ct. 1812 Duplin Co.]

p. 552   MARY J.(JANE) BEST & ELIZABETH BEST of Duplin Co. to STEPHEN GRAHAM (co. not given), 20 Dec 1813, for $125 (acreage not given) a tract known by the name of Piney Woods, or Persimmon Tract, it being their part of a 300A tract coveyed by JOSEPH DICKSON to their father WILLIAM BEST dec'd dated 20 May 1782. Wit: ALEXANDER McGOWEN & MARY GRAHAM. Jan. Ct. 1814

p. 553   D.(DAVID) GILLESPIE & JO.(JOSEPH) GILLESPIE, exrs. of the LW & T of JAMES GILLESPIE dec'd to JAMES RAPHAEL, 22 Apr 1807, for $662, 310A belonging to JAMES GILLESPIE dec'd in 4 tracts to wit: (1) 100A on the WS of the Northeast Branch of Cape Fear River between ANTHONY MILLER'S land, a place called Clark's Folly, beg. at a black gum in the river swamp, joining STEPHENS' clearing & ANTHONY MILLER; (2) 72A granted to MICHAEL & ROBERT DICKSON, beg. at a water oak on the 1st line of sd. patent standing at the S end of the dividing line made between MAJOR CROOM & WILLIAM STOAK; (3) 98A patented by JAMES GILLESPIE & situated as the before mentioned, beg. at a pine his own corner by his field, joining STOAK'S line, PHILIP SOUTHERLAND'S corner by Hill Swamp; (4) 40A beg. at a water oak on the river & runs out with MICHAEL & ROBERT DICK-SON'S line, to a pine on GILLESPIE'S line. Wit: JOSEPH DICKSON, ROBERT (R) STONE. Apr. Ct. 1813.

p. 555   EDWARD ALBERTSON of Duplin Co. to CONSIDER BUSHEE of Lenoir Co.,
19 Aug 1813, for $60, beg. at a pine WINDEL DAVIS' corner on the NS of the Great
Branch & runs with his line to a dead pine sd. DAVIS' corner, to a pine DAVIS' &
BUSHEE'S corner, joining SAMUEL SOWELL'S line & ELLIS' line. Wit: SAMUEL
DAVIS, JOHN (Ŧ) STEWART. Oct. Ct. 1813.

p. 555   JOHN (X) GOFF (SENR.) to BENNET FELLOW, both of Duplin Co., 24
Dec 1807, for $1,016 lawful money of N. C. 290A on the SS of Goff's Mill Creek,
beg. at a poplar in or near the mouth of a small branch, incl. the planta. & mill
where he formerly lived. Wit: MAURICE FENNEL, JOHN MATTHIS. Jan. Ct.
1813.

p. 557   JOHN SULLIVENT to ANDREW GUFFORD, 14 Nov 1797, for 60 pds.
specie, 125A between the Northeast & Goshen, on or near Ned's Marsh, beg. at a
pine an old corner, a little N of the main road, joining ROBERT SULLIVANT'S, to
a water oak in the S Branch, joining BULLARD & ELKANEY SULLIVANT. Wit:
OWEN O'DANIEL, URIAH SULLIVENT, HAMPTON SULLIVENT. July Ct. 1806.

p. 558   MICHAEL BONEY of Hanover Co. (New Hanover) to JOHN E. HUSSEY of
Duplin Co., 13 July 1811, for $125 lawful money 360A on the NS of Limestone
Swamp, beg. at a white oak a corner of a 140A survey granted to JOSEPH T.
RHODES, joining JACOB RHODES' line, between the White Oak & Bear Pocosin,
joining LOFTEN QUINN, being land granted to JOSEPH T. RHODES by patent dated
21 Sep 1785 & by him conveyed to JACOB RHODES who conveyed to MICHAEL
BONEY. Wit: JOHN COOPER, L. HOUSTON. Oct. Ct. 1813.

p. 559   ELIZABETH (X) JONES (co. not given) to her son JOHN JONES (co. not
given), 1 Oct 1813, deed of gift for "love & friendship" all goods & chattels, household furn. & kitchen furn. Wit: JOHN R. MILLER, JAMES MARTENDEL. Oct.
Ct. 1813.

p. 559   NEWMAN (N) EDWARDS to JAMES RHODES (SENR.), both of Duplin Co.,
23 Oct 1812, for $100 lawful money of the U. S. 150A on the ES of the Northeast of
Cape Fear River & NS of Little Limestone & BS of Wild Cat Branch, beg. at a holly
at the run of Wildcat Branch MATTHEW EDWARDS' corner, to a small pine on the
NW edge of Cuffee Branch, thence JAMES WHALEY'S line, to a sweet gum at Little
Limestone, to the mouth of Wild Cat, patented by JOHN BRITTON 21 Sep 1785.
Wit: JOHN B. COX, JOHN E. HUSSEY. Jan. Ct. 1813.

Numbers refer to page
numbers in the deed books
and not to the page num-
bers in this book. Names
of persons appearing in
separate deeds on the same
page of the deed book are
indicated by a (2).

-A-

ADAMS, 1A 136,331; 4A 520;
 Andrew 3A 318; Benjamin
 3A 318,381
ADKINSON, John 1A 61,513;
 3A 335
ADKISON, Thomas 1A 500,548
ALBERSON, D. 3A 515; David
 4A 273,325,335; E. 4A
 394,396; Ed. 4A 190,396;
 Edward 3A 21,513,515,
 556; 4A 8,144,186,207,
 216,273(2),284,307,383,
 389,392,393,458,468;
 Edwd. 4A 79,325; John
 1A 255,314,316; 3A 107,
 442; Marry 3A 163; Saml.
 1A 320; 3A 64; 4A 325;
 Samuel 1A 255,486; 3A
 442,457; 4A 141,256,273;
 Samuel Jr. 3A 109; Sarah
 4A 273; William 1A 486;
 3A 64,402,409,457,552;
 4A 8,104,141,325; Wm.
 3A 21,265
ALBERTSON 3A 218; Edward
 4A 555; Edwd. 3A 455;
 William 3A 243; Wm. 3A
 276,301; 4A 180
ALDEN, 4A 97; Roger 3A
 167,505
ALDERMAN, Daniel 1A 92,94,
 352,356; 4A 161; David
 1A 356,481; 4A 161;
 Elisha 4A 161; John 1A
 267; 4A 364,518; John
 Jr. 4A 518; Sarah 1A
 481; 4A 161
ALEXANDER, Nathaniel 4A
 75; Nathl. 4A 353
ALLAN, Henry 1A 433
ALLEN, Eliazer 1A 121;
 Henry 1A 171; 3A 359;
 4A 24; Henry Sr. 1A 284;
 James 4A 390; John 4A
 485; Leavin 3A 195;
 Sarah (Mrs.) 1A 121;
 Vine 4A 120; William 1A
 125; 3A 332; Wm. 3A 15
ALPHIN, William 4A 89
ANCRUM, John 3A 42,120,
 179,367
ANDERSON, Sarah 1A 375;
 Thos. 3A 197; William
 1A 375
ANDREWS, Abraham 1A 151,
 153; 3A 88,144,352; Mary
 3A 321
ANTHRAM, John 3A 236
ARMSTRONG, 4A 114,127,475;
 Alexander 1A 103,294;
 4A 114,119; Alex. 3A
 251; Alexr. 1A 478; Ed.
 3A 246; 4A 37; Edward
 3A 357; 4A 207,377,399,
 401,506; John 1A 61,117,
 457,533; Thomas 1A 474;
 Thos. 1A 529
ARTHUR, Gideon 4A 327
ASBURY, Geo. L. 4A 429;
 Zilpha 4A 8

ASHE, Samuel 1A 260
ATKINS, John 1A 167,285,
 415,463; 3A 493
ATKINSON, Thomas 3A 288,
 420
AUSTIN, John 3A 351
AUSTON, John 1A 59; 3A 52
AVER, John 3A 17; 4A 120
AVERS, John 3A 256; John
 Senr. 3A 255
AYRES, Thomas 3A 548
AYRS, Thomas 4A 433

-B-

BAILES, 1A 495
BAILS, Nelly 1A 505
BAKER, 3A 231; James 1A
 507; Thomas 1A 450
BALES, 3A 401; David 3A
 135
BALEY, James 3A 85
BALLARD, John 1A 547
BALLERD, P. 1A 114
BANNERMAN, George 3A 40;
 Phebe 3A 40; Robert 3A
 40
BARBER, Absalom 3A 395;
 Thomas 3A 366,395,396
BAREFIELD, Jesse 1A 188;
 Solomon 1A 182; Stephen
 1A 182,190,232,502
BARFIELD, 3A 147,414; 4A
 56,530; Ann 4A 315;
 Anna 4A 319; Frederick
 1A 99,232,377,383,399,
 497; 3A 309; 4A 61,90,
 439,513; Fredk. 1A 495;
 3A 9; J. 3A 90; Jesse
 1A 99,182,190,237,327,
 412,420,502; 3A 105,296,
 349,437,483; 4A 90,193,
 219,513; John 1A 199,
 405,412; 3A 95; J. W.
 4A 39; L. 4A 386; Lewis
 1A 409,536,538; 3A 95,
 125,437,552; 4A 141,164,
 173,267,286,320,325,335,
 376,379,439,477,541;
 Lewis Jr. 4A 315,319,
 320,470; Lewis Sr. 4A
 315,319,470; Polly 4A
 320; Solomon 1A 420;
 Stephen 1A 99,192,328,
 441; 3A 95,278,401; 4A
 342,365; Theophilus 4A
 236; Wright 4A 320
BARNARD, Tho. 4A 181;
 Thomas 4A 160
BARNES, 3A 125,188; 4A
 294; Lewis 1A 136,226,
 374,405,536,538; 3A 318,
 381,489; Richard 3A 355
BARNET, John 1A 110; 4A
 458; Stewart 3A 26
BARNETT, 3A 457
BARNS, 4A 303
BASDEN, Lybern 3A 31
BASS, Andrew 1A 30,105;
 3A 73,126,233; Hermon
 1A 30,105; Nedham 4A
 433; Uriah 3A 206; Widow
 1A 105; 3A 233
BATCHELDER, William 3A 185
BATCHELDORE, John 3A 386
BATTLE, Frederick 4A 272;
 Lott 4A 272
BATTS, James 3A 388; 4A
 151,456; John 3A 88,388;
 Nathan 4A 449
BAZIN (BAZEN), David 3A
 490

BEAGLIN, Nathan 4A 147,148
BEARFIELD, Frederick 1A
 155; Jesse 1A 155,192,
 420; Stephen 1A 192,420
BEASLEY, Austin 3A 335
BEATTY, William H. 4A 495
BEBBERRT, Jacob 1A 178
BEBERET, Jacob 1A 180
BEBERRT, Jacob 1A 176
BECK, 3A 90; Caleb 3A 90;
 Elizabeth 3A 6; J. 3A
 90; John 1A 122,123,252,
 273,400,515; 3A 6,12,22,
 67,198,417,512; 4A 249,
 379,441,455; John Jr. 1A
 64,515; 3A 6; John Sr.
 1A 271; Stephen 1A 271;
 3A 6; 4A 249; William
 1A 123,252,273,399,400,
 550; 3A 6,67,547; 4A 163,
 249,343,473; William Jr.
 1A 550; 3A 6,269,512,
 544; 4A 160,261; William
 Sr. 3A 512; 4A 473; Wm.
 1A 515; 3A 286
BEESLEY, 1A 174,509; 3A
 327; Abraham 1A 103,174,
 176,478,507; 4A 131,475;
 Abram 4A 114; Austen 1A
 172; Austin 1A 17,38,103,
 294,298,478,507,509; 4A
 156; Auston 1A 19; 3A
 56,362; 4A 247; Mary 1A
 17; Solomon 1A 19,172,
 294; 3A 106,251; Thomas
 3A 106
BEHURST, Wm. 3A 512
BELL, 1A 208; Archabald
 1A 257; Benjamin 3A 161;
 Frederick 1A 69,258,491;
 3A 9,133,533; George 3A
 493; Jane 4A 33; John 1A
 367; 4A 33; Orson 1A 208;
 3A 361,510; Thomas 4A 33
BELLOON, Michl. 4A 219
BELLOT, 1A 530
BENNET, Martha 4A 347,348;
 Thomas 1A 220; 3A 355;
 4A 343; Thomas Jr. 4A
 177,405
BENNETT, Geo. 4A 455; Thomas Jr. 4A 304; Thomas
 Sr. 405
BENTON, 3A 225,502; Alex-
 ander 3A 110,116,298;
 Joshua 3A 116,220,296,
 298; William 3A 296,298
BEST, 4A 99; Absolam 4A 96;
 B. 4A 206; Benja. 3A 77;
 4A 255; Benjamin 1A 276;
 3A 174,300,376,378; 4A
 106,145,188,204,245;
 Benjm. 1A 387; Benjn. 4A
 106; Catharine 4A 502;
 Elizabeth 4A 99,552;
 Henry 3A 305; 4A 204,536;
 Howel 3A 351; John 1A
 243; 4A 98,106,245,262;
 Mary Jane 4A 552; Sarah
 4A 255; William 1A 448;
 4A 552; Wm. 1A 74; 3A 65
BEVAN, Joseph 1A 164; 3A
 379; William 1A 164
BEVENT, John 4A 468
BEVERLY, 4A 315; Robert
 1A 405
BEVIN, Joseph 3A 138
BIRD, Robert 1A 312; Sutton
 1A 448
BIRK, Christopher 1A 489
BISHOP, Henry 3A 493;
 Hillery 4A 16,54;

BISHOP con't.
John 4A 360; Robert 1A
213,427,463; 4A 170,216;
Robert Jr. 4A 69; Willis
4A 216
BIZZEL, Arthur 1A 217; 3A
243; Hardy 4A 455; James
3A 243,355; 4A 10,441,
455; William 1A 198; 4A
545
BIZZELL, 4A 545; James 3A
175; Jesse 4A 173; Will-
iam 1A 45; Wm. 4A 173,184
BLACKLEDGE, Richard 1A 398
BLACKMAN, Edmd. 1A 430;
Edmund 1A 64
BLACKMORE, 4A 255,395
BLACKSHER, Elisha 1A 316
BLAIR, George 1A 377; Jean
1A 327,377; 3A 85
BLAKE, 3A 130,192,357; 4A
152,274,332; Francis 3A
186,208; 4A 83; John 3A
359; Joseph 3A 475;
Joshua 1A 242,266; Tho-
mas 1A 488; Walter 3A
475
BLAKLY, John 3A 238
BLAKS, James 1A 34
BLANCHARD, Jedediah 4A
369,371; Jedidiah 3A 291;
Noah 4A 532; Reuben 4A
532; Ur. 3A 291; Urh.
3A 297; Uriah 3A 292;
4A 535; Uriah Hinton 3A
291,297
BLAND, James 1A 267,437,
443; William 1A 267; 3A
389; 4A 40,382,518;
William Jr. 4A 364; Wm.
4A 518
BLANK, 3A 389
BLANSARD, Jedediah 3A 199
BLANSHARD, 1A 198,390;
Jedediah 3A 517; Urh.
1A 86; Uriah 3A 57
BLANTON, 3A 490; John 1A
92,94,170,344,437,447,
481; 4A 201; Joshua 1A
443; 4A 33,445; Richard
4A 370
BLIZARD, John 4A 407,408,
409
BLIZZARD, 4A 210,445;
Ezekiah 3A 196; Hezekiah
1A 525; 3A 2,425; 4A 190;
John 4A 480; Richard 1A
525
BLOODWORTH, 3A 334; David
1A 474,529; John 4A 87,
88; John D. 4A 88; Timo-
thy 1A 162
BLOUNT, 3A 510; 4A 155;
Annis 1A 480; 3A 336;
Benjamin 1A 375; Need-
ham 4A 153,155; 4A 339;
Warren 1A 246,375,480;
3A 336,417
BLUDWORTH, John 4A 375;
John D. 4A 140,160,217,
218,219,276,356,375;
Junius 4A 217,218,219
BLUNT, Warren 3A 309
BOEN, Elijah 3A 434
BONEY, 4A 424,454; Daniel
1A 277; 3A 444; 4A 139;
Jacob 1A 260,379,552;
3A 127,186,192; 4A 51,
112,201,361,370,490;
James 3A 192; 4A 283,
490; John 1A 300,379,541,
552; 3A 221,412,480; 4A
112,137,152,176,242,355;
Michael 4A 32,253,355,

BONEY con't
Michael con't. 368,558;
Wemberk 1A 324; Wembirk
1A 539; William 3A 361;
4A 242,490; Wimbark 1A
379; 3A 412; Wimbeck 1A
58; Wimberk 4A 242;
Wimberk Sr. 4A 242; Wim-
bret 3A 186; Wimbrick
4A 139,152,361; Wright
4A 283,355
BONNEY, John 1A 164
BONY, Jacob 1A 452
BOON, 3A 291
BORDEN, Levi 3A 512; 4A
160,473,491
BOSTICK, Charles 1A 34;
3A 209,477; 4A 290;
Charley 4A 372
BOURDEAUX, Isaac 3A 475;
Israel 1A 499
BOURDEN, 1A 217; 4A 228;
B. 3A 528; 4A 149; Baker
1A 45,237,489; 3A 52;
4A 267,336; Benjamin 4A
17,336; Bryan 4A 10,278,
292,316,545; Catherine
4A 17; Henry 4A 17,336;
James 3A 488,517; 4A
369,371; Nicholas 1A
198; 3A 52; 4A 10,278,
292; Readen 4A 75; Read-
in 4A 278,292; Samuel
1A 237,372; 4A 369,371;
Samuel Jr. 4A 10; Samuel
Sr. 4A 17
BOURN, James 1A 134
BOWDEN, Baker 1A 237; 3A
105,416; 4A 108; Bryan
3A 336,433; 4A 10; Henry
4A 43; James 4A 90,197;
James Baker 4A 491;
Nicholas 4A 90,143,545;
Readen 4A 90; Reading
4A 513; Samuel 1A 237,
372,407,434,445; 3A 399;
Samuel Jr. 4A 197; Sam-
uel Sr. 4A 17
BOWEN, Aaron 3A 334;
Clifton 1A 39,92,214,
344,467; 3A 28; Dan 1A
356; 4A 381; Daniel 1A
164; Danl. 3A 334; Eli-
jah 1A 9,84,92,94,110,
223,323,356,418,486; 4A
176,468; Elisha 3A 260;
James 3A 282; Joseph 4A
175; Mark 4A 234; Nancy
4A 123; Stephen 1A 415;
William 1A 134; Wm. 3A
260
BOWING, Widow 1A 110
BOWSER, Elizabeth 3A 279
BOWZER, 3A 82; Emanuel 1A
171; Emmanuel 3A 17; 4A
120; Henry 3A 505; Luke
3A 112
BOYD, Arthur 1A 243; Eph-
raim 1A 115,243; William
3A 34
BOYET, Absalam 1A 339;
Absalom 1A 545; Absalum
1A 374; Ephraim 4A 206;
James 3A 381; Jones 1A
405; 4A 294; Martha 4A
255; Rhodey 1A 545;
Samuel 1A 401; William
1A 246
BOYETT, Absalom 4A 180;
Absolem 3A 460; Michael
4A 536
BOYT, Arthur 4A 245;
Ephraim 4A 245; William
3A 306; Wm. 3A 157

BRACK, 3A 43
BRACKSTON, Nathan 4A 228
BRADDY, Stephen 1A 133,
213,254
BRADLEY, 4A 343; John 1A
45,88,192; 4A 177,340,
441; John Jr. 3A 421;
John Sr. 3A 421; Richard
1A 45; 3A 137,285,294;
Richd. 3A 417; Simon 4A
304,340; Thomas 1A 372,
445,489; 3A 397
BRADLY, James 1A 504;
Richard 1A 504
BRADSHAW, Benjam. 4A 124
BRALY, John 1A 28
BRANCH, 4A 155; A. 4A 410;
Archelaus 4A 477; Arche-
laus Jr. 4A 531; Arche-
laus Sr. 4A 531; Archi-
bald 4A 79; Arthur 4A
531; Azariah 3A 375;
Benjamin 3A 273; Bryan
3A 528; Burrel 1A 237;
Burrill 1A 237; Eze. 4A
410; Jesse 3A 43; 4A 542;
Matthew 4A 155; Sally 3A
528; 4A 210; Sarah 3A
528; William 4A 155,441
BRAY, John 4A 526; Joseph
1A 201,261; 4A 126,145,
527; Joseph Sr. 1A 1,21,
201,337
BRICE, 4A 58,358; Francis
1A 151,415,454,463,487,
529; 3A 493; George 4A
299,355; John 1A 329;
4A 299; Joseph 4A 36,37,
114,213
BRICKELL, T. H. 4A 299
BRINSON, Hillary 3A 366,
395,396,438,461; Hillery
4A 19; Isaac 3A 279;
John 3A 279
BRISSEE, Francis 4A 489
BRITTON, John 4A 275,559
BROADHURST, William 4A 163
BROCK, 4A 58,353,410; Bar-
net 1A 157; 4A 58; Bea-
sant 3A 110,298; Besant
3A 414,501; Celia 4A 48;
David 4A 58,135,269,352;
James 4A 168; Jesse 1A
141; 3A 298,463,501;
John 1A 180,454; 4A 48,
58,262,269; Lewis 1A 43;
3A 440; 4A 168,454;
Penelope 4A 269; Robert
1A 50; 3A 298,309,393,
501; Stephen 4A 116;
William 4A 168
BROOK, Robert 3A 309
BROOKS, Jonathan 4A 2;
Joseph 1A 308; 4A 327,
460,487; Luves 3A 440;
Tho. 4A 60
BROWN, Benjamin 4A 518;
Charles 1A 367,471,554;
Christopher 3A 107;
Hannah 4A 221; Isaac 4A
281,285; Jacob 1A 137,
284; 3A 245; 4A 372,508;
Jacob Jr. 3A 520; 4A 302;
Jacob Sr. 4A 302,498;
Jesse 1A 257,414; 3A
216; 4A 281,285; John
1A 257; 3A 216; 4A 281;
Redick 4A 130; Stephen
3A 376,438; 4A 126,188;
Stephen Jr. 4A 19; Thomas
3A 541; 4A 101,309;
William 3A 208; 4A 36,
87,88,317,537
BROWNING, William 4A 266

BRUMLEY, 3A 205; Micajah
1A 510,535
BRYAN, 3A 297; 4A 261;
Austen 3A 213; 4A 64;
Austin 1A 329; 3A 537;
Auston 3A 520; 4A 243;
Bartrew 1A 6; John 3A
203; 4A 85; J. T. 4A
273,365; Kedar 1A 61,62,
102,500,513,548; 3A 50,
65,203,288,297,420;
Lewis 3A 369; Nicholas
1A 57,175,433; 3A 195,
415; Patrick 4A 271; Rig-
dom 1A 399; Walter 1A
16; 3A 249; Watty 3A 406
BRYANT, Nicholas 1A 433;
4A 374; Timothy 4A 333;
Walter 1A 16; 3A 226
BRYCE, Francis 1A 167
BULLARD, 4A 104,557; Re-
bekah 1A 88; William 3A
117,182,275; 4A 465
B(U?)LLARD, Wm. 3A 165
BULLS, Henry 1A 364
BUNTING, D. 1A 235; David
1A 551; John 1A 454
BURCH, Christopher 1A 208,
215,220; 3A 133,151,153,
397,485; Joseph 1A 215
BURDEAUS, 3A 186
BURGWIN, 4A 332; John 3A
475
BURNAM, William 1A 252
BURNHAM, 4A 236; William
4A 261
BURNS, Bartholomew 3A 156
BURNSIDE, John 4A 399
BURNUM, William 1A 122
BURTON, Charles 1A 263;
John 1A 263; Prisilla
1A 529; Thomas 1A 263;
3A 79,331,469; Watson
1A 305; 4A 306; Widow
1A 79,474; William 1A
28,263; 3A 469,479
BURWELL, 4A 72
BUSBEE, 3A 515
BUSH, 4A 25,393; Bib 3A 6;
Bibb 3A 375; Bibby 1A
340,544; Bibey 4A 307;
John 4A 110,118,464;
Richard 1A 385; William
1A 38,174; 4A 118
BUSHEE, 4A 186; Consider
3A 515; 4A 190,555
BUTLAR, Elias 3A 26
BUTLER, Christopher 3A
386; Elias 3A 374; Jacob
3A 353; James 4A 136,
442
BUTON, Sarah 1A 188
BYRD, Benjamin 4A 82; John
4A 153; Micajah 3A 71;
Michael 4A 153; Nancy
4A 82; Pearcy 4A 82;
Robert 1A 441,480; 3A
336; Sutton 1A 108; 3A
34; William 4A 82; Zil-
pha 4A 82

-C-

CAISE, Wm. 1A 379
CALEB, John 1A 480
CALL, Isaac 4A 333
CAMPBELL, 3A 334; 4A 370;
Hugh 3A 249
CANADA, Archibald 4A 279;
Joseph 1A 51
CANADAY, Joseph 1A 397;
4A 388; Thomas 3A 350,
531; 4A 322

CANADY, John 3A 493; Mat-
hew 1A 290; 3A 351
CANNADAY, Thomas 4A 54
CANNON, 1A 542; Abraham
3A 297; 4A 506; David
1A 62,69,219,239,420,
471,505; David Jr. 1A
182,185; David Sr. 3A
306; Dennis 1A 61,62; 4
A 506; Edward 3A 305,
306; Elizabeth 1A 257;
Henry 1A 347; 3A 48,203,
382,430; 4A 61,127,417;
William 1A 347; 3A 382
CARAWAY, James 3A 167
CARLETON, John 3A 28; Thos.
3A 28
CARLTON, David 1A 509; 3A
54,57,324,335; 4A 114,
119,127,131,247,279,367,
475; John 1A 509; 3A
106; 4A 217; Peter 3A
106,109; 4A 33,119,364,
475,518; Shadrack 4A
131,475; Thomas 1A 294,
298,507; 3A 106,335;
4A 60,229; William 3A
353
CARR, Archabald 1A 359;
3A 315; Archibald 3A
285,335; 4A 421,426,461;
David 4A 497; James 1A
229,274,310,336,358;
3A 35; John 1A 159,229;
4A 454; Samuel 1A 261;
Thomas 1A 35; William
1A 229,235,285; 3A 332,
372,481,482; 4A 24,207,
226,460,497; Wm. 1A 551
CARRAWAY, Susanna 4A 524
CARRELL, Hardy 4A 175;
Willis 4A 27,175
CARROL, Elisha 1A 457;
Hardy 4A 27
CARROLL, Hardy 1A 150
CARTER, 3A 141,206,318;
4A 215,216; Agustus 3A
446; Alexander 3A 550,
556; 4A 79,97,190,273,
284,307,392,393,394,396,
402,481,520; Constant
4A 79; David 3A 425; 4A
4; Edward 1A 133,255;
3A 107,116,425,442,536;
4A 5,307,462; John 1A
122; 3A 220; Leah 4A
393; Manuel 3A 513,536;
4A 28; Rachael 3A 425;
4A 462; Silas 3A 220,
350,414; 4A 138,373;
Solomon 1A 133,134,213,
331,397; 3A 2,196,260,
276,302,318,425,426,
513,550; 4A 4,396,401,
432,513,520; Willie 4A
428
CARTRIGHT, Claudius 1A 344
CARTWRIGHT, 4A 545;
Claudius 1A 447
CASE, William 3A 475
CASEY, Micajah 4A 434;
Wm. 4A 434
CASTELLOW, 4A 340,343
CASWELL, D. 3A 479; Gov.
1A 448; Richard 1A 42,
51; 3A 545; 4A 454;
Winston 3A 35
CAUMAN, Samuel 1A 344
CHAIRMAN od Duplin Co.
Ct. 1A 114
CHAISTEN, Richard 3A 39
CHAMBERS, 1A 425; Alex-
ander 3A 176,177; Ann
4A 324; James 1A 205,

CHAMBERS con't
James (con't) 476,477;
3A 177,344; 4A 89,329,
362; John 1A 499; 3A
344,372; 4A 31; Samuel
4A 72,329
CHAMBLEE, Joshua 1A 372
CHAMBLES, Joshua 3A 298;
Nathaniel 3A 298
CHAMBLESS, Joshua 3A 363,
399
CHASON, Benjamin 4A 518
CHASSON, Richard 1A 300
CHASTEN, Benjamin 3A 486;
4A 135,367; Joseph 3A
486; Mrs. 4A 135; Rich-
ard 3A 78,391,486; 4A
135; William 4A 135
CHASTON, Richard 3A 158
CHERRY, 4A 97; George 4A
184; Lemuel 4A 173,184;
Samuel 4A 338; William
4A 177; Willis 4A 45;
Wm. 3A 485
CHUBBUCK, Jeremiah 1A 220
CHURCHWELL, James 4A 138;
William 3A 63,188,404;
4A 138
CLARING, Stephen 1A 432
CLARK, 4A 22; Anne 3A 130;
Daniel 1A 471,502; David
1A 471; 3A 292; James
4A 113; John 1A 550;
John Innis 3A 61; Thomas
1A 369,371; 3A 61,130;
William 3A 238
CLARKE, James 4A 22; John
1A 515
CLARKSON, Mathew 3A 167
CLUGSTON, 1A 302; Robert
1A 159
COKWELL, Benjamin 1A 86
COLE, Elizabeth 3A 88;
Robert 1A 485,526; 3A
88; 4A 97; Thomas 4A 6
COLLENS, Charity 3A 193;
Thomas 3A 193; William
3A 193
COLLINS, Charity 3A 371;
Jesse 1A 500; William
3A 371,465
COMMINS, 3A 221
CONNELY, Cullen 3A 354
CONNER, James 3A 493
CONNERLY, 3A 483; 4A 528;
Cullen 1A 182,420,480,
508,512,530; 3A 510; 4A
25,339; John 1A 182,420;
Owen 3A 533
COOK, 3A 82; Daniel 3A 5,
158,391; Henry 4A 207;
James 1A 170; Jesse 3A
349; John 1A 39,171,242,
258,266,324,325,433; 3A
17,59,158,161,216,256,
332,361,391,471,534; 4A
84,120,424; John Jr. 3A
5; 4A 120; John Sr. 3A
5,17,533; 4A 120; Joseph
1A 57; Reuben 3A 471;
Richard 3A 471; Richard
3A 471; Thomas 3A 471;
William 3A 179; Wm.
Cullen 4A 434
COOLEY, Edward 1A 425
COOPER, Benjamin 3A 27;
4A 309; Frances 1A 332;
George 1A 115,387; 3A
27; George Jr. 1A 332;
George Sr. 1A 332; J.
4A 206; John 1A 387; 3A
27,54,240,540; 4A 558;
John Jr. 4A 188; John
Sr. 4A 188; Joseph 3A

COOPER con't
Joseph (con't) 27,57;
Richard 1A 27,332,380,
387
CORBED, James 4A 160
COSTON, James 3A 499; 4A
31
COTTELL, Robert 3A 144;
Thos. 3A 144
COTTLE, Josiah 3A 537;
Robert 3A 537
COTTON, Jesse 3A 518
COVENTON, Levin 3A 172
COVINGTON, Lavin 3A 321;
Phillip 3A 185
COWPER, William 4A 479
COX, 4A 197,274,353;
Andrew 4A 362; Ann 1A 8;
Charles 1A 8,180; Jesper
1A 308; John 1A 187; 3A
17,75; John B. 4A 559;
Joseph Jr. 1A 361; 3A
75; Moses 3A 31; Peggy
4A 362; Robert 1A 33;
Samuel 4A 226; Solomon
3A 31,263; 4A 241,388;
William 4A 61
CRANFORD, Beneter 4A 367
CRAWFORD, 3A 486; John 1A
222
CREECH, 4A 167; Benjn. 4A
167; Edward 4A 86; Mary
4A 86; Sally 3A 502;
Sarah 4A 86; William 3A
502; 4A 86,363
CREEK, William 3A 501
CROOM, Ab. 4A 219; Jesse
1A 194; Joshua 1A 145;
Lott 3A 318; 4A 386;
Major 1A 145,374,432,
545; 3A 460; 4A 553;
Major Jr. 1A 432; Will.
1A 545; William 3A 437
CROSBY, Charity 1A 487;
Wm. 1A 487
CRUMPTON, 4A 358; Thomas
1A 39,214; 3A 189
CRUPTON, Thomas 3A 28
CUMINGS, James 4A 355
CUMMINGS, 3A 192; 4A 487;
Elizabeth 4A 82,537;
Thomas 1A 11,219
CUMMINS, 3A 186; Aaron 4A
305; George 4A 305;
Thomas 4A 305,327

-D-

DAFFIN, Darlin 4A 519
DAIL, Abel 4A 256; Eliza-
beth 4A 256; Thomas 3A
498; 4A 543,544
DALE, Abel 3A 455; Thomas
3A 455
DANIEL, Alexander 3A 124,
136,273; Jeptha 3A 137,
349; John 3A 417,421;
Owen 1A 195; William 1A
188; 4A 304
DANNELL, Robert 3A 369
DARDEN, Charles 3A 331;
Jesse 1A 513; 3A 288
DARELL, John 3A 197
DAVICE, John 3A 105
DAVIE, William R. 3A 479;
W. R. 4A 172
DAVIS, 3A 197,199; 4A 371,
411; David 1A 170,350;
Dolphin 1A 454; Eliza-
beth 1A 319; James 3A
349; Jonathan 1A 170;
Nathan L. 3A 547; 4A
384; Phillip 3A 369;
Rachel 3A 515; 4A 186;

DAVIS con't
Saml. 4A 394; Samuel 3A
513,536; 4A 5,186,216,
370,389,401,402,458,462,
468,481,512,513,555;
Simon 1A 327; Sm. 4A
237,399; Windel 1A 255;
3A 349; 4A 462,555;
Windell 3A 107; Windol
4A 186
DAVISON, 4A 399
DAUGHERTY, George 1A 28
DAWSON, 3A 318; Isaac 1A
386; 3A 318,425; 4A 89,
386,401,462,520
DEAL, Abel 4A 256,522;
Caty 4A 522; Isaac 4A
256; Mary 4A 256
DEAVER, John 3A 105,425
DEBREWHL, 4A 315
DEBRUHL, 3A 498; Edward
Cornwallace 1A 383
DELANY, 4A 509
DEMPSEY, Jno. 4A 511
DEVAN, Thomas Jr. 1A 162
DEVANE, Frances 4A 161;
James 4A 38,182,214;
John B. 4A 38; Thomas
4A 218; William 4A 87,
88,217; Wm. 4A 38,160
DEVER, John 1A 241; 4A
396
DEVOUR, John 1A 241
DICKSON, 1A 172; 3A 223;
4A 177; Alex. 1A 258;
Alexander 1A 19,302,303,
317,448; 3A 362,458,545;
4A 110,415,464,526,527;
Alexr. 1A 358; 3A 251;
4A 446; Ann 1A 358;
Anne 3A 72,138; Dorathy
1A 303,317; Edward 1A
9,13,39,102,226,310,400,
510; 3A 54,57,93,127,
130,138,205,256,440;
4A 266; J. 3A 479,481,
482; James 1A 19,165,
187,199,203,226,303,
317,358,361; 3A 11,28,
106,172,250,251,322;
4A 25,110,118,182,221,
446,459,464; James Jr.
3A 9,62,457; 4A 446;
James Sr. 4A 446; Jane
1A 24,447; Jas. 4A 268;
Jno. 1A 53; Jo. 3A 306;
John 1A 50,125,191,427;
3A 3,62; 4A 36,446,497;
Jones 3A 351,540; 4A
118,335,340,368; Joseph
1A 19,24,39,100,103,
105,170,171,205,210,
214,223,226,243,274,
290,300,302,306,307,
308,329,344,359,430,
447,478,510,541,542,
548,554; 3A 5,22,38,42,
65,72,82,174,189,190,
213,229,251,263,265,
300,306,322,324,327,
356,359,378,391,409,
440,458,461,466,485; 4A
172,272,340,343,440,
545,552,553; Joseph Jr.
3A 336,361; Joseph Sr.
3A 376; L. 4A 155;
Lewis 3A 19; Michael 1A
145,432; 3A 62; 4A 415,
553; Robert 1A 53,125,
145,159,165,178,191,302,
303,305,306,307,317,324,
325,336,358,404,432,499;
3A 62,65,415,486; 4A 10,
246,415,446,459,464,497,

DICKSON con't
Robert (con't) 553; W.
1A 20,50,105,112,114,
191,192,208,214,302,306,
312,353,410,441,508,512,
530; 3A 19,30,256; Will-
iam 1A 306,307,312,400,
420,435,462,530; 3A 3,9,
12,65,87,419,421; 4A 246,
262,340,343,446,459,545;
William Jr. 3A 9,24; Wm.
3A 22,199,263,279,382,
407,409,457,462,528,547;
4A 193,340,439
DILLARD, Theophilus 4A 471;
Thos. 4A 295
DIXON, Benajah 4A 138
DOBBS, Arthur 1A 474
DOBSON, 4A 294; Hezekiah
3A 389; James 1A 228,
331,409; Mary 3A 188,381;
Rebeckah 3A 381
DODD, David 3A 65
DONNELL, Robert 3A 235
DONOHOES, Dormon 3A 212
DORHERTY, George 3A 256
DORSEY, L. 3A 285
DOUGLAS, 4A 25
DOUGLESS, John 1A 66
DRAPER, 1A 88; Thomas 1A
30
DREW, Anthony 3A 533; 4A
27; George 3A 198;
Samuel 4A 458
DRY, William 3A 120,367
DUFF, 1A 452; Benjamin 4A
233; John 1A 162,418;
William 1A 162
DUGLESS, John 1A 117
DUKES, Joseph 1A 166,285
DULANEY, Benjamin 3A 453
DULANY, Ben 1A 361; 4A 479;
Benjamin 1A 382; 4A 260
DUNCAN, 4A 202,288,473;
Edmond 1A 241; 3A 100,
232; 4A 43,286,494; Ed-
mund 1A 30,105,195,241;
3A 97,232,233; Edmund Jr.
1A 195; 3A 97,100,541;
4A 43; Edmund Sr. 3A 100;
Ezekial 4A 207; George
3A 97,100,233,541; 4A
43; Jacob 4A 286; William
1A 30,88,195; 3A 94,97,
100,175,232; 4A 43,63,92
DUNKAN, Emd. 3A 522; George
3A 105; Isaac 3A 510;
4A 25,173,184; Jacob 4A
92,241; Stephen 4A 336;
William 3A 105; 4A 92,
214
DUNKIN, William 3A 447;
4A 441
DUNN, 3A 78; James 4A 133;
Lam. 1A 27,102; Lemon
1A 27; Martan 3A 78;
Phil. T. 3A 167; Saml.
4A 473; Samuel 3A 450;
4A 22,133; William 4A
22,133
DUNNIN, John 3A 172
DURAL, Daniel 4A 365;
David 3A 278; 4A 363;
John 3A 278; 4A 342,365
DUREL, David 4A 342
DURRELL, John 1A 190

-E-

EASON, 3A 512; 4A 473
EDMUNDSON, Bryan 4A 440
EDWARDS, 1A 164; 3A 192;
Matthew 3A 81,499; 4A
21,275,559; Nathaniel 3A

EDWARDS con't
Nathaniel (con't) 215;
Newman 4A 275,559; Oba-
diah 4A 406; Obediah 1A
98; William 1A 342
EGERTON, William 1A 210
ELIOT, John 3A 348; 4A
236,347; Mary 3A 348;
4A 347
ELLIOT, Elizabeth 1A 77;
William 1A 77,448; 3A 34
ELLIS, 4A 555; Benjamin
4A 423; James 1A 98,289;
4A 469; Mary 4A 469
ELLISON, Jesse 3A 147
ENZER, Amboras 1A 23
ENZOR, Amboras 1A 266;
Ambrose 1A 242,323
ERWIN, Edward 4A 157;
Martin 4A 157
EVANS, Benjamin 1A 329;
David 3A 534; 4A 231;
James 1A 159,165,263,
324; 4A 85; Jas. 1A 74;
John 1A 360,440; 3A 96;
4A 37; Lamuel 3A 158;
Margaret 4A 419; Obadiah
4A 101,221; Sam 3A 93;
Saml. 3A 255; Samuel 3A
96,391; 4A 201; Thomas
3A 96,354,534; 4A 231;
Thos. 3A 229
EVARS, John 1A 28
EVENS, John 3A 109; Obe-
diah 3A 303,311
EVERS, Elizabeth 1A 16;
John 1A 16; 3A 5,96,534;
4A 231,404; John Jr. 1A
16; John Sr. 3A 255;
Robert 1A 314
EZEL, Henry 3A 161
EZZEL, Hancel 4A 442
EZZELL, Benjamin 1A 130,
298; Reuben 1A 38;
William 3A 212

-F-

FAISON, Henry 1A 515; 4A
534; Kilby 1A 72,377;
James 1A 23,72; 4A 534
FANNING, John 3A 172
FARIOR, Bryan 4A 498;
David 4A 501; Fredk. 4A
501; John 4A 214,216,
501; John Jr. 4A 498,
501; John Sr. 4A 498;
William 4A 498,501
FARIS, William 3A 475
FARLES, Elisha 1A 544
FARRIER, John 1A 552;
Mary 1A 414; William 1A
488; Wm. 1A 414
FARRIOR, B. 4A 299; Bryan
4A 456,501; Bryant 3A
352,390; 4A 243; James
1A 427; John 1A 137,
427,439,450; 3A 1,3,
245,246,249(2),352,356,
357,359,390,431,438; 4A
96,97(2),186,187,456,
480; John Jr. 4A 282;
John Sr. 4A 282,360;
William 1A 34,137,427,
439,444,488; 3A 1,3,
216,246,308,356,357,
359,390,520; 4A 243;
373; Wm. 3A 245
FAUNAU, Hall 1A 374
FELLOW, Bennet 4A 555
FENLEY, Thomas 3A 474
FENNEL, Edmond 4A 445;
Edmound 4A 375; Edward
4A 219;

FENNEL con't
Maurice 4A 87,88,160,
213,219,375,445,555;
Nicholas 1A 151,153,
415,469
FINLEY, Thomas 3A 462
FLEMING, Alexander 3A 77
FLEMMING, Alex. 3A 235;
Alexander 3A 181,199;
Allen 3A 462; James 3A
462; John 3A 462
FLEMMON, 3A 235; James
1A 380
FLEMMONS, 3A 518; 4A 14
FLOWED(?), William 3A 303
FLOWERS, 4A 236; John 4A
92,214; William 1A 187;
3A 243
FOLEY, 3A 177; Dennis 1A
185; Flood 1A 5; 3A 18;
J. B. 4A 329,426; Jede-
diah 3A 270; Jedediah
B. 4A 329; Jerediah B.
3A 176; Jerediah Bass
3A 18,314,315; John 1A
217,388; 3A 18; 4A 108,
491,545; Stephen 3A 18
FOLSOM, 1A 469; 3A 493;
Benjamin 4A 329; Jere-
miah 3A 103; William
1A 167,415,526; 3A 103
FONVILLE, John 4A 549;
Sarah 4A 549
FOULSOM, Jeremiah 1A 463;
William 1A 463
FOUNTAIN, 3A 88; Henry
3A 356,431; 4A 97;
Henry Jr. 3A 144; Henry
Sr. 3A 144; Mary 4A 151;
Nathan 3A 356,431,539;
4A 151,272,311,507;
Nathaniel 4A 97
FRANK, 4A 114,475; John
4A 388
FRANKLIN, Edward 4A 183
FRANKS, 3A 11
FRAZAR, George 1A 515;
William 3A 39
FRAZER, George 1A 64
FRAZOR, 3A 6
FREDERICK, Andrew 1A 465;
Betsy 4A 448; Felix 1A
48,77,225,364,367,448;
3A 407,451; J. 4A 36;
James 4A 473,502; Jane
4A 99; Nancy 4A 448;
Peter 3A 331; 4A 473;
William 1A 225; 3A 303,
311,364; 4A 98,99,101,
221,448,528; Wm. 3A 60;
Wm. Jr. 4A 210
FRYAR, William 3A 142
FULSAM, Benjamin 1A 136
FULSOM, William 1A 469
FUSSEL, Benjamin 1A 230,
418; 3A 434; 4A 232,
234,293
FUSSELL, 1A 223; Benjamin
1A 162; 3A 429; Jacob
1A 162

-G-

GAINES, Adin 3A 220
GARDNER, James 3A 50
GARIS, Sikes 3A 329
GARNER, James 4A 406;
Nathan 4A 81,93,524;
Needham 4A 81,93,143;
Simeon 4A 81,93,143,
278,292; Wiley 3A 548;
4A 93
GARRAS, John 3A 275

GARRASON, Adonijah 1A 226;
Ebenezar 1A 549; Ephraim
1A 210; Thos. 3A 63
GARRIS, 3A 211,329; Sikes
3A 393
GARRISON, 1A 191; 3A 88;
Adonijah 1A 324,325; 3A
415,449; David 4A 246;
Ebenezar 1A 34,137,444,
488; 3A 245,359,390,537;
Thomas 3A 56,75,415,419,
449; 4A 85,374
GATLIN, Jno. 4A 513
GAUGH, Charles 3A 537;
John 3A 520
GAVEN, Charles 3A 351
GAVIN, 1A 35
GEORGE, Daniel 4A 84; David
3A 188; Jesse 3A 96,444,
480; 4A 112,139
GIBBON, George 1A 542
GIBBONS, George 3A 391;
Stephen 4A 120
GIBBS, 3A 153; 4A 545;
Barsheba 3A 320; Charles
3A 521; 4A 76; John 1A
185,198,220,334,335,
459,462; 3A 153,156,416;
John Jr. 3A 485; 4A 76;
John Sr. 3A 521; 4A 76
GIDDENS, John 3A 231
GILLESPIE, 4A 509; Archi-
bald 3A 3,493; 4A 262;
Borthick 1A 359; Borth-
wick 4A 258; David 4A
229,274,351,354,553;
James 1A 117,166,205,
210,305,345,377,430,432,
454,498; 3A 3,42,203,
351,446; 4A 11,21,37,
184,229,262,354,553;
Jams. 1A 268; Jo. 4A
258; Joseph 3A 351,540;
4A 181,184,229,354,451,
553; Susan 4A 184;
William 4A 274
GILLMAN, Henry 1A 161,222,
235
GILMAN, Henry 1A 300; 3A
446,486; John 3A 158,
229,279; 4A 490,523
GILMORE, Jacob 4A 210,377,
445,522
GILSTRAP, Peter 3A 335
GLISSON, A. 3A 221; Abra-
ham 1A 11,102,205,219,
535; 3A 126,205; 4A 488;
B. 3A 501,502; 4A 411;
Brinkley 1A 505; Bryan
4A 30,95,111,312,331,
410,411; D. 1A 185,198,
410; 3A 8,50,220; 4A
127; Daniel 1A 30,353,
457,508,512; 3A 35,45,
50,69,166,182,336,401,
475,547; 4A 30,411,465,
477,480,488,531,543,544;
Daniel Jr. 4A 544; Danl.
1A 337,530; 3A 51; Danl.
Jr. 4A 543; Denis 1A 11;
Dennis 1A 476,477; 3A
319; Frederick 1A 141;
Herring 4A 488; Jacob
3A 276,302,479; 4A 300,
407,409; John 3A 92,319,
402; 4A 107,411; John
Jr. 4A 297,300; Lewis
4A 107,311,409; Mary
4A 149; Micael 3A 92;
Michael 1A 149,255,314,
316,476,477; 3A 2,21,
84,276,319,328,455; 4A
215,216,411,512; William
4A 149,399,408; Wm. 4A
405

193

GOAFF, Charles 1A 157
GOAR, John 1A 243
GODDIN, 3A 218
GODWIN, 4A 256; William
1A 194; 4A 409
GOFF, 3A 84,88,455; 4A
30,33,111; Charles 1A
487; 3A 249,406; 4A 151;
Gregory 3A 218,276;
John 1A 47; 3A 138,142,
215; 4A 381,555; John
Sr. 3A 507; 4A 1,80;
Lewis 1A 80; Sally 3A
142; Thomas 4A 1,183,
445; William 1A 9,13,47
GOODING, John 4A 221; Mary
4A 221
GOODMAN, 1A 3; Elizabeth
4A 458,468; Harry 3A 35;
Henry 1A 126,182,232,
334,335,420,462; 3A 35,
72; James 1A 126; Jacob
3A 100; Rachel 1A 182,
420; Timothy 1A 182,420;
3A 35; 4A 458,468;
William 1A 334,335,459;
3A 399; Willm. 1A 462
GOODWIN, S. 4A 374; William
4A 107
GOOF(?), John 3A 379
GOORE, Jonathan 4A 45,318;
John Sr. 4A 45,318;
William 3A 157
GORE, 3A 300; Frances 3A
306; John 3A 157,305,
306; 4A 227; Jonathan
3A 157,306,378; William
3A 306; 4A 227
GOUFF, John 3A 520
GRADDY, Alexander 1A 385,
386; Alexander Sr. 4A
376,386; Alexr. 3A 320;
Dm. 4A 191; Durham 3A
92; Elizabeth 1A 134;
Frederick 3A 218; 4A 495;
Fredk. 1A 385,386; 3A
92; Henry 3A 64,77,320;
John 1A 386; Lewis 1A
149,194; William 1A 134,
182,385,386,420; 3A 92,
145; 4A 465
GRADY, 4A 462; A. 4A 29,
411; Abner 4A 515; A.
Jr. 3A 551; 4A 132,515;
Alexander 3A 262; 4A 4,
297; Alexander H. 4A
515; Alexander Hampton
4A 515; Alexander Jr. 3A
551,552,554,555; 4A 5,
29,504,515; Alex. Jr.
4A 376,515; Alexr. O.
4A 515; Anne 4A 515;
A. Sr. 3A 551,555; 4A
132; B. F. 3A 85,87(2),
88,90; Charity 4A 253;
Durham 3A 552; 4A 251,
253,254; Elisabeth 3A
536; Elisha 3A 552; 4A
251,253,254; Elizabeth
4A 254; Eunice 4A 515;
F. 3A 552; 4A 515; F.
3A 552; 4A 515; Fred.
4A 144; Frederick 3A
265,286,319,551,552,555;
4A 132,251,253,254,315,
325,376; Frederick
(Sadler) 4A 315; Frede-
rick Sr. 4A 320,376;
Fredk. 4A 320,386;
Fredk. Sr. 4A 315,504,
515; H. 3A 493,555; 4A
123,216,297,392,393,493,
504,513; Henry 3A 258,
260,261,262,489,500,536,

GRADY con't
Henry (con't) 550,551,
552,554,556; 4A 4,5,29,
132,215,284,302,303,
376,386,394,396,408,410,
465,493,495,515,520;
James 3A 261; 4A 315,
376; Jas. 4A 515; John
3A 258; 4A 29; John T.
3A 260; 4A 515; Nancy
4A 504; Tho. 3A 554;
4A 29; Thomas 3A 536,
550; 4A 5,488; Whitfield
4A 515; William 3A 262,
265,276,282,551,555;
4A 411; Winnifred 4A
504; Wm. 4A 376,386,488,
520; Wm. Jr. 1A 385
GRAHAM, Edward 3A 303,311;
Mary 4A 477,479,552;
Sarah 4A 479; Stephen
4A 98(2),99,479,552
GRANT, Stephen 4A 273
GRAY, Harry 1A 398; John
1A 377; Lodwick 4A 307;
Stephen 3A 513; 4A 307;
Thomas 1A 64,398,430,
441,494,515; 3A 6,90;
4A 545; Thos. 1A 401,
462,494; W. 1A 462
GREEN, David 1A 58,59,
213; 4A 313; John 1A
59,131; 4A 239; Joseph
1A 515; 4A 67,163; Reu-
ben 1A 197; Ro. G. 4A
163; Thomas 1A 482,483;
Timothy 4A 239
GREER, Daniel 3A 286;
David 1A 425; 4A 42,103,
179; John 1A 276;
William 4A 226
GREGG, Frederick 1A 180
GREGORY, Arthur B. 4A 65;
Etheldred 4A 116; Fran-
cis 1A 521; Hardy 1A
547; Jesse 1A 547; Lott
4A 168,388,432; Mrs. 4A
169
GREIGS, Frederick 3A 267
GRIEG, William 1A 208
GRIGGS, Frederick 4A 508
GRIMES, Bathsheba 3A 414;
Charles 3A 42,89,112,
179,236; 4A 413; Hugh
3A 506; James 1A 250;
3A 105,156,232,414,506;
4A 482,494; Jas. 3A 42;
Jesse 3A 522; 4A 465,
500,531; Joseph 1A 248,
250,345; 3A 89,112,506;
4A 6,83; Lewis 3A 506;
4A 203,373; Nancy 3A
73,165; Sampson 1A 248,
250; 3A 73,163,165,182,
414,522; 4A 268,379,
389,465,482,500; Thomas
Sr. 3A 506; William 3A
506; 4A 500
GRIMSLEY, James 3A 518
GUFFIRD, Andrew 1A 75
GUFFORD, 3A 273; 4A 431;
Andrew 1A 67,155,228,
243; 3A 114,126,147,276,
296,302,309,455,463;
4A 429,531,557; J. 3A
502; 4A 199; James 1A
67,228; 3A 258,350,501;
4A 95; Stephen 1A 67,
155; 3A 218,243,276,
302,455; 4A 56,95,107,
199,297,300,312,331,
409,480,538
GULLY, 4A 177,405; Jesse
3A 353; 4A 304,343;

GULLY con't
John 4A 210,304,377,445;
William 3A 353
GURGANUS, Uriah 1A 27;
Wiley 1A 18
GUY, 3A 510; Lemuel 4A
390; Samuel 3A 20,451;
Thomas 3A 131,133;
William 1A 410; 3A 131,
133,361,510,539; Wm. Jr.
539

-H-

HACKLEY, Joshua 1A 443
HAIN, John 3A 90
HAINES, William Harris 3A
94
HAINS, 1A 64; John 1A 494
HALL, Abraham 4A 260; Asa
4A 4; David 1A 39,214;
3A 28; Drew 4A 285; Drury
3A 209; Edward 4A 390;
Isaac 3A 148; 4A 38,182,
276,398; J. 3A 500,528;
4A 480; James 1A 284;
3A 308; 4A 127,146,182,
241,248,262,309,338,390,
438; James Jr. 4A 290;
Jas. 4A 449; Jno. B. 3A
477; Lewis 4A 48,72;
William 1A 332,380,387,
417; 3A 3,27,263,308,
493,527; 4A 118; William
Jr. 3A 510; 4A 25;
William K. 3A 514;
William Sr. 3A 158,391;
4A 415,417,459; Wm. Sr.
4A 25
HALLY, Henry 1A 445
HALSEY, Ann Sophia 4A 313;
Benjn. 3A 328; H. 3A
328; Henry 3A 250,254;
4A 179,313; William H.
4A 313
HALSO, Henry 1A 33; John
1A 33,98,289; 3A 76,338,
340; 4A 46,265; Mary 1A
289; Ruth 3A 76; Stephen
1A 33; 3A 76
HAMES, William Harris 1A
88
HANCHEY, 4A 129,309; Jacob
1A 79,210,474,529; 4A
246; Martin 1A 539; 3A
406; 4A 424; Moses 1A
161,235; 3A 453
HANCHY, Martin 3A 93,152;
3A 256; 4A 124
HANCOCK, Sarah 3A 465;
Stephen 3A 431,465; 4A
19
HANDCOCK, Stephen 3A 193
HANES, Willis 4A 518
HANKS, John 1A 232
HARDESTY, Benjamin 3A 448;
Delilah 4A 296
HARDIE, Joseph Spears 4A
219
HARDY, Jesse 3A 349
HARGROVE, John 3A 544
HARLEY, Howard 4A 161
HARP, 1A 395
HARPER, Blaney Jr. 4A 90;
Charles H. 4A 90
HARREL, 4A 446
HARRELL, Cader 1A 125;
Henry 3A 213; 4A 64;
James 4A 64,124,129,454;
Jacob 3A 213; 4A 64,135;
Kedar 4A 118
HARRIS, Amos 4A 47; Amos
Johnston 4A 279; Casen
1A 5,82; Cason 4A 203;

194

HARRIS con't
Edward 1A 119; John 4A
434,437; Susanah 4A 61;
Uriah 4A 425,433;
William 3A 50,541; 4A
425; Zacheriah 4A 434;
Zechariah 4A 436
HARRISON, Cason 3A 341
HARROLD, James 3A 130
HART, John 1A 502; 3A 349;
Richard 3A 116,375;
Richard Sr. 3A 375
HARTWELL, Danl. 3A 240
HASE, George 4A 433
HASON, Alisia(?), 3A 263
HATCH, Benjamin 3A 518;
4A 14; Sally 3A 518
HATCHER, 3A 291; Hancock
1A 70; 3A 288,292;
Handcock 1A 236,513
HAWKINS, 1A 452; 3A 396;
4A 233; Gideon 3A 366,
396,438; John 4A 234,
293; Sarah 3A 395; W.
4A 512,513; Will 4A 519,
520; William 4A 454,460,
517,518(2),523; Uzial
3A 366; Uzziel 3A 395,
396
HAYNES, John 4A 249
HAYS, George 3A 548
HAYWOOD, John 4A 374;
Stephen 4A 374
HEARING, Samuel 4A 428
HEARS, George 1A 156
HEATH, James 1A 103,174,
478; 3A 322,251; Thomas
1A 174; 3A 327
HEDGES, 3A 412
HEIRS, James 3A 344
HENDERSON, Thomas 4A 357
HENNECY, Elizabeth 4A 80
HENNESY, David 3A 142
HENNESEY, John 3A 142
HENNET, 3A 397
HENRY, R. 4A 137
HERRING, 3A 443; A. 3A
522; Abraham 3A 273;
Alex. 4A 277; Alexander
3A 145; Alexr. 4A 143,
528; Arthur 1A 50,85;
3A 64,84,114,117,147,
276,298,302,402,501; 4A
8,104; Arthur Sr. 3A
273,402; Benjamin 1A 95;
3A 64,110,206,296,502;
4A 86,363,407; Benjamin
Jr. 3A 501; 4A 167;
Benjamin Sr. 3A 501,502;
4A 167; Charity 1A 95;
Daniel 1A 85; 3A 211,
273; 4A 8; Elisha 4A
340,343; James 1A 42,
88,155; 3A 206,488;
John 1A 194; Joseph 1A
72; Lewis 3A 125; 4A
81,267,334,465; Mary 3A
123; Michael 3A 123,125;
Samuel 1A 252; 3A 545;
4A 195,425,428,433,434,
436,437; Sarah 3A 296;
Simon 3A 488; Stephen
1A 85,530; 3A 9,123,
165,273,275,314,375,
503; 4A 8,95,104,429,
431,440,465,531; Stephen
B. 4A 441; Whitfield
3A 273; 4A 429; William
4A 465; Wm. 4A 95,436;
Wm. H. 4A 180
HERRINGTON, 1A 11; Joab
1A 219
HERVY, Stephen 3A 509

HICKS, Abner 3A 288,297;
D. 3A 291; Daniel 1A 66,
70,383; 3A 292; Daniel
Jr. 4A 532; Danl. 1A
236; James 4A 532;
Robert 1A 513; 3A 288,
291; Serene 1A 236;
Thankful 1A 2,51; Thomas
1A 70
HIGGINS, Charles 3A 544
HIGHSMITH, William 4A 382
HILL, Felix 3A 220; Felix
K. 3A 514,544; 4A 39,
163,169,384,473; Felix
Kenan 3A 269,472; Hicory
3A 192; James 3A 547;
James K. 4A 384; Jane
3A 514,547; 4A 39; Jas.
K. 4A 489; John 1A 115,
119,268,499,523; 3A 45,
56,63,166,220,242,261,
269,402,409,450,514,
547; 4A 39; Micajah 1A
64,494; 4A 249; Thomas
1A 112,115,230,280,364,
465; 3A 434,528; Thos.
3A 220; Will 4A 98,216;
W. L. 1A 430; Wm. 4A
373
HINES, 1A 319; 3A 110;
4A 86; Augustin 3A 107;
Benjamin 3A 114; Charity
3A 270; Charles 1A 69,
258,491; 3A 533; Chloe
3A 125; Daniel 1A 319;
3A 123,140; Isaac 1A
90,255,319,320,405,486;
3A 72,107,109,129,140,
141,143,201,276,442,
542; 4A 52,380; Isaac
Jr. 1A 255; Joel 3A 542;
4A 52,334,377; Lewis
1A 90,91,97,320; 3A 124,
136,230,518; 4A 14,267;
Rachel 3A 270; Solomon
1A 70; William 1A 75;
3A 114,129,143; 4A 516;
Willis 3A 517; 4A 14;
Wm. 3A 270
HINNARD, 1A 64
HODAM, George J. 4A 452,
482; George Jornegan
4A 500; George Journegan
4A 202
HODESON, Joseph 1A 487
HODGES, 4A 61; B. 4A 67;
Benjamin 3A 514,522;
4A 61,143,177,491,494;
Benjn. 4A 405; H. 4A
494
HODGESON, Aaron 1A 16,
487; 3A 93,446; 4A 305;
Joseph 4A 68
HODOM, George Jernigan
3A 156
HODUM, Geo. J. 4A 107;
George J. 4A 203; George
Jernigan 3A 341
HOLDEN, 1A 305; 4A 332;
Alexander 1A 358; 4A
118,446; Jeremiah 1A
336,358; John 1A 336;
4A 68
HOLDON, Alexander 3A 362;
4A 110; Jeremiah 1A
336; Jno. 3A 213; John
1A 205,336,369,371,433;
3A 15,221; Thomas 3A
221
HOLLAMAN, Wm. 4A 524
HOLLAN, James 3A 389
HOLLAND, James Jr. 4A 294;
James Sr. 4A 294
HOLLEY, Henry 1A 372,504

HOLLIDAY, Th. 4A 138
HOLLINGSWORTH, 3A 179; 4A
97; Elizabeth 1A 429;
Henry 1A 130,150; 4A 27;
Jacob 1A 429; 3A 213;
James 1A 150; Sarah 1A
429; Stephen 1A 329; 3A
102,213; 4A 64,198;
William 1A 329; 4A 198,
265; Wm. 3A 539; Zebulon
1A 284,427; 3A 359; 4A
175
HOLMES, Gabl. 3A 12
HOLMS, George 1A 279; Lewis
1A 100
HOMES, George 1A 491
HOOD, B. Robin 4A 249
HOOKS, 4A 352; Ann 4A 153,
165,169; C. 3A 146,438,
463,533; 4A 22,153,215,
238,489,528,545; Ch. 4A
165; Charles 1A 312; 3A
19,198,279,430,514; 4A
18,41,169,179,309,415,
494; Charles (infant) 3A
19; Charles Jr. 4A 133;
D. 3A 522; 4A 270,277,
528; David 3A 361,547;
4A 18,41,61,153,155,271;
Hillary 1A 515; Kitty 3A
146; Robert 1A 439; 3A
288; Ruth 1A 439; Susanah
1A 363; 3A 430; 4A 143;
Susannah 1A 439; Thomas
1A 30,105,541; 3A 19,
146,382,430; Thos. 3A
285
HOOPER, Anne 3A 61; George
3A 45; Thos. H. 3A 61
HOOTEN, Ann 1A 456; Char-
les 1A 456
HORN, Jeremiah 1A 14
HORNE, Joseph 1A 377
HOUSE, James 3A 14,85;
Rachel 3A 14
HOUSEMAN, John 3A 165,206
HOUSEMON, John 1A 377
HOUSMAN, 3A 276,302; 4A
132; John 3A 18,92,182,
243,270,314,315; 4A 465
HOUSTON, Ann 4A 493;
Catharine 3A 493; Cathe-
rine 4A 448; Edward 1A
1,268,499; 3A 35,324,
342; 4A 442; Geo. Eust.
3A 460; George E. 4A
449; Griffeth 1A 21;
Griffith 1A 499; 3A 35;
James 4A 423; John 3A
491,493; 4A 313,423,448;
L. 4A 558; Mary 3A 342;
4A 442; Rebeckah 4A 442;
S. 4A 182,313; Sam. 3A
491; Saml. 1A 20; 3A
209,382; Samuel 1A 268,
309,498,499; 3A 66,72,
261; Samuel Jr. 1A 201;
William 1A 499; 3A 35;
4A 41; William A. 4A
103,313; William Jr. 1A
287; William Sr. 1A 1,
20,21,268; Wm. A. 4A
530; Wm. Ann 4A 493
HOWARD, Jesse 3A 243; Saml.
1A 11; Samuel 1A 24
HOWE, Wm. 4A 37
HOWELL, John 1A 369,371
HOWSMAN, John 1A 364
HUBBARD, William 1A 20,21;
3A 35,66,218,243,286;
4A 313
HUBBERD, William 4A 141
HUDGENS, 4A 488; William
4A 488

HUDGESON, 3A 322
HUDGINS, William 4A 111, 502
HUPHAM, Jno. 4A 182,317, 482; John 4A 35,80,82, 140,160,272,276,305, 356,375,381; Nancy 4A 381
HUGHS, Rachel 4A 369,371
HULET, Henry 4A 122,388; Jeremiah 1A 397
HUMPHREY, John 4A 21
HUNTER, 3A 39; 4A 352; Ed. 4A 321; Hogan 3A 351; 4A 188,306; Howel 4A 281; Isaac 1A 131,243, 261; 3A 242,303,311,486; 4A 99,101,221; Isac 1A 429; James 4A 491; Job 3A 351,465; 4A 509; John 4A 99,127,224,262,311, 321,324,480,506,549; Nicholas 1A 53,79,261; 3A 65; Sarah 3A 376; William 1A 401,404; 3A 376,458,465; 4A 415; William Jr. 4A 21; William Sr. 3A 539; 4A 19,281; Wm. 3A 230
HURST, 1A 489,502; A. 4A 163,238,258; Andrew 3A 514,547; 4A 395; James 1A 388,392; 4A 10,108, 545; James Jr. 1A 388; 4A 545; James Sr. 1A 388,545; John 3A 71(2); Sarah 1A 550; William 1A 122,123,252,400; 3A 421; 4A 395; William B. 4A 521 (see 3A 512 Wm. BEHURST)
HUSK, 1A 502
HUSKE, John 1A 551
HUSSEY, John E. 4A 130, 388,558,559
HUTCHESON, Joseph 1A 450
HUTCHINSON, Joseph 3A 89
HYSMITH, Daniel 1A 267

-I-

INGRAM, John 4A 545
IVEY, 3A 381; C. 1A 430; 3A 420; Claborn 3A 332; Curtis 1A 72; 3A 332; John 1A 412; Leah 3A 52; Robert 1A 331; 3A 123, 125; Sarah 3A 332
IVY, C. 1A 513
IZZEL, Hancel 4A 442

-J-

JACOBS, 4A 92
JAMES, 3A 303,311; 4A 98, 101,114,119,221,415, 475; Abraham 4A 136,442; Charles 1A 467; 3A 32, 138,149,452; 4A 114,119, 127; Danl. 4A 212; Edward John 3A 446; Elias 1A 318,430,467; 3A 32, 186; 4A 442; Gabriel 4A 99; George 3A 167; H. 4A 247; Isaac 3A 5,226, 256; 4A 84,404,424; Jacob 3A 212; James 1A 117,159,430,457,474, 529; 3A 303,458; 4A 415; Jno. 3A 96; John 3A 65; Joseph 1A 270,318; 3A 32; Nicanor 4A 68,404, 503; Thomas 1A 219,298; 3A 56,203,205;

JAMES con't
Thomas E. 4A 415,417; Thos. Jr. 3A 225; William 1A 230; 3A 429,434; William Jr. 4A 298; William Sr. 4A 212
JERNAGAN, Elisha 1A 198, 390; Jesse 1A 108
JERNIGAN, Danl. 4A 107; Elisha 3A 528; James 4A 107; Jesse 1A 401; 3A 181,240; John 3A 528; 4A 210; Sally 3A 528; Thomas 1A 401
JOCELYN, Saml. R. 3A 45, 120; Samuel R. 3A 367
JOHN, Thomas 3A 15
JOHNES, Saml. 3A 261
JOHNS, 3A 276; Isable 1A 474,529; John 1A 474, 529; 3A 246; 4A 498
JOHNSON, Amos 3A 448; Benjamin 3A 34; John 4A 218; Thomas 1A 90; William 3A 448; 4A 332, 413
JOHNSTON, 1A 327; 3A 212, 220,437,513; 4A 81,168, 173,237,332,411; Abraham 4A 187,191,288; Amos 1A 439; 3A 87,252,443; 4A 279; Ben 1A 102; Benjamin 1A 359,510,523,533; 3A 20,351; 4A 229,258, 421; Benjm. 3A 471; Francis 1A 58,59,533; 3A 261; Gabriel 1A 529; Hannah 1A 359; Henry 4A 29; Jacob 3A 477; James 4A 539; John 1A 58,359,377,510,535; 3A 21,67,85,180,258,285; 4A 40,184,223,229,399, 419,421,426,461,484; John Jr. 1A 535; Jonathan 4A 183,272; Joseph 1A 58; 3A 1,193; 4A 461, 462; Lewis 3A 361; Matthew 3A 148; Peregrim 1A 494; Peregrine 4A 249; Rachel 4A 246; Reuben 1A 88,100; 3A 94; 4A 187,191,473,545; Richard 4A 1; Robert 4A 96; Robert C. 3A 505; Robert Charles 3A 167; Samuel 1A 167,194,327, 377,415,463; 3A 21,85; Thomas 1A 102,510,533, 535; 3A 205; 4A 116, 168,484; William 3A 79, 252,443; 4A 332
JOINER, Benjamin 4A 318; James 3A 205; William 3A 34
JONES, 1A 329; 3A 375,402; Abe 3A 185,187,321; Anthony 1A 56,126,136,182, 420,536,538; 3A 135,404, 489,528; 4A 49,210,522; Anthy. 1A 409; Augustin 3A 507; 4A 88; Austin 4A 445; Bennet 4A 347, 348; Cordeal 3A 172; Daniel 3A 506; David Jr. 1A 510; Dempsey 3A 172; Elijah 1A 182,105; 4A 286; ELISHA 1A 126; 4A 288; Elizabeth 4A 559; Evan 1A 371; Evans 3A 208; Frederick 3A 404; 4A 49; James 3A 60,518; 4A 14; Jesse 4A 279, 451; John 1A 321; 3A 182,

JONES con't
John (con't) 483,498; 4A 49,71,322,496,539, 559; John Sr. 4A 49,522; Lewis 3A 135; 4A 132, 538; Lidia 3A 145; Martha 3A 348; Mary 4A 49; Moses 1A 523; Nancy 4A 73; Sally 4A 347,348; Saml. 1A 536,538; Samuel 1A 136,405,536; 3A 125; 4A 49,97,123,294,302, 303; Shadrack 3A 483; Solomon 4A 49,445,494; Stephen 1A 126,241; 3A 105,135,321,349,384,393; 4A 71,73,539; Susannah 4A 348; Thomas 3A 141, 226,483,498; William 1A 16,28; 3A 15,17,182; 4A 120,139; William Watts 4A 120,139
JONSON, Reuben 1A 88
JOURNEGAN, 3A 510; Elisha 4A 210; James 4A 202, 208,373,452; Jesse 4A 210; John 4A 210; Ralph 4A 452; Zilpha 4A 210
JURKES(?), Charles 3A 45

-K-

KAY, John 3A 50; Richard 3A 50
KEAN, Richard 3A 245
KEATHLEY, John 3A 30
KEATON, A. 3A 515; Al. 3A 201
KEEN, Richard 1A 137; 3A 216; 4A 456
KEITHLEY, Elizabeth 3A 13; John 3A 13,85; Jonathan 3A 84,140,141,147,455; 4A 237; Richard 4A 237, 256
KELLY, John 1A 548
KENAN, 3A 51; 4A 238,461; Ann 3A 149; Catherine 1A 257; Daniel 4A 355,399; Daniel L. 4A 85,247,338, 357,368,448,480; Daniel Love 3A 539,548; 4A 164, 207,390,449,491; D. L. 3A 314; 4A 22,182,401, 521; Felix 1A 246,257, 264,274,276,292,380,515, 533; 3A 24,45,48,49,303, 402,514,547; 4A 229,238, 384,419; James 1A 121, 205,401,435,499,523; 3A 20,65,73,82,118,119,126, 158,166,205,212,286,297, 314,354,376,391,402,450; 4A 114,172,247,368,390; Jas. 3A 246; 3A 242; 4A 96; Love 4A 67; Michael J. 1A 72; 3A 20; Michael Johnston 1A 523; M. J. 3A 149; Owen 4A 390; Susanah 3A 314; Thomas 1A 43,205,225,523; 3A 126,440,449,510; 4A 247, 454; Thos. 3A 212; William 1A 115,243,257, 367; 3A 24,50,51,166, 199,235,238,402,450,472, 518; 4A 14; Wm. 1A 119, 121
KENARD, Michael 3A 417
KENEDY, Joseph 4A 274
KENNARD, Nathaniel 1A 494
KENT(?), Elizabeth 1A 91, 97
KERNEGAY, George 1A 105

KETHLEY, John 4A 195;
Jonathan 4A 256; Rachel
4A 237
KIBBLE, 1A 383; James 1A
383
KILLEBREW, Buckner 1A 327,
328; 3A 13,14,85; 4A
219; Mary 3A 14
KILPATRICK, Ezler 4A 262
KING, 4A 236,249; Benjamin
4A 480; Bennajah 4A 300;
Charles 3A 71,90; 4A
236,249,496; David 3A
389; 4A 28,79; Jinnea
4A 496; Levin 1A 400;
Nancy 4A 496; Nathan 1A
515; Stephen 1A 3; Thos.
4A 132
KINNARD, James 4A 249,439;
Nathaniel 1A 123; 3A
198; 4A 439
KITHLEY, John 3A 14(2);
Jonathan 4A 544
KITHLY, Jonathan 4A 543
KNIGHT, William 1A 242,
266,323,360; Willm. 1A
130
KNOWLES, 3A 148; Elizabeth
4A 232; Emanuel 4A 232;
James 4A 232; John 1A
467; 3A 379; Robert 1A
323; William 1A 467; 4A
137
KNOWLS, William 4A 176,
234,293
KNOX, 1A 507; 3A 335;
Robert 1A 102
KORNEGA, Jacob 1A 195;
John 1A 195; 4A 43
KORNEGAY, 1A 188,190,192,
327; 3A 342,552; 4A 187,
191,195,219,325,363,
365; Abraham 1A 147; 4A
75,524; Abram 4A 63;
Abram Sr. 4A 39; B. 3A
480,481,482,483,485,498;
4A 14,30,49,104,158,202,
228,352,428; Basil 3A
541,542,545,547,548; 4A
39,43,49,52,75,164,173,
286,288,295,539; Bryan
4A 63,73,524; Charity
4A 399; Daniel 3A 30;
Danl. 3A 541,548; 4A 92;
David 3A 294; 4A 42,179,
488; Elizabeth 4A 144;
George 1A 147,328; 3A
30,233; 4A 43,75,107,286,
434; George F. 4A 132,
144,297,300,312,331,409,
515; George Fisher 4A
144,311; George Jr. 3A
541; George Sr. 3A 541;
Henry 3A 483; 4A 71,73,
286,524; Isaac 4A 300,
311,312,325,331; J. 3A
548; 4A 383; Jacob 1A
182,241; 3A 97,483; 4A
63,75,288; Jacob Sr. 4A
286,524; John 3A 97,541;
4A 71,73,286,288,491;
Joseph 3A 402,512; 4A
39; Js. 4A 89; Luke 4A
63,524; Martin 4A 63;
Mary 3A 61; 4A 524;
Nancy 4A 524; Robert 3A
548; William 3A 64,84,
276; 4A 141,335,409;
William Jr. 4A 39,311,
538; William Sr. 4A 311;
Wm. 3A 261; Wm. Jr. 4A
42,407
KORNEGUS, John 1A 195
KORNEGY, George 4A 436;

KORNEGY con't
George Sr. 4A 195; John
3A 447; Martin 3A 447;
William Sr. 4A 144

-L-

LAMBIRTH, Samuel 3A 335
LAND, Renatus 3A 252,263;
Robert 4A 279
LANE, Alexander 1A 115,
243; James 3A 49,292;
William 3A 369
LANEAR, Benjamin 3A 42;
Jacob 3A 42
LANGSTON, 4A 158; Absalom
1A 90,91,97
LANIER, 3A 89; Benja. 3A
340; Benjamin 1A 39,214,
289; 3A 28,120,236,367;
4A 97,265; Benjamin Jr.
3A 338; Benjn. 3A 236;
Burwell 3A 240; Byrd 1A
487; 3A 236; 4A 504;
Elizabeth 3A 87; 4A 265;
Hosea 4A 289; Isom 4A
289; Jacob 1A 485; 3A
236; James 3A 76,87,338,
340; 4A 46,265,279,289,
311,332,406,504; Jesse
1A 289; 4A 265,279;
John 1A 33,289,485,487;
3A 76; 4A 6,46,265,279,
406; Lewis 3A 340; 4A
265; Mary Ann 4A 265;
Tho. 3A 509,525; Thomas
3A 503; Stephen 4A 374
LANNEARE, Byrd 1A 35
LARRANCE, 4A 186
LASSESFRA, 3A 233
LASSITER, Jacob 4A 90
LASSITTER, Jacob 4A 513
LAWHAUN, Jacob 4A 409
LAWS, Andrew 1A 137,404
LAWSON, Christopher 3A
230,235,518; 4A 8,14,97,
123,157,315,432,493,542;
Christopher Jr. 4A 542
LAYCOCK, William 1A 128
LEA, Joshua 4A 128
LEADE, Wm. 3A 199
LEARY, Job 3A 404
LEBERRY, Rawley 4A 269
LEDDON, Benjamin 3A 59
LEE, 3A 328; Joshua 1A 6,
414; 3A 216
LEIGH, Durham 1A 316; 3A
536; 4A 5,394; Phillip
3A 218
LESTER, Robert 1A 393
LEWIS, Anthony 1A 51,321,
520; 3A 344,374; 4A 322;
Frederick 3A 38,322;
Jane 4A 362
LIDDON, Benjamin 3A 118,
119,223; 4A 438; Benjm.
3A 253; Benjn. 3A 181,
460; Sarah 3A 118,119
LIGHTFOOT, W. 1A 435
LILLINGTON, George 4A 377
LITTLE, John 1A 25,170,
296,297,447,481
LIVINGSTON, Ann 3A 240;
John 3A 240
LOCHON, Jacob 4A 41
LOCKHART, 3A 39; James 1A
79,128,308,345,450,513;
James Jr. 1A 345; Jas.
1A 80; Lillington 1A
345
LOFTEN, Giles T. 4A 346
LOFTIN, Giles Thomas 4A
193
LORD, William 1A 498

LOVE, Daniel 3A 365,472;
Danl. 3A 57; James 1A
274,276; 3A 472; Kenan
3A 48,49,57,126,288,324,
365,449,472,474; Laugh-
lin 1A 307; Michl. 3A
57; Nathaniel 3A 279;
Susanah 3A 472; William
3A 472
LYTLE, Archabald 3A 119;
Archibald 3A 118

-M-

MADDRAY, Starling 3A 198
MAGEE, John 1A 34,137,257,
488,552; William 1A 137,
488
MAINER, Elender 3A 117
MAINOR, John 3A 117; 4A 407
MAIRSES, Richard 1A 364
MALLARD, Daniel 1A 423; 4A
509; Elijah 1A 423; 3A
364,385; 4A 302; George
1A 165,166,423; 3A 364;
James 4A 460; John 1A
285,290,423; 3A 453;
Joseph 1A 290; 3A 364,
468; 4A 274; William 4A
68; Wm. 4A 475
MALONE, T. 4A 172
MALPAS, Hardy 1A 410
MALPASS, 4A 494; Hardy 1A
491
MALPUS, Hardy 1A 258; 3A
533
MANNING, Lydia 3A 371;
Moses 3A 371,438,465; 4A
147,148,216,357,469;
Merit 3A 371; Merrit 3A
540; 4A 357
MANOR, 3A 341; William 3A
117
MARCER, William 1A 18
MARCHANT, John 1A 325
MARTENDEL, James 4A 559
MARTIN, 3A 518; 4A 14;
Abraham 4A 371; Alex. 4A
352,461,473; Alexander
1A 201; 3A 197; Alexr.
1A 337; Christopher 1A
367,380,387,554; 3A 27,
77,145,230; 4A 371; Gov.
1A 48,448; Lewis 3A 145,
235
MARTINDALE, Henry 3A 477;
Samuel 3A 374
MASBURN, Matthew 4A 504
MASHBERN, Christopher 3A
187
MASBURN, James Jr. 3A 477
MASON, Mathew 1A 3
MASSEY, Bethia 4A 89;
Stephen 4A 89
MASTERS, Christopher W. 4A
221
MATCHET, Edward 1A 143;
Jane 1A 476,477; John 1A
136,143,268,476,477,499;
3A 63,176,223,251,261,
314,324,342; William 3A
208,440
MATCHETT, John 3A 177; 4A
329,352; John Jr. 4A 329;
Thomas 4A 72; William 3A
176,177
MATHEWS, Jacob 1A 242,266,
440; 3A 362; James 3A
442; John 1A 360,440; 3A
362; Rice 3A 434
MATHIS, Arthur 4A 189;
Jacob 3A 4A 136,156,189;
Jacob Sr. 4A 156; Joseph
4A 156; Mary 4A 537;

MATHIS con't
William 4A 60,189
MATTHEWS, Arthur 1A 150,
440; Jacob 1A 360; 4A
60; Jacob Jr. 4A 60;
Rice 1A 47,365; William
4A 60
MATTHIS, Edmund 4A 136;
Jacob 4A 47; Jacob Jr.
4A 47; Jacob Sr. 4A 189;
James 4A 458; John 3A
161,490,503,507,509,
525; 4A 37,189,217,375,
555,189
MAXWELL, 1A 405; 4A 302;
A. 4A 389,482; H. 3A
415; 4A 97; Henry 3A
419; Hugh 3A 75; 4A 98,
358,449,494,527; James
1A 166,235,523; 3A 314,
372,489,539; 4A 114,145,
302,303,327,446(2),464
MAYNER, William 3A 147
MEARS, Richard 1A 465,550
MEDFORD, Jesse 3A 374
MEEKS, Jacob 3A 381; Reu-
ben 3A 255
MENON, Michael 3A 61
MERCER, Absalom 1A 18;
Joseph 4A 338; Joshua
4A 18; William 1A 18,
41,254,321; Wm. 4A 322
MERCHANT, John 1A 324
MEREDITH, 1A 350
MEREDY, Alexander 4A 46
MERETT, Philip 4A 442
MERRADITH, Nathaniel 1A
197
MERRIT, Charles 1A 130,
150,298; 3A 335; Ezekial
4A 276; George 1A 443;
Jacob 1A 6; Levi 4A 213;
Mikel 1A 6; Nathaniel
1A 14; Nathiel 1A 156;
Nothial 1A 6; Nothiel
1A 14; Robert 1A 6,156,
350,437; William 1A 14
MERRITT, Charles 4A 175;
Phillip 4A 442; Robert
3A 212; William 4A 442
MESSER, 3A 113; John 1A 55
MESSOR, William 3A 374
MIDDLETON, 3A 514; 4A 415;
David 1A 108,542; 3A 8,
285,300,354,446; 4A 184;
Isaac 4A 126,321,324;
James 1A 165,172,210;
3A 251,306,364,376,453,
469,486; 4A 321; James
Sr. 1A 542; 3A 300,378;
Jas. 1A 108; Mary 4A
321; Robert 4A 106;
Samuel 4A 188,324; Sarah
1A 542; Stephen 3A 376,
468
MILLARD, 3A 153; 4A 76;
Bennitt 4A 149; Hezekiah
3A 151,355,417; 4A 149;
Hezk. 4A 415; Jacob 1A
220; 3A 151; Jesse 3A
151,399,485; 4A 149,405;
Mary 4A 149
MILLER, 4A 407; Anthony
1A 55,136,139,359,425,
432,526; 3A 113,286,324,
351,493; 4A 42,553;
Anthy. 1A 136; Charles
1A 309; 3A 254; 4A 530;
Cs. 4A 42; Elizabeth 3A
254; 4A 19; George 1A
136,268,425,499; 3A 95,
261,322,324,342; 4A 18,
41; George Jr. 3A 254;
Jacob 1A 220; Jesse 4A

MILLER con't
Jesse (con't) 177; John
1A 53,128,210,264,306;
4A 246,421,451,526;
John Jr. 1A 143; John R.
4A 559; John Sr. 1A 264;
Justice 1A 488; Justis
1A 444,552; Mary 1A 309;
Richard 1A 393; 3A 324;
Robert 1A 159; 3A 38;
Sarah 1A 309; Stephen
1A 425,523; 3A 35,53,
54,55,276,322,324,342,
479; 4A 42,72,179,258,
329,461; Thomas 4A 446;
Winneford 3A 53
MILLS, Elizabeth 1A 382;
Hick 1A 41,161,382; 3A
156; 4A 260; James 1A
417; 3A 60,354; Leonard
3A 144,182,354; Nancy
3A 486; Raley 1A 69;
Rawley 1A 258,491,491;
3A 361,510,533; Stephen
4A 233,234,298,472
MINCY, Bryan 3A 523
MINON, Michael 3A 61
MINSEY, 4A 197,228
MINSHEW, Bryan 4A 197,342,
365,471; Jacob 4A 158;
Patsey 4A 197
MITCHELL, Ann 4A 537;
David 1A 454; William
3A 118,119
MIZEL, Levi 3A 448; Luke
3A 448; Mark 3A 448;
William Sr. 3A 448
MIZELL, Levi 3A 450; 4A
110; Levy 3A 355; Luke
3A 355,450; Mark 3A 450;
William Jr. 3A 355;
William Sr. 3A 355,450;
Wm. 4A 110
MIZZEL, William 3A 250
MOBLEY, 4A 107,408; Alex.
4A 413; Alexander 3A
112; Mordecai 3A 112; 4A
413; William 1A 476;
3A 319
MOLPHER, 4A 203
MOLTEN, Abraham 1A 115,121,
246,401,535; 3A 205,376,
378,449,452,466; 4A 45,
318,484; Abraham Jr. 1A
287; 3A 181; Abraham Sr.
3A 72,205,466; 4A 484;
Abram 3A 56,472; Eliza-
beth 3A 72; Jno. 1A 535;
John 1A 361; 3A 72;
John Treadwell 3A 72;
Michael 3A 205,238,303,
466,474; Michl. 3A 311;
Mr. 1A 108; Sarah 1A
219; 3A 466; Tho. 4A
252; Thomas 4A 67,391;
Zilpha 3A 72
MOLTON, Thomas 4A 98,181
MONDS, Sally 4A 482;
William 4A 482
MONK, J. 4A 182
MONTFORD, 1A 405
MOOR, John 1A 225,367;
3A 407; Moses 3A 240;
Widow 1A 465; William
1A 225,429,448
MOORE, Austin 1A 364,465,
550; Auston 3A 301;
Betsey 1A 550; James 1A
112,257,465; 3A 279;
John 1A 112,364,465;
4A 528; Maurice 4A 153,
155; William 1A 225,429,
448; Willis 1A 504
MORAN, J. 3A 285

MORGAN, A. 4A 279; Aaron
4A 11,37,184,227,229,
358; James W. 4A 37;
W. P. 4A 479
MORISEY, Geo. 1A 499;
George 1A 430
MORRIS, Charles 3A 547;
4A 384; Easter 1A 66;
James 1A 66,208,399,400,
410,420,471; 3A 131,133,
166,450,471; 4A 201
MOSELEY, Sampson 3A 152;
4A 503; William 3A 475
MUMFORD, 3A 113,374; 4A
322,542; Charles 1A 139,
526; Elizabeth 3A 404;
Mills 1A 201,337,409;
3A 101,125,317,389,404;
4A 180,322
MUND, 3A 265; 4A 10
MUNDS, Richard 1A 133,134;
Sally 4A 379; Sarah 4A
379; William 4A 379
MUNK, Jacob 4A 87; Mary
1A 75
MURDOCK, Ann 3A 458; David
1A 268,499,554; 3A 67,
223,261,311; 4A 101,419,
221,461,462; Elizabeth
3A 311; 4A 101,221;
Hannah 3A 311; James 3A
311; 4A 101,221; Mary
3A 303,311; 4A 101,221;
William 3A 311; 4A 101,
221
MURPHEY, Timothy 1A 120
MURPHY, 3A 505; Daniel 3A
495,496,503,509; 4A 37,
502,523; John 3A 279;
Timothy 1A 57,128,175;
3A 503,509,525; 4A 398;
William 3A 503,509,525
MURRAH, James 4A 305
MURRAY, 1A 395,439; 4A
459; Archibald 4A 491;
Arthur 3A 79; 4A 2,413;
Asa 4A 6,32,84,122,253;
Daniel 3A 79,495,496;
Jacob 3A 493; James 1A
355; 3A 15,61,144,249(2);
4A 122,212,520; James Jr.
1A 355,395; 3A 79,226;
James Sr. 1A 355,395;
Jesse 1A 355; Nicanor
4A 520; Sarah 3A 448
MURROW, James 1A 363,382;
John 1A 41,382; 3A 95,
113; John Jr. 4A 223;
William 1A 321

-Mc-

McALEXANDER, Hugh 3A 52,
324
McALLISTER, Malcom 4A 381
McCALEB, Annis 3A 336;
Archibald 3A 311; Daniel
3A 336; Gilbert 3A 336;
4A 155; John 3A 336
McCALEP, 4A 155
McCALLAP, Gilbert 1A 312
McCALOP, Gilbert 4A 153
McCANN, 4A 305
McCANNE, 3A 6; 4A 343; H.
3A 372,505; 4A 64,224;
Hugh 1A 79,264,551; 3A
39,179,227,267,537; 4A
31,114,352,353,390,415,
456; Hugh Jr. 3A 229;
Hugh Sr. 3A 67; John 3A
495,496; 4A 266; Natha-
niel 1A 325; 3A 12,22,
67; 4A 353; Nathanl. 1A
167; Nathl. 3A 227,461;

McCANNE con't
 Nathl. (con't) 4A 353;
 Thomas 3A 67,227,229;
 William 1A 72,345; 3A
 78,102,406; 4A 32,68;
 William Jr. 3A 15,78,
 227; William Sr. 3A 227;
 Wm. 3A 144,158,226,255;
 4A 266; Wm. Sr. 3A 67
McCARTY, Florence 4A 497
McCAUM, Neithnel 1A 469
McCULLAR, 3A 288; Henry
 3A 292
McCULLOCH, 1A 62,236; 3A
 9,64,291,297; 4A 311,
 461,528; Alexander 3A
 526; 4A 42; Alexr. 1A
 339,374; George 3A 276,
 402; H. 3A 533; Henry
 1A 58,59,69,70,72,108,
 117,208,225,258,268,
 271,347,434,523; 3A 35,
 67,133,474; 4A 164,493;
 Henry E. 1A 515; Henry
 Eustace 1A 72,112,143,
 239,465,491,513,523;
 3A 336; 4A 61,155;
 Henry Ustus 3A 303; John
 1A 302; 3A 38,458; 4A
 415; John Jr. 4A 415;
 Mary 3A 311; 4A 101,221;
 Mr. 1A 274,276,533;
 Thomas 3A 175
McCULLOH, Catherine 1A
 434; Henry 1A 1,20,21;
 John 1A 159; Penelope
 1A 434
McCULOCH, Mr. 1A 53
McCURDY, William 4A 238
McDALE, Jeremiah 3A 172
McDONALD, Archad. 1A 544
McFARLIN, James 3A 220
McGANUS, Jones 4A 298
McGEE, 3A 65; 4A 119,475;
 Holden 3A 221; 4A 114,
 127,417; Holder 4A 127;
 John 1A 377,444,450;
 3A 89,245,263,308,357,
 359,537; 4A 282,456;
 Thomas 4A 417,526;
 William 3A 246,537; 4A
 101,127,179,221
McGOWAN, William 1A 430
McGOWEN, Alexander 4A 552;
 Edward 4A 357; George
 4A 464; James 4A 146;
 John 4A 11,391; William
 4A 440,506; Wm. 1A 305
McINTIRE, 1A 404; 3A 75,
 351; 4A 461; A. 4A 181,
 252,309; Andrew 1A 290;
 3A 3,225,229,311,406;
 4A 101,223,224,262,391,
 509; James 1A 166,285;
 3A 225,229; Nancy 3A 311
McKEE, Robert 3A 475
McLAIN, Archibald 3A 45
McREE, 1A 16; 3A 93,249,
 406; 4A 112; Robert 3A
 152; 4A 503; William
 3A 52,324,342

-N-

NANCE, Daniel 1A 72
NATHERCUT, William 4A 260
NEALE, John 1A 393; John
 Jr. 1A 393; 3A 180
NEELE, John 1A 393
NEELEY, Andrew 1A 156
NEELY, Andrew 1A 443
NEIL, John 1A 145,166;
 John Jr. 3A 342

NETHERCUT, Loftis 4A 157;
 Lofton 3A 489; Renn 3A
 113; William 1A 139,
 321,526; 3A 113
NETHERICK, William 1A 41
NEW, 3A 547; 4A 202; David
 4A 4; John 1A 119; 3A
 73,126,269; 4A 203,384;
 Margaret 1A 119; William
 3A 192
NEWEL, Jesse 4A 436
NEWELL, Nathan 1A 342
NEWKIRK, Abraham 1A 51,
 167,292,469; 3A 103; 4A
 262,274; Henry 1A 51,
 292; 4A 299,355; Killis
 4A 58,299
NEWSOM, David 3A 55
NEWTON, 1A 208; Abraham
 1A 296,297,352; 3A 215,
 507; 4A 35,36,161; 4A
 183,213,214,217,381,495;
 Eleanor (Mrs.) 4A 528;
 Enoch 4A 214; Jacob 1A
 296,352; James 1A 352;
 4A 161(2),528; John 1A
 77; 3A 451; Joshua 1A
 352; Lois 1A 296,297,
 352; Louis 1A 296; Major
 4A 528; Mrs. 4A 528;
 Patrick 1A 77,364,465,
 550,551; 4A 528; William
 1A 77,491; 3A 361,510;
 4A 528; Wm. 1A 69
NICHOLS, John 1A 399,420
NICKENS, Jonathan 4A 190
NICKSON, Jonathan H. 4A
 392
NIELSON, Alex. 1A 547
NIXON, Danl. 3A 300
NORMAN, Richard 4A 324;
 Thomas 3A 45
NORMENT, Tho. 3A 269;
 Thomas 3A 8,24,48,49,
 50,51,63,166,175; 3A
 238,361,365,449,472;
 Thos. 3A 27,56
NORRIS, 4A 187,332; Isom
 4A 1,404; Jesse 1A 28;
 3A 93,231; 4A 122,191;
 Patrick 1A 45; Reuben
 4A 84,129,231

-O-

OATES, James 1A 122; Jesse
 1A 3; Lowhamah 1A 3;
 Wyatt 1A 122
OATS, 3A 6; Samuel 1A 239
O'DANIEL, Al. 4A 409;
 Alex. 1A 85; 4A 167,
 300,408; Alexander 4A
 297,409,538; Charity
 1A 412; O. 4A 386,470,
 493; Owen 1A 99; 3A 64,
 84,97,265,270,273,275,
 276,302,426,479; 4A 42,
 123,179,208,300,315,
 319,320,392,399,429,
 530,541,557; William
 1A 85,95,99,188,190,
 327,412; Wm. 1A 486
OLIVER, 4A 193; Francis
 1A 215,217,388,390,392;
 3A 43,52,58,137,294,
 363,397,399; 4A 173,
 440; Frans. 1A 407,434,
 489,525; 3A 153,416;
 Isaac 3A 239; John 3A
 239; 4A 78,286; Sarah
 1A 392; 3A 239; 4A 78
OSBURN, Jo. 3A 510
OSBURNE, Joseph 4A 346

OUTLAW, 1A 248; 3A 73,84,
 126,182,201,265,273,457;
 4A 104,376,465,531;
 Alexander 3A 129,143,
 282; 4A 104; Alexd. 4A
 402; Edward 3A 109,129,
 143,488; Edwd. 3A 276;
 George 1A 388,390,525;
 3A 18,126,270,314; 4A
 108,491; James 1A 268,
 405,499,544; 3A 85,109,
 118,119,129,143,145,201,
 261,262,276,282; 4A 52;
 Jesse 4A 199,203,494;
 John 3A 500(2); 4A 52,
 410; Josiah 3A 341; 4A
 208; Lod. 4A 373; Sally
 4A 251
OVERTON, Thomas 3A 12,22

-P-

PADGET, Benjamin 4A 259;
 James 3A 158; Joab 1A
 261,427; 3A 113,359,499;
 John 3A 499
PAGE, John 4A 218
PARADIN, Susanah 3A 185;
 William 3A 187; Wm. 3A
 185
PARKER, 3A 43; Alexander
 3A 516; 4A 293; Amos 1A
 329; 4A 151; Amous 3A
 388; Ann 3A 516; 4A 51;
 Daniel 3A 135,401,498;
 Elisabeth 3A 388; Hardy
 3A 82,423; 4A 24; Isaac
 1A 103,478; 4A 114,475;
 John 1A 157,164,363,427,
 433; 3A 82,135,401,431,
 498,516; 4A 368; John
 Sr. 4A 51,293; Jonathan
 1A 47,549; 3A 401; Peter
 3A 135,401,498; Richard
 1A 80; Robert 3A 523;
 Solomon 1A 80,329; Sus-
 annah 3A 43; William 1A
 141; 3A 43,58,516; 4A
 51; Wm. 4A 293
PATERSON, James 1A 292,
 454; Jane 1A 454
PATTERSON, Betsey 3A 421;
 James 3A 205; 4A 45,318,
 484
PEACOCK, Jesse 3A 235,518;
 4A 14; John 1A 260; 3A
 192; Theophilus 3A 452
PEAL, David 4A 197,228;
 John 4A 197,471; Nathan
 4A 228; Robert 4A 228,
 365
PEALE, John 4A 471
PEARCE, 4A 118; Archibald
 1A 457; Charles 4A 259;
 Joseph 3A 87; Parker 1A
 98,289; Snoden 3A 386;
 Snodon 1A 248; 4A 377
PEARSALL, Anne 3A 322,324;
 Ed. 4A 329; Edward 1A
 143; 3A 243; 3A 351,
 539; 4A 11,335,399,419,
 421,426,440,461,462,
 497; Edwd. 1A 30; 3A 35;
 Ferabe 3A 54; J. 1A 300,
 302,554; 3A 177,229,500;
 4A 421,440; James 1A 30,
 105,114,128,143,159,171,
 210,261,302,337,430,457,
 513; 3A 53,54,55,176,
 177,263,303; 4A 329,407,
 415; Jas. Jr. 3A 534;
 Jeremiah 1A 43; 3A 176,
 177,180,229,344,440;
 4A 224,329; Zilpha 1A
 159

199

PEARSE, 4A 99; Archa. 3A
112; Snoden 3A 112
PERKINS, Martha 1A 53
PHAREZ, 4A 25
PHEBUS, James 1A 452
PHILIPS, Thomas 3A 451
PHILLIP, John 1A 401
PHILLIPS, Benjamin 3A 300,
378; John 3A 300,378,
391; 4A 126,145,188;
Tho. 4A 204; Thomas 3A
300,378; Thos. 3A 486
PHILLMAN, William 1A 178
PHILLMET, William 1A 180
PHILYAW, Martin 3A 477
PHIP, Thomas 1A 225
PHIPPS, Thomas 1A 448
PHIPS, Deborah 1A 456;
Thomas 1A 48,448
PICKET, 3A 89,537; 4A 151;
Dawson 3A 102; Henry 1A
80; 3A 213; James 1A 79,
363,397,549; 3A 213; 4A
83,507; James Sr. 3A
102; Sihon 3A 112; Solo-
mon 1A 397; 3A 102,213;
Thomas 1A 363; 4A 282;
William 1A 363,439; 3A
89,102,443; 4A 252;
William Jr. 1A 395;
William Sr. 1A 395; Wm.
3A 179
PICKETT, Alexander 3A 520;
Dawson 3A 179; 4A 65;
Esther 4A 504; F. 4A 97,
103,282,498; Frederick
4A 6,83,360; Fredk. 4A
2,332,377; Henry 3A 495,
505,537; 4A 97,151,507;
James 3A 179,388,495,
496,505,520,537; 4A 64,
65,151,373,501; John 3A
496; 4A 65; Patty 4A
360; Sihon 4A 507; Solo-
mon 1A 329,179; 4A 65,
198; Thomas 3A 520;
William 1A 355; 4A 6,65,
97,282; William Jr. 3A
179; William Sr. 4A 413;
Wm. 4A 377
PICKITT, William 4A 2
PICKNER, John 4A 132
PICKSON, John 3A 554
PIDCOCK, John 1A 552
PIERCE, William Alex 3A
314
PIPKIN, Archelaus 4A 380;
Arthur 1A 398; Elisha
4A 380; Isaac 4A 380,
539; Jesse 1A 133,255,
319; 3A 141,201; 4A 380;
John 3A 140,141; Lewis
3A 140
PITMAN, 1A 552; Arthur
1A 35; Dempsey 1A 35
PLAT, Adam 1A 417
PLATT, Adam 1A 161,222,
235,280,283,365; 3A 127;
4A 266
POLLOCK, William 3A 450;
4A 172,536; William
Ward 3A 57,288,354;
Wm. 4A 27
POMPHREY, Carter 4A 215
POOL, George 3A 233
POPE, Readin 4A 90
PORTER, 1A 552; Alex. 1A
294; Alexander 1A 509;
Henry 4A 189,367; John
1A 260,505
PORTERVENT, Sarah 4A 537
POTTER, 1A 452
POWEL, 4A 249

POWELL, 1A 108,305; 3A 90,
226; 4A 236; Abraham 3A
34; Britain 4A 140; Eli-
jah 1A 267; Elisha 4A
161,356; Geo. 3A 255;
George 1A 187; 3A 15;
4A 68; Hardy Sr. 1A 267;
4A 40; Jacob 3A 157,306;
John O. 3A 303; John
Osbon 3A 311; John Os-
burn 4A 221; Lewis 4A
141; Rachel 1A 267;
Starling 3A 198; Stephen
1A 246; Patrick 1A 305,
457
PRAIRSES, Weston 3A 349
PRESCOAT, 3A 460; Richard
1A 339,374
PRESCOT, 1A 545
PRESCOTT, Richard 3A 526
PRICE, 4A 228; Barbara 4A
49; James 3A 474; Nat-
haniel 4A 49,197; Tho.
4A 75
PROWSE, John 1A 215
PULLARD, Nicholas 1A 285
PUMFREY, Silvanus 1A 316
PUMPHREY, Silvenus 4A 512;
Solomon 3A 2
PUMPHRY, 4A 481; John 3A
2; Sylvanus 3A 536; 4A
5,394

-Q-

QUIN, Abner 1A 139,321; 3
A 113; Caleb 1A 139; 3A
113; David 3A 362;
James 3A 174; John 3A
261; Thomas 1A 321; 3A
95; Thos. 4A 28; Abner
3A 374; 4A 322
QUINN, Ann 4A 354; Catha-
rine 4A 145; Loften 4A
48,274,388,465,477,558;
Loftin 4A 116,168;
Nancy 4A 291; Thos. 4A
69; Thomas 1A 520,521,
522; 3A 374; 4A 48,216,
241,322; Thos. 1A 545;
3A 31; 4A 116

-R-

RAINER, John 4A 265
RAMSEY, Isaac 3A 253
RAPHAEL, James 3A 314,
315; 4A 509,517,553;
Jas. 3A 527
RAPHEL, Southy 3A 285
RATLEFF, Samuel 3A 78
RATLIFF, Samuel 3A 64,
276,402; 4A 477,530
RAWLINGS, James 1A 350,
481,483; 4A 207
RAWLINS, James 1A 94; 4A
226
READ, A. 1A 268; Andrew
1A 380
REARDON, James 3A 59,157,
239,306,407,547; 4A 18,
41,45,318,355,384,545,
549
REATHERFORD, John 3A 412
REAVES, 3A 541; Adam 3A
94; Hardy 1A 88,279,
489; 4A 425,437; Tho.
4A 425
REED, Andrew 1A 393
REES, David 1A 17; Sabra
1A 17
REEVES, Adam 1A 195; 3A
231,233; Hardy 1A 215;
4A 436; Jesse 3A 233;

REEVES con't
John 3A 231,232,233
REGISTER, Jesse 1A 310;
Thos. 3A 148
REM(?), Richard 3A 357
REVES, Hardy 4A 433; Tho.
4A 437; William 4A 425
RHODES, Benjamin 1A 2; 4A
296; Elizabeth (Taylor)
1A 407,434; Henry 3A 120,
367; Jacob 1A 2; 3A 11;
4A 296,558; James Sr.
4A 559; James Thomas 4A
61; Jno. Felix 4A 423,
442; John 1A 407,434;
John Felix 4A 355; Joseph
T. 1A 2,222,284,417,429,
454; 3A 31,156,267,491;
4A 19,21,61,248,290,296,
355,372,388,508,558;
Joseph Thomas 3A 11,245;
Jos. T. 4A 241; Taylor
4A 336; William 4A 336
RICHARDS, John 3A 38; 4A
502,521
RIGBY, 4A 110; William 3A
174; 4A 118,126; William
Jr. 3A 174; William Sr.
3A 174
RIGSBEE, 1A 172; William
1A 19,226
RIVENBARK, 1A 548; 3A 203;
Frederick 1A 230,500;
3A 288,420,434; 4A 227;
John 1A 230,277,379;
Simon 3A 423,429; William
Wright 4A 226; Wm. W. 4A
234,239; W. W. 4A 398
RIVENBERG, 3A 186; 4A 212
ROADS, 1A 395; J. 1A 43
ROBERDS, Richard 1A 319
ROBERTS, 1A 42,441; 4A 197;
Henry 3A 369; John 3A
488,517,549; 4A 228,369,
371,380,511; Mary 3A 124,
136,201; Richard 1A 194;
3A 124,136,140,201;
Right 3A 201; William
1A 84; 3A 116,549; 4A
307; Wright 3A 124,136
ROBESON, John 3A 24; Wm.
1A 267
ROBINSON, 3A 514; John 3A
409; Thomas 4A 382; W.
4A 36,96
ROCHELS, Eatherent 1A 270
RODGERS, 1A 133; James 1A
294
ROGERS, 3A 129,201,455; 4A
197,228; Anne 3A 38; Asa
4A 57,149; Eleazer 1A
485; Isabella 3A 327;
Isaiah 4A 57; James 3A
38,327; 4A 367; James
Williams 3A 276; James
Wm. 3A 265; Job 3A 38,
322,327; Joel 4A 57;
John 1A 141,459; 3A 43;
John Sr. 3A 58; Mark 4A
261,535; Matthew 3A 251;
Nicholas 3A 38,327; 4A
527; Peleg 3A 38,327,
544; 4A 367; Peleg Sr.
1A 285; Randolph 3A 369,
488; Samuel 1A 86,194;
3A 369; 4A 256; William
3A 218; 4A 259
ROINGTON, Job 1A 11
ROLINS, Robert 1A 437
ROLLINGS, James 1A 482
ROLLINS, Edward 1A 182,420
ROOTS, John 1A 42
ROUCE, John 4A 191

ROUSE, 3A 349,402; 4A 236, 246; Alexander 3A 73, 402,554; 4A 132; Andrew 1A 306; 3A 419; Elizabeth 1A 74; Elizabeth Mary 1A 74; George 3A 419; Henry 4A 129,249; John 4A 373; Martin 1A 191; Phillip 1A 74,191, 306; Solomon 4A 249
ROUTLEDGE, 3A 223; Esther 1A 143; Nicholas 1A 131, 143,167,469; Sarah 3A 118,119; Th. 4A 24,329; Th. Jr. 3A 223; Tho. 3A 446; Thomas 1A 222,264; 3A 65,260,303,311,426, 479,481,482,556; 4A 11, 16,101,221,284,393,396, 419; Thomas Jr. 1A 417; 3A 332,466; Thomas Sr. 3A 118,119,225,332; 4A 16,438; Thos. 1A 112, 404; 3A 52; Thos. Jr. 3A 181; William 1A 143; 3A 118,119; 4A 421; William Jr. 3A 332
ROWAN, Matthew 1A 180
RUNCHEY, Adam 1A 187
RUTHERFORD, 1A 404,541; 3A 93; 4A 16,112; Brock 3A 75; John 1A 79; 4A 242
RYAN, James 1A 197,350

-S-

SALMON, Daniel 3A 233
SANDERFER, Joseph 4A 249
SANDERS, Daniel 4A 513; Richard 3A 550; 4A 4
SANDLIN, Nicholas 3A 446; 4A 243,501
SARLS, Major 4A 437
SASSER, Joel 3A 100
SAUNDERS, Alexander 3A 103,252; 4A 535
SAVAGE, Arthur 1A 53,306, 307; 3A 423,429; Francis Sr. 1A 53; Love 3A 419; 4A 246; William 1A 53; Wm. 1A 277
SCARBOROUGH, Jesse 3A 520; Miles 4A 93
SCARLES, Major 3A 545
SCREWS, James 4A 147,148; Jesse 4A 147,148; John 4A 193,316,346; Joseph 4A 147,148
SEARLES, Major 4A 342
SELLARS, Benjamin 3A 232; John 4A 35; Jacob 1A 14, 156
SHACKLEFORD, 3A 357,390
SHARPLES, W. 1A 35,62
SHARPLESS, William 1A 182, 239
SHAW, C. 4A 139; Colin 4A 160; John 3A 8,334; William 3A 182
SHEFFIELD, 1A 336; Isom 3A 362; John 1A 504; 3A 349; Lincoln 1A 308
SHELTON, Rebeckah 3A 305; Thomas 1A 405,409; 3A 101,305,306,317,381; 4A 180; Thos. 3A 389,452
SHEPARD, Elijah 4A 83; Thomas 4A 415,417
SHEPHERD, John Baptist 1A 274,276,535; Mornen 1A 276; Thos. 4A 37; William 3A 311
SHEPPARD, John B. 1A 332

SHIVERS, William 3A 114
SHOALER, John 3A 238; Levi 4A 83; Moses 3A 238
SHOLAR, 4A 377; Isom 4A 332; Levi 4A 332; Moses 4A 83
SHOLDERS, Moses 1A 485
SHOLER, John 3A 386; Moses 3A 443
SHUFFIELD, 3A 195,227; 4A 353; Amos 3A 195; John 1A 388; 4A 316,346,487, 545; Lincoln 3A 520
SHUFFLE, Amos 4A 253
SHUFIELD, John 4A 545
SIKES, Cader 4A 494; Frederick 4A 10,489; Joseph 4A 489; W. 3A 514,522; Willis 4A 163,489
SILIVENT, John 3A 270
SIMMONS, Daniel 4A 295; Wm. 4A 295
SIMPSON, Elizabeth 4A 114, 127
SINGLETON, David 3A 215; Richard 1A 270
SIRL, Robert 4A 365
SKIBBOW, Henry 1A 352; 3A 371; 4A 357,469
SLOAN, David 1A 24,199, 203,229; 3A 251; 4A 1, 129,484; Edward 1A 425; Gibson 3A 505; 4A 485; John 1A 336; 3A 332; 4A 24; Robert 1A 336; 3A 221,324; 4A 327,485,487; Robt. 3A 227
SLOCUMB, David 1A 494; Samuel 1A 64,400,494
SMITH, 1A 143; 3A 125,147; 4A 30,111,138,541; Ambros 4A 51,214; Ambrose 3A 32; 4A 495; B. 4A 373,374; Benj. 4A 216, 374; Benja. 4A 373; Benjamin 1A 435; 4A 97; Benjm. 4A 98; Curling 3A 146,160,248,382,409; 4A 426; David 3A 437; Dorothy 3A 184; Drew 4A 493; Elijah 3A 523,526; 4A 530,541; Fred. 4A 399,470; Frederick 1A 136,254; 3A 286; 4A 18, 41,42,103,477; Frederick Jr. 4A 386,530; Frederick Sr. 4A 12,42,386, 477,493,530; Fredk. 4A 319; Geo. 1A 538,545; George 1A 110,136,194, 228,314,316,339; 3A 218,258,286,318,319,385, 389,455,460,526,536; 4A 5,42,123,141,157,256, 319,394,470,512; George Jr. 1A 339; 3A 56,254, 285; George Sr. 1A 331, 536; 3A 63,98,101; 4A 542; Isaiah 3A 184,489; 4A 302,303; Ivey 4A 305; James 3A 151,282; Jesse 4A 42; John 1A 544; 3A 196; 4A 236,383; Jones 4A 42; Joseph 1A 429; Keziah 4A 302,303; Lewis 1A 405; 3A 98, 125,184; 4A 542; Nathan 4A 305; Reading 3A 184; Richard 4A 489; Samuel 4A 228; Seliathe 4A 530; William 1A 194, 314,316; Zacheus 4A 530
SMYTH, 3A 490; David 3A 21,72; 4A 411;

SMYTH con't
James 3A 21,513; 4A 411; John 4A 389; ·Sam. 4A 481; Samuel 4A 411; Stephen 1A 467; 3A 434; William 4A 537
SMYTHE, Samuel 4A 30
SNEAD, Wm. 4A 496
SNELL, Stephen 3A 71
SNIPES, 1A 155; 3A 296; Ben 4A 56; Bengemon 3A 114; Benjamin 1A 228; 3A 117,270,273; 4A 8,104, 431,531; Benjamin Jr. 4A 104; Joseph 4A 8,104; Kitty 4A 8,104; Nancy 4A 8,104; William 4A 8
SOLOMON, 1A 30
SORRELL, William 4A 389
SOUTHERLAND, 3A 493; 4A 202,203,208; Daniel 1A 167,292; 3A 216,238,263, 352,357,390,440,446,520; 4A 58,243,299,309,456, 498; Danl. 3A 246; David 4A 170; George 4A 238; Henry 4A 58; Jane 4A 238; John 1A 285; 3A 24, 248,382,430; 4A 238,395; Patience 1A 526; Philip 4A 553; Phill 1A 167, 285,290,415,423,463; 3A 364,385,415,419,453,468, 469,527; 4A 16,54,170, 246,479,509; Phill Jr. 3A 531; 4A 69,216,268, 322,477; Phill Sr. 4A 243; Polly 3A 469; Robert 1A 51,151,153,463; 3A 156,254,331,350,440,531; 4A 69,170,243,383; Robin 1A 526; Samuel 3A 520; W. 4A 268; William 1A 167,213,225,363,415,423, 463,469,499,552; 3A 42, 103,279; 4A 262,355,392; Wm. 3A 327
SOWELL, F. 3A 26; Samuel 1A 84,110; 3A 26,31,103, 254,328,374; 4A 186,322, 383,389,458,468,555; Shadrack 3A 103; Shadrick 1A 84,110; William 4A 383
SPANN, Samuel 3A 475
SPEARS, John 3A 100; 4A 539
SPENCE, Elisha 4A 316; Isaac 3A 349,397; 4A 71, 193,288,316,346; Timothy 3A 61,156,349; 4A 379, 465
SPENCER, Saml. 1A 377
SPIKERMAN, Lewis 3A 420
SPILLER, James 3A 69
SPITTER, James 4A 390
SPIVEY, Nathaniel 3A 220
STAFFORD, Josiah 1A 331; 3A 188,258,381
STALLING, Shadrack 3A 82
STALLINGS, John 3A 481, 482; 4A 1,152,176,183, 212,242,364,398,485,518; L. 3A 161; 4A 80; Meshack 1A 283,365,418; 3A 354,434,475; 4A 232, 283; S. 4A 247,398; S-adrack 3A 189; Shadk. 1A 260; Shadrack 1A 9, 13,199,203,230,281,310, 369,371,418,452,552; 3A 20,61,130,190,192,334, 423,507; 4A 96,183,229, 247,358; Shadrick 1A 24;

STALLINGS con't
William 4A 96,183,358
STALLINS, Meshack 1A 223,
230,280; Shadrack 3A 475
STANDLEY, James 1A 237;
John 1A 42; Moses 1A
340,342; 3A 260
STANFORD, Samuel 3A 351,
510; 4A 25,459,464
STANLEY, 4A 90,396,513;
Moses 4A 143
STEPHENS, 4A 553; Wm. 1A
123
STEVENS, Loammi 3A 71;
John 3A 129; William 1A
252,273
STEVENSON, M. 4A 101
STEWART, Barnet 4A 307;
Daniel 4A 291; James 3A
550,556; 4A 4,284,291,
392; John 3A 26; 4A 402,
448,555; Patrick 1A 274,
276
STOAK, William 4A 553
STOAKES, 4A 358; Andrew
4A 188; Arthur 3A 385;
Henry 3A 160; William
4A 36
STOAKS, Amey 3A 364; Ar-
thur 3A 364; William
Jr. 3A 189,190
STOCKS, Fereby 4A 535
STOKES, Arthur 1A 166,
261,290; Henry 1A 380;
Read G. 3A 109; Reading
3A 52; William 1A 145,
432
STONE, 4A 18; D. 4A 97;
David 3A 61,481,482; 4A
96,97,103,186,187,214,
215,372; Philip 3A 518;
4A 158; Phillip 4A 14;
Robert 1A 178; 4A 553
STRAHORN, Moses 1A 520
STREE, Wm. 4A 401
STREET, Edward 4A 231;
Edwd. 4A 503; William
4A 32,503
STRICKLAND, Absalom 1A
165; 4A 114; Absolam
4A 475; Matthew 4A 131;
Richard 4A 131,475;
Sarah 4A 131
STRICKLING, Absolem 3A
106; Absolom 3A 106,109;
Charles 3A 106; Richard
3A 109; Sarah 3A 106,109
STRINGFIELD, Joseph 1A
267; 4A 40
STROUD, Abel Croom 3A 317;
4A 180; Arthur 3A 101,
317; Lewis 4A 432; Lot
3A 317; Lutson 1A 374,
545; 3A 98,101; 4A 93
STUCKCA, John 3A 94
STUCKEY, John 1A 239; 3A
166,450; Lewis 3A 8
SULAVANT, John 3A 114
SULIVAN, 3A 501; 4A 8,452;
Dickson 4A 268; Hampton
4A 410; John 4A 410;
John Sr. 4A 379,410;
Michael 3A 126; 4A 379;
Widow 4A 452; William
3A 126
SULIVANT, John 1A 67; 4A
203
SULIVEN, Frederick 3A 341;
Lee 3A 22; William 3A
22; Wm. Jr. 3A 341;
Wm. Sr. 3A 341
SULIVENT, Hampton 4A 208;
John (Little) 4A 379;
John Sr. 4A 431; Lewis
4A 431

SULLIVAN, 1A 50; Daniel
4A 494; Elizabeth 1A 5;
Hampton 4A 482; John 1A
5; 3A 393; 4A 208; John
(Little) 4A 482; John
Sr. 4A 482; Lee 3A 240;
Michael 4A 482; Milley
4A 482; Penelope 4A 269;
Sally 4A 482
SULLIVANT, Bryant 4A 199;
Dickson 4A 500; Elkaney
4A 557; John 4A 104;
Robert 4A 557
SULLIVEN, John 1A 75,82;
John Jr. 1A 82,88; Tabi-
tha 3A 409; William 1A
82,88; 3A 409
SULLIVENT, 3A 275,298,315;
Caleb 3A 163,165; Elk-
anah 3A 163; Hampton
4A 557; John 3A 165,285,
309; 4A 557; John (Lit-
tle) 3A 163; John Sr.
3A 163; Michael 3A 163,
165; Robert 3A 163,433;
Uriah 3A 285; 4A 557
SUMMERLIN, Rachel 4A 8;
Siller 4A 8
SUTTON, 4A 386; Benjamin
3A 349,549; 4A 373;
Joseph 1A 405; 4A 401
SWEATMAN, 3A 190; 4A 358;
William 3A 189
SWEENEY, Morgan 3A 31
SWEENY, Morgan 1A 226
SWEETMAN, Wm. 4A 253
SWETMAN, William 4A 333
SWINSON, 4A 118,170,446;
Ebenezer 3A 322; 4A 367;
Jesse 1A 347,349,445;
3A 397; 4A 17,199,202,
269; John 1A 141; 3A
43; 4A 119; Jonas 4A 81;
Richard 4A 322; Theophi-
lus 1A 136; William 4A
487

-T-

TANNER, Samuel 1A 188,
190,319,327; 3A 197; 4A
342,363,365,380; Thomas
1A 190
TARREN, 3A 515
TATE, Robert 4A 283;
William 4A 462
TAYLOR, 3A 297; Adam 4A
259; Catherine 1A 407,
434; Dempsey 1A 82;
Elizabeth 1A 334,335,
459,462; George 4A 495;
Jacob 1A 220,495,497;
3A 48,232,353; 4A 177,
473; James 1A 90,383,
495,497; J. L. 4A 101;
Jno. 3A 523; John 3A
526; 4A 294; John Louis
4A 221; John Valentine
1A 236,513; 4A 172;
Jonathan 1A 64,88,95,
494; 3A 196,198,314,
399,426; 4A 249; Jos.
4A 294; Joseph 3A 523,
526; Thomas 1A 126,237;
4A 210,445; William 1A
141,237,334,335,407,
434,459,462; 3A 231,
523,526; Wm. 1A 372
TEACHEY, 3A 480; Daniel
1A 277,539,541; 3A 412,
444; Daniel Sr. 3A 412;
4A 242; Danl. 4A 64;
Elizabeth 1A 539; Jacob
3A 152,444; Jacob Jr.4A

TEACHEY con't
Jacob Jr. (con't) 129;
John 1A 539; T. 4A 152;
Timothy 1A 539; 3A 412,
444; 4A 32,112,137,370,
503; Timothy Sr. 4A 242
TEACHY, Daniel 1A 128,379,
452; 3A 127,152; Timothy
3A 11,361
TEAGUE, William 1A 30
TEEL, Moses 1A 5
TELMONT, William 1A 205
THALLEY, 4A 353; John 4A
145
THALLY, Andrew 1A 121; 3A
17,195; 4A 327,487; John
1A 121; 3A 187,221,486;
4A 31,327
THIGPEN, Allen A. 4A 260;
Annice 4A 260; Brythal
4A 241,260; Dicy 4A 260;
Job 1A 98,427,439; 3A
42,249,359; 4A 151,272,
507; John 3A 31; 4A 130,
241,248,260; Joseph 3A
31; Miles 4A 151; Wiley
4A 248,260; Willie 4A
130
THOMAS, 3A 332,514; 4A 460;
Archibald 3A 477,531;
4A 54,130; George 3A 517;
4A 371,432,458,468;
Isaac 3A 182; 4A 130;
Jhonathan 1A 456; Jonat-
han 1A 48; 3A 305,306;
4A 255,459; Lewis 1A 48,
108,115,243,246,448,456,
478; 3A 34,239,305,306,
353,409,452; 4A 61,124,
231,238,255; Lewis Ashton
3A 491; Mary 4A 458,468;
Nathaniel 3A 67; Philip
3A 172; William 1A 521;
3A 156,254,531; 4A 130;
William Jr. 3A 156,531;
William Sr. 3A 156,531;
4A 54,130
THOMPSON, 3A 297; Benjamin
3A 318,375; 4A 401;
David 1A 62,70; 3A 292;
Elizabeth 3A 301,375;
Jacob 3A 79; James 1A 72,
513,548; 3A 288,292,420;
4A 172,521; John 1A 340;
4A 399; John C. 3A 301;
John Carter 3A 375;
Lawrence 4A 4; Mary 3A
301; Nichodemus 3A 112,
263; 4A 413; Nichodemus
Jr. 3A 79; Sanders 3A
549; Solomon 3A 79;
Thomas 3A 79; William
1A 70; 3A 292,301,318,
375; 4A 401
THOMSON, B. 4A 399; Eliza-
beth 3A 320; John 3A 318;
4A 399
THORN, Richard 3A 279
TILLMAN, Stephen 1A 166
TINER, James 4A 491; Lewis
3A 533; 4A 177,491
TIPLER, George 4A 98,99,
448; Jane 4A 448
TITTERTON, Thomas 3A 375
TOMSON, John 1A 340
TORRANS, Alexr. 1A 523;
Elizabeth 3A 20; James
1A 523
TREADWELL, John 3A 72
TREWHITT, James Blount 3A
98
TREWIT, 3A 317; James
Blount 3A 101,389
TRUET, 4A 180

TRYON, William 3A 149
TUCKER, Amos 4A 47; David
1A 23,360,440; 3A 161;
4A 60,136,156,189;
Henry 3A 475; John 1A
23,360; William 4A 47
TURBUVILLE, Joseph 1A 64
TURNAGE, 4A 173; Fanny 4A
339; Jesse 3A 542; 4A
158,334; Treacy 3A 153;
4A 339; William 3A 542;
4A 52; Zachariah 3A 43,
58,399; 4A 339; Zache-
riah 3A 153,181,363,433
TURNEGE, 4A 17
TURNING, Jesse Jesse 4A 52
TUTLE, Hophgiban 4A 481
TUTON, William 3A 288,354,
472,544; 4A 521
TWILLEY, 4A 509; Robert
1A 43; 3A 493
TYLER, Moses 1A 372

-U-

UNDERHILL, William 1A 122;
3A 288,417; 4A 316,346
UZZEL, Elisha 3A 206
UZZELL, Thomas 1A 432;
Thos. 1A 405

-V-

VANN, John 3A 525; 4A 36,
398; John Jr. 3A 509;
Mary 3A 205; Scott 3A
525; Steven 3A 205
VENTRESS, George 3A 188
VINING, 1A 390; William
1A 392; 4A 545

-W-

WADE, 4A 538; James 3A
542; 4A 384; Joseph 3A
421; Obadiah 1A 545;
Obediah 3A 460; Vicey
3A 137
WADKINS, Leavin (Levin)
1A 217,246
WAHH, John 1A 454
WAIDE, Jacob 4A 69
WALKER, 4A 477,530; Car-
leton 4A 313; James W.
4A 114; John 1A 281,318;
3A 32; Robert 3A 372;
4A 477
WALLACE, 4A 232; Andrew
1A 57,175,178; 3A 362;
J. 1A 268; Jacob 3A 256;
4A 508; James 1A 176,
178,180,457,499; 3A 267;
4A 362,508; James Jr.
1A 178; Jeremiah 4A 508;
Stephen 4A 362
WALLER, 4A 241,248; Elijah
3A 308; 4A 248; John 1A
103; 3A 81; John Jr. 1A
435; Leven 3A 499; Na-
than 3A 81,87; 4A 11,
279,289,290,296,465,482;
Nathaniel 4A 362; Nathen
1A 243
WALLICE, Jeremiah 4A 302
WALTERS, Henry 3A 61
WARD, 1A 208,383; Cha. 3A
190; Charles 1A 1,21,59,
248,264,268,423,499,
544; 3A 261,468; 4A 384,
479,509; Chas. 1A 136,
300,425; James 1A 347,
349; 3A 146,409; 4A 45;
John 1A 508,512,530; 3A
131,409; 4A 169,392;

WARD con't
Luke 1A 353,512,530; 3A
131,133; 4A 165; Mary 1
A 375; 3A 291; Matthew
3A 147,542; 4A 52; Oba-
diah 4A 521; Phillip 1A
375; 4A 528; Saml. 1A
208; Samuel 1A 50,88,
100,239,258,505; 3A 94,
166,298,309,393,450,
463,501; 4A 373; Sarah
1A 375; Sarah A. 4A 509;
William 1A 239,454; 3A
288,291,292,507; 4A 33
WARDE, Cha. 3A 189
WARREN, Robert 1A 64,494;
3A 90,198; 4A 249;
Trecy 3A 153
WATERS, John 1A 478; 3A
138,149,251,379; 4A 119;
Needham 4A 261
WATKINS, 4A 76; Betsey 4A
277; Daniel 4A 534;
David 4A 534; James 3A
61,181,294,363,399,433,
521; 4A 76,87,108,158,
270,271,272,277,491;
Jas. 4A 78; Jesse 4A
56,57,87,108,545; Jno.
4A 79,272,455; John 1A
35; 4A 56,57,87,108,545,
549; Jos. 3A 416; Lavin
3A 59,151,153; 4A 549;
Leaven 3A 463; Leven
3A 416; Levin 1A 215,
388,390,392,525; 3A 517;
4A 56,57,76,79,108,149,
267,491,545; Levin Jr.
4A 57,149; Peter 3A 463,
470; 4A 267; Polly 4A
270; Sarah 4A 545,549;
William 3A 521; Wm. 4A
56
WATSON, 4A 434; Ezekial
3A 545; 4A 436; John
4A 471; Redick 3A 525
WEBB, Samuel 4A 404;
Thomas 4A 509
WEEDING, John 1A 55; 3A
374
WEEDINGS, John 1A 321
WEEKS, Sabra 1A 17; Tho-
mas 1A 17
WELCH, 1A 121
WELLS, 3A 158,391; Alex-
ander 4A 368,485,537;
Boney 4A 233; Elizabeth
4A 537; Frederick 1A
171,270,281,433; 3A 440;
4A 24,368,537; Fredk.
3A 226; Henry 1A 128;
Jacob 1A 9,13,128,161,
280,283,365,509; 3A 5,
82,189,190,192,324,423,
516; 4A 51,112,201,233,
298,368,398,472,485,
537; Jacob Jr. 1A 452;
3A 361; 4A 242; Jacob
Sr. 4A 24; Joseph 1A
136; Martin 1A 433;
Nathaniel 3A 39; Thomas
3A 208; 4A 537; William
1A 13,199,203,223,310,
365
WELTS, Joseph 4A 329
WEST, Daniel 4A 27,175,
534; James 4A 534;
Samuel 1A 467
WESTBROOK, 3A 309,463,
470; Dempsey 1A 495,
497; 3A 211,298,329,
384,393,501
WESTEN, 1A 237

WESTON, 1A 217,248,250,
502; Absalom 3A 18,73;
Absolam 4A 465; Absolom
3A 182; Benjamin 4A 286;
Bentley 4A 477; Bently
4A 542; Reuben 1A 215,
372,504,505; 3A 182,397;
4A 465
WETTS, Elizabeth 3A 229;
Joseph 3A 229
WHALEY, Isaac 3A 81; 4A
285; James 3A 31,431;
4A 19,275,559; Samuel
3A 31,477
WHEEDEN, John 1A 18; 4A 313
WHITBEE, James 4A 145
WHITE, Hays G. 4A 495;
Robert 4A 248; W. 3A 479;
Will 4A 103,172,186,187,
352,353,373,374(2);
William 4A 96,97(2);
William M. 4A 12; Wm.
4A 214,215,372,373; Wm.
M. 3A 480,481,482; 4A
173,187; Zachariah 3A 534
WHITEHEAD, 4A 336,463;
Edward 3A 470; Jacob 4A
455; John 1A 237,248,
250,505; 3A 211,278,329,
384,393,414,470; 4A 164,
491
WHITFIELD, 1A 97; 3A 21,
230,276,483,541; 4A 75,
365; Bryan 1A 147,405,
412; 3A 125,199,201,206,
243,437; 4A 219,342,365;
Constantine 1A 126,182,
420; 3A 53,54; Edmd. 4A
369,371,380,516; Edmond
4A 511; Hatch 4A 511,
516; James 3A 53,54; Jas.
4A 197; Jo. 3A 13,14;
John 3A 110; Jos. 3A 278;
4A 81,465; Joseph 1A 149;
4A 8,49,195,363,495;
Lewis 1A 340; 4A 511;
Luke 3A 143; Needham 3A
235,518; 4A 14,363,371,
511,516,518; Nm. 1A 147;
William 1A 42,188,328,
340,377,399,412; 3A 13,
197; 4A 22,133,428,434,
516,518; William Jr. 1A
42,149; 3A 14; William
(Minor) 1A 327,328;
William Sr. 1A 147,192,
327; 4A 511; Wm. 1A 328,
340,342,471; 3A 273,500;
Wm. Jr. 3A 488,517; 4A
14
WHITMAN, 3A 527; 4A 16,
309; Ann 4A 503; Condrick
1A 263; 3A 469; Conrad
4A 479; David 4A 68,424;
James 4A 122,424,503;
John 1A 222,417; 3A 152,
226; 4A 1,68,424,503;
John Jr. 4A 68,122,124,
129,503
WIGGINS, 1A 122; 4A 236,
249; Thomas 1A 122,123,
279; 3A 417
WILDER, 3A 438; Joel 1A
414; 3A 461
WILKINGS, Michael 4A 436;
Willis 3A 393
WILKINS, David 4A 260;
James 3A 110; John 3A
145; M. 3A 542; Michael
3A 109; 4A 63,195,428;
Michall 1A 42; William
1A 91,97,320,383,497;
Willis 3A 110,211,329,
384,393

WILKINSON, 3A 51; Eliza-
beth 3A 69; Elizabeth
Ann 4A 146; Harriet 4A
146; James Clark 4A 146;
John 3A 69; 4A 72,119,
146,223,306,448; Mary
4A 448; Mary Jane 4A
146; Robert 1A 77,353,
491,512,530; 3A 69,407;
W. 3A 292; William 1A
271,491; 3A 69,407;
William Sr. 1A 491,551;
3A 75; W. Sr. 3A 69
WILLAFORD, Elisha 3A 534
WILLEFORD, Benton 4A 6;
Elisha 3A 256; William
3A 236
WILLIAMS, 1A 66; 4A 114,
151,475,531; A. 4A 352;
Aaron 1A 197,280,281,
283,296,297,318,352,483;
3A 32,127,166,253,379;
4A 266,333; Amos 3A 81;
Anny 4A 317; Antho. 4A
180; Anthony 1A 405; 3A
101,317,425; 4A 462,542;
Aron 1A 482; B. 4A 353,
373,461,462,479; Ben.
1A 229; Benjamin 1A 61,
62,270,548; 3A 203,297,
480; 4A 12,173,434; Bur-
well 4A 315,320; Byrd
3A 40; 4A 232,317,472;
Chaplain 1A 520,521,522;
Charles 3A 522,523; 4A
342; Cloe 1A 439; Com-
mander 3A 262; Daniel
1A 208; Danl. 1A 279;
David 1A 25,318,437; 3A
32,490; 4A 160,213,214,
375; Dd. 4A 398; Dorathy
1A 172; Edward 4A 449;
Edy 3A 523; 4A 342; Elee
1A 117; Elizabeth 4A 8;
Esther 3A 288; Ezekial
3A 260; Fountain 4A 28,
116; Francis 3A 350; 4A
204,206,536; Frederick
1A 197,281; 3A 148;
George 1A 276; 3A 160;
4A 426,449,461; Hill 3A
438; Hopkin 4A 16; Hop-
kins 4A 518; Humphry 4A
399,401; Jacob 1A 520,
521,522; 3A 75,95,261,
267,285,286; 4A 72,426,
442; James 1A 61,103,
117,342,478; 3A 98,101,
125,203,260,318,375,489,
493,540; 4A 119,198,324,
449,475; James Jr. 3A
404; James Sr. 1A 172;
Jeremiah 1A 157; 3A 267;
4A 151; Jesse 3A 460,
523,526; 4A 21,198,541;
John 1A 8,25,318,337,
339,374,439,520,521,522,
545,552; 3A 32,40,160,
371,426,490; 4A 69,181,
216,249,252,317,319,357,
449,470,472; John Jr.
3A 40; John Sr. 3A 40;
Joseph 1A 25,70,102,
264,270,296,297,318,
350; 3A 32,434,440,474;
4A 51,67,229,317; Joseph
Jr. 1A 318; 4A 317;
Laben 3A 209; Lemuel 3A
1; 4A 21; Lewis 4A 116,
432; Mary 3A 379,420;
Nancy 4A 198; Richard
1A 8,151,153,157,226;
3A 371; 4A 110; Robert
1A 61,66,276; 3A 351;

WILLIAMS con't
Robert (con't) 4A 96;
Saml. 1A 62; Stephen
1A 8,25,98,153,435,450;
3A 527; 4A 309; Theophi-
lus 1A 66,69,72,75,99,
188,190,192,208,258,
316,327,328,399,410,
412,429,462,502; 3A 50,
67,166,450,533; Tho. 3A
275; William 1A 385,
542; 3A 425,551,554,555;
4A 4,29,132,462; Wm. 4A
415; Zilpha 4A 232
WILLIAMSON, John 1A 383
WILLIFORD, 3A 87; Benton
1A 450; 3A 89; 4A 504;
Elisha 3A 386
WILLIS, Frederick 3A 440;
George 1A 323; Jacob 3A
419; Jonathan 1A 323
WILLSON, 4A 49; Alexr. 1A
182,185; Andrew 1A 274;
John 1A 350,482,483;
Joseph 1A 8,157,176,178,
180; 3A 446
WILSON, 4A 32; Andrew 1A
131; Jas. 1A 440; John
3A 522,528; 4A 78,143;
Michael 3A 457; Thomas
4A 334
WINDERS, 3A 506,528; Ed-
ward 3A 73,397; James
1A 347,349; 3A 24,146,
430; 4A 45,169; John 1A
250,347,349,372,445;
3A 18,73,156,314,409;
John Jr. 1A 250; John
Sr. 1A 445; Joseph 1A
349
WINFIELD, 4A 197; Joseph
1A 86; 4A 396
WINNANTS, Peter 1A 513
WITHERINGTON, Barney 4A
513; Daniel 4A 513
WOLF, Charles 3A 90; 4A
249
WOOD, Daniel 4A 239;
Frederick 4A 275; Henry
4A 275; Jacob 3A 540;
Jhon 1A 28; Mary 4A
259; William 4A 259
WOODARD, James 3A 58
WOODS, Freeman 4A 101;
Hannah 4A 101,221
WOODWARD, Elisha 1A 287;
3A 438; 4A 290; James
3A 43; John 1A 2,55,
137,257,287; 3A 245,250,
357,359,438; 4A 281,456;
John Sr. 3A 216,438
WOOLF, Charles 1A 494
WOOTEN, Allen 3A 258; 4A
458,468; Shad. 4A 458,
468; Shadk. 4A 141;
Shadrack 3A 55; William
3A 55
WORLEY, 4A 97; Frederick
4A 493; Jane 1A 499;
Jean 1A 499; Loften 1A
55; Loftis 1A 254,339;
3A 56,184,254; 4A 42,
530; Nancy 4A 493;
Readick 4A 386; Redick
4A 470,530,541; Thomas
1A 55; 4A 42,319,470
WORSLEY, John 3A 63;
William 4A 123
WRAY, William 3A 282
WRIGHT, D. 4A 155,549;
David 3A 8,20,66,248;
4A 149,379,522,528;
Elizabeth 1A 452; James
1A 77,353,452,465,508,

WRIGHT con't
James (con't) 512,530;
3A 131,133,407; 4A 165,
399,528; John 1A 217,
312,441; Mary 1A 271;
Tho. 4A 229; Thomas 1A
312,498; 3A 8(2),24,42,
50,51,56,66,120,182,263,
265,270,279,286,303,311,
367,426,438,450,547; 4A
141,261,465; Thos. 3A
48,226,245,324,407

-Y-

YOUNG, 1A 515; James 4A
219; Peter 3A 516; 4A 51

WHITFIELD con't
  Doll 3A 54; Doratha 3A
  53; Furney 3A 14; Jack
  3A 53; Jacob 3A 14,53;
  Jimmima 3A 53; Linay 3A
  13; Millia 3A 14; Peg
  3A 53; Penny 3A 54; Rose
  3A 14; Winney 3A 14
WILKINSON, Dizey 1A 551;
  Lew 4A 146; Luce 4A 146;
  Milley 4A 448; Mint 4A
  146; Sylvia 4A 146; Tom
  3A 69; Virgil 4A 146
WILLIAMS, Abram 3A 540;
  Bob 3A 253; Chloe 3A 350;
  Fanny 4A 252; Hamlet 1A
  462; Hannah 1A 399;
  Jenney 3A 253; Jerry 4A
  252; Linkham 4A 375;
  Lydia 1A 462; Roger 3A
  522; Sam 4A 252; Thener
  1A 399
WILSON, Chloe 3A 522;
  Fillis 4A 143; Judy 4A
  78; Lintz 4A 143; Vio-
  let 3A 522
WOOD, Abram 3A 540
WOOTEN, Harry 3A 55; Mary
  3A 55; Pegg 3A 55
WORSLEY, Friday 3A 63
WRIGHT, Harry 3A 8; Roger
  3A 56

FIRST NAMES ONLY

The following are first
names only. No surnames
were found in the records.

_____, Abraham 3A 92
GEORGE II. 1A 454; 3A 133
GEORGE III. 1A 117
_____, Henry 3A 388
_____, Hezekiah 3A 414
_____, James 3A 442
_____, Reuben 3A 533
_____, Richard 3A 125
_____, Ruth 1A 363 (see
  also 1A 439)
_____, Thomas 3A 89

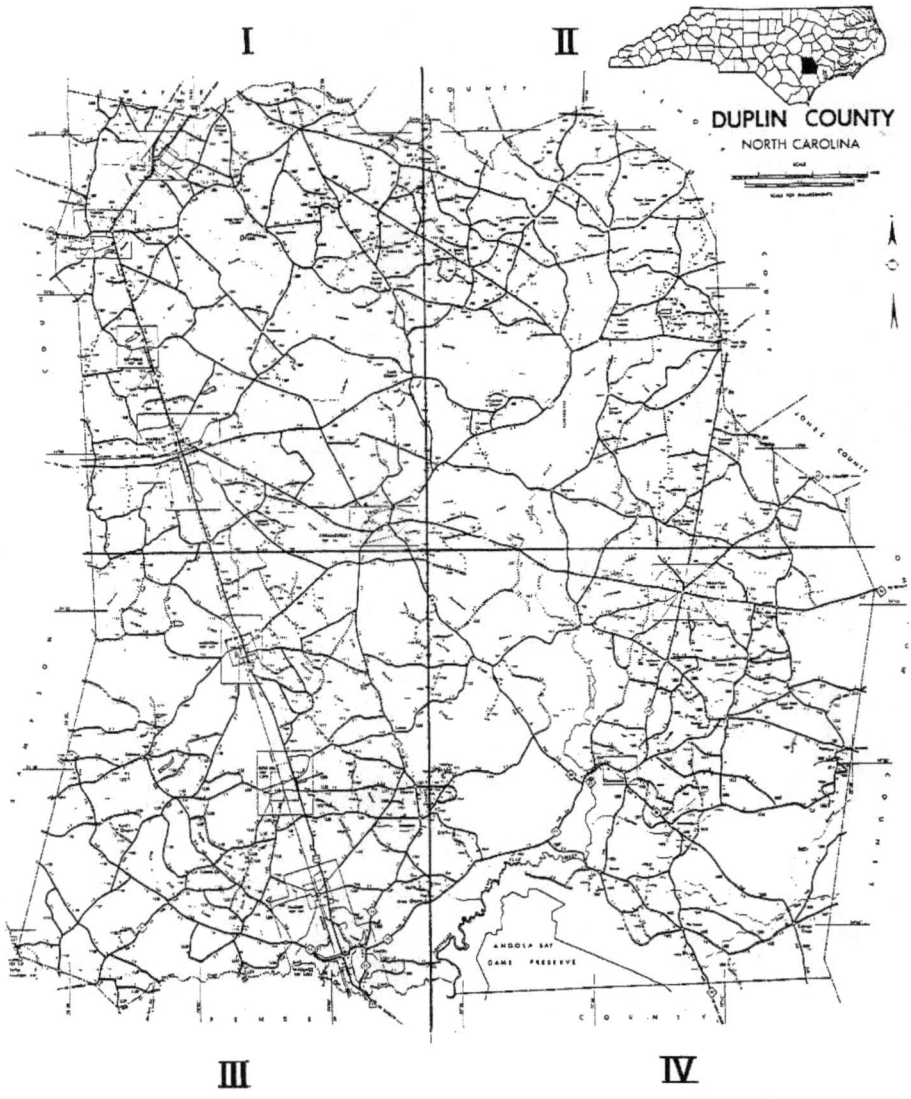

I

II

DUPLIN COUNTY
NORTH CAROLINA

III

IV

I

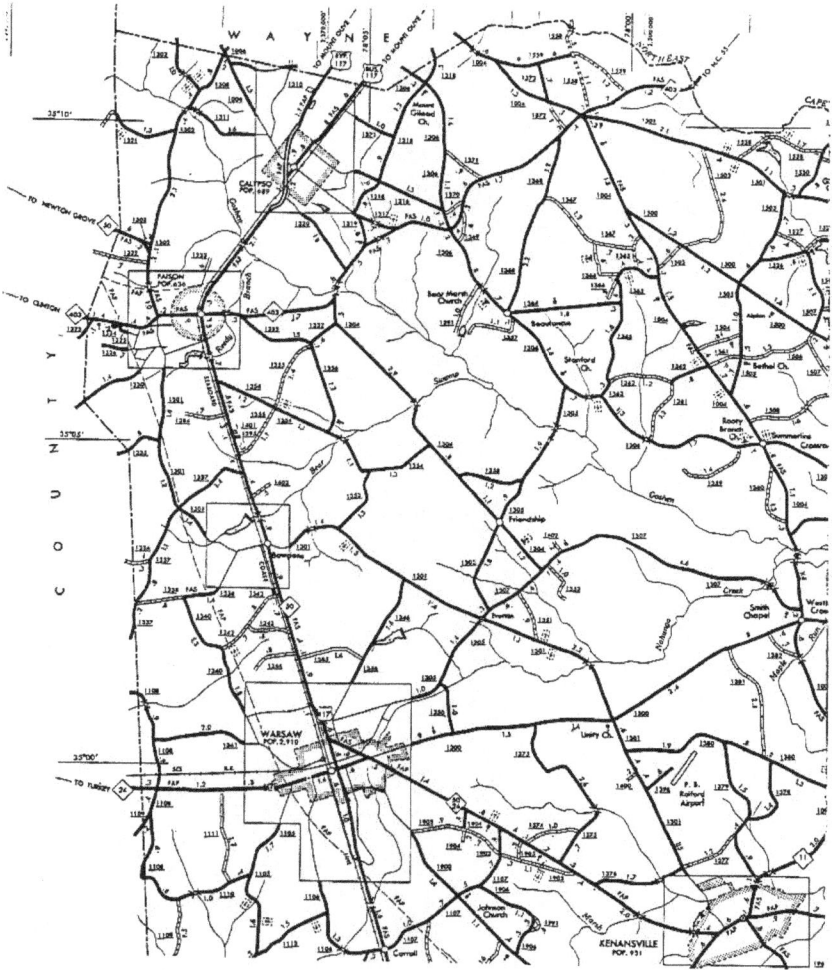

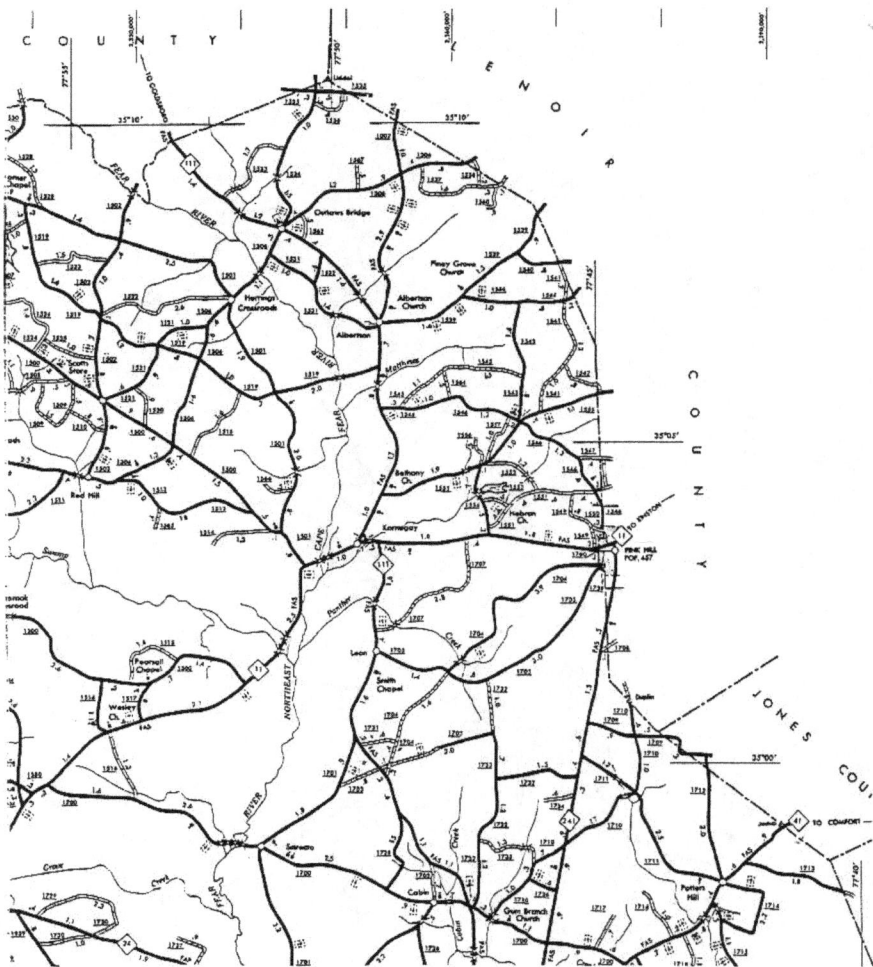

III

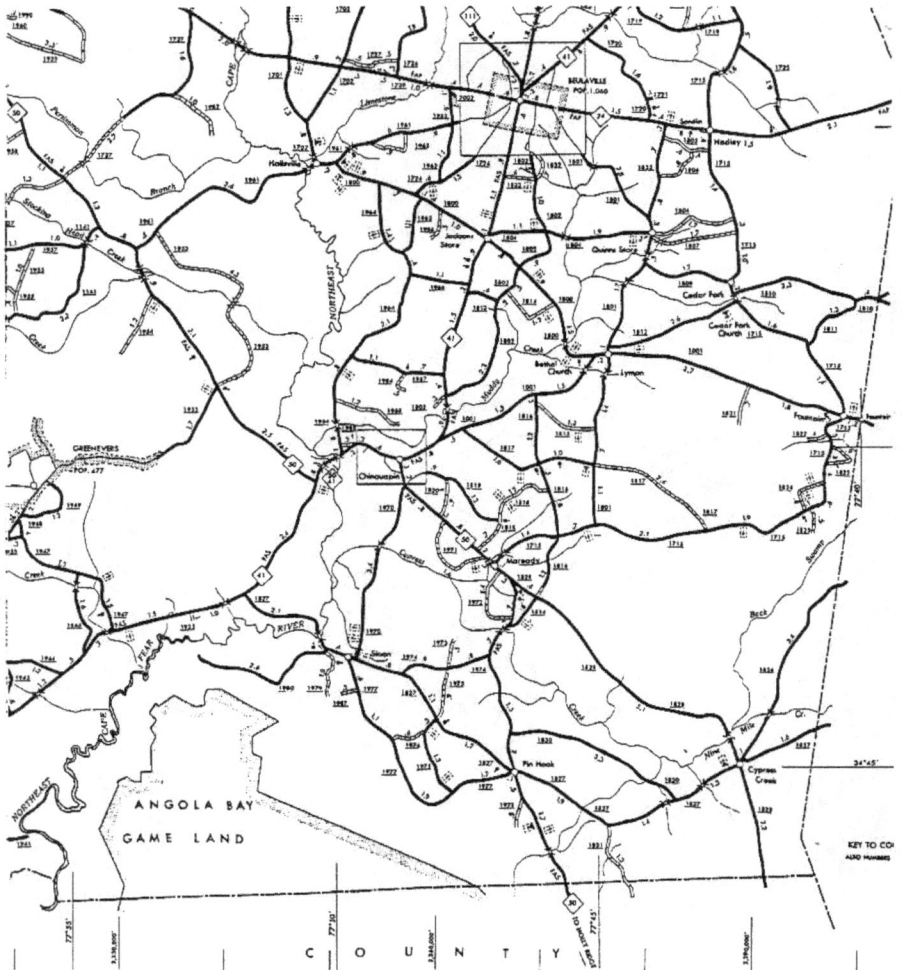

IV

www.ingramcontent.com/pod-product-compliance
Lightning Source LLC
Chambersburg PA
CBHW021903020426
42334CB00013B/451